National Wildlife Federation®

FIELD GUIDE TO
BIRDS
OF NORTH AMERICA

D0168192

National Wildlife Federation®

FIELD GUIDE TO
BIRDS
OF NORTH AMERICA

Written by Edward S. Brinkley

Foreword by Craig Tufts, NWF Chief Naturalist

Photographs supplied by VIREO,
The Academy of Natural Sciences

STERLING
New York / London
www.sterlingpublishing.com

Dedication

A written dedication could never adequately express the deep debts of gratitude I owe hundreds of fellow birders, family members, and friends over the past 40 years. Birding as a passion can be pursued solitarily, but my happiest times birding have been with mentors, friends, and field-trip participants—millions of small moments in which birds' appearances seemed to stop time itself and to fuse us all together in wonder and astonishment. Above all others, my parents, Stanworth and Kate Brinkley, gave me the encouragement and support I needed to grow as a person and as a birder, learning the difficult balance of curiosity and caution, tenacity and modesty, hope and discernment that it takes to be a modern birder. Their warmth, their guidance, and their generosity are more than a person dare hope for from a parent; but their example of lives lived with humor and humility—more even than their infectious belief in the dignity and intrinsic worth of others—resonates in and inspires all who have known them. It is to them that this book is dedicated, and to my earliest, most cherished mentors—Susan Taylor Hubbard, Gisela Adele Grimm, Rebecca Old White, Floy Cooper Burford, and YuLee Ruff Larner—who taught me that for a life in birding to be fulfilling, one must first be a naturalist and a natural historian, a lover of beauty and of people. I have been very fortunate to know people of such good will and great spirit. —*Ned Brinkley*

Published by Sterling Publishing Co., Inc.
387 Park Avenue South, New York, NY 10016

© 2008 by Andrew Stewart Publishing, Inc.

Distributed in Canada by Sterling Publishing
c/o Canadian Manda Group, 165 Dufferin Street,
Toronto, Ontario, Canada M6K 3H6

Distributed in the United Kingdom by GMC Distribution Services
Castle Place, 166 High Street, Lewes, East Sussex, England BN7 1XU

Distributed in Australia by Capricorn Link (Australia) Pty. Ltd.
P.O. Box 704, Windsor, NSW 2756, Australia

Library of Congress Cataloging-in-Publication Data

Brinkley, Edward S.
    National Wildlife Federation field guide to birds of North America /
written by Edward Stanley Brinkley.
        p. cm.
    Includes index.
    ISBN-13: 978-1-4027-3874-6 (alk. paper)
    1. Birds—North America—Identification. I. National Wildlife Federation.
II. Title
QL681.B75 2007
598.097—dc22

For information about custom editions, special sales, premium and corporate purchases, please contact Sterling Special Sales Department at 800-805-5489 or specialsales@sterlingpub.com.

National Wildlife Federation® name and logo are trademarks of National Wildlife Federation and are used, under license, by Andrew Stewart Publishing, Inc.

NATIONAL WILDLIFE FEDERATION

The mission of the National Wildlife Federation is to inspire Americans to protect wildlife for our children's future.

Protecting wildlife through education and action since 1936, the National Wildlife Federation® (NWF) is America's largest conservation organization. NWF works with a nationwide network of state affiliate organizations, scientists, grassroots activists, volunteers, educators, and wildlife enthusiasts— uniting individuals from diverse backgrounds to focus on three goals that will have the biggest impact on the future of America's wildlife.

Connect People with Nature

NWF is committed to volunteer and education programs that connect people to nature and wildlife. NWF publications like *Ranger Rick, Your Big Backyard, Wild Animal Baby,* and *National Wildlife* educate adults and children of all ages about nature and conservation. The **Backyard Wildlife Habitat**™ program teaches individuals how to create habitat that supports wildlife in their own backyards and provides people with an easy yet effective way to practice their conservation values at home. The **Green Hour** encourages kids to go outside to experience nature for one hour each day. Education programs like **Campus Ecology** and **Earth Tomorrow** bring together students from diverse backgrounds, teaching them leadership skills to become America's next generation of conservation leaders.

Protect and Restore Wildlife

Loss of habitat due to oil and gas drilling, urban sprawl, and deforestation is a major threat to the future of America's wildlife. NWF works tirelessly to obtain permanent protection for critical habitat areas—areas that are essential to the recovery of species populations such as wolves, salmon, and the Florida panther.

NWF's work also includes protecting lands like the pristine Arctic National Wildlife Refuge, the vanishing wild areas of the western United States, and the green forests of the Northeast. Water and wetland protection programs focus on restoring the Great Lakes, the Snake River, the Florida Everglades, Louisiana's coastal wetlands, and the Northwest's Puget Sound. In addition to working to restore these habitats today, NWF fights for expanded Clean Water Act protection and campaigns for smarter water and land management for the future.

For more than 30 years the Endangered Species Act (ESA) has been the primary tool for conserving endangered and threatened species and their habitats. NWF is committed to upholding the full protection of the ESA, despite attempts to weaken it.

Confront Global Warming

Global warming heats up the atmosphere, which causes glaciers to melt, sea levels to rise, water temperatures to creep up, precipitation patterns to change, and droughts and storms to become more extreme. It is the single biggest ecosystem emergency we face today. Scientists predict that unless we act, one-third of wildlife species in some regions could be headed for extinction within the next 50 years.

NWF recognizes this dire situation and is taking action now to help halt global warming. Working with members, state affiliates, and partners, NWF mobilizes grassroots activists to push for state and national policies that reduce emissions of heat-trapping pollution. By providing good science and public outreach tools, NWF educates Americans about smart, efficient energy use.

The National Wildlife Federation relies on Americans from all walks of life, of all political and religious beliefs, of all ages to advance our mission: *protecting wildlife for our children's future.* Visit www.nwf.org or call 800-882-9919 to join us today!

Contents and Visual Key to the Bird Groupings

Ducks, Teal, Shoveler, Wigeons, Pintails, Scaup, Eiders, Scoters, Goldeneyes, Mergansers, Geese, Brant, Swans

Guillemots, Murres, Razorbill, Murrelets, Dovekie, Auklets, Puffins

Pelicans, Tropicbirds, Gannet, Boobies, Frigatebird, Cormorants, Anhinga

Albatrosses, Petrels, Shearwaters, Fulmar, Storm-Petrels

Jaegers, Skuas, Gulls, Kittiwakes, Terns, Noddies, Skimmer

Foreword

All of us who are passionate about the natural world cannot help but be aware of its changing landscapes and climates. For anyone in North America who seeks to combine observations of these ongoing natural changes in the environment with enjoyment of the outdoors, there are few better resources than this superb new field guide to the birds of North America. The natural histories of the hundreds of bird species included in the guide are tied directly to the health of the habitats they seek, whether the birds are overwintering guests in our backyards, migrant passersby following our rivers, coastlines, or forest tracts, or nesting pairs with very specific needs for food and cover.

It is important that a bird guide, like any book concerning natural history, include the most up-to-date information. Bird populations and distributions fluctuate, sometimes quite rapidly, in the face of the earth's changing climate. In addition, as the scientific community's knowledge of our feathered wildlife increases, information—from thirty, ten, or even five years ago—becomes outdated. Where to find a particular species, when to look for it, or even what to call it are just some of the aspects of birding that are constantly changing. There is, then, much to learn in this guide for all birders, from beginners venturing out on their first field trip to long-time birding enthusiasts who know every bird likely to pass through their region.

The *National Wildlife Federation Guide to Birds of North America* describes more than 750 species of birds and displays them in their natural habitats in some 2,100 stunning color photographs. Four-color range maps give users a quick and accurate indication of bird distribution at any season. Each species of bird comes alive through descriptions of its behavior, vocalizations, and habitat preferences. The comprehensive, well-illustrated introduction offers a thorough overview of the natural history of birds, including flight, plumages, songs, and migration, as well as tips on how to watch and identify birds. A conservation section covers the biggest threats to bird populations and details how birding can be an opportunity for involvement in important citizen-science programs.

My excitement for this new guide goes beyond its content and design to an appreciation of its author, Ned Brinkley. A lifelong birder, Ned is a product of both his love for birds and the guidance and mentoring he received from his parents, friends, and fellow birders in southern Virginia and beyond. Ned serves as editor for the highly respected journal of bird distribution *North American Birds;* he is also well known as a guide of birding excursions in the Americas and beyond. In this book, Ned combines his very significant skills in writing and editing with his zeal for birds and birding.

Like Ned Brinkley, I am a birder because of some innate need for the natural world in my life, spawned from the love, time, and knowledge passed on to me by my parents, neighbors, and peers. Putting a name to a bird empowers us, and directs us to use our knowledge. I can guarantee you that my copy of this guide will enjoy a rich, much traveled life. You, too, will come to think of it as an indispensable partner. When you pick up a copy for yourself, pick up an extra or two, for your daughter or grandson or perhaps a child around the corner who may want to put a name to a bird or three. It may be the best investment you've ever made.

Craig Tufts
CHIEF NATURALIST,
NATIONAL WILDLIFE FEDERATION

Introduction

A common thread connects those of us who watch birds, whether in our backyards or in remote rain forests: the desire to know, to understand, and to identify the creatures we observe. Birding has grown in popularity like no other outdoor activity in modern times and now ranks just after gardening and walking, claiming tens of millions of enthusiasts on this continent alone. Many excellent field guides treating the identification of birds in North America (here defined as the continent north of Mexico and the Caribbean) are currently in print. Most of these use illustrations that stress distinguishing characteristics, or "field marks," of the species. This guide relies on photographs to cover the birdlife of North America. Within its pages, hundreds of compelling, crisp, and unretouched images by

When studied closely, even subtly plumaged birds, such as this Tricolored Heron, can reveal a remarkable palette of pigmentation in plumage, eyes, bill, and skin.

today's top avian photographers convey the aesthetic appeal and intrinsic beauty of each species. The accompanying captions and text are intended to communicate in a concise manner the information necessary for identifying and fully appreciating these remarkable creatures.

Scope and Arrangement of This Guide

When creating a bird field guide, the most difficult decisions are also the most basic ones: which species to include and how to present them in relation to one another. More than 1,000 bird species have been reported in North America north of Mexico—too many to cover in depth in a portable field guide. Most guides, therefore, do not cover some of the more rarely seen birds, particularly escaped captives and species not reported every year in North America. Every new field guide must also take into account recent changes in the status and distribution of North American birds and those likely to occur in the future.

This guide covers all of North America's regular breeding birds—approximately 580 species—as well as an additional 180 or so nonbreeding species that regularly or occasionally visit North America. In recent years, several tropical and subtropical species formerly quite rare north of Mexico have become regular visitors, some of them even nesters, in U.S. border states; many of these are included in this guide because of this recent increase in their extralimital records (records of occurrence outside of a species' normal range).

However, this guide does not cover most species that have been recorded only a few times in North America, including nearly 100 Eurasian species seen occasionally or rarely on Alaska's Bering Sea islands and Aleutian Islands (islands close to Siberia where visiting birders also carry field guides to Eurasian birds). Of the 80 families of birds recorded in North America, five are not treated in this guide: Old World flycatchers (family Muscicapidae, 7 species recorded),

The family Upupidae is represented in North America by one record of Eurasian Hoopoe from Old Chevak, Alaska, in 1975.

hoopoes (Upupidae, 1 species), pratincoles (Glareolidae, 1 species), thick-knees (Burhinidae, 1 species), and accentors (Prunellidae, 1 species). The first three have been recorded only as vagrants to Alaska; there is a single record of Double-striped Thick-knee *(Burhinus bistriatus)* from Texas in 1963; accentors are represented by a few records of Siberian Accentor *(Prunella montenella)* in Alaska and western North America.

The American Ornithologists' Union (AOU) is the international body that maintains the official checklist of wild birds recorded in the Americas, *The American Ornithologists' Union Check-list of North American Birds*. This field guide generally follows the AOU's nomenclature for the birds of North America—that is, the English and scientific names the organization designates as correct for those species. The AOU arranges the checklist in phylogenetic order, a linear sequence that attempts to represent evolutionary relationships among birds, with closely related species grouped more closely together; the first species in the checklist are thought to be the most ancient, the last the more recently evolved. Ornithologists revise the accepted sequence of the list from time to time. Because of recent discoveries based on DNA analysis and other biochemical evidence, the

longstanding placement of loons at the beginning of the list (through most of the 20th century) has changed. More changes will likely occur in the future.

This guide does not rely strictly on the AOU's sequencing of species; the birds are sometimes grouped according to basic similarities that pose identification problems for beginning birders. See "About the Guide" (page 31) for more information on groupings and sequencing of the species.

Classification

Birds are egg-laying, feathered vertebrates in the class Aves (Latin for "birds"). They are divided into orders (recognized by the suffix "-iformes"), large groupings that include many different birds that appear to be close evolutionary relatives. For example, the order Pelecaniformes includes pelicans, tropicbirds, cormorants, darters, frigatebirds, boobies, and gannets, all of which have completely webbed feet and specialize in eating aquatic prey. Orders are divided into families (suffix "-idae"); within families there are often subfamilies ("-inae"). Families are further divided into genera (plural of genus) and species.

A species is traditionally defined as a population of like organisms capable of breeding together and producing fertile offspring. Every species is assigned a scientific name, which consists of a genus name (a taxonomic rank that may include one or dozens of different

The breeding grounds of the extinct Labrador Duck (male shown) were never discovered; the last individual was reported in 1875.

species) and a species name. For example, Northern Bobwhite is a bird (class Aves) in the order Galliformes and the family Odontophoridae; it is placed in the genus *Colinus* (derived from a Central American word for "partridge") and given the species name *virginianus* (from Virginia); the scientific name *Colinus virginianus* identifies this species unambiguously to any ornithologist in the world.

Subspecies are geographically distinct populations, or "races," of a species that

The distinctive *ridgwayi* subspecies of Northern Bobwhite, Masked Bobwhite, is an endangered bird of northern Mexico. A few hundred also persist in southern Arizona at Buenos Aires National Wildlife Refuge.

show different characteristics; they are assigned a three-part scientific name, called a trinomial. The trinomial of the distinctive northern Mexican subspecies of Northern Bobwhite known as "Masked Bobwhite" is *Colinus virginianus ridgwayi.* The subspecies found in much of the Southeast is *Colinus virginianus virginianus* and is called the "nominate" subspecies because it was the first to be scientifically named and described. (Nominate subspecies bear the same subspecies name—in this case, *virginianus*—as the

species name.) When referring to multiple subspecies, this guide often uses the shorter word "taxa" (plural of taxon).

Ongoing changes The classification of genera and species is often revised to reflect new information and changing opinions. Many populations of birds (especially gulls, waterfowl, and hummingbirds) regularly hybridize—that is, they interbreed with other species—and some produce hybrid young capable of breeding. Some species hybridize so readily with other species that in certain areas hybrids may actually be more common than either parent species. Modern ornithologists see instances of hybridization not as a troublesome fly in the ointment but as fascinating evidence of the ongoing process of speciation, in which various populations evolve and interact and over time may give rise to new species.

Every year, somewhere in the world, ornithologists elevate a subspecies of bird to the level of full species. As this guide was in production, the four smallest subspecies of Canada Goose were split into a full and separate species under the English name Cackling Goose and the scientific name *Branta hutchinsii.* Species are also regularly combined (or lumped), becoming a single species; the former species are then often designated as subspecies. For example, in 2005 White Wagtail and Black-backed Wagtail were combined as one species, White Wagtail.

Just before this guide went to press, the AOU voted to split Blue Grouse into two species: Sooty Grouse, *Dendragapus fulginosus* (displaying male shown here), of the Pacific region, and Dusky Grouse, *Dendragapus obscurus* (illustrated on page 172), found in the Interior West.

Parts of a Bird

It is not necessary to have a detailed knowledge of the anatomy and morphology of birds to be a competent birder, but it is important to be thoroughly familiar with the parts of a bird's visible plumage, or its feathers. The major groups of feathers are the remiges (flight feathers of the wing), rectrices (tail feathers), coverts (feathers that cover the bases of the remiges and rectrices, both above and below), upperparts (mantle, scapulars, and upper surface of the folded wing), and underparts (throat, breast, belly, flanks, vent, and undertail coverts). It is also necessary to know the terms for the markings of the head and for the parts of the bill (beak).

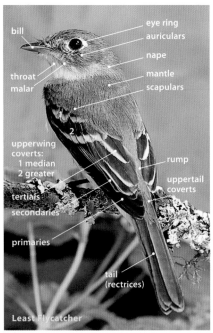

Least Flycatcher

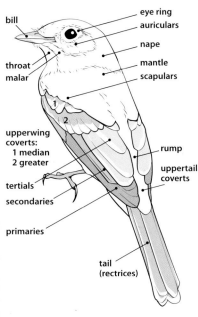

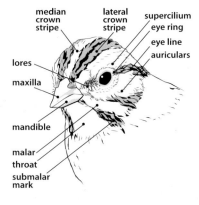

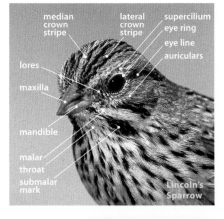

Lincoln's Sparrow

Birders often use less formal terms to identify features of a bird: cheek, forehead, chin, wrist, arm, hand, frontlet, cap, bib, eye patch, cowl, and others. Consult the Glossary (page 502) for definitions of these terms.

crown
lores
supercilium
auriculars
bill
nape
scapulars
mantle
malar
throat
upperwing coverts:
1 median
2 greater
tertials
secondaries
primaries
breast
side
tail
(rectrices)
belly
flank
uppertail
coverts
undertail
coverts
vent
tarsus
toes

Chipping Sparrow

crown
lores
supercilium
auriculars
bill
nape
scapulars
mantle
malar
throat
upperwing coverts:
1 median
2 greater
tertials
secondaries
primaries
breast
side
tail
(rectrices)
belly
flank
uppertail
coverts
undertail
coverts
vent
tarsus
toes

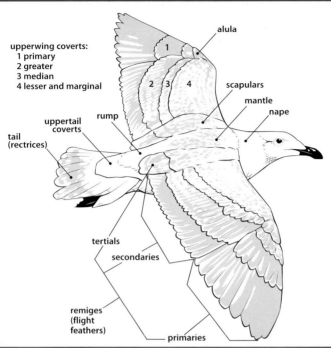

upperwing coverts:
1 primary
2 greater
3 median
4 lesser and marginal

alula

scapulars

mantle

nape

rump

uppertail
coverts

tail
(rectrices)

tertials

secondaries

remiges
(flight
feathers)

primaries

upperwing coverts:
1 primary
2 greater
3 median
4 lesser and marginal

alula

Great Black-backed Gull
(immature)

scapulars

mantle

nape

uppertail
coverts

rump

tail
(rectrices)

tertials

secondaries

remiges
(flight
feathers)

primaries

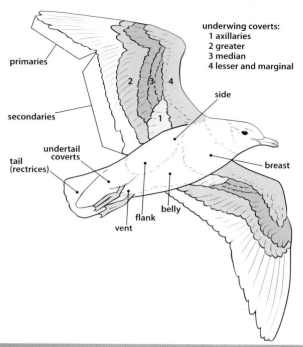

primaries

underwing coverts:
1 axillaries
2 greater
3 median
4 lesser and marginal

2 3 4

1

side

secondaries

undertail
coverts

tail
(rectrices)

breast

vent

flank

belly

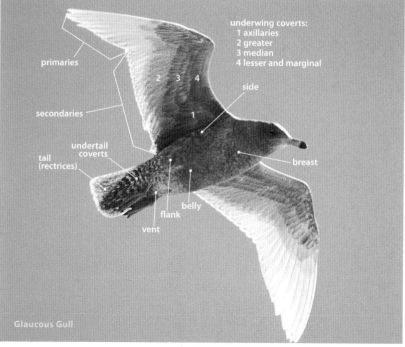

primaries

underwing coverts:
1 axillaries
2 greater
3 median
4 lesser and marginal

2 3 4

1

side

secondaries

undertail
coverts

tail
(rectrices)

breast

vent

flank

belly

Glaucous Gull

Plumage and Molt

A bird's feathers (its plumage) are made from keratin, the same substance found in human fingernails. Though durable, feathers become worn and must be replaced regularly. The process of feather replacement is called molt, and almost all birds molt at least some feathers at least once a year. Very large birds, such as eagles and pelicans, can have complex, irregular molts that last for months. Most birds, however, have regular, predictable molts that occur usually over a few weeks during a period when they are not nesting or migrating.

Large birds, such as this Bald Eagle, may not attain their definitive adult plumage for five or more years; most passerines and shorebirds acquire adult plumage by their second year and most gulls by their fourth.

Immature Plumages

Some birds hatch with a downy coat of feathers, but most—especially passerines (perching birds)—hatch naked and acquire their first coat of contour feathers, called juvenal plumage, in their first month or so. In most species, fledglings are young birds with newly acquired juvenal plumage that are just leaving the nest; they often still have a few traces of natal down. Juveniles are young birds that have fledged and are still in their juvenal plumage. Some species, such as most warblers and sparrows, hold juvenal plumage for a relatively short time, molting into the next plumage after just a few weeks. Others, such as gulls and shorebirds, retain juvenal plumage for several months, although the appearance of the plumage changes considerably during this time through wear.

Plumages that follow juvenal plumage are attained by either a complete molt (of all feathers) or a partial molt (often just of body feathers and coverts). Some species, such as the ptarmigan, undergo several partial molts annually, producing a variety of plumages over the course of a year. Because molt can differ significantly even in closely related species, it can be difficult to apply consistent terminology to plumages and the molts that produce them. This guide uses the "life-year" system, which is closest to how human age is marked. A bird in its first-fall plumage or its first-winter plumage is still in its first year of life: less than 12 months old. These plumages differ from juvenal plumages but in many cases retain some juvenal feathers.

European Starling in fresh autumn plumage (left) is neatly speckled and shows brown covert edges. With wear (right), it appears darker and has green and purple sheens; this is the plumage in which most starlings breed.

Adult Plumages

Most passerines attain adult plumage (sometimes called definitive plumage) around or just after their first full summer, at about one year of age; larger nonpasserines often take longer, usually reaching maturity of their plumage by the second or third year (some large birds do not attain adult plumage for nearly a decade). As birds near adult plumage, they usually resemble adults more and more closely. (The term "subadult" refers to a bird whose plumage is nearly, but not quite, that of an adult; the term "immature" applies more broadly to any bird that has not acquired its adult plumage.)

Adults of a great many species of birds acquire breeding plumage (also called alternate plumage) just before the breeding season, and most hold this plumage for about half the year. Breeding plumage is usually more striking than nonbreeding plumage (or basic plumage), especially in males. Most birds molt into their breeding plumage, but some species—such as European Starling—attain their breeding appearance by a gradual wearing of feather edges from their autumn plumage.

Species in which males and females show different plumages for at least part of the year are said to be sexually dimorphic. In many such species, males in breeding plumage are more colorful or more strikingly patterned than females. Male ducks bear a bold or colorful plumage for most of the year and molt into a very plain plumage, called an eclipse plumage, for only a few weeks in summer. Males in eclipse plumage sometimes resemble females (these briefly held plumages usually are not illustrated in this guide).

Plumage Variation

Some widespread bird species show a tremendous variety of colors and markings. If these variations occur in relatively regular and predictable patterns, as they do in Song and Savannah Sparrows, they may lead to the designation of subspecies. However, variation in some species' plumages does not show such patterns. Snow Goose and Rough-legged Hawk, for example, have different plumage morphs, or forms, which are considered not subspecies but simply color variants. Species that show different color morphs that do not relate to age or sex are said to be polymorphic in plumage.

Individual birds can also show aberrant (atypical) plumages; these include leucism (with unusually pale or whitish plumage, either overall or in certain feathers), melanism (with unusually dark plumage), and albinism (with no pigment; such birds are starkly white and have pink eyes and legs). Even more rarely, a bird will display a strong suffusion of yellow (xanthism) or red (erythrism) in the plumage.

Albino birds, such as this American Robin, lack pigmentation in eyes and legs as well as plumage. The feathers appear white, the eyes and legs pink.

Leucistic birds, such as the Common Tern at lower right, have normal pigmentation in the eyes and often some feathers; if mostly white, they usually show a hint of the normal plumage pattern.

How to Identify Birds

When faced with a bird in the field, a birder first takes note of its key distinguishing features, or "field marks"—overall size and shape, bill structure, plumage (the markings on head and body)—and its actions. Many birds can be identified by the colors and patterns of their plumage alone, but plumages can be difficult to assess in the field. Distance, tricky lighting, individual variation, and damage from staining, oil, or simple wear and tear (old feathers often become sun-bleached and bedraggled) can lead to the absence or obscuring of field marks. Therefore, even before studying a bird's plumage in detail, a birder takes note of its size and structure.

The structural features of the head and the size and shape of the body provide crucial information for the identification of many species. It is usually possible to "narrow down" the identity of a bird in the field to just a few possibilities by determining its overall proportions: Is the body slender or thickset? Are the neck and legs long or short? Are the wings short, broad, and rounded or long, narrow, and pointed? How many toes are on the foot?

Some birds can be identified by a distinctive structural feature, such as the spatulate bill of Roseate Spoonbill.

Oftentimes, the bird's bill alone is enough to narrow down the identification: Is it thin or heavy? Long or short? Narrow or broad? Because size can be hard to judge in the field at any distance, even on a nearby bird, it can be useful to compare the size of the bird in question to that of birds around it, if possible.

Birds in Action

Experienced birders learn quickly to identify birds by their actions as well as their structure and plumage. A feeding Wilson's Phalarope, for instance, can be picked out quickly by its habit of racing around wildly after flying insects, an action seen in few other shorebirds. Phoebes regularly dip or flare the tail more noticeably than do smaller flycatchers. Many species hold themselves in distinctive postures when feeding or resting, and these postures can be clues to identification. For example, Broad-tailed Hummingbirds often perch in a less upright position than Rufous Hummingbirds. Sometimes a change in posture can confuse an observer: a roosting owl may appear quite compact when undisturbed but stretch into an elongated "concealment posture" when an intruder approaches; Lesser and Greater Scaup usually sleek the plumage of the head when foraging, which eliminates the small corner at the rear of Lesser's head, a key distinguishing feature of these very similar species.

Birds in flight Flying birds, especially when seen from a distance, can be particularly difficult to identify. Although it can be relatively easy to identify large, slow-flying birds, passerines in flight are often quite challenging, especially for the beginning birder; in fact, some species of warbler and sparrow have never been photographed well in flight.

When you are beginning to identify birds in flight, first get to know the species well when they are not flying. Learn a bird's overall shape and plumage characteristics

Identification of flying birds is often difficult, but many species are readily distinguished by a few key features. Great Egrets, such as this nesting bird, can be told from smaller egrets by their large size, black legs and feet, and heavy yellow bill. All herons and egrets retract the neck in flight, while cranes fly with the neck extended.

when it is relatively still, then watch as it flies off. Once the bird is in flight, study its overall shape, including its various wing shapes, the cadence of its wingbeats, and the features of its plumage that show up clearly at a distance. Because these aspects of flying birds are difficult to convey in still photographs, they are best learned with patience and practice in the field. A few behavioral traits of flying birds are easy to spot; for example, a large, dark, crowlike bird flying in the distance can often be identified as a raven rather than a crow if it makes "somersaults" in midair.

As you observe the birds, get into the habit of taking good notes on what you see. Keep a journal of notes and field sketches and take photographs, and refer to your journal and photos often to build your knowledge. Good note-takers also find that they recall details more easily; the process of recording notes helps fix them in the memory.

Identifying Birds by Ear

One of the greatest pleasures, and challenges, of birding is learning to identify birds by their distinctive vocalizations. Birds give both songs and calls, and they also make sounds with the wing and tail feathers and the bill, particularly when courting.

Most North American birds, including this Prairie Warbler, learn their songs in their first year. Tyrant flycatchers, by contrast, have innate songs—that is, they know them from birth.

Songs Male birds use songs both to attract mates and to define and defend territories. They usually repeat a song often and sometimes couple it with a flight display; a few species sing mostly on the wing. In a number of species, including some wrens, cardinalids, and blackbirds, females also sing, usually a quieter or weaker version of the male's song (although some females sing vigorously and some sing a very different song than the male's). Most birds sing only during the breeding season and most intensely in the early morning. Songs of a species may vary both individually and regionally. Some species have enormous repertoires: Brown Thrashers sing more than 100 distinct song types. Many flycatchers and warblers have a secondary song, given mostly at predawn or dusk and presumably directed mainly at rival males.

Calls Birds of all ages and sexes give many calls, short vocalizations used to maintain contact, beg for food, solicit courtship or copulation, warn of predators, or scold intruders in their territory. Some calls are distinctive and instantly recognizable, while others sound quite similar to calls of other species and are thus less useful for field identification. Most North American passerines "learn" their songs from their parents or others of their species. The vocalizations of flycatchers, by contrast, are innate (known from birth); their songs are sometimes very similar to their call series (this is especially true in the kingbirds).

The best way to learn vocalizations and other sounds birds make is to watch them court and sing, listen carefully, and then write down your own notations or phonetic transliterations or humorous mnemonic jingles—something that will stay with you. A fellow birder once said that he never failed to recognize a Summer Tanager singing because it says, to his ear: "Peanut butter, peanut butter, peanut butter, your mama." To supplement field study of songs, many birders record birds with a sound recorder or video camera or listen to recordings of bird vocalizations on videos, compact discs, or web sites.

Limits of Field Identification

It is not possible to identify every bird in the field. Young Allen's and Rufous Hummingbirds, for instance, are essentially identical, only distinguishable with the bird in hand. There are also individual birds that stump even proficient birders. These include birds that have unusually pigmented plumage, bills or legs that differ in color from most of their species, or broken or deformed bills. Innately aberrant birds are usually rare, except in shorebirds and gulls, two groups in which atypical individuals are often observed.

Some bird species show remarkable variety in plumages, particularly those that have many subspecies (although most subspecies of North American birds show only minor differences from each other). The subspecies of some birds show clinal differences, meaning that a change in one characteristic or another varies gradually over a broad geographic area. No field guide can depict all possible plumages of all North American birds—besides the many subspecies (this guide depicts some of the more distinctive ones) are countless individual birds that differ noticeably from typical individuals of their species or subspecies. (Anyone who has spent a day observing thousands of Herring Gulls can confirm this point.)

Hybrids—the offspring of two different species—are often impossible to identify with certainty in the field. Hybrid birds, of course, do not belong to a single species, nor do they always show characteristics that are clearly intermediate between the parent species. Across much of the continent hybrid birds are rather rare, but there are certain well-known zones of hybridization (such as the Pacific Northwest, the Canadian Rockies, and the Great Plains) where they are more common. To further complicate matters, hybrids often breed

"Olympic Gull," a hybrid of Glaucous-winged and Western Gulls, is seen in the Pacific Northwest.

Aztec Thrush is a species normally found only in mountains of Mexico; this vagrant male was photographed in Arizona.

with nonhybrids, resulting in young called backcrosses. In such situations, identification is difficult or impossible, sometimes even with a study of DNA.

Vagrancy in Birds

A species' known, expected geographical range is usually a useful clue in an identification, but the appearance of vagrants, birds far out of their typical range, complicates matters. Most vagrants reported in North America are birds that have strayed a few hundred miles out of range but that breed within North America; all such species are depicted in this guide. A small minority of vagrants come from Eurasia, South America, or Africa, and these species are usually not depicted.

The study of bird vagrancy is relatively new. Some theories suggest that vagrants have a faulty navigation system and confuse, for example, north and south, leading them to migrate northward instead of southward in the fall. Most such strays are long-distance migrants, often passerines or shorebirds that spend the winter in tropical regions of the world. Other vagrants have been blown off course by weather systems; for example, European Golden-Plovers returning to Iceland in spring sometimes make landfall in Newfoundland because of strong easterly winds. Some vagrants are transported to North America on large ships; on rare occasions hummingbirds, rails, and even owls have been found in large shipments of plants. Seabirds—especially the tubenoses, such as petrels and shearwaters—are particularly prone to wander far out of range; there are few barriers to their travel over the open ocean, and strong weather systems such as hurricanes can also displace them great distances.

In some cases, vagrants may be pioneering individuals or flocks of birds that are testing out new breeding or wintering areas; they may remain in areas well out of range and establish breeding populations or become part of a growing wintering population.

Reporting vagrants Birders relish the sight of a new or unusual species in their area. Anyone might discover a vagrant species, sometimes just by looking out a window and seeing something unfamiliar. Vagrants are of special interest to ornithologists because they contribute to the collective picture of a species' natural history, including range expansion, responses to weather and climate, and migratory patterns. All states and most provinces have bird records committees that keep track of, review, and archive reports of rare birds; such committees are grateful to receive well-documented reports of unusual species or subspecies. Upon finding an unusual-looking bird, then, it is a good idea to take notes as well as a video or photographs, in order to study the bird in detail afterward and so that others can review the notes and images.

Natural History of Birds

Habitats

A habitat may be defined as the environment or ecological community where an animal or plant normally lives. Like mammals, birds occupy the full range of habitats in North America, from High Arctic pack ice to the Chihuahuan Desert of Mexico and the Southwest. North American habitats can be characterized by their dominant plant communities and/or geological features. Habitats encompass both broad, general types, such as hardwood or coniferous forests, and finer distinctions, such as oak-hickory or maple-basswood hardwood forests and subalpine mixed conifer forest. Many widespread bird species, such as Ovenbird, nest in all types of hardwood forests, but other species require very specific habitat types to survive. Red-cockaded Woodpeckers nest only in longleaf and loblolly pine savannas of the Southeast. Such habitat specialists are usually the species in greatest need of conservation attention; some are considered vulnerable to extinction.

In a varied landscape such as this one at Denali National Park, Alaska, different species of birds might be found in the riparian areas (along the river), the grassy fields, the various forest communities, and the more barren alpine areas.

A region of the country may contain a nearly uniform habitat type, such as the shortgrass prairie that stretches from the Panhandle of Texas to southeastern Colorado; but most regions support multiple habitats. Peninsular Florida, for example, embraces the Everglades, mangrove and subtropical forests, and prairies. (For more information on regions and habitats, consult the Bird Conservation Regions map at http://www.nabci-us.org/bcrs.html.)

Aquatic habitats Birds occupy many aquatic habitats, including riparian areas (along rivers) and lakes, ponds, swamps, and marshes. Saltwater pelagic (oceanic) and littoral (nearshore) habitats are home to a great variety of seabirds, some of which—including the alcids, tubenoses, and tropicbirds—spend many consecutive years at sea before coming to land to nest. Within these aquatic environments there are distinct habitats where birds congregate. On the ocean, some of these are defined by currents, such as the Gulf Stream and the California Current, others by submarine topography, such as the continental shelf, where the continental landmass drops off steeply. The shelf is cut by canyons that create upwellings of seawater that draw prey items to the surface. Some seabirds are specialized foragers in these offshore habitats: Audubon's Shearwater is most numerous around large rafts of pelagic algae, home to many small fish and other prey. Gadfly petrels, by contrast, may roam vast areas of ocean in search of less concentrated prey, such as cuttlefish and squid.

Habitats of migratory birds Migratory birds and birds that make irregular movements out of their core ranges may occupy many different habitat types over the course of a year. Migrating species have both breeding and wintering grounds, as well as intermediate stopover or staging sites, areas with adequate food resources that allow them to fatten up for their onward journey. Habitats used during migration and in winter do not always closely resemble those of the nesting grounds. For example, many Neotropical migrant species winter in Caribbean mangrove forests, the lushly forested montane slopes of eastern Mexico, or the diverse forests of the Andes or Amazon Basin—habitats that are quite different from the forests of the North where they breed. In addition, adverse weather conditions such as fog, rain, contrary winds, or storms can force migrants to land in habitats they might not otherwise occupy: migrating birds are often seen in tiny city parks and cemeteries or on ships and offshore oil-drilling platforms.

The varied diet of Greater Roadrunner includes insects, spiders, scorpions, snakes, lizards, small birds, rodents, fruit, seeds, and carrion.

Adaptation to habitat Bird species adapt to their habitats in remarkable ways. Some desert species, for instance, have never been observed drinking water: they apparently draw the moisture they need from seeds or insects. In Arctic regions, ptarmigan survive winter storms by roosting inside snowdrifts. The seafaring albatrosses may remain airborne for days at a time, "sleeping" on the wing by shutting down parts of the brain not needed for flight. Some species are capable of adapting well to human environments when their natural habitats are destroyed by development: in the Southeast, Black Skimmers and many species of tern have nested on the flat roofs of shopping malls, which replace their usual beach nesting areas.

Foraging

When not resting or preening, birds are usually searching for food. Birds often forage in challenging environments: White-throated Swifts zoom far above the clouds, chasing tiny insects and spiders aloft, while Common Murres dive for small fish hundreds of feet below the ocean surface. Most birds specialize in their foraging methods to some degree, and some are easily identified by them. Dowitchers, for instance, feed by rapid,

regular jabs of their long bill into muddy substrates, a rhythmic "sewing machine" motion that permits their identification as dowitchers even at a distance. When trying to identify a small woodland bird, one can often narrow down the possibilities by noting whether it gleans from twigs and leaves (as do many warblers), plucks from the outermost tips of branches while clinging (parids), hover-gleans from needle clusters (kinglets), picks from bark crannies (nuthatches), or excavates from holes in bark made by blows of the bill (woodpeckers).

Many species of birds that share a common habitat employ different foraging techniques or exploit different food resources. Trogons, cuckoos, and the larger vireos, for instance, all move slowly through the forest canopy, watching for caterpillars and other insects and capturing prey by gleaning or a quick sally; their size differences, however, ensure that they compete very little, as the larger species take prey too large for the smaller birds to eat and do not take the smaller prey.

Some bird species forage cooperatively. Roadrunners kill rattlesnakes in pairs, and Harris's Hawks hunt rodents in small teams. Foraging woodland birds often travel in mixed-species flocks, or guilds, led by parids.

Storing food A few species—notably shrikes, parids, corvids, and some woodpeckers and owls—store, or cache, food for later consumption. Species that forage heavily on pine nuts, such as Clark's Nutcracker, hide thousands of nuts and are able to remember these locations for long periods of time. Several acorn-eating woodpeckers often store nuts in "granary trees."

Breeding
Most bird species breed just once or twice a year, during their breeding season. Males often have more brightly colored plumages and sing more frequently at this time.

Courtship Birds employ a great variety of courtship strategies before nesting, including songs, flight and ground displays, and offerings of food and sometimes nests or burrows. Songbirds (passerines) tend to stake out territories and sing to entice females. In several species of grouse and shorebirds, males gather together in a lek and display collectively for females, engaging in a variety of dancing and drumming behaviors. Truly flamboyant courtship displays are not uncommon in North American birds: cranes, prairie-chickens, ptarmigan, several grouse, and Wild Turkey put on the most spectacular shows; some woodpeckers, raptors, hummingbirds, and swifts also have remarkable elements in their displays.

Mating and nesting Many bird species are monogamous: the male and female remain together throughout at least one breeding season and usually raise the young together. Less common mating systems include polygyny (males with multiple female mates) and polyandry (females with multiple male mates). Many birds employ variations of these systems.

Birds lay their eggs in nests, burrows, or nest-scrapes from below ground level (Burrowing Owl) to the tops of trees (Bonaparte's Gull). Their nesting grounds range from backyards to tiny, rocky islands far out in the Pacific Ocean. Small landbirds usually nest solitarily within a territory, while many waterbirds nest in colonies. Some birds lay their eggs in other birds' nests, a strategy known as brood parasitism (Brown-headed Cowbirds do so exclusively, thus engaging in obligate brood parasitism); they allow the host parents to raise their single nestling, which may eject other eggs from the nest after hatching.

The chicks of some species hatch naked and blind and are called altricial young; others—notably galliform and shorebird chicks—are precocial, born feathered and sighted and able to scamper around and feed themselves just minutes after hatching. Parental care varies tremendously among bird species, but most parents feed, protect, and care for their young until fledging—that is, when the young bird is able to fly and leave the nest. In some species, including cranes and several corvids, the young stay with their parents for nearly a year or longer as they learn migratory routes and foraging strategies.

In spring, Lesser Prairie-Chickens and related species form leks, aggregations of displaying males that attract females; the females observe the males carefully for evidence of good health and vigor.

Flight is an activity that often requires high degrees of attentiveness and athleticism. Peregrine Falcon, thought to be the fastest species of bird on Earth, contends with strong g-forces when pulling out of a hunting "stoop," as shown here. Peregrines may dive toward prey at speeds nearing 200mph (320km/hr), then swoop sharply upward after striking prey.

Flight

All North American bird species (with the exception of the extinct Great Auk) are capable of flight—a feat that looks effortless but is in fact a complex activity, crucial for a bird's survival, that requires learning, skill, and athleticism. Birds take to the air by flapping the wings, spreading the wings into a strong wind, or dropping from a perch while opening the wings. Flapping creates thrust, or forward momentum, and this enables the wings to create lift: air flowing over the top of the wings moves faster than air flowing below the wings, making the air pressure above the wings lower and thus lifting the wings and the bird with it. Birds show many other adaptations for flight: light, hollow bones, streamlined bodies and bills, and tails that serve as rudders for steering.

Wing shape Wing shape varies markedly among bird species, even closely related ones. The aspect ratio of a bird's wing is the relationship of its length to its width. Birds with relatively short, wide wings have a low aspect ratio, whereas birds with long, narrow wings have a high aspect ratio. Such a technical term may seem unnecessary for field identification, but its implications for flight are readily apparent in the field: birds whose wings have a low aspect ratio, such as the alcids, flap their wings rapidly and seldom glide, while those with a high aspect ratio, such

as albatrosses, may not have to flap for hours at a time. A bird's ability to fly is also influenced by its wing-loading: the relationship between its weight and its total wing area. Albatrosses, which are very heavy and have rather narrow wings, have relatively little overall wing area and thus high wing-loading; it takes a stiff breeze to keep these birds aloft. In contrast, many raptors have lower wing-loading—they are rather light-bodied and have long, wide wings—which permits them to soar (stay aloft with relatively little flapping) or to kite (hang over one spot with minimal flapping) under a variety of conditions.

Hummingbirds are known for their ability to hover in one spot, a manner of flying that requires enormous energy resources; they are also the only birds able to fly backward, a feat made possible by the configuration of the joints and musculature of the wings. Dippers, alcids, and many shearwaters, which inhabit aquatic environments, use their broad, short wings for underwater propulsion. Swifts adjust their scythe-shaped wings almost constantly in flight, which gives them the aerodynamic agility they need to capture tiny airborne insects.

Migration

In the narrow sense, migration indicates a regular, usually annual movement of a bird or other creature from one area to another. Many species of birds make

Evangeline Beach, Nova Scotia, is one of North America's many traditional stopover sites, where millions of migrating birds, such as these Semipalmated Sandpipers, feed and rest.

regular migrations between breeding and wintering areas, driven by the presence of food and favorable climate in different places at different times of year. Literally billions of birds migrate to and from (and within) North America each year, mostly in spring and fall. Birds exert tremendous energy while migrating, and they rely on both favorable winds and updrafts to ease their passage. Such conditions are found especially in the mountains, where winds strike the ridges and are deflected upward, causing lift. Many species that nest on land are not adapted to aquatic environments and thus do not like to be caught out over large bodies of water while migrating; concentrations of migrants seeking pathways that avoid water crossings are often seen along coastlines (of lakes, rivers, and oceans), on islands, and at the tips of peninsulas.

At a few places in North America, it is possible to stand and watch migrants passing in almost uncountable numbers: on occasions, over a million American Robins have passed Cape May Point, New Jersey, in a day, and similar counts of Short-tailed Shearwaters have been seen passing offshore of Gambell, St. Lawrence Island, Alaska. Most passerines migrate at night, passing over large areas in a single

evening, detected only by their calls (or with radar technology).

In the past, biologists described four basic "flyways" of migrants in North America, especially for waterfowl. Modern ornithologists recognize that migratory pathways and overall strategies for migration are not so simple to describe. Neotropical migrants travel to tropical areas—from Mexico and the Caribbean south to temperate South America. Most Neotropical migrants are passerines, but various raptors, shorebirds, seabirds, nighthawks, and cuckoos also migrate through or to the tropics. Short-distance migrants generally remain within North America, most of them migrating earlier in spring and later in fall than Neotropical migrants. Some species move in response to unfavorable conditions, whether a crash in food resources or a period of inclement weather. These movements are sometimes called facultative migrations or, in some cases (as with northern finches and owls), irruptions. Birders often call these movements "influxes," "invasions," or simply "flights."

How birds navigate to their final destination—often to the same acre where they were raised—is not well understood. Birds use a variety of visual cues, such as the sun when migrating by day or the stars when migrating by night, to orient themselves so they fly in the appropriate direction for their destination. Some species are known to use the earth's electromagnetic fields or polarized light to orient themselves while migrating. Some birds, such as geese and cranes, begin migrating with their parents and apparently learn specific routes from them and others in the flock; such birds probably recognize and follow certain rivers, ridges, and coastlines. Migratory skills in most species, however, appear to be innate rather than learned. In most migrants, hormonal changes triggered by the changing length of daylight stimulate migratory behavior.

Conservation

The primary reasons for declining populations of birds across North America are the loss and degradation of many of their habitats. This has been caused largely by human activities; development, modern agricultural methods, overharvesting of natural resources, and pollution are among the serious threats to natural habitats across North America.

There are well-documented examples of birds that have suffered steep population declines as a result of pollution. Peregrine Falcons were reduced almost to extinction in the middle of the 20th century because of eggshell thinning caused by the pesticide DDT. Hundreds of thousands of seabirds (and other marine animals) have been killed by oil spills from large tankers. Loons and other northern-nesting species declined precipitously from the effects of acid rain, which has damaged forests and wetlands in the Northeast.

The banning of DDT in 1972, as well as of other organochlorine pesticides in the United States, led to the recovery of many bird species from near-extinction. But such pesticides are still legal in other parts of the world, including some parts of South America where many North American species winter. And in the United States and Canada, intensive use of other pesticides by the agricultural industry has resulted in death and severe genetic damage to many vertebrates.

Following is a general discussion of conservation issues of some habitats in North America and how they affect bird populations. In addition, the introduction to each bird group notes conservation concerns, and a list of bird conservation organizations appears on page 508.

Forests Harvesting, fragmentation, and degradation of forests have caused severe declines in many bird populations. For example, in the Southeast, Red-cockaded Woodpeckers are endangered, largely due to the loss of old-growth pine forests, and Ivory-billed Woodpeckers, which once thrived in old-growth lowland forests, may be extinct (sight reports of this species still exist; see page 273). A subspecies of Spotted Owl that depends on the rapidly dwindling old-growth forests of the Pacific Northwest is listed as threatened. Countless woodland birds are negatively affected by heavily fragmented forests (which are unsuitable for species of interior woods) and by replanted woodlands that lack the diversity of natural forests. Strip-mining, mountaintop removal, and construction have replaced woodlands with human-modified environments useful to only a minority of bird species.

Prairies and grasslands Most of the vast prairies that once covered central North America and teemed with birdlife were converted to agricultural use more than a century ago, and modern agricultural practices, including applications of toxic pesticides, herbicides, and rodenticides, continue to degrade the few remaining native grasslands of the Great Plains. Likewise, the more aggressive methods of modern cattle ranching have destroyed vital riparian corridors and open-country habitats and have encouraged the rapid spread of invasive plant species, degrading and destroying habitats used by prairie-chickens, sage-grouse, and other birds.

Wetland and ocean habitats Agricultural activity and development in North America since colonial times have resulted in the draining of tens of millions of acres of freshwater wetlands, and many populations of waterfowl and other species that rely on these habitats have plummeted perilously over the years. It was not until the early 20th century that American governments began taking measures to preserve freshwater wetlands; but these habitats are still quite endangered and fragile, beset by pesticide and fertilizer pollution, drought, and invasive alien species. In coastal areas, development has forced colonial waterbirds and many shorebirds into smaller and smaller breeding areas, and these are subject to frequent disturbance by recreational boaters and beachcombers. Offshore, a staggering array of pollutants—abundant garbage discarded at sea, mercury and other heavy metals, and oil spills—plague seabirds and marine mammals. Seabirds also suffer from the overfishing of key prey species, and thousands are killed in gill nets and on long-lines. Some populations, especially of larger tubenoses, are declining at alarming rates.

Global warming The burning of fossil fuels to produce energy has produced excessive carbon dioxide in the atmosphere and caused the gradual warming of both atmosphere and oceans, a phenomenon commonly referred to as global warming. The consequences of this to birdlife (as well as human life) could be catastrophic in the relatively near future. Already in the Arctic—where the polar ice cap is melting and sea ice is much less extensive than in decades past—there are signs of ecosystem collapse. The rise in sea level predicted to occur in fewer than 100 years could eliminate the Florida Everglades, along with many islands, beaches, and salt marshes used by millions of nesting birds. Rising temperatures would radically alter many other habitats and allow tree diseases and insects to invade regions previously too cold for them. Global warming has already resulted in outbreaks of tree pests, severe forest fires, and the invasion of shrubs into what was once tundra—breeding habitat for dozens of bird species.

Getting Involved in Bird Conservation

From the earliest days of the conservation movement, birders have led the way. They have worked to protect birds' habitats, protest unsustainable killing of birds, and fight the poisoning of the environment that led to near-extinction of many species we now take for granted in North America. Populations of Bald Eagles, Peregrine Falcons, Brown Pelicans, and many other birds have recovered, but there are still hundreds of species faced with declining populations and habitats.

Birders seeking to contribute to bird conservation should join bird conservation organizations, read their newsletters and magazines, and watch for opportunities to help out locally or beyond. At the local level, bird clubs and Audubon Societies are always active in wildlife-oriented activities and in legislative initiatives. It can be extremely gratifying to work within these organizations to help create or preserve local habitat, build nest boxes, or raise money for bird conservation. Taking action on the national or international level may consist of participating in letter-writing or fund-raising campaigns, lobbying efforts, or even education and outreach projects in distant parts of the world.

Simply going out and watching and identifying birds—as well as counting them carefully—can contribute to a whole host of citizen-science projects that are maintained on Web sites. Long-term projects on the Internet include:

eBird   www.ebird.org
Christmas Bird Count   www.audubon.org/bird/cbc-mbr-pwrc
North American Breeding Bird Survey   www.mbr.pwrc.usgs.gov/bbs/
Project FeederWatch   www.birds.cornell.edu/pfw

About the Guide

This guide covers all species of birds that breed in or regularly visit North America north of Mexico, as well as many of the rarer visitors. The species are generally grouped and ordered according to the checklist of the American Ornithologists' Union (AOU)—that is, beginning with what are thought to be the most ancient families and continuing in phylogenetic sequence to the more recently evolved. However, to aid beginning birders in some of the more common identification problems, the guide often diverges from the AOU's order. In most of these cases, birds with similar structural features, especially the shape of the body and bill, are grouped together; for example, the unrelated Great Blue Heron and Sandhill Crane—both tall, grayish birds with a long neck and a long, pointed bill—are shown together to better illustrate their differences. Unrelated birds with similar color, size, habits, or habitat are also sometimes juxtaposed. See the Contents (pages 6–9), which incorporates a **Visual Key to the Bird Groupings.**

Group introduction essays Each section of the guide begins with an introductory essay that gives general information on the group, including which families the species belong to, physical characteristics common to the group as a whole, and general information on habitat, foraging and breeding behaviors, and conservation.

Names and measurements The common and scientific names of the species follow those given by the AOU. The length (L), from bill to tail tip, and the wingspan (WS), from wingtip to wingtip, are given in both English and metric measurements.

Captions and labels For most of the species covered, the guide includes photographs of the plumages you are most likely to observe in North America. These can include breeding and nonbreeding adults, male and female (if distinguishable in the field), various nonadult plumages (labeled as juvenile, immature, subadult, 1st fall, etc.), and some of the more distinctive subspecies. The majority of the photos are labeled to indicate the plumage. In cases where the specific plumage of a bird cannot be determined from a photograph, as in many of the tubenoses, the image is not labeled. Species that show clinal variations often have geographic labels to indicate where the photo was taken. Captions indicate identifying features of the species as well as features that distinguish it from similar-looking birds.

Text The information provided for each species is intended to aid in identification and in understanding the species' natural history and distribution. The text may discuss winter and summer habitats, unique behaviors, diet and foraging techniques, courtship and nesting strategies, physical characteristics, and comparisons with similar-looking species. The descriptions and transliterations of the songs and calls give a rough idea of the species' primary vocalizations. Many of the descriptions mention the pitch of a song or call, which can range from almost inaudibly high (as in the end of the Blackburnian Warbler's song) to almost inaudibly low (as in the owl-like hooting of a displaying Dusky Grouse). Musical terminology is occasionally employed: "crescendo" and "decrescendo" for sounds that grow increasingly louder or softer, "modulated" for burry, buzzy, or scratchy sounds (as opposed to "pure-toned" or "sweet" or "clear"), and "syncopated" for songs that seem to have irregular rhythms or unexpected stresses.

Range maps The maps indicate typical North American ranges of the species, including winter and summer ranges and migration routes. Rare or extralimital occurrences are shown in some cases. See the key to the range maps on the inside flap of the guide's front cover.

How to Bird

"Birding" is more than a passing interest in birds; it is a fascination with them that combines appreciation of their aesthetic appeal with intellectual curiosity about their identification, behavior, and habitats. Birding can combine scientific discovery, adventure, and athleticism. Most people know that birding involves watching birds, but there are many refinements to the simple act of raising a binocular.

Getting Started

Many people who watch birds begin at home by putting up a few bird feeders and watching the dozen or so (or in rural areas many more) species that come to visit. Some backyard birders also create habitat for birds by supplying native plants, roost and nest boxes, and water sources. It is useful to purchase a few books on birds and birding, such as field guides, books covering the status and distribution of local birds, and books on such specific subjects as bird feeding, behavior, and bird families.

Most birders find that they learn a great deal when they go out birding with others, whether on an organized group trip, such as with the local Audubon Society chapter or bird club, or just with a few friends. Groups of birders share their knowledge and provide different perspectives, which can help accelerate the learning process. Many local groups offer free or low-cost field trips or guided trips. Professional tour groups offer package birding excursions to all corners of the planet, from Arctic islands to Amazonian rain forests.

Binoculars and Scopes

Finding a good binocular is a crucial step toward becoming a proficient birder. Reliable binoculars sell for about $200, while the best cost more than $1,000. Many a birder has been stunned to look through a high-quality binocular and see the incredible clarity, color transmission, and image size that the finest glass provides: birds that seemed unidentifiable brown blobs suddenly appear as miniature works of art, with intricate and colorful patterns. To perceive the finest details of a bird's plumage—whether for the purposes of identification or aesthetic pleasure—a high-quality binocular is a necessity.

Most birders use a 7-, 8-, or 10-power binocular, which means that the bird appears seven to ten times larger than it does to the naked eye. The lower powers are easier to hold steady and provide a wider field of view, which makes it easier to locate a bird and stay with it. Binoculars also are labeled according to the size (in millimeters) of the objective lenses (the larger lenses at the end); a 7 x 42 binocular is thus a 7-power binocular with 42mm objective lenses. In general, objective lenses should measure in the 40–50mm range to provide optimal light for binoculars in the 7- to 10-power range.

In areas where birds may be more distant, such as marshes, beaches, and mudflats, many birders use spotting scopes mounted on tripods to get close-up views. Birding festivals, common in many states, can be good places to compare the different kinds of binoculars and spotting scopes.

It is important to field-test a binocular before purchasing it. A binocular should feel good to hold and to look through (both with and without eyeglasses) and should provide the ability to focus quickly on both flying and close-perched birds.

Logistics

A birding excursion can be a spontaneous junket to a nearby woodland, mudflat, or marsh or a carefully planned trip farther afield. In either case, it is important to take along a guide book and a good map of the area, and, as with any outdoor trip, to wear proper clothing for the weather and pack food and water, insect repellent, and an emergency first-aid kit. It is wise not to travel alone to more remote areas.

Time of year In most places, the greatest variety of birds is observed during periods of migration, when many species are on the move. Spring migration is best for seeing Neotropical migrants heading northward in their bright breeding plumages. Autumn migration provides opportunities for studying the more subtle plumages and for finding vagrants. Summer is the time for nesting birds. In winter, a challenging time for birding in many parts of North America, such boreal species as Rough-legged Hawks, Northern Shrikes, owls, and finches may appear well south of their usual haunts.

Time of day "The early bird gets the worm" is an adage that can apply equally well to "early birders." Many birds, especially passerines, are particularly active during the first few hours of daylight—probably because they are hungriest at this time of day (birds are often most conspicuous when they are foraging). Often there is another burst of foraging activity in late afternoon after the heat of the day has passed. Many species of birds, however, can be studied throughout the day; these include waterfowl, shorebirds, and many other nonpasserines.

Weather A rule of thumb for experienced birders is "Bad weather often brings 'good' birds." Birds are deeply affected by weather. For example, migratory birds rely on southerly winds to bring them north in spring and on northerly winds for their passage southward. When birds encounter winds that are contrary to their needs (such as a cold front in spring), they often stop migrating suddenly; during these times large numbers may descend into small areas to wait for more favorable weather, a phenomenon birders refer to as "fallout." Hurricanes are strong enough to drive pelagic birds as far inland as the Great Lakes. It is difficult to predict how bird movements will be affected by weather events, but increasingly scientists are using radar technology to monitor this, and a trove of information on the subject can now be found through the Internet.

Stealth To identify a bird, one must see it well. As a general rule, birds do not like rapid movements or loud noises and will flush or otherwise avoid them. In order to watch birds closely, it is necessary to keep talking and movements to a minimum. Successful birders avoid shuffling their feet in leaves or gravel and keep as quiet and still as possible. They dress in a way that minimizes their visibility to birds but maximizes comfort in bad weather or buggy environments, avoiding colorful or "noisy" clothing, such as squeaky shoes and ponchos. A portable, three-legged stool is handy in areas where it may be necessary to wait and listen for long periods, and a blind (a concealing enclosure) is helpful for close views in open areas. It is important to be stealthy when approaching birds; on a mudflat, beach, or other open expanse, a sidling or zigzagging, stop-and-start course works better than a direct route, as it allows the birds time to adjust to the presence of intruders. In aquatic environments, a small flat-bottomed boat, canoe, or kayak creates minimal disturbance, sometimes allowing for close views of shy species.

Competence and patience Identification of birds by sight and recognition of them by sound are only two components of what one might call birding "competence." Learning bird distribution by habitat and season, becoming familiar with nesting habits, working out how weather influences birds, and predicting where food resources will concentrate birds are all aspects of basic competence in birding.

Probably the single most important quality in any naturalist, though, is patience. Patient scanning of the sea, sky, or trees may be tedious, especially if few birds seem to be around, but to become a proficient birder, it is necessary to watch the environment carefully over relatively long periods of time, often several hours. The perceptive and patient birder can be privileged to witness phenomena that no one else has seen or described before.

Ducks

Ducks are placed with geese and swans in the family Anatidae, the waterfowl. They are medium-sized birds with stocky bodies, webbed feet, usually short tails, and often flat bills. Most show pronounced sexual dimorphism in plumage for most of the year, with males more strikingly colored and patterned. (Males of most species molt for a brief time after mating into a duller "eclipse plumage.")

All ducks live in or near aquatic habitats, where they forage for aquatic vegetation, fish, insect larvae, and crustaceans. A few species also venture into cultivated lands to eat grain.

Tree ducks—here represented by the whistling-ducks and Wood and Muscovy Ducks—often roost or nest in trees. They feed by picking food from the water's surface or by submerging their heads. Whistling-ducks feed mostly at night, Wood and Muscovy Ducks by day.

Dabbling ducks *(Anas),* like tree ducks, rarely dive for food; they feed either by "dabbling" with the bill to pick items from the water's surface or by "tipping up"—reaching below the surface, tail in the air. Some use their bills to strain water and mud or to strip seeds from vegetation.

Diving ducks form a diverse group that includes the bay ducks, sea ducks, mergansers, and stiff-tailed ducks. All forage by diving underwater, sometimes to considerable depths. They swim with wings closed, propelled by their feet, which are set farther back on the body than in dabbling ducks. Bay ducks *(Aythya),* also called pochards, forage in open waters. Male bay ducks may be recognized by their striking glossy red, purple, or green heads. Sea ducks include Long-tailed and Harlequin Ducks, scoters, and eiders, which feed around rocky shores on shellfish, and the goldeneyes and Bufflehead, which are more widely distributed inland in winter. Mergansers have a long, narrow bill, with sawlike serrations for grasping slippery prey. Stiff-tailed ducks are represented in North America by Ruddy and Masked Ducks, both small, stocky species with tails that are often cocked upward.

Most ducks nest in remote northern lakes and marshes and migrate southward for the winter; they are highly gregarious, sometimes forming winter flocks in the thousands. Courtship, usually occurring through winter and into spring, involves calling, exaggerated head movements, and flight displays by males or by both sexes.

Despite continuing work by conservation groups, most ducks are in decline in North America, with the exception of Green-winged Teal and Gadwall.

Adult Black-bellied Whistling-Duck, showing the distinctive gooselike neck typical of whistling-ducks.

Mallards and other dabbling ducks "tip up" to forage below the water's surface.

Diving ducks, such as this Bufflehead, are strong divers and underwater swimmers.

Geese and Swans

Snow Goose has both dark and light morphs; the dark morph is often called "Blue Goose."

Geese (*Chen, Anser,* and *Branta*) and swans (*Cygnus*) are also members of the family Anatidae, the waterfowl. Like ducks, geese and swans have stocky bodies, webbed feet, and usually short tails. They differ in their bills, which tend to be deeper at the base, and in their size: most geese are larger than ducks, and swans are enormous—up to 5' (1.5m) long, with a nearly 7' (2.1m) wingspan. Unlike ducks, geese and swans are usually not sexually dimorphic in plumage, although many species show marked differences in size and voice between the sexes. Snow and Ross's Geese are unique among the world's geese in showing plumage polymorphism: both have a light morph, a dark morph, and several intermediate plumages.

Swans and geese eat aquatic vegetation, and most geese also graze on land on short grasses and grains. Like dabbling ducks, they don't dive while foraging, but their long necks enable them to reach deeper underwater when dabbling or tipping up.

Most swans and geese nest on tundra or remote western lakes and marshes; introduced populations of Canada Goose also nest in urban areas. Courtship displays in swans and geese are minor or absent, as pairs usually mate for life. In autumn most northern-nesting geese and swans migrate southward to gather in huge flocks at traditional wintering grounds, often on agricultural lands.

Dozens of nonnative waterfowl species are kept in zoos and private collections; of these, many have escaped captivity, although few have become established as nesting birds in North America. (One exception is Mute Swan, introduced to North America from Europe.) These escapees from captivity can make it difficult to discern patterns of occurrence of rare Eurasian species, such as Whooper Swan, Falcated Duck, and Baikal Teal.

Adult Emperor Goose. Populations of this species appear to be declining in Alaska and Siberia.

Swans and geese, like ducks, have long been hunted as game birds, and their populations declined in the twentieth century because of overharvesting as well as habitat loss. Hunters joined forces with conservationists to reverse these trends, and wildlife refuges and new management practices now protect waterfowl and their habitats. As a result, most North American geese and swans now have stable or increasing populations.

Black-bellied Whistling-Duck

Dendrocygna autumnalis
L 21"/53cm   WS 30"/76cm

A common, increasing resident of the Gulf coast states, Black-bellied Whistling-Duck inhabits freshwater marshes, swamps, and ponds. It nests mostly in tree cavities near the water. Vagrant flocks are sometimes found far north of the species' normal range. White-faced and West Indian Whistling-Ducks, Neotropical species rarely reported, are probably escapees. **VOICE** An accelerating, wheezy whistling, usually consisting of 4 notes in rapid succession; often delivered in flight.

adult

red bill

chestnut breast and back

black belly

white in wings diagnostic in all plumages

black underwings, white in upperwings

juveniles

gray bill

distinctive gooselike shape

lacks rich colors and patterned upperparts of Fulvous Whistling-Duck

Fulvous Whistling-Duck

Dendrocygna bicolor
L 19"/48cm   WS 26"/66cm

Fulvous Whistling-Duck is a local and declining species in Gulf coast states, mostly in warmer months, and a vagrant elsewhere. It is often seen in flocks. This species nests next to freshwater ponds, sometimes in tree cavities, and winters in freshwater marshes and ponds in Central America. It is seen less frequently in trees than is Black-bellied Whistling-Duck and dives for food more readily. Juveniles are plain like Black-bellied but lack white in the wings. **VOICE** Similar to Black-bellied but thinner.

adult

chestnut barring in dark back

caramel-colored head and body

adults

wings black above and below, in striking contrast to buffy underparts

(white tail base visible from above)

Wood Duck

Aix sponsa
L 18½"/47cm   **WS** 30"/76cm

Wood Duck is common and widespread in wooded swamps in the East but more local in the West. It nests in tree cavities and in artificial duck boxes, often over water. In winter it is found on ponds and swamps throughout the Southeast, mostly near the coast in the West. This species eats seeds and nuts, especially acorns and hickory nuts. **VOICE** Male: when flushed a thin, upwardly inflected *jweeeeep*. Female: a loud, crescendo *oooWEEK!* Also gives quacking and piping whistles.

adult male

crest, intricate head pattern

(in flight; note long tail, downward-pointed bill)

eclipse male

retains faint head pattern

adult female

white eye patch

compare female *Anas* ducks

white-stippled flanks

Muscovy Duck

Cairina moschata
L 28"/71cm   **WS** 43"/1.1m

This large Neotropical species is a rare permanent resident in southern Texas, most often seen near Falcon Dam (on the Rio Grande). It nests in tree cavities and nest boxes over bodies of fresh water. Domestic varieties are widespread, and small populations of feral birds, which are partly or mostly white, occur in many states. Muscovy Duck eats plant matter, fish, termites, and many aquatic invertebrates. Its flight is ponderous and steady, like that of a large goose. **VOICE** Not often heard; quiet quacks and grunts.

adult male

glossy black with brilliant white wing coverts

subadult male

browner than adult male (female and juvenile also browner)

domestic birds show varied piebald patterns

Mallard
Anas platyrhynchos
L 23"/58cm   WS 35"/89cm

Mallard is a common nester from coastal Arctic tundra south through wetlands of much of the lower 48 states and is also found in suburban and urban settings, where feral birds abound. It winters in diverse habitats, from marshes and lakes to city ponds, chiefly in the lower 48. Hybrids with other *Anas* ducks are common, complicating identification of some individuals. The subspecies *diazi,* called Mexican Duck, is resident in New Mexico, Arizona, and western Texas. Mexican Ducks and Mallards interbreed, producing intergrades. **VOICE** Familiar quacking, most often from female; female also gives descending series of raspy, "laughing" quacks.

adult male

iridescent green head, white collar

yellow bill; rich brown breast

(extremely large individuals often seen in parks are descendants of domestic birds)

adult female

irregular dark markings on orange bill

more contrasting plumage than female Mottled and American Black Ducks

white outer rectrices

adult male

white borders on blue speculum visible in flight (compare American Black Duck)

eclipse male

molting and eclipse males similar to female but with yellow or olive bill

Mexican Duck (*diazi*)

darker crown and eye line and duskier face than Mottled

(dark tail and undertail like Mottled, unlike nominate Mallard)

male and female similar, but female has more olive and orange tones in bill

American Black Duck

Anas rubripes
L 23"/58cm   WS 35"/89cm

This very dark duck is common in eastern wetlands, although it declined severely in the second half of the 20th century. It nests in saltwater and freshwater marshes and on lakes and ponds, often near wooded areas, and winters in the southeastern and south-central U.S. in many habitats, from wooded swamps and riparian marshes to salt marshes and bays. Hybrids with Mallard are relatively frequent, a situation of some concern to conservationists. **VOICE** Quacking similar to Mallard but usually shorter and raspier.

adult male
dark yellowish bill
lightly streaked throat without buffy tones (compare Mottled Duck)

adult female
feathers of upperparts lack pale edges
darker, colder color than Mottled Duck or Mallard
female and juvenile have dusky bill with olive tones

lacks white borders on violet speculum (compare Mottled Duck and Mallard)
adult female

brilliant white underwing coverts similar to Mallard and Mottled Duck, but with greater contrast to body
adult male

Mottled Duck

Anas fulvigula
L 22"/56cm   WS 30"/76cm

Mottled Duck replaces American Black Duck in Florida and the western Gulf coast. This species inhabits mostly coastal marshes and ponds but is increasingly found inland. An introduced population in South Carolina hybridizes with Mallard. **VOICE** Familiar quacking similar to Mallard.

adults
buffy head, unstreaked throat (compare American Black Duck)
rich brown edges to covert and body feathers
dark spot near bill in lower face
(bluish speculum lacks white borders)
no white in tail (compare Mallard)

Blue-winged Teal
Anas discors
L 15½"/39cm **WS** 23"/58cm

This small duck occurs in many habitats south of the tundra; it nests on shallow lakes in prairies, farmland, and grasslands, and winters on lakes, rice fields, and other wetlands. Like other teal, Blue-winged feeds mostly on seeds of aquatic vegetation. Females and eclipse males are similar to Cinnamon Teal. **VOICE** Varied: a piping *keep,* like Long-billed Dowitcher (from female); a weak single quack, sometimes in descending, "snickering" series (mostly from female); scratchy yelps; froglike barks; a shoveler-like *thk.*

adult male

male always dark-eyed (compare Cinnamon Teal)

white facial crescent and flank patch

powder blue wing patch similar to Cinnamon

adult female

broken eye ring

adult male

more contrasting head pattern than female Cinnamon

flanks and coverts more crisply patterned than in Cinnamon

Cinnamon Teal
Anas cyanoptera
L 16"/49cm **WS** 22"/56cm

Cinnamon Teal is a strikingly plumaged western species seldom seen east of the Mississippi River. This species nests in freshwater marshes and on lakes at many elevations, usually west of the prairie-parkland habitats of most dabbling ducks. It winters in southern Texas and California, mostly in coastal freshwater habitats, and in Mexico. Hybrids with Blue-winged Teal are often reported. **VOICE** Male: a grating, mechanical-sounding rattle and a shoveler-like *chuk.* Female: a weak quack similar to Blue-winged.

adult male

vivid rust plumage

male always red-eyed (compare Blue-winged Teal)

adult male

white underwings similar to Blue-winged

adult female

plainer face and longer, more shoveler-like bill than female Blue-winged

richer brown overall than Blue-winged; flanks have indistinct or no pattern

Northern Shoveler

Anas clypeata
L 19"/48cm WS 30"/76cm

This distinctive duck breeds mostly in the Interior West, nesting on well-vegetated, shallow freshwater lakes with muddy edges. It winters in freshwater and some brackish habitats in the southern and coastal U.S. and Mexico. To eat, it sifts mud and water with its wide bill, straining out tiny invertebrates and plant matter. Northern Shoveler is the most territorial of all North American dabblers. **VOICE** Male: a nasal *thk* or *thk-thk,* like the sound made by an air pump. Female: a gabbling quack, often doubled; rougher and deeper than other teal.

adult male

green head, white breast, rusty sides

spatulate bill distinctive in all plumages

adult female

similar to female Cinnamon Teal, but with larger bill, more contrasting plumage

large head and bill easily seen on flying birds

blue forewing patch

adult males

Garganey

Anas querquedula
L 15½"/39cm WS 24"/61cm

This Eurasian teal is a vagrant to freshwater marshes and lakes of North America. Because the male holds its breeding plumage only briefly, the species is not commonly kept in captivity, and so most reports likely represent wild strays. From July through late winter, males resemble females but show more pronounced facial markings: a dark eye line and a dark line below the eye. **VOICE** Most calls similar to Cinnamon and Blue-winged Teal, including shoveler-like calls. Male gives an odd rattle.

adult male

white supercilium

(silvery blue-gray upperwing coverts, seen in flight)

purple tones in cheek

long scapulars

sharp break between white belly and dark breast

adult female

dark eye patch and eye line; diffuse dusky patch in cheek

Gadwall

Anas strepera
L 20"/51cm **WS** 33"/84cm

Gadwall is a wigeon-sized duck that nests in freshwater marshes and on lakes and impoundments, mostly in open country, and winters in similar habitats in the southern U.S. and Mexico. Gadwall's range has expanded to include the Atlantic coast and the northwestern U.S. An agile aerialist, it flies swiftly in tight flocks. Courting males perform complex displays, including aerial chases. **VOICE** Several common calls: a Mallard-like quack (female); a sweet, squeaky piping; a flat, nasal *map* (male).

adult male

pale, rusty-edged scapulars

gray tertials

white inner secondaries (prominent in flight)

black tail coverts

adult female

plumage more strikingly patterned than female Mallard

dark bill with narrow orange sides

contrasting white belly patch

Green-winged Teal

Anas crecca
L 14"/36cm **WS** 23"/58cm

The abundant Green-winged Teal nests chiefly on freshwater ponds and lakes from tundra to prairies; in winter it forms flocks in varied saltwater, brackish, and freshwater habitats. A Eurasian subspecies *(crecca),* sometimes called Common Teal, visits Bering Sea islands; it is very rare elsewhere in North America, found mostly on the coasts with American Green-wingeds *(carolinensis).* **VOICE** Male: a high, thin peeping call (usually from feeding flocks). Female: weak, descending series of quacks in a burry "whiskey voice."

adult male, American

dark rufous and "teal" green head

white bar on side of breast

lacks breast bar

white scapular stripe

adult male, Eurasian

adult female

dark head and throat

(both sexes show green speculum with pale borders in flight)

creamy stripe near tail in all plumages

American Wigeon

Anas americana
L 20"/51cm   WS 32"/81cm

The widespread American Wigeon nests near small lakes and marshes in open and semiopen habitats. In winter it is found on freshwater lakes, brackish estuaries, and saltwater bays with aquatic vegetation. Wigeons often feed around swans and diving ducks, stealing plants those species bring to the surface. Pale greater upperwing coverts are visible on females in flight (lacking in female Eurasian Wigeon). **VOICE** Male: a wheezy, piping, 2–3 syllable whistle. Female: a low, growling *grrrrr;* also a quack.

adult male

iridescent green eye patch

cream forecrown

adult female

adult male and female

white axillaries (compare Eurasian)

black border at bill base on female and juvenile (compare Eurasian Wigeon)

Eurasian Wigeon

Anas penelope
L 20"/51cm   WS 32"/81cm

Small numbers of this Old World species are seen among flocks of American Wigeons, regularly near the coasts and more rarely inland, mostly in the cooler months. The adult male in eclipse plumage is rufous on the head, breast, and sides (unlike Cinnamon Teal). Hybrids with American Wigeon are often reported. **VOICE** Male: a wheezy single *whew* or *wichoo,* more strident than American Wigeon. Female: similar to American but more mechanical and grating.

adult male

gray back noticeable in wigeon flocks

rich orange-red head, yellowish forehead

duskier under-wings than American

adult female, rufous morph

head more rufous than American

adult males

lacks black border at bill base (compare American Wigeon)

(gray morph like American, but more uniform breast and throat)

Northern Pintail

Anas acuta
L 21"/53cm (female); 25"/64cm (male)
WS 34"/86cm

Northern Pintail is a stunning dabbling duck that is declining in numbers. It breeds from the tundra southward, largely in Alaska, Canada, and the Great Plains, nesting in open country around rivers, marshes, and lakes. Like other dabbling ducks, pintails court with vigorous gesturing of the head and erratic paired flights, the male uttering a repeated "burp whistle." Pintails winter in a variety of inland and coastal wetlands, from river margins to marshes and swamps to estuaries. Flocks of flying birds often form lines (smaller dabbling ducks usually fly in irregular formations). This species is relatively shy and wary, feeding mostly in the evening and at night. Northern Pintails nest quite early in spring, some even before ice has broken on rivers and lakes. **VOICE** Male: a tremulous, tooting whistle, often doubled. Female: nasal quacking, higher and softer than Mallard.

adult male

long, elegant, distinctively patterned neck

very long tail

adult female

unmarked, uniformly colored head

gray bill

marbled plumage

long tail

pale belly (contrasts with darker underwings in flight)

adult female

long tail and neck in flight (like whistling-ducks)

broad pale edge to secondaries

White-cheeked Pintail

Anas bahamensis
L 17"/43cm   **WS** 26"/66cm

White-cheeked Pintail is a tropical American duck that strays rarely to the Southeast, where it is seen most frequently in Florida. Some North American sightings are probably of birds that have escaped from collections. Over its Caribbean range this species frequents mangrove swamps, brackish and saltwater lagoons, and freshwater marshes and ponds. It feeds on plant matter, especially seeds and algae. **VOICE** Male: a low piping. Female: a weak, short *kwek* or *kek*.

adult

white cheek, pale tail, and red in bill distinctive

Canvasback
Aythya valisineria
L 21"/53cm   WS 29"/74cm

The largest North American bay duck, Canvasback is declining but still relatively common. This species breeds from the lower tundra of Canada into the prairie marshes of the northern Great Plains; it winters mostly on coasts and in the southern U.S. on lakes, bays, rivers, and lagoons, often in large flocks and sometimes with other bay ducks. **VOICE** Male: usually silent; in display a gargling gobble with occasional peeping. Female: a burry, braying call, repeated.

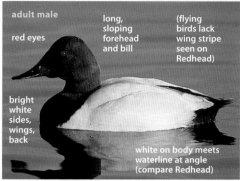

Redhead
Aythya americana
L 19"/48cm   WS 29"/74cm

Redhead breeds in open country from Alaska and central Canada into the northern Great Plains, Great Basin, and similar settings, and winters mostly on brackish tidal water and freshwater rivers and lakes. Like several other duck species, Redhead can be a brood parasite, laying its eggs in the nests of other Redheads or other species, even those of gulls, coots, or rails. **VOICE** Male: in display a cheerful *rrrruuuurrrr*, rising then falling in pitch. Female: a quiet, guttural grunt.

Ring-necked Duck
Aythya collaris
L 17"/43cm WS 25"/64cm

Ring-necked Duck breeds mostly in the boreal forest belt, where it nests near freshwater ponds in open country and forests. It winters in diverse freshwater situations, including marshes, lakes, and borrow pits. In flight, both sexes show a weak gray wing stripe (unlike scaup or Tufted Duck). The maroon ring around the male's neck can be seen only under optimal conditions. **VOICE** Male: in display a rapid series of syncopated piping, sounding like Morse code. Female: a rapid series of strident, modulated quacks.

adult male
distinctive bill pattern
strongly peaked rear crown
white bar on side of breast

adult female
strong white eye ring
unique head shape, like male
white band on bill

Tufted Duck
Aythya fuligula
L 17"/43cm WS 25"/64cm

A visitor from Eurasia, mostly to northern coastal areas in winter, Tufted Duck is found on freshwater lakes and on bays and other saltwater bodies. Young and eclipse males show shorter tufts, as do hybrids, which can complicate identification of some individuals. In flight, both sexes show extensive white in the remiges, like Greater Scaup. **VOICE** Male: in display a nervous, erratic, high-pitched bubbly piping and a *wheeoo* call. Female: a short, grating *quer!* and various raucous or growling quacks.

adult male
clean white flanks (grayer in first-winter male)
long tuft
dark back

adult female
short tuft
dark back (compare grayer back of female scaup)
broader black tip to bill than on scaup
(most show much less white at bill base)

Greater Scaup

Aythya marila
L 18"/46cm   WS 28"/71cm

Greater Scaup nests mostly alongside ponds and lakes in tundra and taiga, and winters on coasts, usually on salt water, where Lesser Scaup is often less common. Head shape differences in scaup are best studied when birds are relaxed or asleep, not feeding. Though Greater is closely related to Lesser Scaup, hybrids are unknown—perhaps because the two species are so similar. **VOICE** Male: in display an exuberant *whup-WHOOP-DEE-DOO!* Female: a guttural, grating, ravenlike growl, along with clucking noises.

adult male
broad-tipped bill
rounded head

adult female
rounded head

brighter white on inner primaries than Lesser

large bill; extensive white on face

Lesser Scaup

Aythya affinis
L 17"/43cm   WS 26"/66cm

Lesser Scaup breeds farther south than Greater Scaup, from tundra into the prairies and Great Plains. It winters largely in freshwater environments and is found inland in larger numbers than Greater. If lakes freeze in winter, large numbers may move to seacoasts. Unlike other bay ducks, scaup eat mostly invertebrates rather than plants. **VOICE** Male: in display a bizarre chorus of irregular gulping, gagging, bouncing, and clucking sounds. Female: mostly a short, harsh, repeated *argh argh.*

adult male
peaked rear crown on resting birds
narrower bill than Greater

adult female
peaked rear crown
smaller bill, less white on face than Greater

white on inner primaries less intense than on Greater

Common Eider

Somateria mollissima
L 25"/64cm   WS 39"/99cm

Common Eider breeds on rocky coasts and Arctic tundra shores and winters along seacoasts. It is fairly common on the Atlantic coast south to New York, rarer southward; in the West it is very rare south of Alaska. Four North American subspecies differ mostly in bill color, shape, and females' plumage tones. In the eastern subspecies *dresseri*, males resemble Hudson Bay *sedentaria* in having greenish yellow bills; females have more rufous tones. In the 2 Arctic taxa, *borealis* and *v-nigrum*, females are plain brown and males have vivid yellow or orange bills. **VOICE** Male: a gentle, somewhat gurgly cooing, rising and falling in inflection. Female: low, guttural *ko-ko-ko-ko-ko* calls.

adult male, Hudson Bay *(sedentaria)*

"long-nosed" appearance distinctive in all plumages

white back (unlike King Eider) visible from a long distance

white breast (unlike Spectacled Eider)

adult female, Hudson Bay *(sedentaria)*

facial feathering extends to nostrils (compare female King)

evenly barred flanks

adult female, eastern *(dresseri)*

more richly colored than any other female or young male eider

plumage has rich rufous tones

1st winter male

like female but more uniformly colored, bill more olive-yellow

(breast turns white in first winter)

transitional male

molting birds highly variable; seen in summer

bill shape best identifying mark

adult male

white back (black on King Eider) and breast contrast with dark belly and tail

King Eider

Somateria spectabilis
L 22"/56cm WS 35"/89cm

The striking King Eider is abundant in northern parts of its range but scarce south of Alaska and Canada. It breeds on inland and coastal tundra of the High Arctic and winters along far-northern seacoasts, south of heavy sea ice. Most observed well south of typical range are females or young males. **VOICE** Male: in display a low, crooning, dovelike call; in flight frequently a low croaking. Female: low, guttural *ko-ko-ko-ko-ko* calls similar to female Common and Spectacled Eiders.

adult male | orange and red "royal crown" unmistakable | black back (white on Common Eider)

pearly blue crown and nape, pale green cheek

orange on maxilla in first winter diagnostic

adult female | upturned gape creates "smiling" expression

1st winter male

facial feathering does not reach nostrils (compare Common Eider)

V-shaped crescents on flanks

Spectacled Eider

Somateria fischeri
L 21"/53cm WS 33"/84cm

Local and declining in Alaska, Spectacled Eider breeds in coastal tundra and winters in the Bering Sea in polynyas, small areas of open water in sea ice. **VOICE** Male: in display a low, cooing *r-Rooo.* Female: low, guttural *ko-ko-ko-ko-ko* calls.

adult male and female | male black-breasted, unlike other eiders

"spectacles" of both sexes distinctive in all plumages

Steller's Eider

Polysticta stelleri
L 17"/43cm WS 27"/69cm

Relatively rare and declining in Alaska, Steller's Eider nests near pools in coastal tundra, often far inland, and winters along seacoasts, especially near river mouths. **VOICE** Male: growls and a soft croon. Female: growling, guttural calls.

adult female and male | male's eye patch and green tuft on nape unique

female identified by bill and head shape, eye ring, blue speculum

White-winged Scoter
Melanitta fusca
L 21"/53cm   WS 34"/86cm

This large duck (close to the size of Common Eider) breeds on freshwater ponds and lakes in the far-northern boreal forest belt and tundra of western Canada and Alaska, and winters on coasts; a few transients are found inland (many on the Great Lakes). Its size and white secondaries distinguish it from smaller dark-winged scoters and from female eiders. **VOICE** Not often heard; calls include a trebled quack, a squeaky clucking, a thin whistle, and a bell-like cry (from courting male).

adult male | white eye crescent | distinctive bill shape | white secondaries

culmen structure of adult male unlike any other duck

adult female

larger than Black and Surf Scoters | white in wing often visible at rest

Black Scoter
Melanitta nigra
L 19"/48cm   WS 28"/71cm

The widespread Black Scoter nests near small lakes in boreal areas and winters mostly on bays and open ocean, especially near rocky coasts. It often forms aggregations of hundreds or thousands, in which the sounds of calling birds and whistling wingbeats are tremendous. **VOICE** Male: most often irregular piping and a sad-sounding, down-slurred *peeeeer,* reminiscent of Dusky-capped Flycatcher. Female: a nasal, burry *ggrrraaa,* sounding like a door with rusty hinges.

plumage entirely black

orange "knob" at bill base

adult male

1st winter male

like female but with orange on maxilla

adult female

pale cheek and neck contrast with dark crown, nape, breast

compare Surf Scoter, Redhead, Ruddy Duck

Surf Scoter
Melanitta perspicillata
L 20"/51cm   **WS** 29"/74cm

The unique bill of the male Surf Scoter makes it one of North America's most impressive drakes. It is a common breeder in far-northern corners of the continent and is often seen in very large wintering flocks on ocean coasts, where it feeds heavily on shellfish. The wings of adult male scoters make a pleasant whistling sound in flight. This species seldom flies in lines as other scoters do. **VOICE** Male: a short, gargling note. Female: a hoarse, grating croak, sometimes doubled.

adult male

black and white "skunk" pattern on head; white eyes

distinctive black, white, orange, and red bill

1st winter male

faint markings on bill and head

distinctive deep bill base similar to male; feathering along culmen

distinct dark cap with white patches in face unique

adult female

Harlequin Duck
Histrionicus histrionicus
L 16"/41cm   **WS** 26"/66cm

With its intricate pattern of cinnamon and cobalt blue, the adult male Harlequin Duck is a "must-see" of North American birding. This species breeds along fast-flowing rivers in northeastern Canada and the Pacific Northwest and in mountainous areas of the West; it winters around rocky areas and headlands on ocean coasts, rarely inland. Despite their striking plumage, males blend well with their rocky, whitewater habitats. **VOICE** Male: a creaky, whistled *pwee!* Female: a quacking, staccato chatter.

adult male

black-bordered white stripes on head and breast

white spot at ear

long, pointed tail

male appears dark at a distance

adult female

round white spot behind ear distinctive

small bill, bulbous head, thick neck (compare scaup, scoters)

Common Goldeneye
Bucephala clangula
L 19"/48cm   **WS** 26"/66cm

Like most North American diving ducks, Common Goldeneye breeds chiefly in Canada and Alaska in the boreal forest belt, nesting in tree cavities near freshwater lakes and streams. It winters in saltwater and freshwater habitats. Hybrids with Barrow's Goldeneye are often reported. Young male Commons can show a facial crescent like Barrow's. **VOICE** Male: a nasal, burry *zip-HERE!*, given mostly in display with head thrust over back. Female: an annoyed-sounding, croaking quack, often given in flight.

adult male

green head with circular spot at bill base

shows more white above than Barrow's Goldeneye

adult female

distinguished from female Barrow's by more sloping forehead and larger bill, with little or no yellow (yellow mostly near tip of maxilla)

Barrow's Goldeneye
Bucephala islandica
L 18"/46cm   **WS** 28"/71cm

Barrow's Goldeneye has been recorded in much of North America but is numerous only in the Pacific Northwest, western Canada, and Alaska. This species nests in tree cavities near water, sometimes at high elevations in the Rocky Mountains, and winters mostly along northern ocean coasts. There are few confirmed records away from typical range. In flight, both sexes show less white in the upperwings than Common Goldeneye. **VOICE** Male: a 2-part croaking. Female: a croaking quack similar to Common.

adult male

purplish head, with white crescent at bill base

dark plumage extends down side of breast (unlike Common)

unique head shape: flat crown, steep forehead; bulging lower nape

adult female

dome-shaped head similar to male; richer brown than female Common

mostly yellow bill shorter than Common (rare female Commons show nearly as much yellow in bill in winter)

Long-tailed Duck

Clangula hyemalis
L 16"/41cm; male to 21"/53cm with tail
WS 28"/71cm

One of North America's most charismatic waterfowl species, Long-tailed Duck (formerly known as Oldsquaw) is elegant in plumage, structure, and vocalizations alike. It breeds in the northernmost Canadian and Alaskan tundra, usually near small ponds or streams, and winters in flocks on northern ocean coasts and the Great Lakes. A series of molts results in a variety of plumages in both sexes. This species can dive to depths of 200' (60m) in pursuit of shellfish. **VOICE** Male: a yodeled *ow-A-LOU-ET!* call, one of the most memorable sounds of the Far North; this call is also often heard from flocks on calm days in winter. Female: a short, husky quacking call, often repeated.

adult male, spring

pink on maxilla (adult males only)

white face, black head and breast

brown back, rusty-edged scapulars

adult male, winter

white head, tan face, brown neck patch

(brown lower breast)

white body and scapulars, dark wings

adult female, summer

white eye patch

(white under tail and on flanks)

juvenile

gray-brown back, crown, and lower cheek patch

similar to winter female but paler

adult male and adult female, winter

female has brown crown and lower cheek patch on white face

flying flock resembles alcid flock

dark underwings in both sexes

Common Merganser
Mergus merganser
L 25"/64cm **WS** 34"/86cm

Common Merganser is a locally common, very large duck that breeds chiefly near woodland rivers and lakes in Canada, southern Alaska, and the Northwest. It winters on freshwater lakes and large rivers, rarely on salt water. In some males the plumage below has a pale pink cast in optimal light. **VOICE** Male: in display chaotic, gabbling, guttural clucking sounds in chorus. Female: a low, harsh, grunting quack similar to goldeneye females, given especially in flight.

adult male

narrow red bill

green head

brilliant white below

adult female

rufous head with neat crest

crisp division between gray breast and rufous head

white chin sharply defined

Red-breasted Merganser
Mergus serrator
L 23"/58cm **WS** 30"/76cm

A common, medium-sized merganser, Red-breasted breeds almost entirely in northern Canada and Alaska, nesting next to lakes and rivers in the boreal forest and tundra. The species winters on the Great Lakes and on open salt water along ocean coasts and the Gulf of Mexico, where flocks often forage by "herding" fish into shallows. The exaggerated postures of courting males can be seen in late winter, before migration. **VOICE** Very rapid quacking; displaying male gives a strange, mechanical-sounding "sneeze."

adult male

shaggy crest

rusty breast

extensive white in wings

males (top two) dark-breasted

adult female

brownish head with shaggy crest

white on throat not sharply defined (compare Common Merganser)

Hooded Merganser
Lophodytes cucullatus
L 18"/46cm **WS** 24"/61cm

Hooded Merganser breeds farther south than the larger mergansers, nesting in tree cavities in woodland areas, usually near water. It winters in wooded swamps, on freshwater marshes and lakes, and on brackish rivers and estuaries, even in urban settings. Males raise and lower the crest both in courtship and during conflicts. **VOICE** Male: in display a loud, descending, snoring *AHH-WAAAAAAARRR* (sounding like a leopard frog), ending with a popping *PUK!* Female: a short, burry *burrp!*

adult male
(flying birds look very slender)
black-bordered fanlike crest (here raised)
rufous sides
2 black bars at side of breast

adult female
brown crest
narrow bill
gray body
(flies with rapid, shallow wingbeats, showing black and white pattern in secondaries)

Bufflehead
Bucephala albeola
L 14"/36cm **WS** 21"/53cm

This diminutive relative of goldeneyes breeds mostly near fresh water in cavities excavated by Northern Flickers. It winters on freshwater lakes and rivers and sheltered saltwater bays. Bufflehead is named for its disproportionately large head; "Buffalo-head" and "Butterball" are local names. These ducks eat a wide variety of insects, crustaceans, and plant matter. **VOICE** Male: in display an excited, hoarse, irregular whooping. Female: a short *grrr*, often given in flight in the nesting season.

adult male
large white patch on rear of head
black back and white sides distinctive
smaller than mergansers, with less ornate plumage
appears tiny and black and white in flight
adult female/ 1st winter male
small and dark, with oblong white cheek patch
(eclipse male similar)

Ruddy Duck

Oxyura jamaicensis
L 15"/38cm   **WS** 18"/46cm

A common bird of western prairies and plains, Ruddy Duck nests on freshwater lakes with vegetated edges, making a nest of floating vegetation. It winters, often in large flocks, on lakes and rivers and sometimes estuaries and brackish or saltwater bays. Unlike other diving ducks, Ruddies often arrive on the nesting grounds unpaired. **VOICE** Male: in display a comical, mechanical-sounding series of accelerating, staccato popping noises, ending in a squirrel-like *bweh*. Female: a short, nasal *yahhn*.

adult male

stiff tail often raised

shiny chestnut body

blue bill

male retains white cheek in winter (compare Black Scoter)

adult female

single dark cheek stripe

Masked Duck

Nomonyx dominicus
L 14"/36cm   **WS** 17"/43cm

This rare and irregular visitor to southeastern Texas and Florida is very difficult to spot: it hides among water lilies and other vegetation, in ponds that are heavily overgrown with aquatic vegetation or in rice fields. Exceptional vagrants have occurred far north of this species' normal tropical American range. Displaying males inflate the neck like a balloon, then bounce the bill while calling. **VOICE** Not often heard; low popping sounds and high piping calls, sounding like foraging baby chickens.

adult male

black face

blue bill with dark tip

long, stiff tail

adult female

double-striped face

plumage richly marbled with rufous

Brant
Branta bernicla
L 25"/64cm **WS** 42"/1.1cm

Brant is an attractive small goose that is local in its distribution on coasts and rather uncommon inland during migration. It breeds in High Arctic tundra and winters in bays and salt marshes. Two subspecies breed in North America: the lighter-bellied *hrota* (American Brant), which winters in the East, and the darker-bellied *nigricans* (Black Brant), which winters in the West. Both subspecies have been recorded as vagrants in the continent's interior and on the "opposite" coasts from their normal range, almost always in Brant flocks. A Eurasian subspecies, *bernicla* (Dark-bellied Brant), has been recorded a few times in the East; adults differ from Black Brant in having smoky gray upperparts and belly, with very little white in the flanks. Identification of a stray or unusual-looking Brant is complicated by the presence of a population that nests in Canada's Parry Islands and winters in Puget Sound, Washington; this population, called "Gray-bellied Brant," is not yet recognized as a subspecies and appears to be intermediate between American and Black Brant in most respects. **VOICE** A rolling *crrok;* also a guttural, gravelly gabbling, often given by flocks in flight.

adult, American Brant *(hrota)*

black "stocking" on neck and breast contrasts with brown body

adult, Black Brant *(nigricans)*

white neck crescents connect across throat (unlike eastern birds)

blackish brown lower breast and belly contrast with white flanks

juvenile, American Brant *(hrota)*

lacks neck crescents

pale sides more uniform than adult

immature, Black Brant *(nigricans)*

like adult but coverts show neat pale tips

(most juveniles have uniformly sooty sides; often lack neck crescents)

flocks often lack classic V formation of other goose species

Canada Goose

Branta canadensis
L 30–48"/76–122cm
WS 50–61"/1.3–1.5m

Canada Goose is a common breeder
from the interior of Canada and Alaska
south through most of the U.S., nesting
near wetlands of many sorts, even in
urban settings. It winters on farmland,
in wetlands, and on golf courses.
Nonmigratory populations in suburban
areas are introduced. In large flocks,
aberrant individuals with white flecking
are often seen. **VOICE** A familiar yelping
honk, delivered singly or in accented
pairs; hissing at nest.

Cackling Goose

Branta hutchinsii
L 22–30"/56–76cm
WS 42–50"/1.1–1.3m

In 2004 ornithologists "split" the four
smallest subspecies of Canada Goose
into a separate species, Cackling Goose.
This species breeds in tundra and winters
on farmland and in wetlands. Most
subspecies are readily recognized by their
small stature and small bill compared to
Canada Goose; there is some uncertainty
about how to separate the smallest
Canada Goose subspecies (*B. c. parvipes*)
from *taverneri* Cackling Goose. **VOICE**
Similar to Canada Goose but higher-
pitched.

Greater White-fronted Goose

Anser albifrons
L 28"/71cm   **WS** 53"/1.3m

This goose is common in much of the West. It breeds in Arctic tundra and muskeg and winters in open plains and estuaries. The Greenland subspecies *flavirostris*, rare in the East, shows an orange-yellow rather than pinkish orange bill. Mated pairs often migrate northward with young of the previous one or two years. **VOICE** Squeaky, high-pitched, descending honking with "laughing" quality.

adult

white feathering around bill (acquired in first winter)

barred and speckled belly

orange feet and legs

immature

paler than dark-morph Snow Goose, without "grin patch"

little or no white feathering around bill

dark tail (unlike Snow Goose)

(Bean and Pink-footed Geese, Eurasian vagrants, have mostly dark bills)

pinkish orange bill in American subspecies (orange-yellow in Greenland subspecies)

Barnacle Goose

Branta leucopsis
L 27"/69cm   **WS** 50"/1.3m

This very rare visitor from Greenland and Europe is usually seen in company with Canada Goose. Barnacle Goose nests on cliffs in the Arctic, and most make transoceanic flights to western Europe in winter. Some seen in North America are escapees from captivity, but many are probably from Greenland, where populations are increasing. Apparent hybrids with Cackling or Canada Goose have been reported. **VOICE** A high-pitched, short, squeaky yelp; higher and shorter than Cackling Goose.

adult

white face

black neck and breast

Snow Goose
Chen caerulescens
L 30"/76cm **WS** 55"/1.4m

Very common and increasing over its range, Snow Goose breeds in far-northern Arctic tundra south to Hudson Bay. It winters in farm fields and marshes of the southern U.S. in flocks of many thousands that often include smaller numbers of Ross's Geese. There are two subspecies: Greater *(atlanticus)*, seen in the coastal mid-Atlantic states in winter; and the very widespread Lesser (nominate, including the common dark morph, "Blue Goose"), which is closer in size to Ross's but still larger. Dark-morph Greater Snow Geese are rare. **VOICE** A contented *rauw,* given when feeding; a higher-pitched, often doubled honk—*eenhk!*—when agitated or in flight.

adult

dark "grin patch" in heavy bill

face often stained yellow (from foraging)

immature

facial feathering curved at bill base (compare Ross's Goose)

variably grayish; darker than immature Ross's

adult, "Blue Goose" (nominate)

white head

white undertail coverts (unlike Emperor Goose)

immature, "Blue Goose" (nominate)

dark head

(gray tail, white underwing coverts best seen in flying bird)

adult

black primaries visible in flight (similar to Ross's)

Ross's Goose

Chen rossii
L 25"/64cm   **WS** 44"/1.1m

Ross's Goose breeds in High Arctic tundra of Canada and winters mostly in marshes and farm fields west of the Mississippi. Small numbers are noted annually in the East, usually among Snow Geese, with which Ross's occasionally hybridizes. A rare dark morph shares structural features with the white morph. **VOICE** Similar to Snow Goose but higher-pitched.

adult   small bill lacks "grin patch" and often shows lavender patch at base (compare Snow Goose)

head and face usually snow white, lacking yellow staining seen on Snow

smaller and with shorter neck than Snow

immatures   straighter facial feathering at bill base than Snow

similar to adult, but with dusky bill, crown, and sometimes back (but always whiter than immature Snow)

adult, dark morph

dark neck, crown, sides, and back contrast with pale belly, upperwing coverts, and face (unlike dark-morph Snow)

adult Ross's (with adult Snow Goose, right)

shorter neck, smaller head and bill than Snow Goose, often apparent in flying birds

Emperor Goose

Chen canagica
L 26"/66cm   **WS** 47"/1.2m

Emperor Goose, a scarce and local species of western Alaska, breeds in coastal tundra and tidal marshes and winters almost entirely along the Alaska Peninsula and nearby islands; it is recorded very rarely south of Alaska on the Pacific coast. **VOICE** A high-pitched double honk similar to Snow Goose.

adult   blackish throat and foreneck contrast with white head and back of neck

gray body has scaly pattern, bluish tones above

white tail (all plumages)

orange legs

(juvenile has sooty head, white eye ring)

Tundra Swan
Cygnus columbianus
L 52"/1.3m **WS** 65"/1.7m

Tundra Swan is a locally common breeder, chiefly in coastal High Arctic tundra, and is uncommon away from traditional wintering grounds and migratory routes. It winters on lakes and estuaries, mostly in the lower 48 states, feeding in open waters, marshes, and croplands. The American (nominate) subspecies is known as Whistling Swan; a Eurasian subspecies, Bewick's Swan *(bewickii)*, is a rare visitor in North America, usually found among flocks of Whistling Swans. Voice and bill shape are the best clues for distinguishing this species from Trumpeter Swan. First-year birds are difficult to distinguish, but immatures molt their dusky plumage in winter, so they look much whiter than young Trumpeters by late winter. **VOICE** In flight a loud, rolling, high-pitched whooping, very different from Trumpeter Swan; also a soft but grating *kruk-kruk*.

adult,
Whistling Swan

smaller and more
delicate than other
swan species

immature,
Whistling Swan

reddish
bill edged
in black

pale grayish
brown
plumage,
molted in
winter

adult,
Bewick's Swan

rare visitor
from Eurasia

Trumpeter Swan, Whistling Swan (American subspecies of Tundra Swan), and Bewick's Swan (Eurasian subspecies of Tundra Swan) are very similar in appearance: large and white with a black bill. Adults are best distinguished by differences in bill shape and the amount of yellow on the lores or base of the maxilla.

Trumpeter Swan adult
Black maxilla straight at gape; forehead feathers form V-shape; no yellow on lores; angle of bill at lores looks more open, less pinched, than in Whistling.

Whistling Swan adult
Black maxilla curved at gape; forehead feathers form U-shape; less yellow on lores than Bewick's (15 percent lack yellow).

Bewick's Swan adult
Extensive yellow on base of maxilla. Whooper Swan, also a Eurasian vagrant, similar but much larger.

Trumpeter Swan

Cygnus buccinator
L 60"/1.5m WS 80"/2m

Formerly listed as endangered, Trumpeter Swan is now increasing, though its population still numbers only about 30,000. It nests in muskegs and in remote western parks with large lakes, and winters on coasts near breeding areas in the Pacific Northwest and Interior West. Trumpeters have been introduced in states to the east and now occasionally appear in states along the Atlantic and Gulf coasts. **VOICE** Diagnostic; low-pitched honking, sounding like a trumpet.

adults

heavier bill and longer neck than Tundra Swan

immatures

bill reddish with extensive black

dusky plumage retained through first winter (unlike Tundra Swan)

Mute Swan

Cygnus olor
L 60"/1.5m WS 75"/1.9m

Mute Swan is an introduced European species that nests and winters on ponds, lakes, and marshes from southern New England to Virginia in the East; around Victoria, British Columbia; and in scattered locations in the Midwest. Birds escaped from captivity are observed commonly. The species can be aggressive toward other waterbirds and even people; this has led to their removal from the wild in some areas. **VOICE** A hoarse, raucous trumpeting, heard only occasionally; also hissing on territory.

adults

knobbed orange bill

(wings often held raised above back)

curved neck

long, pointed tail

immature

lacks pronounced "knob" on bill

dark brownish plumage (some much paler)

Loons

Loons are members of the ancient family Gaviidae, fossils of which date back tens of millions of years. They are heavyset diving birds with daggerlike bills that they use to spear fish, crustaceans, and other aquatic prey. Like grebes, loons have feet set far back on the body, an adaptation for agile pursuit of prey under water. The larger species may spend more than a minute below the water's surface and dive to depths of several hundred feet.

Common Loon with chick; both parents feed the young, even after they fledge.

Loons nest on remote lakes or sheltered coastlines in Canada and Alaska; Common Loon also nests in the northern United States. Their elaborate courtship displays involve synchronized swimming, chasing, and bill movements, and males and females also give a variety of yodeling, quacking, and whinnying calls. In autumn loons migrate southward to winter on large lakes and ocean coasts, where they can sometimes be observed in large, loose flocks; Yellow-billed Loon is usually seen singly, especially in the lower 48 states.

Common Loon, which nests on boreal lakes farther south than other loons, faces a host of conservation problems: acidification of the lakes, development (resulting in pollution of the lakes and disturbance by recreational boaters), and poisoning by ingestion of lead sinkers used in fishing tackle.

Grebes

Grebes are members of a group of birds (family Podicipedidae) that probably arose in South America millions of years ago. They share qualities with both waterfowl and loons, but they have toes that are lobed rather than webbed; tails so tiny as to be almost invisible; and fluffy, almost furlike plumage in the flanks and undertail. The bills of grebes also differ from those of other diving birds, varying from blunt and pointed in the unique Pied-billed Grebe to stiletto-like in Clark's and Western Grebes. Grebe bodies are well adapted to hunting underwater for fish, crustaceans, and other aquatic prey; smaller species can regulate their buoyancy and submerge without diving by compressing the body plumage.

Grebes nest on freshwater lakes and ponds. Their courtship displays involve bobbing and bowing, and pairs of some species engage in an almost balletlike footrace across the water's surface. In fall grebes in northern areas leave the nesting grounds for coastal and inland wintering grounds to the south.

Some grebe populations have declined in recent decades. Horned Grebes have disappeared from the northern prairie pothole country, and at Mono Lake, California, the flocks of Eared Grebes that once numbered more than a million are lately reduced to less than 200,000.

Western Grebe with chicks. Young birds ride on their parents' backs, even underwater.

Identification of Loons

Loons are often seen from a long distance, resting on the water or actively feeding, and a spotting scope is useful for studying them. The colorful and boldly patterned breeding plumages usually present little difficulty for identification; nonbreeding plumages, however, require careful study. Concentrate on the head, neck, and bill, paying attention to pattern as well as overall shape. Size can be hard to judge at a distance.

The two largest species, Common and Yellow-billed Loons, have massive, blocky heads and heavy bills. Pacific and Arctic Loons are intermediate in overall size, with medium-sized bills and bulky necks that seem to blend into their rounded crowns. Red-throated Loon is slender and slender-billed, like a grebe. Common, Pacific, and Arctic Loons usually hold the bill parallel to the water's surface; Red-throated and Yellow-billed Loons normally tilt the bill upward.

Loons in Flight

Flying loons can be difficult to identify, but the different shapes and flight styles of the species provide useful clues for identification. The larger two loon species fly with slow wingbeats and hold the wings perpendicular to the body. The smaller three species fly with more rapid wingbeats, holding the wings slightly swept back from the body.

Common and Yellow-billed Loons look enormous in flight, with broad wings, heavy heads, and large feet trailing well beyond the tail. Pacific and Arctic Loons are quite difficult to distinguish from each other in flight; look for Arctic's white flanks. They differ from the larger loons in their more compact shapes and less obvious trailing feet, and they are larger and more substantial and appear darker overall than the slimmer, paler Red-throated Loon. Red-throated often carries its slender neck well below the level of the body in flight, raises and lowers its head, and moves its head from side to side, unlike other loon species. It also raises the wings quite high in flight and has a noticeably deeper wingstroke than other loon species.

Grebes in Flight

Loons can be confused with larger grebes in flight, but the grebes always show much white in the wings, visible even at a distance: all have white secondaries, and the larger species have some white upperwing coverts as well. Their white wing patches, as well as their very thin necks, make grebes distinguishable from loons under most conditions.

Common Loon

Gavia immer
L 32"/81cm **WS** 46"/1.2m

Common Loon's eerie vocalizations and striking breeding plumage have made it a symbol of the wild North. This species nests on large lakes throughout the boreal forest and tundra; most winter on the seacoasts, with a few found on interior reservoirs. Concern for declining populations in the Northeast led to a groundswell of public support for this species, including formation of the Loon Rangers (who protect breeding sites) and the North American Loon Fund. Because Common is the most widespread of the loons, it is the loon to study for comparison with the others, especially in nonbreeding plumage: it is slightly smaller and less heavily built than Yellow-billed Loon but has a heavier neck and bill than the three smaller species. **VOICE** Territorial call a piercing yodeled *wheea-whee,* given 3 times, introduced by a rising wail. Contact call an elklike bugling. Alarm call a tremulous whinnying sound.

breeding adult

checkerboard pattern on back and scapulars

dark, heavy head and bill

nonbreeding adult/ subadult

bill can look pale but culmen always dark and curved

dark side of neck shows uneven border

juvenile

similar to winter adult but back and coverts show neat pale fringes

breeding adult

large head and feet

broad wings

Yellow-billed Loon

Gavia adamsii
L 35"/89cm **WS** 49"/1.2m

The rare Yellow-billed Loon nests by tundra lakes and rivers and winters on the coast, mostly in Canada. Single birds are seen south to California, and there have been fall and winter records, mostly of juveniles, at lakes in landlocked states and as far south as Brownsville, Texas. **VOICE** Calls similar to Common Loon but deeper.

breeding adult

strikingly heavy, ivory bill; culmen always straight

more white on back than Common Loon, and heavier head (eyes appear smaller)

juvenile

(nonbreeding adult similar but more uniform above)

outer half of culmen pale

paler overall than Common

Pacific Loon

Gavia pacifica
L 25"/64cm   WS 36"/91cm

Pacific Loon, formerly considered a small subspecies of Arctic Loon, nests on tundra lakes. It winters, often in large aggregations, along Pacific shores and is seen more often in deeper offshore waters than are Common or Red-throated Loons. Fall, winter, and spring records from interior lakes and the Atlantic coast are few but increasing. **VOICE** Territorial call a mournful, rising yodel, *oo-looEEE*, repeated. Contact call a low *kwao*, similar to Arctic but higher.

breeding adult

paler nape, smaller bill than Arctic Loon

lines on sides of neck do not meet lines on breast

juvenile

gently rounded crown

dark side of neck not broken by white

most show dark throat strap

(nonbreeding adult more uniform above)

nonbreeding adult

more heavy-bodied and much darker than Red-throated

dark flanks (white in Arctic Loon)

head and neck often look very dark against white chin

Arctic Loon

Gavia arctica
L 27"/69cm   WS 40"/1m

This Eurasian species breeds in North America only on Alaska's Seward Peninsula and vicinity. It closely resembles the smaller Pacific Loon in all plumages but always shows white above the waterline at the flanks, most extensively when resting (Pacific may show white along the waterline, especially when preening its sides or when body plumage is fluffed over the wings). **VOICE** Territorial call a high-pitched, rising *oo-oooowwEEE*, repeated. Contact call a rising wail, *waooow*. Many other quacking, shrieking, and cawing calls.

breeding adult

darker nape and heavier bill and head than Pacific Loon

lines on neck meet lines on breast

white on flanks can be hidden by waves

nonbreeding adult/subadult

heavier head and bill than Pacific Loon

juvenile

white flank patch usually obvious

Red-throated Loon
Gavia stellata
L 25"/64cm **WS** 36"/91cm

Red-throated Loon breeds in tundra, where it nests on small ponds and forages in larger water bodies, flying back and forth with much calling. It winters mostly along ocean coasts, often in large aggregations, and is rare inland away from the Great Lakes. Unlike the larger loons, it can launch into flight from land. Nonbreeding adults and juveniles may be mistaken for grebes. **VOICE** Territorial call a mournful, descending wail, *weeeoow;* also a rapid, raspy quacking, given mainly in flight on breeding grounds.

adult

small, with slender neck

bright rusty throat and eyes contrast with gray face

thin bill often uptilted

nonbreeding adult

soft gray crown and back of neck

white in front of eyes

dark gray back with neat white marks

(stark white underparts)

nonbreeding adult

dark gray above

smaller feet than Common

slender neck and wings recall grebes, but lacks white in upperwings

extensively white neck and face

Red-necked Grebe
Podiceps grisegena
L 18"/46cm **WS** 24"/61cm

This medium-sized grebe nests on marshy ponds in tundra, boreal forests, and northern prairies, and winters on coasts and in smaller numbers on the Great Lakes. It differs from small grebes in its heavy head and bill, but it may be confused with loons and with the "swan grebes" (Clark's and Western), which are larger and have longer bills. Displaying birds raise crown feathers into a striking "toreador's cap." **VOICE** Territorial call a series of strident, staccato piping calls; also rapid, muffled quacking.

adult

white cheek contrasts with reddish neck, black cap

blunt bill always shows yellow

nonbreeding adult

gray auriculars framed by white foreneck, throat, hindcheek

bill longer than Horned Grebe, shorter than Western Grebe

black crown fades to gray in face

(first-winter bird has paler eyes)

Western Grebe

Aechmophorus occidentalis
L 25"/64cm **WS** 24"/61cm

Western Grebe nests in colonies on prairie sloughs and shallow lakes bordered by rushes, where in impressive courtship displays pairs of birds rear up on their feet and rush in perfect synchrony across the water's surface. Most winter in coastal waters; some are found on interior lakes and rivers. Clark's and Western Grebes have a long, thin neck and are often called "swan grebes." **VOICE** Breeding birds very vocal: territorial male gives a reedy, screechy *krrri-KRRII;* female answers with *kri-DEE.*

adult

dark of crown extends below eyes (area around eyes paler in nonbreeding plumage)

bill olive-yellow with dusky edges

courting adults

"rushing ceremony" performed by pair, or by 2 males to attract female's attention or in rivalry

Clark's Grebe

Aechmophorus clarkii
L 25"/64cm   **WS** 24"/61cm

The elegant Clark's Grebe nests on lakes and in marshes of the Great Plains and Great Basin, and winters on lakes in the Southwest and California and along the southern Pacific coast. Until 1981 Clark's was considered a light morph of Western Grebe, but the two species seldom hybridize. Clark's often forages farther from shore on lakes than Western, but Western ranges farther offshore on the ocean than Clark's. **VOICE** Similar to Western Grebe but simpler and often single-syllabled.

adult

white of face extends above eyes

white of neck more extensive than on Western (best viewed on bird facing away)

bill bright yellow with orange tone

paler overall, especially on sides, than Western

"weed ceremony" courtship display, also performed by Western

hybrids and backcrosses of Clark's and Western Grebes show intermediate characteristics: this bird has head and bill similar to Western, but more extensive wing stripe like Clark's

adults

Horned Grebe
Podiceps auritus
L 14"/36cm   **WS** 18"/46cm

Horned Grebe breeds on northern lakes and sparingly in prairie pothole country farther south, where it is declining. In winter sizable numbers may be seen along ocean shores and on coastal bays and rivers. Smaller numbers winter on interior lakes; if lakes freeze suddenly, Horned and Red-necked Grebes make escape flights to seek open water and sometimes become grounded. **VOICE** Nesting bird gives rapid, nasal twittering calls, often with irregular tempo and tone.

breeding adult

golden head plumes extend fully over sides of crown

white-tipped bill

rusty plumage of flanks extends to neck

usually has hint of gold above eye, rust in neck

nonbreeding adult

pale loral spot

molting adult

pale-tipped bill

mostly white auriculars and neck; black on nape very narrow

Eared Grebe
Podiceps nigricollis
L 13"/33cm   **WS** 16"/41cm

The gregarious Eared Grebe nests in colonies on freshwater lakes and winters on freshwater bodies and at sheltered coastal saltwater sites. Its small bill is ideal for seizing small insects and crustaceans, its chief prey. Populations at traditional locations in California have declined steeply in recent years. Molting Horned Grebes can be mistaken for Eared: Horned often has rust in neck; Eared never does. **VOICE** Territorial call a repeated, high-pitched, hiccuping *wwee-KIP!* Nesting bird often gives chattering twitter like Horned.

breeding adult

golden plumes sparse and splayed across cheek

shape of head and neck unique

thin, black-tipped bill

black neck (compare Horned Grebe)

nonbreeding adult

often raises wings, revealing fluffy tail coverts

dusky bill tip

nonbreeding adult

often shows peaked crown

dark lores

dusky auriculars and foreneck

Pied-billed Grebe

Podilymbus podiceps
L 13"/33cm **WS** 16"/41cm

This widespread grebe nests on ponds and lakes with emergent vegetation and winters on freshwater bodies and protected saltwater bays. Shier and less gregarious than other grebes, it often sinks out of sight when spotted—thus its local names "Sink Peter" and "Helldiver." **VOICE** Breeding male loud and vocal; territorial call a rapid, accelerating then decelerating series of *coo* or *caow* calls, broken by drawn-out *whaa* calls.

breeding adult

dark eyes, white eye ring

warm brown with olive or rusty tones

short, black-banded bill

nonbreeding adult

bill structure and "fluffy" plumage very different from small ducks

(lacks wing stripe in flight of other small grebes)

Least Grebe

Tachybaptus dominicus
L 9"/23cm **WS** 11"/28cm

Least Grebe inhabits freshwater marshes and lakes of southern Texas; nesting pairs may temporarily establish themselves in small flooded fields and ditches where aquatic insects are abundant. Although nonmigratory, the species does wander, and strays have turned up in several southern states. **VOICE** Pair in duet gives nasal, rapid, descending titters, slowing toward end. Contact call an unbirdlike, nasal *bean,* with comical cartoon sound-effect quality.

breeding adult

tiny

brilliant yellow eyes

slaty plumage

nonbreeding adult

retains yellow eyes all year

paler head, throat, bill than breeding birds

often raises wings, revealing cottony tail coverts

Auks, Murres, Puffins, and Kin

The murres, murrelets, auklets, auks (Razorbill and Dovekie), puffins, and guillemots of the family Alcidae—commonly called "alcids"—are marine birds with relatively short wings, webbed feet, and well-insulated, compact bodies. Perfectly suited to a life spent in cold, rough seas, alcids are awkward, almost penguinlike, on land and come to shore mostly to nest or when ailing. This family shows great diversity in bill structure and in size, ranging from the petite Least Auklet,

Alcids such as this adult Pigeon Guillemot use both feet and wings when foraging, appearing to "fly" underwater.

the world's smallest alcid (3 oz/85g), to the extinct, flightless Great Auk (11 lbs/5kg). Alcids have countershaded plumages that help them escape notice of both aerial and marine predators. Some species show different plumages in summer and winter; puffins and auklets sport head plumes and brightly colored bills in breeding dress, which they shed after nesting. Birds in this group can be confused with ducks, grebes, and loons at a distance, but their shape and distinctive manner of flight—low to the water, with rapid wingbeats—quickly distinguish them from other waterbirds.

Alcids dive for their prey, using both their wings and feet for propulsion and steering. The larger species, which feed on fish and squid, can dive to depths of 600′ (180m); smaller species may dive to 150′ (45m) for copepods, small jellyfish, and plankton. While some species stay close

Great Auk, once found on islands from eastern Canada to Scotland, was the largest alcid. By 1800 the last Canadian colony, on Funk Island, had been eliminated by hunters, who took eggs, chicks, and adults for food and bait. The species was last seen in 1844.

to land year-round, most feed in pelagic waters during the nonbreeding season.

Alcids nest mostly on the ocean's edge in cliffs, rock crevices, or burrows; many Marbled Murrelets nest high in coniferous trees and often well inland. Most larger species nest in colonies, while smaller species, such as Kittlitz's Murrelet and the guillemots, are solitary nesters. Some smaller alcids, including Xantus's Murrelet, are strictly nocturnal on the breeding grounds, which helps them avoid predators such as gulls. Courtship among alcids may involve loud braying calls and much movement of the head. Puffins and auklets show off their bills and head plumes in displays. Ancient Murrelets sit in trees and "sing" above their burrow entrances. After fledging, young birds take to the ocean, often accompanied by a parent. Young birds may spend up to eight years on the open ocean before returning to the breeding colonies. Like most pelagic birds, alcids exhibit strong natal philopatry, returning to the area where they were hatched.

The habits and habitats of alcids put them in the way of many dangers at sea, such as predatory fish. But by far the greatest threats to their survival are manmade: hundreds of thousands have been killed by oil spills and other pollution or by entanglement in gill nets.

Black Guillemot
Cepphus grylle
L 13"/33cm   **WS** 21"/53cm

This medium-sized alcid inhabits rocky seacoasts in the northern Bering Sea and the eastern High Arctic through New England, straying rarely to mid-Atlantic states in winter. Most remain near land. Unlike other Atlantic alcids, which can form large aggregations, Black Guillemot is seen mostly singly or in pairs. Courting adults call often, revealing brilliant scarlet mouth-lining. Arctic populations appear almost snow white in winter. **VOICE** Very high-pitched squeaks and whistles on nesting grounds.

breeding adult

velvety black plumage

white wing coverts

vermilion feet

juvenile

barred wing coverts

white underwing coverts in all plumages

compare smaller Long-billed Murrelet

(nonbreeding adult similar, but with whiter head, breast, coverts)

Pigeon Guillemot
Cepphus columba
L 14"/36cm   **WS** 23"/58cm

Pigeon Guillemot is widespread in western North America. It can be found year-round along ocean shorelines from western Alaska through central California, although it becomes much more localized in fall and winter. This species is often seen around kelp beds and rock jetties, diving to the sea floor to probe rocks and vegetation for prey. Dusky underwing coverts always distinguish flying birds from Black Guillemot. **VOICE** Squeaky, almost rodentlike twittering very similar to Black Guillemot.

breeding adult

black bar in white wing patch (compare Black Guillemot)

breeding adult

dusky gray underwings in all plumages

juvenile

most show heavy barring on coverts, back, underparts

(nonbreeding adult similar, but with whiter head, breast, coverts)

Common Murre
Uria aalge
L 17"/43cm   **WS** 26"/66cm

Common Murre is a large, long-billed alcid of cold coastal and pelagic waters. This species is abundant in the Pacific and less numerous and more restricted in range in the Atlantic. It nests in large colonies on rocky cliff ledges along oceans and bays, usually among other alcids. Like Thick-billed Murre, Common Murre can dive to depths of 500' (150m) in search of small fish such as capelin and sand lance. It prefers to forage in ice-free seas, where it spends its first 5 or 6 years before returning to colonies to breed. In winter Common Murre can be difficult to distinguish at a distance from Razorbill, which also has white on the face; differences in bill structure are clear at close range. Like other alcids, murres are vulnerable to oil spills, which have killed many thousands. **VOICE** A low-pitched, grating, booming *URRRRRRrrrrrr*, descending, and a bleating sound; heard only on nesting grounds.

breeding adult

thinner bill than Thick-billed Murre

brown cast to head and neck (compare Thick-billed)

sides and flanks usually show indistinct streaks

breeding adult, "bridled" morph

recorded only in Atlantic and Alaska

breeding adult

(dusky axillaries, white in other larger alcids)

shorter tail than Razorbill (feet often visible)

head, bill look more slender in flight than Thick-billed

Razorbill nonbreeding adult

white on face recalls Common Murre, but bill much deeper

nonbreeding adult

curved black line extends from eyes

swims with tail down (Razorbill often cocks tail up)

more white in face than Thick-billed

Thick-billed Murre

Uria lomvia
L 18"/46cm   **WS** 28"/71cm

This bulky, far-northern counterpart to Common Murre nests on narrow cliff-sides in northern Canada and Alaska. In winter Thick-billed Murre strays out of range more often than Common; it is more regularly found far out to sea and exceptionally inland, as a vagrant in large lakes. Adults feeding young may fly over 100 miles (160km) in a day searching for prey. **VOICE** A booming roar similar to Common Murre but lower in pitch and more jarring; heard only on nesting grounds.

breeding
adult

uniformly blackish
above (compare
Common Murre)

heavier bill than
Common; most
show prominent
white line in
maxilla

whiter flanks than
Common (few
streaks usually
concealed)

nonbreeding
adult

less white
in face than
Common

1st year

smaller
bill than
adult

darker face and nape
than Common; flanks
unstreaked or less streaked

Razorbill

Alca torda
L 17"/43cm   **WS** 26"/66cm

Razorbill nests on rocky cliffs in eastern Canada and winters in the Labrador Current south to North Carolina; it is sometimes seen in flocks of hundreds, both from shore and well out to sea, but is usually seen singly or in small groups. Clad in striking tuxedo-like black and white, displaying adults open their unusual bills to reveal vivid yellow mouth-lining. Razorbills dive for up to a minute, chasing prey as deep as 400' (120m). **VOICE** A piglike, rattling grunt in short series of even duration, given on nesting grounds.

breeding
adult

white
brow line

similar
in size to
murres

unique, deep,
laterally
compressed bill
with white bar

(see photo of
nonbreeding
adult on p. 74)

breeding
adult

heavy
head

long tail usually
conceals feet

juvenile's bill smaller
than adult's, deeper
than murres'

Marbled Murrelet

Brachyramphus marmoratus
L 10"/25cm   WS 16"/41cm

Marbled Murrelet ranges from Alaska to central California and is found singly, in pairs, or in small groups along the coast or just offshore. Its remarkable nesting habits were only recently discovered: most nest high above the ground on large limbs of old-growth conifers, sometimes more than 40 miles (64km) from the ocean. As with other small alcids, adults feed their young at night. **VOICE** Very vocal, even away from nest site; calls include a series of high-pitched *kleeeee* sounds.

Long-billed Murrelet

Brachyramphus perdix
L 10"/25cm   WS 17"/43cm

Long-billed Murrelet, in 1996 recognized as a separate species from Marbled Murrelet, breeds only in northeastern Asia. Unlike Marbled, it has an extensive record of vagrancy into the interior and even to the Atlantic coast from October to December. Look for these vagrants especially at inland reservoirs and lakes; in the Pacific Northwest, look for Long-billed on the ocean in August and September. **VOICE** Call a distinct, incisive *keer*, higher and noticeably shorter than Marbled.

Marbled Murrelet breeding adult — rich brown overall, with darker face and crown — dark outer rectrices (unlike Kittlitz's) — bill longer than Kittlitz's, shorter than Long-billed

Marbled Murrelet nonbreeding adult — white scapulars contrast with dark upperparts — wings can conceal pale sides

Marbled Murrelet nonbreeding adult — white nape framed by black face and shoulder bar — pale flanks often visible (compare larger murres)

Long-billed Murrelet nonbreeding adult — narrow white eye arcs — black nape often shows faint pale spot — (breeding adult like Marbled, but paler throat, less richly colored upperparts) — lacks black shoulder bar and white nape of Marbled

Dovekie
Alle alle
L 8"/20cm   **WS** 15"/38cm

This tiny alcid of the Far North forages on copepods in the Greenland and Labrador Currents; it is often seen from shore in eastern Canada and New England in winter. Most Dovekies observed in North American waters nest in Greenland, where colonies numbering in the millions cover rocky islands and headlands. A few pairs probably nest on Alaska's St. Lawrence Island. This species occasionally "wrecks" on the coast, usually during strong onshore winds. **VOICE** A short, high-pitched trilling call, heard on nesting grounds.

breeding adult

tiny

heavy bill relative to size (compare murrelets)

black head

nonbreeding adult

white of throat extends behind auriculars

often appears to lean forward in water

nonbreeding adult

rapid, whirring wingbeats

dark mask; dark half-collar

dark underwings

Kittlitz's Murrelet
Brachyramphus brevirostris
L 10"/25cm   **WS** 17"/43cm

Kittlitz's Murrelet is a permanent resident of Alaska and is almost never recorded elsewhere in North America. The species nests on bare ground above the tree line near mountain summits, usually on a north-facing slope, often on glacial moraines well away from seacoasts; it winters near its nesting areas and forages near glacial outflows. Populations of Kittlitz's currently appear to be in steep decline. **VOICE** Not often heard; basic calls include a trebled quack, a low moan, and a squeaky clucking.

breeding adult

paler than Marbled, with shorter bill and white outer rectrices and undertail coverts

(most adults show more golden-brown tones above)

breeding adult

white belly (unlike Marbled) best seen in flying bird

nonbreeding adult

very white face surrounds dark eye

tiny bill

Xantus's Murrelet
Synthliboramphus hypoleucus
L 9½"/24cm   **WS** 15"/38cm

Xantus's Murrelet is found in ocean waters off California; it is seen more often in inshore waters than Craveri's, usually singly, in pairs, or with young. This murrelet nests in ground cavities or hollows on offshore islands and sometimes uses rabbit holes or burrows of Burrowing Owls. The Mexican subspecies *hypoleucus,* a rare fall visitor to Pacific coastal waters, shows a whiter face than the California subspecies *scrippsi.* **VOICE** Often gives a single whistled call, sometimes in series, at sea or near nesting areas.

Craveri's Murrelet
Synthliboramphus craveri
L 9½"/24cm   **WS** 15"/38cm

Craveri's Murrelet is an endemic breeder on rocky islands in the Gulf of California and the Pacific off Baja California. It occasionally visits offshore waters of southern California in late summer and fall. Like Xantus's Murrelet, Craveri's sits low in the water, making it hard to see the more extensive dark mark on the sides of the breast; but in flight this mark is often more noticeable than the dark underwings. Craveri's total population is probably less than 20,000 birds. **VOICE** Not often heard; a dry, insectlike trilling at nest.

Ancient Murrelet
Synthliboramphus antiquus
L 10"/25cm   WS 17"/43cm

Ancient Murrelet is named for the wreath of white feathers, like white hair, that rings the crown of breeding adults. This small alcid nests in terrestrial crevices in hillsides and forests but is otherwise entirely maritime, favoring nearshore waters of Alaska and the Pacific Northwest. It is a rare vagrant to interior lakes in late autumn. As in Xantus's Murrelet, young accompany their parents to sea when they are 2 days old. **VOICE** Nesting adult gives mostly short, high-pitched notes, rattles, and trills.

breeding adult

pale bill

white in brow

blue-gray back contrasts with black and white plumage

black face and throat

white below extends almost to nape

breeding adults

pale bill

gray back

juvenile

like adult, but lacks white in brow

Cassin's Auklet
Ptychoramphus aleuticus
L 9"/23cm   WS 15"/38cm

A common small alcid of Pacific shores, Cassin's Auklet nests in colonies in burrows and recesses on rocky islands and headlands. It is often seen in large numbers and ranges well out to sea, especially in winter in the California Current and its upwellings, where zooplankton, shrimp, fish, and small squid form most of the diet. In some areas adults defend burrows year-round. **VOICE** A low-pitched croaking sound on nesting grounds; large colonies sound like a chorus of frogs.

breeding adult

pale eyes

mostly gray, with white eye arc

tiny

pale spot in base of mandible

(juvenile similar, but with darker eyes)

nonbreeding adult

appears small, compact, sooty gray in flight

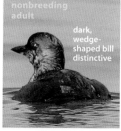

nonbreeding adult

dark, wedge-shaped bill distinctive

Crested Auklet

Aethia cristatella
L 11"/28cm **WS** 17"/43cm

This common small auklet of Alaska and Siberia nests coastally in crevices among boulders above the high-water mark. It winters gregariously on open ocean, largely in the Bering Sea, sometimes among Least and Parakeet Auklets. As in the other ornate auklets of the Pacific, its bill color becomes a dusky brownish orange in winter. Adults exude chemicals that have a tangerine-like scent—apparently to repel parasites. **VOICE** Various short barking, honking, moaning, and grunting calls on nesting grounds.

breeding adults

multiple dark plumes in crest; 1 white plume in face (several in Whiskered Auklet)

(young birds and nonbreeding adults have similar pale eyes but smaller crest and bill)

Parakeet Auklet

Aethia psittacula
L 10"/25cm **WS** 18"/46cm

Parakeet Auklet is a Bering Sea species seen chiefly in Alaska. It nests in coastal areas in crevices and under fallen rocks, places where snow cover can delay nesting until late June. Unlike smaller auklets, Parakeet Auklet does not nest in colonies but is found in scattered pairs. It winters far out to sea in the North Pacific, where it feeds mostly on krill. This species is usually observed singly or in small groups. **VOICE** Nesting adult gives shrill, tremulous squeals and rough, syncopated barks.

breeding adult

pale belly

lacks plumes in crest (compare Crested Auklet)

(nonbreeding adult similar, but with duskier bill, paler throat)

breeding adult

only auklet with white belly and orange bill

breeding adult

broader, more rounded wings than other *Aethia*

Whiskered Auklet

Aethia pygmaea
L 8"/20cm **WS** 14"/36cm

The little-known Whiskered Auklet breeds only in Alaska's Aleutian Islands, hiding its nest in inaccessible sea-cliffs, often under overhangs or rocks. It forages for small crustaceans and other invertebrates in tidal rips of inshore waters and winters at sea near the nesting grounds. The species has been recorded once in Washington but otherwise never south of Alaska. Like other auklets, it has an expandable throat pouch for transporting food back to the nest. **VOICE** Nesting adult gives high-pitched mews and paired calls, often in long series.

breeding adults

combination of crest and multiple facial plumes distinctive (reduced in nonbreeding plumage)

(white crissum, unlike Crested Auklet)

Least Auklet

Aethia pusilla
L 6"/15cm **WS** 12"/30cm

The world's smallest alcid and probably the most numerous seabird nesting in the Bering Sea, Least Auklet is restricted to Alaska and Siberia, where it nests in enormous colonies on rocky islands and coastal sites. Like its larger relatives Crested and Whiskered Auklets, it remains in Siberian and Alaskan waters during the nonbreeding season, but it is seen in larger flocks. Both gulls and falcons prey on Least Auklets. **VOICE** A chattering, screechy, ternlike trill, heard only at nest colonies.

breeding adults

tiny

tiny white plume behind eyes

light to heavy mottling below

breeding adults

dark and light extremes

(juveniles and nonbreeding adults white below)

Rhinoceros Auklet

Cerorhinca monocerata
L 15"/38cm   WS 22"/56cm

The unusual bill of Rhinoceros Auklet sports a hornlike projection in the breeding season. This large auklet is a widespread Pacific coastal nester from Alaska south to California; it winters in coastal areas mostly south of Canada. Like its close relatives the puffins, Rhinoceros Auklet excavates burrows in soft soil and often lines its nest. When foraging, it chases small fish (especially sardines) toward the surface to concentrate them. **VOICE** A series of growling and lowing, cowlike sounds at nest.

breeding adult

distinctive "horn" on bill (acquired in late winter, lost after breeding)

facial plumes

juvenile

thick bill

gray underwings (like puffins)

darker eyes, paler underparts than adult

Tufted Puffin

Fratercula cirrhata
L 15"/38cm   WS 25"/64cm

Tufted Puffin, the only black-bellied member of its genus, is widely distributed during the breeding season from Alaska south to central California. Its preferred nest sites are burrows and crevices on remote rocky headlands and islands, especially where slopes are steep. This species winters at sea, usually solitarily and often far offshore. Like other puffins, it sheds the outer part of the bill in winter. **VOICE** A low, moaning growl at nest.

breeding adult

unique golden head plumes

nonbreeding adult

adult sheds head plumes and part of bill after breeding

(juvenile has smaller, dull olive-yellow bill)

Atlantic Puffin

Fratercula arctica
L 12"/30cm **WS** 21"/53cm

One of the world's most familiar alcids, Atlantic Puffin nests chiefly on rocky coasts in Maine and the Canadian Maritimes, excavating burrows in grassy areas on cliff-tops; its colonies have become significant tourist attractions. Puffins spend their first 4 years far out at sea over deep waters, returning in their fifth or sixth year to nest. They can dive to depths of 200' (60m) but usually go no deeper than 100' (30m). **VOICE** At nest an intermittent low groaning, reminiscent of a distant motorcycle.

breeding adult

distinctive orange, blue, and yellow bill

nonbreeding adult

after breeding season, colorful outer layers of bill shed and face becomes dusky

---

Horned Puffin

Fratercula corniculata
L 15"/38cm **WS** 23"/58cm

The highly pelagic Horned Puffin is named for the leathery dermal spike that projects above the eyes in breeding adults. This species nests in small colonies around cliffs and islands in Alaska and British Columbia, using both burrows and rocky crevices, often the same site each year. It winters well out to sea in the North Pacific, where it feeds on squid and lanternfishes. A few are seen as far south as California almost annually. **VOICE** Low-pitched, rumbling calls in rhythmic phrases at nest; unlike other puffins.

breeding adult

deep yellow and orange bill (gray and orange in winter)

white belly

breeding adult

orange feet obvious in flight

"football" shape in flight (like Atlantic Puffin)

rounded but narrow wings, like other puffins

Pelicans, Cormorants, Boobies, and Allies

American White Pelican has a wingspan of nearly 9' (3m), equal to that of a California Condor.

A diverse set of families makes up the order Pelecaniformes: the pelicans (Pelecanidae), cormorants (Phalacrocoracidae), darters (Anhingidae), tropicbirds (Phaethontidae), boobies and gannets (Sulidae), and frigatebirds (Fregatidae). All pelecaniforms have completely webbed feet and feed largely on fish and other aquatic prey. All but the tropicbirds nest in colonies, some of which can involve many thousands of birds with nests only a few inches apart. The ternlike tropicbirds are the smallest of the order, with wingspans of a mere 3' (1m); American White Pelican, with a nearly 9' (3m) wingspan, is almost as heavy as a swan.

Pelecaniforms have evolved to exploit both marine and freshwater habitats. Some are specialized foragers; the fish-spearing Anhinga, for example, is limited to freshwater lakes and swamps. Others, such as Double-crested Cormorant, forage equally well in rivers, ponds, and ocean. The most pelagic of the pelecaniforms are the tropicbirds; they spend most of their lives over the open ocean, diving from great heights in the air to seize fish, squid, and cuttlefish. Boobies, gannets, and Brown Pelican also dive on fish from the air, mostly in marine environments, often near land. Magnificent Frigatebird swoops

Blue-footed Boobies use their brightly colored feet in courtship displays.

over the ocean's surface to pluck prey items or harasses other seabirds and steals their catches. Cormorants swim on the surface, diving under to seize fish and crustaceans. American White Pelican lowers its 5-gallon bill pouch into the water as it swims to trap fish, crayfish, and other prey.

Courtship among pelecaniforms is often spectacular. Sulids perform graceful, dancelike promenades, point their bills skyward, and use their brightly colored feet—brilliant red, blue, or yellow in the tropical boobies—in exaggerated displays. Breeding male cormorants and pelicans attract females with colorful gular pouches and head or flank feathering and also engage in loud calls, posturing, and wing movements. Male boobies often present females with tokens, such as rocks or feathers; male darters, cormorants, and pelicans may offer gifts of nesting material. The display of Magnificent Frigatebird takes the prize: the male inflates an enormous, cherry red gular sac like a great balloon and clatters his long bill as the female looks on.

North American pelecaniform populations are generally stable, and some are even increasing steadily, such as those of Double-crested Cormorant and Brown Pelican, two species that have recovered remarkably well after the banning of DDT.

Identification of Pelecaniforms

Shape, locomotion, and behavior offer important clues to the identification of pelecaniforms. Cormorants and anhingas, for example, are superficially similar—both long-bodied, long-necked, surface-diving birds—but they display many differences in shape, movement, and foraging manner.

When foraging, an Anhinga sinks slowly into the water and often exposes only the head and part of the neck, keeping most of the body submerged—something cormorants never do.

Cormorants dive like loons, plunging headfirst. Great and Pelagic Cormorants often leap upward, almost clearing the water before submerging; Double-crested dives without the leap.

Cormorants in Flight

Brandt's, Pelagic, and Double-crested Cormorants can often be seen from shore on the Pacific coast. Overall size and shape of head and neck help distinguish these species on the water or in flight.

Double-crested shows the most robust form, with long, rather broad wings and a heavy neck that is kinked in flight. Brandt's also looks large and full-winged, but its wings and tail both appear shorter than those of Double-crested, and it usually holds its neck straight, not kinked.

Pelagic is very different, with its slender head, long, thin, snakelike neck, and long, narrow wings. Red-faced Cormorant, sometimes confused with Pelagic where the two are found together in coastal Alaska, has fuller wings and a heavier, more distinct head.

Aerial Divers

Diving behavior differs among the aerial plunge-divers: the tropicbirds, boobies, and gannets. These pelagic birds are often seen at great distances over the ocean; their differences in structure and behavior provide good clues for identification.

Boobies, especially the smaller species, can be distinguished from gannets by their narrower wing shape and their style of diving for prey: boobies often dive at shallow angles, whereas gannets usually dive from directly above prey. Tropicbirds are easily confused with Royal Tern at a distance (especially younger tropicbirds that lack the long tail streamers of adults); both tropicbirds and terns dive from high in the air, but tropicbirds typically close the wings, plunging into the ocean like a large dart. Tropicbirds' wingbeats are also more rapid than the wingbeats of most terns (recalling pigeons).

Brown Pelican
Pelecanus occidentalis
L 50"/1.3m   WS 81"/2m

After the banning of DDT in 1972, Brown Pelican made a stunning comeback from near-extinction; large numbers again populate the Gulf and Pacific coasts, and the species' Atlantic range has expanded to include Maryland and Virginia. In recent years a few have even wandered well inland. Unlike American White Pelican, Brown Pelican plunge-dives for fish. **VOICE** Low grunting, rarely heard; begging nestlings in crèches give distinctive piping and moaning sounds, by which adults identify them.

juvenile and breeding adult

pouch turns reddish in breeding Pacific adults (dark brown in Atlantic birds)

juvenile grayish brown above, with pale belly

juvenile

enormous size, long bill, and long, wide wings distinctive

(adult plumage acquired in third year)

American White Pelican
Pelecanus erythrorhynchos
L 62"/1.6m   WS 108"/2.7m

This pelican nests in colonies at boreal lakes, prairie sloughs, and marshes, largely in the Great Plains and Great Basin; its wetland winter habitats include sheltered saltwater bodies. It forages by scooping fish and other prey from the water while swimming, often working cooperatively in flocks. Like Brown Pelican, White travels in flocks and often soars. This species has increased steadily in recent decades and is often found out of range. **VOICE** Nesting bird gives low-pitched croaking. Nestling gives short, nasal barks.

breeding adult

(bill plate absent in nonbreeding adult and juvenile)

one of the largest and heaviest of American birds

(adult's crown and nape turn sooty after chicks hatch)

adults

size and shape unmistakable in flight

white tertials and humerals (compare Wood Stork, Whooping Crane, Snow Goose)

Red-billed Tropicbird
Phaethon aethereus
L 37"/94cm   WS 44"/1.1m

A solitary species of deep, usually warm ocean waters, Red-billed Tropicbird is typically seen well out to sea in the Gulf Stream, the Gulf of Mexico, or off southern California. Tropicbirds fly with quick, deep, even wingbeats. Like other tropicbirds, Red-billed flies rapidly and rather high, covering large areas of ocean in search of squid and other prey, which it captures by plunge-diving. The rare **Red-tailed Tropicbird** *(P. rubricauda)*, recorded off California, is similar in size. **VOICE** A harsh, ternlike screech.

dark primary coverts make black of primaries extend well into carpal joint

barred above

Red-billed Tropicbird adult

black primary coverts

Red-billed Tropicbird juvenile

mostly white, with red central rectrices

(juvenile shows barring in back, coverts, rump; white primaries; black maxilla)

Red-tailed Tropicbird adult

White-tailed Tropicbird
Phaethon lepturus
L 30"/76cm   WS 37"/94cm

White-tailed Tropicbird, the smallest of its family, nests in cliffs and crevices on Caribbean islands, visiting the Gulf of Mexico and Gulf Stream in the warmer months. The adult's bill varies from greenish yellow in Pacific populations to orange in Bermuda nesters. Most North Atlantic adults have a peach, golden, or apricot wash on the tail. Young birds appear rather tiny and narrow-winged, much smaller and slimmer than the heavyset Red-billed Tropicbird. **VOICE** A high, piping *krreeek!*

adult

heavy greenish yellow bill (orange in Atlantic)

distinct black bar extends from tertials nearly to carpal joint

black outer primaries (but not their coverts)

chick near fledging

juvenile

plumage has narrow black edges above

slimmer bill, wings, body than Red-billed, and dorsal markings more sparse

lacks black in primary coverts

Northern Gannet

Morus bassanus
L 37"/94cm   **WS** 72"/1.8m

Northern Gannet nests on cliffs in large colonies (called gannetries) in maritime Canada and winters mostly off the mid-Atlantic states, often well out to sea. Few avian assemblages in the Atlantic rival the blizzardlike spectacle of thousands of gannets feeding over the ocean, plunging rapidly from up to 90' (27m) in the air to seize fish from below as they rise from their dive. The gannet is essentially a boreal booby; its bill and head show structural differences from warm-water sulids, and these are useful for identification at close range. Juveniles and subadults are sometimes mistaken for the smaller boobies or even for albatrosses, which are slightly larger and have a very different bill structure. Gannets apparently mate for life and return each year to the same small nest site, to which they add a layer of seaweed and grass before laying their eggs. As in other boobies, adults feed their young regurgitated fish. **VOICE** Feeding bird gives a low, modulated *arrgh,* repeated rhythmically, especially when preparing to dive on prey. Birds taking off and landing at colonies give similar but softer calls.

adult

golden wash on head

dark primaries visible on resting bird

greenish stripes along toes (compare Masked Booby)

adult

white with black primaries and primary coverts

3rd year (with adult)

subadult shows black and white ("piano keys") pattern in upperwings

gannetry

juvenile

sooty gray-brown overall, with small pearl gray speckling on head, breast, coverts

(in flight, note white in uppertail coverts and axillaries)

distant sitting bird may resemble a loon

Masked Booby
Sula dactylatra
L 32"/81cm   **WS** 62"/1.6m

This large tropical sulid nests in North America only at the Dry Tortugas, islands located 70 miles (112km) west of Key West, Florida; small numbers, usually singles, are seen annually in the Gulf of Mexico and the Gulf Stream, where flying fish are preferred prey. The broader-winged Northern Gannet also winters (and rarely summers) in these waters; use care when distinguishing subadult plumages of these species: in all plumages, Masked Booby shows white in the outer underwing coverts, whereas first-year gannets have only white axillaries. **VOICE** Nesting bird gives startling, donkeylike calls and loud whistles.

extensive black in remiges and rectrices apparent on resting bird

dark "mask" of skin circles bill

pale legs and feet (compare Northern Gannet)

adult

juvenile

dark head contrasts with white collar, pale bill

adult

entirely dark remiges

compare shape and head of smaller Red-footed Booby

Blue-footed Booby
Sula nebouxii
L 32"/81cm   **WS** 62"/1.6m

A rare, irregular visitor to western states from Mexican breeding areas, Blue-footed Booby is more likely than other boobies to stray inland. Vagrants are often tame and approachable (this is one reason for the name "booby"). Rare "flights" of boobies to large lakes and reservoirs of the Southwest most often involve juveniles and subadults; such visitors often remain for weeks or months. **VOICE** Nesting bird gives gooselike honks and high-pitched whistles, the latter mostly from adult male.

adult

speckled head

brown above, pale below

brilliant sky blue legs and feet

juvenile   dark head and bill

mostly white underparts

dull blue-gray feet

adult

narrow wings

white rump, pale head

Red-footed Booby

Sula sula
L 28"/71cm **WS** 60"/1.5m

Red-footed Booby is an almost annual visitor to Florida's Dry Tortugas, where up to 4 individuals have been seen in a day; it is a vagrant elsewhere in North America. This is the smallest and most graceful of the American sulids, almost reminiscent of a large tropicbird. Juveniles are dark and acquire either dark or light plumage as they age. Adult Pacific birds usually have dark tails, whereas adult Atlantic birds always have white tails. Juveniles are similar to Brown Booby but appear more slender, with a longer tail and narrower wings, as well as dusky pink-orange (not very pale yellow) legs and feet. Red-footed nests in trees and readily perches on ship railings or riggings, sometimes traveling great distances as a ship-rider. **VOICE** Nesting bird gives guttural gobbling and harsh, piping shrieks.

adult, Pacific, light morph

black remiges like Masked, but more slender in body and wings

tail often black in Pacific populations

adult, Atlantic, light morph

golden wash on head

brilliant coral red feet

subadult, Pacific, light morph

often shows dusky breastband (unlike Brown Booby)

pinkish orange feet (dusky yellow in Brown Booby)

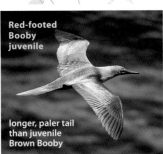

Red-footed Booby juvenile

longer, paler tail than juvenile Brown Booby

upperwings more uniform than Red-footed

Brown Booby juvenile

paler underwing coverts than juvenile Red-footed

adult, Pacific, dark morph (brown-tailed)

tan head and underparts, brown upperparts, and brown (or sometimes white) tail

much paler than Brown Booby

Brown Booby
Sula leucogaster
L 30"/76cm **WS** 57"/1.4m

In the U.S., Brown Booby is found regularly only at the Dry Tortugas. Like other tropical sulids, it may disperse far from its nesting grounds in summer and fall; strays of both the Caribbean (nominate) and the Pacific *(brewsteri)* subspecies have turned up well north of usual range. The species hunts small fish with agile, low-angle dives, often in shallow inshore waters. Resting birds perch on channel markers, buoys, and pilings. (A juvenile is shown with Red-footed Booby, p. 90.) **VOICE** Similar to Blue-footed Booby.

adult female

chocolate brown above and on breast

yellow facial skin

white belly

vivid yellow legs and feet

adult male, Pacific — pale gray wash on head (unlike Atlantic adult)

adult male, Atlantic — bluish gray facial skin

mostly white underwing coverts (on both sexes)

Magnificent Frigatebird
Fregata magnificens
L 40"/1m **WS** 90"/2.3m

With its long, narrow wings and tail and long, hooked bill, Magnificent Frigatebird is distinctive in flight. Frigatebirds nest in colonies in mangroves and forage over salt water, pirating fish from other seabirds and following fishing vessels to take advantage of discarded fish. Single birds can wander far from range; other species of frigatebird (Great and Lesser Frigatebirds) have turned up as vagrants in North America, so use caution when identifying vagrants. **VOICE** Displaying male makes clacking noises with bill; high, thin, harsh chirping sounds at nest.

adult male, displaying

gular pouch inflated (seen around nesting areas)

adult female

dark body and head contrast with white breast

juvenile

white head and part of breast

Double-crested Cormorant

Phalacrocorax auritus
L 32"/81cm   **WS** 52"/1.3m

By far the most widespread cormorant in North America, Double-crested nests in colonies along ocean coasts and lakeshores in many areas, and winters along coasts and in lowland areas of the Southeast, Southwest, and Rio Grande valley. Populations have dramatically increased since the banning of DDT in 1972, leading to concerns that cormorants may start crowding out other colonial nesters and about their overconsumption of juvenile fish; the latter fear has turned out to be unfounded. This species provides a standard by which to compare other cormorant species: Great is bulkier and larger, while Neotropic and the three Pacific species are less bulky and thinner through the head and neck. Adult cormorants have distinctive plumage, but juveniles of most species vary in coloration below, from very dark blackish brown to almost white. The structure of the head, neck, and bill; the shape of the gular skin; and tail length are useful features to study. **VOICE** Nesting bird gives low, guttural croaks and moans. Nestling makes piping sounds.

adult

terminal end of gular skin less acutely pointed than in smaller Neotropic Cormorant

gular and loral skin extensively orange

immature

gular skin rounded at terminus; orange loral skin (lacking in Neotropic)

pale underparts, similar to immature Neotropic

heavier proportions than Neotropic

breeding adult

holds neck crooked in flight

tail shorter than Neotropic, longer than Brandt's

wings longer and more pointed than Brandt's and Pelagic Cormorants

breeding adult

wispy crest (white in many western birds)

plumage of throat rounded where it meets gular skin (compare Great Cormorant)

Neotropic Cormorant
Phalacrocorax brasilianus
L 26"/66cm   WS 40"/1m

Neotropic Cormorant is smaller and more slender than Double-crested Cormorant, with which it is often seen on inland freshwater lakes and sheltered coastal waters in Texas, New Mexico, and Arizona. In recent years, vagrant individuals have increased at scattered locations in the Great Plains and the Mississippi River drainage. Unlike other cormorants, Neotropic occasionally dives on prey, mostly fish and crustaceans, from the air or a perch. **VOICE** Nesting bird gives piglike croaks and low, squabbling noises.

breeding adult

gular skin bordered with white in breeding bird; terminates in sharp angle

immature

delicate build, dark (not orange) loral skin, and sharp terminus to gular skin (compare Double-crested)

longer-tailed than Double-crested

Great Cormorant
Phalacrocorax carbo
L 36"/91cm   WS 63"/1.6m

Great Cormorant nests at rocky coastal sites in New England and Canada and winters southward regularly to the Carolinas, almost exclusively on salt water. It is usually seen singly or in small groups, less often in close aggregations of several dozen. This species is often seen in the same vicinity as the more numerous Double-crested Cormorant, but it is relatively rare inland. **VOICE** Nesting bird gives nasal croaks and low, nasal, bleating calls, descending in tone.

adult

white plumage of throat narrows to point within yellow gular skin (compare Double-crested)

massive bill and blocky head; thicker neck than Double-crested, and black (not orange) loral skin

head, neck, flanks have white feathering in high breeding plumage

immature

belly and throat distinctively white

Pelagic Cormorant
Phalacrocorax pelagicus
L 26"/66cm **WS** 39"/99cm

Pelagic Cormorant is strictly a saltwater species and is almost never found inland. It is less gregarious than Brandt's Cormorant, with which it overlaps in range extensively, and is usually seen in small groups or singly. Like Brandt's, Pelagic can forage well out to sea and dive deeply, to at least 120' (35m). But Pelagic prefers inshore waters, where it forages mostly near the sea floor. **VOICE** Nesting bird gives croaking grunts; birds in territorial disputes give unusual *sssssss* calls.

nonbreeding adult

crown appears flat; lacks tuft of breeding adult

(immature similar)

thin, always dark bill

slender neck often appears contorted

breeding adult

tufted head

green gloss on body

long tail

purple gloss on neck

white on flanks

Brandt's Cormorant
Phalacrocorax penicillatus
L 34"/86cm   **WS** 48"/1.2m

A gregarious cormorant of rocky Pacific coastlines and islands, Brandt's is similar in size to Double-crested but has slightly shorter wings and tail, a dark bill, and a more slender neck and head. Like Double-crested, Brandt's is often seen in flocks, but it does not wander inland and tends to fly low over water in long, single-file formations. Compared to the other Pacific cormorants (Pelagic and Red-faced), Brandt's has a larger, heavier head, neck, and bill. **VOICE** Nesting bird gives low, guttural croaking.

nonbreeding adult

crown appears rounded

sturdier head and neck, shorter tail than Pelagic Cormorant

pale buffy feathering borders gular skin (which turns vivid blue in high breeding condition)

immature

no orange in bill or facial skin (unlike Double-crested)

gular skin surrounded by pale plumage

pale tan or brownish below (compare Pelag

Red-faced Cormorant

Phalacrocorax urile
L 30"/76cm WS 46"/1.2m

This little-studied species of Alaskan coasts and islands is sometimes called a "shag," as are all slender-necked cormorants, including this species' close relative Pelagic Cormorant. Red-faced Cormorant forms larger aggregations than Pelagic, both at colonies—which are set on cliffs among other seabirds—and during the nonbreeding season. Red-faced builds sturdy, tidy nests of grass and seaweed (much neater than those of other species) on rock ledges. **VOICE** Nesting bird gives low, thrumming croaking.

breeding adult

red face (duller in winter)

yellowish bill, unique among cormorants, visible at a great distance

immature

pale bill with yellow cast

neck and underparts have brown tones

Anhinga

Anhinga anhinga
L 35"/89cm WS 45"/1.1m

Anhinga is the only American represen-tative of the darters, a widespread tropical family of freshwater-foraging diving birds. Though darters are superficially similar to cormorants, their pointed bill and very slender head and neck are more reminiscent of herons; like herons, they spear prey, usually while swimming with only the head and neck visible above the water. Anhinga makes a bulky stick nest in trees, mostly over water. During courtship, the skin around the male's eyes takes on a clear cerulean color. **VOICE** A dry, guttural rattle or series of abrupt rattles and grating, nasal, heronlike croaks.

adult male

intricate pale pattern in upperwing coverts and scapulars

long, daggerlike bill and very long tail (unlike cormorants)

adult female/ juvenile

very long neck and tail produce very different flight profile from cormorants

pale brown head, neck, breast

Tubenoses

"Tubenose" is a collective term for four closely related pelagic seabird families grouped in the order Procellariiformes: the goose-sized albatrosses (Diomedeidae); the gull-sized shearwaters, fulmars, and petrels (Procellariidae); the much smaller storm-petrels (Hydrobatidae); and the diving-petrels (Pelecanoididae), found only in the Southern Hemisphere. Tubenoses have stout bodies and heads and webbed feet for swimming (and diving, in some species). They are named for their tubed

Courtship among Laysan Albatrosses involves a complex series of exaggerated poses, each accompanied by different vocalizations or bill sounds.

nostrils, or naricorns—specialized parts of the bill used both to detect scents and to extrude salt extracted from seawater by the salt glands. Because they can drink salt water, tubenoses are able to spend years at a time at sea. Their pelagic habits are also aided by buoyant plumages and, in most cases, aerodynamic wing structures, supreme adaptations for harnessing breezes and traveling great distances with minimal expenditure of energy. Recently, an albatross fitted with a satellite transmitter was found to travel 13,670 miles (22,000km) around the world in 46 days; several others are known to have circled the globe twice in 18 months!

Tubenoses feed on a great variety of marine organisms, from plankton (eaten by the smallest species) to squid (by the largest) and many types of crustaceans, fish, cephalopods, and carrion in between. Their keen senses of sight and smell guide them to food; some species forage at night, relying on bioluminescence in their prey. Most tubenoses seize prey at the water's surface with strong, sharp-edged bills that have a hooked unguis (nail) at the tip of the maxilla. Several shearwaters, such as the abundant Sooty Shearwater, readily dive to moderate depths—up to 60′ (18m)—using both wings and feet to pursue prey underwater.

Tubenoses nest in colonies mostly on remote oceanic islands far from familiar birding locations. Most of the smaller species, such as storm-petrels, enter and leave burrows only at night in order to avoid predators. Northern Fulmar nests high on cliffs in the Arctic, in an area of almost perpetual daylight, where it discourages predators by expelling a stream of stomach acid.

Courtship among tubenoses usually involves paired flights at sea and around the breeding grounds (these can take place both day and night) and allopreening, in which members of a pair preen each other's plumage. Albatrosses, which mate for life and may live to be 75 years old, have a more elaborate set of courtship displays than the smaller species: male and female perform a series of calls and fantastic, stylized postures in a specific sequence. After courtship and copulation, tubenoses return to sea for a period, to gain weight needed to produce their single egg.

Like other marine birds, tubenoses are threatened by pollution of many sorts (plastic debris has been found in the stomachs of many species), oil spills, overharvesting of prey species, and long-lining, a fishing practice that threatens several larger petrels and albatrosses with extinction in the near future.

Identification of Tubenoses

The majority of tubenoses are pelagic species and as such are rarely seen near shore; most people encounter them while at sea. The bills of all tubenoses have tubed nostrils but differ in length, depth, and shape. On pelagic birding trips, tubenoses are often lured close with food, and their different bill structures can then be observed.

naricorn

culminicorn

nail

Black-footed Albatross

Trinidade Petrel

Wedge-tailed Shearwater

Leach's Storm-Petrel

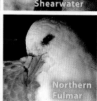

Northern Fulmar

Albatrosses, the largest tubenoses, have large bills made of multiple plates. The naricorns are located on opposite sides of the bill. (In the smaller tubenoses the naricorns join at the base of the culmen.) The culminicorn, a distinct plate located along the top ridge of the culmen, is brightly colored in some albatrosses, such as Yellow-nosed. Shearwaters have long bills, like albatrosses, but their bills are less deep. Petrels and fulmars have shorter, stubbier bills. The culmen of all tubenoses ends in an arched, sharp nail (unguis) that is used for tearing prey and gripping slippery catches like squid. The nail is bulbous in some species (Northern Fulmar) and heavily hooked in others (Black-capped Petrel). In small petrels (such as Cook's and Bermuda), the nail blends more with the rest of the bill. Storm-petrels all have very small bills; there are subtle differences in length and depth, but these are rarely useful for species identification.

Tubenoses in Flight

The flight behavior of tubenoses varies according to wind speed, but, as with raptors, a seabird's various flight styles can be learned with patient, repeated observation. A bird's wing shape is directly related to its manner of flight.

Black-browed Albatross

Audubon's Shearwater

The wings of albatrosses are very long and rather narrow, a shape that is described in aerodynamic terms as having a very high "aspect ratio" (the relationship of length to width). Tubenoses with such wing shapes fly in long, graceful arcs, following a roller coaster–like path, and flap only occasionally (less so in higher winds).

The wings of Audubon's Shearwater, by comparison, are short and wide and have a lower aspect ratio but a higher "wingloading"—the relationship between body weight and overall wing area. Thus Audubon's tends to flap rapidly between glides, although when winds are brisk it is able to gain more lift and flaps much less.

Laysan Albatross

Phoebastria immutabilis
L 32"/81cm   **WS** 79"/2m

Laysan Albatross nests in vast colonies on remote islands, mostly the Northwestern Hawaiian Islands, and forages in deep waters across the North Pacific. It is rarely seen near shore except when nesting. Its population of about 874,000 would seem to make it an abundant species, but its numbers have declined sharply in the past decade, mostly a result of the longline fishery. Laysan has hybridized with Black-footed Albatross. **VOICE** Moaning and piping sounds from courting adults; low grunting sounds from feeding birds at sea.

adult

white head, underparts, tail coverts

brown tail and upperwings

white primary shafts

adult

underwing coverts variably mottled with white and brown

Yellow-nosed Albatross

Thalassarche chlororhynchos
L 32"/81cm   **WS** 79"/2m

Yellow-nosed Albatross is a rare visitor to the North Atlantic and Gulf of Mexico, often to inshore waters. It normally inhabits the temperate South Atlantic, nesting on Tristan da Cunha and Gough Islands (the subspecies *bassii* nests on islands in the Indian Ocean). Black-browed (shown on p. 97) is the only other albatross reported in the western North Atlantic; at a distance, either species could be mistaken for a large gull. **VOICE** Brays and grunts from courting adults; croaks from feeding birds at sea.

adult

slender wings, brown above and white with narrow dark border below

adult

adult has yellow "nose" (culminicorn)

Black-footed Albatross

Phoebastria nigripes
L 32½"/83cm WS 80"/2m

Black-footed Albatross is the Pacific albatross most likely to be observed near shore. It often gathers in large numbers to scavenge prey around fishing boats, particularly squid-fishing trawlers. Like Laysan Albatross, Black-footed nests chiefly in the Northwestern Hawaiian Islands, forming large, dense colonies. The world population of about 278,000 birds appears to be declining by about 10% every decade. **VOICE** Moans, whinnies, quacks, and whistles from courting adults; squeals from squabbling birds at sea.

adult

brown; white around bill

white in tail coverts acquired in about 7th year

adult

older birds paler, especially on head

subadult

younger birds lack white in tail

narrower wings than Short-tailed Albatross, and gray (not pink) bill

Short-tailed Albatross

Phoebastria albatrus
L 37"/94cm WS 88"/2.2m

Short-tailed Albatross nests on the island of Torishima, Japan, and the Senkaku Islands, China. It is an annual visitor to the northeastern North Pacific and Bering Sea off Alaska and is recorded with increasing frequency farther south off the Pacific coast. Single birds occasionally visit Midway Island in the central Pacific. Short-tailed is still considered critically endangered, with a population of only 1,840 birds in 2004. **VOICE** A mooing, braying sound and various groaning sounds from courting adults.

adult

large

white plumage has extensive black above

golden head

pink bill has pale blue tip

subadult

like adult but brownish nape (adult plumage attained in 12–20 years)

juvenile

recalls Black-footed but has larger, pink bill and broader wings

Black-capped Petrel

Pterodroma hasitata
L 16"/41cm **WS** 37"/94cm

This agile aerialist, North America's most
frequently observed gadfly petrel, is
often seen in small flocks over deep Gulf
Stream waters. Like other *Pterodroma*,
Black-cappeds are observed on land
only rarely, when hurricanes drive them
inshore or inland. The species presumably
nests only in mountain cliffs of the
Dominican Republic, Cuba, and possibly
the Lesser Antilles. It is considered
endangered. **VOICE** Low- and high-
pitched, tremulous moans and wails from
courting adults; calls heard only rarely
at sea.

extensive
white collar
and uppertail
coverts

black
cap

heavy
bill

some show
M pattern in
upperwings

narrow
black ulnar
bar in white
underwings

stark white
below

cap shape variable
(some extend to
back, eliminating
white collar)

Bermuda Petrel

Pterodroma cahow
L 15"/38cm **WS** 35"/89cm

Bermuda Petrel, or Cahow, was thought
to be extinct between 1630 and 1950;
it is one of the world's rarest seabirds,
with only 35 pairs on Bermuda in 2005.
Since 1995 a few have been observed
annually off North Carolina in spring and
summer. Some individuals are entirely
dark above, showing no white in the tail
coverts. **VOICE** Adults in antiphonal
courtship give a high, quavering
oooooooooo-EEK! and a deep, gravelly
aaaaawwwww-AK!; also a puppylike
squeal.

limited white in
uppertail coverts; gray
cowl (compare Black-
capped)

body and wings
slimmer than Black-
capped, more like Fea's

narrow
wings

wide, black
ulnar bar

small bill

Trinidade Petrel

Pterodroma arminjoniana
L 14½"/37cm WS 37"/94cm

The graceful Trinidade Petrel nests on a few small islands in the Atlantic and Indian Oceans. Single birds, light and dark morphs and intermediate plumages, have been observed mostly in the Gulf Stream off North Carolina between spring and fall. All forms can be confused with jaegers and shearwaters, but Trinidade flies in buoyant, steep arcs. This species is sometimes combined with Herald Petrel of the Pacific. **VOICE** Similar to other Atlantic gadfly petrels; also a squeal similar to Northern Flicker.

light morph

most show broad ulnar bar in pale underwings; some have dark underwings

light morph

dark morph

compare "archer's bow" wing shape to shearwaters and jaegers

rich dark brown below, with silvery bases to remiges and greater primary coverts (compare dark jaegers)

Fea's Petrel

Pterodroma feae
L 15"/38cm WS 34"/86cm

Fea's Petrel is a small gadfly petrel of the Macaronesian islands off western Africa. North American records, all of solitary birds, are associated with Gulf Stream waters between Nova Scotia and South Carolina. The pale uppertail usually contrasts with the back, a pattern shared only with the very rare Zino's Petrel of Madeira, which is smaller-billed and not yet recorded in North America. **VOICE** Similar to Bermuda Petrel but with mournful downward inflection.

pale gray cowl rather than cap (compare Bermuda and Black-capped Petrels)

many have dark eye patch

heavy bill

mostly slaty underwings contrast with pale belly

M pattern in upperwings

most show pale uppertail coverts

Galapagos Petrel/ Hawaiian Petrel

Pterodroma phaeopygia/sandwichensis
L 17"/43cm   **WS** 39"/99cm

In 2002 the two subspecies of Dark-rumped Petrel were recognized as distinct but very similar species: Galapagos Petrel and Hawaiian Petrel. Birds of this complex have recently been recorded as rare visitors to waters off California between May and October; it is not yet clear whether they are visitors from the Galápagos, Hawaii, or both, but Hawaiian birds are suspected in most cases. **VOICE** Barking, growling, grunting, and squealing calls; the repeated, low-pitched *oo-AH-oo* of Hawaiian Petrel lends the species its Hawaiian name, 'Ua'u.

Galapagos Petrel

dark above

long wings and tail

Galapagos Petrel

black cowl

heavy bill

ulnar bar narrows toward axillaries

Murphy's Petrel

Pterodroma ultima
L 15½"/39cm   **WS** 38"/97cm

Murphy's Petrel is named for seabird researcher Robert Cushman Murphy. Small numbers of this little-known tropical petrel have recently been observed in deep water off the West Coast, mostly in spring. The species may be confused with dark shearwaters, Northern Fulmar, jaegers, or other brown Pacific gadfly petrels in or near its range, such as Solander's, Kermadec, and Great-winged Petrels. **VOICE** Accelerating *boo* calls similar to Boreal Owl, gull-like cries, and undulating, long hoots.

mostly brown with gray cast above

pale chin and face

tail often appears wedge-shaped

grayish brown overall with pale around base of bill and in primary bases

Mottled Petrel

Pterodroma inexpectata
L 14"/36cm **WS** 32"/81cm

Mottled Petrel is one of several transequatorial migrant seabirds that migrate from nesting islands off New Zealand to forage in the rich waters off Alaska in summer. It is occasionally observed far off the Pacific coast in autumn. Its species name derives from the "unexpected" discovery of one in upstate New York in 1880. **VOICE** On breeding grounds a series of high-pitched excited *ti* and *kik* notes (similar to other small gadfly petrels), along with a throaty, quavering *urrrrrr-WIK!*

pale uppertail coverts contrast with dark rump

compact, stocky body; often appears short-tailed

(dorsal M pattern usually apparent; depends on wear and angle of light)

dark gray belly patch visible from great distance

broad black ulnar bar stands out in white underwing

heavier bill than Cook's Petrel

Cook's Petrel

Pterodroma cookii
L 11"/28cm **WS** 27"/69cm

Cook's Petrel is probably the most numerous of its genus found off the Pacific coast, usually well offshore, in its nonbreeding season (May–October). It is much smaller than other North American gadfly petrels; the similar Stejneger's Petrel, recorded a few times off California, has a much darker crown that contrasts sharply with the pale gray mantle, unlike in Cook's. Cook's may also be confused with small gadfly petrels not yet recorded in North America. **VOICE** Similar to Mottled Petrel but higher-pitched.

distinct dark eye patch (rare Stejneger's Petrel has blackish cap extending to eyes)

pale gray above, with dark M pattern in wings

gray uppertail coverts contrast with black tips of central rectrices

white outer rectrices; black in Stejneger's

nearly white underwings

very pale crown

Manx Shearwater
Puffinus puffinus
L 13½"/34cm **WS** 33"/84cm

This chunky, small shearwater of cool waters nests in the northern North Atlantic and winters off temperate South America. Its long migration makes it one of the most widely distributed of American shearwaters; it has recently even turned up in increasing numbers in the Pacific. **VOICE** On breeding grounds, a cacophonous low growling interspersed with highly modulated, high-pitched yelping, rhythmically repeated; other nasal, whining, and wailing calls. A colony of calling adults has a comical sound.

contrasting blackish brown above, white below through undertail

white wraps around back of dark auriculars

dark face framed by white in rear (compare Audubon's Shearwater)

white undertail coverts often visible on birds swimming away

looks longer-winged and shorter-tailed than Audubon's, recalling a small Greater Shearwater

Audubon's Shearwater
Puffinus lherminieri
L 12"/30cm **WS** 27"/69cm

The petite Audubon's Shearwater forages mostly in tropical waters, especially in the Gulf Stream. It is associated with the pelagic drift community, organisms that live among rafts of gulfweed (algae of the genus *Sargassum*), and can often be observed foraging by diving into the algae and swimming underwater with open wings. In flight Audubon's flaps rapidly between glides, especially in low winds. **VOICE** Nasal mewing and twittering calls from nesting bird; not often heard at sea.

long tail, short wings (compare Manx Shearwater)

dark above

no white behind dark auriculars (compare Manx)

slender bill

dark undertail coverts

Black-vented Shearwater
Puffinus opisthomelas
L 14"/36cm **WS** 34"/86cm

This species breeds only on islands off the Baja California peninsula; it is often abundant close to the southern California coast from fall through spring. Its flight is rapid and choppy, much like that of Manx Shearwater, with which it was formerly combined as a single species. Like Manx, Black-vented Shearwater dives readily for food, is not strongly attracted to boats, and gathers in large flocks in the nonbreeding season. **VOICE** On breeding grounds a moaning growl and hissing, braying, wailing, and snoring calls.

dark undertail coverts (compare Manx Shearwater)

head often looks dark at a distance

underparts often have sooty brown cast

dusky brown at sides of neck, almost meeting across upper breast

lacks distinct facial pattern and blackish upperparts of Manx

often appears dusky brown overall when sitting on water

Wedge-tailed Shearwater
Puffinus pacificus
L 16"/41cm **WS** 39"/99cm

The tropical Wedge-tailed Shearwater is widespread in the Indo-Pacific basin and numerous off western Mexico. It has been recorded about a dozen times off California, and both dark and light morphs have been seen. Its long tail and wings give this medium-sized shearwater a distinctive shape in flight. **VOICE** A variety of rising and falling moaning, wheezing sounds from courting adults; call sometimes likened to a child's crying.

dark morph

long tail usually held closed (making wedge shape hard to see)

uniformly brown (slightly paler below), with gray bill

dark or intermediate morph

brown overall, but paler tan-brown below

(greater upperwing coverts often appear paler in flight)

dark morph

slender gray bill

Pink-footed Shearwater
Puffinus creatopus
L 19"/48cm   **WS** 43"/1.1m

Pink-footed Shearwater breeds on islands
off Chile and spends the nonbreeding
season (spring–fall) off the Pacific coast.
Its plumage shows much variation, with
some individuals more dusky below. Aside
from the paler-faced Streaked Shearwater,
a vagrant to the West Coast, Pink-footed is
the largest shearwater in the North Pacific.
In flight Pink-footed looks less buoyant
and agile than Buller's Shearwater. **VOICE**
A nasal, bleating *nyyeeehhh* at sea;
nesting birds give a syncopated series of
low hoots on different pitches.

uniformly dark
brown upperparts

languid wingbeats
compared to
smaller species

pinkish bill has
dusky tip

pale underwings
with variably
dark lesser and
median coverts
and axillaries

Cory's Shearwater
Calonectris diomedea
L 20"/51cm   **WS** 45"/1.1m

Cory's Shearwater nests on islands in
the eastern Atlantic and feeds in pelagic
waters of the temperate Atlantic from late
spring through autumn, preying on small
baitfish driven to the surface by larger fish.
Cory's is often found in flocks with Greater
or other shearwaters; it is occasionally
observed from land, during migration
or when prey moves inshore. **VOICE** A
low, owl-like *hoooooo,* nasal *ooooooo-IK*
and *awwwww-IK* calls, and low growling
sounds from courting adults; nasal
bleating from feeding birds at sea.

long, lanky wings
and labored
flapping produce
loping flight style
in light winds

molting birds often
have pale area in
upperwings

heavy yellow
bill, unlike other
shearwaters

long, broad
wings

pale underwings
bordered in
brown

world's largest
shearwater

Buller's Shearwater

Puffinus bulleri
L 18"/46cm **WS** 38"/97cm

Buller's Shearwater nests on New Zealand's offshore islands and passes through Pacific coast waters in late summer and fall. It appears long-tailed and long-winged in flight as it executes long glides between graceful wingbeats. Though not generally attracted to boats, it often investigates flocks of birds gathered around boats. Flocks sometimes gather where prey is plentiful. This species was recorded off New Jersey in 1984. **VOICE** Various rhythmic howling, wailing, and braying sounds.

distinctive dark crown, primaries, and most coverts against pale gray back and secondaries (compare gadfly petrels)

appears long-tailed and long-winged

sleek appearance in flight recalls gadfly petrels

long tail

soft white below, with gray cowl and gray edges to underwings

Greater Shearwater

Puffinus gravis
L 18"/46cm   **WS** 42"/1.1m

The striking Greater Shearwater nests on Tristan da Cunha and Gough Islands in the South Atlantic and spends the summer and autumn in the North Atlantic, where it is especially numerous around the Canadian Maritimes and off New England. In flight it is distinguished from Cory's Shearwater by its smaller size and snappier wingbeats. This species dives well and is often attracted to boats. **VOICE** High-pitched howling from courting adults; nasal, bleating whines, similar to Cory's, from feeding birds at sea.

dark brown above

distinct long, black cap

often white in uppertail coverts

long, thin, dark bill

strong contrast between upperparts and underparts

(compare Black-capped Petrel)

heavy brown mottling on underwings and belly

Sooty Shearwater
Puffinus griseus
L 18"/46cm **WS** 39"/99cm

In the Pacific, Sooty Shearwater sometimes forms flocks of more than a million birds; it is often seen from land. This species dives and swims well underwater, sometimes to depths of 30' (9m) or more, as it forages for anchovies and other small fish. Its flight tends to be direct, with rapid bursts of flapping and graceful glides. Unlike dark gadfly petrels (genus *Pterodroma*), Sooty has a long, slender bill. **VOICE** Breeding bird gives repeated series of moans, brays, and catlike wails, rhythmic and varied in tone.

uniformly sooty brown above

flies with rapid wingbeats and brief glides

appears to have longer neck and flatter head than Short-tailed, with sloping forehead and longer bill

variably patterned underwings, with silvery sheen

"longer" head and heavier bill than Short-tailed

Short-tailed Shearwater
Puffinus tenuirostris
L 17"/43cm **WS** 38"/97cm

Like its close relative Sooty Shearwater, this is an abundant bird, with a population of perhaps 23 million around Australia. Short-tailed Shearwater spends the summer off Alaska, where enormous flocks are seen in the Bering Sea into September and October, before passing southward off the Pacific coast during fall and winter. The species is very difficult to distinguish from Sooty Shearwater. **VOICE** A series of screeches, cackles, and wails similar to Sooty Shearwater but more rapid and jerky.

very slender wings

less projection of body ahead of wings than in Sooty

small, rounded head; shorter, more slender bill than Sooty

often unpatterned underwings, mostly lacking silvery sheen of Sooty

appears short-necked, with rounded head and steep forehead

sometimes shows dark head; can also show pale chin like some Sooty Shearwaters

Flesh-footed Shearwater
Puffinus carneipes
L 17"/43cm **WS** 41"/1m

Flesh-footed Shearwater, a scarce visitor from Australia and New Zealand to Pacific coastal waters, resembles a dark version of Pink-footed Shearwater. Its pale feet and legs are difficult to see at sea, but the pale bill contrasting with dark overall plumage is visible from a long distance. Beware confusing this species with a melanistic (dark) Pink-footed or with vagrant species such as Great-winged and Parkinson's Petrels. **VOICE** Nesting adult gives rising, nasal, strident *ooo-hoo* and *ooo-hooah* cries.

uniformly brown (secondaries here catching light)

heavy, pale pink bill has dusky tip

pinkish legs sometimes visible

uniformly dark brown below (remiges look paler in direct light)

slightly smaller than Pink-footed Shearwater

pale bill contrasts with dark plumage, including underwings

Northern Fulmar
Fulmarus glacialis
L 19"/48cm **WS** 42"/1.1m

This stocky, thick-billed tubenose nests on cliffs in Arctic and subarctic regions and winters at sea in cold currents. Fulmars fly with bouts of stiff flaps on open wings with much gliding in between (compare the more buoyant flight style of gulls). Atlantic birds are mostly white-headed, pale below, and gray dorsally. Pacific birds range from pale whitish to very dark gray-brown overall. Fulmars are strongly attracted to chum and carrion. **VOICE** A rapid, almost ducklike quacking on nesting grounds.

Pacific, dark morph

medium to dark gray

wingtips appear more rounded than in shearwaters

(some birds browner and much darker, recalling Flesh-footed Shearwater)

Atlantic, pale morph

thick bill with prominent naricorns (compare gulls and shearwaters)

gray tail (unlike gulls)

white-headed and gray above (sometimes mottled gray with bluish hue)

Band-rumped Storm-Petrel

Oceanodroma castro
L 9"/23cm   WS 17"/43cm

This storm-petrel is fairly common during summer in deep waters of the Gulf Stream and Gulf of Mexico. Its nearest nesting grounds are islands of the eastern North Atlantic. Compared to Leach's Storm-Petrel, Band-rumped tends to fly more directly, in wide, roller-coaster arcs; its wing shape appears fuller and broader, less sharply angular in the carpal joint, and almost scythelike in overall shape. **VOICE** At colonies adult gives squeaks that sound like a wet finger rubbed on a windowpane.

recalls Leach's but lacks deep fork in tail, carpal bar less buffy and less extensive, and wing shape less angular

narrower white area in uppertail coverts than Wilson's

flight less erratic than Leach's, more dynamic than Wilson's

less white in flanks/undertail area than Wilson's, but more than Leach's

heavier bill and longer wings than Wilson's

feet never project past tail tip (unlike Wilson's)

Leach's Storm-Petrel

Oceanodroma leucorhoa
L 8"/20cm   WS 18"/46cm

A bird of deep water, Leach's Storm-Petrel is rarely seen from land away from its nesting areas, where it is strictly nocturnal. The species is often compared to nighthawks because of its angular wing shape and bounding, erratic flight, with deep wingstrokes and frequent changes in direction. Individuals with dark uppertail coverts are common in the Pacific, unknown in the Atlantic. **VOICE** Adult gives a rapid, rollicking *pup-prrtl-DEE-didldo* in flight over colonies and a nightjarlike, purring call on nest.

deep fork in tail

buffy carpal bar broader than Band-rumped

white uppertail coverts usually broken by dark line (rarely so in Band-rumped)

very little white in flanks

flight rather erratic, recalling nighthawks

forked tail

long, pointed, angular wings

pale buffy carpal bar

Wilson's Storm-Petrel

Oceanites oceanicus
L 7½"/19cm **WS** 16"/41cm

An abundant breeder in Antarctic and subantarctic regions, Wilson's Storm-Petrel spends the nonbreeding season (April–September) in the North Atlantic. It is the most common storm-petrel in the Atlantic and should be carefully studied by beginning birders in order to more easily recognize other species. In direct flight it resembles a swallow and often courses low over the water, its even flapping interspersed with frequent short glides. When feeding, it dangles and patters its long legs on the water while fluttering in place. In high winds, Wilson's often arcs above the water's surface, as larger storm-petrels routinely do in lighter winds. Wilson's gathers in large flocks where its prey, mostly plankton, is concentrated and often mixes with other storm-petrels. It is attracted to chum. **VOICE** Doubled or repeated *ark* notes, whiny and harsh, from courting adults; squeaky *keep* notes from feeding birds.

wings lack angularity of Leach's, scythe shape of Band-rumped

white uppertail coverts form broad band

feet project well beyond tail tip

prominent whitish carpal bar (especially evident in fresh plumage)

white of uppertail coverts extends well into flanks and undertail area (unlike Band-rumped, Leach's)

many birds in Northern Hemisphere show extensive wing molt

feet project well beyond tail (unlike larger storm-petrels)

feeds by pattering on surface of water and picking food (larger storm-petrels rarely patter)

White-faced Storm-Petrel

Pelagodroma marina
L 7½"/19cm **WS** 17"/43cm

The distinctive White-faced Storm-Petrel has a unique flight style: on broad wings held out like sails, it glides between the waves, bouncing kangaroo-like with its long legs and large feet off the water's surface, flapping only occasionally with shallow, fluttering wingbeats. This species is a scarce late-summer and autumn visitor to offshore waters from the Carolinas to New England; most records are of solitary birds. **VOICE** A repeated, mournful, descending *ooooo* at nest.

distinctive shape and face pattern

long legs, yellow feet

Black Storm-Petrel

Oceanodroma melania
L 9"/23cm WS 19"/48cm

Black Storm-Petrel breeds between May and December only on islands off southern California and Baja California and is a common sight there in warmer months; it winters mostly from Baja California to Peru. This very large storm-petrel is most easily identified when flying: its slow, deep wingbeats are more similar to Black Tern than to smaller dark storm-petrels such as Ashy or dark-morph Leach's. **VOICE** A ringing, grating *tuckaree t-tuk-a-rooo!* from breeding adult.

long, forked tail

long, broad wings have broad, buff-brown carpal bar

robust body and head, bulkier overall than Ashy or Leach's Storm-Petrel

uniformly dark brown, except for paler carpal bar

Ashy Storm-Petrel

Oceanodroma homochroa
L 8"/20cm WS 17"/43cm

A species that breeds only on islands off the California coast, Ashy Storm-Petrel is most often seen during the warmer months, when it forages, often in flocks, relatively close to shore. Careful study of this common species will help in distinguishing other dark storm-petrels: it has shallower, more rapid wingbeats than Black and more direct flight than Leach's. The ashen tones in its plumage and its paler underwings can be detected in optimal light. **VOICE** Adults in burrow give a purring duet similar to Leach's and an excited, high-pitched *kri-ih whee-PU, ki-krr* over colonies at night.

ashen tones can be seen in good light

contrastingly pale greater underwing coverts

much larger than Least, smaller and more slender than Black, with longer tail and narrower wings

pale underwing coverts (visible in good light at close range), unlike Black

ashen tones in head, back, uppertail coverts (visible in optimal light)

carpal bar less buffy and less extensive than in Leach's

Least Storm-Petrel

Oceanodroma microsoma
L 5¾"/15cm **WS** 13"/33cm

Least Storm-Petrel is an endemic nester on islands off Baja California and a summer and autumn visitor to California waters. Its tiny size, very dark brown plumage, and low, erratic flight make it easy to mistake for a bat or a swift, but its deep wingbeats are unlike either. **VOICE** Series of high-pitched, accelerating *krri* calls from breeding adults at colonies.

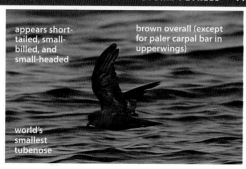

appears short-tailed, small-billed, and small-headed

brown overall (except for paler carpal bar in upperwings)

world's smallest tubenose

Wedge-rumped Storm-Petrel

Oceanodroma tethys
L 6"/15cm **WS** 14½"/37cm

A tiny Pacific storm-petrel of South American islands, Wedge-rumped Storm-Petrel is a rare visitor to California waters in the nonbreeding season (August–January). **VOICE** Twittering, purring notes at colonies; sharp, squeaky notes at sea, rarely heard.

tiny and compact

extensively white uppertail coverts almost reach tip of short tail

overall shape and wingbeats recall Least Storm-Petrel (very unlike Wilson's)

Fork-tailed Storm-Petrel

Oceanodroma furcata
L 8½"/22cm **WS** 18½"/47cm

Fork-tailed Storm-Petrel is the only storm-petrel with pearl gray plumage; its wing coverts and the area around the eyes are contrastingly dark. Though a strong flier, its wingbeats appear delicate. Fork-tailed is associated with cold currents; it nests in colonies from Alaska to northern California and is seen only rarely off southern California. The dark eye patch and pale plumage make it easy to confuse resting birds with phalaropes. **VOICE** Squeaky, twittering calls from nesting adult.

pale gray above

dark eye patch

forked tail

appears darker in low light

wingtips often appear rounded

underwing coverts darker than remiges

Gulls, Terns, Skimmer, and Kin

Parasitic Jaegers chase other larids (here an Arctic Tern) to steal their prey or food.

Jaegers, skuas, skimmers, gulls (including kittiwakes), and terns (including noddies) are often grouped into a single family, Laridae. All larids are small to medium-sized waterbirds with webbed feet and relatively long wings. The group includes very familiar birds, such as the gulls that wheel around the seashore or above fast-food franchises, as well as pelagic species rarely observed on land in North America, such as the skuas. Black Skimmer differs markedly from other larids (and all other birds) in its outsized bill, with mandible longer than maxilla. In 2006, the American Ornithologists' Union moved jaegers and skuas into their own family, Stercorariidae.

The so-called "seagull" is represented on this continent by no fewer than 30 species, from the world's largest, the goose-sized Great Black-backed Gull, to the world's smallest, the dove-sized Little Gull. Bill size and shape in gulls is very much tied to body size: larger species have heavier, deeper bills, while the smallest gulls have rather thin, ternlike bills. Terns are less adaptable than gulls in most respects, and they also show relatively less diversity in structure and plumage. The mostly dark-plumaged jaegers and skuas recall birds of prey: jaegers, with their pointed wings and swift flight, resemble falcons; skuas, with their heavy bodies and bills and aggressive manner, recall hawks.

Larids show a remarkable range of foraging techniques. Most gulls are adapted to seizing fish or other prey from the water's surface; others pick fruit on the wing, flycatch, dig for grubs and worms,

and even drop shellfish onto rocks to break them open. Few birds are better adapted to manmade environments than gulls, which forage in an astonishing array of places: city parks and streets, landfills, sewage treatment plants, agricultural fields, and hydroelectric plants, to name only a few. Most terns forage by diving, but some also flycatch insects or pick prey from the water's surface. Skimmers forage by lowering the mandible into the water when flying and snapping the bill shut upon sensing prey. Jaegers and skuas derive much of their food in the manner of raptors, either through direct predation of small mammals and birds or by stealing food from other birds. Like gulls, jaegers and skuas are omnivores.

Most larids nest in colonies, sometimes very large ones, though the jaegers, skuas, and larger gulls often nest solitarily and defend large territories. Most species nest on the ground or on sea-cliffs, with little in the way of a true nest; a few, such as noddies and Bonaparte's Gull, nest in trees. Courtship usually consists of ritualized posturing, parading, and calling; some species make offerings of small fish or other items. Gulls, particularly the larger species, have "long calls" that they use in a variety of contexts, including pair-bonding. Both parents feed their young.

Gull populations are mostly stable or increasing. Terns and Black Skimmers, however, are vulnerable to a variety of disturbances at nesting colonies, and productivity in several species of tern is considered low.

Identification of Larids

The array of species and plumages in a large flock of gulls and terns can overwhelm the inexperienced birder. A first step in larid identification is to make separate "scans" for differences in overall size, bill structure, upperparts color, and leg color, and thus begin to separate the flock into species. In gulls study eye color and wingtip pattern, which vary among individuals in a species but can provide additional

Herring, Great Black-backed, and Glaucous Gulls

information. It is important to learn the extent of variation within a species. First-winter Herring Gulls, for example, vary in body and bill sizes and plumage, and adults vary in leg color, eye color, head markings, and wingtip patterns.

The family Laridae presents numerous identification pitfalls. Juvenile gulls of the largest species are darker than adults (some quite dark brown), and most have dark bills; they can be mistaken for jaegers or skuas, which also have dark bills (except when very young). Juvenile Heermann's Gull, for example, is sooty brown overall and easily mistaken for a jaeger; its initially dark bill acquires a pale base within a few months, which separates it from older jaegers.

Identifying gulls is further complicated by hybridization, especially among four-year gulls (see p. 120). In some areas, hybrid gulls and their backcrosses are abundant. In the coastal Northwest, for instance, Glaucous-winged x Western Gull hybrids outnumber the parental types, and other hybrids are also common. Many hybrids show characteristics that are intermediate between the parent species; some hybrids cannot be identified.

Larid Bills

The larger larids—skuas, Black Skimmer, and large gulls—have heavy bills, and the smallest species (Least Tern and Little Gull) have thin or short bills. Most gulls have moderately long but rather deep bills in which the culmen curves

gently at the tip; terns and some small gulls have more slender, pointed bills. Male gulls tend to be larger than females, and their bills are correspondingly heavier. The smaller species in the many confusing "gull pairs"— Franklin's and Laughing, Iceland and Thayer's, Little and Bonaparte's, California and Herring— nearly always have a more delicate (shallower and sometimes shorter) bill. The same is true of "tern pairs," such as Elegant and Royal, Arctic and Common, and White-winged and Black. Runt individuals and small females can have bills that are quite small for the species; a petite Ring-billed Gull, for instance, may resemble a Mew Gull.

Jaeger and skua bills have a fairly strong nail at the end of the culmen (like the bills of tubenoses). The extent of the nail and the size and position of the gonys (the point on the mandible where the two sides fuse, usually visible as a slight downward-projecting point) relative to the rest of the bill differ among the jaegers. Pomarine Jaeger has a heavy, skualike bill with a distinct gonys and a relatively small nail. The bill of the intermediate Parasitic Jaeger has a slighter gonys, and the nail occupies about a third of the bill overall. The diminutive Long-tailed Jaeger has the smallest bill, with the nail extending almost half the bill length and the gonys almost at the bill's midpoint. The two skuas also differ in bill size, with Great having a thicker bill than South Polar.

Western Gull

Heermann's Gull

Parasitic Jaeger

South Polar Skua

Parasitic Jaeger
Stercorarius parasiticus
L 19"/48cm WS 42"/1.1m

Parasitic Jaeger nests in coastal tundra of northern Canada and Alaska and migrates, mostly along the Pacific and Atlantic coasts, to wintering grounds that stretch from California and the Carolinas to South America. This species is often seen in pursuit of terns, from which it pirates fish; it is the only bird whose diet consists almost solely of prey taken from other birds. Like the other jaegers, Parasitic lives at sea in the nonbreeding months, but it is typically the most numerous jaeger in nearshore waters and is thus a benchmark species to learn well for comparison with the others. Parasitic is intermediate in size and structure between Pomarine and Long-tailed Jaegers: it lacks the heavy-headed, broad-winged, and barrel-bellied appearance of Pomarine but is more substantial—more falconlike and less ternlike—than Long-tailed. **VOICE** Various querulous fussing and piping calls; a nasal *ayy-ERR!*, heard mostly on breeding grounds.

breeding adult, light morph

nape and sides of neck washed with yellow-gold, as in other adult jaegers

most show 3–5 white primary shafts

wings broader and darker brown than Long-tailed; central rectrices shorter

breeding adult, light morph

cap less extensive than Pomarine

diffuse breastband

breeding adult, intermediate morph

pale plumage above maxilla (unlike other jaegers)

medium brown throughout, with darker cap

streaked nape

warmer, more rufous tones above (unlike Long-tailed)

pale juvenile, worn

adult, dark morph

dark brown with golden nape

Long-tailed Jaeger
Stercorarius longicaudus
L 22"/56cm **WS** 40"/1m

A slender, graceful seabird, Long-tailed Jaeger nests in upland tundra of northern Canada and Alaska and migrates, mostly well offshore, to wintering areas off South America. Because of its remote nesting grounds and pelagic habits in the nonbreeding months, this is the least familiar of the three jaegers. In flight it appears narrow-winged and somewhat long-tailed compared to the others, even without the elongated central rectrices of breeding adults. Its delicate wingstrokes are often likened to those of a tern. Breeding adults are always light (no dark morph); juveniles range from very dark to very pale. Both adults and subadults have a strong gray component to the back and wings, unlike other jaegers. Like the larger jaegers, Long-tailed is a kleptoparasite, pirating prey from other birds, but it forages for itself to a greater extent and even eats berries before commencing fall migration. **VOICE** A high-pitched, strident *kiii-iuw,* sounding uncannily like Red-shouldered Hawk; also a sharp *yip,* a rolling *kriiiw,* and various nasal calls similar to Parasitic but higher.

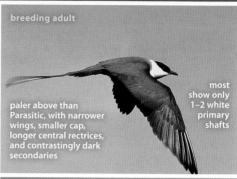

breeding adult

paler above than Parasitic, with narrower wings, smaller cap, longer central rectrices, and contrastingly dark secondaries

most show only 1–2 white primary shafts

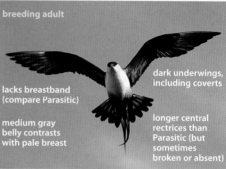

breeding adult

lacks breastband (compare Parasitic)

medium gray belly contrasts with pale breast

dark underwings, including coverts

longer central rectrices than Parasitic (but sometimes broken or absent)

pale juvenile

pale, unstreaked nape

bill almost half black

lacks warm tones above of Parasitic

outer 2 primary shafts white

subadult

adultlike plumage acquired in second year, but coverts and underparts still heavily barred

intermediate juvenile

tips of central rectrices rounded and blunt (pointed in Parasitic)

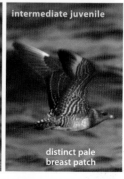

intermediate juvenile

distinct pale breast patch

Pomarine Jaeger

Stercorarius pomarinus
L 21"/53cm **WS** 48"/1.2m

Pomarine Jaeger is a nomadic species of High Arctic regions, nesting in coastal tundra where lemmings, its chief prey, are abundant. The species winters on open ocean waters, where it is often seen harassing gulls for food. Of the three jaegers, Pomarine is most likely to be confused with a skua: it is large-headed, heavy-bodied, and wide-winged, with extensive white in the primaries and the bases of the underprimary coverts. The word *pomarinus,* from the Greek for "lid-nosed," refers to the sheath of feathering over the base of the maxilla. **VOICE** Calls include a nasal, rising *jeeep* and various fussing calls, lower-pitched than smaller jaegers; a gruff *gark* sometimes heard at sea.

breeding adult, light morph

extensive white in primaries

cap extends far down face

long, spoon-shaped central rectrices

dark, well-defined breastband

breeding adult, dark morph

entirely chocolate brown, with dusky, diffuse cap

pale bases to primary coverts in underwings (unlike smaller jaegers)

nonbreeding adult, light morph

all tail coverts barred black and white

extensive white in primaries and bases of underprimary coverts (unlike small jaegers)

subadult, light morph

broader wings, more extensive cap than smaller jaegers

subadult, light morph

adultlike plumage acquired in second year, but coverts and underparts still heavily barred

juvenile, dark morph

most juveniles are dark (very rarely pale-headed) and lack rufous tones of most Parasitics

heavy, deep hooked bill

heavily marked sides

Great Skua

Stercorarius skua
L 22"/56cm **WS** 54"/1.4m

During the nonbreeding season, Great Skua inhabits Atlantic pelagic waters south to North Carolina, where most birds are presumably from breeding grounds in Iceland and the Faroe Islands; a few nonbreeders also spend the summer off eastern Canada. This powerfully built seabird regularly attacks birds larger or heavier than itself, either pirating their food or killing them. It is often attracted to gull flocks around fishing boats. **VOICE** A very short, nasal *eehnc,* heard mostly on breeding grounds.

adult/subadult

smaller than Herring Gull, but heavier-bodied

skuas fly with strong, deep wingbeats and surprising speed and agility

adult/subadult

gold and rufous streaks above

dusky cap

broader wings than Pomarine Jaeger, with more white in primary bases above

adult/subadult

short, broad tail

South Polar Skua

Stercorarius maccormicki
L 21"/53cm **WS** 52"/1.3m

South Polar Skua nests in Antarctica—it is the only bird ever recorded at the true South Pole—and migrates northward to spend its nonbreeding season (May–October) in pelagic waters. Like Great Skua, it ambushes shearwaters and gadfly petrels, eating food disgorged by its startled victims. The rare light morph is distinctive among skuas. Intermediate- and dark-morph birds resemble juvenile Great Skua and also Brown Skua (possibly a vagrant in Nova Scotia). **VOICE** A short, nasal *haaar,* mostly on breeding grounds.

adult, intermediate morph

most show golden or blond streaks in nape

mostly brown plumage lacks rufous tones

light morph

adult, intermediate morph

most of body paler than wings

bill often clearly smaller than in Great Skua

(subadult very similar; fresh juvenile shows unique pale gray tones)

white in primary bases as in Great Skua, but lacks cinnamon tones in upperparts

wings darker than body

Gull Plumages and Molts

Gulls hatch with a fuzzy coat of natal down and molt through several plumages before attaining adult plumage. Molts usually take several months to complete. Most of the smaller species of gulls are "two-year" gulls: they hatch in the breeding season of one calendar year and mature in the next (in just over 12 months). Intermediate-sized gulls, such as Ring-billed, generally take three calendar years (just over two full years) to attain adult plumage and thus are "three-year" gulls. Most of the largest species, such as Herring Gull, are adults at just over three years of age—a span of four calendar years; these are "four-year" gulls. (There are exceptions: the tiny Little Gull and the large Yellow-footed Gull are three-year gulls, and medium-sized Heermann's Gull appears to be a four-year species.) As adults, gulls undergo partial molts of head and body feathers twice a year, in spring and fall. They molt their flight feathers once a year, after breeding (Franklin's replaces its flight feathers twice a year); gulls in summer appear ragged, as their worn remiges and rectrices are replaced.

Bonaparte's Gull
1st winter

Bonaparte's Gull
winter adult

Two-year Gulls

Two-year gulls, such as Bonaparte's, have striking dorsal patterns in the juvenal plumage, and almost all of them (Ivory Gull and Red-legged Kittiwake excepted) show a prominent carpal bar or dark secondary coverts as juveniles. Soon after they are flying well, they molt the head and body feathers, along with some coverts, which produces *first-winter plumage,* also called first-basic plumage. (First-winter plumage is similar to juvenal plumage and often depicted in this guide instead of juvenal.) The head and body feathers are then molted again in spring, resulting in *first-summer plumage,* or first-alternate plumage. (First-summer plumage, usually similar to first-winter plumage, is not depicted in this guide.) The whole plumage, including remiges and rectrices, is replaced in the autumn of the birds' second year, resulting by wintertime in *adult nonbreeding plumage,* or definitive basic plumage. In spring, the birds again molt head and body feathers to attain *adult breeding plumage* (definitive alternate plumage), including in some smaller gulls a dark hood.

Three-year Gulls

Three-year gulls in North America include Ring-billed Gull and the exceptional Little and Yellow-footed Gulls (noted above), plus Mew, Franklin's, Laughing, and Black-tailed Gulls. Juvenile three-year gulls are not as strikingly marked as the two-year species; they are generally more brownish above and lack the neat carpal markings of the smaller species, although Little Gull shows very contrasting markings above. The progression of plumages in three-year gulls is the same as for two-year gulls, but the three-years take about a year more than two-year gulls and undergo two additional molts to attain adult nonbreeding plumage. (Their additional plumages—second winter and second summer—are similar to adult plumage and are not depicted here.) One difference between the subadult or near-adult plumages and adult plumages of this group can be seen in the primary tips: adults (except for Black-tailed Gull) have either white tips to the primaries or white "mirrors" (spots of white near the tip); most younger birds lack these.

Four-year Gulls

Four-year gulls, represented here by Herring Gull, include the larger "white-headed" gulls—that is, those that have pure white heads (no hoods) in adult breeding plumage. The nonbreeding (winter) plumages of many of these species are very similar to breeding plumages except for darker markings in the head, which can be moderate flecking to very heavy mottling. Gulls

Ring-billed Gull juvenal plumage (in transition to 1st winter)

Ring-billed Gull 1st winter

Ring-billed Gull 2nd winter

Ring-billed Gull breeding adult

in this group have nine different plumages, compared to the seven plumages of three-year species and five plumages of two-year species. The plumages of four-year gulls can be challenging for the beginner. Their names are rendered just as those for two-year and three-year species—(juvenal, first winter/first basic, first summer/first alternate)—but they extend another year, into a third winter and third summer, before adult plumage appears. When learning the plumages of four-year gulls, it is easiest to begin with adult plumages, learn first-winter plumages next, and then tackle the plumages in between. The second- and third-winter plumages are the scarcest in any given flock (because of survivorship) and often resemble the adult closely enough to be recognizable once that plumage is learned well.

Herring Gull juvenal plumage

Herring Gull 1st winter

Herring Gull 2nd winter

Herring Gull 3rd winter

Herring Gull breeding adult

Little Gull

Larus minutus
L 11"/28cm   WS 24"/61cm

Little Gull, a widespread Eurasian species, occasionally nests in lakeside habitats in Canada. In the nonbreeding season, it is normally observed singly or in small numbers in flocks of Bonaparte's Gulls, on large lakes and rivers or open ocean; adults are readily distinguished by their mostly slaty underwings; shorter, rounded wings; and gray rather than white primaries above. Second-winter birds often show some slaty gray in the outer primaries. **VOICE** A very ternlike *kiiw, kik, ki-dew*, singly and in rolling, stuttering series.

breeding adult

rounded wingtips

short, thin bill

dark gray underwings with white trailing edge

1st winter

dusky hindcrown (compare Ross's Gull)

upperwings more extensively black above than other small gulls

short tail

nonbreeding adult

smaller than Bonaparte's Gull, with shorter, white-tipped wings (no black) and short, thin bill

Ross's Gull

Rhodostethia rosea
L 13"/33cm   WS 33"/84cm

The slender Ross's Gull of eastern Siberia has nested occasionally beside tundra lakes in northern Canada and Greenland. Eastbound fall migrants are seen along the northern Alaskan coast, presumably heading for wintering grounds in the pack ice. Winter adults (which usually lack the collar of breeding birds) and first-winter birds may be confused with Little Gull, but note structural differences between the two. **VOICE** Breeding bird gives a nasal *yi-KIH*, rapidly repeated; also single *kik* calls and series similar to Little Gull.

breeding adult

narrow wings medium gray below, with wide white trailing edge (compare Little Gull)

wedge-shaped tail (difficult to see) unique among gulls

1st winter

extensive black in upperwing coverts and outer primaries

breeding adult

small, stubby bill

black collar; crown often appears peaked

pink wash below (often hard to see)

Bonaparte's Gull
Larus philadelphia
L 13"/33cm **WS** 33"/84cm

This abundant small gull nests in lakeside trees in muskeg and boreal forests and migrates in the nonbreeding season to the Great Lakes, ocean coasts, and lower Mississippi River valley. Large flocks gather to feed on small fish, especially where the fish are concentrated by currents or driven to the surface by larger predatory fish. Unlike larger species, Bonaparte's is rarely seen at landfills. **VOICE** Most calls ternlike; a high, nasal *kiier* and a low, rattling growl, *kerrrr,* especially from feeding flocks.

breeding adult

white outer primaries and black primary tips visible above and below

entirely black bill (compare Black-headed)

longer wings and bill than Little Gull

1st winter

coverts have brownish cast (black in Little)

nonbreeding adult

white outer primaries (unlike Little, Ross's Gulls)

dusky auricular patch (as in other nonbreeding hooded gulls)

similar to Black-headed above but smaller, with smaller bill and narrower wings

---

Black-headed Gull
Larus ridibundus
L 16"/41cm **WS** 40"/1m

This Eurasian species nests as near as Iceland and can be fairly common on coasts in Newfoundland in winter; it is uncommon to rare south of New England and very rare inland. Black-headeds are usually found flocking with smaller Bonaparte's or larger Ring-billed Gulls. First-winter birds differ from Bonaparte's in darker inner primaries above and below and a heavier, bicolored bill. **VOICE** A low, screechy, grating *rauwww* or *reeahh;* also many guttural, ternlike calls *(kiw, ki-di-di, kik).*

breeding adult

black hood, often with brownish cast

white nape, unlike Bonaparte's

reddish bill, larger than Bonaparte's

1st winter

bicolored bill

dusky inner primaries (unlike Bonaparte's)

nonbreeding adult

coral red bill and legs

underside of primaries contrastingly dusky, except for outermost (unlike Bonaparte's Gull)

Franklin's Gull

Larus pipixcan
L 15"/38cm   **WS** 36"/91cm

This delicate hooded gull nests in large colonies in marshes of the northern Great Plains and Great Basin and migrates in fall to southern South America. Because it is a long-distance migrant, Franklin's Gull strays far out of range regularly; wanderers are often seen among other gulls on the coasts and at large inland reservoirs. Sabine's is the only other American gull to undertake a transequatorial migration. **VOICE** Call a high, mewing, almost yelping *kioow;* long call like Laughing Gull but higher.

breeding adult

more delicate than Laughing Gull, with shorter wings, more white in primary tips, more petite bill, wider white eye crescents

breast and belly often have pink cast

breeding adult

black wingtips have white inner border, unlike Laughing

nonbreeding adult

"hangman's hood" with wide white eye crescents (compare nonbreeding Laughing)

Laughing Gull

Larus atricilla
L 16"/41cm   **WS** 40"/1m

The Gulf and Atlantic coasts would not be the same without the far-carrying call of Laughing Gull. This species nests in coastal salt marshes and winters on coasts; postbreeding birds from Mexico visit California in large numbers. Strays are apt to turn up anywhere gulls concentrate in the lower 48 states; hurricanes may drive hundreds into the interior. **VOICE** Calls include an animated *kow,* a higher *kiw,* and a lower *kow-kow-kow;* long call an accelerating then slowing series of *hah* calls, with laughing quality.

breeding adult

differs from Franklin's in longer legs, longer, more decurved bill, longer wings with less white in primary tips

usually narrower white eye crescents than Franklin's (wide extreme shown here)

juvenile

white uppertail coverts contrast with brown plumage, dark tail

nonbreeding adult

whiter head, longer legs and wings than Franklin's

Sabine's Gull
Xema sabini
L 14"/36cm **WS** 33"/84cm

The distinctive Sabine's Gull (discovered in Greenland in 1818 by Edward Sabine) breeds on High Arctic tundra. The species' long migration to South America makes it a candidate for appearance anywhere in North America, especially in fall at large lakes or offshore. It can be common in fall off the West Coast and may be seen rarely from shore; in the Atlantic, it is rare and highly pelagic. This gull is unusual in performing distraction displays (like shorebirds) and courtship feeding (like terns). **VOICE** A harsh *kiiew* or *kirrr*.

breeding adult

charcoal gray hood ringed in black

short black bill has yellow tip

long, white-tipped primaries

juvenile
adultlike dorsal pattern (but brown, not gray, coverts)

dark-tipped, forked tail

breeding adult

(adult and juvenile show similar upperwing pattern, unusual in gulls)

contrasting wedges of black, gray, and white in upperwings

Black-legged Kittiwake
Rissa tridactyla
L 16"/41cm **WS** 36"/91cm

Black-legged Kittiwake nests in large, bustling colonies on seaside cliffs in Alaska and maritime Canada; it winters in pelagic waters and is seldom seen on beaches or inland. This species often investigates gull flocks around boats. A smaller relative, **Red-legged Kittiwake** (*R. brevirostris*), breeds on cliffs on islands off Alaska and winters in Alaska's Pacific waters. **VOICE** Call a sharp, nasal, barking *awk* or *kwak;* long call a raucous, rolling *ki-i-da-wak!* Red-legged's calls much higher-pitched.

Black-legged Kittiwake adult

unmarked yellow bill

slender wings

black wingtips lack white markings

Black-legged Kittiwake juvenile
dark nape collar

pronounced dark M pattern above

Red-legged Kittiwake adult

proportionately larger head, smaller bill, and darker upperparts than Black-legged

Ring-billed Gull

Larus delawarensis
L 17"/43cm WS 48"/1.2m

Ring-billed Gull nests in colonies on islands in lakes and off coasts, and winters on coasts and in farm fields, parking lots, and reservoirs. It feeds largely on fish but also takes worms, fruit, refuse, rodents, and carrion. It is more robust and heavier-billed than its close relative Mew Gull. Hybrids with Franklin's and Laughing Gulls are documented. **VOICE** Varied calls: a sharp *kyow,* a higher, plaintive *ki-ew,* and a lower *khow* or *how;* long call protracted: a set of high-pitched *ki-ew* calls followed by clucking and 2 more *ki-ew* calls.

breeding adult

pale iris

very little white in tertials and scapulars

heavier bill than Mew Gull, with distinct ring

nonbreeding adult

nape faint stippled wit brow

juvenile

(distinct tail-band, unlike American Mew)

adults have much black in primaries (compare Mew)

(first-winter birds lose brown in head and underparts by autumn)

more coarsely marked coverts and underparts, darker primaries than Mew

---

Mew Gull

Larus canus
L 16"/41cm WS 43"/1.1m

Mew Gull breeds in taiga, nesting near water in trees or on the ground, and winters on the outer Pacific coast. Its small size and bill and rounded head recall the smaller kittiwakes, but its plumages are closer to Ring-billed Gull. Adults of the European subspecies *canus,* rare in the East, are similar to the American *brachyrhynchus* (shown here), but first-winter *canus,* like Ring-billed, has a tailband. **VOICE** Calls include a high, descending *kii-ew* and a snappy, barking *kyap;* long call a rolling, laughing series of calls.

breeding adult

more delicate and slightly darker above than Ring-billed Gull; broad, white crescents on tertials and scapulars

dark eyes

(nonbreeding adult often shows faint bill ring and extensive mottling on head)

1st winter

paler primaries, covert pattern less jagged than Ring-billed

breeding adult

larger white spots in outer primaries than Ring-billed, almost touching white on next inner primary (except in *canus*)

California Gull

Larus californicus
L 21"/53cm **WS** 54"/1.4m

California Gull nests in colonies on lakes in the northern Great Plains and Great Basin, and winters mostly along the Pacific coast. It may be detected in large mixed gull flocks by its size and bill shape: intermediate between the smaller Ring-billed and larger Herring Gulls. A gull monument in Salt Lake City, Utah, commemorates this species' role in saving Mormon settlers' crops from a grasshopper infestation in 1848. **VOICE** Calls similar to Herring Gull but higher, rougher, and more modulated; long call more nasal.

breeding adult

smaller bill and head than Herring Gull

bill not heavy or bulbous (compare Herring)

more robust than Ring-billed

1st winter

pink bill has black tip

dark greater coverts form band

nonbreeding adult

bill has even, pencil-like width

larger bill than Ring-billed, often with black mark at gonys but also with red mark, lacking in Ring-billed

---

Herring Gull

Larus argentatus
L 25"/64cm **WS** 58"/1.5m

The widespread Herring Gull nests mostly on small islands in lakes, from the tundra into boreal forests, as well as in colonies on Atlantic coastal islands. Remarkably adaptable, it can forage even during harsh winters in varied habitats, from pelagic zones right to the base of the Rocky Mountains; it readily visits landfills with other gulls. Hybridization with many large gull species has been reported. **VOICE** Varied calls include a rich *kyow,* a lower *how,* and a higher *kier;* long call a slow, high trumpeting with long introductory note.

breeding adult

pale gray above; extensive black in primaries

heavier head and bill than California and Thayer's Gulls

medium pink legs and feet

nonbreeding adult

primaries have more black than Thayer's, less than California

head often heavily mottled

juvenile

plumage variation extreme

plumage and base of bill gradually lighten during first winter

similar to Western Gull but with paler plumage, slimmer bill (also compare Thayer's)

Glaucous Gull

Larus hyperboreus
L 27"/69cm WS 60"/1.5m

Glaucous Gull nests on cliffs, tundra, and small islands in the High Arctic almost as far north as there is land; most winter along icy coasts of Alaska and Canada, with smaller numbers on the Great Lakes and in coastal New England. In plumage this species most resembles Iceland Gull, but it is larger and heavier; it is larger than Herring Gull, with a heavier bill. Hybrids with Herring are often reported. **VOICE** Common call a surprisingly high-pitched, thin *kiew*, higher than Herring; long call like Herring but more gravelly.

adult — yellow iris

unmarked white wingtips (also rarely seen in *kumlieni* Iceland Gull)

heavy bill has mostly parallel sides

winter adult shows little or no streaking in head

less primary projection than Iceland

1st winter

heavy build

broad wings

remiges translucent from below

juvenile

heavy pink bill has distinct black tip

neatly patterned beige and buff tones (sometimes pure white)

whitish primaries

Glaucous-winged Gull

Larus glaucescens
L 26"/66cm WS 58"/1.5m

This large gull breeds and winters on coasts; it may also be seen inland during winter in eastern Washington. Typical adult and first-winter birds can be distinguished from Western and Glaucous Gulls by the wingtips (paler than Western, darker than Glaucous); Glaucous-winged hybridizes with both species (and with Herring Gull), complicating identification of many individuals. It is slightly more delicate in build than Western. **VOICE** Similar to Western but lower-pitched and slower, with wooden quality.

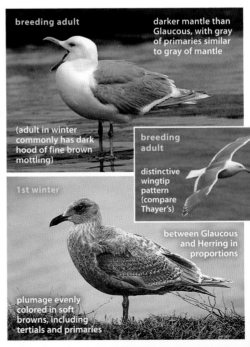

breeding adult

darker mantle than Glaucous, with gray of primaries similar to gray of mantle

(adult in winter commonly has dark hood of fine brown mottling)

breeding adult

distinctive wingtip pattern (compare Thayer's)

1st winter

between Glaucous and Herring in proportions

plumage evenly colored in soft browns, including tertials and primaries

Iceland Gull

Larus glaucoides
L 22"/56cm **WS** 54"/1.4m

Iceland Gull nests on cliffs in southern Baffin Island and adjacent areas, and winters mostly in maritime Canada and New England and along the St. Lawrence Seaway. A "white-winged" gull, along with the larger Glaucous and similar Thayer's Gulls, it shows mostly pale remiges when seen from below. Iceland Gulls in North America are of the subspecies *kumlieni*, in which adults usually show dusky tones in the primaries. **VOICE** Calls mostly similar to Glaucous and Herring Gulls; long call has squeaky quality.

nonbreeding adult *(kumlieni)*

usually appears more delicate than Thayer's, especially in bill and head

primaries have dusky gray, not blackish, marks

1st winter   stocky body, but long wings give graceful appearance

petite head and small, dark bill

looks shorter-legged than Thayer's

juvenile

some have "coffee and cream" pattern on tertials, tail, primaries (compare Thayer's)

Thayer's Gull

Larus thayeri
L 23"/58cm **WS** 55"/1.4m

Thayer's Gull is thought to breed only on cliffs in remote northern Nunavut and northwestern Greenland; it winters on the Pacific coast and is rare and irregular elsewhere. One of the most enigmatic of North American endemic birds, Thayer's has been considered a form of both the similar Herring and Iceland Gulls. Some individuals, possibly hybrids with Iceland Gull, are unidentifiable to species. **VOICE** Short and long calls similar to Herring Gull but lower and less rich and musical.

breeding adult

adult usually has black of primaries restricted to outer webs and tips

smaller than most Herring Gulls

colder gray above than Iceland Gull, with black (not dusky) in wingtips

nonbreeding adult

black outer webs of outer primaries give striped look

juvenile

often similar to Iceland but tertials have brown centers; primaries and tailband darker brown

(some individuals much darker, very close to Herring but more delicate build)

Western Gull

Larus occidentalis
L 25"/64cm **WS** 58"/1.5m

This is the large, heavy-billed, dark-backed gull often seen on Pacific beaches or islands, its year-round habitat. Birds of the nominate subspecies of Western Gull, seen mostly north of Monterey, California, are paler above and darker-eyed than the more southerly subspecies *wymani*; there is much overlap between these darker and lighter taxa, and variation is gradual. Hybrids with Glaucous-winged Gull are common, even outnumbering parental types around Puget Sound, Washington (the northern 190 miles/300km of this species' range is considered a hybrid zone); hybrids can resemble Thayer's Gull but are larger, with much heavier bills. Like Glaucous-winged and other large coastal gulls, Western sometimes drops shellfish onto pavement to open them, a behavior that is learned. **VOICE** Long and short calls similar to Herring Gull, but notes of long call lower and less sweeping.

breeding adult
(wymani)

unstreaked head, even in winter

extensive tertial and scapular crescents

(nominate subspecies paler above and with dusky head in winter)

white secondary edges form border on folded wing

pink legs

juvenile

heavy head

(pale rump area contrasts with dark back, unlike Herring)

large, heavy-tipped, dark bill (compare Herring)

dark plumage similar to Herring

3rd winter

adult and subadult broad-winged

outermost primary has 1 white mirror

long secondaries have extensive white tips

Yellow-footed Gull

Larus livens
L 27"/69cm **WS** 60"/1.5m

A little-known gull that breeds in colonies on islands in the Gulf of California, Yellow-footed Gull visits southern California's Salton Sea mostly during the nonbreeding season and is very rare elsewhere in the state. This species resembles the Western Gull subspecies *wymani* in structure and plumage but has vivid yellow legs. The similar Kelp Gull, probably a closer relative, has duller legs with a greenish cast. **VOICE** Long and short calls different from Western: lower-pitched and with odd nasal quality.

breeding adult

very similar to Western but with longer neck, heavier head and bill

legs and feet yellow by second winter

Great Black-backed Gull

Larus marinus
L 30"/76cm WS 65"/1.7m

This is the world's largest gull, usually identified by its girth and stature alone. It breeds in coastal colonies and winters mostly on the coast, but also on the Great Lakes. Other large dark-backed gulls are vagrants in Great Black-backed's range— Kelp, Slaty-backed, and Western—so use care in identification. Great Black-backed has recently increased as a vagrant to the Gulf coast and interior states. **VOICE** Calls low: a strident, hoarse *khow* or *kahaow* and an annoyed-sounding *how;* long call slower and chestier than Herring Gull.

breeding adult

goose-sized

blackish mantle; primaries only slightly darker

(nonbreeding plumage has little or no head streaking)

dull pinkish legs and feet, often with ashen cast

1st winter

heavy head, bill, and overall build

head, underparts, base of tail very pale, contrasting with wings, bill, tailband

broad wings

Lesser Black-backed Gull

Larus fuscus
L 21"/53cm WS 54"/1.4m

Once considered a rarity in North America, Lesser Black-backed Gull (subspecies *graellsii*) is now a regular visitor in the nonbreeding season to the Atlantic coast and Great Lakes and a rare but annual visitor to the West. Adults are readily recognized by their dark upperparts and yellow legs (most large gulls are paler above with pink legs; California Gull has a greenish cast to the legs). **VOICE** Calls varied, like "Herring with a head cold"; long call nasal, lower and more rapid than Herring.

breeding adult

charcoal gray upperparts contrast with black of primaries

smaller and slimmer than Herring, with longer wings giving more graceful look

vivid yellow legs

nonbreeding adult, worn

"salt and pepper" speckles on head

1st winter

recalls Herring, but wings and body more slender; white uppertail coverts and base of tail contrast with black tailband; and greater upperwing coverts darker

Ivory Gull

Pagophila eburnea
L 17"/43cm **WS** 37"/94cm

This gull of the High Arctic seems a living fragment of the ice floes that are its year-round environment. It nests on cliffs of Baffin Island and other islands of northern Nunavut, and winters around the pack-ice edge, where it forages ternlike for small fish, scavenges carrion and polar bear kills, and even eats seal feces. Strays in the Great Lakes, New England, and southern California attract throngs of bird enthusiasts. This gull is declining in North America. **VOICE** Calls plaintive and descending; a soft *kew*, often in series.

adult

gleaming white

yellow bill has greenish base, orange tip

jet black legs

juvenile

unique dorsal speckling

juvenile

sooty face

dark-tipped remiges and coverts

Heermann's Gull

Larus heermanni
L 19"/48cm **WS** 51"/1.3m

After breeding in Mexico, Heermann's Gull visits coastal California in large numbers, with smaller numbers farther up the coast. It is often seen attempting to steal fish from Brown Pelicans and other seabirds. Young birds, with their dark plumage and sleek, long wings, are easily confused with jaegers but usually lack white. This species is a very rare vagrant in the East. **VOICE** Short calls include low, nasal *eeow, err,* and *yi* notes, often in series; long call a distinctive rapid, gabbling laugh, sounding muffled.

breeding adult

the only dark-bodied North American gull with white head and red bill

2nd winter

bill turns from yellowish to red at base

gray feathers replace uniformly sooty brown juvenal plumage

head takes on "salt and pepper" appearance

nonbreeding adult

Rare Gulls

Gulls from other continents are reported every year in North America, and many birders seek them out, carefully poring over gull flocks. Not all rare gulls are identifiable to species, in part because of hybrids and backcrosses, in part because of individual variation. In reporting rare species, such as those shown here, it is important to take photographs and to encourage others to view the bird.

YELLOW-LEGGED GULL
Larus (cachinnans) michahellis
L 24"/61cm **WS** 57"/1.4m

Chiefly a Mediterranean species, Yellow-legged Gull has been reported a few dozen times between Atlantic Canada and Texas. It was once considered a form of Herring Gull, which it resembles; adults have yellow legs and feet, rare in the American subspecies of Herring.

KELP GULL
Larus dominicanus
L 23"/58cm **WS** 53"/1.3m

Kelp Gull, from the Southern Hemisphere, was once thought to be a subspecies of Lesser Black-backed Gull; it is heavier-bodied and -billed, duller-legged, and darker above. This species has nested on islands off Louisiana in the Gulf of Mexico, where it hybridizes with Herring Gull. Pure Kelps are very rare in North America; they have been recorded otherwise only in Texas, Indiana, Colorado, and Maryland.

SLATY-BACKED GULL
Larus schistisagus
L 25"/64cm **WS** 58"/1.5m

Slaty-backed Gull is slightly larger than Kelp Gull. It has bred several times in Alaska but is chiefly a Siberian species known mostly as a vagrant in North America, mostly on the Pacific coast but rarely also the Atlantic and Gulf coasts.

BLACK-TAILED GULL
Larus crassirostris
L 18"/46cm **WS** 47"/1.2m

Another eastern Asian species, Black-tailed Gull, shows patterns of vagrancy in the East similar to those of Slaty-backed Gull; it is rarer on the West Coast. In flight the adult's jet black tailband is diagnostic.

Yellow-legged Gull adult

very similar to Herring Gull, but darker above and with vivid yellow legs

Kelp Gull adult

similar to Western Gull subspecies *wymani,* but legs dull yellowish green

larger and more robust than Lesser Black-backed

Slaty-backed Gull adult

slaty upperparts with broad white trailing edge to remiges

primary pattern has extensive white

similar size or larger than Herring Gull, with more robust appearance

Black-tailed Gull adult

similar size to Ring-billed Gull, but longer-winged and darker above

long bill has black ring, cherry red tip

Brown Noddy

Anous stolidus
L 15"/38cm   **WS** 32"/81cm

Brown Noddy nests at Florida's Dry Tortugas. It is remarkably scarce away from the eastern Gulf of Mexico and is observed very rarely in the Gulf Stream north of southern Florida. Like Black and White-winged Terns, noddies feed by swooping to the water's surface and picking, rather than plunge-diving; their chief prey are small, minnow-sized fish. Unlike juvenile Black Noddy, juvenile Brown lacks white in the crown, which comes in slowly over the first year and is often indistinct well into the bird's second year. **VOICE** An unusual low, mechanical rattle, *urrrrrr*, at colonies; begging young give a more ternlike *koweeek!*

adult

larger than Black Noddy, with heavier body and bill

adult

long tail appears rounded when spread (notch in center sometimes visible)

wider-winged than Black

(when worn, upper-wing coverts look contrastingly pale)

Black Noddy

Anous minutus
L 13½"/34cm   **WS** 30"/76cm

A small tropical tern observed almost annually at Florida's Dry Tortugas, Black Noddy resembles a small, darker version of Brown Noddy but has a longer, finer bill. Many individuals observed at the Dry Tortugas are subadults, which are less uniformly colored than adults, often showing worn, pale brown upperwing coverts. Unlike Brown Noddies of similar age, juvenile and subadult Blacks show a well-defined white forecrown. **VOICE** Similar to Brown Noddy but higher.

adult

blackish in fresh plumage (worn birds can appear brownish)

bill proportionately longer and more slender than in Brown

smaller than Brown Noddy, with smaller-looking head

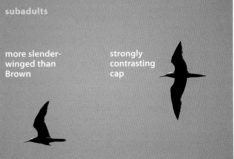

subadults

more slender-winged than Brown

strongly contrasting cap

Sooty Tern
Onychoprion fuscatus
L 16"/41cm   **WS** 32"/81cm

Sooty Tern nests in North America mostly at Florida's Dry Tortugas and sparingly on other islands in the Gulf of Mexico. Nonbreeding and postbreeding birds forage widely in the Gulf and the Gulf Stream. Foraging flocks often follow schools of large predatory fish and will soar to great heights to watch for them. Tropical storms and hurricanes typically displace Sooty Terns far inland. **VOICE** A nasal *a-weda-wed* (often remembered "wide-a-wake," a mariner's name for this bird), a nasal *urEEur,* and a skimmerlike *ip.*

adult   origami-like angularity and sharp plumage contrasts

juvenile   (told from distant noddies by pale underwing coverts)

pale-edged coverts

adult   dark remiges contrast starkly with coverts

greater wing area than Bridled Tern

adult   less white in tail than Bridled Tern

Bridled Tern
Onychoprion anaethetus
L 15"/38cm   **WS** 30"/76cm

Bridled Tern nests sparingly in the Florida Keys. Nonbreeding and postbreeding birds are common in the Gulf of Mexico and in the Gulf Stream north to the mid-Atlantic states; most are observed there in late summer and early fall. Bridled Tern hunts in floating rafts of marine algae *(Sargassum)* for small fish and invertebrates; it is often seen perched on flotsam, especially boards, along tide lines. Some follow schools of feeding fish, as does Sooty Tern. **VOICE** A querulous *wheeep?,* heard at sea.

adult   grayish brown above (Sooty blackish)

white "bridle" extends beyond eyes (unlike Sooty Tern)

(shows much more white in tail, when spread, than Sooty)

subadult, molting

most observed in U.S. appear pale-headed from a distance

juvenile

pale brown back and coverts with neat, white edges

Black Tern
Chlidonias niger
L 9½"/24cm WS 24"/61cm

Black Tern breeds in interior marshes, lakes, and sloughs, where it builds a floating nest of vegetation, and winters mostly in South America. In migration, it is often found far out to sea in the Gulf Stream and Gulf of Mexico; large numbers of nonbreeders also summer in the Gulf. Breeding adults are black-bodied, with slaty gray wings; all other plumages are pale below, with a dark hindcrown and auricular spot. **VOICE** Calls very low-pitched, including a nasal, harsh *kiw,* a trilled, staccato *kididiw,* and similar.

breeding adult

blackish head and body with dark gray wings

older juvenile

uniformly gray upperparts (unlike White-winged)

nonbreeding adult

wings and back darker than White-winged Tern; black "ear muffs" more extensive, and darker

(dark "spur" of plumage extends from nape to side of breast)

White-winged Tern
Chlidonias leucopterus
L 9½"/24cm WS 23"/58cm

This Eurasian vagrant is most often recorded in Atlantic states; it frequents freshwater lakes and impoundments, mostly between spring and early autumn. On 3 occasions, the species has been found paired with Black Terns in North America, but no hybrids have been observed. Nonbreeding adults are similar to first- and second-winter plumages: chalky white overall, with much paler wings and tail above and below than Black Tern. **VOICE** Similar to Black Tern but usually even lower.

breeding adult

velvety black plumage and underwing coverts contrast with white upperwings and tail

usually found with Black Terns

red legs

molting adults/ subadults

white rump distinctive

nonbreeding adult/ subadult

paler above than Black Tern and entirely white below; lacks dark "spur" of plumage at side of breast

Tern Plumages and Molts

The plumages of most terns are deceptively simple—white below and pale gray above, with a dark cap, a mostly white tail, and some dark pigmentation in the primaries. The patterns in these features, however, vary in confusing ways because of the complex molts in terns. An understanding of these molts is important for identification.

Common Tern young juvenile

Common Tern older juvenile

Common Tern 1st summer

Common Tern winter adult

Common Tern is widespread and the species to which other medium-sized terns are often compared. Like other terns, Common holds a juvenal plumage for a short time. By autumn the brownish back and covert edges of this plumage have worn to gray, and the body plumage begins to molt into first-winter (or first-basic) plumage, a plumage fully acquired on the South American wintering grounds.

Many subadult birds stay the year in South America, but a few return in spring to North America in a first-summer plumage, which resembles a nonbreeding adult in the head but a late-summer adult in wing wear (the molt schedule of these subadults is still a few months behind that of adults). By the next year's second-summer plumage, many Common Terns look like full adults, but some retain white flecking in the head and belly or a trace of a carpal bar. Most Commons reach full adulthood and begin breeding in their third calendar year, at about two years of age. Adult breeding (or alternate) plumage and adult nonbreeding (basic) plumage alternate throughout the tern's life.

Common Tern undergoes two incomplete molts of its remiges per year, as opposed to the single complete molt of most larids. It molts the inner primaries in late summer after breeding and then resumes southward migration. The remaining remiges are molted through midwinter; once this molt is complete, the inner primaries that were new in September have become worn, so they are replaced before the birds set out for the Northern Hemisphere, as are the body, head, and other feathers, to bring the bird into full breeding plumage.

When it arrives at the nesting areas, then, an adult Common Tern has fresh inner primaries but older outer primaries. Both sets of feathers are fresh enough to look pale from above; this pale appearance is caused by tiny barbules that show up as a powdery patina on the feathers. As the nesting season wears on, the barbules wear off, so that the older outer primaries show up as contrastingly darker than the paler, younger inner primaries. By contrast, Arctic Tern has a complete molt of the remiges, and the primaries look evenly pale on birds in North America.

Royal Tern
Thalasseus maximus
L 20"/51cm **WS** 41"/1m

The far-carrying call of Royal Tern is a familiar sound near Gulf and Atlantic barrier beaches, where this species nests in large colonies, feeding on fish and crustaceans. It also winters on coasts and is seen as a vagrant farther inland, often after hurricanes. As beaches are developed, colonies have been increasingly limited to dredge-spoil islands. The structure of the bill is important in identifying large terns; adult Royals occasionally have a cherry red bill. **VOICE** A burry, rolling *kaarREEK!* or *kaarRA!* and various *eek* and *keek* calls.

breeding adult

shaggy, short crest

deep orange bill, rather heavy through gonys

bill heavier than Elegant, less heavy than Caspian

lacks rosy tones of breeding Elegant Tern

nonbreeding adult

less black in primaries below than Caspian

white forecrown

juvenile

stout, yellowish orange bill

coverts, remiges, back heavily marked

Elegant Tern
Thalasseus elegans
L 17"/43cm **WS** 34"/86cm

Elegant Tern nests in large colonies in southern California (the largest colony of this species is at Isla Rasa, Mexico). After breeding, birds disperse widely up the coast to forage in coastal waters. Vagrants have been observed inland and on the Atlantic and Gulf coasts. Elegant is smaller than Royal Tern, with a thinner bill and narrower wings; the angle at the carpal joint may appear more acute, closer to Sandwich Tern, with which it has hybridized on rare occasions. **VOICE** Most calls similar to Sandwich Tern but lower.

breeding adult

(often shows rosy tones in underparts in breeding plumage)

long, slightly decurved bill, often paler at tip

nonbreeding adult

appears sleeker than Royal in flight, with narrower wings

nonbreeding adults

droopy crest distinctive in all adult plumages, much longer than in Royal Tern

Caspian Tern

Hydroprogne caspia
L 21"/53cm　**WS** 50"/1.3m

The husky, heavy-billed Caspian Tern is the largest tern in the world. It nests in colonies at traditional locations on large lakes or estuaries but will colonize new areas where prey, mostly small fish, are abundant. Many migrants pass over land to wintering grounds on the Gulf coast or farther south; family groups can be heard calling overhead at night, the juvenile's whistled "groveling" call answering the adult's raucous screech. **VOICE** Adult gives a very harsh, raspy *rrrrreOW,* juvenile a high *whe-wheeoow!*

breeding adults

deep, black cap

heavy, deep red bill, dusky near tip

plumage very pale overall

juvenile

like adult but with dark bars in coverts, mantle, tertials

nonbreeding adult

retains most of cap, but crown stippled with white

extensive black in primaries below (compare Royal)

broad wings; slow, strong wingbeats

Sandwich Tern

Thalasseus sandvicensis
L 15"/38cm　**WS** 34"/86cm

This slender tern of beaches and barrier islands often nests among Royal Terns. In winter it withdraws to Florida, the Gulf coast, and the Caribbean. Like Elegant Tern, Sandwich appears narrow-winged in flight; adults look starkly white above, similar to the smaller, more compact Gull-billed Tern. Cayenne Tern (subspecies *eurygnatha* of Sandwich) is a rare visitor from South America; it has a yellowish bill. **VOICE** A rising *kareek!* or *keerip!* similar to Royal but higher and harsher; also an abrupt *krow.*

breeding adult

smaller than Royal, larger than Common Tern

long, thin, dark bill with yellow tip unique

nonbreeding adult

white forecrown

primaries darker than in breeding plumage (as in most white *Sterna*)

juvenile

neatly marked above with black and dark brown

legs and bill turn from yellowish orange to black, usually soon after fledging

Common Tern

Sterna hirundo
L 14"/36cm WS 30"/76cm

Common Tern nests near interior lakes and rivers and along coasts on barrier islands. Because it molts on wintering grounds, it is seldom observed in its nonbreeding plumage in the U.S. On western Alaskan islands, the subspecies *longipennis* is a regular visitor; adults are darker than mainland Commons, with a long black bill and darker legs. **VOICE** Varied high, grating calls, including a quick *kik,* a rising *krrrrri* (often in rapid series), a squeaky *kirrIH,* and a harsh *KRII-ah.*

breeding adult

upperparts slightly darker than Arctic Tern

wingtips extend beyond tail tip

longer legs than Arctic

juvenile

darker overall than Arctic, with heavy, dark carpal bar

breeding adult

wide dark border to primaries below

breeding adult

primaries darken late in breeding season

Forster's Tern

Sterna forsteri
L 14"/36cm WS 31"/79cm

This widespread and versatile tern nests in salt marshes and on barrier beaches and islands in lakes and prairie sloughs. It is often compared to Common Tern; adults are larger, longer-tailed, and paler and have a silvery white sheen above. Adults molt into nonbreeding plumage in late summer; most have a distinctive eye patch by late August, though some retain dark feathers in the nape later, thus resembling Common. **VOICE** Similar to Common but lower and with rattling quality.

breeding adult

silvery sheen above

tail projects well beyond wingtips

orange bill base and legs (more reddish in Common and Arctic Terns)

breeding adult

very long tail; bright white underparts (compare Common, Arctic)

older juvenile

black eye patch

(nonbreeding adult similar)

(young juvenile extensively buffy above)

Arctic Tern

Sterna paradisaea
L 15"/38cm **WS** 31"/79cm

Arctic Tern makes the longest migration of any bird, traveling some 20,000 miles (32,000km) round-trip from its northern nesting areas over pelagic waters to its wintering grounds in the Antarctic. It is regularly observed in the Pacific and scarce in the Atlantic south of New England. In flight, Arctic has an ethereal quality, created by its slow downward wingstroke, brilliant white underwings, and unmarked pale gray upperwings. **VOICE** Similar to Common Tern but higher, harsher, and less musical.

breeding adult
paler above but often darker below than Common, with shorter bill and shorter legs

tail projects beyond wingtips

young juvenile

brown tones quickly lost

short legs and bill

(older juveniles very pale)

1st summer

rarely seen

dark carpal bar, short legs

breeding adult

narrow dark trailing edge to primaries below (compare Common)

Roseate Tern

Sterna dougallii
L 12½"/32cm **WS** 29"/74cm

This striking cosmopolitan species breeds in the Florida Keys and along the coasts of Atlantic Canada and the Northeast. It is a relatively rare migrant elsewhere, presumably on its way to wintering grounds in northeastern South American waters. Breeding adults are often washed with rose below; they may recall a tiny tropicbird—brilliantly white, with a long tail—but their quick, shallow wingbeats are distinctive. **VOICE** Some calls—like *kiew!*—similar to Common Tern; also a rapid, flat *kiVIT!* and a plaintive *cheVI.*

breeding adult

strikingly pale overall, often with rosy bloom below

very long tail

black bill (base becomes reddish in summer)

breeding adult

whitish overall, with dusky outer primaries and dark cap

juvenile

mantle and coverts have neat, dark subterminal marks, recalling larger juvenile Sandwich Tern

Gull-billed Tern
Gelochelidon nilotica
L 14"/36cm WS 34"/86cm

Gull-billed Tern is a scarce coastal species of the Southeast and southern California, rarely recorded out of range; it winters from the Gulf of Mexico through South America. Unlike other terns, which plunge-dive for fish, Gull-billed takes insects on the wing and plucks invertebrates, fish, and small frogs from shallow water and mudflats. It occasionally flocks with other tern species but is most often seen apart, in pairs or family groups. **VOICE** A distinctive, nasal *didididididi* and a rising *diWOOT!*

breeding adults

pale overall, with contrasting black cap, bill, legs

very long-winged

black bill heavier than in small terns

breeding adult

distinctive shape in flight: short-tailed and long-winged, with short, blunt bill

juvenile

faint mask

pale bill and legs darken quickly

stocky and pale gray overall

buffy brown color in mantle and coverts lost by autumn

Aleutian Tern
Onychoprion aleuticus
L 14"/36cm WS 30"/76cm

Aleutian Tern breeds on coasts in Siberia and Alaska, and a few have been recorded in British Columbia in late spring; it apparently migrates through eastern Asia to winter in the South Pacific, probably in pelagic waters. Among Arctic Terns, with which it often nests in loose associations, Aleutian appears much darker, and its white forehead stands out. Juveniles are also distinctive, with extensive rufous on the sides and covert edges above. When nesting, Aleutian is much less aggressive than Arctic. **VOICE** A musical, unternlike *rididid*.

breeding adult

darker than Arctic Tern, with distinct white forehead, entirely black bill

breeding adult

secondaries dark from below

belly often appears dark

Least Tern

Sternula antillarum
L 9"/23cm **WS** 20"/51cm

The truly tiny Least Tern breeds along coasts and on islands along major rivers. In recent years it has nested on flat, gravel roofs of shopping malls, sometimes in large numbers. Its slender body, narrow wings, and jerky wing action are like those of no other seabird. Least forages for small fish, usually near the coast; small numbers are often observed far out to sea in the Gulf Stream and Gulf of Mexico, where they forage along seawater fronts. **VOICE** Calls include a high *kiDEEK* and nervous, rapid, squeaky tittering.

breeding adult

white forehead

outer 2 primaries dark

small, yellow bill

extremely small and slender body and wings

juvenile

1st year

dark primaries and carpal bar (absent in similar nonbreeding adult)

scaly appearance above

Black Skimmer

Rynchops niger
L 18"/46cm **WS** 44"/1.1m

Black Skimmer is the sole North American representative of its subfamily, Rhynchopinae—the only birds in which the mandible is longer than the maxilla. Like terns, their closest relatives, skimmers specialize in foraging for fish. Unlike terns, skimmers feed mostly at night, especially when falling tides concentrate fish in shallows. They forage by lowering the mandible into the water while flying and snapping the bill shut upon detecting prey. **VOICE** A nasal, yapping, puppylike *ip;* also a series of vibrating nasal calls.

breeding adult

distinctive bill and plumage unmistakable

(nonbreeding adult shows pale collar)

red legs

juvenile

juvenile

unique foraging method

like adult but with brown, pale-edged upperparts, orangish yellow legs

Wading Birds

"Wading birds," as the term is used in the pages that follow, are long-legged waterbirds of six families: herons, night-herons, egrets, and bitterns (Ardeidae); ibises and spoonbills (Threskiornithidae); storks (Ciconiidae); flamingos (Phoenicopteridae); cranes (Gruidae); and Limpkin (Aramidae). The first three families are placed in the order Ciconiiformes, which also includes the vultures of the Americas. The others are

Snowy Egret's courtship display includes fanning its abundant nuptial plumes.

only distant relatives of herons and their allies: cranes and Limpkin are in the order Gruiformes, which also includes the much smaller rails; flamingos are usually placed in their own order, Phoenicopteriformes. Most wading birds live in wetlands, from mudflats to marshes to swamps. They are largely carnivorous, eating aquatic vertebrates and invertebrates, although cranes also include acorns, fruit, and grains in their diet. Some species are highly specialized in their prey selection or foraging methods; others prey on a variety of animals using diverse techniques.

American Flamingo, showing the distinctive bill shape of its family.

Herons and egrets are the most familiar members of the family Ardeidae. These birds are often seen posed elegantly at the edge of a pond or stream, watching for fish and frogs. They spear prey with lightning-quick jabs propelled by strong muscles in their long necks. Cattle Egret is exceptional among ardeids in that it forages mostly in fields, following livestock or tractors that stir up insects, its chief prey. Bitterns nest in freshwater or brackish marshes, where they often stay hidden in reedbeds and are hard to find. Night-herons forage extensively at night, as their name implies, but are still usually easier to detect than the bitterns. Most ardeids nest in colonies in trees or reedbeds. Courtship involves a variety of stylized postures, garrulous calls, and, in some species, a display of specialized, wispy breeding, or nuptial, plumes called "aigrettes" (the French word for these feathers that gave rise to the English name "egret"). After the breeding season, both adults and young birds may wander widely in search of food; by autumn most herons and egrets begin migration toward southern-tier states or the tropics.

Ibises and spoonbills are specialized foragers, as their unusual bill shapes indicate. They usually sweep their bills from side to side in shallow water, creating currents that dislodge aquatic prey. Ibises also forage by touch in mud or soft soil, using their long, curved bills to extract worms, crayfish, small fish, and amphibians. Both spoonbills and ibises have been found wandering far from their typical ranges, especially in recent years.

Wood Stork and the enormous Jabiru, a vagrant from Central America, are the only native storks found in the United States.

Like spoonbills, they have unfeathered heads and feed by touch in shallow water. To hunt, they lower the bill into the water and snap it shut upon sensing prey (mostly fish); their reaction time can be remarkably fast, with Wood Stork measured at 0.03 seconds. Like other wading birds, storks sometimes appear far out of range in summer and fall; some will remain for weeks in an area, especially where drying ponds concentrate fish.

The United States has very few wild flamingos, at most a few dozen in Florida's Everglades, but flamingos may turn up in southern states, both escapees from captivity (and these include other species such as Lesser, Chilean, and Greater Flamingos) and wild wanderers from their West Indian range. Flamingos have highly specialized, angular bills with lamellae, or filters, that allow them to sift through mud and water to feed on tiny insects, crustaceans, algae, and other food. They usually forage by lowering the bill into shallow water while standing, although their webbed feet also make them good swimmers. Flamingos display in tight groups, turning their bills back and forth, stretching their legs, and raising their wings to reveal black remiges. Their nests are muddy mounds built on the ground.

Cranes have inspired humans for millennia with their extraordinary courtship displays: they perform exuberant

Jabiru, a huge tropical stork, has been recorded in Texas on at least eight occasions.

dances that involve leaps, bows, dips, and wing movements and are accompanied by rolling, bugling cries. Cranes forage by walking slowly with the bill near the ground and pecking and probing at a variety of prey and vegetable material. They nest solitarily, often in large territories in bogs or marshes. Young cranes stay with their parents through their first winter and spring, learning migration routes and foraging techniques.

Limpkin might be mistaken for a bittern or young night-heron, but its decurved bill is a clue that it is related to rails. A closer look at the bill—with its right-hand curve and a twist at the mandible tip—reveals its specialized purpose: to extract the aquatic apple snail, the mainstay of this species' diet, from its shell. Nesting Limpkins tend to defend territories, as rails do, but they sometimes form loose "colonies." Limpkins wander northward on rare occasions, possibly in response to drought.

Most ardeid populations are relatively stable, but other wading birds have not recovered from past losses, particularly Whooping Crane and Wood Stork, whose numbers plummeted by 90 percent in the last century.

Courting Sandhill Cranes leap and bow, seeming to dance in display. This species' breeding range is expanding eastward.

Great Blue Heron

Ardea herodias

L 46"/1.2m **WS** 73"/1.8m

Casual observers often refer to this large, stately wader as a crane. In fact, Great Blue Heron is the largest of the North American ardeids, readily identified by its massive bill, blue-gray or dark gray plumage, and overall structure. Great Blue is found in nearly every sort of habitat other than deserts. It preys mostly on fish but also eats reptiles, amphibians, and birds (such as small rails), and will even hunt rodents in dry fields. In southern Florida a white subspecies, Great White Heron (*occidentalis*), is common along the coast; the white-headed Würdemann's Heron is an intergrade between Great Blue and Great White. **VOICE** A very loud, jarring *raaak!* or *raaannk!* and other guttural calls.

breeding adult

black feathers above eyes border white crown

heavy bill

blue-gray plumage

Würdemann's Heron adult

like Great Blue, but with white head

breeding adult

courtship display

juvenile

dark cap

dark gray plumage

pale throat

black remimes contrast with paler coverts (unlike Sandhill Crane)

breeding adult

flying herons retract neck (compare cranes)

Great White Heron (*occidentalis*)

pale legs (compare Great Egret)

heavy, straw-colored bill

Sandhill Crane
Grus canadensis
L 44"/1.1m   **WS** 75"/1.9m

An elegant bird of open habitats such as prairies, meadows, tundra, and agricultural fields, Sandhill Crane gathers in spectacularly large flocks at traditional locations across the continent's interior during the nonbreeding season. North American subspecies range from the smallest, Lesser (nominate), which nests in tundra, to Greater *(tabida),* which nests in southern Canada and the northern U.S. The subspecies *pulla,* known as Mississippi Sandhill Crane, has a population of just over 100 individuals and is listed as endangered. **VOICE** A rolling, guttural, bugling *a-KRRRRRRRR,* often repeated.

Great Egret
Ardea alba
L 38"/97cm   **WS** 51"/1.3m

Great Egret is a familiar sight in wetland habitats across most of the U.S. but is relatively rare in Canada. It is nearly as tall as Great Blue Heron but much lighter and more delicate. In high breeding condition, adults sport vivid grass green loral skin and long nuptial plumes, or aigrettes, on the back. This remarkably adaptable species has recovered well from the plume-hunting era. **VOICE** Similar to Great Blue but uninflected, lower, and less resonant; breeding bird gives ducklike gabbling.

Sandhill Crane adult

red forecrown, white cheek

gray plumage, often with abundant rusty feathers

Sandhill Crane juvenile

lacks red forecrown

often quite rusty overall

forages by walking and pecking through fields

Sandhill Crane adult

extends neck in flight (compare herons)

remiges not darker than coverts

Great Egret breeding adult

long, yellow bill

long neck

more than a foot taller than Snowy Egret

dark legs and feet

Snowy Egret
Egretta thula
L 24"/61cm WS 40"/1m

The delicate Snowy Egret is chiefly a bird of coastal and interior wetland habitats; small populations are also seen around wetlands in the Great Basin, western Great Plains, and central valleys of California. Adults in high breeding condition (held only for a few weeks) sport crimson loral skin, tangerine feet, and abundant nuptial plumes—wispy feathers on the back and breast. Snowy Egrets were hunted for these plumes, used to adorn hats in the early 20th century; outcry against this practice launched modern bird conservation. **VOICE** Common call a grating *rrrow;* also drawn-out croaking from squabbling birds and braying and guttural sounds from breeding birds.

Snowy Egret breeding adult

much smaller and more light-bodied than Great Egret

yellow lores

legs partially project past tail in flight (compare Cattle Egret)

black legs, yellow feet

Snowy Egret juvenile

yellow lores

yellow legs have dark edge (nonbreeding adult similar)

(some show paler legs and bill)

Little Egret
Egretta garzetta
L 25"/64cm WS 41"/1m

Little Egret is a rare visitor from Eurasia and Africa to the Atlantic coast from Newfoundland to Virginia in spring and summer. It differs from the very similar Snowy Egret by its larger size; longer, heavier bill and thicker legs; usually slate gray lores; and, on breeding adults, 2 long head plumes. **VOICE** Most calls similar to Snowy; breeding bird gives rapid gobbling sounds.

Little Egret breeding adult

lores usually gray (sometimes yellowish in breeding season)

long, heavy bill

thick, dark legs (compare Snowy Egret)

nonbreeding adult

gray lores

(juvenile similar)

Little Egret breeding adult

2 long, thin head plumes

long breast feathers

Little Blue Heron

Egretta caerulea
L 24"/61cm   **WS** 40"/1m

This small egret of southeastern marshes and swamps is unusual among ardeids in having a white juvenal plumage before taking on the slaty blue and violet-maroon breeding plumage of adulthood; birds molting into adult plumage are nicknamed "calico herons." Juveniles are similar to young Snowy Egrets but have distinctive narrow gray tips to the primaries, grayish lores, and dull greenish legs. Little Blue usually stalks prey slowly, preferring shallow fresh water. **VOICE** A nasal *eehhhhh.*

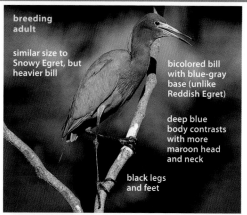

breeding adult

similar size to Snowy Egret, but heavier bill

bicolored bill with blue-gray base (unlike Reddish Egret)

deep blue body contrasts with more maroon head and neck

black legs and feet

juvenile

olive-gray bill and lores

dusky primary tips (visible in flight)

greenish legs and feet

transitional

mottled white and grayish blue

Cattle Egret

Bubulcus ibis
L 19"/48cm   **WS** 35"/89cm

Cattle Egret is often seen in farm fields, where it feeds on insects disturbed by animals or machinery and sometimes rides the backs of cattle or horses. It forages, bathes, and nests in wetlands. This egret, native to the Old World, colonized the Americas in the 20th century. Unlike other egrets (except Reddish), the young have a dark bill; on adults the bill becomes cherry red at the height of courtship. **VOICE** Nesting bird gives a short, gravelly *ehh* and nasal, grating quacking.

breeding adult

smallest of the white ardeids

fulvous plumage in crown, breast, back

short, yellow legs

juvenile

dark bill (gradually turns yellow)

dark legs

adult

compact shape in flight

toes just project past tail

Tricolored Heron

Egretta tricolor

L 26"/66cm WS 36"/91cm

Tricolored Heron forages in coastal salt marshes mostly singly or in mixed flocks of egrets. Like Reddish and Snowy Egrets, it often chases small fish and other prey through shallow water. Adults in high breeding condition are unmistakable, with cerulean lores and bill, magenta eyes, a violet and cobalt blue neck, and butterscotch aigrettes. Once abundant in the Southeast, this species appears to have declined sharply in recent decades. **VOICE** A nasal, ibislike *ehhhhhh*, less modulated than similar Little Blue Heron.

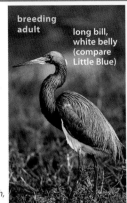

breeding adult

long bill, white belly (compare Little Blue)

juvenile

much magenta in neck and coverts

adult

contrasting white belly and underwing coverts in flight

Green Heron

Butorides virescens

L 17"/43cm WS 26"/66cm

This small heron of wooded swamps, streams, and ponds is rarely found among flocks of other herons; it forages in secluded locations, stalking small fish, tadpoles, and amphibians from a perch just above the water's surface. A cryptic bird, Green Heron is usually detected by its alarm call, given when flushed. The species is strongly migratory and may turn up almost anywhere. **VOICE** Agitated bird often gives a soft clucking sound; flight/alarm call familiar: a piercing *skiew!* or *skyow!*

breeding adult

rusty neck

green cast to back and coverts

dark cap (can be raised as crest)

small and dark

juvenile

streaked neck

coverts have pale tips and edges

Reddish Egret
Egretta rufescens
L 31"/79cm   WS 47"/1.2m

Reddish Egret, a striking species restricted mostly to Florida and coasts of the Gulf of Mexico, is one of the most active and animated foragers among the ardeids; it is often seen chasing fish in zigzag patterns across saltpans and shallows with its wings open. Adults have both a white and a dark morph, and both morphs can be found in the same brood. Though younger birds bear resemblance to other *Egretta*, their foraging behavior, white eyes, and heavy, uniformly dark gray legs distinguish them. **VOICE** Not often heard away from nest site; a short, nasal *uhhh*, *eh-eh*, or *uh-oh*, sounding constricted.

breeding adult, dark morph
slaty plumage
cinnamon head and neck
gray legs have steel blue cast
bicolored bill

breeding adult, white morph
heavy, bicolored bill
gray legs

juvenile, dark morph
unusual chalky tones above

breeding adult, dark morph
adults in high breeding condition have shaggy russet head and neck feathers, often distended
animated foraging in shallow water

juvenile, white morph
heavy dark bill and dark lores
heavy, gray legs (compare Little Blue Heron)

adult, dark morph
canopy foraging: lures fish into shade created by wings

American Bittern
Botaurus lentiginosus
L 29"/74cm   **WS** 43"/1.1m

American Bittern's booming territorial call—a memorable sound of the American wilderness—lends the species its folk name "thunderpumper." It forages mostly in freshwater habitats, hunting amphibians, crayfish, and fish with uncannily slow movements. When alarmed, some point the bill skyward, attempting to blend in with the reeds. **VOICE** Advertising males produce a resonant *ooooohnk-A-doonk!*, repeated for long periods; nocturnal flight call a nasal *arrk*, sometimes doubled.

adult

dark crown and malar (unlike night-herons)

heavyset and cryptically colored

distinct broad brown streaks below

adult

more pointed wings and darker remiges than juvenile night-herons

Least Bittern
Ixobrychus exilis
L 12"/30cm   **WS** 17"/43cm

The smallest member of the heron family, the shy Least Bittern inhabits reed beds in fresh and brackish marshes, chiefly in the eastern U.S. It is normally seen perched or climbing around in tall reeds, quietly watching the water's surface, or in flight to and from its nest. The loral skin of breeding males flushes a vivid carmine color. Courtship is rarely observed. **VOICE** Territorial male repeats a soft, insistent *coo-co-co-co-co* from cover; alarmed bird gives a series of rapid *kik* calls; nocturnal flight call a froglike *garc!*

adult male

tiny (smaller than Clapper Rail)

black back and crown

buffy chestnut wing coverts

adult female

patterned like male, but colors more muted

Black-crowned Night-Heron

Nycticorax nycticorax
L 25"/64cm   WS 44"/1.1m

Though widespread in wetland habitats, the retiring, nocturnal Black-crowned Night-Heron is observed less often than are diurnal herons and egrets. Night-herons forage mostly between dusk and dawn but will also take prey during the day. Black-crowned is an omnivore, even taking small nestlings of other birds. During the day, it roosts communally or singly in dense vegetation, where it can often be observed closely. **VOICE** Alarm and flight calls an abrupt *wok!*

breeding adult

black crown and back

pale below

(legs turn rich pink at height of breeding)

only toes project beyond tail in flight (compare Yellow-crowned)

juvenile

darker overall and thicker-necked than Yellow-crowned

yellow on bill

indistinct streaks below

large white spots on coverts

Yellow-crowned Night-Heron

Nyctanassa violacea
L 24"/61cm   WS 43"/1.1m

Yellow-crowned Night-Heron is a scarce inhabitant of salt- and freshwater marshes and inland riparian habitats. Its heavy, deep bill is adapted for dispatching fiddler crabs, blue crabs, and crayfish; like Black-crowned Night-Heron, it also takes vertebrate prey. Both species stalk prey slowly, like American Bittern (with which the young are often confused) or the smaller Green Heron. **VOICE** A sharp *kwok!*, flatter and higher than Black-crowned.

breeding adult

white cheek, yellow crown

slate gray plumage

heavy bill

dark bill

small white spots on coverts

(remiges contrast with paler coverts in flight)

distinct streaks below

juvenile

long legs (feet project well beyond tail in flight, unlike Black-crowned); legs yellow outside of breeding season

White Ibis
Eudocimus albus
L 25"/64cm **WS** 38"/97cm

White Ibis, a hallmark of the coastal Southeast, is found in lowland wetlands: salt marshes, riverbottom swamps, and shallow lakes and ponds. It uses its long bill to probe in mud for crayfish, worms, and amphibians and to take small fish. Like other waders, White Ibis may wander well out of range during warmer months, young birds more often. Introduction in Florida of Scarlet Ibis, a South American species, has led to hybridization; hybrids are a pinkish salmon color. **VOICE** A rather quiet, low-pitched, nasal *uhhh* or *ehhh*.

breeding adult

brilliant red face, bill, legs

breeding adult

dark wingtips

juvenile

brown head, neck, upperparts gradually turn white

Limpkin
Aramus guarauna
L 26"/66cm **WS** 40"/1m

Limpkin is a tropical wading bird most closely related to rails but as tall as a medium-sized egret. In North America Limpkin is restricted to Florida, where its eerie call rings from freshwater marshes, hammocks, and wooded swamps. It has a long neck and a long, decurved bill, an adaptation for hunting large snails of the genus *Pomacea,* its preferred prey in Florida. **VOICE** A haunting, rolling, grating wail, *krreeeeeeeerrr!* or lower *krrrow!;* also a sharp, low *tchk,* a rolling *kyrrr,* and cranelike chattering and clucking sounds.

adult

dark brown with white spots

(juvenile slightly paler above)

slightly decurved bill

long, dark, heavy legs (compare night-herons, American Bittern)

Glossy Ibis
Plegadis falcinellus
L 23"/58cm **WS** 36"/91cm

Glossy Ibis is fairly common in marshes near the coast in some areas but scarce inland. It uses its decurved bill to sweep through shallow water or to probe into soft substrates, such as wet farm fields, where it preys on earthworms. Because both Glossy and White-faced Ibises have been detected far out of range and have occasionally hybridized, use caution and rule out hybrid derivation in vagrant individuals. **VOICE** Feeding bird gives a reedy, nasal *urrh;* similar sounds, more rapidly repeated, heard at colonies.

breeding adult — dark eyes

dusky face bordered with narrow, pale blue lines

dark maroon plumage with iridescent green and purple coverts

rather dark legs

adult

less heavy-bodied than cormorants in flight; longer bill

juvenile

plain-faced

not distinguishable from juvenile White-faced

lacks iridescent colors of adult

White-faced Ibis
Plegadis chihi
L 23½"/60cm **WS** 37"/94cm

In the American West, White-faced Ibis is most often associated with flooded fields and freshwater marshes and ponds. It is slightly larger and heavier than Glossy Ibis; breeding adults are distinguished mainly by their white facial feathering, striking red eyes (also on nonbreeding adults), and rosy loral skin. Most adults also show reddish legs, especially at the "knees." Juveniles are indistinguishable from juvenile Glossy Ibises. Both dark ibises have expanded their ranges in recent decades. **VOICE** Very similar to Glossy.

breeding adult

(nonbreeding adult retains red eyes; young birds begin to acquire red eyes as early as their first autumn)

white border to red facial skin — red eyes

red "knees"

Roseate Spoonbill
Platalea ajaja
L 32"/81cm   WS 51"/1.3m

With its spoon-shaped bill and vivid plumage, this gaudy tropical wader of southern Texas, Louisiana, and Florida is unique among North American birds. As the bill shape suggests, spoonbills are specialized foragers, taking shrimp and other small prey in shallow water. Their vivid plumage colors are derived from chemical components of this prey. Spoonbills occasionally wander out of range and may forage readily in atypical habitats. **VOICE** Breeding bird gives cooing, braying, and piping sounds; also ibislike *urrr* calls, often in series.

breeding adult

greenish facial skin

deep pink wings with long scarlet marginal coverts

spoon-shaped bill

(orange tail most apparent in flight)

juvenile

pale rose-pink wings

spoon-shaped bill

American Flamingo
Phoenicopterus ruber
L 47"/1.2m   WS 60"/1.5m

Despite the ubiquity of captive flamingos at theme parks and plastic flamingos on suburban lawns, the wild American Flamingo is a magnificent sight in Florida Bay, where a few can be found in fall and winter. To forage, this stately, slender bird lowers its large bill into the water and strains water and mud for blue-green algae, diatoms, insect larvae, and small fish and shellfish. Juveniles lack the pink pigmentation adults acquire through this diet. Because other flamingo species occasionally escape from captivity, use care when identifying all flamingos. American Flamingo is sometimes combined with *P. roseus*, of the Old World, as a single species, "Greater Flamingo." **VOICE** A gooselike honking.

adults

fluorescent pink overall, most intense on coverts, head, neck

long, thin legs and neck

subadult

pale grayish plumage with dark remiges

(juvenile darker gray-brown)

adult

dark remiges

flies with outstretched neck, like spoonbills

Wood Stork

Mycteria americana
L 40"/1m WS 60"/1.5m

Wood Stork is a denizen of southern wetlands, where it forages most readily in drying ponds with high concentrations of fish and other prey. To feed, it lowers its heavy bill into the water and, upon sensing prey, snaps it shut with lightning speed. Most tall wading birds are called "storks" colloquially, but Wood Stork is the only true stork found in North America, aside from the much larger Jabiru, a tropical species known only as a vagrant to Texas. Wood Storks wander far out of range on rare occasions, sometimes as far north as Canada. **VOICE** Courting adults at colonies clatter their bills and hiss.

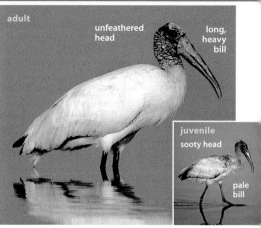

adult

unfeathered head

long, heavy bill

juvenile
sooty head

pale bill

adult

entirely black remiges (compare flight profile and remiges of American White Pelican)

yellow feet

Whooping Crane

Grus americana
L 52"/1.3m WS 87"/2.2m

This critically endangered species breeds only in Wood Buffalo National Park in northern Canada; it winters on the Texas coast in salt marshes and near oak mottes, feeding on aquatic invertebrates, fish, amphibians, and acorns. In 1940 only 22 Whooping Cranes survived in the wild. In 2004, 194 were counted in Texas; migratory and nonmigratory wild Whoopers are now established in Florida. **VOICE** A rolling, trumpeting *ba-KOOOO!* with varying inflections, often repeated.

adult

red crown and malar

large white "bustle" (tertials)

much taller than herons and egrets

very long, dark legs

juvenile

rusty-toned plumage gradually turns white

adult

black primaries visible in flight

Rails, Gallinules, Coots, and Kin

The family Rallidae is represented in North America by six breeding species of rail (including Sora) and by one species each of gallinule, moorhen, swamphen, and coot. These small to medium-sized birds somewhat resemble chickens, having rotund bodies, chickenlike feet, and a strutting gait, but they are most closely related to cranes and Limpkin and are classed with them in the order Gruiformes. Rallids are generally secretive, retiring birds with complex plumage patterns that make them difficult to see in the dense marshes most inhabit; the species that tend to forage more often in the open—such as American Coot, Purple Gallinule, and Common Moorhen—lack such cryptic coloration. In structure, rails may appear plump, but they are able to compress their bodies laterally and thus run quickly through dense vegetation. All rallids swim well; coots have specialized lobed toes with flanges that help them swim and dive nearly as well as a duck, and they are the only North American rallid species apt to be found in flocks like ducks. Purple Gallinule and the introduced Purple Swamphen have exceedingly long toes that enable them to walk on floating vegetation.

Corn Crake is a Eurasian rail species recorded 27 times in eastern North America as of 2005.

Rails and their relatives forage in aquatic habitats by picking and probing for small invertebrates and vertebrates; most species also incorporate plant matter in their diet. Like the smaller rails (often referred to as "crakes"), coots and moorhens have short, blunt bills best suited for picking up small prey or taking seeds and aquatic vegetation; the longer-billed species are better at probing into mud for small crabs or similar prey.

In courtship, the males of most rallid species strut and show off wings, flank patterns, and undertail coverts to the females. While courting rallids are seldom observed, they are quite often heard. Their calls serve to keep a pair in touch with one another and to maintain territories. Nests are constructed of plant material and are usually well hidden within a marsh. Rail chicks are semi-precocial and are usually blackish (and thus confused with adult Black Rails on occasion). They follow their parents until they fledge, roosting at night in the nest in which they were hatched or in a nursery nest constructed by the parents. After breeding, most rallids in temperate areas migrate southward for the winter. Some are hunted as game birds.

When seen flushing from a marsh, a rallid may seem to have hectic, sloppy wingbeats that barely keep it airborne before it drops back into the vegetation. This impression is misleading: rallids are very strong fliers, and they have colonized remote oceanic islands reached by few other birds. Their strong flight makes them capable of remarkable feats of vagrancy; several species that have been recorded extralimitally in the United States and Canada include Spotted Rail and Paint-billed Crake from the American tropics and Eurasian Coot, Baillon's Crake, and Corn Crake from Eurasia.

Although most rallid populations appear stable, Black Rail and King Rail have small, declining populations. The reasons for these declines are not well known.

Black Rail

Laterallus jamaicensis
L 6"/15cm **WS** 9"/23cm

Black Rail inhabits grassy marshes on outer coasts and wet meadows and marshes inland. It is a difficult bird to observe; unless pushed by tidal waters, it stays in deep cover and rarely flies. Black Rail is easiest to hear when other wetland creatures are less vocal. The chicks of most rails are blackish—a common source of confusion. **VOICE** Territorial song a distinctive *KI-KI-krrrrr;* pair gives a Least Grebe–like trill; male gives low growls, barks, and whinnies; female gives a low *cococo* and a sneezy *kyew!*

adult
chestnut nape
red eyes and short, black bill
black with white speckles above, rich gray below

adult
short tail often cocked
underparts show bluish gray sheen in good light

Yellow Rail

Coturnicops noveboracensis
L 7"/18cm **WS** 11"/28cm

This secretive bird nests in wet meadows and shallow marshes from the prairies to the tundra edge, and winters in saltwater and brackish marshes, rice fields, and wet fields with standing fresh water. It is rarely seen in flight except when flushed, but it occasionally clambers up into bushes to take refuge from floodwaters. Flying birds are readily told from larger Soras by their white secondaries. **VOICE** Territorial song a Morse code–like series of dry *tik* calls, usually in sets of 2 or 3 (sounding like rocks tapped together).

adult
bright buff-yellow streaks against dark upperparts
richer yellow below than young Sora
white secondaries distinctive
nonbreeding adult
like breeding adult but bill, face, underparts, and upperpart streaking more tan-buff than yellow; legs duskier
(juvenile similar but has mostly dark bill, finely spotted nape and crown)

Sora

Porzana carolina
L 8½"/22cm WS 14"/36cm

Sora is a small, adaptable crake that nests from grassy-edged tundra ponds to prairie sloughs to marshes of the southern Great Basin. Many winter in marshes of the South. Sora seems less secretive than the smaller Black and Yellow Rails, often visiting marsh edges to feed, preen, bathe, or sun. Like most rails, it appears to fly weakly when flushed. In fact, it is a fast, powerful flier. **VOICE** Both sexes give a loud, descending whinny, recalling Eastern Screech-Owl; also an inquisitive *kerrEE?* and a loud *eeek!*

adult

often cocks tail, showing white undertail coverts

short yellow bill surrounded by black face

soft blue-gray neck and breast

juvenile

bill has olive tones

upperparts have pale streaks (finer than Yellow Rail)

lacks black face and gray breast of adult (compare Yellow Rail)

Virginia Rail

Rallus limicola
L 9½"/24cm WS 14"/36cm

Virginia Rail breeds in upland freshwater marshes and coastal salt marshes; most winter coastally in fresh- and saltwater environments. Like other long-billed rails, it flies often and regularly walks around in the open. To avoid predators, this species may dive and swim underwater, propelled by its wings. **VOICE** A descending series of accelerating grunts recalling King Rail but more nasal, almost like laughing call of Mallard; a rapid *kek kek kek kedek kedek kedek* on one pitch; a very harsh, fussing *kik-ki-krrrrrrr,* similar to Clapper Rail.

adult

long bill

rich chestnut upperwings

dark gray face contrasts with crown, nape, throat

much smaller than King Rail

adult with chick

all rail chicks are black (often confused with Black Rail)

juvenile

hint of adult's face pattern

mostly dark bill

grayish to pale pink legs

grayish black sides and back, with rufous tones in scapulars and tertials

Clapper Rail

Rallus longirostris
L 14½"/37cm **WS** 19"/48cm

This chicken-sized rail inhabits mostly salt marshes year-round, where it forages, often conspicuously, along the edges for marsh crabs and other invertebrates. More than other true rails, it is often seen with young in tow during the breeding season. Clappers are often called "marsh hens" by hunters. **VOICE** A dry, staccato, accelerating series of *kek* (clapping) sounds; also a descending series of grunts, drier than Virginia, and a harsh *ga-ga-ga-ga-grrrrrrr*, similar to Virginia. Calls mostly at dusk and dawn.

adult, Atlantic *(crepitans)*

gray overall, with faint buff tints below

colors and face pattern less striking than much smaller Virginia and slightly larger King Rails

juvenile, Atlantic

duller than adult

adult, San Francisco Bay *(obsoletus)*

olive-brown above, rufous tones below

western and western Gulf taxa more warmly colored than Atlantic birds

---

King Rail

Rallus elegans
L 15"/38cm **WS** 20"/51cm

King Rail is a North American endemic species that has declined with the draining of freshwater marshes, its preferred year-round habitat. It is closely related to Clapper Rail, and hybrids have been recorded where ranges overlap in brackish environments. Like Clapper, King is rather bold and often seen in the open, sometimes with young; still, it is far more often heard than seen. **VOICE** Mostly similar to Clapper but slower, chestier, and richer, particularly the deep "grunt" call, used in part as a contact call.

adult

rich rufous above and below

dark centers on mantle, upperpart coverts, scapulars (compare western subspecies of Clapper Rail)

juvenile

similar to Clapper but coverts more rufous

Common Moorhen

Gallinula chloropus
L 14"/36cm **WS** 21"/53cm

Common Moorhen is locally common in the Southeast and Southwest, where it prefers extensive freshwater marshes. Eastern populations are strongly migratory. Moorhens forage mostly in marshes or while swimming near cover, usually reed beds; they may also be seen walking on dry land like gallinules and coots. They are strong swimmers, though their toes lack lobes or webbing. **VOICE** A rolling, high-pitched, nasal trumpeting with a piteous quality, slowing toward end; also a high *keek!*, similar to Purple Gallinule.

breeding adult

olive-brown back and wings contrast with slaty body

red frontal shield

red, yellow-tipped bill

white outer undertail coverts and flank stripe often visible

(compare Northern Jacana, p. 214)

juvenile

bill dusky, becoming yellowish

yellowish legs (duller in coots)

dull gray below (compare coots)

nonbreeding adult

plumage and bill duller in fall and early winter

American Coot

Fulica americana
L 15"/38cm **WS** 24"/61cm

American Coot is hardly rail-like in behavior: it regularly swims in the open on freshwater ponds and marshes, diving for aquatic vegetation and invertebrates. Coots routinely walk onto pondside suburban lawns to pick at vegetation and insects; their large, lobed toes are well-suited to both water and land. The similar Eurasian Coot is a vagrant to Canada and Alaska. **VOICE** Single grunting, trumpeting, and clucking notes, often with a nasal or grating quality; male gives higher calls, female lower, more guttural calls.

adult

whitish bill has rusty subterminal band

dark rusty frontal shield

slaty gray; head darker than body

juvenile

gray above, pale below, with ivory bill (compare Common Moorhen)

1st winter

lacks frontal shield

toes have broad, lobed flanges for swimming

Purple Gallinule
Porphyrio martinica
L 13"/33cm **WS** 22"/56cm

The colorful Purple Gallinule frequents freshwater environments with abundant floating vegetation. Some winter in Florida, but most migrate to the tropics in autumn; a few disoriented migrants turn up out of range each year as far away as Canada and South Africa. With their long toes, gallinules walk well over aquatic vegetation and even land on tree limbs, unlike coots and moorhens. **VOICE** Various high-pitched clucking notes, rather chickenlike, often in series; also a higher *keek!*

adult

sky blue frontal shield

red and yellow bill

grass green above, electric purple below

long, yellow legs and toes (obvious in flight)

juvenile

olive above, pale below

tawny cast to sides, head, neck

Purple Swamphen
Porphyrio porphyrio
L 18"/46cm **WS** 39"/99cm

A very large rail native to the Old World, Purple Swamphen is common very locally in southeastern Florida around Broward County, where it was introduced in the late 1980s. It is relatively tame, walking around pond edges, lawns, and golf courses with little regard for people. Its adaptability to human-altered environments suggests that populations may thrive and spread. Records outside of Florida (such as in Delaware) are assumed to be escapees rather than vagrants from the Old World. **VOICE** A comical, nasal *eeh!* and various grunting, clucking, trumpeting, squeaking, and chirping calls.

adult
(*poliocephalus*)

gray head

most Florida birds appear to be of the southern Asian subspecies *poliocephalus*, sometimes split as Gray-headed Swamphen

large, dusky red bill and frontal shield

red legs, long toes

Quail, Grouse, Turkey, and Kin

The "gallinaceous" (chickenlike) birds in the order Galliformes are represented in North America by three families. In the family Odontophoridae are the quail, including Northern Bobwhite. Phasianidae contains grouse, sage-grouse, prairie-chickens, ptarmigan, and Wild Turkey, as well as the introduced Old World pheasants, peafowl, partridges (including Chukar), guineafowl, and Himalayan Snowcock. The tropical American family Cracidae has just one species in the United States, Plain Chachalaca, whose range barely crosses the border into southernmost Texas.

A female Spruce Grouse with chicks. Galliform chicks are precocial, able to forage just after hatching.

Galliforms are largely ground-dwelling birds that peck at the ground for food much in the manner of chickens. Most are compact and sturdy, with strong feet for walking and scraping the ground; some have long tails, but most are short-tailed and short-legged. Although galliforms are capable of flight, most run rather than flush; Plain Chachalaca is a talented tree-climber and has a long hind toe adapted for arboreal life.

Greater Sage-Grouse in flight, showing the rounded wing shape of gallinaceous birds.

All natural habitats in North America—including forests, fields, prairies, tundra, and bare mountaintops—are home to one or more species of chickenlike birds. Scaled and Gambel's Quail thrive in the arid Mojave, Sonoran, and Chihuahuan Deserts, where temperatures over 115° F (46° C) are not rare, and Rock Ptarmigan is a permanent resident in northern Nunavut, where temperatures can drop as low as –60° F (–51° C). Each species is well suited to its environment; ptarmigan, for example, have thick, insulating plumage, including feathered legs and feet, while desert-dwelling quail conserve water in their organs with remarkable efficiency. Galliforms feed mostly on plant matter, especially seeds and buds, and also eat insects and other invertebrates.

Galliforms are sexually dimorphic in plumage. The more highly ornamented males possess, depending on the species, eye combs, wattles, air sacs on the neck, "beards" of feathers on the breast, pinnae (feathers that look like rabbit ears when raised), crests, and topknots. Males flaunt, raise, or inflate their adornments during elaborate, cacophonous courtship displays. Most galliforms build nests in concealed places on the ground; cracids nest in trees. Chicks are precocial and forage for themselves just after hatching.

Many populations of galliforms are declining rapidly, not so much from hunting losses (many are game birds) as from destruction or alteration of their habitats. Several species have lost well over 99 percent of their precolonial populations and continue to decline, especially the sage-grouse, prairie-chickens, and Northern Bobwhite.

Exotic Game Birds

Dozens of species of game birds and "ornamental" birds in the order Galliformes have been imported to North America. Of those species released into the wild, Chukar, Gray Partridge, and Ring-necked Pheasant have established thriving populations here; such factors as inhospitable climate, predators, diseases, and overhunting have prevented others from becoming widely established. Nevertheless, many species of exotic galliforms are observed in North America after they escape (or wander off) from captivity or are released for hunting purposes.

Some of the gallinaceous birds introduced in North America differ markedly from their wild counterparts in the Old World. Ring-necked Pheasant is native to Asia, but most that breed in North America are descendants of birds produced in captive crossbreeding programs in the 19th century in England that involved different subspecies (mostly those known as "Blackneck" and "Chinese Ringneck"). Every year new Ring-necked Pheasants are released in North America for hunting; these released birds can show much variation in plumage. Green Pheasant (*Phasianus versicolor*) of Japan, which has mostly dark green body plumage and was once considered a subspecies of Ring-necked, is occasionally released for hunting but no longer breeds in North America.

Common Peafowl (*Pavo cristatus*), called "peacock" by most people, is a southern Asian species uncommon in the wild but frequently observed on farms, parklands, and estates worldwide. Females are much plainer than the stunning males and lack the enormous tail.

Helmeted Guineafowl (*Numida meleagris*), native to Africa, is prized less for its appearance than for its habit of eating ticks. Feral guineafowl are known to breed in the wild in the southern United States and appear not to be dependent upon humans for food in some areas.

Red-legged Partridge (*Alectoris rufa*), a native of western Europe, is similar to Chukar but smaller. The species has no self-sustaining population in North America; it is bred in captivity, both for food and to release for hunting.

The tiny **Japanese Quail** (*Coturnix japonica*), smaller than Northern Bobwhite, is also occasionally released, though less so now than in the past. It might be confused with a small rail or the young of larger galliforms.

Northern Bobwhite
Colinus virginianus
L 10"/25cm **WS** 13½"/34cm

The male Northern Bobwhite's ringing territorial song is heard spring through summer in farmlands and brushy fields. Bobwhites are mostly seen foraging slowly on the ground for seeds and insects. After breeding, they form coveys that roost at night in tight circles with each bird facing outward. This species is declining in most areas, mostly owing to land-use changes. **VOICE** Male's song a loud, whistled *perWHEET! (bobWHITE!)*, often with introductory notes. Many other calls—*WHEEdle, puraKEE, whoi, kid*—some in series.

adult male

plumage variable; darkest in Florida and westernmost part of range

white supercilium and throat with distinct dark borders

adult female
similar to male but throat and supercilium buff-orange

Montezuma Quail
Cyrtonyx montezumae
L 9"/23cm **WS** 15"/38cm

This quail inhabits stony upland areas with scattered oaks and grassy cover; in these sun-dappled environments the male's striking "harlequin" plumage provides excellent camouflage. Birds are often detected by their foraging sounds—they dig with their large feet for bulbs, nuts, and insects. Unlike most quail, they do not form large coveys after breeding but travel in pairs or family groups. **VOICE** A descending, quavering, mechanical-sounding whistle; many other calls, including an inquisitive *wurr* and a low *wepp*.

adult male

unique head pattern

streaked with straw-buff above, polka-dotted below

adult female

upperparts streaked and barred

heavy, deep bill

strong legs and feet

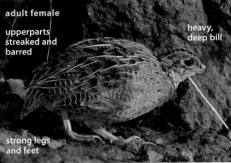

Chukar

Alectoris chukar
L 14"/36cm   **WS** 21"/53cm

Introduced as a game bird from Eurasia in the late 1800s and later, Chukar is now relatively common across most of the Great Basin; it inhabits arid montane environments, especially rocky canyons, slopes, and cliffs. Like other partridges, Chukars form coveys in winter that forage, usually on the ground, on seeds, leaves, insects, and fruit. The smaller Red-legged Partridge, also from Eurasia, is seen much less frequently. **VOICE** A repeated, nasal *chuKAR,* often begun with rapid, syncopated, clucking notes; alarm call *witoo!*

adult

off-white throat with black border

soft blue-gray above

barred sides

Gray Partridge

Perdix perdix
L 12½"/32cm   **WS** 19"/48cm

In farm country of the northern Great Plains and former prairies of the Great Lakes regions, the introduced Gray Partridge is an uncommon and often inconspicuous bird, found especially where hedgerows and other plantings provide cover. Modern agriculture and the loss of shelterbelts appear to have contributed to this species' decline. Gray Partridge is native to Eurasia. **VOICE** Rapid, scratchy, sometimes clucking sounds; recalls a pheasant's crowing but quieter and more mechanical-sounding.

adult male and female

female less richly colored than male, lacks belly patch

male has rich chestnut belly patch, tawny throat and supercilium

(in flight, Gray Partridge and Chukar show rusty tail)

Gambel's Quail

Callipepla gambelii
L 10"/25cm   **WS** 14"/36cm

Gambel's Quail is a widespread resident in canyons and deserts, especially in the southern Great Basin and Sonoran Desert. It has also adapted to suburban areas and sometimes visits feeders. Gambel's is more arboreal than bobwhites, feeding on fruit and seeds in trees and large cacti and roosting in bushes or trees. Its populations decrease notably during droughts. **VOICE** Male sings a repeated *hup WAAY ha ha.* Nasal calls include an inquisitive *whaaoo,* a sharp *u-wik,* and a collared-dove-like *hehh.*

adult male

rich ruddy crown

unspotted nape

black forehead (compare California Quail)

black belly patch; creamy "cummerbund"

adult female

similar to male but with smaller topknot, weak facial pattern

California Quail

Callipepla californica
L 10"/25cm   **WS** 14"/36cm

This adaptable species occupies chaparral, sage scrub, woodlands, farmland, and suburbs, especially near water. Like other quail, it forms coveys in the nonbreeding season that forage, often conspicuously, on hillsides and field edges and even in backyards with sufficient cover. In these coveys, one bird acts as sentinel, giving an alarm if it spots a predator. **VOICE** Male's song a familiar, ringing *hup WAAY ho* (often remembered *chi-CA-go*) with talkative quality. Calls include a nasal *waaay* and *uk* and sputtering clucks.

adult male

dark crown, less ruddy than Gambel's

buff forehead (compare Gambel's)

heavily patterned nape and belly

adult female

topknot very small

browner than Gambel's

patterned forehead, nape, belly

brown sides (female Gambel's has chestnut sides)

Scaled Quail
Callipepla squamata
L 10"/25cm **WS** 14"/36cm

Scaled Quail ("blue quail" or "cottontop" locally) is an animated species of arid grasslands, from the Tamaulipan brushlands and Chihuahuan and Sonoran Deserts north into prairies fringing the Rocky Mountains. It occasionally hybridizes with Gambel's Quail; hybrids may resemble muted Gambel's but have a more "scaly" appearance. **VOICE** Contact call a singsong *tuck-too,* endearing but rough, repeated 6–7 times; also an abrupt *WEEER,* a shrieking *wok!,* a high *cheepee,* and a low *kut-kut.*

adult male

short-tufted, gray-brown head contrasts with "scaly" plumage

adult female

less bluish in breast and nape than male

back and underparts have bluish cast

(southern Texas subspecies *castanogastris* has chestnut belly)

Mountain Quail
Oreortyx pictus
L 11"/28cm **WS** 16"/41cm

This striking and little-studied species inhabits brushy, wooded mountains, especially pine-oak woodlands with manzanitas and other undergrowth at elevations of up to 10,000' (3,000m). Many move into foothills in late autumn. Because Mountain Quail often forages in dense cover and "freezes" at signs of danger, it is usually seen by chance. For the best opportunity for a sighting, search near streams and springs and along remote roads early in the day. **VOICE** Male gives a hoarse, far-carrying *waAARK!*

adult male

head plumes longer in male

rusty throat bordered with white on sides

strongly barred flanks

adult female

rusty crissum, flanks, throat

Willow Ptarmigan

Lagopus lagopus
L 15"/38cm **WS** 24"/61cm

Willow Ptarmigan is an abundant species of tundra plains and taiga, especially with thickets of dwarf willows, and can also be found in Arctic mountain ranges up to the tree line. Like Rock Ptarmigan, Willow occasionally irrupts south of its usual range in winter; there are a few records from the lower 48 states, all in the northern tier. Ptarmigan are grouse adapted for life in extremely cold environments. Their dense plumages provide superb insulation, and their feet are fully feathered, enabling them to walk on top of newly fallen snow. To stay warm, all ptarmigan dig burrows in snowbanks for roosting at night or during storms. Ptarmigan are best known, however, for their system of molts: a complete molt in fall that produces a snow white plumage; a partial spring molt into courtship or breeding plumage; and a second partial molt in summer into a mostly brown plumage. All of these plumages blend well with their respective habitats: snow-covered in winter, patches of snow in spring, and a complex palette of browns, rusts, and greens in summer. Ptarmigan eat mostly seeds, buds, and other plant matter; young also eat insects and spiders. **VOICE** Male's courtship calls are varied, talkative phrases, mostly nasal in quality and highly entertaining; both sexes give low clucks.

adult male, spring

red eye combs conspicuous in courtship and in clashes between males

rich rufescent head and neck contrast with white body (spring male Rock Ptarmigan dirty white overall)

adult male, summer

wings, back, tail mottled brown and rufous

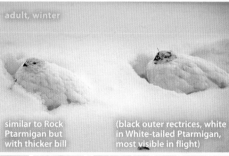

adult, winter

similar to Rock Ptarmigan but with thicker bill

(black outer rectrices, white in White-tailed Ptarmigan, most visible in flight)

adult female, summer

when threatened, fans tail and raises salmon-red eye combs

adult female, summer

very similar to Rock Ptarmigan but has larger bill

heavily barred

Rock Ptarmigan

Lagopus muta
L 14"/36cm   **WS** 23"/58cm

Rock Ptarmigan inhabits inhospitable High Arctic tundra barrens, offshore islands, and areas above the tree line in western Canada; it is the only bird species that spends its entire life on tundra. Males are energetic and comical in courtship displays: they fly above a female, march in circles, spread wings and tail, raise the eye combs, and call continuously. Females closely resemble Willow Ptarmigan but have smaller bills. **VOICE** Displaying male gives a mechanical-sounding rattle, followed by a sound like steam escaping.

very dark above, with white throat

bill smaller than Willow Ptarmigan

(mainland birds less blackish above)

adult male, summer (western Aleutians)

adult male, winter

black outer rectrices (like Willow Ptarmigan)

dark eye line unique to this species (but lacking in female)

male raises eye combs in courtship and conflict

White-tailed Ptarmigan

Lagopus leucura
L 13"/33cm   **WS** 22"/56cm

White-tailed Ptarmigan breeds in several montane locations in the lower 48 states, but it is perhaps the least familiar ptarmigan to birders, as most of its range is restricted to western Canada and southeastern Alaska. Like Rock Ptarmigan, it frequents barren, rocky areas above the tree line, especially near streams; both species descend to lower elevations in winter. White-tailed forages by browsing in low vegetation, eating mostly leaves and buds of alpine plants. **VOICE** Displaying male gives staccato clucking.

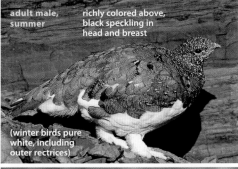

adult male, summer

richly colored above, black speckling in head and breast

(winter birds pure white, including outer rectrices)

adult female, summer

dark speckles with yellow tints, little rufous

(summer adults show white outer rectrices in flight)

Spruce Grouse
Falcipennis canadensis
L 16"/41cm **WS** 22"/56cm

The "fool hen" of the boreal forest, Spruce Grouse occupies dense spruce, fir, pine, and hemlock woods north to the muskeg; it is among the most approachable of birds in a habitat where many species appear unperturbed by humans. This species feeds mostly on evergreen vegetation, especially new shoots, and forages inconspicuously in trees. The subspecies in the Rockies and Cascades (*franklinii*) has a different display from the nominate. **VOICE** Displaying male gives low (almost inaudible) hooting.

adult male (nominate), displaying

rufous-buff rectrix tips

smaller than Dusky Grouse, with distinct black throat and breast

(subspecies *franklinii* similar but with white tips to uppertail coverts)

rufous adult female

(some much grayer overall)

relatively short tail (compare Dusky Grouse)

barred rather than speckled below

Dusky Grouse/ Sooty Grouse
Dendragapus obscurus/fuliginosus
L 20"/51cm **WS** 26"/66cm

The shy, subtly plumaged birds of western pine and fir forests known as Blue Grouse were split into two species in 2006. The Pacific coastal species, Sooty Grouse (*D. fuliginosus*, p. 13), lacks whitish markings above and has fewer rectrices than the interior species, Dusky Grouse. The two differ in courtship displays, but both are most easily located by the male's display calls in spring. **VOICE** Displaying male gives low, owl-like hooting, sounding like air blown across the top of a jug.

adult male, Dusky, displaying

air sacs inflated and eye combs raised in display

brown and slate-colored overall, with pale stippling in flanks

(Sooty shows yellow air sacs and paler rectrix tips)

adult female

long tail and neck; speckled below (compare Spruce Grouse)

noticeably larger than Spruce Grouse

Ruffed Grouse

Bonasa umbellus
L 17"/43cm   **WS** 22"/56cm

Ruffed Grouse is an elusive species of mixed and deciduous woodlands. Like other grouse, it forages, mostly on the ground, on buds, leaves, seeds, and berries; it also eats insects, invertebrates, and even some amphibians. In a unique display, the male mounts a fallen log and struts, fanning its tail and raising crest and neck ruffs, then beating its wings with increasing rapidity to produce a very low drumming sound. Populations show large fluctuations from year to year. **VOICE** Sharp clucking.

rufous adult

strong rufous tones to upperparts and tail

heavily barred flanks in some individuals

adult male, displaying

drumming sound produced by rapid wingbeats

grayer adult

(plumage varies from rusty to brown to pale gray)

short crest and dark neck ruff often visible

Himalayan Snowcock

Tetraogallus himalayensis
L 18"/46cm   **WS** 25"/64cm

Between 1963 and 1979, some 2,025 Himalayan Snowcocks—a large Asian species of montane habitats—were released in mountainous areas in Nevada (of the 6 subspecies, the dark nominate form was introduced). A few hundred birds persist there, especially in the Ruby Dome/Thomas Peak area; intrepid birders hoping to see this large species travel into this remote, roadless country on foot, by horseback, or even by helicopter. **VOICE** Displaying male gives loud, fluting whistle; also various chuckling clucks.

adult

pale head has rusty stripes

heavy, decurved bill

scalloped pattern on breast

white primaries (conspicuous in flight)

Greater Prairie-Chicken

Tympanuchus cupido
L 17"/43cm   **WS** 28"/71cm

Millions of Greater Prairie-Chickens once dotted the vast tallgrass prairies of the Midwest and Great Plains, and their booming communal courtship displays enchanted early naturalists. With more than 99% of their habitat now destroyed, prairie-chickens have become scarce. Heath Hen, the Atlantic coastal subspecies, became extinct in 1932; the small Attwater's Prairie-Chicken of Texas (subspecies *attwateri*) now numbers fewer than 50 in the wild. **VOICE** Displaying male makes loud whooping, cackling, and hooting sounds.

adult male, displaying

darker overall than Lesser Prairie-Chicken

orange air sacs, inflated during display

adult female

darker than Lesser

strongly and evenly barred below

Lesser Prairie-Chicken

Tympanuchus pallidicinctus
L 16"/41cm   **WS** 25"/64cm

Lesser Prairie-Chicken is a rare, declining resident of dry shortgrass prairies of the southern Great Plains. Like Greater Prairie-Chicken, it gathers before dawn in leks (communal displaying groups). Males raise earlike feathers (pinnae), droop the wings, inflate air sacs on the neck, dance, and vocalize constantly—one of the most captivating sights of the American wilderness. Lesser begins the display with tail-fanning (Greater fans the tail throughout the display). **VOICE** Displaying male gives wild, rapid, descending cackling and tooting calls.

adult male, displaying

slightly smaller than Greater Prairie-Chicken (but larger than Attwater's) and paler, blending with more arid habitats

adult female

like Greater but less robust and paler

narrower belly bars than Greater

Sharp-tailed Grouse
Tympanuchus phasianellus
L 17"/43cm **WS** 26"/66cm

Sharp-tailed Grouse is found in open prairie and steppe habitats with scattered deciduous trees and shrubs; it sometimes moves into recently burned open areas at the edges of boreal forest and muskeg. Like ptarmigan, this species digs snow burrows to keep warm during cold or foul weather. Males display on leks, arriving before sunrise. **VOICE** Displaying male gives bewildering variety of raucous gobbles, hoots, shrieks, and squeaks, supplemented by a loud purring sound made by rapid stamping of the feet.

adult male, displaying

pale, graduated tail distinctive

purple air sacs inflated in display

adult

less richly colored upperparts than ptarmigan, more finely marked than prairie-chickens

(pale tail base visible in flight)

Ring-necked Pheasant
Phasianus colchicus
Male **L** 35"/89cm **WS** 31"/79cm

An Asian species of open habitats, Ring-necked Pheasant has been released in North America since colonial times for game hunting. Its populations are self-sustaining mostly in agricultural areas, especially with varied croplands, hedgerows, and drinking water. Males display with beating wings and loud calls, often attracting several females. The sexes often segregate in winter. Many related taxa have been introduced; some look quite different. **VOICE** Displaying male gives an explosive, crowing *owaAAK!*

adult male

most often seen form has white collar, green head, copper body

very long tail has distinct bars

(many darker taxa without collars have been introduced)

adult female

long tail

buff-brown overall with dark markings (compare Sharp-tailed Grouse)

up to 14" (36cm) shorter than longer-tailed male

Greater Sage-Grouse

Centrocercus urophasianus
Male L 28"/71cm WS 38"/97cm

A rapidly declining species endemic to the vanishing sagebrush plains and foothills of the West, Greater Sage-Grouse feeds largely on the leaves and buds of sage and similar native plants. This species' display, in leks of up to 80 birds, is stunning: males puff out breast feathers, fill large, wobbly air sacs, spread the tail, strut, and call continuously. In some areas, this species moves to lower elevations in winter. **VOICE** Displaying male makes several wing noises, then gives 2 odd, gulping *OOP-ull-goop* sounds.

adult male, displaying

larger than Gunnison Sage-Grouse, with darker tail and shorter head plumes

adult female

striking marbled pattern above

large bill; white throat

female up to 6" (15cm) smaller than male and about half the weight

black belly patch

Gunnison Sage-Grouse

Centrocercus minimus
Male L 22"/56cm WS 30"/76cm

Gunnison Sage-Grouse is an endangered species, with a total population of probably less than 4,000; only one group remains in Utah and six in Colorado, the largest numbering about 3,000 birds in Colorado's Gunnison Basin. This species depends on large areas of big sagebrush *(Artemisia tridentata)* for survival. **VOICE** Displaying male gives 9 or 10 hooting gobbles on one low pitch, interspersed with 3 wing noises; very different from display of Greater Sage-Grouse.

adult male, displaying

(female 4"/10cm smaller than male, and about half the weight)

broader white bars in tail, longer head plumes than Greater Sage-Grouse

(female resembles female Greater but smaller and tail appears paler)

Wild Turkey

Meleagris gallopavo
Male L 46"/1.2m WS 64"/1.6m

Wild Turkey prefers swamp forests and upland and montane forests with oaks in the East, and arid mesquite scrub, oak woodlands, chaparral, and pinyon-juniper woodlands in the West. Large flocks are often seen foraging in farm fields in the nonbreeding season; displaying leks form in early spring from these flocks. Turkeys usually roost in trees at night. **VOICE** Displaying male ("tom") gives a vigorous, descending gobbling; other calls include a high, clear yelp, a repeated high *hike*, and chickenlike noises.

adult male, displaying

buffy or copper tail tip (white in western subspecies and domestic birds)

naked, blue and red head; plumage has iridescent copper, blue, and green sheens

adult female

resembles male but less ornate

smaller than male (by up to 10"/25cm), usually apparent in flocks

Plain Chachalaca

Ortalis vetula
L 22"/56cm WS 27"/69cm

Plain Chachalaca inhabits brushy woodlands and their edges, typically woodlands with hackberry and mesquite near water, where it nests in trees. It is more arboreal than other game birds, often dashing through the canopy with great speed and agility. At dawn and dusk, flocks of chachalacas chorus loudly from roosting areas. An introduced population thrives on Sapelo Island, Georgia. **VOICE** Entire flock gives a loud, grating *JA-CHA-LAK!* in staggered "singing rounds." Birds disturbed by predators give loud, wooden-sounding alarm calls.

adult

olive-brown above, buffy below, with darker head

tail has narrow white tips

(compare turkey, grouse; also Greater Roadrunner, p. 253)

adult

red gular skin most evident during breeding season

Vultures and Diurnal Raptors

During a long car trip through just about any open habitat in North America, one is likely to see a few hawks or vultures soaring above the fields, perched watchfully on a telephone pole, or eating prey or carrion on the ground. Thirty-two species of diurnal raptors—including hawks, eagles, kites, Northern Harrier, and Osprey (family Accipitridae) and falcons and Crested Caracara (Falconidae)—nest in North America, and another eight species have been reported as vagrants from Mexico or Eurasia. California Condor and the two vultures found north of Mexico (Cathartidae) are often considered "honorary raptors," as they forage and migrate in the skies much like raptors; however, their evolutionary relationships with raptors are unclear and they seldom take live prey.

Red-tailed Hawk, like other diurnal raptors, tears its prey into small pieces before eating.

Diurnal raptors, usually recognized by casual observers as "hawks" or "eagles," are birds of prey with hooked bills and talons adapted for killing prey and tearing into flesh. (Owls are also birds of prey, but most owls hunt nocturnally.) Their speed and skill when hunting have been a source of wonder for humans since our earliest written history. Some species of diurnal raptors supplement their diet with carrion, especially under adverse conditions or when prey is scarce.

Steller's Sea-Eagle, the largest raptor in North America, is a rare visitor to Alaska from Siberia.

Members of the family Accipitridae, often called accipitrids, range greatly in size—from the tiny Sharp-shinned Hawk, with a wingspan of less than 24" (50cm), to the mighty Steller's Sea-Eagle (a vagrant in North America), the world's largest eagle, with an 8' (2.5m) wingspan. Because accipitrids have evolved to exploit different prey resources, they differ greatly in shape as well as size. Harriers and White-tailed Kite have elegant, long wings and tails, perfect for coursing over meadows and marshes in search of rodents; the similarly shaped but more aerial Mississippi and Swallow-tailed Kites hunt dragonflies in midair. Hook-billed Kite, which feeds mostly on arboreal snails, and Osprey, which eats mostly fish, also have distinctive wing shapes related to their specialized foraging strategies. The three accipiters (genus *Accipiter*) are relatively long-tailed like kites, but they have broader, shorter wings better adapted for hunting in closed environments such as thickets and forests, where they pursue mostly birds. The buteos (genus *Buteo*) and their relatives in the Southwest (Common Black-Hawk, Harris's Hawk) all have broad wings and relatively short tails for harnessing warm, rising air (thermals). With little effort, these birds can remain aloft most of the day as they watch for prey on the ground; their vision is up to eight times more acute than a human's. Most buteos also hunt well from perches, such as fence posts, treetops, or cliffs.

Falcons are renowned for their speed and grace in the air, which many feel are unrivaled in the world of birds. True falcons (genus *Falco*) range in size from the petite American Kestrel to the stocky Gyrfalcon, but all are somewhat similar in shape. Their long, pointed wings and moderately long tails are adapted for rapid acceleration and maximum maneuverability when pursuing prey, whether aerial insects, shorebirds, or ptarmigan. Crested Caracara, a distinctively patterned relative of falcons, is quite different in shape, its long legs and heavy, deep bill suited for flexible foraging strategies that include walking on the ground to scavenge carrion. Like caracaras, vultures and condors have strong legs and bills for gaining access to carcasses of dead animals, which form almost their entire diet. Their naked heads are an adaptation for feeding on carrion, which can quickly soil feathers and spread disease. Turkey Vulture is known to have such keen senses of smell and vision that Black Vultures appear to follow them to dead animals.

Courtship among diurnal raptors involves paired flights above a territory; male buteos, Golden Eagles, and accipiters also perform display flights that consist

Peregrine Falcons take mostly avian prey in dazzling, high-speed dives (or "stoops"), often from high in the air.

of exaggerated, slow wingbeats or abrupt, swooping dives. These aerial acrobatics also serve as warnings to other members of the species not to pass through the nesting territory. All accipitrids build nests of vegetation, usually twigs and sticks. Larger falcons nest on bare cliffs or ledges and smaller falcons nest in cavities (American Kestrel) or old nests of crows, ravens, or other raptors (Aplomado Falcon and Merlin). Vultures and condors usually nest in caves or cliff recesses. Most diurnal raptors migrate southward in winter or make some sort of movement away from the nesting area after breeding, especially when prey becomes scarce.

Because raptors are "apex predators" (at the top of their food chain) that feed largely on vertebrates, they have been subject to repeated poisoning in modern times: pesticides such as DDT become increasingly concentrated in fish and other prey items as they work their way up the food chain, and their levels reach lethal proportions in the top predators. Peregrine Falcon, Osprey, and Bald Eagle were threatened with extinction by the early 1970s, due to eggshell thinning and premature hatching caused by DDT. Local reintroductions and efforts by conservationists to ban DDT and other organochlorine pesticides in North America have brought these and other species back from the brink of extinction.

Ospreys catch fish in swift dives, usually after spotting prey while hovering.

Raptors in Flight

Raptors and vultures in flight challenge birders to become proficient at identification from afar. Shape, flight style, and plumage characteristics are often evident enough to distinguish species, even at great distances, especially among the very large birds and the very small. The raptors intermediate in size between the smallest and the largest, however, require careful study. The six species shown below can be confused with each other in various ways, even though they are not all closely related.

Peregrine Falcon's long, pointed wings often jut forward at the wrist, for a "crossbow" silhouette. Peregrine has a shorter tail than Mississippi Kite, and its fleet, fluid wingstrokes are unlike the more delicate, buoyant actions of the kite.

Mississippi Kite has long, pointed wings and a slender body. Despite its smaller size it can resemble a Peregrine Falcon when seen at a distance or in silhouette, but unlike falcons, kites twist and fan the long tail often when foraging.

Prairie Falcon is regularly mistaken for Peregrine over the continent's western interior. Prairie differs in its small size and its shape: it is more evenly slender of body and less pointed in the primary region (the outer portion of the wings).

Gyrfalcon, despite its larger size, is also sometimes taken for a Peregrine; it has much broader wings overall, and its wingtips often look barely pointed. With its very heavy body and broad tail it can resemble a soaring buteo.

A soaring juvenile **Northern Goshawk** can be confused with an immature Red-shouldered Hawk: both have a long, broad, banded tail, rather long, full, tapered wings with a slight bulge in the secondaries, and streaky underparts.

Red-shouldered Hawk juvenile is distinguished by the pale crescents at the base of the primaries. Compared to Northern Goshawk, its wingtips are more square-cut and less tapered, its wings are fuller, and its tail is not as long.

Buteos exhibit many differences related to subspecies, morph, and age. Given the extreme variation in plumage in species such as Red-tailed Hawk, it is wise to learn the basic shapes of the various buteos. In the species shown below, soaring adults (illustrated) have shorter tails and rather shorter, broader wings than immatures, and the difference in shape between adults and immatures can be substantial. Buteos can change flight behaviors rapidly, altering the appearance of the wing shape.

Red-tailed Hawk (here a rufous morph) has full, wide wings and a broad tail. In soar, its wings usually show a bulge through the secondaries; the wings of other buteos seldom impart such an impression of breadth.

Ferruginous Hawk is large-bodied, like Red-tailed, but its wings lack the bulging secondaries and appear longer overall, more tapered, and pointed in the "hand." Ferruginous usually does not fan the tail broadly; Red-tailed often does.

Rough-legged Hawk can recall a slender version of Ferruginous (and both species have a dark morph), but its tail and wings appear longer, more graceful, and less broad in the "arm" (a hawkwatcher's term for the wing's inner portion).

Swainson's Hawk looks longer-tailed and more slender-winged than other buteos, especially as an immature. In full soar, the wings appear to curve gently along the trailing edge to a neat point that is accentuated by the dark remiges.

Red-shouldered Hawk can look somewhat lanky in the wing when immature, but adults look full-winged, and their wings have more gently rounded trailing edges than the wings of the larger and bulkier Red-tailed.

Broad-winged Hawk is a relatively small buteo with proportionately wider wings that come to a broad point in the outer primaries. A soaring Broad-winged, with tail and wings fully spread, has a compact shape all its own.

Turkey Vulture

Cathartes aura
L 27"/69cm   WS 69"/1.8m

The sight of a Turkey Vulture gliding over open country is a familiar one from deserts to mountain canyons and also in some cities and suburbs. As it soars over the terrain, tilting slowly back and forth and only occasionally flapping (Black Vulture flaps rapidly between glides), Turkey Vulture uses its keen sense of smell to locate carrion even when it is covered or in dense woods. In fall thousands migrate southward; many western birds winter in the tropics. **VOICE** Rarely heard; nesting bird hisses and gives nasal barks.

adult
naked red head
brownish black plumage overall
wings and tail project beyond body

juvenile
grayish head gradually turns red

adult
long, upswept wings, long tail (Black Vulture's shorter)
(compare barred remiges of Zone-tailed Hawk)
toes fall well short of tail tip
silver sheen to remiges below

Black Vulture

Coragyps atratus
L 25"/64cm   WS 58"/1.5m

Black Vulture often rises later in the morning than Turkey Vulture and may actually follow that species, which has a far superior sense of smell, to discover carrion. The two show very different shapes in flight and while roosting or feeding on the ground. Both spread their wings while roosting to warm up, especially in the early morning. Both species, informally called "buzzards," are slowly expanding their range northward. **VOICE** Rarely heard; nesting bird hisses and groans.

adult
sooty gray head (all ages)
thinner bill, much shorter wings and tail than Turkey Vulture

adult
shorter wings and tail than Turkey Vulture
pale area in primaries
toes almost touch tail tip

California Condor
Gymnogyps californianus
L 47"/1.2m   **WS** 108"/2.7m

By modern times, the great California
Condor, which had once roamed much
of the West, was found only in southern
California. By 1987, all 27 birds that
survived were in captive breeding
facilities, the others having been shot
illegally or poisoned by lead ammunition
in carrion. As of 2004, through captive
breeding, 105 California Condors had
been released into the wild in Baja
California, California, and Arizona and
are once more breeding there. Lead shot,
however, continues to kill birds. **VOICE**
Similar to vultures.

adult

naked, pinkish orange head

enormous

juvenile

grayish head, legs, underwing coverts

adult

white underwing coverts (darker in juvenile)

large wing area provides great stability in flight

Osprey
Pandion haliaetus
L 23"/58cm   **WS** 64"/1.6m

Once threatened with extirpation by DDT
in North America, Osprey is now a familiar
sight on lakes, bays, and rivers, and its
huge stick nests are conspicuous on
buoys, channel markers, and large trees.
Osprey (colloquially called "fish hawk")
hunts by hovering over the water, then
plunging down to grasp fish with open
talons lined with spicules (barbs). In fall
migration hundreds can be seen passing
hawkwatch sites en route to wintering
areas. **VOICE** Piercing whistled notes,
heard mostly around nest.

adult with nestlings

short crest

dark eye stripe

dark brown above, white below

adult

flies on bent wings

some show brownish "necklace"

underwings mottled brown and white

Northern Harrier
Circus cyaneus
L 20"/51cm   **WS** 42"/1.1m

Northern Harrier is the only North American representative of a cosmopolitan genus. Harriers specialize in open habitats—tundra, meadows, prairies, farm fields, marshes, and the like—where they are expert mousers. They course low over the ground, often just above the grasses or reeds, rocking side to side on upswept wings, then dropping straight down on rodents. Their wings, body, legs, and tail are distinctly long and slender, all perfectly adapted for flying over and foraging in high grasses. Unlike other diurnal raptors, harriers have an owl-like facial disc, which presumably helps them detect prey by ear. Some appear to migrate in rain and under cover of darkness, unusual among hawks. Like falcons, harriers do not hesitate to make long water crossings when migrating. When rodents are especially numerous, this species is often polygynous (males mate with multiple females); males bring food to the nests of multiple mates. **VOICE** Male gives a rapid series of high-pitched *keeh* calls. Female and young give a whining *seeeuw*.

adult male

narrow wings white below with dark on secondaries and outer primaries

pale gray head

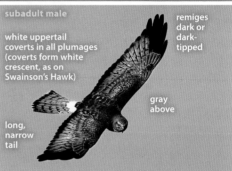

subadult male

white uppertail coverts in all plumages (coverts form white crescent, as on Swainson's Hawk)

remiges dark or dark-tipped

gray above

long, narrow tail

juvenile

facial disc, as in owls

warm rust-orange body

adult male

long legs, wings, tail obvious on sitting birds

adult female

lacks rufous tones of juvenile

pale eyes (not dark as in young birds)

banded remiges, streaked breast, speckled underwing coverts

Crested Caracara

Caracara cheriway
L 23"/58cm **WS** 50"/1.3m

The striking Crested Caracara, a tropical relative of falcons, is numerous in the U.S. only in deserts and grasslands of Texas, where it is called "Mexican eagle." Like vultures, it flies in search of carrion during the warm part of the day, though not soaring at great heights; it also hunts live prey from low perches, as hawks do. Unlike vultures, Crested Caracara has long legs that are well suited for walking. **VOICE** A nasal, guttural, growling rattle, sounding almost mechanical; call may be the source of the bird's Guarani name, *traco-traco*, from which the name "caracara" is derived.

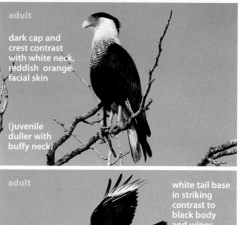

adult

dark cap and crest contrast with white neck, reddish orange facial skin

(juvenile duller with buffy neck)

adult

white tail base in striking contrast to black body and wings

white in neck and primaries

long tail, wings, head; easily told from distant ravens and vultures by white in head and tail

Hook-billed Kite

Chondrohierax uncinatus
L 16"/41cm **WS** 33"/84cm

Hook-billed Kite is found in the Lower Rio Grande valley of Texas, where perhaps a few pairs per year raise young on the river's north side. Like many raptors, it is most conspicuous at midmorning, soaring as the air warms and thermals rise. Its heavy, hooked bill is adapted for feeding on arboreal snails; piles of snail shells beneath a tree often reveal its presence in forests. The scarce dark morph, which is mostly blackish, has nested only once in the U.S. **VOICE** A high-pitched, descending chatter, far-carrying and with a laughing quality.

adult female, light morph

rusty barring on coverts and underparts

banded remiges and rectrices (similar to Red-shouldered Hawk)

adult male, light morph

unusual wing shape: "pinched" at body, broad and rounded at tip

adult male, light morph

heavy bill

belly barred with gray (rusty in female)

broad tailband

Swallow-tailed Kite
Elanoides forficatus
L 23"/58cm   **WS** 48"/1.2m

The elegant Swallow-tailed Kite is like no other American bird of prey. It occupies southeastern pine forests, wooded savannas, hammocks, and other wetlands with scattered trees. This species hunts dragonflies, small reptiles, and birds, often eating small prey while soaring. Like other highly migratory kites, it can show up hundreds of miles out of range, especially in spring. Breeding pairs sometimes associate with nonbreeders, which may assist in feeding young. **VOICE** A very high-pitched, thin *kwi-kwi-kwi-kwi!*

adult

white body and coverts, black remiges and rectrices

elongate wings and tail

adult

(juvenile similar but washed with buff on head and breast; shorter-tailed)

white head looks small for body

very long tail and wings

upperparts inky black with bluish gloss

Snail Kite
Rostrhamus sociabilis
L 17"/43cm   **WS** 46"/1.2m

Snail Kite (formerly Everglades Kite) is a widespread Neotropical species found in wetlands of southern Florida. It feeds almost exclusively on aquatic apple snails *(Pomacea paludosa)*, its slender, hooked bill perfectly suited to prizing them from the shell. These kites frequently roost communally, often among Anhingas. Snail Kite is endangered in North America, its numbers reduced mostly by habitat loss. **VOICE** A series of mechanical-sounding, rattling, unbirdlike calls, reminiscent of a large frog.

adult male

glossy bluish black plumage

sharply hooked bill

adult male

broad-ended wings and broad tail; white tail base in all plumages

adult female/subadult male

pale throat and supercilium

mottled below

(juvenile similar but heavily streaked below)

Mississippi Kite

Ictinia mississippiensis
L 14½"/37cm **WS** 35"/89cm

This kite inhabits prairies and agricultural land and forages mostly for large, aerial insects such as cicadas and dragonflies. Where prey is abundant, Mississippi Kites may occur in considerable numbers and nest in close proximity. Spring migrants may wander as far north as southern Canada. In recent years, nesting pairs have been discovered well north of historical range, in Virginia, Illinois, Iowa, and Colorado. **VOICE** A thin, high-pitched, rising *ssseew-EE;* also a 2-part, piping *ssee-seeuw,* descending, sometimes in many-syllabled tremolo.

adult
darker blue-gray above
pale gray below

adult
white secondaries visible at great distance

adult
long, pointed wings

long, dark, squared tail

(juvenile similar but tail barred, underwings mottled)

distinguished from Peregrine Falcon by more buoyant flight, short outer primary

White-tailed Kite

Elanus leucurus
L 16"/41cm **WS** 42"/1.1m

White-tailed Kite prefers open country—agricultural fields, rangelands, and grasslands—where it hunts mostly mice and large insects. Unlike most North American raptors, this species "hover-hunts": hovering with its wings beating rapidly before dropping to seize prey. The smaller American Kestrel and the larger Red-tailed Hawk also hover-hunt. In recent decades this species has declined over some of its range, but it has increased lately on the West Coast. **VOICE** A high, piping *wheeow;* a much harsher, 2-part *whee-AK;* and grating chatters.

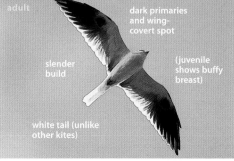

adult
dark upperwing coverts contrast with gray and white plumage

adult
dark primaries and wing-covert spot

slender build

(juvenile shows buffy breast)

white tail (unlike other kites)

Accipiter Identification

North American accipiters—Sharp-shinned Hawk, Cooper's Hawk, and Northern Goshawk—can be tricky to identify while on the wing. Size can be unreliable, because it is difficult to judge the size of birds in the air, especially among species exhibiting such pronounced sexual dimorphism in size (for example, female Sharp-shinned Hawk is nearly as large as male Cooper's Hawk). Hawkwatchers concentrate on four aspects of flying birds: tail, wings, head, and belly.

Tail

The tails of the three species are all relatively long, but they are differently shaped and patterned. Sharp-shinned Hawk has the shortest tail of the three, with a squared end that often shows a central notch. Cooper's Hawk has a long, narrow tail by comparison, usually with a broad, rounded end that shows a fairly wide pale terminal band. Northern Goshawk's tail appears shorter and broad by comparison and has four dark zigzag bands when seen from above (the others have three bands). There are exceptions, including some Sharp-shinneds with rounded tails and rare Cooper's with squared tails.

Wings

The wings of accipiters differ as well: Sharp-shinned and Northern Goshawk have rather broad or full-looking wings for their sizes, with a sinuous S-curve along the trailing edge, while Cooper's Hawk has narrower, lanky-looking wings that taper more gradually toward the tip. Sharp-shinned flaps its wings quickly, Cooper's employs slower and more graceful wingbeats, and Northern Goshawk uses deep and impressively slow strokes.

Head

Sharp-shinned's head looks quite small and neckless, with eyes set in the middle. Cooper's Hawk has a large, long, and flexible head, with eyes set farther forward (and unlike the other accipiters, immature Cooper's tends to have a tawny nape). Northern Goshawk's stout head recalls a buteo's.

Belly

The belly is an important identifying feature of immature birds: Cooper's has a very pale, almost unmarked lower belly, while Northern Goshawk and Sharp-shinned are heavily marked from the breast well into the belly.

Northern Goshawk

Accipiter gentilis
L 23"/58cm   **WS** 43"/1.1m

Northern Goshawk is a retiring raptor of coniferous and mixed woodlands. It is large and relatively heavy-bodied but an agile hunter, taking prey as large as grouse and hares. Adult females are especially aggressive around nests and have been known to attack intruding humans from behind. This species is confused regularly with Cooper's Hawk and young Red-shouldered Hawks. **VOICE** A strident *wheeee-ah*, descending; also a *k-kle-kle-kle-kle* chatter, higher and slower than Cooper's.

adult
striking white supercilium
gray barring below
slaty above
tail long like other accipiters but with broader base

adult
very broad wings and tail compared to Cooper's Hawk (recalls Gyrfalcon)

juvenile
broad wings have S-shaped trailing edge
heavily streaked belly, flanks, undertail, underwing coverts
broad tail shows pale borders to black bands

Cooper's Hawk
Accipiter cooperii
L 17"/43cm **WS** 33"/84cm

Cooper's Hawk preys on small birds, often making swift surprise attacks at bird-feeding stations. Because of similar bold raids on domestic poultry, this species was once shot as a "chicken hawk," and a bounty was paid for it; this practice was ended in the mid-20th century. Cooper's is a very common sight in autumn migration, as well as in deciduous and mixed woodlands. **VOICE** A nasal *kih*, much lower-pitched than Sharp-shinned Hawk, usually given in long, staccato, chattering series.

adult
pale nape gives capped look
heavier legs and head, longer tail than Sharp-shinned Hawk

juvenile
long wings
long tail has broad, white tip
heavy head
sparse streaks on white belly (most very lightly marked)

adult
trailing edge of wings often straight
broader tail base than Sharp-shinned

Sharp-shinned Hawk
Accipiter striatus
L 12"/30cm **WS** 24"/61cm

This tiny hawk of forests and their edges resembles a small version of Cooper's Hawk. It preys on small birds, often at backyard feeders, and also sometimes takes other small vertebrates. As with Cooper's, large numbers are seen from many hawkwatch sites. Unlike Cooper's, Sharp-shinned appears to be in a long-term population decline, for reasons that are not clear. Both species can breed in their first spring, at just under 1 year of age. **VOICE** A very high-pitched series of *kir* notes with a chattering quality.

adult male
rusty cheek contrasts with crown, but nape dark (looks less "capped" than Cooper's)
tiny
smaller bill and head, thinner legs than Cooper's

adult female
nearer in size and appearance to Cooper's
square-tipped tail has dusky, not white, edge

juvenile
small head barely projects beyond carpal joint
heavily marked below
square-tipped tail

Common Black-Hawk

Buteogallus anthracinus
L 21"/53cm WS 50"/1.3m

Common Black-Hawk is anything but common in the U.S.: it inhabits only a few forested riparian valleys and canyons in the Southwest and western Texas, and its population, probably never large, appears to have declined. Throughout their tropical range, Common Black-Hawks are tied to waterways, where they forage on crayfish, fish, small mammals, and amphibians. Males display over territories with deep, butterfly-like wingbeats. **VOICE** Sharp whistles and shrieks reminiscent of Osprey.

adult

yellow facial skin

long, yellow legs

adult

extremely broad wings

single black subterminal tailband

juvenile

slimmer wings and longer tail than adult; finely banded remiges and rectrices

Zone-tailed Hawk

Buteo albonotatus
L 20"/51cm WS 51"/1.3m

In pine-oak woodlands, especially in foothills, canyons, and mountains, Zone-tailed Hawk typically soars lazily in the updrafts along ridges, foraging mostly for terrestrial vertebrates and small birds. In flight it has an uncanny resemblance to Turkey Vulture and will even mingle with vultures while hunting; such mimicry may disguise it from prey. Juveniles are similar in shape but have fine barring in both the remiges and rectrices. **VOICE** A high-pitched, bloodcurdling *whheeeeeeer*, descending.

adult

shows 1 broad white tailband and narrow pale rectrix tips (compare Common Black-Hawk)

yellow cere and orbital ring

more slender body than Black-Hawks

adult

long, narrow wings and tail

contrasting remiges barred (unlike Turkey Vulture)

single white tailband

blackish plumage overall, with soft gray cast

adult

tailband visible from above (on juveniles tail appears black from above)

Harris's Hawk

Parabuteo unicinctus
L 21"/53cm WS 46"/1.2m

This unusual species of deserts, brushy savannas, and arid woodlands is most closely related to buteos and Common Black-Hawk. Unlike other American raptors, it breeds year-round and often forms polyandrous groups (2 males, 1 female). Harris's Hawks also sometimes form communal groups of 4 or 5, usually including young from previous broods, that defend the nest and feed the young. They may hunt collectively for large rodents. **VOICE** A strange, grating, nasal *eeehhhhhhhh*, similar to a caracara.

adult · yellow facial skin · chestnut upperwing coverts and thigh feathers · very long tail and legs

adult · dark, broad wings · (juvenile similar in shape, heavily streaked below, with barred remiges) · rich chocolate brown body and wings · chestnut underwing coverts · long tail; very wide black tailband

White-tailed Hawk

Buteo albicaudatus
L 23"/58cm WS 50"/1.3m

The coastal prairies, Tamaulipan scrub, and ranchland of southeastern Texas form White-tailed Hawk's northern limit. This species soars at relatively high altitudes through much of the day. It hunts from perches and the air, taking mostly small rodents and also reptiles, amphibians, birds, and insects. It is occasionally seen hunting along the advancing edge of a grass fire. Juveniles are very dark with white on the breast. **VOICE** A distinctive, high-pitched *wheee-ak, whe-AK, whee-AK* (male); *ah-KUT, ah-KUT, ah-KUT* (female).

adult · powdery gray above with pale chestnut upperwing coverts · white below · long legs · wingtips extend past tail

adult · broad wings; often kites · single black tailband

juvenile · pale patch on breast · often rich brown below

juvenile · long, broad wings pointed at tip and pinched at body · pale, dark-tipped tail

Broad-winged Hawk

Buteo platypterus
L 16"/41cm **WS** 34"/86cm

Broad-winged Hawk hunts small vertebrates and insects inside the canopy cover of deciduous and mixed woods. During migration, flocks sometimes numbering in the thousands are observed in eastern and central North America. A rare dark morph (dark brown flecked with chestnut) nests chiefly in western Canada; it is told from a dark-morph Short-tailed Hawk by the broad, dark tips to the remiges and very wide tailband. **VOICE** A ringing, thin, high-pitched, far-carrying *pweeeee!* or *pe-eeeeee!* or *pip-peeeee!*

adult · small buteo · brown above, chestnut barring below · 1 white tailband visible

adult · dark-tipped remiges · wings appear full but rather short, especially in full soar

juvenile · "paring knife" wing shape similar to adult, but tail finely banded, underparts variably spotted

Gray Hawk

Buteo nitidus
L 17"/43cm **WS** 35"/89cm

Gray Hawk is found in the Lower Rio Grande valley of Texas and in southeastern Arizona in riparian forests, especially with cottonwoods and sycamores, and nearby open areas. It hunts from a low perch for insects and small vertebrates. Juveniles differ from juvenile Broad-winged Hawk in a longer tail, white rump band, and strong face pattern (a bolder supercilium and dark eye line). **VOICE** A drawn-out, high-pitched, descending *wheeeeeeeer;* similar in quality to Red-shouldered Hawk, but call single, not repeated.

adult · longer-tailed than small buteos · medium gray above, pale gray below · 2 white tailbands

adult · differs from Broad-winged in more rounded wingtips and more and narrower tailbands · gray-barred body · flight accipiter-like, with rapid flapping and gliding

Short-tailed Hawk

Buteo brachyurus
L 15"/38cm **WS** 35"/89cm

This dimorphic buteo occupies a great variety of habitats within its large tropical range. It has a small population in Florida (and also Arizona and possibly Texas), where it inhabits mangrove forests, cypress swamps, pine savannas, and mixed woodlands, especially near water; the few Arizona birds inhabit montane pine forests. Short-tailed's diet is unusual for a North American buteo, consisting mostly of birds; it captures prey in sudden stoops while soaring slowly over the trees, often in semiopen areas along the edge of a woodland. This species, once rarely seen perched and considered shy in Florida, is either increasing or becoming more tolerant of humans, as it is now a relatively common sight in southern Florida. Most Florida birds appear to move southward to winter in southernmost Florida and the Keys, but the extent of migration in the species is not well known. Dark morphs outnumber light morphs in the U.S. **VOICE** A long, high-pitched *keeeeyaaah*, intermediate in quality between Swainson's and Broad-winged Hawks.

adult, light morph

strikingly white below

chestnut patch often visible at sides of upper breast where breast meets brown "helmet"

faintly banded tail

adult, light morph

chestnut nape

white below with dark-tipped remiges

dark "helmet"

juvenile, dark morph

heavily speckled underparts and underwing coverts, strongly banded remiges (compare dark-morph Broad-winged)

immature, light morph

buff supercilium and lower cheek (unlike Broad-winged)

sparse streaking on sides of upper breast (unlike Gray)

adult, dark morph

speckled coverts

wingtips more rounded than Broad-winged (in which dark morph is rare)

evenly banded tail

Red-shouldered Hawk

Buteo lineatus
L 17"/43cm **WS** 40"/1m

Red-shouldered Hawk is a small buteo of mature deciduous and mixed forests, wooded swamps, and their margins; it is often found near fresh water, where it hunts a wide variety of prey, including amphibians, reptiles, rodents, snails, and fish. This hawk has 5 subspecies that vary mostly in size and plumage coloration; some are intensely ruddy, as in California, others (especially in Florida) much paler. In the California subspecies, *elegans,* juveniles closely resemble adults. In all other subspecies juveniles are sometimes confused with young accipiters (Northern Goshawk and Cooper's Hawk) or with Broad-winged Hawk; Red-shouldered differs from all in showing primary crescents (but beware molting Broad-wingeds) and from Broad-winged in showing more rounded wingtips and banded secondaries. **VOICE** An insistent, descending *eeee-errrrrr,* more pure-toned and less harsh than Red-tailed Hawk; often imitated by jays.

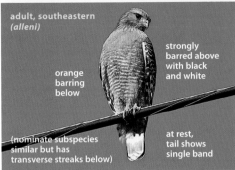

adult, southeastern *(alleni)*

strongly barred above with black and white

orange barring below

(nominate subspecies similar but has transverse streaks below)

at rest, tail shows single band

adult, California *(elegans)*

solid orange breast

(Texas subspecies *texanus* also richly colored)

adult, South Florida *(extimus)*

pale gray head

underside of body and underwing coverts lightly washed with rufous

adult

rusty upperwing coverts ("shoulders")

boldly barred greater coverts and secondaries

adult

strikingly banded tail and remiges

juvenile, eastern (nominate)

translucent primary crescent

longer wings and tail than Broad-winged Hawk (compare also larger accipiters)

longer tail, narrower wings than adult

Swainson's Hawk

Buteo swainsoni
L 21"/53cm   WS 52"/1.3m

A delicate buteo of western grasslands, prairies, and other open habitats, Swainson's Hawk forages on insects and rodents from the air as well as on the ground; it sometimes follows plowing operations in agricultural areas. Most birds are typical light morphs, but the species shows a wide variety of darker rufous and dark brown plumages. Flying Swainson's Hawks of all ages and morphs can be readily identified by their characteristic long, tapered, rather pointed wings, somewhat reminiscent of a harrier. All plumages but the darkest adults also show a white crescent in the uppertail coverts, similar to harriers' but smaller. **VOICE** Rather similar to Red-tailed Hawk but weaker and less emphatic.

adult, light morph

white throat

dark chestnut bib

slender body

adult, light morph

pale coverts contrast with dark remiges

longer-winged than Broad-winged

weakly banded tail

juvenile, light morph

dark remiges

buff-caramel cast to body and underwing coverts

wing shape almost harrier-like

subadult

white crescent at tail base (compare Northern Harrier)

adult, darker morph

dark rufous body

pale undertail coverts

molting subadult, darker morph

outermost 3 primaries fresh (adult feathers)

mottled below

Red-tailed Hawk

Buteo jamaicensis
L 22"/56cm   WS 50"/1.3m

Red-tailed Hawk is the most variable and widespread North American raptor. There are some 7 subspecies north of Mexico that range in body plumage from almost snow white to quite blackish below; the many morphs in between vary mostly in plumage patterns. The reddish tail and husky, full-winged shape of adults are recognizable throughout Red-tailed's range (although the subspecies *harlani* is divergent in both structure and plumage). All subspecies hunt mostly rodents from perches or in the air. Red-tailed Hawk is an abundant species, found in virtually every habitat, from tundra to forest, desert to marsh; as such it is a point of reference for other raptors, buteos in particular, and an important hawk to study. Most subspecies intergrade where ranges meet. **VOICE** A familiar, piercing, descending *kee-eerrrrrrr*, often given on the wing.

adult, eastern
(*borealis*)

prominent white markings in scapulars

vivid rusty red tail

adult, eastern
(*borealis*)

full wings

dark marks in belly and underwing coverts

juvenile, eastern
(*borealis*)

narrower wings and longer tail than adult

belly band

banded tail lacks rusty color

adult, eastern
(*borealis*)

more white spotting above than on western adults

juvenile, eastern
(*borealis*)

much white spotting in scapulars

unfeathered legs (compare Ferruginous and Rough-legged Hawks)

brownish tail has narrow black bands

Subspecies

East of the Mississippi River, observers see mostly the *borealis* Red-tailed (shown on the facing page), which is brown above and pale below, usually with a variable, mottled belly band. Florida birds *(umbrinus)* are similar but smaller. West of the Mississippi, subspecies of Red-tailed Hawk show great plumage variety. The southwestern *fuertesi* looks most like eastern birds but is lighter, and adults show little or no belly band. *Calurus* (western) and *alascensis* (Alaska) are the most variable in body plumage, with individuals that range from a dark chocolate brown to light morphs that approach eastern birds in appearance. In the prairies and plains, a pale morph of *borealis* (once called *kriderii*) is ghostly white below, with only the tips of the rectrices showing a pinkish salmon cast; small numbers of this subspecies winter east of the Plains. Unlike any of the other subspecies, *harlani*—once considered a full species, Harlan's Hawk—has no brown or reddish tones in the plumage: its morphs are either light or dark, with a mostly white, faintly barred tail. Small numbers of *harlani* and *calurus* are observed east of the Mississippi every year.

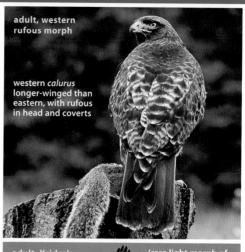

adult, western rufous morph

western *calurus* longer-winged than eastern, with rufous in head and coverts

adult, Krider's Hawk (pale morph of *borealis*)

(rare light morph of *harlani* similar but with uniformly dark upperparts, dirty white tail)

typical Red-tailed shape, but mostly white underparts, much white on upperparts

whitish tail sometimes has salmon cast

adult, western rufous morph

rufous chest, dark belly

paler tail shows faint banding

adult, southwestern

like eastern subspecies but paler overall

very pale below

adult usually lacks strong belly band

Range of Harlan's Hawk

adult, Harlan's Hawk *(harlani)*, dark morph

more compact shape than other subspecies

blackish (not brown) below

no red in tail

(often has white streaks in breast)

Rough-legged Hawk
Buteo lagopus
L 21"/53cm **WS** 53"/1.3m

Rough-legged Hawk is a large buteo of the Arctic, nesting mostly from the tree line northward and preying almost exclusively on rodents. In winter birds visit open habitats in southern Canada and the lower 48 states in numbers that vary greatly from year to year; these fluctuations, as in Snowy Owl and other Arctic species, are probably tied to both nesting success and prey availability. Most seen far south of usual range are juveniles. Rough-legged hunts gracefully on the wing, often hovering over marshes or fields; it sometimes perch-hunts from small branches on the outer crown of a tree, unlike Red-tailed Hawk. Red-tailed has much larger, unfeathered legs and feet. **VOICE** A high, descending *wheeee-eer*, less grating and more nasal than Red-tailed.

juvenile, light morph

straw-colored chest

large chocolate belly patch

this plumage most often seen well south of range

white tail has dusky terminal band

adult male, light morph

rare well south of range

feathered tarsi; smaller feet than Red-tailed

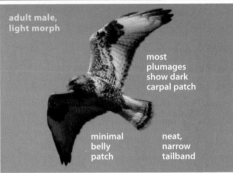

adult male, light morph

most plumages show dark carpal patch

minimal belly patch

neat, narrow tailband

adult female, light morph

like juvenile but with more distinct tailband

juvenile, dark morph

pale head

mottled brown and black below

indistinct tailband (adult male blackish, with distinct band)

adult, dark morph

more common in East than West

gape extends only to a point even with eye pupil (unlike Ferruginous)

Ferruginous Hawk

Buteo regalis
L 23"/58cm WS 56"/1.4m

The largest North American buteo, Ferruginous Hawk has an almost aquiline presence; large-billed and heavy-headed, wide-bodied and full-winged, it might be mistaken for an eagle, especially in the rarer dark morph. The species is restricted to dry open habitats, especially deserts and grasslands, where it hunts small mammals from the air or a low perch. More than most buteos, Ferruginous Hawk spends a great deal of time on the ground. This species is distinctive in all plumages, showing very white remiges (with dusky tips) and pale rectrices from below. **VOICE** A very high, thin, piping *wheeee-errrr*, descending, with a somewhat plaintive quality.

adult, light morph

gape extends beyond eye pupil

light tail

upperparts and leg feathering brilliant rufous

adult, light morph

heavy, long, pointed wings

pale below with dark wingtips, thighs, covert markings

tail shows salmon cast

juvenile, light morph

like adult but leg feathering pale; indistinct tailbands

(young juveniles may show only pinfeathers on tarsi, making them look unfeathered)

adult, dark morph

heavier in body, head, bill than Rough-legged and Red-tailed

very long gape

underparts and coverts usually have chestnut tones

tail pale with gray cast

molting subadult, dark morph

pale, unbanded tail (unlike Rough-legged Hawk)

Bald Eagle

Haliaeetus leucocephalus
L 34"/86cm **WS** 80"/2m

This large, powerful raptor lives almost anywhere on the continent where there is water. Though still listed as threatened in the U.S., Bald Eagles have steadily increased in number since the banning of the pesticide DDT. The species is now a common sight along rivers and coastlines where it was absent or rare in the 1970s. Bald Eagle feeds mostly on fish and waterfowl and sometimes takes carrion. Adults, with brown body and wings and white head and tail, are unlikely to be confused with any other species, although similar Old World sea-eagles—White-tailed Eagle and Steller's Sea-Eagle—have been recorded in Alaska. Juveniles are mostly brown but easily told from any plumage of Golden Eagle by their whitish underwing coverts and their very different shape in flight. Adult plumage is attained around age 5 (sixth calendar year), and between juvenal and adult plumages there are 4 highly variable subadult plumages (2 shown here) attained through partial molts. These are usually called first-basic through fourth-basic plumages. **VOICE** Surprisingly high, thin twitterings and chirps, often in stuttering series.

adult

white tail and head contrast with brown body

striking yellow bill and feet

juvenile

dark with white underwing coverts

nonadults have wider wings than adult because secondaries are longer

juvenile, worn

(first basic similar but shows molt in secondaries)

very white in wings and body

2nd basic

extensive white in head and tail

mottled belly

4th basic

narrow wings, like adult

still shows some traces of white in wings, black in tail

Golden Eagle
Aquila chrysaetos
L 35"/89cm **WS** 84"/2.1m

The awe-inspiring Golden Eagle is found in remote habitats from tundra to desert, mountains to marshes. It hunts relatively large birds and mammals—as large as herons and marmots—from the air, dropping directly onto prey from great heights. Eagles of the genus *Aquila* are related to buteos but are larger with longer wings, and they soar with greater stability. Most juveniles show extensive white at the bases of the remiges and rectrices, while adults are distinguished from Bald Eagle by their tawny nape and upperwing coverts. **VOICE** High, thin, barking *yep!* or *key-ep!* calls, sometimes in series; not often heard away from nest.

adult

gold tones in coverts and nape often visible at a great distance

enormous body and feet

juvenile

wings appear to bulge in secondaries (secondaries shorter in adult)

white in tail base and bases of remiges

adult

stoops on prey from high in the air, lowering talons just before striking

juvenile

white in bases of remiges variable, sometimes absent

adult feeding nestlings

eagles build large stick nests (Golden often nests on cliffs)

adult

pale bar in upperwing coverts

usually lacks white in tail

narrower wings than juvenile because of shorter secondaries

American Kestrel

Falco sparverius
L 10½"/27cm   WS 23"/58cm

American Kestrel, one of the most colorful of the world's raptors, is a diminutive falcon of open habitats. Kestrels nest in cavities excavated by woodpeckers, particularly Northern Flickers, but they also accept artificial nest boxes. They breed most readily in open habitats with plentiful hunting perches. Like shrikes, kestrels are expert mousers, and they also take small birds, bats, insects, reptiles, and even fish on rare occasions. They perch, often on a fence post or utility wire, for long periods watching for prey; they will also hover over areas where prey has been sighted. Upon spotting prey, they fly swiftly to it, swoop, and pounce. In poor light, it can be difficult to see the distinctive colors of American Kestrel, and in flight it may be mistaken for Merlin, which has a more compact shape and a shorter tail with (usually) strong black and white banding. For reasons not yet clear, this species is experiencing a rapid population decline in the East. **VOICE** A rapid series of high-pitched *kli* calls.

adult male

strong face pattern with 2 black stripes

pinkish salmon back contrasts with bluish upperwings and crown

female

bold face pattern

upperparts and tail barred and banded with brown and rust

adult male

brilliant rufous tail has black band

adult male

often observed hover-hunting on rapidly beating wings

female

evenly banded remiges and rectrices

heavily marked belly

Merlin

Falco columbarius
L 12"/30cm   **WS** 25"/64cm

This small falcon nests in boreal forests and muskeg (recently also in cities and towns) and winters mostly on the coasts and in the Great Plains. Merlins pursue birds and insects on the wing, accelerating to incredible speeds and snatching prey with great agility. The paler subspecies, Richardson's Merlin *(richardsoni),* nests in the prairies; the very dark Black Merlin *(suckleyi)* is seen mostly along the Pacific coast. **VOICE** Similar to American Kestrel but lower-pitched and harsher.

adult male (nominate)

steely gray above

weak face pattern

heavily marked with brown below

adult male (richardsoni)

soft gray upperparts

much paler below than nominate, especially the face

adult male

shaped like American Kestrel, but darker below and with shorter tail banded black and white

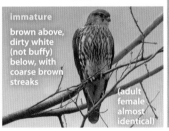

immature

brown above, dirty white (not buffy) below, with coarse brown streaks

(adult female almost identical)

Aplomado Falcon

Falco femoralis
L 16"/41cm   **WS** 44"/1.1m

The striking Aplomado Falcon is found in remote yucca-studded deserts and grasslands of southern New Mexico and far-western Texas, where it is rare and endangered. It has been reintroduced in coastal savannas of southern Texas, where it nested in centuries past; as of 2004, almost 1,000 falcons had been released, resulting in about 40 nesting pairs and 125 fledged young. This species hunts birds and insects on the wing or from perches. **VOICE** A series of sharp *kek* calls given in series.

adult

bold supercilium

long wings and tail, giving distinctive silhouette in flight

white breast, dark belly, orange lower belly and crissum

Peregrine Falcon

Falco peregrinus
L 18"/46cm **WS** 40"/1m

Once on the brink of extinction in North America, Peregrine Falcon has made a slow comeback since the banning of the pesticide DDT in 1972. At least on the Atlantic and Gulf coasts, the species may be seen in healthy numbers during autumn migration, when thousands move southward toward wintering areas. This powerful, streamlined falcon hunts flying birds from the air, stooping at great speed—up to 186 mph (300km/h)—on birds as large as Mallards and striking them downward with the talons. Compared to Gyrfalcon, Peregrine has narrower, more pointed wings; a narrower, longer tail; and dark (not pale) remiges that show less contrast with the underwing coverts. The subspecies *tundrius* nests in the Arctic; *anatum* nests south of the tree line; many intermediate birds are the result of reintroductions. **VOICE** Agitated bird gives harsh, nasal *rehh* calls in series.

adult *(anatum)*

steely blue-gray above; black "hangman's hood" contrasts with yellow orbital ring and cere

adults of all subspecies pale below with dark barring; *anatum* has tawny-rufous wash on breast

long wings reach tail tip

large, yellow legs and feet

adult *(tundrius)*

similar to *anatum* but black "sideburns" more distinct; breast white, without tawny tones

barring in underwing coverts and on belly

long tail; long, pointed wings

compare shape of Mississippi Kite

adult *(tundrius)*

contrasting pale gray rump

"crossbow" silhouette

juvenile *(tundrius)*

bold, buffy supercilium

brown above

buffy streaked with brown below

juvenile *(pealei)*

very dark subspecies of coastal Pacific Northwest

similar birds in East a result of reintroduction programs

Gyrfalcon

Falco rusticolus
L 22½"/57cm **WS** 57"/1.4m

Gyrfalcon is a relatively rare raptor of Arctic habitats; it only occasionally leaves the northern reaches of Canada and Alaska. It hunts birds as large as geese, usually simply by chasing them down. The world's largest falcon, it averages twice as heavy as Peregrine Falcon. The species varies in color, from white to very dark brown birds. Most adults in North America are lead gray above, and juveniles are medium brown above. **VOICE** A repeated, rising, very nasal *rrreeee-ehhh*, lower and slower than Peregrine.

adult, gray morph

usually lightly marked below

barred above

wings do not reach tail tip

juvenile, gray morph

gray cere and orbital ring (yellow in adult)

dark wingtips and checkered underwing coverts contrast with pale remiges

broad, heavily barred tail

Prairie Falcon

Falco mexicanus
L 17½"/44cm **WS** 39"/99cm

A falcon of open habitats and canyon lands, Prairie Falcon hunts rodents and birds by shallow-angled swoops from low to the ground, rather than by the high-altitude stoops of Peregrine Falcon. Young Peregrines can look very similar to Prairie Falcon but have longer, darker tails and never show Prairie's underwing pattern. Prairie Falcon is almost unknown east of the Mississippi River and appears to be declining in many areas of the West. **VOICE** Similar to Peregrine but a bit higher.

adult

distinctive head pattern

pale brown above

wings do not reach tail tip

juvenile

similar to adult but more heavily streaked below; adult more spotted or barred

adult

pale belly, remiges, and rectrices contrast with black axillaries and greater coverts (compare young Peregrine)

Shorebirds

Shorebirds are closely related birds of open-country and shoreline habitats. They are represented in North America by seven families, though some are only rare visitors. The largest family, the sandpipers (Scolopacidae), includes sandpipers (the smallest of these are called "peeps"), yellowlegs, redshanks, greenshanks, curlews, dowitchers, phalaropes, snipe, woodcocks, tattlers, godwits, turnstones, stints, knots, Willet, Whimbrel, Sanderling, Dunlin, Ruff, and Surfbird. Of some 75 species recorded in North America, 36 are known to have bred on the continent; one, Eskimo Curlew, is likely extinct.

Sandpipers show extraordinary diversity in size and shape. They are usually brown, white, and rust, although some are more dapper. In phalaropes, females are more brightly colored than males, a reverse sexual dimorphism that is rare among birds; the more cryptically plumaged males incubate the eggs and tend the young. Sandpipers rely on touch and smell when foraging. The smaller species pick around in open habitats for tiny invertebrate prey, while larger species probe more deeply into mud or sand to extract much larger prey. Many shorebird species feed near one another on mudflats or pond margins. Phalaropes often forage on lakes and ponds by spinning in circles to create a vortex that brings tiny prey items to the surface.

The other large shorebird family, Charadriidae, contains plovers and lapwings; 16 species have been recorded in North America, and 11 species breed regularly here. As a rule, plovers have shorter, thicker bills than similarly sized sandpipers, and they tend to forage more in the manner of American Robins: running for short distances, then pausing, looking, and listening before extracting small invertebrate prey from the substrate.

Several smaller families of shorebirds have bodies and bills adapted for more specialized foraging. The oystercatchers (Haematopodidae) are husky birds with powerful bills designed to crack open mollusks. They are found almost exclusively on outer coasts, where their prey is readily available. The stilts and avocets (Recurvirostridae) are elegant, long-legged shorebirds with striking plumages and slender bills; the upwardly curved bills of avocets are adapted for sweeping insect larvae and other small organisms from the water. Northern Jacana, in the tropical family Jacanidae, has extremely long toes, similar to a gallinule's, and can walk on floating vegetation.

Once an abundant breeder in northern Canada, Eskimo Curlew was hunted to extinction; it was last reported in 1963.

Shorebird courtship displays involve rhythmic calling, posturing and parading on the ground, and sometimes aerial activity such as flying in circles while calling (as in woodcocks) or diving earthward (as in snipe). Most shorebirds are monogamous, although phalaropes practice polyandry (females have multiple mates), and several species are polygynous (males have multiple mates).

The conservation status of most shorebirds is complex and in many cases poorly known. Species with small populations are of great concern, but documented declines in more numerous species such as Semipalmated Sandpiper, Red Knot, Sanderling, and Whimbrel have raised red flags in recent years.

Identification of Shorebirds

Identification of shorebirds can be quite complicated. Among the factors to consider are time of year, habitat and location, and molt. Shorebirds can display extensive variation within a species, particularly among juveniles and molting birds. Spotting scopes aid in obtaining detailed views of the birds' plumage and structure, which is usually necessary for identification.

Western Sandpiper, dull juvenile

Western Sandpiper, juvenile

Timing and Location

Most shorebirds that nest in Alaska and Canada begin their southward migration toward stopover and wintering grounds soon after nesting, as early as the third week of June. Adults leave the nesting areas earlier than juveniles (young of that year), and from late June through much of July most of the shorebirds seen on mudflats in the lower 48 states are adults.

By late July juveniles of several species begin to appear in the flocks, and by the middle of August they usually predominate. In late summer to autumn, it is easy to distinguish between adult and juvenal plumages of most shorebirds: adults show worn, splotchy-looking feathers, especially in the coverts and tertials; juveniles show uniformly fresh coverts and remiges that often have crisp, pale borders, giving them a neatly spangled, scalloped, or scaly appearance above. In autumn juveniles, if not recognized as such, can be mistaken for adults of another species.

Plumages and Molt

Molt in shorebirds is similar to molt in their nearest relatives, the terns and gulls. Adults molt twice per year, between brighter breeding plumage and duller nonbreeding plumage (also called alternate and basic plumages, respectively). Molting birds exhibit transitional plumages, in which aspects of different plumages are apparent.

Over a period that can extend from January into April, adults attain breeding plumage

through a partial molt of body, head, and some covert feathers, and make their northward migration to breeding grounds. Their complete molt (all feathers) into nonbreeding dress occurs just after breeding, usually August into November, along with the migration southward to staging and wintering sites.

Juveniles begin a partial molt of head and body feathers into their first-winter plumage soon after they reach staging areas on the coast (midsummer into the autumn months).

By spring, adults have molted into breeding plumage again and returned northward to nesting areas. In some species, first-winter birds do not migrate to the breeding grounds with adults but stay in wintering areas. There they undergo a partial molt into first-summer plumage; this plumage varies among species and individuals: it can look very much like first-winter plumage or nearly as bright as adult breeding plumage. (The subadult first-winter and first-summer plumages are not illustrated in this guide.)

Molts are protracted and differ among species: some molt on migration, others afterward, others both during and afterward. Adult Long-billed Dowitchers, for example, appear to undergo a complete molt at stopover sites in the interior of the continent before moving to coastal wintering areas. Adult Short-billed Dowitchers do not begin to molt their flight feathers until they reach coastal wintering areas. Thus a dowitcher in wing molt seen away from the coast is almost certainly a Long-billed.

American Golden-Plover
Pluvialis dominica
L 10½"/27cm **WS** 26"/66cm

An American Golden-Plover standing in its dry tundra breeding habitat, ringed by blooming rhododendrons, may be one of the Arctic's most captivating sights. Large flocks migrate through North America's interior, stopping on farm fields, prairies, and dry lakebeds; smaller numbers are seen on coastal mudflats and beaches. Once a prized game bird, this species is now rather uncommon. **VOICE** Calls include a high, thin, hesitant *suweeet?* and *queedle;* weaker and higher than Black-bellied Plover.

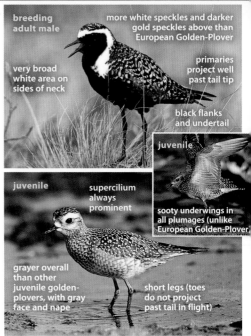

breeding adult male

more white speckles and darker gold speckles above than European Golden-Plover

very broad white area on sides of neck

primaries project well past tail tip

black flanks and undertail

juvenile

sooty underwings in all plumages (unlike European Golden-Plover)

juvenile

supercilium always prominent

grayer overall than other juvenile golden-plovers, with gray face and nape

short legs (toes do not project past tail in flight)

Pacific Golden-Plover
Pluvialis fulva
L 10¼"/26cm **WS** 24"/61cm

Pacific and American Golden-Plovers were once combined as Lesser Golden-Plover. This species nests on moist tundra of Siberia and western Alaska, preferring lower elevations and wetter habitats with higher vegetation than American Golden-Plover. It migrates to Hawaii and the South Pacific, sometimes flying more than 2,000 miles (3,220km) nonstop. A few winter on the West Coast, especially in California, in short-grass fields and marsh edges. **VOICE** A high *chu-EET,* like American Golden-Plover but lower.

breeding adult male

primaries project just past tail

narrow white plumage continues from neck to flanks and undertail

longer legs, longer bill, larger yellow-gold markings than American

breeding adult female

more muted than male; white sides and flanks, unlike American

juvenile

longer bill than other golden-plovers

brighter, more uniform gold than American

long legs (toes project past tail tip in flight)

Black-bellied Plover

Pluvialis squatarola
L 11½"/29cm **WS** 29"/74cm

Black-bellied Plover typically nests on dry tundra ridges near water and winters on mudflats, coastlines, and wet farm fields. Migrants turn up along muddy or sandy coastlines and on lakes or farm fields, often in large numbers during inclement weather. Black-bellied is more thickset than its close relatives the golden-plovers, with a small hind toe (lacking in the golden-plovers). **VOICE** Call a rich, sweet, slurred *pleeooohee,* falling then rising; golden-plover calls have 2 rather than 3 components.

breeding adult

recalls golden-plovers but larger, with heavier bill and white crown and dorsal markings

juvenile

heavier body and bill than golden-plovers; rarely shows gold tones

nonbreeding adult

all plumages have white underwings, tail, wing stripe, and jet black axillaries, striking in flight

European Golden-Plover

Pluvialis apricaria
L 10½"/27cm **WS** 26"/66cm

During spring migration over the North Atlantic from Africa to Iceland, small flocks of European Golden-Plovers are occasionally blown off course by storms and end up in Canada's Atlantic Provinces. Flocks are most often seen in April in eastern Newfoundland near the capital, St. John's. There are no reports of this species from New England, but it should be looked for there. **VOICE** Calls include a thin, squeaky, rising *dui,* a monotonous *sieu,* and a plaintive *doo-deer* that rises then falls. All golden-plovers have fluting songs.

breeding adult

fine, greenish gold speckles above

sides and undertail extensively white

short-legged, pot-bellied look (compare other golden-plovers)

nonbreeding adult

tones less rich than juvenile; weaker facial pattern than other golden-plovers

juvenile

indistinct facial markings and small bill

rich, brassy gold colors in dense pattern

short legs (toes do not project past tail in flight)

Semipalmated Plover
Charadrius semipalmatus
L 7¼"/18cm **WS** 19"/48cm

This versatile little plover nests on tundra mostly north of the tree line, normally in open areas with sand or gravel substrates; some nest in northern forested areas where coasts and river systems provide similar habitats. In migration and on wintering grounds, "Semis" utilize flat open areas, from dry, plowed farm fields to coastal mudflats; they adroitly pick insects and pull worms from the ground. The species is named for the partial webbing between the front toes. **VOICE** Calls a squeaky *chuWEEP!* and a low *kiwip*.

breeding adult

white eyebrow line absent or weak (compare Common Ringed Plover)

thinner breastband, larger bill than Common Ringed

nonbreeding adult

mostly dark bill

thin yellow orbital ring (lacking in Common Ringed)

juvenile

narrow pale feather edges above

lower edge of "mask" meets maxilla in all plumages

brown breastband

Common Ringed Plover
Charadrius hiaticula
L 7½"/19cm **WS** 10½"/27cm

Common Ringed Plover overlaps in range with Semipalmated Plover in Canada's eastern Baffin and nearby islands and on Alaska's St. Lawrence Island. It is a rare visitor to the Canadian Maritimes, New England, and islands off Alaska. The two species are readily distinguished by their calls; webbing between toes is only slightly less in Ringed. A smaller Eurasian species, Little Ringed Plover, is a very rare spring visitor to the Aleutians; breeding adults show a yellow eye ring. **VOICE** Call a mellow, melancholy *per-reer* or *powee*, lower than Semipalmated Plover.

breeding adult

thinner-based bill, wider breastband, more prominent white eyebrow than Semipalmated Plover

juvenile

lower edge of "mask" meets gape in all plumages (compare Semipalmated)

Wilson's Plover

Charadrius wilsonia
L 8"/20cm **WS** 20"/51cm

Wilson's Plover (formerly Thick-billed Plover) is strictly a coastal species, found along Atlantic and Gulf shores; it nests on open sandy beaches and barrier islands where there are nearby tidal mudflats for foraging. Most winter in the tropics and Florida. There are very few records from landlocked states; most of these occur in spring. Birds of the subspecies *beldingi*, from western Mexico, visit California on occasion. **VOICE** Most calls very high and sharp, including a quick *kip* and *kittr* and a sweet, rising *queet*.

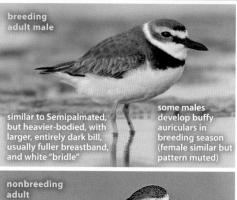

breeding adult male

similar to Semipalmated, but heavier-bodied, with larger, entirely dark bill, usually fuller breastband, and white "bridle"

some males develop buffy auriculars in breeding season (female similar but pattern muted)

nonbreeding adult

upperparts notably paler than Semipalmated

thicker bill and heavier breastband than sand-plovers, Mountain Plover

---

Killdeer

Charadrius vociferus
L 10½"/27cm **WS** 24"/61cm

The widespread Killdeer usually nests in agricultural areas, but it tolerates many habitats with stony substrates—from gravel bars in rivers, to urban rooftops, to driveways. In winter Killdeer form large flocks in farm fields. As its scientific name indicates, this "vociferous" species calls frequently. Nesting birds perform elaborate "broken-wing" distraction displays when the nest is approached too closely. **VOICE** Calls loud and insistent: *deee, deedeedee, kill-DEEAR,* and a rolling chatter.

breeding adult

long tail strikingly orangish above (best seen in flight)

double breastband

(nonbreeding plumage essentially identical)

breeding adult and chick

red orbital ring visible at close range

chick has 1 breastband

Snowy Plover

Charadrius alexandrinus
L 6½"/17cm   **WS** 17"/43cm

Snowy Plover, known elsewhere in the world as Kentish Plover, nests along the margins of Inland alkaline lakes and on sandy beaches along the Gulf of Mexico and Pacific coast, where it blends in well with its surroundings. Most winter along ocean coasts. Like Piping Plover, Snowy forages on open mudflats. Pacific coast populations of this species are listed as threatened in North America. The U.S. population numbers just over 20,000 as of 2004. **VOICE** Call a rising, rolling or trilled *dooorEET!* with nasal quality, and a low *krup*.

breeding adult

black patch behind eyes

thinner bill than Piping Plover

black legs

1st winter

most populations slightly darker above than Piping Plover

pale pinkish to grayish legs

Piping Plover

Charadrius melodus
L 7¼"/18cm   **WS** 19"/48cm

The pale Piping Plover is a bird of similarly pale habitats year-round, mostly sandy beaches on the ocean and Great Lakes and drying alkaline lakebeds and river sandbars in the Great Plains. This endangered North American endemic has suffered from the loss of Atlantic coastal habitats to development; nesting birds that remain are often disturbed by beachgoers and predators. Efforts to minimize such disturbance have helped stabilize some populations. **VOICE** A soft, high-pitched *pee* or *pee-lo*.

breeding adult male

black-tipped orange bill, pale face

black neck ring (partial in some males); black border to "bridle"

orange-yellow legs (here with bands)

chick very pale, with yellow legs

nonbreeding adult

paler face and thicker bill than Snowy Plover

yellowish legs

Mountain Plover

Charadrius montanus
L 9"/23cm **WS** 23"/58cm

This subtly plumaged plover breeds on the Great Plains and winters on farm fields, desert flats, and high plains. Its habitats may be quite barren, with very short grass or no vegetation, and it favors areas overgrazed by cattle, which resemble those grazed by bison herds in centuries past. Like many other birds that nest in the shortgrass prairies of the Great Plains, its populations have declined drastically since European settlement and continue to decline. **VOICE** Calls unobtrusive: a rough *krrk* and a low *qurt*.

breeding adult

uniformly brown above

dark loral spot and crown

unbanded breast (compare Wilson's Plover)

nonbreeding adult

(stark white underwings readily apparent on flying birds)

paler head markings than breeding adult

Lesser Sand-Plover

Charadrius mongolus
L 7½"/19cm **WS** 22"/56cm

Lesser Sand-Plover, also called Mongolian Plover, is an Asian species that regularly visits Alaska's Aleutians and other islands, mostly in spring; it has nested in western Alaska on rare occasions. Lesser is otherwise very rare on the Pacific coast and a vagrant elsewhere in North America. It forages on mudflats much like Semipalmated Plover. The very similar but slightly larger Greater Sand-Plover has been recorded once in California. **VOICE** Call a low, rattling *rrktk*.

breeding adult

black mask, white frontlet

rich orange-rufous on breast extends to nape, set off from white throat by narrow black line

nonbreeding adult

lacks white collar of smaller plovers

larger than Semipalmated Plover, with larger bill and longer, dark (not yellow) legs

(juvenile similar but with buff-apricot wash on breast)

Eurasian Dotterel
Charadrius morinellus
L 8¼"/21cm WS 23"/58cm

This Old World species nests irregularly in western Alaska on dry upland and montane tundra, often near scree fields. It is a vagrant to Pacific coast states, seen mostly in shortgrass prairies and agricultural fields among other plovers. The combination of soft gray upperparts, white breastband, and cinnamon belly is unique among American shorebirds; females are slightly more richly colored than males. **VOICE** Call a high, clear, sometimes quavering *peee*, often in series; also a trill sounding like end of Dunlin's song.

breeding adult female | "harlequin" face pattern | small bill

(males do most of incubation and are less brightly colored)

white breast-band (present to some degree in all plumages)

juvenile

mottled above

faint breastband and head pattern

yellow legs

Northern Lapwing
Vanellus vanellus
L 12½"/32cm WS 33"/84cm

A Eurasian plover of grassy pastures, agricultural fields, and mudflats, Northern Lapwing is a vagrant to Atlantic coast states and provinces, recorded only a few times inland in North America. Most birds are found singly, in company with Killdeer, in late fall or winter. **VOICE** A shrill, nasal *eeee, eee-eer, eeee-wee, eeeooo*, and similar, usually falling in tone.

breeding adult | long crest

dark upperparts have magenta, purple, green sheens

(shorter crest in juvenile and nonbreeding adult)

orange-buff undertail coverts

Northern Jacana
Jacana spinosa
L 9½"/24cm WS 20"/51cm

The only member of the family Jacanidae recorded north of Mexico, Northern Jacana is a vagrant to southern Texas and more rarely to southeastern Arizona, found on freshwater bodies with floating vegetation. Jacanas are called "lilytrotters" for their ability to walk on this vegetation, aided by their long toes. **VOICE** Staccato chirping or fussing calls, often in series.

juvenile | dark eye line

brown above, white below

extremely long legs and toes

adult

long, yellow bill; yellow frontal shield

rich chestnut-copper

(brilliant saffron remiges visible in flight)

American Oystercatcher

Haematopus palliatus
L 17½"/44cm WS 32"/81cm

The husky American Oystercatcher nests on sandy beaches and barrier islands. It forages in intertidal areas, salt marshes, rocky coasts, and tidal guts for oysters, clams, mussels, crabs, and limpets. It also eats worms, sometimes visiting flooded farm fields near nesting areas. Hurricanes sometimes displace single birds far inland; the few that visit California are from Mexico. Eurasian Oystercatcher, a vagrant to Canada, is blackish above. **VOICE** A high, piping *queep!* and longer *queer,* often in rapid, rolling series.

adult

black hood

brown above, white below

stout, red-orange bill

chick

dark bill gradually acquires color

adult

looks heavy-headed and broad-winged in flight

Black Oystercatcher

Haematopus bachmani
L 17½"/44cm WS 32"/81cm

This striking shorebird is endemic to the rocky intertidal zone of the American Pacific coast and is a permanent resident in most of its range. It is usually observed in family groups that forage along islands and open coastlines, where tides expose shellfish and other marine life clinging to rocks and where tide pools often contain potential prey items. Hybrids with American Oystercatcher have been recorded in California. Like many shorebirds, oystercatchers swim fairly well. **VOICE** Very similar to American.

adult

dark overall

heavy, red-orange bill

juvenile

paler above than adult, with pale spots on coverts

dusky-tipped bill

Greater Yellowlegs
Tringa melanoleuca
L 14"/36cm **WS** 28"/71cm

Greater Yellowlegs breeds in marshy areas of the boreal forest and muskeg, and winters in varied aquatic habitats. It mostly picks or chases invertebrates and small fish and may also feed by swinging its bill back and forth in the water. In mixed flocks, it is often this sentinel species that sounds the alarm when a predator or person approaches, pumping its head and calling loudly. **VOICE** Call an insistent, whistled *deer deer deer,* with notes distinct and descending.

transitional (molting) adult

longer, stronger, more upturned bill than Lesser

juvenile

2-toned bill (also in winter adult)

gray-stippled breast

breeding adult

underparts more strikingly marked than Lesser

Lesser Yellowlegs
Tringa flavipes
L 10½"/27cm **WS** 24"/61cm

One might expect Lesser Yellowlegs to be a pint-sized version of Greater, but this is a distinctly different bird: it breeds farther north, winters farther south, gathers in larger flocks, is more partial to freshwater environments, and tolerates closer approach by people. Lesser Yellowlegs forages like Greater, often racing around after prey in shallow water, and may also swim like phalaropes in deeper water. Yellowlegs were prized game birds in the 19th century. **VOICE** Call a sharp, high *tew tew,* often thinner and lower than Greater.

transitional (molting) adult

more delicate than Greater

straight bill only slightly longer than head

juvenile

entirely dark bill

dusky breast

more neatly marked and darker above than winter adult

breeding adult

underparts less heavily marked than Greater

Solitary Sandpiper
Tringa solitaria
L 8½"/22cm **WS** 22"/56cm

Solitary Sandpiper nests in trees near marshy and boggy areas in the boreal forest and muskeg, using old nests of songbirds. It is usually solitary, but small, loose groups may be seen during migration to the tropics, typically along the edges of secluded muddy ponds, streams, or marshes. The similar Green Sandpiper, recorded in Alaska, has mostly white uppertail coverts and rectrix bases. **VOICE** Call similar to Spotted Sandpiper but higher: a thin, sweet *pee-eet* or *peepeepee;* also a short *pip.*

breeding adult

dark and compact

darker above than Lesser Yellowlegs, with shorter, olive legs

(often raises wings after landing, revealing black underwings)

juvenile

prominent eye ring in all plumages

teeters and bobs tail when walking, like Spotted Sandpiper

breast and head have sooty brown wash

Wood Sandpiper
Tringa glareola
L 8"/20cm **WS** 20"/51cm

Wood Sandpiper is seen regularly in migration in Alaska's western Aleutian Islands, where it has nested on rare occasions; it is rarer on St. Lawrence Island and the Pribilofs and a vagrant elsewhere in North America. This unobtrusive species might pass unnoticed among flocks of shorebirds gathered in freshwater ponds, but it differs markedly from American *Tringa* species, sized like a Solitary Sandpiper but patterned more like a yellowlegs. **VOICE** Call a high, whistled *pwee,* very similar in pitch to Long-billed Dowitcher.

breeding adult

slightly smaller than Solitary Sandpiper, with more patterned upperparts, paler underwing coverts, white-based rectrices

plumage pattern like Lesser Yellowlegs, but smaller with more buffy spotting above

juvenile

supercilium strong beyond eyes

large, buff-gold spots above

diffuse streaking at sides of breast

rear of body appears truncated compared to yellowlegs

Willet

Tringa semipalmata
L 15"/38cm **WS** 26"/66cm

The two subspecies of this large shorebird lead different lives: the smaller, darker nominate subspecies, Eastern Willet, nests in and near Atlantic and Gulf coast salt marshes, while Western Willet *(inornatus)* is a bird of wet prairies and fields in the Great Plains and Great Basin. Both winter on ocean coasts and forage for shellfish. **VOICE** Song a rolling, repeated *pee-weel-willet!*, higher and more rapidly delivered in Eastern. Calls, often in series, include a strident *kiw* or *keer*, a talkative *kah hah*, and a loud *wheap!*

breeding adult, Eastern (nominate)

slightly larger than Greater Yellowlegs but much stockier (compare godwits)

dark, heavy barring below

gray legs

(Western *inornatus* larger and more lightly marked)

nonbreeding adult
heavier bill and build than yellowlegs; smaller than godwits

very plain overall

adult

prominent white in tail and wings

Spotted Redshank

Tringa erythropus
L 12½"/32cm **WS** 25"/64cm

Spotted Redshank is a Eurasian bird that rarely visits Alaska's offshore islands and is a very rare vagrant elsewhere. The adult's rich black breeding plumage is distinctive, and from May through July its red legs become black. The leg color of juveniles varies from green-yellow to pale orange. Juveniles and nonbreeding adults can be confused with yellowlegs; some Greater Yellowlegs have similar, intensely orange legs. **VOICE** A burry *chu-weet*, recalling Semipalmated Plover; also a strident, ternlike fussing.

breeding adult

black with white speckling above

white eye arcs

dark legs

nonbreeding adult

base of mandible red (never so in yellowlegs)

dull reddish legs

(juvenile similar)

Buff-breasted Sandpiper

Tryngites subruficollis
L 8¼"/21cm **WS** 18"/46cm

The delicate Buff-breasted Sandpiper nests mostly in northern Nunavut on tundra ridges, often near water. Males displaying in leks expose their silvery underwings, puff up their breast feathers, and move about like windup toys. When migrating through the Great Plains, flocks feed on invertebrates in dry farm fields, shortgrass prairies, turf farms, and airports. **VOICE** Song a series of dry *tic* notes. Call a grating *krreep,* similar to Pectoral Sandpiper, or a low *chup.*

adult, displaying

short, dusky bill

white underwing coverts striking in flight and display

mostly unspotted buffy underparts

pale buffy face unpatterned except for stippled crown

juvenile

feathers have dark centers with pale edges, giving scaly look above

rather long, yellow legs

Ruff

Philomachus pugnax
L 11"/28cm **WS** 21"/53cm

Of all Eurasian shorebirds that visit North America, Ruff is the species most widely reported. Found at freshwater ponds, usually with extensive muddy or grassy margins, Ruff forages in deeper water and more actively than Pectoral Sandpiper, with which it is often seen. Females, called reeves, are noticeably smaller than males; their breeding plumage is usually lightly mottled with black, as if in molt. In flight, both sexes show white, oval-shaped patches on the sides of the rump. **VOICE** A nasal, skimmerlike *ehh-deh;* rarely heard.

breeding adult male, displaying

distended "ruff" may be russet, black, or white

bare skin on face

displays mostly at breeding leks, rarely on migration

juvenile

scaly appearance above

long tertials

buffy wash overall

nonbreeding adult male

unique body and bill shape

long tertials

orangish legs and bill base (here mud-covered); leg color highly variable

Whimbrel

Numenius phaeopus
L 18"/46cm **WS** 32"/81cm

This stout curlew nests mostly on Arctic tundra; it winters on coastal marshes, tidal mudflats, and sandy and rocky beaches, which also serve as stopover sites during migration. During stormy weather, flocks often touch down in wet farm fields or freshwater ponds. Whimbrel usually forages on invertebrates by shallow probing or picking. Two white-rumped subspecies from Eurasia are rare coastal vagrants. **VOICE** A series of loud, liquid whistles on one pitch.

breeding adult

striped head

long, decurved bill

evenly marked underparts (compare Bristle-thighed Curlew)

fresh adult

rump and underwings uniformly warm brown (compare Bristle-thighed)

Bristle-thighed Curlew

Numenius tahitiensis
L 17½"/44cm **WS** 32"/81cm

A seldom-seen species that nests only in upland, hilly tundra of western Alaska, Bristle-thighed Curlew stages in that state's Yukon-Kuskokwim River delta and then migrates 2,500 miles (4,000km) over water to Hawaii and islands of the South Pacific. There birds feed on crustaceans and even albatross eggs and molt into a flightless state, unique among shorebirds. In Alaska, berries and insects form part of this species' late-summer diet. **VOICE** Call a loud, clear *tweeep!*, sounding like a whistle used to hail a taxi.

adult

similar shape to Whimbrel, but shows stark white belly and buffy tail

(bristlelike feathers around thighs difficult to see)

adult

underwing coverts have cinnamon tones

rich yellow-buff rump and tail

unmarked flanks and belly

Upland Sandpiper

Bartramia longicauda
L 12"/30cm   **WS** 26"/66cm

The declining Upland Sandpiper breeds in open grasslands, prairies, farm fields, and pastures and in tundra. Its curlewlike display is memorable: frequent tremulous whistling calls given high in the air while on fluttering wingbeats. Migrating birds visit drier fields and plains, where they walk with a jerky gait in search of invertebrates, especially insects. **VOICE** Song a rolling whistle, rising then falling (often called a "wolf whistle"). Call a rapid, fussy series of bubbly notes, sometimes heard overhead at night during migration.

breeding adult

like a tiny curlew in plumage but with shorter, straight bill, thinner neck, longer tail

eyes appear large in pale face

breast patterned with neat dark chevrons

often perches on posts

juvenile

more scaly appearance above than adult

long, thin neck gives "pinhead" look

breeding adult

long tail projects far past wingtips

Long-billed Curlew

Numenius americanus
L 23"/58cm   **WS** 35"/89cm

This stately wader nests in dry grasslands, pastures, sage flats, and prairies of the Great Basin and Great Plains, where it forages mostly for insects. Many winter on outer U.S. coasts, foraging for worms, crabs, and other marine life. Eurasian and Far Eastern Curlews, Old World species, are vagrants to North America; Eurasian has a white rump and underwings, Far Eastern has barred underwings. **VOICE** Song a series of whistles recalling Upland Sandpiper but more complex. Call a high, thin, rising *kliiiii* or *kuh-liiiii*.

adult female

bill much longer than Whimbrel, head lacks stripes

(sleeping bird with tucked bill recalls Marbled Godwit)

(juvenile has much shorter bill)

adult male

underwing coverts and remiges have cinnamon and buff tones (lacking in all Eurasian curlew species)

Hudsonian Godwit
Limosa haemastica
L 15½"/39cm   **WS** 29"/74cm

Hudsonian Godwit is an uncommon and local nester on coastal tundra and muskeg; it is usually seen in numbers only at its staging areas in Canada's James Bay, the southern Great Plains, Cook Inlet, Alaska, and the upper Texas coast. This godwit forages by probing deeply in mud for invertebrates. It is thought that many "Huds" perform a nonstop migration from James Bay over the East Coast and thousands of miles of ocean to their South American wintering grounds. **VOICE** Call a high, thin *kleew* or *kwi-KWI!*

breeding adult

smallest godwit

deep chestnut below contrasts with paler neck and face

(mostly black tail and white uppertail coverts visible in flight; white wing stripe narrower than in Black-tailed Godwit)

juvenile

buff-edged coverts above

slightly upturned bill

breeding adult

black underwing coverts in all plumages, unique among godwits

---

Black-tailed Godwit
Limosa limosa
L 16½"/42cm   **WS** 29"/74cm

This rare stray from Siberia and Europe is striking in any plumage, from the rich orange breast and neck of breeding males to the striking black tail and white coverts and underwings of nonbreeders. In North America most are found singly in marshy, freshwater environments. The Icelandic subspecies *(islandica)*, recorded in the East, is richly colored below in breeding plumage. **VOICE** Call a high, nasal *di-deer, ki-de-dew* or descending *kiier* (many variations), and a rhythmic, repeated *wicka wicka wicka.*

nonbreeding adult

very similar to nonbreeding Hudsonian Godwit but larger, with straighter, longer bill

best told by wing pattern

nonbreeding adult

white underwings with wide white wing stripe unique (compare Willet

breeding adult (islandica)

straight bill

vivid orange head and neck; barred belly

juvenile

breast and neck have strong buff cinnamon wash

Bar-tailed Godwit

Limosa lapponica
L 16"/41cm **WS** 30"/76cm

The Siberian subspecies *(baueri)* of this godwit breeds on dry upland tundra of western Alaska, where its musical song mixes with Whimbrel's fluting song. Small numbers are seen annually in the Pacific Northwest; most make nonstop flights over the Pacific to winter in Australia and New Zealand. Both *baueri* and the western Eurasian *lapponica* are rare visitors to brackish and saltwater environments of the Atlantic coast. **VOICE** Calls include a nasal *keer, kweep, keek,* and *kidear kidear kidear,* lower than Hudsonian Godwit.

nonbreeding adult

tail barring often visible on foraging birds

dark centers of feathers give streaky appearance above

strong supercilium

(juvenile similar but buffier, with patterned tertials)

breeding adult male *(baueri)*

richly rufous

no barring on breast (other godwits show some ventral barring in breeding plumage)

nonbreeding adult *(lapponica)*

white tail has narrow dark bars

mostly white underwings (barred in *baueri*); lacks wing stripe

Marbled Godwit

Limosa fedoa
L 18"/46cm **WS** 30"/76cm

This lovely buff and cinnamon sandpiper nests in pastures and prairies of the northern Great Plains, especially near wetlands, where it eats mostly earthworms and insects and also probes for plant tubers. In the nonbreeding season, birds gather at traditional sites in coastal bays and marshes and forage on tidal mudflats for marine organisms. **VOICE** Calls solid, often strident, with yelping quality, including repeated *kehr, kew-der, YIHdihkah,* and *awick* notes.

nonbreeding adult

warm buff-brown tones in all plumages, like curlews

lacks white in tail and wings (unlike all other godwits)

breeding adult

neatly barred sides

very long bill has pinkish orange base

breeding adult

underwings with cinnamon and buff tones unique

Surfbird

Aphriza virgata
L 10"/25cm WS 25"/64cm

The heavyset Surfbird breeds above the tree line in Arctic montane tundra, especially in rocky areas, where it blends in well with the lichen-covered stones. In winter it rarely strays from rocky habitats of the outer coasts and can be found foraging among turnstones, tattlers, and oystercatchers for invertebrates in the intertidal zone. Migrants are sometimes seen on sandy shorelines. Surfbirds winter coastally from southern Alaska to southern Chile. **VOICE** Calls include soft squeaks and chips.

breeding adult

mottled gray above, with peach-rufous scapulars

short, yellowish legs

Surfbird in flight with Black Turnstone (low

nonbreeding adult

pale eye ring

thick bill has pale base to mandible

gray, with speckled belly

Wandering Tattler

Tringa incana
L 11"/28cm WS 26"/66cm

This shorebird of rocky shorelines forages nimbly at the surfline, bobbing and rocking its head and tail almost constantly. Tattlers breed above the tree line in Arctic mountains, usually not far from streams. Despite this species' epic migration (as far as Australia), migrants rarely turn up out of range. The similar Gray-tailed Tattler visits Bering Sea islands and is a vagrant to the American Pacific coast; it is best distinguished by its call, a rising *tu-weet!* **VOICE** Call a trilled *deedeedeedee*, like a distant Whimbrel.

breeding adult

speckling in supercilium behind eyes

neat zigzag barring below

(Gray-tailed paler overall; barring below finer and more limited to breast)

nonbreeding adult

white half-supercilium

gray overall

black lores

dull yellow legs

(best told from Gray-tailed by call)

Black Turnstone

Arenaria melanocephala
L 9¼"/23cm **WS** 21"/53cm

Black Turnstone is well camouflaged on the wet, stone-studded tundra and sedge meadows of coastal Alaska, where it nests, and the dark, rocky shores of the Pacific coast, where it spends the nonbreeding season. Turnstones use their stout, slightly upturned bills to overturn shells, seaweed, and other beach debris in search of invertebrates; this species forages for limpets, mussels, and barnacles, shattering or prizing them open. **VOICE** Similar to Ruddy Turnstone but higher and drier; also a musical trilling *treeeeereeeeree.*

breeding adult

"salt and pepper" supercilium

mostly blackish, with white belly

white patch at base of bill

(see flight picture with Surfbird, p. 224)

nonbreeding adult

grayish to dull orange-pink legs, duller than Ruddy Turnstone

mostly sooty and unpatterned head and breast

Ruddy Turnstone

Arenaria interpres
L 9½"/24cm **WS** 21"/53cm

A widespread shorebird of many habitats, Ruddy Turnstone nests chiefly on coastal far-northern tundra and winters on beaches and rocky ocean coasts. Most forage like Black Turnstone in beach wrack and on rocky shores; this adaptable species may also be seen begging for breadcrumbs with Ring-billed Gulls, eating earthworms in plowed farm fields, taking small crustaceans on mudflats, and picking through trash at garbage dumps. **VOICE** Call an incisive *kyew!* or *ki-du!* and a protracted, low rattle.

breeding adult

brilliant ruddy tones above

"harlequin" head pattern

breeding adult

complex white, black, and ruddy pattern above

juvenile

ruddy and black tones of breeding adult replaced by browns

orange legs

(nonbreeding adult similar)

Semipalmated Sandpiper

Calidris pusilla
L 6¼"/16cm **WS** 14"/36cm

This is the most abundant eastern peep on any given beach, impoundment, or mudflat. Millions of "Semis" nest in the Canadian and Alaskan tundra, and most make their way to traditional stopover sites in the Canadian Maritimes, New England, and mid-Atlantic states, where they fatten up for their migration over open ocean. **VOICE** Calls a low, rough *krup* and a higher *chit;* often gives a descending series of tittering, nasal *dee* calls when foraging.

breeding adult

stout, thick-tipped bill

less spotted below than Western Sandpiper

plumage tones mostly brown; scapulars and tertials have uniformly dark centers

juvenile

dark cap and auriculars

scapulars have only faint rusty color

uniformly scaly upperparts

Western Sandpiper

Calidris mauri
L 6½"/17cm **WS** 14"/36cm

The well-named Western Sandpiper nests only on coastal tundra of Alaska and Siberia, stages in spring in vast numbers in the Copper River delta of southern Alaska, and winters on coasts throughout the Americas. In nonbreeding plumage, Western can closely resemble Semi-palmated Sandpiper, which usually has a shorter bill. Western's long, droopy bill, heavier at the base and tapered at the tip, often recalls the larger Dunlin. **VOICE** Call a high, short, scratchy *cheet,* higher than Semipalmated.

breeding adult

long, droopy bill

bright rufous-orange coverts, scapulars, auriculars, cap

nonbreeding adult

very similar to Semipalmated but with longer bill, paler auriculars

juvenile

paler overall than Semipalmated, especially the face

contrasting scapulars strongly black and rufous

Red-necked Stint

Calidris ruficollis
L 6¼"/16cm **WS** 14"/36cm

This Asian peep is rarely seen in North America. It is a rare nester on coastal tundra of western Alaska, an uncommon sight among other small shorebirds on Alaska's offshore islands in migration, and a vagrant on Atlantic and Pacific coasts as well as inland. Most records away from Alaska have been of birds in full or partial breeding plumage, which is distinctive but similar to Little Stint. **VOICE** Call a high, somewhat raspy *chriit*, lower than Western Sandpiper.

breeding adult

scapulars and some coverts orange-rufous

bright orange-rufous hood has speckled border

black legs

juvenile

bill usually very fine and tapered

very similar to Semipalmated Sandpiper, but brighter above, less capped, no webbing between outer toes, and longer primary projection

more scapular/covert contrast than in Little Stint, with less distinct, pale mantle "braces"

Little Stint

Calidris minuta
L 6"/15cm **WS** 14"/36cm

Little Stint, a Eurasian species rarely seen in Alaska's Aleutians and other Bering Sea islands, is a vagrant in spring and summer among other peeps in the lower 48 states. Little Stint favors more open habitats than the similar Least Sandpiper. In North America, spring and early summer vagrants are adults; all records after August have been of juveniles. Juveniles resemble juvenile Red-neckeds but have tertials edged in rufous and a mantle edged with a pale buffy line. **VOICE** Call a sharp, high *stit* or similar in short series.

breeding adult

fine, slightly drooping, short bill

foxy orange coverts and tertials

white throat (unlike Red-necked Stint)

breeding adult

pale orange face and sides of breast

speckled orange wash on breast (unlike Red-necked)

similar in size to Least Sandpiper

Least Sandpiper
Calidris minutilla
L 6"/15cm **WS** 13"/33cm

Least Sandpiper breeds across a large swath of Alaskan and Canadian tundra and muskeg. In migration, it visits varied habitats, including muddy pond edges, rivers, wet farm fields, and fish hatcheries. It stays at the periphery of mudflats, where it picks at the surface for food. This is the only peep with yellow legs other than Temminck's and Long-toed Stints, both vagrants to Alaska. At rest and in flight, Least looks smaller and darker than Semipalmated Sandpiper. **VOICE** Call a distinctive, high, trilled *preep* or *krreep!*

breeding adult

tiny, with dark brown plumage

thin, fine-tipped bill

posture often seems crouched

darker mousy brown above than other peeps

nonbreeding adult

yellow legs

juvenile

brilliant chestnut and rufous feather edges above

bill usually shows droop at tip; breast washed with buff

greenish cast to yellow legs

Spotted Sandpiper
Actitis macularius
L 7½"/19cm **WS** 15"/38cm

Spotted Sandpiper bobs the rear half of its body as it forages, much like a waterthrush, and flies with stiff, shallow wingbeats. The species has one of the widest breeding distributions of any American shorebird; it nests in open or partly wooded areas near water. Migrants and wintering birds occupy many habitats, from breakwaters on ocean coasts to the edges of inland rivers and reservoirs. **VOICE** Call a sweet, rising *pwee!*, often doubled; lower and slower than similar call of Solitary Sandpiper.

breeding adult

spotted below

white eye ring broken by black eye line; long, white supercilium

nonbreeding adult

actively chases insects

juvenile

unspotted below

coverts have neat buff and brown barring

(similar Common Sandpiper, a vagrant to Alaska, has longer tail and broad white base to wing stripe)

White-rumped Sandpiper
Calidris fuscicollis
L 7½"/19cm **WS** 17"/43cm

White-rumped Sandpiper nests chiefly on wet tundra in Nunavut. In fall it heads to wintering grounds in southern South America, undergoing one of the longest migrations of any shorebird. It stages in spring in the Great Plains before passing northward back to the Arctic. This species and Baird's Sandpiper stand out among smaller peeps because their longer wings project noticeably beyond the tail. **VOICE** Call a short, faint squeak, *tseek,* with electric quality.

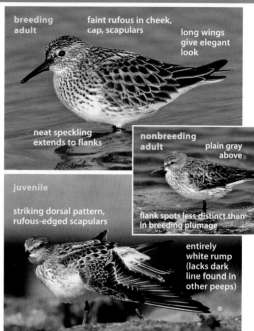

breeding adult
faint rufous in cheek, cap, scapulars
long wings give elegant look
neat speckling extends to flanks

nonbreeding adult
plain gray above
flank spots less distinct than in breeding plumage

juvenile
striking dorsal pattern, rufous-edged scapulars

entirely white rump (lacks dark line found in other peeps)

Baird's Sandpiper
Calidris bairdii
L 7½"/19cm **WS** 17"/43cm

This graceful peep nests on dry Arctic tundra as far north as there is land. It is sometimes referred to as a "grasspiper" because it prefers drier habitats than other peeps, especially dry lakebeds, fields, and dry alfalfa fields. Migrants are also found along mudflat edges, rice crops, sewage treatment ponds, and flooded fields. Unlike other peeps, migrating and wintering birds can be found at very high elevations. **VOICE** Call a coarse *kreep,* much lower than Least Sandpiper and with Pectoral's harshness.

breeding adult
unstreaked supercilium
dark blotches in scapulars
(unmarked belly, unlike White-rumped)

juvenile
uniformly scaly appearance above
long wings
buff-tan cast above and on breast

Pectoral Sandpiper
Calidris melanotos
L 8¾"/22cm   WS 18"/46cm

Pectoral Sandpiper is named for its strong breast markings, which displaying males expand tremendously by using an underlying air sac. This species nests on wet tundra in Canada and northern Alaska. During migration and in winter it prefers muddy and grassy meadows to mudflats, where it can hide from view, much like snipe. Males are notably larger than females, as in Ruff. **VOICE** Song a series of low, hollow hoots given in flight. Call a harsh, modulated *krrrt* or *chrrp*, sometimes *kreep* (lower-pitched in male).

breeding adult

larger than peeps

sharp contrast between patterned breast and white belly

yellow legs

typical juvenile

like adult but neater pale edges to feathers above

bright juvenile

upperparts like Sharp-tailed, but "pectoral" pattern below

Sharp-tailed Sandpiper
Calidris acuminata
L 8½"/22cm   WS 18"/46cm

Sharp-tailed Sandpiper is the stunning Siberian counterpart to Pectoral Sandpiper, occupying similar breeding habitat and wintering in the South Pacific. In North America it turns up mostly in fall, favoring marshy or grassy freshwater sites, including wet farm fields, sewage treatment ponds, and turf farms. Most of the vagrants seen are in juvenal plumage; use caution when separating Sharp-tailed from bright juvenile Pectorals. **VOICE** Call a sweet *chreep* or *weep,* less modulated and higher than Pectoral.

breeding adult

bold, white eye ring; rufous cap

speckling on breast often extends to flanks as chevrons

juvenile

supercilium widens behind eyes (compare Pectoral)

bright buffy breast with diffuse streaks, lacking sharp break of Pectoral

more brightly colored than most Pectorals, with neat rufous cap

Rock Sandpiper

Calidris ptilocnemis
L 9"/23cm   **WS** 17"/43cm

The little-known Rock Sandpiper nests on dry tundra near the coast. The nominate subspecies breeds on the Pribilof Islands and winters mostly at Cook Inlet, Alaska; the mainland subspecies *(tschuktchorum)* winters in rocky coastal habitats south to central California. Thousands of "Rocks" use the Yukon River delta as a stopover site before and after the breeding season. **VOICE** Song a run-on series of modulated trills in short, paired phrases, less complex than Purple Sandpiper. Calls similar to Purple.

breeding adult
(nominate)

pale buff-rufous
scapulars

black belly
patch

(mainland subspecies
smaller and much
darker overall)

nonbreeding
adult

gray above, paler
below; gray
speckling on breast
more distinct than
in Purple

very similar to Purple
but with greenish
yellow legs and bill base

Purple Sandpiper

Calidris maritima
L 9"/23cm   **WS** 17"/43cm

Like its close relative Rock Sandpiper, this species might be called a "rockpiper": it is almost never seen away from rocky coastal habitats. Purple nests on rocky upland tundra and in winter frequents inhospitable shorelines swept by storms. It is very rare inland, except at several sites in the eastern Great Lakes in fall. In fresh nonbreeding plumage, purple tones in the mantle, scapulars, coverts, and tertials are evident in optimal light. **VOICE** Short calls low and coarse, most like Dunlin but lower: a sharp *kreep, kreesh,* and *kip.*

breeding
adult

very dark
overall

shaped like
Dunlin and Rock
Sandpiper, but
lacks belly patch
and rusty tones

nonbreeding
adult

violet
highlights in
upperparts visible
in good light

very similar to
Rock Sandpiper
but with orange
legs and bill base

Dunlin

Calidris alpina
L 8¾"/22cm WS 17"/43cm

Dunlin, once known as Red-backed Sandpiper, breeds in marshy tundra and winters in large flocks on coastal mudflats. This species uses its long bill to probe methodically in mud, much like the smaller Western Sandpiper. After breeding, the subspecies *pacifica* (from western Alaska) migrates to the West Coast, *hudsonia* (northern Canada) to the East, and *arcticola* (northern Alaska) to Asia. **VOICE** Song, often heard from spring migrants, a descending series of buzzy trills. Call a buzzy *kreeer* or *jeeer*.

breeding adult

striking bright brick red above

long, drooping bill

black belly patch

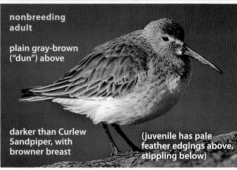

nonbreeding adult

plain gray-brown ("dun") above

darker than Curlew Sandpiper, with browner breast

(juvenile has pale feather edgings above, stippling below)

Curlew Sandpiper

Calidris ferruginea
L 8¾"/22cm WS 18"/46cm

The rich brick orange plumage and namesake curved bill of Curlew Sandpiper distinguish this Eurasian vagrant species. It nests on wet tundra, mostly in Siberia (rarely in Alaska), and winters on coastal mudflats and lakeshores, mostly in Africa and Asia. Juveniles and winter adults, rare in North America, have plumages and foraging techniques similar to Dunlin. In flight, Curlew shows a white rump, like Stilt Sandpiper, but also a thin white wing stripe, absent in Stilt. **VOICE** Call a gentle *krriip* or *kererip,* less modulated than Dunlin.

breeding adult

decurved bill

rich rusty orange below

longer legs than Dunlin lend a more stately appearance

juvenile

strong supercilium

pale overall, with scaly upperparts

nonbreeding adult

generally paler above than Dunlin

entirely white rump (broken by dark line in Dunlin)

long, dark legs (compare Stilt Sandpiper)

Stilt Sandpiper
Calidris himantopus
L 8½"/22cm **WS** 18"/46cm

This relatively scarce American shorebird nests on wet coastal tundra in northern Canada and adjacent Alaska, and winters on mudflats and ponds in the tropics. Breeding plumage is distinctive, but juveniles and nonbreeding birds are often mistaken for Lesser Yellowlegs or dowitchers. Stilt Sandpiper forages like (and often with) dowitchers, probing deeply while standing in rather deep water, aided by its long legs. Like Curlew Sandpiper, Stilt has a white rump. **VOICE** Call a high, muffled *kyeer!* or *keew!*

breeding adult

droop in outer part of bill

rufous in crown and auriculars

nonbreeding adult

pale legs

coarsely barred below

recalls Curlew Sandpiper but head, breast, upperparts darker, more contrasting

juvenile

recalls Dunlin but paler gray above, with stronger supercilium

olive-yellow legs (unlike Curlew Sandpiper)

Red Knot
Calidris canutus
L 10½"/27cm **WS** 23"/58cm

Red Knot breeds locally on upland tundra barrens of Nunavut and northern Alaska, and winters on coastal mudflats. It has suffered severe population declines (by as much as 80%) at migration stopover sites in Delaware Bay, possibly a result of the overharvest of horseshoe crabs, whose eggs fuel its almost nonstop flight to its nesting grounds. Great Knot, the only larger *Calidris,* is a vagrant to Alaska and the Pacific coast from Asia. **VOICE** Calls nasal; a low, rising *pwee-way* and a singsong *go-way,* second part lower and repeated.

breeding adult

stout body and bill

brownish gray above

pale rufous-orange below

nonbreeding adult, worn

very pale gray, especially rump, tail, underwings (fresher plumage darker gray)

juvenile

ghostly gray with neat scaly pattern above (compare Ruff)

Red-necked Phalarope

Phalaropus lobatus
L 7¾"/20cm   **WS** 15"/38cm

This phalarope is a widespread breeder on lakeside tundra in Alaska and Canada. Most migrate directly to the open ocean off southern Canada, where they stage on their way to pelagic wintering grounds farther south; large numbers are also seen at some inland locations. Red-necked and Red Phalaropes are the only pelagic shorebirds, although many species are seen at sea during migration. Foraging birds on ponds often spin in circles, creating a vortex that concentrates tiny prey. **VOICE** Call a short, sharp, high *vik!*

breeding adult female

white chin framed by dark head and vivid red neck

buff stripes on blue-gray back

(adult male's plumage less vivid)

upperparts darker and more streaked than Red Phalarope

transitional juvenile

feathers edged rufous above; a few gray feathers of first-fall plumage coming in

juvenile

Wilson's Phalarope

Phalaropus tricolor
L 9¼"/23cm   **WS** 17"/43cm

Wilson's Phalarope nests south of the other phalaropes, principally in prairie marshes of the northern Great Basin and Great Plains. On migration, it is found mostly in western and central parts of the continent on saline and freshwater ponds and lakes. Most winter in South America. Like other phalaropes, Wilson's picks small invertebrates from the water's surface, but it dashes around shorelines more actively, even catching flying insects on foot. **VOICE** Call an almost ducklike, nasal *whemp* or a more booming *whoop*.

breeding adult female

back has deep gray and cranberry tones

(adult male's plumage less vivid)

striking head pattern; rich peach wash on neck

dark legs

nonbreeding adult

very pale; races around quickly

transitional juvenile

upperparts have neat pale edges

pale face, dark cap, and long, thin, straight bill

yellow legs

(shows white rump in flight)

Red Phalarope

Phalaropus fulicarius
L 8¼"/21cm   WS 17"/43cm

Red Phalarope nests mainly on wet coastal tundra of the High Arctic and winters in pelagic waters. Like other High Arctic nesters that are pelagic in the nonbreeding season—Long-tailed Jaeger and Sabine's Gull, for example—Red is seen inland only rarely during migration. This species is called "whalebird" for its habit of picking parasites from the backs of great whales. **VOICE** A high, sharp *keep!*, more musical than Red-necked Phalarope.

breeding adult female

thick, yellow bill

rich gold stripes above

dark cap, red neck and underparts

(adult male's plumage less vivid)

nonbreeding adult

transitional juvenile

paler and more uniform gray above than Red-necked, with stockier body and bill

like Red-necked Phalarope, but bill thicker, especially at tip, and body heavier

Sanderling

Calidris alba
L 8"/20cm   WS 17"/43cm

Almost any visitor to sandy ocean beaches in the U.S. in spring, fall, or winter sees this small, pale sandpiper foraging at the water's edge, racing back and forth with the waves while probing for invertebrates exposed by receding waters. Sanderling nests mostly in northern Nunavut on dry tundra with scattered rocks, usually near water; it migrates quickly to the coasts, making inland stops mostly at larger lakes. Migrating flocks seen over the ocean can be taken for phalaropes. **VOICE** Call a short, sharp, emphatic *kit* or *kvit*.

breeding adult

(compare smaller stints)

black scapular and mantle feathers have bright rufous edges; head and breast have black spots, rufous wash

nonbreeding adult

ghostly gray above, paler than Red Phalarope

juvenile

contrasting gray and black pattern above, snow white below

(extensive white wing stripe visible in flight)

heavy, black legs

Short-billed Dowitcher

Limnodromus griseus
L 11"/28cm **WS** 19"/48cm

Short-billed Dowitcher seems an incongruous name for a long-billed bird, but its bill is shorter than that of Long-billed. This species nests in muskeg and mossy tundra and forages in salt marshes, mudflats, and, less often, freshwater habitats. Three distinctive subspecies occupy disjunct ranges in Alaska *(caurinus)*, the prairie provinces *(hendersoni)*, and Quebec *(griseus)*. **VOICE** Song a rich, burry *gree-doi, gree-doi, gree-doi oi gree-doi*. Call a sharp *tututu*, more rapid than call of Greater Yellowlegs.

breeding adult *(griseus)*

nonbreeding adult

paler flanks and paler overall than Long-billed

spotty pattern in orange foreneck

white belly

(caurinus similar)

juvenile

vivid markings above; tertials have rufous edges and bars

breeding adult *(hendersoni)*

unspotted foreneck

most colorful subspecies in breeding plumage: heavily marked with gold above, rich orangish below

---

Long-billed Dowitcher

Limnodromus scolopaceus
L 11½"/29cm **WS** 19"/48cm

Long-billed Dowitcher breeds on wet coastal tundra and winters on freshwater ponds. Like Short-billed Dowitcher, it forages with rapid "sewing machine" motions, probing deeply in mud for invertebrates. Call notes distinguish the dowitchers; patterns of the scapulars (in breeding adults) and tertials (in juveniles) are also diagnostic. **VOICE** Song like Short-billed but phrased differently: *pee-peet, peeter-WEEtoo, wee-too*. Call a sweet, high *keek!*; feeding birds give quiet contact calls, unlike Short-billed.

breeding adult

dark scapulars have rufous barring, white tips

throat has dark speckling

brick orange extends from face to vent

(fresh spring adults often show crisp dark feather edges below)

nonbreeding adult

tail shows more black than white (unlike Short-billed)

juvenile

tertials leaf gray with narrow pale edges

less colorful than Short-billed

Wilson's Snipe

Gallinago delicata
L 10½"/27cm **WS** 18"/46cm

Wilson's Snipe breeds in bogs, meadows, and marshes, and winters in muddy fields, ditches, and marshes and along waterways. Breeding males perform a "winnowing" flight display, with pulsating sounds produced by the outer tail feathers. Wilson's was once combined with Common Snipe, a regular visitor to Alaskan islands from Eurasia (the smaller Jack and Pin-tailed Snipe have also been recorded there). **VOICE** Song a loud, pulsing, repeated *WEEKa* or *kik*. Call a very scratchy, unmusical *tzehp*.

adult

head and back boldly patterned in pale yellow-gold and brown

(juvenile very similar)

adult

very heavy barring on sides (compare dowitchers)

striking pattern blends well with muddy fields and marshes

American Woodcock

Scolopax minor
L 11"/28cm **WS** 18"/46cm

American Woodcock is such a singular shorebird that it has inspired a wealth of colloquial names, including "timberdoodle," "bog-sucker," and "night partridge." It nests in wet mixed and deciduous woodlands near open meadows and streams. In early spring males rise at dusk to perform aerial display flights: they fly in circles, producing twittering wing noises, and give a comical call when alighting back on the meadow runway. **VOICE** Call a very short, very nasal *bzzzt*.

adult

large eyes aid in nocturnal flying and foraging

long, pliable bill very sensitive, specialized for extracting earthworms

adult

orange-buff below; cryptic dead-leaf pattern above for camouflage

American Avocet

Recurvirostra americana
L 18"/46cm WS 31"/79cm

American Avocet nests colonially or singly on shallow freshwater lakes and sloughs, and winters, often in sizable flocks, in saltwater and freshwater environments. Migrants are uncommon but may turn up almost anywhere in proper habitat. Avocets search for insect larvae and other aquatic invertebrates by sweeping the bill along the water's surface. When threatened, they often cooperate in elaborate distraction displays and aerial mobbing. **VOICE** A reedy, wooden *weep!*, lower than stilts and less often in series.

breeding adult male

(female's bill more strongly recurved)

black and white wings; burnished orange head and neck

transitional adult (juvenile similar)

striking white secondaries and scapulars

nonbreeding adult

off-white or gray head and neck

Black-necked Stilt

Himantopus mexicanus
L 14"/36cm WS 29"/74cm

The elegant Black-necked Stilt is found year-round in shallow ponds and marshes, mostly in freshwater and brackish environments. Like avocets, stilts eat mostly tiny invertebrate prey, but they usually forage by picking prey singly with their long, thin, pointed bill. Stilts often serve as sentinel species for other shorebirds, alerting them to intruders with noisy calls. A similar Eurasian species, Black-winged Stilt, has been recorded in Alaska. **VOICE** Very vocal; a sharp, yipping *vik!* or *wik!*, often in long series.

adult male

long, slender, red legs and black and white plumage unmistakable

(adult female has brownish back, contrasting with black neck; juvenile has brown upperparts, including coverts, tinged with buff in youngest birds)

Pigeons and Doves

Pigeons and doves (family Columbidae) are represented in North America by 12 breeding species, three of which are not native, and six vagrants from Eurasia or tropical America. One native species, Passenger Pigeon, became extinct in the early 20th century. Most columbids are medium-sized, stocky birds with small heads, short, thin bills, medium-long tails, and short legs. The ground-doves and Inca Dove (genus *Columbina*) are much smaller birds than those in the genera *Patagioenas* (Band-tailed, Red-billed, and White-crowned Pigeons), *Zenaida* (Mourning and White-winged Doves), *Columba* (the introduced Rock Pigeon), *Streptopelia* (the introduced Eurasian Collared-Dove and Spotted Dove), and *Leptotila* (White-tipped Dove). Quail-doves, in the tropical American genus *Geotrygon,* are very plump-looking, terrestrial doves that resemble quail; two species are very rare vagrants in the United States.

Once possibly the most abundant bird species on the planet, Passenger Pigeon was hunted to extinction by European settlers in the New World; the last individual died in 1914 in the Cincinnati Zoo at age 29.

Most North American columbids have rather plain plumage that is countershaded gray or brown above and paler below. The very dark tropical Red-billed and White-crowned Pigeons are exceptions, and many species have pink or green tints or iridescent colors in the nape. Rock Pigeons, those urban dwellers known to most people as simply "pigeons," show a wide variety of plumage types that are derived from many centuries of captive breeding. Many individuals seen in North America, however, exhibit the species' ancestral phenotype—that is, the way wild Rock Pigeons still look today on the cliffs of Scotland. "Ringed Turtle-Dove," which also shows plumage variation, is not a true species: it was bred by aviculturalists (people who raise and breed captive birds) from doves of the genus *Streptopelia.*

Pigeons and doves are found mostly in open habitats, from deserts to prairies to city parks; a few thrive in forested habitats. They forage on the ground and in trees for seeds, fruits, and nuts. Perhaps because of their high-fiber diet, most species consume large amounts of water; they drink by siphoning, as through a straw, continuously (other birds dip the bill and let gravity deliver the water to the stomach).

In the United States, columbids court and breed through much of the year, and courting males are easy to observe as they strut, bow, coo, and make display flights over the nesting area. All species build sloppy-looking stick nests in trees or bushes in which they lay just one or two eggs. After the breeding season, some species gather in rather large flocks, and at least four species are migratory—Mourning and White-winged Doves and White-crowned and Band-tailed Pigeons.

The larger pigeons and doves are considered game birds and are hunted in the nonbreeding season. Passenger Pigeon became extinct at least in part because of excessive hunting. This pigeon may once have been one of the world's most numerous bird species, its population estimated in the billions well into the early 19th century, when flocks were said to "darken the skies." No North American columbid is currently considered endangered, although population declines in Common Ground-Dove and Band-tailed Pigeon in some areas are of concern to conservationists.

Band-tailed Pigeon
Patagioenas fasciata
L 15"/38cm **WS** 26"/66cm

Band-tailed Pigeon inhabits coastal and montane forests, usually of oak or pine oak. Unlike Rock Pigeon, it tends to forage high in trees, concealed from view, and is often first detected when flushed: on takeoff, its wings noisily clap together. Flocks wander widely in search of seeds, acorns, and fruit and may gather in numbers where food is plentiful; birds occasionally wander far out of range and often eat at bird feeders, especially in fall and winter. **VOICE** A low, repeated *hoo-whoo*.

adult

large and dark

red eye ring, white half-collar

subtle rose tones below

yellow bill and legs

dark remiges contrast with pale coverts above

dark band, pale tip in tail

juvenile

uniformly gray

base of bill paler than tip

dark remiges (also in adult)

Rock Pigeon
Columba livia
L 13"/33cm **WS** 28"/71cm

The familiar pigeon of cities and farms, Rock Pigeon (formerly Rock Dove) has spread successfully since its introduction from Europe in colonial times. Its nests are found on buildings and bridges and in quarries. Centuries of domestication have produced a wide variety of plumages, from slaty to fawn-colored to pure white, as well as many piebald varieties; but the ancestral phenotype of this species still exists. **VOICE** A low, rolling *bbrrrrra-co-coooo*, rising in middle, then falling, rapidly repeated.

adult, ancestral phenotype

dark bill has white cere

dark edges of remiges and coverts form 2 black crescents on folded wing

pale gray above and below, with darker head

flocks often contain many variants (unlike other pigeo

adults

mixed flocks usually show a variety of plumages, from mostly white to tawny to mostly sooty birds

White-crowned Pigeon

Patagioenas leucocephala
L 13½"/34cm WS 24"/61cm

White-crowned Pigeon reaches its northern limit in southern Florida, especially in mangrove and other moist subtropical forests of the Keys, where it is mostly a permanent resident. It is usually seen flying rapidly between wooded areas; it feeds in trees on berries and fruit and rarely walks on the ground. Because this species is not hunted in Florida, it can often be closely approached. Some Florida birds appear to winter in the West Indies. **VOICE** A repeated *hoo-whoo-hoooo,* often introduced by a long *hoooo.*

adult

blood red, pale-tipped bill

rich sooty color overall, with contrasting white crown

juvenile

paler than adult; white crown and iridescent feathers on nape acquired in first year

uniformly dark rectrices

Red-billed Pigeon

Patagioenas flavirostris
L 14"/36cm WS 25"/64cm

The retiring Red-billed Pigeon is found in native woodlands along the Rio Grande. It usually stays concealed in treetops, where it feeds on fruits, and is often first seen when flushed from a tree; but the best time to spot this bird may be early morning, when it sits out to warm itself in the rising sun. Flying birds resemble dark Rock Pigeons but look larger-headed. **VOICE** A loud *whoo-ooo! who-wh-wh-wh-whoooooo,* mostly on one pitch, second part repeated. Call a gruff, growling *whoo-uf!*

adult

pale eyes, red orbital ring

soft gray overall, with extensive maroon tones in head, neck, upperwing coverts, and underparts

pale bill has reddish base

adult

yellow on bill tip discernible from some distance

Mourning Dove

Zenaida macroura
L 12"/30cm **WS** 18"/46cm

Mourning Dove is a common sight in open habitats south of the boreal forest from mountaintops to deserts, especially farmland and suburbs. It feeds on seeds, almost always on the ground. This species breeds year-round in southern parts of its range, producing up to 6 broods a year. Though many Mourning Doves withdraw from the northern Great Plains and southern Canada in winter, this species is not often observed in its diurnal migration. The spread of Eurasian Collared-Dove through North America appears to be reducing the abundance of Mourning Doves, especially in urban areas, but more study is needed to determine this. **VOICE** A despondent-sounding *hooooOOOhh-whoo-whoo-whoo*, first part rising, then on lower pitch.

Mourning Dove adult — "beauty mark" below auriculars — pale orbital ring — black-spotted coverts and tertials — no white in wings — long tail

adult — tapered tail shape — black and white in rectrices, easily seen on landing bird

Mourning Dove juvenile — easily mistaken for ground-dove or Inca Dove but larger, with longer tail

Spotted Dove

Streptopelia chinensis
L 12"/30cm **WS** 21"/53cm

In 1917 Spotted Dove, a species of southern Asia, was introduced in the Los Angeles area. It spread rapidly during the 20th century, nesting as far north as Bakersfield, California; in recent decades, however, this species has begun to decline and has become harder to find away from its strongholds in urban and suburban Los Angeles. **VOICE** A scratchy *ho-hooo-hoo*, weaker than Eurasian Collared-Dove.

Spotted Dove adult — dark brown above, paler below, with rose tones — half-collar speckled black and white

Spotted Dove juvenile — similar to young Mourning Dove but some rose tones in head and breast — lacks spotting in nape

White-winged Dove

Zenaida asiatica
L 12"/30cm **WS** 19"/48cm

This large, conspicuous dove is common in southwestern deserts, brushlands, canyons, and foothills. It forages in trees and cacti for fruit and eats at feeders. A nonmigratory Florida population has recently become established and appears to be spreading. In spring and fall, wanderers are found out of range, some as far north as southern Canada. **VOICE** A memorable *rrro-hoo-hooo-hooo (who cooks for you)* on one pitch; also syncopated short *coo* notes followed by longer *hoos,* alternately rising and falling.

adult · rich lazuli orbital ring, red eyes

white in upperwing coverts visible in folded wing (obvious on flying birds)

stronger mark below auriculars than on Mourning Dove

adult

juvenile

like adult but duller, especially eyes and orbital ring

white-tipped tail not tapered, shorter than Mourning Dove

often drinks nectar at flowers

Eurasian Collared-Dove

Streptopelia decaocto
L 13"/33cm **WS** 22"/56cm

In the mid-1970s, Eurasian Collared-Doves escaped from an aviary in the Bahamas; by 1978 some had dispersed to Florida. The species has since multiplied and spread into North America, especially into suburbs of the South and West; it is expected to be abundant across the continent in a few decades. A smaller, paler avicultural form, "Ringed Turtle-Dove," is often seen in southern states, and some birds in North America appear to be of mixed derivation. **VOICE** A harsh *ho-hooo-ho,* repeated; also a nasal *haaow.*

adult · distinct black half-collar

tan plumage, paler above than Mourning Dove

grayish undertail coverts contrast with white outer rectrices

juveniles

adult

from below, appears large and pale in flight, except for grayish undertail coverts and black in base of rectrices

(from above, brownish back and inner wings contrast with gray secondaries and dark primaries)

Common Ground-Dove
Columbina passerina
L 6½"/17cm WS 11"/28cm

Common Ground-Dove is a scarce, declining species over much of its range. It forages terrestrially on small seeds and favors brushy areas and thickets, although it will also forage in open areas with nearby cover. The species becomes much scarcer in midwinter in Arizona, which suggests that some birds probably withdraw southward into Mexico. In flight the wings of ground-doves give a subtle, insectlike clicking, typical of many *Columbina*. **VOICE** A rising, 2-part *ooo-ooop*, repeated in monotonous, rapid succession.

adult male and female, eastern

short bill with orange-red base

male has blue cast to nape

narrow dark edges on crown, nape, breast feathers

juvenile

like Mourning Dove but much smaller and shorter-tailed, with rufous in primaries

adult male, western

paler and much less richly colored than eastern

scapulars lack spots (found in Ruddy Ground-Dove)

(underwing coverts and primary bases bright rufous in flight)

Ruddy Ground-Dove
Columbina talpacoti
L 6½"/17cm WS 11"/28cm

The striking Ruddy Ground-Dove is mostly seen in fall and winter, usually among small flocks of Common Ground-Doves or Inca Doves in ranchlands with brushy areas. Unlike Common, Ruddy shows black underwing coverts in flight (both sexes). This species has spread slowly northward from Mexico and by 2003–2004 had nested in Arizona and California; more evidence of U.S. nestings will likely be discovered. **VOICE** Similar to Common Ground-Dove but more rapid and with extra syllable.

adult male, eastern (rufipennis)

males of eastern Mexican subspecies (vagrant to Texas) more richly colored than western *eluta*

adult male, western (eluta)

black spots in scapulars

lacks scaly appearance to feathers of breast and nape (found in Common)

Inca Dove
Columbina inca
L 8½"/22cm **WS** 11"/28cm

Inca Dove is found in Texas, the desert Southwest, and, increasingly, brushy areas of the southern Great Plains. Most are seen around towns and farms where seeds and water are available. Unlike ground-doves, it eats at feeders routinely. Inca Dove is relatively scarce in natural habitats other than riparian corridors near settlements. It is sensitive to cold and many birds often roost huddled together. **VOICE** A 2-part *oh-houp,* slightly descending and repeated often, rendered "no hope" for its melancholy quality.

adult

wings produce rattlesnake-like rattle in flight

(rufous primaries and patterned tail similar to short-tailed *Columbina*)

long-tailed

adult and nestling

adult has red eyes

(juveniles have plainer, less scaly plumage than adults and yellowish eyes)

White-tipped Dove
Leptotila verreauxi
L 11½"/29cm **WS** 18"/46cm

White-tipped Dove is the only North American representative of its genus, which contains 10 other tropical American species. It reaches its northern limit in scrubby habitats and dry forests of southernmost Texas; a few have reached Florida's Dry Tortugas, probably from Mexico. This shy bird is usually seen walking away through brushy cover. It feeds on seeds and berries and sometimes forages in trees. Flying birds look short-tailed and dark-winged. **VOICE** A low, mournful *wh-whooo-oooo* on one pitch.

adult

red orbital ring

faint tones of magenta and sea green in hindcrown and nape

snowy white chin and forecrown

juvenile

lacks pronounced orbital ring and nape colors of adult

white tips to outer rectrices (all ages)

Parrots and Parakeets

Parrots and parakeets (and macaws) are members of the family Psittacidae, which includes about 360 species worldwide. While psittacids vary in body shape—from the slender, long-tailed parakeets to the stout-bodied, short-tailed parrots—all have strong, curved maxillas for opening fruits, seeds, and nuts. They typically are highly social, nest in cavities, and have loud, far-carrying calls. Most New World species have green plumages with other colors in the wings and head. The only native representative from temperate North America, Carolina Parakeet, is now extinct. A few Mexican species have been detected in border areas: Thick-billed Parrot was formerly resident in Arizona (it is now confined to the highlands of Mexico), and at least some of the Red-crowned Parrots and Green Parakeets that nest in southernmost Texas are probably of wild provenance.

The southern United States is home to many exotic psittacids (more than 90 species recorded), nearly all of which are escapees from pet owners. Many *Amazona* species are resident nesters in Florida and California, and the striking

Once common in the Southeast, Carolina Parakeet has been extinct since about 1940.

Chestnut-fronted Macaw now nests in Florida. In addition to these Neotropical species, psittacids from Africa and Australasia, such as Budgerigar, Cockatiel, and various lovebirds and cockatoos, are also often observed. North America lacks the natural habitats in which most exotic psittacids evolved, and the birds depend on urban and suburban environments to provide their food—mostly from exotic fruit and nut trees—and nesting and roosting areas. Unlike the tropical species, Monk Parakeets are adapted to living in temperate climates and can be observed year-round in many large cities, even as far north as Chicago.

Because they are found mainly in developed environments, parrots and parakeets tend not to displace native birds from their niches, as some other introduced birds have done (European Starling, for instance). Conservationists, however, are concerned about the potential spread of avian diseases by parrots to native birds and about the very real damage to native populations of parrots posed by the caged bird trade. Many species of psittacids worldwide have become endangered, and several even extinct, because of this trade.

Black-hooded Parakeet nests locally in Florida.

Red-crowned Parrot

Amazona viridigenalis
L 12"/30cm WS 25"/64cm

A native of Mexico, Red-crowned Parrot inhabits urban, agricultural, and forested areas. It is found in the U.S. in southern California, Texas, and Florida. These parrots are highly gregarious, flying between communal roosts and feeding areas and delivering raucous calls in early morning and late afternoon. At other times of day the species is less conspicuous, as it feeds or rests within foliage. **VOICE** Various talkative, grating calls when perched; in flight a piercing, high-pitched call followed by 3 or 4 much lower, abrupt *klaak!* calls.

adult

full red cap

red in secondary coverts

Red-lored Parrot

Amazona autumnalis
L 12½"/32cm   WS 26"/66cm

This widespread species, also called Yellow-cheeked Parrot, is seen in small numbers often in Texas and occasionally California and Florida. Its status is not well understood, owing to confusion with young Red-crowned Parrots. Red-lored is a native of evergreen and mixed forests from Mexico to Brazil; it is often found in well-vegetated suburban neighborhoods of the U.S., where it sometimes roosts with other species of *Amazona*. **VOICE** Calls high and raucous, similar to Red-crowned but with a more shrieking quality.

subadult

similar to juvenile Red-crowned but darker bill, extensive bluish crown

(adult has yellowish cheeks)

Amazona parrots have broad, rounded wings

wing pattern like Red-crowned, with blue-tipped remiges and red in secondary coverts

subadult

Yellow-headed Parrot

Amazona oratrix
L 14"/36cm   WS 28"/71cm

This robust native to Mexico and Belize is popular with pet owners, and escapees have established small breeding populations in Florida. Single birds and pairs are often seen in Texas and southern California, where breeding has also occurred. In 2005 it was estimated that fewer than 7,000 birds remained in the wild, the decline a result of illegal trapping and destroyed habitats. **VOICE** Calls include a resonant, rolling, talkative *ahrrra, kiya-ha-ha,* and *ho-oh-oh;* less raucous-sounding than smaller *Amazona*.

adult

yellow on head variable but reaches eyes even in juveniles

subadult

less extensive yellow on head than adult

White-fronted Parrot
Amazona albifrons
L 9½"/24cm **WS** 23"/58cm

White-fronted Parrot nests sparingly in Florida, where there are fewer than 30 pairs, and California, where it is seen in pairs or small flocks. It flies on trembling wingbeats just over the trees—unlike larger *Amazona*, which often fly high in the sky. The species is native to Central America from western Mexico to northwestern Costa Rica. **VOICE** Shrill calls with laughing, screeching quality, *ki-ah-hah-hah* and similar.

adult

(extensively blue remiges and red primary coverts visible in flying birds)

yellowish bill; white forecrown bordered by blue crown, red around eyes

Thick-billed Parrot
Rhynchopsitta pachyrhyncha
L 16"/40cm **WS** 33"/83cm

Once an irregular visitor to forests of southern Arizona and New Mexico, Thick-billed Parrot has not been recorded in the U.S. since 1938, although there was one sighted in New Mexico in 2003, possibly a stray from northwestern Mexico, where this species is a declining endemic. A reintroduction program in the Chiricahua Mountains, Arizona, in the 1980s was not successful. **VOICE** A gentle, talkative *ahhr* and *a-ha-ha-ha,* soft for a parrot.

adult

black bill

green overall, with red in leading edge of wings and red forehead extending back as supercilium

(yellow underwing bar, long tail and wings visible in flight)

Monk Parakeet
Myiopsitta monachus
L 11"/28cm **WS** 19"/48cm

Monk Parakeet builds enormous, round stick nests, unique among the world's parrots, that house several nesting pairs; the nests are placed in trees or on telephone poles, often around electrical transformers. This species is native to South America; North American populations, derived from escapees, are locally common in several midwestern and eastern states and scarce in the West. **VOICE** A high-pitched, thin *krii* or *grii,* grating but short; often heard around nest.

adult

gray face and throat

pale bill

blue in remiges

large colonial nests unique among psittacids

Green Parakeet
Aratinga holochlora
L 12½"/32cm   WS 21"/53cm

Found in urban groves and gardens, Green Parakeet is a common resident of southernmost Texas, its population probably a mix of escaped captives and wild colonists from northeastern Mexico. Greens are also widespread in Florida and California, along with other mostly greenish *Aratinga* parakeets (sometimes called conures)—especially Mitred, Red-masked, Dusky-headed, and Blue-crowned Parakeets; some have established small local populations. **VOICE** A rolling, grating, high-pitched chatter.

uniformly green; some have red flecks in head

no blue in remiges (compare Monk Parakeet)

White-winged Parakeet
Brotogeris versicolurus
L 9"/23cm   WS 15"/38cm

White-winged Parakeet is rare and local in southern Florida and southern California, found mostly in suburbs and city parks. It was formerly combined with Yellow-chevroned Parakeet as Canary-winged Parakeet. Native to South America, this species appears to be declining in North America, though it was fairly common through the 1980s; fewer than 100 pairs are thought to remain. **VOICE** A clipped, rising *kleer* or *kler,* often doubled or trebled.

adult

white in secondaries and inner primaries sometimes visible in folded wing, always striking in flight

darker green plumage than Yellow-chevroned, lacking yellow tones

yellow greater secondary coverts like Yellow-chevroned, but primary coverts white, not yellow

Yellow-chevroned Parakeet
Brotogeris chiriri
L 9"/23cm   WS 15"/38cm

Yellow-chevroned Parakeet is locally uncommon in southern Florida and southern California, where a few hundred pairs persist in parks, orchards, suburbs, and wooded areas. Hybrids with White-winged Parakeet have been observed in Florida; use care when identifying individual birds. **VOICE** Similar to White-winged Parakeet.

adult

no white in remiges (compare White-winged)

yellow greater upperwing coverts visible on resting bird

Cuckoos, Anis, and Roadrunner

Cuckoos, anis, and roadrunners are members of the family Cuculidae, an ancient group of birds with no close relatives among other bird families. Cuculids are long-tailed, medium-sized birds; with their relatively short legs and zygodactyl feet (two toes point forward, two backward), they are best suited for perching, though Greater Roadrunner is terrestrial. Most cuculids are found in warmer climes, even in deserts; Black-billed Cuckoo

Unlike some Old World cuckoos, which are brood parasites, Black-billed Cuckoo (shown here) and other American species typically raise their own young.

ranges well north into Canada to the edge of the boreal forest. In addition to the six regular nesting species found in North America, Oriental and Common Cuckoos (of Eurasia) have occasionally turned up on Alaskan islands.

In plumage, cuculids show remarkable diversity, from the coal black simplicity of the anis, to the countershaded plumage and patterned tails of cuckoos, to the streaky camouflage of roadrunners. They generally have curved, short bills, although the bills of anis are very deep and those of roadrunners are rather long. Their bills suit their diets well: cuckoos forage on caterpillars, including large, hairy caterpillars few other birds eat; anis eat a wide variety of seeds, fruits, insects, and reptiles; and roadrunners take prey as large as adult rattlesnakes, kangaroo rats, and sparrows. Anis and cuckoos are stolid foragers, peering around slowly while perched and then making a swift sally out to snare prey. Roadrunners are sometimes stealthy when hunting but also use direct pursuit; when running down lizards they can achieve speeds of up to 25 miles per hour (40km/hr). Roadrunners sometimes capture prey by teamwork; for example, when confronting a poisonous snake, one bird distracts the snake while the other strikes. When taking live prey, cuculids tend to dispatch the prey and then soften it by beating it against a branch or, in the case of roadrunners, a stone.

Courtship among cuculids is a rather simple affair, with the male calling and chasing the female and offering food, which is often exchanged during copulation. All species make sloppy-looking stick nests similar to those of doves, and their young hatch asynchronously, like those of owls. North American cuculids tend to rear their own young (some Old World species are brood parasites); even on the rare occasions when they lay their eggs in the nest of another bird species, they feed all the nestlings, along with the host parents. Anis sometimes nest communally, and the young remain with their parents for at least six months after hatching, working as nest helpers to feed the next brood. Cuckoos are long-distance migrants to Central and South America. Anis move much shorter distances: Groove-billed Ani repairs into Mexico, while Smooth-billed Ani is mostly sedentary in Florida.

The conservation status of the cuckoos is difficult to assess, as they wander widely in search of local outbreaks of tent caterpillars, their preferred prey. In the desert Southwest, Yellow-billed Cuckoo is tied to riparian corridors and is very scarce. Smooth-billed Ani was once common and widespread in Florida but is now found only sparingly in the southeastern part of the state.

Groove-billed Ani
Crotophaga sulcirostris
L 13"/33cm **WS** 17"/43cm

Groove-billed Ani is found mostly in
the Rio Grande valley of Texas, in scrub,
agricultural areas, and riparian thickets.
This species is not strongly migratory, but
most birds withdraw into Mexico for the
winter, and vagrants can turn up far out
of range. Anis forage for insects, small
reptiles, and fruit by hopping around in
dense grass or shrubs and sometimes pick
parasites from cattle and horses. **VOICE**
A repeated, high-pitched whistle, *PEE-ooo,*
with loud, sharp opening and descending
end.

adult

mandible weaker and shallower than in Smooth-billed Ani

even rows of grooves in maxilla (lacking in immature)

compare larger grackles

Smooth-billed Ani
Crotophaga ani
L 14"/36cm **WS** 18"/46cm

This West Indian native was once common
in southern Florida; it is now very scarce
there, mostly because its open-country
and scrub habitats have been largely
developed, and modern agricultural
practices have reduced its insect prey.
Smooth-billed Ani also eats lizards,
snails, and plant matter. Breeding occurs
in groups; monogamous pairs within a
group lay eggs in a communal nest and
defend a common territory. **VOICE** A
rising, whistled, querulous *quuuur-LEEK!,*
with emphatic ending.

adult

nape feathers show broader glossy edges than on Groove-billed Ani

maxilla has high arch, rarely with faint grooves

heavier mandible than Groove-billed and noticeable angle at gonys

Black-billed Cuckoo

Coccyzus erythropthalmus
L 12"/30cm **WS** 18"/46cm

Like Yellow-billed, Black-billed Cuckoo inhabits open woodlands, especially where tent caterpillars are abundant; but it visits scrub and mixed woods more often. Black-billed is generally scarcer than Yellow-billed and breeds farther north. This species takes a variety of food, including small fish, mollusks, and berries. Young birds have a bitternlike response to intruders: they point the bill skyward and remain motionless on their perch. **VOICE** A soft, persistent *cucucu, cucucucucu,* sometimes in irregular Morse code–like pattern.

adult

slimmer than Yellow-billed, with more delicate dark bill

red orbital ring

(flying birds show little or no rufous in primaries)

gray undertail; rectrices have narrow white tips

yellowish orbital ring

buffy wash on throat

juvenile

Yellow-billed Cuckoo

Coccyzus americanus
L 12"/30cm **WS** 18"/46cm

This widespread woodland cuckoo is especially common near outbreaks of tent caterpillars, its primary prey; it also takes insects, birds' eggs, and tree frogs. Its long song, heard on summer afternoons, is said to be a harbinger of rain, thus its local names "rain bird" and "rain crow." Populations of this species appear to be in decline. **VOICE** An accelerating series of staccato *kuk* notes, followed by decelerating *kdpow* notes; also a slow, mournful series of throaty *coo* notes on one pitch or descending slightly.

adult

(flying birds show extensive rufous in primaries)

yellow bill

striking undertail pattern

young juvenile

short, slaty bill

more white in undertail than Black-billed

Mangrove Cuckoo
Coccyzus minor
L 12"/30cm **WS** 17"/43cm

Mangrove Cuckoo is a widespread Neotropical species that breeds in southernmost Florida and, like Black-billed and Yellow-billed Cuckoos, migrates to the tropics for the winter. Winter reports from Florida indicate that at least some birds are resident. In the U.S. this species inhabits principally mangrove and other subtropical hardwood forests of the Florida Keys; in the tropics it frequents a wide range of habitats, from arid scrub to wet montane forests. **VOICE** A low-pitched, hoarse, nasal *ow ow ow aw aw*, last 2 notes lower and slower.

adult

black maxilla, yellow mandible

dark mask

slightly smaller than other cuckoos, with heavier bill

grayer above than Yellow-billed, with no rufous in primaries

cinnamon underparts distinctive

striking undertail pattern

Greater Roadrunner
Geococcyx californianus
L 23"/58cm **WS** 22"/56cm

This unusual cuculid is a symbol of the desert Southwest and southern Great Plains. Roadrunners live mostly on the ground, but they fly well and often hunt from or sunbathe on low perches. When chasing prey—lizards, rodents, and small snakes—they can attain speeds of 25 mph (40km/h). At night their body temperature lowers, an adaptation for coping with cool desert nights; they warm up with the morning sun. **VOICE** Male's song a mournful, descending series of about 8 long *coo* notes.

adult

bare skin around eyes

long tail

streaked above and on throat and breast (compare Plain Chachalaca)

adult

sunbathing, with feathers ruffled

Owls

North American owls are placed in the families Strigidae (typical owls) and Tytonidae (barn owls); these two families are relatively closely related and have as their nearest of kin in North America the nightjars and nighthawks. Owls vary greatly in size, but all have strong, hooked bills and talons (suited for capturing, killing, and eating live prey), eyes adapted for foraging at night, and broad, usually rounded wings.

Nocturnal owls use their keen hearing to locate prey, but diurnal species, such as this Northern Hawk Owl, hunt visually. Owls swallow prey whole.

Ecologically, owls are rather like hawks: they are widespread and found in virtually every habitat, even heavily urbanized areas; the smallest species prey on large insects, the largest on small mammals; and their plumages are composed mostly of browns, rusts, black, and white. Owls, however, have several morphological differences from hawks that are related to their nocturnal activities. They have a round facial disc that focuses sound waves to their very sensitive ear openings. The ear openings of some species, such as Great Gray Owl and Barn Owl, are strongly asymmetrical, which permits them to pinpoint the location of rodents tunneling under deep snow or hidden beneath grasses on moonless nights. Many species have "horns" (ear tufts) that, along with cryptic plumages, help camouflage them as they roost by day. Like hawks, owls have keen vision, but the eyes of most owls are specially adapted for gathering light in order to hunt at night. Night-hunting owls also have tiny serrations in the edges of the outer primaries, which make their flight almost inaudible. They hunt by stealth in flight, usually taking prey on the ground; many species are adroit hunters in thick cover, particularly those that eat birds, such as pygmy-owls. Owls usually swallow prey items whole, later regurgitating a pellet of the bones, fur, and other indigestible parts.

Many owls time their breeding to coincide with peak abundance of prey. Larger species make bulky stick nests in trees or on cliffs (Barn Owl also nests in barns and other structures), while smaller owls nest in cavities. Some species take readily to nest boxes, which they also use for daytime roosting. Flammulated and Elf Owls are Neotropical migrants, and Barn and Short-eared Owls regularly leave northern parts of their breeding range; most species, however, are sedentary or irrupt southward in "flight years," mostly when prey is scarce in the breeding range.

Populations of many owls appear to be declining. Burrowing Owl, usually found in the West in prairie-dog towns or ground squirrel colonies, has suffered because of eradication of those rodents. Spotted Owls have been victims of habitat loss, especially of the heavily logged old-growth coniferous forests of the Pacific coast.

Burrowing Owl in threat posture.

Nighthawks and Nightjars

Nighthawks and nightjars (family Caprimulgidae) are members of a large family found across the world in tropical and temperate regions. Most are familiar only in their voices, which ring out on spring evenings, or as a set of glowing orange-red eyes seen in the headlights on country roads at night. Their colloquial name, "goatsuckers," derives from the folk belief that some species drink the milk of goats.

In conflict and courtship, caprimulgids (here Common Poorwill) often spread wings and tail, revealing contrasting markings.

Caprimulgids are medium-sized, slender birds, usually with rather long wings and tails, short but very broad bills, and very short legs. Their plumages have complex patterns of dark browns, black, and white, which help them blend into their environment and escape detection by predators. Their cryptic coloration and nocturnal habits recall owls, which are their nearest relatives. Owls, however, have much larger, stronger feet and heavier bills, even those species that eat mostly flying insects, the chief food of caprimulgids.

Lesser Nighthawk with newly hatched chicks.

Nighthawks (genus *Chordeiles,* page 266) are found only in the Americas; they differ from nightjars (most in *Caprimulgus,* page 268) in having longer, more pointed wings that lack barring, paler bellies, and crepuscular feeding habits (they feed at dawn and dusk). They are often seen flying overhead in open habitats, even in cities, hawking insects much like a bat or swallow. Nighthawks are diurnal migrants and congregate in large flocks when migrating; nightjars are solitary, nocturnal migrants. Most caprimulgids winter in the tropics.

With few exceptions, caprimulgids forage in flight. Nighthawks tend to fly higher than nightjars, coursing back and forth above treetop height and seizing insects with their wide gapes. Nightjars often perch-hunt, fluttering up from the ground or a horizontal tree limb upon spotting a moth or other insect. Nightjars have well-developed rictal bristles, stiff hairlike feathers that probably serve a tactile function and help guide prey to the mouth.

The rarely seen courtship displays of nightjars consist of males spreading the tail and wings to reveal areas of white and often distending the white throat, while calling. Common Nighthawks are often observed in display: the male calls and dives suddenly from high in the air, pulling up into a large, U-shaped arc and making a loud wing noise at the bottom of the dive. All caprimulgids nest on the ground (or a flat rooftop, in the case of some Common Nighthawks), using a shallow scrape rather than building a nest.

Population trends in caprimulgids are poorly understood, but several sets of data indicate a widespread decline in Common Nighthawk and in Whip-poor-will.

Barn Owl

Tyto alba
L 16"/41cm   WS 42"/1.1m

A widespread but usually scarce species, Barn Owl can be found in almost any open habitat in which prey and nesting sites are available, from deserts to farms to marshes. It preys on mice and other rodents. Barn Owl is strikingly pale below and sometimes mistaken for the diurnal Snowy Owl, but its buff and gray upperparts, dark eyes in a white facial disc, and long legs set it apart from other American owls. This species is strictly nocturnal and rarely observed in flight even at dusk. **VOICE** A bone-chilling, screeching hiss, often given in flight; similar to begging cries of fledglings of many larger owls but usually with less nasal quality.

adult male

facial disc has dark caramel-colored border

dark eyes

pale below

adult

distinguished in flight from Short-eared Owl by broader, shorter wings, lack of strong carpal patch, and projection of feet well beyond tail

adult female

underparts have buffy or tawny wash, especially on breast (some males also have this)

nestlings

young hatch at different times for up to 2 weeks

Short-eared Owl

Asio flammeus
L 15"/38cm **WS** 38"/97cm

This sleek owl frequents open habitats—such as savannas, grasslands, agricultural fields, marshes, and prairies—and may gather in large numbers where rodents are abundant. It hunts mostly at night but often by day, coursing low in mothlike flight until it spots prey, then dropping suddenly. Displaying males ascend high in the air, drop quickly, and make up to a dozen loud wing claps. **VOICE** A high, hoarse, nasal screech—*rrrreeeeer-reee!*—often followed by a doglike *yap;* courting male gives quiet, rapid hooting.

adult

tiny ear tufts, hard to see

streamlined body

brown and straw-colored above

(darker birds of Caribbean origin sometimes seen in southern Florida)

adult

belly and underwings much lighter than Long-eared Owl

breast and carpal patch darker than Barn Owl

Long-eared Owl

Asio otus
L 15"/38cm **WS** 36"/91cm

A darker woodland counterpart to Short-eared Owl, Long-eared Owl tends to be much more secretive and nocturnal, rarely foraging before dark. When seen flying in moonlight, its darker underparts and jerky, stiff-winged flight separate it from the mothlike meandering of the paler Short-eared; both species show a pale patch in the primaries above. In winter both species pass the day in communal roosts, usually in conifers. **VOICE** Various flat, monotonous hoots, sharp barks, whoops, and spooky moaning sounds.

adult

large, long ear tufts near top of head (not at sides)

orange facial disc has dark internal borders (compare Great Horned Owl)

narrow posture typical of roosting bird

Great Horned Owl

Bubo virginianus
L 22"/56cm WS 44"/1.1m

A large, powerful owl, resident in all habitats from the tundra edge to deserts and into tropical America, Great Horned fills the ecological niches occupied during the day by Red-tailed Hawk. Emerging at dusk, it surveys an open area from a favorite perch for just about any prey—skunks and opossums, snakes and scorpions, other owls, and birds as large as grouse and American Bittern. It can take prey weighing up to three times its weight. In flight this owl recalls a *Buteo* hawk, but it has a more compact wing shape and more robust body. Plumage color varies from almost blackish brown in Pacific coastal birds to almost ashen white in some interior populations. All populations are similarly shaped and have unique "horns" on the sides of the head, not on the top of the head, as in other American owls. **VOICE** Familiar duet of paired adults consists of low hooting, accelerating at first, then closing with 2 longer *hoos*. Smaller males give lower-pitched calls.

adult, eastern

prominent ear tufts on sides of head

plumage color varies geographically

eastern birds show russet facial disc

adult, western

some western populations are browner overall than eastern birds, with gray facial disc

nestlings, southwestern

adult, eastern

very broad wings and tail, like *Buteo* hawks

Great Gray Owl

Strix nebulosa
L 27"/69cm **WS** 52"/1.3m

This permanent resident of high-mountain meadows, boreal forest, and muskeg hunts rodents from evening through early morning in fields, swamps, bogs, and burned areas. In winter it often hunts by day, plunging into deep, ice-encrusted snow to capture prey it detects by ear. Generally fearless, it is among the most approachable of birds of prey. When prey is scarce in the North, Great Grays make small "flights" southward. **VOICE** A series of low, muffled hoots, lower than Great Horned Owl.

adult
large head with concentric circles in facial disc; eyes appear small in head
white below face (like Great Horned Owl)
enormous but light-bodied

Snowy Owl

Bubo scandiacus
L 24"/61cm **WS** 52"/1.3m

Snowy Owl replaces Great Horned Owl on open tundra. Lemmings are its preferred prey, and it hunts a variety of other prey, including grebes, ducks, and, when wandering well south of range, gulls. This species is easily observed when it appears in southern areas, as it rests and hunts by day in open terrain. It seems compact, but adult females can weigh over 4 lbs. (1.8kg), almost twice as much as the larger Great Gray Owl. **VOICE** Courting male rarely heard; gives deep, hoarse hooting, a crowlike bark, and a long, reedy screech.

adult male
slightly larger than Great Horned Owl, but much heavier

1st year
white facial disc
sooty markings

adult male
older males nearly snow white
active, agile diurnal hunter

Barred Owl
Strix varia
L 21"/53cm   **WS** 42"/1.1m

Barred Owl's familiar 8-hoot call is heard in mixed woodlands and swamp forests, especially in the South, where it often calls during the day. This species preys on insects and vertebrates and especially favors amphibians. Courting birds, often seen by day, call loudly, open their wings, bow, and wag their heads wildly. **VOICE** A series of loud, clear hoots usually remembered as *Who cooks for you, who cooks for you-alllllllll?*, last hoot drawn out and descending; also guttural, monkeylike chattering and a loud single hoot or *hoo-aw.*

adult

pale facial disc

streaked (not spotted) flanks and belly (compare Spotted Owl)

Spotted Owl
Strix occidentalis
L 18"/46cm   **WS** 40"/1m

Three subspecies of Spotted Owl are found in forested mountain canyons of the Southwest *(lucida)*, the Sierra Nevada (nominate), and old-growth forests of the Pacific coast *(caurina)*. The coastal population is listed as threatened, its habitat steadily reduced by the timber industry; where *caurina* overlaps with Barred Owl (whose range is expanding), it is further threatened by hybridization between the two. **VOICE** A series of 3 loud hoots, second usually doubled; higher and more hesitant than Barred.

adult

smaller and darker than Barred Owl, with darker facial disc and spotted (not streaked) underparts

Boreal Owl
Aegolius funereus
L 10"/25cm **WS** 21"/53cm

This little-known owl of boreal forests and coniferous and mixed high-mountain forests rarely strays far out of range. Like its relative Northern Saw-whet Owl, it roosts by day in thick cover, usually dense copses. Like Northern Hawk Owl and Northern Shrike, it caches small vertebrates for later consumption, warming frozen prey next to its body before eating. Boreal and Northern Saw-whet Owls take readily to nest boxes. **VOICE** A rapid series of hoots, accelerating then decelerating.

adult

heavily spotted crown and back

white facial disc framed in dark brown

pale bill

fledgling

mostly dark brown; distinct white crescents between eyes

Northern Saw-whet Owl
Aegolius acadicus
L 8"/20cm **WS** 17"/43cm

Northern Saw-whet Owl is a small, widespread bird of deciduous and mixed forests. This owl is hard to find: its small size and cryptic plumage allow it to blend in among the branches and brambles where it roosts during the day. Like Boreal Owl, it rarely flushes when found roosting and often ignores observers. Both species prey mostly on mice and small birds. In some years, Saw-whets migrate southward in substantial numbers. **VOICE** A very regular series of high-pitched toots, mostly on one pitch.

adult

brownish facial disc heavily streaked with white

lightly spotted upperparts

underparts heavily streaked with rufous

fledglings

white between eyes

chocolate brown above, warm rust-orange below

Elf Owl

Micrathene whitneyi
L 5¾"/15cm   WS 13"/33cm

The world's smallest owl, Elf Owl is a sparrow-sized, insectivorous species of arid habitats. It breeds in the Chihuahuan and Sonoran Deserts, nesting in cavities in saguaro cacti and telephone poles, and up into adjacent canyons with oaks and sycamores. Like many small owls, this species uses old woodpecker cavities for nesting and can often be seen emerging from these at dusk. **VOICE** A tittering, high-pitched *a-he he he he he he,* with even cadence.

adult

tiny

yellow eyes; white eye crescents

plumage mottled with white, rufous, and pale gray

long, bare legs

Flammulated Owl

Otus flammeolus
L 6¾"/17cm   WS 16"/41cm

A small species of montane pine and oak forests, Flammulated Owl is entirely nocturnal; it spends the day concealed high among pine boughs or in a tree cavity. Like Elf Owl, Flammulated winters in Central America; it is rarely observed on its long migration, but vagrants have been recorded on Florida's Gulf coast and off Louisiana on oil-drilling platforms in the Gulf of Mexico. **VOICE** A surprisingly low-pitched *hoo,* sometimes doubled, often difficult to locate.

adult

small

dark eyes

scapulars, breast, facial disc, and ear tufts usually touched with rufous

adult

ear tufts flat

long wings

adult
concealed on roost

some have little or no rufous

Northern Pygmy-Owl
Glaucidium gnoma
L 6¾"/17cm **WS** 12"/30cm

This owl of well-wooded mountains and foothills preys mostly on songbirds and can take prey as heavy as itself. It is active

by day. Songbirds discovering this species at rest frequently "mob" it, gathering in surrounding branches and giving scolding calls. **VOICE** An even series of high toots, sometimes delivered for long periods.

reddish adult

spotted sides

small

streaked below

long, barred tail

gray adult

spotted (not streaked) crown

Ferruginous Pygmy-Owl
Glaucidium brasilianum
L 6½"/17cm **WS** 12"/30cm

This species is found in brushlands of southernmost Texas and saguaro forests of Arizona. Like the related Northern Pygmy-Owl, it preys mostly on songbirds, which are drawn to its call and frequently mob owls roosting by day. **VOICE** A

regular, repeated, tooting *pwip,* like Northern Pygmy-Owl but usually higher and faster.

Ferruginous Pygmy-Owl adult

small

similar to Northern Pygmy-Owl but with unspotted sides and streaked (not spotted) crown

Northern Hawk Owl
Surnia ulula
L 16"/41cm **WS** 28"/71cm

Northern Hawk Owl is a scarce species in spruce forests and muskeg of Canada and Alaska. A few birds wander farther south in some winters; in rare "flight years" many may appear in the northern U.S. Hawk owls are mostly diurnal foragers: they perch, often for long periods, atop a spruce tree, and strike quickly with rapid, stiff wingbeats, catching prey and swooping back to another perch. **VOICE** Much like Boreal Owl but longer and higher.

Northern Hawk Owl adult

face similar to Boreal Owl but larger

often perches in open

barred below

sexes similar in size (unlike other owls)

long tail

Eastern Screech-Owl

Megacops asio
L 8½"/22cm   WS 20"/51cm

The purring tremolo of Eastern Screech-Owl on calm spring evenings is familiar in diverse habitats: Appalachian highlands, Great Plains river valleys, Carolina sandhills and savannas, Adirondack hollows, and midwestern orchards and suburban parks. The species readily accepts nest boxes and raises young in close proximity to houses when there is sufficient prey—mice, birds, and large insects. **VOICE** Call a descending, high-pitched whinny; tremolo—an even, purring trill—often follows.

adult,
red morph

usually
pale bill

red morph
found only
in Eastern
Screech-Owl

adult
gray
morph

most are gray or red, but
can also show pale gray or
brownish plumages

adult

concealment
posture

Burrowing Owl

Athene cunicularia
L 9½"/24cm   WS 21"/53cm

The only small terrestrial owl in North America, Burrowing Owl nests in burrows and often rests on fence posts by day. Its populations have declined with the loss of its open-country habitat to agriculture and development and with the drastic reduction of black-tailed prairie dogs, which provide burrows. The Florida subspecies *(floridana)* differs subtly from western *hypugaea* in plumage; both taxa have strayed out of range. **VOICE** Male: an odd, endearing, roosterlike *coo-cooo!* Female: a harsh, short screech.

adult, Florida
(floridana)

streaked
crown and
narrow
"eyebrows"
(spotted
crown, wider
"eyebrows" in
western birds)

long
legs

adult, Florida
(floridana)

spotted underwing coverts
(plain in western birds)

fledgling, western
(hypugaea)

pale, unmarked buff
below (Florida birds subtly
marked below)

Western Screech-Owl

Megascops kennicottii
L 8½"/22cm **WS** 20"/50cm

Once combined with Eastern Screech-Owl, this species was accorded full species status in 1981. Western Screech-Owl thrives in varied habitats, from humid coastal forests to southwestern deserts. Where ranges meet in the Great Plains, screech-owls are best distinguished by voice. Western varies greatly in size and plumage; as many as 18 subspecies have been recognized. **VOICE** Distinct pure, high, crescendo *poo* notes that accelerate like a bouncing ball coming to rest; tremolo like Eastern, often broken in middle.

adult

darker bill than Whiskered and Eastern Screech-Owls

vertical streaks dominant on underparts (compare stronger horizontal streaks of Whiskered and Eastern)

(birds of Pacific Northwest, subspecies *kennicottii*, usually brownish, not gray)

Whiskered Screech-Owl

Megascops trichopsis
L 7½"/19cm **WS** 17"/43cm

This Central American species just reaches the U.S. in southeastern Arizona and southwestern New Mexico, where it overlaps in range with the very similar but larger Western Screech-Owl. Voice is the most reliable distinguishing feature between the two. Whiskered tends to favor higher elevations and oak-clad canyons and slopes. Its "whiskers" are stiff bristles on the ends of the facial-disc feathering—very difficult to see in the field. **VOICE** A series of notes similar in pitch to Western Screech-Owl but with irregular Morse code–like cadence.

adult

distinguished from Western Screech-Owl by smaller size and feet, more orangish eyes, paler bill base, and more mottling above

Common Nighthawk

Chordeiles minor
L 9½"/24cm   **WS** 24"/61cm

Its diurnal habits make Common Nighthawk a familiar bird of country and city. Nighthawks are often seen foraging like large swallows for flying insects. Males, in "booming" displays, call loudly and swoop in a great U-shaped arc to just above the ground, then pull upward with a whooshing sound (made with the primaries). This species appears to be declining; fewer have been observed at fall migration monitoring stations in recent years. **VOICE** An abrupt, unbirdlike *bzzzzschrp!*

adult female

female and juvenile lack white throat

much geographic variation in plumage; some birds quite pale, others almost blackish above

adult male

white wing bar very close to base of primaries

primary bases unspotted (unlike Lesser)

adult male

white bar in primaries shows angled edge, far forward of tertial ends (unlike Lesser)

white throat

primaries project beyond tail tip

Antillean Nighthawk

Chordeiles gundlachii
L 8½"/22cm   **WS** 21"/53cm

This bird can be called the ecological "replacement" species for Common Nighthawk across most of the West Indies, where Common does not nest. Antillean Nighthawk nests in the U.S. only in the western Florida Keys and is fairly common from Marathon westward. The smaller size and perhaps more slender wings of this species are apparent only with rare comparisons of Common and Antillean in flight; the two are best distinguished by voice. **VOICE** A sharp, dry *pi-chick* or a rhythmic *pilly-pi-tik!* given in flight.

adult

some show pale gray tertials contrasting with remiges and coverts (also seen in juvenile Common)

adult male

very similar to Common but appears smaller and narrower-winged in direct comparison

Lesser Nighthawk
Chordeiles acutipennis
L 9"/23cm WS 22"/56cm

This slender species of southwestern deserts rarely vocalizes in flight, unlike the larger Common and the smaller Antillean Nighthawks. Lesser tends to forage nearer the ground than does Common; in flight, it appears more graceful and swooping, with more rounded wingtips, and looks much buffier in the belly and underwing coverts. Lesser Nighthawk molts before migrating in fall (Common molts on wintering grounds). **VOICE** Song a low, purring trill; also an odd nasal meowing sound with irregular cadence.

juvenile

buffy throat can be hard to see

sandy brown or gray above, lacking strong contrasts of Common Nighthawk

(adult female shows buffy wing patch, unlike Common)

adult male

white bar in primaries closer to wingtip than in Common

adult male

white throat

buffy spotting in remiges (absent in Common)

primaries just reach tail tip, and white bar in primaries projects past tips of tertials (compare Common)

Common Poorwill
Phalaenoptilus nuttallii
L 7½"/19cm WS 16½"/42cm

The diminutive Common Poorwill inhabits arid environments, from low deserts and sagebrush up into canyons and foothills. It hunts from the ground, often from a rocky outcrop, sallying upward in mothlike flight to catch insects. This species has occasionally been found torpid in rocky crevices in winter—essentially hibernating rather than migrating southward, unusual among American birds. **VOICE** Song a liquid, repeated *purr-WILL-ip,* last part inaudible from a distance.

paler adult

mottled gray above with darker face (white collar often concealed at rest)

darker adult

short tail covered by wings (unlike other nightjars)

rufous banding in remiges sometimes visible at rest

(in flight looks short-tailed and -winged)

Whip-poor-will

Caprimulgus vociferus
L 9½"/24cm **WS** 19"/48cm

Whip-poor-will's ringing song, a familiar night sound in eastern deciduous and mixed woodlands, has made it a favorite of poets from the earliest colonial times. Few know the species well; it is strictly nocturnal, usually seen as a shadow above the trees or a flash of dark with white tail corners lifting up in front of a car. When found on day roosts, however, "Whips" are usually rather approachable. This species times its breeding to coincide with the full moon, when it can forage all night to feed its young; at other times it forages just after dusk and just before dawn. For reasons not known, Whip-poor-will's populations appear to be declining in some areas. Mexican Whip-poor-will, found in Arizona, New Mexico, and western Texas, is often treated as a separate species *(C. arizonae)*. **VOICE** Song a rolling, repeated *rrrip-poor-REEER;* more pure-toned in eastern birds, lower and burrier in *arizonae.*

paler adult — dark median crown stripe — gray scapulars contrast with rest of upperparts

darker adult — nictitating membrane often covers eyes when at rest

male shows distinct white collar in some poses

adult male — rounded crown (unlike Chuck-will's-widow)

outer rectrices have broad white tips (narrower and buffy in females)

often perches on low branches

Buff-collared Nightjar

Caprimulgus ridgwayi
L 9"/23cm **WS** 18"/46cm

Buff-collared Nightjar is recorded in the U.S. only from a few remote rocky canyons of southeastern Arizona and southwestern New Mexico. It is a little-known species, rarely seen and usually detected only by its voice. Buff-collared is a bit smaller than Whip-poor-will (which can show buff tones in the collar) but larger than Common Poorwill. **VOICE** A stuttering, rising *tu tu tu tu TU CU CHEEOO!* Calls include a low *chuck* and rolling *krrrrr.*

adult

fulvous tones in complete collar

more uniform and less coarsely marked above than Whip-poor-will

tail projects less beyond wings than Whip-poor-will

Chuck-will's-widow

Caprimulgus carolinensis
L 12"/30cm WS 26"/66cm

A very large nightjar of pinewoods and farmlands, Chuck-will's-widow is sometimes mistaken in flight for an owl, but its long, rather pointed wings and long tail are distinctive even in silhouette. Although it eats mostly large insects, this species is large enough to prey on warblers and even sparrows, which it captures on the wing and devours whole. **VOICE** Song a far-carrying *tuk-weeoo-WEEDOO!*, first syllable often inaudible at a distance; often incorrectly identified as Whip-poor-will.

gray adult

dark auriculars contrast with gray crown and coverts

appears deceptively small at rest

resting birds appear larger-headed and more flat-crowned than Whip-poor-will

rufous adult female

large size apparent in active birds

fulvous auriculars

rufous in tail unlike other large nightjars

(male has white in outer 3 rectrices)

Common Pauraque

Nyctidromus albicollis
L 11"/28cm WS 24"/61cm

Common Pauraque (pronounced *pow-RAH-kay*) is one of the most widespread of tropical American nightjars; in the U.S., it is found only in the brushy Tamaulipan scrub of the Lower Rio Grande valley of Texas, where it is a common sight and sound in the late evening on sandy backroads. In flight, its very large white patches in the wings, very long tail (white-sided in adult males), and unusually broad wingtips are distinctive, as is its flight behavior, which is erratic and floppy-looking. Unlike other species, pauraques sometimes chase insects on foot. **VOICE** Song a vibrant *pur pur pur-WEEEEEERRR!*, rising then falling.

adult

chestnut auriculars have pale lower border

long tail

heavily spotted coverts and scapulars

adult male

white bar in primaries

buff and brown bands in upperwings

buffy underwing coverts

white outer rectrices striking in flight (not seen on other North American caprimulgids)

(adult female has buff bar in primaries, much less white in tail)

Kingfishers and Trogons

Kingfishers (family Alcedinidae) are heavyset birds with heavy bills and heads but small feet and short tails. Their structure reflects an adaptation for fishing, specifically for plunge-diving from a perch or a hovering position. North American species are blue or green above and white below, with a rufous breast or belly in all but the male Belted and female Green Kingfishers. They eat fish, aquatic crustaceans, and amphibians. Courtship consists of aerial chases and feeding. All North American species nest in burrows excavated in vertical banks.

Trogons (Trogonidae, which includes Eared Quetzal) are long-tailed, medium-sized birds with short legs and short, rather heavy bills. Plumage patterns of males and females are similar, although males are more brightly colored. When foraging, trogons and quetzals sit almost motionless, peering around slowly much

Male Elegant Trogon at nest hole.

like cuckoos. Upon spotting a large insect or small lizard, they fly swiftly to pluck it from a branch. Both trogons and quetzals also readily forage on berries; they nest in old woodpecker cavities. Populations of trogons and kingfishers in North America appear to be stable.

Green Kingfisher

Chloroceryle americana
L 8½"/22cm   **WS** 11"/28cm

Green Kingfisher is smaller and more retiring than the *Ceryle* kingfishers. It is usually seen in rapid flight low over the water or perched motionless on a vine or branch overhanging a pond, stream, or river. In these sun-dappled environments, it can be well camouflaged. This species is often located by its quiet, distinctive call. The white outer rectrices can be apparent on flying birds. **VOICE** An unmusical *ti-kit*, likened to 2 rocks struck together, repeated irregularly in long series or in rattles; also a dry *zzzzsherk* and high squeaks.

adult male

vivid, dark green upperparts and head

very long bill for size

rufous breast

adult female

white collar conspicuous in profile

similar to male but lacks rufous in breast (also absent in juvenile)

Belted Kingfisher

Ceryle alcyon
L 13"/33cm   WS 20"/51cm

Belted Kingfisher, widespread but not numerous, nests north to the tree line in deep burrows in high, exposed banks, especially along rivers, streams, and lakeside bluffs. It readily perches in the open on utility wires, bridges, and fence posts and also hunts from perches, peering into the water for fish. Single diurnal migrants move southward along lakeshores and coastlines in fall. A few winter well north of typical range. **VOICE** A sharp, incisive rattle, *krrrrrrrrrr*, varying in pitch; mechanical and woodpecker-like.

adult female

rufous flanks connected by rufous belly band, unlike adult male

(underwing coverts bright white)

adult male

juvenile

like adult, but with darker crest, more white in coverts and secondaries

slate blue upperparts and head

bluish breastband has rusty undertones in fresh plumage

white collar and underparts

Ringed Kingfisher

Ceryle torquatus
L 16"/41cm   WS 25"/64cm

The heavyset Ringed Kingfisher reaches the northern limit of its range in southernmost Texas, where it forages over open fresh water—from resacas, to rivers, to small urban parks with ponds. Those familiar with Belted Kingfisher are impressed by Ringed Kingfisher's greater girth and louder call; males have a rich rufous belly (white in male Belted). **VOICE** A very loud, mechanical clattering and an explosive *k-KOK!*, deeper and lower than Belted.

adult male

heavy bill has pale, yellow-tinged base

(white underwing coverts)

adult female

more ornate than male

(underwing coverts bright rufous)

white breastband separates blue breast from rufous belly

Elegant Trogon

Trogon elegans
L 12½"/32cm   WS 16"/41cm

The range of Elegant Trogon reaches its northern limit in sycamore and oak forests of southeastern Arizona's canyon country. This relatively shy, sedentary bird is more often heard than seen; it sits motionless, watching for insects and small vertebrates, which it captures in a swift sally. It also eats fruit, especially berries. **VOICE** A low, gruff *kwah, kler,* or *burr* call, repeated in series of a dozen or so, recalling Wild Turkey but more modulated and lower.

adult male

yellow bill, black face, red orbital ring

undertail finely marked with black (uppertail has strong coppery sheen)

rose red belly and undertail coverts separated from green by white breastband

adult female

nests in tree cavities

heavy yellow bill; white mark behind eyes

adult female

brown rather than green upperparts; fainter rose belly than male

Eared Quetzal

Euptilotis neoxenus
L 14"/36cm   WS 24"/61cm

This rare vagrant to southeastern Arizona tends to forage more actively and higher in trees than Elegant Trogon; in fall it is especially attracted to fruiting madrone trees. Its "ears" are wispy plumes behind the eyes, difficult to see in the field. **VOICE** Song a series of tremulous whistles, increasing in volume. Calls include a squeaky, tenuous, rising *weee?* or *suwee?*, usually closing with a sharp *KT!*; a high, quavering Blue Jay–like *kee-yah,* repeated in rapid series on one pitch; and a harsh, rattling, descending *krr-krr-krr.*

adult male

rich green upperparts, head, breast

vivid rose red belly

broad tail appears white below

noticeably larger and heavier-bodied than Elegant Trogon

female

like adult male, but head and breast mostly brownish

Woodpeckers

Woodpeckers (family Picidae) live wherever there are trees or large cacti. They specialize in foraging on trees, usually by removing bark or drilling holes to take insects and their larvae. Some species also eat acorns, which they may store in granary trees for later consumption. Woodpeckers have chisel-like bills suited to scaling bark or creating foraging pits in trees. They have strong feet, with toes usually in a zygodactyl arrangement (two toes pointing forward and two backward), and stiff tails to brace against as they cling to or hitch up trees in small vertical "leaps." Built to extract prey from tight spaces, woodpeckers' tongues are barbed and very long (up to 5"/13cm). Most species use rapid-fire, loud drumming to mark territory and attract and keep in contact with mates. Many species also communicate with descending "fuss" or "whinny" calls. Woodpecker courtship is ostentatious: most species call rapidly, raise the crown feathers, spread the wings while clinging to a tree, and bob rhythmically together. All woodpeckers excavate cavities for nesting; some accept artificial cavities. Many species mate for life. Red-cockaded and Ivory-billed Woodpeckers are endangered, the latter critically; other American woodpecker populations appear to be stable or have had only modest declines.

Female Pileated Woodpecker feeding young.

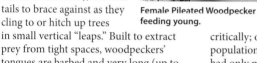

Ivory-billed Woodpecker
Campephilus principalis
L 19"/48cm **WS** 33"/84cm

This majestic woodpecker was a relatively common resident of southeastern forests through early colonial times. Its numbers declined rapidly through the 18th and 19th centuries, largely because it was shot for food, novelties, and specimens, and because old-growth lowland forests, its habitat, were felled for timber. The last unquestioned photographic images of the species were taken in northern Louisiana in 1935. However, sight reports have persisted until modern times, as recently as 1999 near Slidell, Louisiana, and 2005 near Brinkley, Arkansas. Because most sightings of this species pertain in fact to Pileated Woodpecker, observers should take care to document and photograph all suspected Ivory-billeds. **VOICE** Call a nasal *kent*, given in irregular series and likened to calls of Red-breasted Nuthatch; also gives a territorial double-rap: 2 knocks in very quick succession.

adult male

long, heavy, pale yellow bill

red hindcrest (black in female and immature) covered by black forecrest

white stripes extend from face down sides of mantle

white secondaries and inner primaries form white "shield" on back

Acorn Woodpecker

Melanerpes formicivorus
L 9"/23cm **WS** 17"/43cm

Acorn Woodpecker is named for its habit of storing acorns by drilling holes in trees, buildings, or telephone poles to use as granaries. It also often flycatches from trees like Red-headed Woodpecker. This species inhabits oak and mixed forests, often in foothills or mountains, living in groups of up to 16 birds (at least one breeding pair plus earlier offspring). Birds may wander from their territories during years of low acorn production. **VOICE** A strident, nasal *WECK-ah,* repeated; also a nasal, trilling fuss.

clownlike white face with black around bill

adult male

lower throat tinged with yellow

red only in hindcrown, framed in black

(in flight shows white primary bases and white rump; White-headed shows black rump)

adult female

White-headed Woodpecker

Picoides albolarvatus
L 9¼"/23cm **WS** 16"/41cm

This scarce resident of montane pine and fir forests is rarely found below elevations of 4,000' (1,200m). Unlike most *Melanerpes* woodpeckers, which drill holes to store acorns, White-headed forages mostly by flaking off bark in search of insects and spiders; it also feeds heavily on seeds of ponderosa pine, incense-cedar, and sugar pine. In winter males forage alone at higher elevations, sometimes in Coûlter pines. **VOICE** A sharp *kideep!;* fuss high, rapid rattle similar to Hairy and Nuttall's Woodpeckers.

adult male

only white-headed woodpecker

red nape

adult female

lacks male's red nape

white in primary bases striking in flight

Red-headed Woodpecker

Melanerpes erythrocephalus
L 9¼"/23cm **WS** 17"/43cm

A familiar bird of rural and suburban areas, especially in the Southeast, Red-headed Woodpecker prefers woodlands with oak and beech trees. Like Acorn Woodpecker, it stores acorns in traditional granary trees; it also catches insects in flight. This once-common species has declined, owing in part to starlings taking over its nest holes. **VOICE** An abrupt, burry *quearrrr!*, richer and more strident than similar call of Red-bellied Woodpecker; also a harsh fuss.

adult

entirely red head (unique among eastern woodpeckers)

white secondaries and rump striking in flight

juvenile

gray-brown head

barring in secondaries

Lewis's Woodpecker

Melanerpes lewis
L 11"/28cm **WS** 21"/53cm

Lewis's Woodpecker, named after American explorer Meriwether Lewis, is an uncommon resident of open pine and pine-oak woodlands, oak savannas, and cottonwood stands. It forages mostly by flycatching and often perches on telephone wires. Lewis's stores acorns, as do many *Melanerpes,* but only during the nonbreeding season; it does not drill holes for its caches. It sometimes clashes with Acorn Woodpecker over stored food. **VOICE** A quiet *kif*; fuss a high-pitched series of flickerlike *wik* notes.

adult

crimson face

dark plumage has bronze, purple, and green sheen

(plumage, broad wings, and slow, deep wingbeats recall a crow in flight)

juvenile

brownish head and belly

less glossy above

lacks adult's pink belly

Red-bellied Woodpecker
Melanerpes carolinus
L 9¼"/23cm **WS** 16"/41cm

In most of its range, Red-bellied is the only woodpecker that shows a neat zebra-striped pattern across the upperparts. This species has slowly expanded its range northward into wooded habitats and well-treed cities and suburbs. It forages for seeds, insects, and fruits, often hoarding food in tree crevices. In autumn some migrate southward along the coast and in mountains; wintering birds may displace sapsuckers from their sap wells. **VOICE** A mellow, rolling *quurrrr!*, less strident than Red-headed; also a series of rich *chimp* calls.

adult male

entire crown and nape reddish

(aberrant birds with orange-gold nape distinguished from Golden-fronted Woodpecker by barring in rump and tail coverts)

tan crown, reddish nape

in both sexes, central lower belly has red or pink wash (difficult to see); most pronounced in adult male

(juvenile lacks red in nape)

adult female

Gila Woodpecker
Melanerpes uropygialis
L 9¼"/23cm **WS** 16"/41cm

Gila Woodpecker excavates nest cavities in large saguaro cacti of the Sonoran and Mojave Deserts. It also thrives in suburbs with large saguaros and few houses. Pairs defend and reuse their nest cavities from year to year; abandoned cavities become homes for Elf Owls and other desert birds. Like most woodpeckers, Gila is omnivorous, sometimes taking birds' eggs and small lizards. **VOICE** A rolling *quirrrr*, similar to Red-bellied Woodpecker; repeated *wik* notes; and a repeated nasal, tinny *deet* or *deetle*.

adult male

narrow red crown patch

barring in rump and tail

adult female

unmarked brown head

Golden-fronted Woodpecker

Melanerpes aurifrons
L 9¼"/23cm   **WS** 17"/43cm

This tropical woodpecker is found in dry habitats: scrub and dry woods, semidesert mesquite, orchards, riparian washes, and parks. It usually remains in pairs year-round (more sociable *Melanerpes* maintain year-round group territories). This species has hybridized with Red-bellied Woodpecker where ranges overlap. Adults sometimes show a golden wash on the lower belly. **VOICE** A strident, rolling *krrrrrrr*, higher-pitched than Red-bellied; *chimp* calls very similar to Red-bellied, often ending in trill.

adult male

yellow spot at base of bill

red crown, orange nape

adult female

rich yellow nape

tail usually black (compare Red-bellied)

white rump and tail coverts

Arizona Woodpecker

Picoides arizonae
L 7½"/19cm   **WS** 14"/36cm

Arizona Woodpecker, formerly Brown-backed Woodpecker (and once combined with Strickland's Woodpecker of Mexico), is a permanent resident in oak and pine-oak canyons and montane areas of southeastern Arizona and southwestern New Mexico. It feeds on insects and larvae and sometimes fruit and nuts, often near the ground. In winter some move to lower elevations to join foraging guilds of Bushtits, parids, and nuthatches. **VOICE** An incisive *pik!*, similar to Hairy Woodpecker but more tinny; fuss a harsh, descending rattle.

adult male

solid brown above, with large area of white in hindneck

brown-spotted below

adult female

similar to male but lacks red in nape

Yellow-bellied Sapsucker

Sphyrapicus varius
L 8½"/22cm **WS** 16"/41cm

The sapsuckers, even adult males, are among the most difficult to identify of American birds, because of variation in plumages and hybridization. Yellow-bellied, the most widely distributed sapsucker, is found mostly in deciduous and mixed forests. It often winters in the West Indies, unique among American woodpeckers. To trap insects, sapsuckers drill parallel rows of holes in trees to form sap wells, which they maintain and defend. **VOICE** A short, nasal mewing call; many types of fusses.

adult male
red throat framed in black
red crown; white nape
pale marks above more extensive than in Red-naped; back spotting has more buffy-gold tones

white throat
red crown
white nape
adult female

speckled crown
head paler than other juvenile sapsuckers
older juvenile

Red-naped Sapsucker

Sphyrapicus nuchalis
L 8½"/22cm **WS** 16"/41cm

A woodpecker of western montane coniferous forests with birch and aspen, Red-naped Sapsucker barely overlaps in range with Yellow-bellied Sapsucker, although the two species have hybridized. Details of the nape and throat distinguish most adults from Yellow-bellied; juveniles are darker-crowned than juvenile Yellow-bellieds and usually molt into adultlike plumage by early winter (Yellow-bellied often retains brownish juvenal plumage through midwinter). **VOICE** Very similar to Yellow-bellied, perhaps lower-pitched.

adult male
red throat touches long white facial stripe
red crown and throat; black malar
nape usually shows red wash or spot (compare Yellow-bellied)
adult female
pale chin bordered by red
less spotted above than Yellow-bellied; back spotting whitish (not buffy-gold)

Red-breasted Sapsucker

Sphyrapicus ruber
L 8½"/22cm **WS** 16"/41cm

Until 1983 Red-breasted and Red-naped Sapsuckers were considered subspecies of Yellow-bellied Sapsucker. Red-breasted inhabits moist Pacific coastal forests, which are largely coniferous. Hybrids occur where its range overlaps with other sapsuckers; these zones of hybridization appear to be stable, as birds of hybrid derivation are apparently not as successful as nonhybrids. The ranges of the northern and southern subspecies meet around Klamath Lake in southern Oregon. **VOICE** Similar to Yellow-bellied.

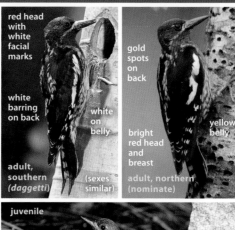

red head with white facial marks

white barring on back

adult, southern (*daggetti*)

white on belly

(sexes similar)

gold spots on back

yellow belly

bright red head and breast

adult, northern (nominate)

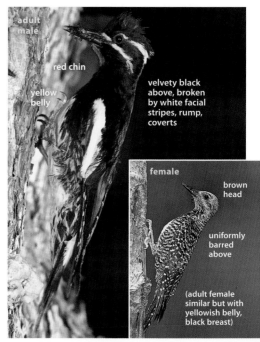

juvenile

head and sides more spotted than other sapsuckers

Williamson's Sapsucker

Sphyrapicus thyroideus
L 9"/23cm **WS** 17"/43cm

This handsome sapsucker inhabits montane forests of lodgepole pines, hemlocks, aspens, larches, and firs. It is unusual among sapsuckers in having pronounced sexual dimorphism. Williamson's defends territories against the smaller Red-naped Sapsucker. Pairs use a traditional nest tree but frequently excavate a fresh cavity each year. Hybridization with other sapsuckers is rare. **VOICE** A hawklike *queeyah!* and repeated flickerlike *wik* notes.

adult male

red chin

yellow belly

velvety black above, broken by white facial stripes, rump, coverts

female

brown head

uniformly barred above

(adult female similar but with yellowish belly, black breast)

Hairy Woodpecker

Picoides villosus

L 9"/23cm   WS 14½"/37cm

Next to Northern Flicker, Hairy Woodpecker is the most widely distributed woodpecker species In North America. Like flickers, Hairy shows much variation in plumage, from dusky populations with flank striping on the Pacific coast, to Rocky Mountain birds with black wing coverts, to southeastern birds with small bills and much white spotting in the coverts. Hairy Woodpecker is a generalist, able to forage and nest in woodlands of all sorts: the northernmost boreal forests, the mountains of Mexico, and almost into the subtropics of Florida. Occasional juveniles showing yellow in the crown could be confused with American Three-toed Woodpecker. **VOICE** A high-pitched, sharp *pik!*, usually louder and much more incisive than Downy Woodpecker; fuss mostly on one pitch.

adult male, eastern

red nape spot

outer rectrices lack barring (most populations)

much larger bill than Downy Woodpecker

adult female, eastern

heavy bill

white below

in both sexes, small black "spur" of plumage at side of breast (absent in Downy)

white-spotted upperwing coverts

juvenile, Interior West

speckled below

lacks white spotting in upperwing coverts (also in adults)

Downy Woodpecker

Picoides pubescens
L 6½"/17cm **WS** 11½"/29cm

Downy Woodpecker is the smallest American woodpecker found north of Mexico. Like Hairy Woodpecker, it shows much geographic variation and occurs in virtually any wooded environment. At only half the weight of Hairy, however, Downy can forage on dry cornstalks and tall weeds. Downy also fares better in suburban settings. Voice is distinctive between the two species. **VOICE** A quick *pikk*, less explosive than Hairy; fuss a high-pitched whinny, often descending. Drum is typically more rapid than Hairy.

adult male

lacks dark "spur" of plumage at side of breast (compare Hairy)

red nape spot

outer rectrices often show black spots

nape lacks red spot

tiny bill, smaller than Hairy

adult female

(Pacific coastal birds sootier below; most western taxa lack white in coverts)

Red-cockaded Woodpecker

Picoides borealis
L 8½"/22cm **WS** 14"/36cm

This endangered woodpecker is endemic to open pine woodlands of the Southeast. Family groups maintain large territories and are uniquely organized, much like a wolf pack, with an alpha pair and several related nest helpers. The species' decline is a result of habitat loss and degradation, fire suppression, and the removal of diseased trees in which they nest. **VOICE** A distinctive, rapid but quiet *krrerr;* fusses starlinglike; some calls high-pitched, similar to Brown-headed Nuthatch.

adult male

red nape spot hard to see

black-bordered white cheek unique

like male but lacks red nape spot

adult female

Black-backed Woodpecker

Picoides arcticus
L 9½"/24cm   **WS** 16"/41cm

Black-backed Woodpecker is a bird of remote boreal and montane spruce-fir forests. It favors recently burned areas of forests and often establishes territories for 6 or more years as the forest regenerates before moving on. This species forages for beetle larvae by flaking off large areas of bark; stripped patches on dead or dying trees are a clue to its presence. **VOICE** A flat *kuk* and a robust, sharp, dry *pink* or *kyeep;* also a harsh, grating fuss.

adult male

yellow crown

violet-blue gloss above

lacks supercilium in all plumages

only black-backed woodpecker with barred remiges

adult female

like male but lacks yellow crown

both sexes show violet-blue gloss above in good light

American Three-toed Woodpecker

Picoides dorsalis
L 8½"/22cm   **WS** 14½"/37cm

This woodpecker inhabits spruce, aspen, and lodgepole pine forests, particularly where there are burned and beetle-infested trees. It forages by flaking off bark. Three-toed shows more geographic variation than Black-backed Woodpecker, mostly in the extent of white in the head and back. Like other year-round residents of boreal forests, it is approachable and is rarely observed out of range. **VOICE** A short, nasal *keemp* or *climp* and a descending, fussy trill.

adult male

3 rather than 4 toes (like Black-backed)

yellow crown

like a small Black-backed but with whitish or barred (not black) back and white supercilium

adult female

crown has white stippling (lacks yellow of male)

(males in the Rockies have almost entirely white back)

Nuttall's Woodpecker
Picoides nuttallii
L 7½"/19cm **WS** 13"/33cm

This small woodpecker is restricted to chaparral with scattered trees, pine-oak and oak woods, and riparian areas of California; it also breeds sparingly in the northwestern corner of Baja California. Nuttall's forages on insects and also fruit and mast. Hybrids with the smaller Downy and Ladder-backed Woodpeckers have been recorded, but Nuttall's is usually territorial against these species. It is not migratory but occasionally disperses up into mountains after the nesting season. **VOICE** A sharp *keep!* or *kideep!* (sometimes 3-noted) and a high, rapid, kingfisher-like rattle.

adult male

red only in hindcrown (compare Ladder-backed)

dark cheek framed in white (unlike Downy or Hairy Woodpeckers)

white spot at base of bill

head pattern like male (but without red)

adult female

Ladder-backed Woodpecker
Picoides scalaris
L 7"/18cm **WS** 13"/33cm

The widespread, adaptable Ladder-backed Woodpecker is associated with lowland pinyon-juniper woods, pine forests, riparian cottonwoods, and deserts of the Southwest. Like other small woodpeckers it often forages by gleaning prey from crevices in bark rather than excavating pits or peeling bark; it also eats cactus fruit, as do Gilded Flicker and Gila Woodpecker. **VOICE** A short, sharp *pik* or *chip,* similar to Downy Woodpecker but lower and richer.

adult male

differs from Nuttall's Woodpecker by more red on crown, whiter face, more spotting on upper back

dusky buff spot at base of bill

outer rectrices more barred than Nuttall's

adult female

Northern Flicker

Colaptes auratus
L 12"/30cm **WS** 20"/51cm

Northern Flicker is a large terrestrial woodpecker found throughout North America, provided there are trees near patches of open ground for foraging on ants, its main food item. The eastern subspecies, Yellow-shafted Flicker (nominate), shows bright saffron-colored remiges and coverts in the underwings, while the western subspecies, Red-shafted *(cafer)*, has rose-salmon tints on the underwings. Like the 3 related sapsucker species, these forms interbreed where their ranges meet, but the zone of intergradation (interbreeding among subspecies) appears to be stable rather than spreading. Though large, flickers are sometimes evicted from their nest sites by small mammals and birds; they have in turn been recorded nesting in old burrows of kingfishers and Bank Swallows. **VOICE** A loud, sustained series of *wik* or *week* notes; also an incisive *queeah!* or *cleeah!*

adult male,
Yellow-
shafted
(nominate)

tan-brown
face and
throat

black
malar
mark

yellow
underwings

white rump
(prominent
in flight)

adult female,
Yellow-shafted
(nominate)

brown face
and throat

like male
but lacks
black malar
mark

adult female,
Red-shafted
(cafer)

like male
but lacks
red malar
mark

adult male,
Red-shafted
(cafer)

mostly
gray head

red malar
mark

reddish
underwings

Gilded Flicker
Colaptes chrysoides
L 11"/28cm **WS** 18"/46cm

Once considered a subspecies of Northern Flicker, the smaller Gilded Flicker is restricted to deserts of northwestern Mexico and southern Arizona, with a small, disjunct population on the California–Nevada border. It resembles Red-shafted Flicker (the western subspecies of Northern Flicker); hybrids with Red-shafted are known but are very uncommon, probably because Red-shafteds do not breed in deserts but in pine-oak woodlands. **VOICE** Like Northern Flicker but higher-pitched.

adult male

differs from Red-shafted Flicker in bright yellow underwings, warm cinnamon crown, oblong spots on lower belly and flanks, and more black on rectrices when viewed from below

adult female

upperparts have narrower bars than Red-shafted; both sexes have paler back

Pileated Woodpecker
Dryocopus pileatus
L 17"/43cm **WS** 29"/74cm

The boldly patterned Pileated Woodpecker inhabits mature forests and suburban areas with adequate supplies of dead trees. It is a versatile forager, hammering into heartwood for beetle larvae, digging up ants, and gorging on berries. Females (see additional photo on p. 273) resemble males but have a dusky forecrown, shorter red crest, and black malar mark. **VOICE** A ringing series of descending, accelerating *dah* notes, with laughing quality; also repeated *wok* calls and nasal yelps around nest.

adult male

very large

bold face pattern

crested

(female has black, not red, mark on malar)

(white underwings and primary bases visible in flight)

adult female

mostly black remiges (unlike Ivory-billed) contrast with white underwing coverts

Swifts and Swallows

Swifts (family Apodidae) are mostly dark, highly aerial birds with slender bodies, long wings, short, stiff tails, and small bills. They have very small legs and feet suited to clinging rather than perching. Swifts forage much like swallows, but their closest relatives are hummingbirds; both groups are placed in the order Apodiformes (from the Greek word *apodos,* meaning "without feet").

Like many other swallow species, Barn Swallow adults often feed their young in brief hovering flight, without perching, particularly after the young leave the nest.

Few birds are as suited as swifts to a life in the open air. They rarely rest during the day—stopping mainly at the nest to feed their young—and spend most of their time high in the air, foraging at rapid speeds for aerial insects and floating spiders. Their ability to flap their wings independently of one another increases their aerial agility, already considerable owing to their long, slim wings, which provide both lift and maneuverability. Swifts inhabit most environments except open desert and tundra. Their paired courtship flights, always accompanied by twittering calls (and sometimes by midair copulation), are familiar signs of spring. They nest mostly in hidden recesses (chimneys in the case of Chimney Swift, caves and crevices behind waterfalls for Black Swift). Nests of the smallest species are half-cups of twigs cemented together and affixed to a vertical surface with saliva; Black Swift makes a horizontal nest of moss and lichen. All North American swifts migrate southward in autumn, and most winter in the tropics.

Swallows (family Hirundinidae), unlike swifts, are passerines (perching birds), and they are regularly seen resting on utility wires, fences, and clotheslines, something that swifts cannot do because of their tiny feet. Swallows are more robust of body and wing than swifts, with larger bills and feet (though both are still relatively small); they also have more colorful plumages, often electric blue, green, or purple above and sometimes with rufous accents. Except for the sexually dimorphic Purple Martin, males and females are similar, though females are often noticeably less colorful. Like swifts, swallows forage by chasing aerial insects on the wing, but their flight appears less erratic. While most forage at lower altitudes than swifts, several swallow species are known to forage very high in the atmosphere. Swallows are often found in open terrain near water; like swifts, they often sip water or even bathe while flying, skimming and splashing low over a lake or river. They nest in recesses, from old woodpecker cavities and nest boxes, to cavities in riverbanks, to spaces in old wharves and farm buildings. Many species nest in colonies: Cave and Cliff Swallows, which form large colonies, attach vertical mud nests to the walls of old barns and caves and, more recently, to the undersides of bridges and overpasses. Purple Martin readily uses martin houses and hollow gourds set out for them. Most North American swallows are long-distance Neotropical migrants.

Populations of swifts all seem to be in gradual decline. It is almost certain that air pollution, habitat loss, and pesticide applications have taken heavy tolls on these and many other insectivorous birds. Swallow populations in North America appear to be stable or even, in the case of Cave Swallow, increasing.

Aerial Birds from Below

Bound to the ground, birders often find themselves looking up at those remarkable aerialists, swifts and swallows. During their migrations, many species mix together in large flocks, and identification of single birds may rest on quick impressions of shape and plumage pattern.

Swifts

Most swifts observed in a given region are of the expected species—Chimney Swift in the East, and the rather dissimilarly shaped Vaux's, White-throated, and Black Swifts in the West. The two *Chaetura* swifts, Chimney and Vaux's, occasionally stray out of range. Vaux's Swift appears more stubby-tailed and -winged in a mixed flock with Chimney Swift and tends not to show Chimney's apparent bulge in the outer remiges (a feature best observed on birds with wings fully extended). Most Vaux's have paler, ashier throats and contrastingly ashy rumps.

Swallows

Adult swallows are often vividly colored and easy to identify, but many juvenile swallows are mousy brown above and lack the distinctive iridescent colors of adults. Adult Barn Swallow is easily identified by its deeply forked tail. Juvenile Barn, however, has a much shallower fork and variable rufous on the throat and can be confused with Cave and Cliff Swallows. Barn Swallow has long, narrow wings that come to a neat point; Cave and Cliff have wider, more blunt-tipped or rounded wings and square tails.

When in flight, the four brown-backed swallows—Bank, Northern Rough-winged, and juvenile Tree and Violet-green Swallows—show quite distinctive shapes. Tree Swallow is the largest of the four and has wide, full wings. Violet-green Swallow, by comparison, looks more slender in both body and wings, and its wings appear proportionately longer. The white sides of the rump are much more extensive on Violet-green Swallow and only narrowly divided down the middle of the rump (in both adult and young birds).

Tree Swallow in juvenal plumage often shows a dusky, indistinct breastband that is sometimes broken in the middle; this can lead to confusion with Bank Swallow—a smaller and daintier species with narrow wings, a rather long tail, and a much more distinct breastband that sometimes has a distinct cusp at the midpoint.

Northern Rough-winged Swallow may seem drab and thus difficult to identify, but in North America it is the only brown-backed swallow in which the breast, throat, and face are washed with brown (buffier in young birds). Its proportions are more like those of Tree Swallow—somewhat broad-winged and short-tailed—but there is no contrast between the throat and head in any plumage. Beware the much larger juvenile Purple Martin, in which the throat is washed with gray.

Tree Swallow, juvenile

Purple Martin, juvenile

Northern Rough-winged Swallow

Bank Swallow

Violet-green Swallow, juvenile

White-throated Swift

Aeronautes saxatalis
L 6½"/17cm   **WS** 15"/38cm

The summer stillness of western canyonlands is often broken by the faint, pleasant screeching of White-throated Swifts as they pass overhead at whiplash speeds, foraging for insects. The only other swifts in North America with patches of white in the plumage are the larger White-collared Swift, which has turned up as far north as Michigan, and White-throated Needletail and Fork-tailed Swift, Asian vagrants to Bering Sea islands. **VOICE** A high-pitched, syncopated, grating chatter.

adult — white throat, breast, edges of secondaries

adult — long, narrow wings; white patches on sides of rump

adult — often looks white-headed from below

Black Swift

Cypseloides niger
L 7¼"/18cm   **WS** 18"/46cm

Black Swift nests in small colonies behind waterfalls and on oceanside and montane cliffs. It has not been recorded in North America after early autumn and is thought to winter in northern South America. This species is noticeably larger and darker than the more slender-winged White-throated Swift, and its wingbeats appear more languid. Common Swift, a rare vagrant from Eurasia, is also mostly dark but has a more deeply forked tail. **VOICE** Call consists of sweet, rich but quick *chip* notes, often in series.

adult — (underparts may show faint, narrow, pale mottling at close range, more so in juveniles)

(pale frontlet)

tail may show shallow fork when closed but not when fanned

often nests behind waterfalls

adult — distinctive shape, with huskier wings and tail than other species

flight less erratic than that of smaller swifts

wider forked tail (hard to see) than White-throated Swift

Chimney Swift
Chaetura pelagica
L 5¼"/13cm WS 14"/36cm

Chimney Swift, the East's only swift, heralds spring in April, arriving in small, chattering, courting flocks. It cements a sloppy-looking stick nest to the side of a chimney or in the cavity of a hollow tree in the woods. In autumn this species gathers at traditional locations into larger and larger flocks, sometimes numbering in the thousands, before migrating southward to wintering grounds in the Amazon basin. **VOICE** A rollicking, exuberant chatter of staccato *chip* notes, usually descending.

adult

throat can be pale cream or dark

medium brown overall, with rump color close to back color

adult

(upperparts show little contrast between back and rump, unlike Vaux's)

typically darker below than Vaux's

wings appear longer and broader than Vaux's, usually with bulge in trailing edge

from below, secondaries look dark (often appear translucent in Vaux's)

Vaux's Swift
Chaetura vauxi
L 4¾"/12cm WS 12"/30cm

Vaux's Swift is scarce and declining, due to extensive logging of old-growth forests, which has left few large, hollow trees for nesting (Vaux's nests only rarely in chimneys). Most are observed singly or in small groups over fir or redwood forests or nearby rivers and lakes. Small numbers may spend the winter in cities near the Gulf of Mexico, but most winter between central Mexico and Venezuela. **VOICE** Call notes similar to Chimney Swift but higher; courting bird gives a chatter-call, stuttering at first, then a rapid trill.

adult

shorter wings and tail than Chimney Swift

usually paler throat than Chimney

trailing edge of wings lacks bulge of Chimney

adult

wingtips often look blunter than in Chimney

often appears paler below than Chimney

Purple Martin
Progne subis
L 8"/20cm   **WS** 18"/46cm

In the East, Purple Martin arrives at its nesting sites as early as January in Florida and by April elsewhere. The eastern (nominate) subspecies nests readily in condominium-style "martin houses"; western *arboricola* uses natural tree cavities and *hesperia,* of southern Arizona, saguaro cavities. In preparation for fall migration, martins gather at staging areas by the thousands. **VOICE** Female at nest gives a bluebirdlike warbling; male a low, liquid, rolling chirping. Calls include a low, harsh *deer-droit,* a sharp *churr,* and rolling twitters.

adult male

resplendent deep purple overall

long, sleek body, large head

adult male

broad, pointed wings almost falconlike

breeding adult female (nominate)

purple crown, back, coverts

charcoal gray around head and breast

breeding adult female (arboricola)

like eastern subspecies but throat, collar, forehead pale

Barn Swallow
Hirundo rustica
L 6¾"/17cm   **WS** 15"/38cm

The adaptable Barn Swallow nests in eaves or ledges of just about any structure, including barns, bridges, docks, and outhouses. A relatively tame bird, it usually returns to the same area each spring. It is a scarce breeder in extreme environments of the Arctic, Southeast, and Southwest and also avoids well-forested areas. Barn Swallow has occasionally nested on its "wintering" grounds in Argentina. **VOICE** Song a squeaky set of phrases, punctuated by drier rattles. Calls a sharp *evit* and a rolling chatter.

adult

deep blue above, pale orange below, with rufous frontlet and throat; some have whitish belly

paler juvenile

white be pale ora throat

adult

long, tapered, pointed wings

darker juvenile

very dusky orange below

long, forked tail has white band

Cave Swallow

Petrochelidon fulva
L 5½"/14cm WS 13½"/34cm

Formerly limited to a few caves and sinkholes in Texas and New Mexico, Cave Swallow began nesting under bridges and overpasses and expanding its range in the 1960s; it is now common over open country in much of Texas. Its nest is a simple cup of mud. In November fast-moving storms may bring scores of Caves to the Great Lakes and East Coast. Nesting birds in Florida are of the nominate race, which has tawnier sides than the southwestern *pelodoma*. **VOICE** Song a remarkably varied concatenation of whistles, squeaks, and purring rattles. Calls include a sweet, high *jeev, tchew,* and *tyew* and drier, finchlike *tjvt* and *swit.*

adult (nominate)

stark contrast between pale orange throat and dark crown

rufous-orange rump (like Cliff Swallow)

adult *(pelodoma)*

dark cap, orange-buff forehead and throat (compare Cliff)

mostly grayish sides

Cliff Swallow

Petrochelidon pyrrhonota
L 5½"/14cm   WS 13½"/34cm

Cliff Swallow is scarce and local in the East, more numerous in the West. This adaptable species uses human alteration of the landscape to its advantage: instead of nesting just on cliffs, a scarce habitat in most areas, it uses barns, bridges, eaves, and old buildings. Single colonies can be huge, holding as many as 3,500 nests. The clearing of eastern forests has probably allowed Cliff Swallow to expand into new open habitats. **VOICE** Song a long series of dry, squeaky sounds and mechanical rattles. Call a low, rough, nasal *rrrrt.*

breeding adults

southwestern subspecies has rufous or rusty forehead, like bird on right (or darker)

dusky throat (compare Cave Swallow)

mud nests are igloo-shaped

adults

adult

white forehead (never in Cave)

bluish back stippled with white

buff-orange rump

flocks often seen gathering mud to make nests

Northern Rough-winged Swallow

Stelgidopteryx serripennis
L 5½"/14cm WS 14"/36cm

This swallow excavates nest burrows in vertical cliffs, banks, dry streambeds, and bluffs with loose, sandy substrates; it has also adapted to manmade structures such as disused drainpipes and openings in bridges, as long as these are set in vertical faces. The species' name derives from the rough edge of the outer web of the outermost primary, a feature difficult to see in the field. **VOICE** Song an irregular series of call notes. Call a low, gravelly *zschp*.

breeding adult

both underparts and head lack sharply contrasting patterns

adult

broad wings; pale bases of remiges; unpatterned head

juvenile and adult

juvenile shows variably rusty upperwing coverts

adult and juvenile brown above, with dusky throat and breast

Bank Swallow

Riparia riparia
L 5¼"/13cm WS 13"/33cm

Bank Swallow nests in colonies, excavating deep burrows in sandy banks, gravel quarries, and road-cuts, usually near water; colonies may have hundreds of tightly spaced burrows. This is perhaps the only North American swallow that does not normally nest on manmade structures. Because of its specific habitat requirements, it is relatively scarce and localized across much of its breeding range. **VOICE** Similar to Northern Rough-winged Swallow but higher-pitched, a buzzy *dzzrt* or *bzzzt*.

breeding adult

small (easy to pick out in mixed swallow flocks)

white throat set off by brown nape, auriculars, breastband

breeding adult

gray-brown back contrasts with darker wings

juvenile

narrow white edge on secondaries, auriculars, forehead

(rump often appears buffy)

Tree Swallow

Tachycineta bicolor
L 5¾"/15cm WS 14½"/37cm

The widespread Tree Swallow nests in both natural cavities and nest boxes. Unlike strictly insectivorous swallows, it eats berries in fall and winter, and flocks of thousands may be seen stripping bayberry bushes of fruit. Most females in their first spring have more brown than green on the upperparts. The similar Bahama Swallow, with a longer, forked tail, has rarely strayed to Florida. **VOICE** Song a short set of sweet whistles ending in low, liquid gurgles. Calls include song components and a low, buzzy *tzzzt*.

breeding adult male

iridescent green-blue back in direct light

dark face and nape contrast with white throat and underparts

adult
dark face, unlike Violet-green

juvenile

nape often pale

sides of rump show little or no white

sooty gray-brown above

dusky, ill-defined breastband

(some first-year females similar)

Violet-green Swallow

Tachycineta thalassina
L 5½"/14cm   WS 13½"/34cm

Violet-green Swallow is a delicate western species that nests in tree cavities, cliff crevices, and nest boxes from Mexican highlands to Alaskan muskegs. It forages high in the air and often high in the mountains, sometimes with swifts. On migration, large flocks often assemble near water bodies. A few winter in California; migrants return to southern nesting areas by late February. **VOICE** Song lacks liquid quality of Tree Swallow. Call a mechanical *tz-tzzzt*, often repeated in a rapid staccato, like sounds from a powerline.

breeding adult male

felt green above

white on face extends above eyes, but lores dark

white at sides of rump visible at a distance

smaller than Tree Swallow

adult male

looks shorter-tailed and longer-winged than Tree in flight

adult female

violet rump

lacks distinct mask of Tree Swallow, more pale plumage in face

(some like adult male)

Hummingbirds

Hummingbirds (family Trochilidae) are extraordinary creatures: they are the smallest of birds, with the smallest of eggs; they are the only birds able to fly backward, and their wings beat faster than any other bird—up to 30 beats per second. All hummingbirds have slender bodies, wings, and bills and very small feet adapted only for perching; however, they are classed not with the passerines (perching birds) but with their distant relatives the swifts in the order Apodiformes.

Male Ruby-throated Hummingbirds often drive females from flowers and feeders.

Male hummingbirds have throat patches (gorgets) of iridescent colors to which ornithologists have given vivid labels—ruby, amethyst, and sapphire. These colors are generated by complex feather structures that reflect certain wavelengths of light but not others. Males use their jewel-like gorgets, and in some species crowns, in courtship displays and territorial clashes; adult females and young males lack full gorgets and are usually more subtly plumaged than adult males.

Hummingbirds forage on flower nectar, using their long, grooved tongues to wick the fluid directly to the throat. Many species are attracted to red flowers that are tubular in structure; manufactured hummingbird feeders that imitate this shape and color attract one or more species almost instantly, whether set out in desert washes or alpine meadows. As a hummingbird sips nectar, it often collects the flower's pollen on its head; cross-pollination occurs as the bird moves from flower to flower. In addition to nectar, hummingbirds eat a great variety of insects and other invertebrates, some spotted from a perch and caught on the wing, others gleaned from foliage, still others picked from the ground or from emerging swarms. Some hummingbirds take tiny insects trapped in sap wells made by sapsuckers.

Male hummingbirds perform dazzling courtship displays: they make steep dives from high in the air, often following up with an aerial dance of side-to-side flying or other acrobatics and much calling and flashing of the gorget. Hummingbird males are promiscuous, mating with as many females as possible within their territory (and even outside it). The males leave the females to construct the nest and raise the young alone.

Many hummingbird species are strongly migratory. Ruby-throated Hummingbird, which breeds as far north as Canada, migrates across the Gulf of Mexico to the Yucatán Peninsula; Rufous Hummingbirds from Alaska may travel as far as the mountains of Mexico. Other species wander widely; at least seven have made their way from the tropics into the United States. In some cases, western species have begun to spend the winter season in the Southeast instead of tropical areas, apparently attracted by feeding stations.

Despite their extraordinary popularity, hummingbirds are some of the least understood of North America's birds from the standpoint of conservation. A few range-restricted species, such as Allen's and Buff-bellied Hummingbirds, are apparently declining because of habitat loss. The population sizes and dynamics of most other species are either unstudied or very poorly known.

Identification of Hummingbirds

More and more hummingbirds are observed far from their typical ranges. There are now records of 16 different species east of the Mississippi, where for generations the only hummingbird likely to be seen was Ruby-throated (with a few Rufous Hummingbirds turning up in fall and winter). This change in the distribution of these birds means that many more people are faced with the complexities of hummingbird identification. The mostly green-backed females and immature birds are far more difficult to identify than adult males, and some, such as female and immature Allen's and Rufous Hummingbirds, cannot be reliably identified in the field.

Black-chinned Hummingbird *(Archilochus)*

Ruby-throated Hummingbird *(Archilochus)*

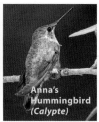

Anna's Hummingbird *(Calypte)*

Costa's Hummingbird *(Calypte)*

Archilochus and *Calypte*

Anna's and Costa's Hummingbirds *(Calypte)* are easily confused with Black-chinned and Ruby-throated *(Archilochus)*. Both Ruby-throated and Black-chinned are smaller and much less robust than Anna's, with slender bodies and necks, when alert, and smaller heads. They are closer to Costa's in proportion but have longer tails that project just beyond the wingtips at rest (wingtips cover the tail tip in Costa's).

Ruby-throated and Black-chinned females and juveniles are very similar. Black-chinned looks more bronzy above and lacks the emerald green shown in Ruby-throated's back and crown. Ruby-throated shows a sharper contrast between the white throat and the crown and

auriculars. The outermost primaries are pointed in female Ruby-throated, more bulbous and curved in Black-chinned. Black-chinned females often have very long bills.

Anna's and Costa's Hummingbirds rarely stray to the East; but westerners often struggle to distinguish silent females and juveniles (Anna's loud call note is distinctive). Costa's is somewhat smaller than Anna's, with a longer, often decurved bill; its shorter tail does not project beyond the wingtips at rest. Costa's has pale, mostly unmarked underparts; Anna's has greenish dusky mottling on the flanks and dusky stippling on the lower throat. Costa's looks pale-faced; Anna's is more dusky and mottled in the face.

Calliope Hummingbird *(Stellula)*

Broad-tailed Hummingbird *(Selasphorus)*

Stellula and *Selasphorus*

Female Calliope and Broad-tailed Hummingbirds *(Stellula* and *Selasphorus*, respectively) are both regularly mistaken for Allen's or Rufous Hummingbirds (also *Selasphorus*), which are often more strongly marked below and show much more extensive rufous in the rectrix bases. Calliope is tiny and short-billed, and its short tail is completely covered by the wings at rest—unlike any of the three *Selasphorus*. A flying Calliope looks compact, even stubby in flight, with its short tail and bill and "pot-bellied" appearance. Broad-tailed Hummingbird is larger than Rufous and Allen's, and its much fuller, broader tail is apparent with close, comparative study. Like Calliope, female and young male Broad-tailed Hummingbirds often show a neatly speckled throat (a "five o'clock shadow").

Ruby-throated Hummingbird

Archilochus colubris
L 3¾"/10cm **WS** 4½"/11cm

Ruby-throated Hummingbird is the only breeding hummingbird in eastern North America. It frequents semiopen habitats south of the boreal forest where flowers are plentiful, including suburbs, parks, and open areas within forests. "Hummer gardens" and feeding stations have made this species a regular patron of backyards and have led to the discovery of a dozen additional hummingbird species in the East, usually seen as single vagrants. **VOICE** Call a short *tew, tzip,* or *t-tip.*

adult male

outer primaries have much narrower tips than Black-chinned

ruby red gorget, black chin (rosy or whitish chin in Broad-tailed)

entirely dark, forked tail

immature male

attains red throat gradually in first year; tail pattern like female

adult female

more vivid emerald green above than Black-chinned, with more contrasting head pattern

Black-chinned Hummingbird

Archilochus alexandri
L 3¾"/10cm **WS** 4¾"/12cm

Black-chinned Hummingbird is a common visitor to backyard gardens and feeders. It nests in more arid country than Ruby-throated Hummingbird, including desert washes and chaparral, as well as in more moist environments like orchards, shaded canyons, and riparian woods. Black-chinned migrates to Mexico in winter, but a few linger at feeders around the Gulf of Mexico and in the Southeast, a recent pattern of occurrence. **VOICE** Similar to Ruby-throated but a bit lower.

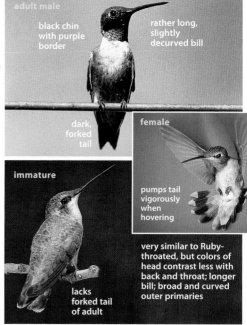

adult male

black chin with purple border

rather long, slightly decurved bill

dark, forked tail

female

pumps tail vigorously when hovering

immature

lacks forked tail of adult

very similar to Ruby-throated, but colors of head contrast less with back and throat; longer bill; broad and curved outer primaries

Costa's Hummingbird

Calypte costae
L 3½"/9cm   **WS** 4¾"/12cm

While some desert species nest during the
nourishing monsoon rains of July, Costa's
nests in the cooler months of February
and March, provided flowers and insects
are plentiful; it and the related Anna's
may be the only hummingbirds seen
in the deserts at this season. In coastal
California, Costa's nests later, in March and
April. Most migrate toward coastal areas,
but a few remain year-round in flower-
rich areas of Arizona. **VOICE** Call a rich,
ringing, sparrowlike *tsit*.

adult male

rich purple
crown, extensive
purple gorget

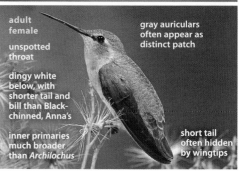

adult
female

unspotted
throat

dingy white
below, with
shorter tail and
bill than Black-
chinned, Anna's

inner primaries
much broader
than *Archilochus*

gray auriculars
often appear as
distinct patch

short tail
often hidden
by wingtips

Anna's Hummingbird

Calypte anna
L 4"/10cm   **WS** 5¼"/13cm

This familiar garden hummer is present
in virtually every lowland and foothill
habitat west of the Sierra Nevada and
Cascades and is also found in southern
Arizona, where it is expanding eastward. It
is a permanent resident through most of
its range, with modest movements toward
the coasts and mountain meadows in the
heat of summer. In winter males court
females with daredevil dives from high
in the air and pendulum-like swaying in
midair. **VOICE** Call a high, short *tsit!*

adult male

extensively
green and gray
underparts

stunning
strawberry
red gorget
and crown

subadult
male

red crown
feathers
appear
within 1
year

compact
shape

tail projects
past wingtips

adult female

shorter bill
than Costa's

a few red feathers
in center of throat

dusky belly, mottled
sides (unlike Costa's)

Rufous Hummingbird

Selasphorus rufus
L 3¾"/10cm   WS 4½"/11cm

Rufous Hummingbird nests in semiopen habitats where woodlands open onto verdant, flower-rich meadows, often near streams. It defends territories against other hummingbirds with inexhaustible energy, driving them out in long chase-flights. The species is best observed at gardens and feeders, where it also dominates. Southward migration begins in late June; many winter in the Southeast, and vagrants are widely reported. **VOICE** Call a sharp, rich *tchup*, relatively low and resonant.

adult male

strongly rufous-orange above and on flanks

dark red gorget

very similar to male Allen's Hummingbird, but usually lacks green tones in back

adult female

almost identical to Allen's; safely distinguished by measurements of outer tail feathers (broader in Rufous)

rectrices next to central pair show narrow tips

(first-year birds similar)

Allen's Hummingbird

Selasphorus sasin
L 3¾"/10cm   WS 4¼"/11cm

Allen's Hummingbird breeds along the Pacific coast, largely in California, where it is common in suburban gardens, riparian woods near meadows, and canyons. Postbreeding migration to Mexico begins in May; birds may return as early as January. The subspecies *sedentarius* on California's Channel Islands and the adjacent mainland is nonmigratory but expanding its range. In courtship, Allen's makes a J-shaped dive, like Rufous, but the display is not repeated and begins with a rocking flight. **VOICE** Calls very similar to Rufous.

adult male

very similar to Rufous but with green upper back (rarely seen in Rufous)

immature

rectrices next to central pair lack narrow tips

adult female

white breast sharply set off by mottled throat with red spots

orange-buff wash on flanks and often in supercilium

almost identical to Rufous

Broad-tailed Hummingbird

Selasphorus platycercus
L 4"/10cm **WS** 5¼"/13cm

The sturdy Broad-tailed Hummingbird favors high-elevation semiopen forests and edges, especially near open fields with abundant flowers. It is often detected by the male's wing noise—a loud, zinging trill that some compare to certain waxwing calls. In August large numbers of migrants may gather in meadows with Rufous Hummingbirds, and the competition for nectar can be impressive. Some migrants stray eastward to winter in Gulf states. **VOICE** Call a high, staccato *tchip*.

adult male

recalls Ruby-throated Hummingbird but larger, with long, broad tail, buff and green sides

female

immature male

white eye ring

throat neatly dotted with green (a "five-o'clock shadow")

rufous in rectrix bases limited to outer feathers

long, broad tail conspicuous; projects well beyond wingtips at rest

Calliope Hummingbird

Stellula calliope
L 3¼"/8cm **WS** 4¼"/11cm

The tiny Calliope Hummingbird is easy to mistake for a large insect as it makes its low, slow movements from flower to flower. Like Broad-tailed Hummingbird, Calliope breeds in montane habitats, usually between 4,000' (1,200m) and the tree line, where nighttime temperatures may drop below freezing even in summer. Southward migration begins in July; migrants can be plentiful in the Rockies and at feeders in lowlands. Calliope is similar to *Selasphorus* but shows little or no rufous in the tail. **VOICE** Call a high, soft *tsip*.

adult male

short, rather straight bill

wine red streaks in gorget bordered by white

adult male

adult female

dark spot in front of eyes, white lores

wingtips extend past tail tip (unlike *Selasphorus*)

sides have buff wash

very short tail

Broad-billed Hummingbird

Cynanthus latirostris
L 4"/10cm **WS** 5¾"/15cm

Broad-billed Hummingbird reaches the northern limit of its breeding range in riparian canyons and foothills of southeastern Arizona and southwestern New Mexico; it is relatively common up to about 5,000' (1,500m) in varied habitats, from mesquite lowlands through higher-elevation stands of oaks, sycamores, and cottonwoods. Breeding birds are observed mostly from March to September; a few winter in the U.S. **VOICE** Call a rattling *tsi-tit,* similar to Ruby-crowned Kinglet.

adult male

red, dark-tipped bill

vivid green, with blue throat and cheek

subadult male

limited red in bill

adult female

strong supercilium; narrow strip of blue in throat with pale border

reddish mandible

pale supercilium over gray mask

uniformly dusty gray below

blue tail in all plumages

White-eared Hummingbird

Hylocharis leucotis
L 4"/10cm **WS** 5¾"/15cm

This striking species of Mexico's pine-oak forests appears in small numbers in similar habitats in southeastern Arizona, usually at feeding stations in summer and very rarely after September. The adult male's vibrant purple head, set off by a snow white supercilium and green body, is stunning but difficult to see except in ideal light. Females resemble Broad-billed Hummingbird but have a shorter, straighter bill, wider supercilium, and speckled belly. **VOICE** Call a high, strong *tsip* or *tseet,* very unlike Broad-billed.

adult male

deep green body, tail, wing coverts

dark (purplish) head with stark white supercilium

adult female

stronger supercilium than Broad-billed Hummingbird

lightly mottled with pale green below

Violet-crowned Hummingbird

Amazilia violiceps
L 4½"/11cm   WS 6"/15cm

In Arizona and New Mexico, Violet-crowned Hummingbird is a summer resident of sycamore and cottonwood groves near streams, especially where there are flowering plants. Where flowers are scarce, Violet-crowned hunts insects in treetops. Its distinctive violet cap can be difficult to see in shadow. Females build nests almost exclusively in Arizona sycamores. **VOICE** Call a flat *tchak,* often in stuttering series.

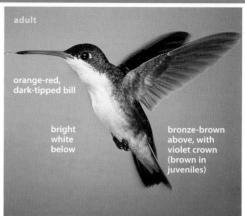

adult

orange-red, dark-tipped bill

bright white below

bronze-brown above, with violet crown (brown in juveniles)

Buff-bellied Hummingbird

Amazilia yucatanensis
L 4¼"/11cm   WS 5½"/14cm

This is the only hummer that nests in gardens, orchards, scrub, and native woodlands of southernmost Texas. Some winter in gardens along the Gulf coast. The related Cinnamon Hummingbird, recorded once in Texas and Arizona, has entirely buffy underparts; the smaller Xantus's Hummingbird has been recorded several times on the Pacific coast. **VOICE** Call a loud, insistent *tsick,* delivered in Morse code–like series.

adult

dark (not rufous) wings

broad-based bill, heavier than Berylline Hummingbird

peach-buff belly, rich rufous tail

Berylline Hummingbird

Amazilia beryllina
L 4¼"/11cm   WS 5½"/14cm

Berylline Hummingbird, a common Mexican species, is a very rare and irregular visitor in small numbers to middle elevations in the mountains of southeastern Arizona, where it has nested a few times. Berylline appears dark in indirect light, and the orangish bill base can be difficult to see, especially in young birds. This species' name is derived from the intense green of the head, similar to that of the gemstone beryl. **VOICE** Call a short, rattling *tddddk.*

immature

green above

(adult's face, throat, breast more solidly green)

rufous in bases of remiges

greenish breast, gray belly

coppery rufous tail

Magnificent Hummingbird

Eugenes fulgens
L 5¼"/13cm WS 7½"/19cm

Magnificent Hummingbird roams widely through shadowy pine-oak montane forests in search of flowers. This species is not quite as heavy as Blue-throated Hummingbird, but it lives up to its name in the adult male's magnificent violet crown and neon green gorget. In autumn vagrants have been found at feeders in the Midwest and East. Records from the Great Basin and Rockies, however, are from late summer. **VOICE** Call a *tchip* note, a bit like Blue-throated but flatter, lower, and less squeaky.

adult male

white spot behind eyes

violet crown hard to see

black belly contrasts with green gorget

adult female

longer bill than Blue-throated; lacks bronze rump and strong head markings

Blue-throated Hummingbird

Lampornis clemenciae
L 5"/13cm WS 8"/20cm

This is the largest North American hummer, found in moist wooded canyons with flowers. It is usually detected by the male's distinctive call note. Blue-throated chases other species from flower patches, flashing and fanning its large, white-tipped tail as it darts about. Plain-capped Starthroat, a Mexican vagrant to southern Arizona mountains, is similar in size, but males show a ruby throat and white flanks. **VOICE** A distinctive high, sharp, squeaky *tseep!* or *tseek!*

long supercilium

blue throat (hard to see) with partial white border

adult male

long, broad tail with extensive white tips to outer rectrices

adult female

prominent supercilium

shorter bill than Magnificent Hummingbird and Plain-capped Starthroat

bronze cast to rump

Green Violet-ear

Colibri thalassinus
L 4¾"/12cm **WS** 7"/18cm

A vagrant from Mexico, Green Violet-ear is the only mostly green hummingbird with a decurved bill likely to show up at hummingbird feeders. This species has reached many midwestern and eastern states and even Alberta, mostly in summer. The reasons for this sharp increase in extralimital records are not known. The much rarer Green-breasted Mango, recorded in Texas and North Carolina, has violet in the tail, and young birds and females have white streaks from throat to belly. **VOICE** Call a dry *tchap*.

adult

green throat and crown set off blue auriculars and breast patch

adult/subadult

banded, bluish tail and violet-blue auriculars and breast patch in both young birds and adults

young birds often have paler undertail coverts

Lucifer Hummingbird

Calothorax lucifer
L 3½"/9cm **WS** 4"/10cm

This hummingbird nests as far north as Big Bend National Park, Texas, where it forages along lower slopes on agave, paintbrush, and penstemon flowers. Postbreeding birds have also turned up at backyard hummingbird feeders in Arizona, New Mexico, and western Texas. Breeding is likely but still unconfirmed in southwestern New Mexico. This is the only pale-bellied hummingbird in North America with a strongly decurved bill (many other species show a slightly decurved bill). Unlike other male hummingbirds, Lucifer displays at the nest. **VOICE** Call a flat, sharp *tchip*.

adult male

violet-magenta gorget extends down sides of neck

long, decurved bill

grayish green sides with buff flanks

tail usually appears long and pointed

adult female

long, decurved bill and broad, buffy supercilium

diffuse breastband

Tyrant Flycatchers

Tyrant flycatchers in North America are part of the enormous family Tyrannidae, which contains more than 400 species; 35 species in 10 genera nest in the United States and Canada, from deserts to boreal forests, and another 10 have been seen as vagrants north of Mexico and the Caribbean. Tyrant flycatchers evolved in the New World tropics, and their diversity there is remarkable. Tyrannidae is the only family of suboscine passerines (a tropical American group that includes cotingas, woodcreepers, and antbirds) that extends northward across the Mexican border. Suboscines, unlike oscines (all other North American passerines), do not learn their songs; rather, their songs are innate.

Flycatchers are upright-perching, small- to medium-sized passerines with typically broad-based bills surrounded by rictal bristles. Their rather long, pointed wings are typical of long-distance migrants (temperate-zone nesters generally migrate to the tropics in winter). Most species are brown, gray, or greenish above and a paler whitish or yellowish below, and many have wing bars. Although some tropical species are strikingly patterned, most flycatchers are subtly plumaged and quite similar to each other.

As their name implies, flycatchers take mostly insect prey, primarily flying insects; fruit forms an important part of the diet in migration and on the wintering grounds for some of the larger species. Larger flycatchers and the pewees, including Olive-sided Flycatcher, usually sit on a conspicuous perch and watch for passing insects, which they fly out and capture with the bill in midair, returning to the same perch. Smaller species tend to show less fidelity to one perch. A few species, especially the phoebes and the larger flycatchers, also take prey from the ground, including spiders, small lizards, and even small birds such as hummingbirds.

Most tyrannids sing to attract mates and mark territory; a few, notably the kingbirds and Vermilion Flycatcher, have

Olive-sided Flycatcher with a white-lined sphinx moth.

striking aerial displays as well. Many species have dawn songs that differ from their daytime vocalizations. Temperate-zone flycatchers make cup-shaped nests, placing them in the fork of a tree or along a limb; Yellow-bellied and Cordilleran Flycatchers sometimes nest on or near the ground. *Myiarchus* species nest in cavities, as does Sulphur-bellied Flycatcher. Several other tropical species, notably becards and kiskadees, make larger spherical nests with side entrances.

Populations of tyrant flycatchers have declined in many areas. The most severe declines appear to be among flycatchers of the genus *Contopus,* especially Olive-sided Flycatcher and the wood-pewees. Several *Empidonax* may also be declining, and one, the southwestern subspecies (*extimus*) of Willow Flycatcher, is federally listed as endangered: its limited riparian habitat supports fewer than 500 pairs. The reasons for declining flycatcher populations probably lie in habitat changes across the Americas, including the fragmentation and destruction of forests and overbrowsing of the forest floor by deer. Other threats include pesticide use and the proliferation of Brown-headed Cowbirds, which are brood parasites.

Identification of Tyrant Flycatchers

Certain tyrant flycatchers, such as the gaudily plumaged male Vermilion Flycatcher and the long-tailed Scissor-tailed Flycatcher, are among the most recognizable of North American birds. The more plain-colored flycatchers, however, are often frustratingly difficult to identify. Experienced birders pay careful attention to details of bill shape, primary projection, plumage color, and vocalizations.

Dusky Flycatcher (Empidonax)

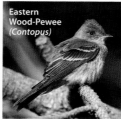
Eastern Wood-Pewee (Contopus)

Eastern Phoebe (Sayornis)

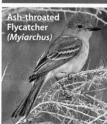
Ash-throated Flycatcher (Myiarchus)

Gray Kingbird (Tyrannus)

Empidonax flycatchers (11 species north of Mexico), known as "empids," are all small birds, 5–6" (13–15cm) in length, that are grayish brown to greenish gray above and paler below and have wing bars and usually eye rings. To identify an empid, take note of its overall plumage colors, primary projection (the distance that the tip of the primaries projects past the tips of the tertials), color and proportions of the bill, shape and tone of the eye ring (if present), and proportions of the body (head and tail). Bills of these species can look remarkably similar; most are short and thin, often with a pale mandible. When observed from below, most eastern empids have broad, spade-shaped bills, as do Pacific-slope and Cordilleran Flycatchers; the western-breeding Dusky, Hammond's, and Gray Flycatchers have narrow bills with a dark tip below.

Contopus flycatchers (4 species, plus 1 vagrant) are slightly larger, measuring about 6–8" (15–20cm). Some *Contopus,* namely the wood-pewees, are easily confused with *Empidonax* flycatchers. Wood-pewees are best distinguished by their relatively long wings, reaching almost halfway down the tail, and long primary projection; they never flick their wings and tail (unlike most empids), and they lack eye rings, which most empids have. The larger, larger-billed *Contopus* species (Olive-sided Flycatcher and

Greater Pewee) are more distinctive; a distant Olive-sided can be mistaken for a kingbird.

Myiarchus flycatchers (4 species, plus 2 vagrants) are larger species, 7–9" (18–23cm) long. All have rufous-edged primaries (and usually rectrices), a yellowish belly, gray tones in the throat and upper breast, and a brown back. Most have bills that are noticeably heavier than those of the small flycatchers, although Dusky-capped Flycatcher has a bill comparable in length to the larger *Contopus.* Identification often requires listening to vocalizations and studying the bird's proportions, pattern of rufous in wings and tail, and other plumage patterns.

Tyrannus flycatchers (9 species, plus 1 vagrant), the kingbirds, are rather heavy-billed, stocky birds that range in size from 8½" (22cm) in Eastern Kingbird to 16" (41cm) in Fork-tailed Flycatcher, including its long tail. Most kingbirds can be correctly identified with careful study. The very similar Tropical and Couch's Kingbirds are best distinguished by vocalizations.

Sayornis flycatchers, the phoebes (3 species), measure about 7" (18cm). These open-country birds have long tails and very plain plumages, lacking eye rings and wing bars. All habitually "dip" or flare the tail, which makes them easy to identify; Gray Flycatcher, an empid, also dips the tail.

Greater Pewee
Contopus pertinax
L 8"/20cm WS 13"/33cm

The sweet song of Greater Pewee, once called Coues' Flycatcher after naturalist Elliot Coues, is heard in deciduous, pine, and mixed montane forests. This bird forages and sings from dead snags in the open and attacks birds (even raptors) and mammals that happen into its territory. It typically forages lower than Olive-sided Flycatcher and higher than Western Wood-Pewee. **VOICE** Song a clear, pure-toned whistle, usually remembered *Ho-SAY ma-REE-AH!;* often begins with *der-dreep* notes. Call a single or multiple *pip.*

adult
large bill has pale orange mandible
dusky gray below

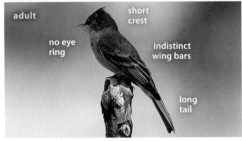

adult
short crest
no eye ring
indistinct wing bars
long tail

Olive-sided Flycatcher
Contopus cooperi
L 7½"/19cm WS 13"/33cm

Olive-sided Flycatcher inhabits boreal forests in the East and open montane and Pacific coastal forests in the West. Like Greater Pewee, it frequents open areas with dead snags for perching, especially burned areas and bogs. Also like Greater Pewee, it is aggressive toward corvids and raptors when nesting and sings a memorable, ringing song. **VOICE** Clear, whistled song immortalized as *Quick! THREEEE BEEERS!;* first note short, then usually long and descending. Call a spirited *pip-pip-pip!,* sometimes a single *pip.*

adult
pale base to mandible
heavier bill than wood-pewees
white throat and center of breast; belly framed by dusky, indistinct streaking

adult
no crest
distinct dark sides to breast
short tail
resembles large wood-pewee or small kingbird

juvenile
dark base to mandible
all ages appear larger, larger-headed, shorter-tailed than wood-pewees

Eastern Wood-Pewee

Contopus virens
L 6¼"/16cm WS 10"/25cm

Eastern and Western Wood-Pewees are essentially indistinguishable in the field and best separated by their songs. Like Greater Pewee and Olive-sided Flycatcher, both forage from a favorite perch; but wood-pewees lack the obvious crest of Greater and starkly contrasting sides of Olive-sided. Their ranges overlap in mid-continent, but hybridization between them has not been reported. **VOICE** Song a rising, whistled *peeeaWEEE*, followed by a downward *PEEoooo*. Calls include a soft *pit* and sweet, rising *purwee*.

adult

more olive
tones above
than Western
Wood-Pewee

mostly pale
mandible

more dusky
below than
Empidonax,
especially
on undertail
coverts

wingtips extend far
past uppertail coverts,
unlike *Empidonax*

adult,
worn

dark head
with partial
eye ring

modest
wing
bars

looks very
sooty in
dim light

juvenile

cinnamon-
buff wing
bars

sides of breast
faintly gray
(compare Olive-
sided Flycatcher)

Western Wood-Pewee

Contopus sordidulus
L 6¼"/16cm WS 10½"/27cm

Wood-pewees breed in deciduous, mixed, and coniferous forests, Western Wood-Pewee more often in coniferous forests. They hunt from exposed perches and build cup-shaped nests (Western's is larger and deeper) on limbs well away from the tree trunk. **VOICE** Song, heard mostly in the very early morning, a high, hasty, rising *t-tew-ti-tip!*, often ending with a harsh, modulated *BEEEurrrrr* and with introductory notes; much less pure-toned than Eastern Wood-Pewee. Calls like Eastern; also a quick *tup* and buzzy *bzew*.

adult, worn

no olive
tones above
(compare
Eastern)

eye ring weak
or absent

adult's bill often
entirely dark but
usually pale at
base of mandible

wood-pewees do
not wag or dip tail,
unlike phoebes
and empids

juvenile

averages sootier
on central breast
than Eastern,
with less white
on throat

some show
underside pattern
similar to Olive-
sided Flycatcher

cinnamon-buff
wing bars

Yellow-bellied Flycatcher

Empidonax flaviventris
L 5½"/14cm WS 8"/20cm

This scarce empid of boreal forests favors coniferous woods around bogs or other wet areas, where it nests on the ground in sphagnum moss or root tangles. Even in the gloom of dark forests, its distinctive plumage is readily apparent. Acadian Flycatcher is not as richly marked below; Pacific-slope and Cordilleran Flycatchers are duller, especially in the wings, and often have a crested look. **VOICE** Song an abrupt, repeated *tsch-prk!* or *tschurp!* Call a sweet, rising *pweee,* much like a wood-pewee.

adult   evenly rounded head

greenish above

prominent, full, often yellowish eye ring

stark contrast between blackish wings and pale wing bars (compare Pacific-slope)

most brightly yellowish *Empidonax*; fresh adult shows green and yellow tones even in shade

juvenile   short tail looks narrow

short bill

wing bars have yellow-buff cast

throat and neck usually dusky (compare Acadian)

juvenile   buffy wing bars

often wags short tail

yellowish cast on throat and belly; breast often olive-washed

Acadian Flycatcher

Empidonax virescens
L 5¾"/15cm WS 9"/23cm

A medium-sized, heavy-billed empid of deciduous and mixed forests, Acadian Flycatcher frequents swamps, streams, or wet patches and often forages at the woodland edge or over water. In ideal light—not too intense or too weak—its greenish back is obvious; worn birds in late summer and fall can appear brownish. Unlike Yellow-bellied Flycatcher, Acadian molts before fall migration. **VOICE** Song an abrupt *sree-PEE!* Calls include high, thin, sneezy notes—*pik, peek, pwee, psit, pweet*—and a lower *whiw.*

adult

greenish back in all plumages, hard to see in strong light

plainer below than Yellow-bellied Flycatcher, with more uniform eye ring, broader tail, less rounded head (looks peaked in rear)

juvenile

greenish above

face and whitish throat washed with dusky olive

thin, complete eye ring

buffy wing bar

long primary projection

Pacific-slope Flycatcher

Empidonax difficilis
L 5½"/14cm WS 8"/20cm

Pacific-slope and Cordilleran Flycatchers
were combined as one species, Western
Flycatcher, until 1989. This species breeds
in moist woodlands with undergrowth; it
is sometimes seen chasing Hammond's
Flycatchers in its territory. **VOICE** Song
of 3 thin notes—*pseet, tsick, tseet!*—
separated by pauses; first note sweet,
second much higher (unlike Cordilleran),
last higher and insistent. Typical male call
like first note of song but longer: a rising,
single-noted *suwheet,* without breaks
(unlike Cordilleran).

adult

averages less colorful, smaller, smaller-billed than Cordilleran

large eye ring, pointed at rear

drab wing bars; rear crown notably peaked and crested (compare Yellow-bellied)

shorter wings and longer tail than Yellow-bellied, giving longer, thinner appearance

adult, worn

much grayer than fresh adult, with narrower wing bars and eye ring

Cordilleran Flycatcher

Empidonax occidentalis
L 5½"/14cm WS 8"/20cm

This flycatcher breeds in montane forests
just east of the Pacific ranges, sometimes
nesting on the ground. Only voice reliably
distinguishes Cordilleran from Pacific-
slope Flycatcher where ranges overlap;
Cordilleran visits drier habitats and may
forage higher in trees, but more study is
needed to determine differences between
the two. **VOICE** Song of 3 thin notes—
pree, tsdup, tseep!—separated by pauses;
first note sweet, second much lower, last
much higher and insistent. Typical male
call an upslurred, sweet *wee-SEET!*

adult

averages more olive and yellow, larger and longer-billed than Pacific-slope, but safely distinguished only by voice

adult

shorter primary projection than Yellow-bellied

tertials and wing and covert edges show little contrast (compare Yellow-bellied)

Least Flycatcher

Empidonax minimus
L 5¼"/13cm **WS** 7¾"/20cm

Least Flycatcher inhabits deciduous, mixed, and coniferous woodlands, often nesting near small breaks in the woods. A pugnacious species, it often chases American Redstarts from its territory. Its round- and large-headed look is similar to Yellow-bellied Flycatcher, but its coloration makes it more easily confused with Alder, Willow, Hammond's, and Dusky Flycatchers. Like Yellow-bellied, Least migrates to tropical wintering grounds before molting. **VOICE** Song a rapid, repeated *ts-pik!* Call a quick *pit.*

juvenile — full eye ring

mandible usually pale

grayish head; greenish back

very short primary projection (makes short tail look longer); shorter, narrower tail and shorter bill than Alder and Willow

adult

small

appears large-headed

differs from Hammond's and Dusky in paler underparts, more contrast in edges of remiges, wider bill

Northern Beardless-Tyrannulet

Camptostoma imberbe
L 4½"/11cm **WS** 7"/18cm

This tropical flycatcher is the only member of its subfamily (Elaeniinae) that nests north of Mexico. It forages quickly through scrubby vegetation and thorn woods, sometimes gleaning insects from bark like a kinglet. A few overwinter in Texas, joining foraging guilds of woodland birds. Beardless-tyrannulets make globe-shaped nests with a side entrance, unlike *Empidonax* flycatchers. **VOICE** Song a distinctive, repeating series of plaintive whistles, *dew dew DEW DEW,* increasing in volume but descending slightly in pitch. Call a high, squeaky *speek.*

adult — crest often raised — faint supercilium

dusky wing bars

very short bill, orange-yellow at base of mandible

adult

can be confused with *Empidonax* flycatchers, but forages more actively, has blunter tip to bill, and lacks rictal bristles (thus its name "beardless")

Alder Flycatcher

Empidonax alnorum
L 5¾"/15cm WS 8½"/22cm

Until 1973 Alder and Willow Flycatchers were combined as Traill's Flycatcher. Both species prefer brushy habitats near water, with Alder more closely associated with alder trees and Willow with willows. Where found together, Alder often takes moister sites, but the two species sometimes clash over territories. Certain identification is only possible with vocalizing birds (or in-hand measurements). **VOICE** Song a very modulated *zzhrreeBEEur* or *zzrrrrrear*. Call a quick *pip*.

adult

averages greener on back and crown than Willow

medium primary projection, like Willow

adult, worn

more distinct eye ring than most Willows

very broad-based bill, like Willow

Willow Flycatcher

Empidonax traillii
L 5¾"/15cm WS 8½"/22cm

Willow Flycatcher, found in brushy areas near water, is usually the plainest and brownest above of all empids. It is distinguished from wood-pewees by lesser primary projection (tips of the primaries just reach the tail base) and less sooty, more contrasting plumage, especially in the wings (but western subspecies are dingy brown above). Unlike wood-pewees, Willow often flicks its tail. **VOICE** Song a sneezelike *rritz-bew!*, often introduced by a lazy, upward *zzhrrink*. Call a loud, slow *whit*.

adult, eastern

more gray-backed than Alder, usually lacks distinct eye ring

broad-based bill, like Alder

adult, western

paler overall than Alder and eastern Willow, with more brown tones above than in eastern adults (all juveniles brownish above)

wing bars and tertial edges duller than in eastern birds

Dusky Flycatcher

Empidonax oberholseri
L 5¾"/15cm WS 8¼"/21cm

The widespread Dusky Flycatcher nests in diverse habitats, including open coniferous forests with undergrowth, montane chaparral and dry brush, and riparian stands of willows or aspens. It is often confused with Hammond's and the paler Gray Flycatchers, which also have narrow bills. **VOICE** Song a repeated series of 3 notes: a quick *tsik*, a rough *bwaay* (or *prrdrt*), and a sweet, rising *prreee*; variable in sequencing of notes. Calls a flat *whit*, given frequently when foraging or alarmed, and a mellow *tew-hic*.

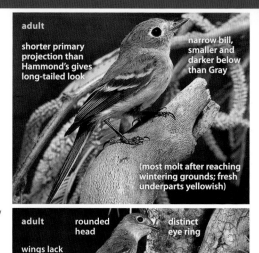

adult

shorter primary projection than Hammond's gives long-tailed look

narrow bill, smaller and darker below than Gray

(most molt after reaching wintering grounds; fresh underparts yellowish)

adult

rounded head

distinct eye ring

wings lack contrasting feather edges

very short primary projection

Hammond's Flycatcher

Empidonax hammondii
L 5½"/14cm WS 8¾"/22cm

This petite, narrow-billed empid nests high in the canopy of mature coniferous forests (unlike Dusky Flycatcher, which fares well in cutover areas). It is closest in plumage to Least and Dusky Flycatchers but has a notably longer primary projection; Hammond's usually shows a gray throat and breast and olive-yellow underparts in fresh plumage. **VOICE** Song a series of repeated phrases, varying in sequence: a quick *tsiip* and rising *surr-ip* followed by a lower, grating *grrrt*. Calls a quick, high *pip* and lower *wiw*.

adult

prominent eye ring pointed at rear

long primary projection makes tail look somewhat short

large, gray head with very small, dark, narrow bill

adult

molts before fall migration; fresh plumage green above, yellowish below

adult

gray throat, olive-yellow belly (compare Least)

narrow, notched tail

Gray Flycatcher
Empidonax wrightii
L 6"/15cm **WS** 8¾"/22cm

Gray Flycatcher is a pale empid of arid sagebrush, open pinyon-juniper and oak-pine woods, and other brushy habitats of the Great Basin and shrub-steppe. When perched, it pumps its tail like a phoebe: a slight, rapid upward flick followed by a slow, downward droop (other empids pump rapidly, beginning with a downward flick). **VOICE** Song a harsh, burry, repeated *jrrrr-rip,* occasionally interrupted with a high, sweet *teew.* Calls include *wiw* and *whit* similar to Dusky, Willow, or Least.

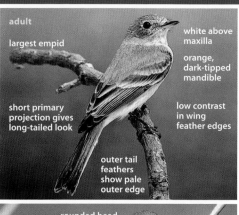

adult

largest empid

white above maxilla

orange, dark-tipped mandible

short primary projection gives long-tailed look

low contrast in wing feather edges

outer tail feathers show pale outer edge

adult, worn

rounded head with modest eye ring

overall grayish to gray-brown

bill narrow when seen from below

Buff-breasted Flycatcher
Empidonax fulvifrons
L 5"/13cm **WS** 7½"/19cm

A little-known species of Mexico and northern Central America, Buff-breasted nests in open montane pine forests, usually near brushy slopes. In the U.S. it is found only in a few mountain ranges of southeastern Arizona and in the Davis Mountains of western Texas. In some years, as few as 20 birds are counted in Arizona. This is by far the most distinctive U.S. empid; adults and juveniles are often vividly colored below. **VOICE** Song an alternating pair of explosive phrases: *pdew!* and *PEEU!* or similar. Call a sharp *pit.*

adult

smallest empid

breast washed with rich apricot

adult, worn

prominent, heavy eye ring

retains some buff-orange wash on breast

Eastern Phoebe

Sayornis phoebe
L 7"/18cm **WS** 10½"/27cm

Eastern Phoebe breeds mostly in open deciduous woods and agricultural areas, especially near water; it builds its nest under bridges, in the eaves of buildings, or even inside open buildings. Phoebes are smaller and more slender than kingbirds and longer-tailed and plainer than the smaller empids and wood-pewees. All three *Sayornis* move their tails when at rest and are often quite tame when approached. Eastern and Black Phoebes are usually seen sitting on a low perch in the open, often near water. **VOICE** Song a series of rising then falling phrases: *sreee ree-bee, sreee reee,* the latter with a burry quality. Call a rich, sweet *tcheep,* quiet and unobtrusive.

Eastern Phoebe adult

dark head contrasts with gray back

lacks eye ring, wing bars

pumps tail

Eastern Phoebe juvenile

like adult but with more yellow wash on belly, more contrast in remiges edges

coverts show off-white margins (compare Black Phoebe)

Black Phoebe

Sayornis nigricans
L 7"/18cm **WS** 11"/28cm

Black Phoebe is found mostly near water in the Southwest, where Eastern Phoebe occurs only as a rare stray. This species nests under eaves and bridges, like Eastern Phoebe, and also in coastal cliffs and canyon walls. It often hunts in streams or rivers, hawking insects actively while moving from rock to rock. **VOICE** Song a series of rising and falling phrases, very thin and sibilant, *srii, srii, syew, srii, syew.* Call similar to Eastern.

Black Phoebe adult

black breast and sides contrast with snow white belly

upperparts darker, more uniform than Eastern Phoebe; rear crown more peaked

Black Phoebe juvenile

like adult but wing coverts show rusty margins

(cinnamon rump)

pumps tail

Say's Phoebe

Sayornis saya
L 7½"/19cm WS 13"/33cm

Say's Phoebe breeds in open country from the far-northern muskeg of Alaska to the sweltering sagebrush habitats of the southern Great Basin. It nests in cliffs and eroding banks as well as abandoned farm buildings. Say's may be confused with female or young Vermilion Flycatchers, which are smaller and usually streaked below. Unlike the other two phoebes, Say's usually flares rather than pumps the tail. **VOICE** Song an alternating series of sweet, whistled phrases: a falling *pidirrreew* and a rising *pidrrrreep*. Call a mournful, slightly descending whistle, *pee-ee*.

Say's Phoebe
adult

largest
Sayornis

dusty gray-brown
above (paler than
other phoebes)

long,
blackish
tail

pale salmon-
colored belly and
vent (juvenile
similar but paler,
with salmon-buff
wing bars)

Vermilion Flycatcher

Pyrocephalus rubinus
L 6"/15cm WS 10"/25cm

Possibly a relative of phoebes, Vermilion Flycatcher likewise prefers open, brushy country near water; like phoebes, it is a tail-wagger. The pale gray plumage and indistinctly streaked underparts of juveniles and females bear little resemblance to the unforgettably incandescent plumage of adult males. **VOICE** Song a rolling *pi-pi-pi-piprrrrt!*, rising then falling; repeated with mechanical regularity, often during slow, butterfly-like display flight. Call a sharp, high *pseep!*

Vermilion
Flycatcher
adult male

dark eye line
connects with
dark back

luminous
vermilion crown,
throat, belly

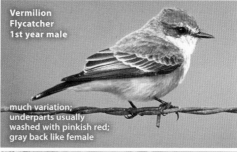

Vermilion
Flycatcher
1st year male

much variation;
underparts usually
washed with pinkish red;
gray back like female

Vermilion
Flycatcher
1st year
female

breast has indistinct
grayish streaks

yellow wash
on vent

Great Crested Flycatcher

Myiarchus crinitus
L 8¾"/22cm **WS** 13"/33cm

The tropical-sounding call of this flycatcher is startling in the dawn chorus of eastern deciduous forests and their edges. Great Crested Flycatcher hunts large insects from perches in treetops and on snags and, like other large tyrannids, also eats berries. It nests in cavities, especially old woodpecker cavities, and accepts nest boxes. **VOICE** Song a series of rising and falling phrases: *queeleep! queelurr, queeleep!* Calls include an abrupt *reep REEEP rip rip!*

adult

large

bushy, brown crest raised when alert

heavier bill than Ash-throated Flycatcher

brighter overall than other *Myiarchus*, with more extensive yellow below

juvenile (crest lowered)

back has olive cast

wing coverts and tertials show broad white edges

sharp contrast between throat, belly, back in fresh plumage

mostly rufous tail

Brown-crested Flycatcher

Myiarchus tyrannulus
L 8¾"/22cm **WS** 13"/33cm

Brown-crested Flycatcher nests in riparian woods, scrub, and hill country of southern Texas and in deserts of the Southwest, mostly in Arizona; it may also be seen in other habitats, including suburbs. The two U.S. populations are of different subspecies; Texas birds *(magister)* average smaller overall than western birds *(cooperi)* and have a smaller bill. **VOICE** Song a descending, tripping *prrrrrit-rill-deer,* usually loudest on first syllable. Calls include an abrupt, woodpecker-like *krrip!* and an emphatic *whip!*

adult

less colorful than Great Crested Flycatcher, with less extensive and duller yellow below

adult

bushy brown crest raised when alert

much shorter primary projection than Great Crested, and lacks wide white margins in tertials

Ash-throated Flycatcher

Myiarchus cinerascens
L 8½"/22cm **WS** 12"/30cm

Like Brown-crested Flycatcher, Ash-throated Flycatcher breeds in open, dry habitats, but it is more widespread. In late autumn a few turn up in eastern states, where they are distinguished from the larger Great Crested Flycatcher by their smaller bill and paler plumage. The very similar Nutting's Flycatcher of Mexico has appeared twice in Arizona and once in California. **VOICE** Song a fussy series of burry, kingbirdlike *ki-breer, krerr,* and *kibrik* notes. Calls a quick *prik* and *prp.*

adult

hindcrown peaked when alert

slightly smaller, paler below, with thinner bill than larger *Myiarchus*

rufous primary edges; white secondary edges

narrow pale margins to tertials

juvenile

some look quite large-billed

less contrast in edges of remiges than adult

tail tip shows hardly any brown from below (adult shows even brown tip)

Dusky-capped Flycatcher

Myiarchus tuberculifer
L 7¼"/18cm **WS** 10"/25cm

This relatively dull, slender *Myiarchus,* whose range barely reaches the U.S., is found mostly in arid, brushy canyons sheltered by oaks. Structurally it is much less bulky than Ash-throated Flycatcher and might even be taken for a phoebe at first glance. **VOICE** Song a series of lazy phrases, trilling and accelerating at end: *preeeer . . . pidew . . . pedeeerrrrrrr!* (last note like a police whistle). Call a plaintive *preeeer,* descending.

adult

appears dark-capped

brownish (not gray) auriculars (compare other *Myiarchus*)

wings and undertail show little or no rufous

wing bars indistinct or absent

appears large-headed and large-billed for size

adult

rufous in tail limited to outer edges, often hard to see

browner face, yellower belly, and more slender bill than larger Ash-throated Flycatcher; less contrast above in edges of coverts and remiges

Western Kingbird
Tyrannus verticalis
L 8¾"/22cm WS 15½"/39cm

Western Kingbird nests from the Great Plains westward, in any open habitat where there are a few trees available for nesting. Like all *Tyrannus*, it is a pugilist, attacking birds that dare enter its territory, diving at and even riding the backs of vultures and hawks. This species is often observed on the East Coast in fall. **VOICE** Song a nasal, sputtering series that rises in inflection, speed, and pitch, then falls quickly: *prip pp prreep pp PREEpoopop.* Calls similarly clipped *spik, pik,* and *kit* sounds.

adult

black tail has distinctive white outer edges (obscure or absent in worn birds)

smallest bill and shortest tail of all yellow-bellied kingbirds

lacks dark gray breast of Cassin's Kingbird, large bill of Couch's and Tropical Kingbirds

adult

all kingbirds have broad wings (longer and more pointed in long-distance migrants)

tail pattern visible on flying birds

Cassin's Kingbird
Tyrannus vociferans
L 9"/23cm WS 16"/41cm

Cassin's Kingbird breeds in scrub, savannas, and open woodlands with pines, oaks, junipers, eucalyptus, and sycamores. It is more richly colored than Western Kingbird, which shares its open-country habitats. At a distance, most are identified by the striking white throat patch and malar set in the deep gray head and breast. **VOICE** Song a series of raspy notes and longer, clearer *keekyer* calls; also a stuttering set of *rah* notes ending in a loud *REEAR!* Common calls include nasal *tew* and *ki-deer* notes and a loud, modulated *chi-QUEER!*

adult

upperwing coverts edged in pale sandy brown (compare Western Kingbird)

dark gray breast contrasts with small white throat patch and yellow belly

dark brown tail has sandy edges and tip

adult

palest birds can be mistaken for Western, but chin and malar contrastingly white

Couch's Kingbird

Tyrannus couchii
L 9¼"/23cm **WS** 15½"/39cm

In the U.S. Couch's Kingbird breeds in southeastern Texas in almost any habitat, including urban areas. Subtle differences in plumage and bill size distinguish this species from the closely related Tropical Kingbird, but voice is the only reliable identifying feature. **VOICE** Song rises and falls like Western Kingbird's song but has fuller, sweeter, slower notes. Calls include a hoarse but sweet *krrreer* and a *kik-ki-kreeer!*, rising then descending. Kingbirds' vocalizations are not easily separated into songs and calls.

adult

bill much larger than Western and Cassin's Kingbirds, averages shorter than Tropical

brown, unpatterned tail

adult

averages greener back, paler brown wings and tail than Tropical Kingbird

Tropical Kingbird

Tyrannus melancholicus
L 9¼"/23cm **WS** 14½"/37cm

One of the most widespread of American flycatchers, Tropical Kingbird—or "TK"—is found from southern Arizona and Texas all the way to central Argentina in just about any habitat, usually near water. In Texas it often nests close to Couch's Kingbirds without conflict. In autumn it turns up as a vagrant along the Pacific coast, even to Alaska. **VOICE** Song differs from other kingbirds; a continuous, rapid series of sweet, rising, staccato notes, with trilling, insectlike rapidity. Calls similarly complex, unlike Couch's Kingbird.

adult

longest-billed yellow-bellied kingbird

yellow of belly merges into pale olive breast (compare Western, Cassin's Kingbirds)

adult

differs from Couch's in longer bill; duller green on back; darker brown wings and tail; usually more masked look; best distinguished by voice

Eastern Kingbird
Tyrannus tyrannus
L 8½"/22cm **WS** 15"/38cm

Eastern Kingbird is not limited to the East; it is absent as a breeder only on the West Coast and in the western Great Basin, where it is a regular vagrant. In late summer and early fall, this feisty bird migrates by day in loose flocks, stopping at traditional roosting areas. As with most long-distance migrants, its wings are long and slender for its size. This species often captures insects by "kiting" into the wind, then dropping quickly. **VOICE** Song a rolling series of sputtering, thin *tiw* and *tsiw* notes. Calls similar to song components.

adult

blackish head contrasts with white throat

dark back has bluish sheen in strong light

black tail has white tip

juvenile

like adult but duller, with paler edges to upperwing coverts and tertials

Rose-throated Becard
Pachyramphus aglaiae
L 7¼"/18cm **WS** 12"/30cm

Rose-throated Becard is usually found in large sycamore trees near water. Like other tropical species with similar ranges, it is scarce in the U.S. and can be hard to find; look for its bulky hanging nest on the outer limbs of trees. Becards are probably closely related to tyrannids. Males and females of the subspecies *albiventris,* which nests in Arizona, are less richly colored than *gravis,* which visits southern Texas. **VOICE** Pair gives a rolling duet of high-pitched notes, accelerating then slowing, sounding like squeak toys; call an energetic *speee!*

adult male

distinctive, with slaty plumage, dark crown, rosy throat patch

rosy throat begins to appear in first year

female

recalls a tiny kingbird but has short, rufous tail and distinct black cap (juvenile and first-year female show rufous back)

Gray Kingbird

Tyrannus dominicensis
L 9"/23cm **WS** 14½"/37cm

Gray Kingbird nests in Florida and is rare elsewhere on the Gulf coast and north to North Carolina. This energetic species makes up in charisma what it may lack in plumage: it spends the day vigorously dive-bombing transgressors in its territory, including humans; foraging omnivorously (even dispatching small lizards); and calling almost constantly, its rolling call inspiring many nicknames. Patient observation of nesting birds may yield views of the ruby red crown patch, used in courtship or agonistic encounters with rivals. All kingbirds have a crown patch (usually red, but yellow in Thick-billed); Grays may reveal theirs more often. **VOICE** Song recalls that of Tropical Kingbird. Call a spirited *pet-CHEERRRY!*

Gray Kingbird adult
paler above than Eastern Kingbird, with much heavier bill

dark mask contrasts with gray crown

adult
long tail appears forked when folded

often perches high in trees or on utility wires

Gray Kingbird juvenile
mask often less contrasting than in adult

pale brownish edges to upperwing coverts

Thick-billed Kingbird

Tyrannus crassirostris
L 9½"/24cm **WS** 16"/41cm

A robust Mexican flycatcher, Thick-billed Kingbird breeds annually in southeastern Arizona and occasionally in western Texas and southwestern New Mexico; it favors riparian sites with cottonwoods and sycamores. Freshly plumaged adults and juveniles are strongly washed with yellow below and easily told from Tropical Kingbird by their dark brown upperparts. **VOICE** Song a stuttering series of *ti* notes, usually with a rolling *twheeeer* toward end. Common call a rising, querulous *purrr-EET?*

Thick-billed Kingbird adult

larger bill than Eastern Kingbird

yellow wash on lower belly and vent

(yellow crown patch rarely seen)

Thick-billed Kingbird juvenile

darkest on crown

usually appears dark brown above

rufous-buff margins to upperwing coverts and remiges (unlike Tropical Kingbird)

Fork-tailed Flycatcher

Tyrannus savana
L 16"/41cm WS 14"/36cm

This slender tropical kingbird strays irregularly across the eastern U.S., mostly in autumn. It is rarely misidentified: even young birds sport an improbably long tail. Birds in the U.S., usually of the nominate South American subspecies, are thought to be "reverse migrants," their migratory orientation skewed by 180°. **VOICE** A series of sputtering notes similar to Western Kingbird and Scissor-tailed Flycatcher. Call a liquid *slik*.

adult

dark head, gray back, white breast

very long tail flaps in breeze, unlike Scissor-tailed Flycatcher

immature

shorter tail than adult; whiter below than Eastern Kingbird, with longer tail

Scissor-tailed Flycatcher

Tyrannus forficatus
L 15"/38cm WS 15"/38cm

The very signature of the southern Great Plains, Scissor-tailed Flycatcher is a kingbird nearly endemic to that region, nesting only marginally into northeastern Mexico. It is a breathtaking bird: a soft pearl gray above, a pink wash on the belly, and often brilliantly rose-pink underwing coverts. This species has hybridized with other kingbirds, including Western and Couch's; hybrids look more like yellow-bellied kingbirds but show more graduated rectrices. **VOICE** Song similar to Western Kingbird but slower; a halting, sputtering *pip pip PAreep!* or similar, repeated. Call a sharp *kip*.

adult

gray above

(belly washed with pink)

long, black and white, forked tail

pink of underwing coverts often visible at bend of wing on resting bird

juvenile

(pale yellow wash below)

much shorter-tailed than adult (tail resembles Western Kingbird)

Great Kiskadee

Pitangus sulphuratus
L 9¾"/25cm **WS** 15"/38cm

Great Kiskadee is named for its loud, far-carrying song. This species is common and widespread in the tropics and in Bermuda (where it was introduced in 1957); in the U.S. it is a permanent resident in the Rio Grande valley and lower Gulf coast of Texas, found in open woodlands and edges near water. Kiskadees rarely stray; they have turned up only exceptionally east to Louisiana and west to Arizona and possibly California. **VOICE** Song an energetic, husky *krik-a-DEERR!*

adult

striking head pattern

heavy body, head, bill; bright saffron yellow underparts

adult

short, brilliant rufous tail

(juvenile very similar)

Sulphur-bellied Flycatcher

Myiodynastes luteiventris
L 8½"/22cm **WS** 15"/38cm

This flycatcher breeds in high-elevation canyons of southeastern Arizona and southwestern New Mexico, with rare strays recorded as far north as southern Canada. Other streaked flycatchers with strong head patterns are vagrants in the U.S.: the smaller, smaller-billed Variegated Flycatcher in Maine and Ontario, and the tiny Piratic Flycatcher in Florida, Texas, New Mexico, and Tennessee. **VOICE** Calls include a nasal, singsong *DEW di drrriup* and agitated squeaks.

adult

brilliant rufous tail contrasts with otherwise streaky brown plumage

adult

white malar and supercilium set off by dark eye line and throat stripe

head pattern unlike other flycatchers

(juvenile very similar)

Shrikes

Shrikes (family Laniidae) are medium-sized passerines of open-country habitats. These birds recall a small jay in overall shape and in fact are possibly related to corvids. Both North American shrike species are plumaged in gray, black, and white; younger birds show browner tones above and faint barring below. Northern Shrike, the larger species, nests in boreal forests and muskeg and is seen regularly only south to the northernmost United States in winter; Loggerhead Shrike nests mostly south of Canada and ranges southward into the deserts of Mexico. Brown Shrike of Eurasia has been recorded eight times as a vagrant to North America, mostly in Alaska.

Northern Shrike with impaled prey item.

Both Loggerhead and Northern Shrikes are regularly confused with Northern Mockingbird, which has much more white in the wings and tail, a more slender bill, and a different flight style that lacks the rapid wingbeats and often undulating path of the shrikes. The black mask of shrikes (absent in mockingbirds) probably functions, like a falcon's mask, to absorb glare in the well-lit habitats shrikes occupy.

Shrikes are unique among passerines in that they feed like birds of prey, taking birds, rodents, and large insects in swift, direct capture much as kestrels do. Their short but powerful bills have a hooked maxilla with a small tomial notch (a tiny toothlike serration), as in a falcon's bill, which they use to dispatch prey quickly, often with a bite to the neck. While shrikes lack the talons of a raptor, having simple perching feet like other passerines, they can tear into prey using their heavy bills. Like owls, shrikes regurgitate pellets of indigestible material. Shrikes cache what they catch, using barbed wire or thorn trees to display prey items; this larder presumably functions both to impress potential mates and to indicate occupied territories. Because they rely on sites where they can impale prey and find hunting perches, shrikes shun grasslands that lack trees, unless manmade features such as utility poles are available.

Courtship among shrikes is not often observed. Both sexes bow and flash the white in their wings and tail, and the male sings a rather sweet, simple song or calls quickly. Territorial disputes look similar, with much posturing and rapid chattering. Shrike nests are simple cups of twigs and grasses set in small crotches in trees. The nests of Loggerhead Shrike are easy to find, often placed in isolated trees near prime feeding areas.

Shrikes are rarely observed in true migration, as most make only facultative movements when prey becomes scarce. Cyclic population crashes of voles in Canada bring hundreds of Northern Shrikes southward into the United States; these flights occur every five years or so with varying intensity.

The few Loggerhead Shrikes that now nest in the Northeast (sometimes designated as subspecies *migrans*) were once uncommon migrants and wintering birds along the East Coast, but this population is all but extirpated. Another subspecies, *mearnsi*, which nests only on San Clemente Island off southern California, is likewise imperiled: just 76 birds remained in the wild as of 2004.

Loggerhead Shrike

Lanius ludovicianus
L 9"/23cm **WS** 12"/30cm

This open-country bird is declining over most of its range. Males impale prey—large insects and small reptiles, amphibians, rodents, and passerines—on barbed wire and thorns to cache food and mark territories (indicating their fitness to potential mates). The 9 subspecies show some geographic variation in plumage, mostly in the darkness of the upperparts and the amount of white in the wings, coverts, and tail. **VOICE** Song a series of harsh paired phrases repeated at precise intervals. Calls include harsh fusses.

adult

darker above than larger Northern Shrike; broader black mask extends above eyes and maxilla

juvenile

mask fainter than adult's

brownish above; tan wing bar and underparts

(faint, fine barring in underparts quickly lost)

Northern Shrike

Lanius excubitor
L 10½"/27cm **WS** 14½"/37cm

Northern Shrike breeds in the taiga of Canada and Alaska; unpredictable numbers visit southern Canada and the lower 48 states in winter, when this species is almost always seen singly. Like Loggerhead Shrike, Northern feeds on insects and small vertebrates; but Northern also takes prey items nearly as heavy as itself, such as waxwings and mockingbirds. It is often concealed in foliage but perches conspicuously when hunting. **VOICE** Similar to Loggerhead but lower-pitched, less harsh and more mimidlike.

adult

narrow mask does not extend above eyes (compare Loggerhead)

pale gray upperparts

pale mandible

juvenile
mask can be quite faint

brownish above, barred below (barring held much longer than in Loggerhead)

adult

less white in wings than Northern Mockingbird

Vireos

Vireos (family Vireonidae) are small landbirds that resemble warblers but have heavier bills and heads. Once assumed to be close relatives of warblers, vireos are now thought to be most closely related to shrikes (the tomial notch near the tip of the maxilla perhaps hints at this relationship) and also to corvids. Vireos have heavier legs than warblers, often with a bluish tone; this can be helpful for identification. In plumage, vireos (genus *Vireo,* a Latin word whose root means "green") are plainer than warblers overall:

Vireos, such as this Warbling Vireo, are sometimes mistaken for warblers or kinglets, which forage by gleaning like vireos but have thinner bills and legs.

mostly olive or gray above and paler below, with touches of yellowish in some species. Most have distinctive markings around the eyes, either "spectacles" or a supercilium, and most have wing bars in fresh plumage.

Like most warblers, vireos forage by gleaning prey from vegetation, from low scrub up through the canopy; they eat insects and their larvae and also, especially during the nonbreeding season, small fruits. While foraging, vireos often seem less animated and more methodical than warblers, scanning from a perch before moving to the next branch; however, smaller vireos, such as Black-capped and White-eyed, seem to be in constant, nervous motion when foraging. Hutton's Vireo closely resembles Ruby-crowned Kinglet and often flicks its wings like a

Adult Red-eyed Vireo, showing tomial notch in maxilla.

kinglet, while Bell's and Gray Vireos use distinctive tail movements while foraging. These actions of wings and tail probably serve to startle prey. Some vireos make short sallies from a perch to pick insects, much as a flycatcher does.

Male vireos sing to advertise territories and occasionally engage in song flights; unlike most passerines, males of some species sing from the nest. Vireo songs are often quite similar, as between Plumbeous and Yellow-throated or Philadelphia and Red-eyed. Philadelphia may actually imitate a Red-eyed's song to keep that species away from its territory. The calls of most vireos (not described in the species accounts) are quite similar and in some cases indistinguishable among species—a descending, raspy, nasal set of scolding calls with a catlike quality. Both sexes guard their territory against intruders. Most vireos make cup-shaped nests that hang on the fork of a small branch; only Gray Vireo regularly nests on top of a branch. All species except Hutton's Vireo migrate southward in winter.

Populations of most vireos are relatively stable across the continent. Black-capped Vireo and the *pusillus* subspecies of Bell's Vireo (called Least Bell's Vireo) are both federally listed as endangered, their numbers reduced by habitat loss and brood parasitism by Brown-headed Cowbird.

Bell's Vireo
Vireo bellii
L 4¾"/12cm   **WS** 7"/18cm

Bell's Vireo inhabits low, thick vegetation near water. In the West it prefers semiarid country with scrub oaks, riparian areas with willows, and stands of mesquite; eastern birds prefer hedgerows and shrubby patches in prairies. Bell's forages actively, its long tail in constant motion. A disjunct California subspecies, Least Bell's Vireo *(pusillus),* is listed as endangered. **VOICE** Rapid, tripping tangle of buzzy notes, increasing in tempo and loudness; first part seems to ask a question, second part to answer it.

adult, western

some individuals uniformly grayish above, lacking greenish tones in rump and back

faint supercilium, eye line, eye ring, and wing bars

when foraging, moves long tail both up and down and side to side

adult, eastern

small and slender

greenish tones above

shorter-tailed than western

yellowish below

Gray Vireo
Vireo vicinior
L 5½"/14cm   **WS** 8"/20cm

Gray Vireo is almost confined to arid pinyon-juniper and oak-juniper scrub and chaparral of the Southwest. A first-time observer might not recognize this plain bird as a vireo; but its bill (heavier than a warbler's, lighter than a sparrow's) is that of a vireo, and its plain gray plumage resembles Bell's and Plumbeous Vireos (those species have 2 distinct wing bars and a stronger facial pattern). **VOICE** Song a monotonous set of 3 sweet phrases—roughly *tree, sweer, dyew*— usually descending in pitch; more rapid than Plumbeous.

adult

wings have brownish cast

short primary projection gives long-tailed look

low contrast between gray head and white throat

(birds in fresh plumage show distinct lower wing bar, faint upper wing bar)

adult, worn

faint pale eye ring and lores

(moves tail when foraging, like Bell's)

very plain

Philadelphia Vireo
Vireo philadelphicus
L 5¼"/13cm **WS** 8"/20cm

In deciduous and mixed forests of central and southern Canada, Philadelphia Vireo overlaps with the similar-sounding Red-eyed Vireo; it is smaller and lighter-bodied than Red-eyed and thus able to forage at the tips of small branches. Fall birds are sometimes mistaken for warblers because of their small bill, bright yellowish tones, and foraging habits. **VOICE** Song similar to Red-eyed but higher and slower.

Philadelphia Vireo adult

dark remiges and crown (upperparts more uniform in Warbling Vireo)

dark loral line (paler or absent in Warbling)

yellow below fades to whitish lower belly

Philadelphia Vireo adult/ 1st fall

head pattern less distinct than Red-eyed Vireo

greenish above, brighter yellow below than on spring birds

bill larger and less pointed than Tennessee Warbler

Warbling Vireo
Vireo gilvus
L 5½"/14cm **WS** 8½"/22cm

In the East Warbling Vireo inhabits deciduous areas with undergrowth, especially lakeside or riparian thickets, willow groves, and poplar stands; in the West it favors edge habitat with alders, cottonwoods, birches, and aspens. It is usually detected by its complex, rapid song, delivered incessantly from inside crown foliage. The nominate subspecies in the East is larger, closer in bulk to Red-eyed Vireo; western *swainsoni* is smaller and more brightly colored (especially fall immatures). **VOICE** Song variable and warbling, often remembered *iggledy-piggledy-piggledy-PICK!* (less continuous and rich-toned in western birds).

Warbling Vireo adult

uniform upperparts, without contrast between crown and back

pale lores

note heavier bill and legs than in warblers

Warbling Vireo adult

narrow pale edges to greater coverts in western subspecies

bluish gray legs, unlike warblers

Red-eyed Vireo

Vireo olivaceus
L 6"/15cm   **WS** 10"/25cm

The most widespread of American vireos, Red-eyed sings throughout the day in well-wooded suburbs and deciduous and mixed forests. Once an abundant species, it continues to decline in many parts of its range, possibly because of brood parasitism by Brown-headed Cowbird, a problem for many passerines. This species consumes much fruit on migration and in Amazonia, where it winters. **VOICE** Song a series of sweet, robinlike phrases of 2 to 4 syllables with singsong quality, repeated rapidly for long periods.

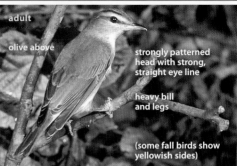

adult

olive above

strongly patterned head with strong, straight eye line

heavy bill and legs

(some fall birds show yellowish sides)

adult

gray cap shows distinct black border

red eyes (brown in first-fall birds)

white breast and belly

(immature tinged brownish above in fall)

Yellow-green Vireo

Vireo flavoviridis
L 6¼"/16cm   **WS** 10"/25cm

This tropical counterpart to Red-eyed Vireo is an occasional breeder in southernmost Texas, usually near ponds or lakes in relatively dense second-growth vegetation. It is also a fall vagrant across the southern tier of the U.S. **VOICE** Song sounds uncannily like a flock of House Sparrows.

adult

distinguished from Red-eyed Vireo by larger, paler bill and gray crown without black border

bright yellow sides, flanks, undertail

Black-whiskered Vireo

Vireo altiloquus
L 6¼"/16cm   **WS** 10"/25cm

A West Indian species, Black-whiskered Vireo breeds north into mangrove forests of southern Florida; it forages mostly in the upper parts of trees and in fruit-laden thickets. **VOICE** Song ringing and articulate like Red-eyed, usually rendered *sweet-John, sweet-John to-whit!*

adult

long bill

like dull Red-eyed Vireo but with grayish "whisker" (submalar line)

(yellowish sides in fresh plumage)

(vagrants seen north to Virginia)

Blue-headed Vireo
Vireo solitarius
L 5½"/14cm **WS** 9½"/24cm

The attractive Blue-headed Vireo inhabits deciduous forests in Canada and deciduous and mixed forests farther south. Many winter north of Mexico, joining foraging guilds of woodland birds in scrubby thickets and woods. Most can be told from Cassin's Vireo by their green back, brightly colored sides, and sharp division between the throat and head. **VOICE** Song similar to Red-eyed Vireo but slower, simpler, sweeter, and higher, with one note often sliding into the next.

adult (nominate)

blue-gray head distinctly set off from white throat and green back

sides strongly washed with yellow-olive

strong wing bars (often tinged yellow)

adult, Appalachian (*alticola*)

grayer-backed than nominate

The "Solitary Vireo" Complex

Three arboreal vireo species—Blue-headed, Cassin's, and Plumbeous—were until recently combined into a single species called Solitary Vireo. All are relatively heavy-bodied and -billed and show pronounced "spectacles" (pale lores and strong eye rings) in all plumages. Their ranges and habitats overlap to some degree, and they can be difficult to tell apart in the field, especially duller immatures or birds in worn plumage. Hybridization among these species, though not documented, could result in birds that are not identifiable to species. Identification of silent vireos away from the typical breeding range should be made with great caution.

Blue-headed Vireo has the most contrasting plumage of the three. It breeds in eastern highlands, the Northeast, and up through central Canada. **Cassin's Vireo,** mainly of the Pacific coast and Northwest, closely resembles a dull-plumaged Blue-headed Vireo, but a bright Cassin's shows less contrast between head, back, and throat. Worn dull spring Cassin's can look like Plumbeous, but Cassin's has less white in the outer rectrices than the others. **Plumbeous Vireo** dwells in the Rocky Mountains and Great Basin. Mostly gray above, it is unlike Blue-headed Vireo, but the brightest birds approach a dull Cassin's in appearance.

Blue-headed Vireo (dull)

Cassin's Vireo (bright)

Plumbeous Vireo

Cassin's Vireo

Vireo cassinii
L 5½"/14cm **WS** 9½"/24cm

Cassin's Vireo is found in mixed forests of spruce, fir, pine, and oak at middle to high elevations in mountains, as well as along the Pacific coast. It resembles Blue-headed Vireo but shows less sharp contrast between the head, throat, and back. Cassin's sometimes flicks its wings when foraging. **VOICE** Song burrier and hoarser than Blue-headed but a bit higher and sweeter than Plumbeous.

Cassin's Vireo adult

gray of head blends into greenish gray back (compare Blue-headed)

thin whitish wing bars weaker than in Blue-headed

secondaries have greenish tinge

Cassin's Vireo adult

drabbest adults similar to Plumbeous but with shades of green in back and secondaries

tertial edges narrower than in Blue-headed

Plumbeous Vireo

Vireo plumbeus
L 5¾"/15cm **WS** 10"/25cm

Plumbeous Vireo frequents wooded slopes and canyons of the Interior West, with pinyon-juniper and ponderosa pine forests its preferred habitats. Fall birds sometimes show olive tones along the sides and a yellow cast to the flanks. Such birds can be told from the dullest Cassin's Vireos by the sharper contrast between the gray head and white throat and the lack of greenish tones in the secondaries. Worn birds resemble Gray Vireo but show a more pronounced pattern in the wing bars and face and do not pump the tail when foraging. **VOICE** Song very similar to Yellow-throated Vireo but less varied; burry, downslurred notes, *churree, chrreet,* and so forth, delivered more slowly than Cassin's or Gray.

Plumbeous Vireo adult

2 strong wing bars (compare Gray Vireo)

strongly "spectacled" look

lead gray head starkly contrasts with white throat

yellow wash limited to flanks

Plumbeous Vireo adult, worn

wing bars and contrast in plumage reduced

Yellow-throated Vireo

Vireo flavifrons
L 5½"/14cm **WS** 9½"/24cm

This vireo is associated with deciduous forest edge habitats, such as stands of oaks near water, swamps, and well-treed parks. Yellow-throated often nests in smaller tracts of forest than the sympatric Red-eyed Vireo, but it is unevenly distributed and is scarce or absent across large areas in its range. Like Blue-headed and Red-eyed Vireos, it forages slowly and deliberately through the canopy. **VOICE** Song a burry, ringing *ee-ahrie, ur-lee,* or similar, repeated every few seconds; many variations in inflection.

adult

yellow on breast and head unique among vireos

very heavy bill

adult/1st fall

green back contrasts with gray rump (Pine Warbler has yellowish rump and often blurry streaks on flanks)

heavier bill and legs than warblers

dullest immature birds resemble Pine Warbler

White-eyed Vireo

Vireo griseus
L 5"/13cm **WS** 8"/20cm

White-eyed Vireo nests in low, brushy habitats, especially thickets near water, but also early successional growth along fields or roads and woodlands with extensive understory. It stays within dense cover when foraging and is usually detected by its ringing song. Subspecies found in southern Texas and southern Florida are markedly duller above. **VOICE** Song a loud, rollicking combination of quick clipped phrases, often remembered as *quick-to-the-rear!,* but very varied; often opens and closes with an emphatic *shick!*

adult

yellow "spectacles" with white eyes distinctive (young birds dark-eyed)

adult, worn

worn birds show narrower wing bars, like other vireos

(immature similar but shows dusky eye color)

Black-capped Vireo
Vireo atricapilla
L 4¾"/12cm **WS** 7"/18cm

The distinctive Black-capped Vireo breeds in scrubby oak habitat of central Texas and Oklahoma. In part because its habitat requirements are so specific—patchy, dense oak scrub, mostly on slopes or eroding areas—the species is rare and listed as endangered, with a population numbering fewer than 10,000 birds. **VOICE** Song a series of short, harsh, phrases that have a fussy quality, repeated rapidly. Contact call *k-dit,* similar to Ruby-crowned Kinglet; also a fussy *zhrreee* and a higher *shreee.*

adult male

white "spectacles" starkly contrast with jet black head

adult female

similar to male but head paler, blending with back

(first-year male similar)

Hutton's Vireo
Vireo huttoni
L 5"/13cm **WS** 8"/20cm

Found in Pacific coastal forests and highland forests of the Southwest, Hutton's Vireo is a permanent resident in woodlands with oaks, pines, and firs. It forages like a kinglet, flicking its wings and moving about restlessly in both low vegetation and treetops. It is not closely related to Ruby-crowned Kinglet but is very similar in appearance. The nominate subspecies (Pacific coast) is greener above than *stephensi* (Arizona). **VOICE** Song unlike other vireos; a simple, up-slurred *surr-EE!* or *jurr-EE!*, repeated all day.

adult, Arizona (*stephensi*)

pale lores and eye ring (broken above eyes)

drab brownish olive

Hutton's Vireo adult, Pacific (nominate)

very like Ruby-crowned Kinglet but with heavier bill and heavier, bluish legs

Ruby-crowned Kinglet adult

black-based secondaries

thin bill

thin, dark legs

Chickadees, Titmice, and Allies

Chickadees and titmice (family Paridae) are small, agile, animated passerines of diverse woodlands—from dwarf willow fens of northern Alaska, to juniper-clad foothills of the Great Basin, to the suburban East. Eleven species breed in North America, and one Eurasian species, Great Tit, has strayed to Alaska. In structure, chickadees and titmice share some attributes: relatively compact bodies, very short, conical bills, and fairly long tails. Chickadees usually have a pale cheek set off by a dark cap and bib. Titmice, larger on average, are gray overall with crests and few other adornments; the exception is Bridled Titmouse, which has a more intricate head pattern. Parids eat a variety of insect matter, seeds, and berries. They cache food, much like a corvid does, for later consumption; this behavior can sometimes be observed at bird-feeding stations, although usually the birds retrieve a seed from the feeder and fly a short distance away to open and eat it. With much coaxing, some species learn to take seeds from the hand.

Carolina Chickadees, like other parids, build nests in cavities, and both parents feed the young.

Parids and their allies do not have elaborate courtship displays. Males sing and feed females, and both sexes investigate potential nest cavities, where they make cup-shaped nests. Many species readily accept nest boxes. Like the other families treated in this section, they have a monogamous breeding system; some apparently mate for life.

Away from feeders, nonbreeding parids forage in family groups or in company with nuthatches, kinglets, small woodpeckers, Brown Creeper, vireos, and warblers. In these groups parids lead the flocks, often announcing the presence of a predator, such as an owl, snake, or hawk, with noisy scolding. Although harassing a predator at close range would seem to be a risky affair, "mobbing" serves to draw the attention of numerous small birds to the location of the predator and probably teaches young birds to recognize potentially dangerous animals. Imitating titmice calls (called "pishing") can be effective in drawing out woodland birds, apparently because titmice are the sentinel species in these mixed-species flocks or "guilds" of woodland birds.

A diverse group of families called "allies" of the chickadees and titmice family (Paridae) are treated in this section of the guide, even though some of these are not currently considered close relatives of parids. Until recently, for instance, Bushtit and Verdin were considered parids, but the latest research suggests that these birds are the sole New World representatives of two Old World families, the long-tailed tits (Aegithalidae) and the penduline tits (Remizidae), respectively. The unusual Wrentit, restricted to California and Oregon, recalls both Bushtit and wrens but appears to be a member of the babbler family (Timaliidae)—also an Old World family with no other representatives in the New World. Brown Creeper, the only North American representative of its family (Certhiidae), and the four species of nuthatch (Sittidae) often join parids in foraging parties during the nonbreeding season, along with many other woodland species. The evolutionary relationships between creepers, nuthatches, and parids are not well understood, and their placement together is based more on their shared habitat and association in the nonbreeding season than on similarities in plumage and structure.

Nuthatches (family Sittidae) frequent much the same woodland habitats as parids, but their structure is quite different. They are stocky birds with long, pointed bills, short tails, and very strong, sizable feet with which they cling to tree bark. Both nuthatches and woodpeckers are "scansorial" birds, adapted to climbing; but unlike woodpeckers, which mostly move upward around a tree, nuthatches move all around the trunk and limbs. Like parids, nuthatches nest in cavities and are not predictably migratory. Red-breasted Nuthatch does stage large-scale fall irruptions from montane and boreal habitats in years when food is scarce.

Brown Creeper (family Certhiidae), resident in many sorts of mature forests, is reminiscent of a tiny woodpecker. Creepers forage up trees with quick, hitching motions made possible by their stiff tails and strong legs. Their thin, decurved bills are weaker than the bills of woodpeckers and better suited for prying tiny prey from bark crevices. Creepers make nests behind loose strips of bark and, like nuthatches, sometimes roost communally in a cavity during cold weather.

Verdin, Bushtit, and Wrentit (families Remizidae, Aegithalidae, and Timaliidae, respectively) are birds strictly of the American West and Mexico and are never observed far from their respective habitats. Verdin most resembles parids, especially chickadees, in structure, with its fine, conical, pointed bill and rotund body and head. Instead of a chickadee-like bib and cap, however, the adult Verdin has a yellow head and thus can be confused with warblers. This species forages by gleaning and, like parids, readily hangs upside down to reach the tips of light branches. It makes a spherical twig nest with a side entrance and apparently builds separate roosting nests as well. Bushtit also resembles parids but has a longer tail and an even smaller bill. Bushtits are most often seen traveling in large groups comprised of several families that hold large communal territories, but they also regularly travel with foraging flocks of other passerines, including parids and warblers. The pendulous nests of Bushtits are often attached to mistletoe. Wrentit is even longer-tailed than Bushtit and has a larger, slightly decurved bill. This species is sedentary; nesting adults form long-term monogamous pair bonds and are believed to remain within their territories for life, as long as the habitat remains suitable.

Of the species in these six families, conservationists have most concern for those with the most restricted ranges, the smallest populations, and the most threatened habitats. High on the list is Wrentit, whose chaparral habitat has been very heavily developed; though this species tolerates some degree of fragmentation, it does not thrive amid intensive development. Range-restricted species, such as Bridled and Oak Titmice, should be monitored over the long term for declines. Brown-headed Nuthatch is a victim of habitat loss in southeastern pinewoods, and Verdin populations in thorn scrub of the Sonoran Desert have declined sharply as that habitat is modified or eliminated. Mountain Chickadee appears to have undergone a recent decline for reasons that are not clear.

Nuthatches are often spotted moving up and down on the trunks and limbs of trees. They eat both seeds, for which they have earned the name "nuthatch," and insects.

Tufted Titmouse

Baeolophus bicolor
L 6½"/17cm   WS 9½"/24cm

This familiar bird of deciduous forests frequents areas with mature oaks, as acorns form a large part of its winter diet (it also visits feeders for seeds). In nonbreeding months it joins foraging guilds of other woodland birds, presumably for safety from predators. Families forage together in winter. Tufted is expanding its range northward. **VOICE** Song a sweet, whistled *peter peter peter peter*, varied in inflection and tone. Calls include a harsh *ray* and *schick-a-day-day*, huskier than chickadees.

adult

gray crest, dark frontlet

paler birds show bluish tones above

adult

largest of its genus (with Black-crested Titmouse)

pale face surrounds large, dark eyes

buffy flanks (sometimes concealed)

Black-crested Titmouse

Baeolophus atricristatus
L 6½"/17cm   WS 9½"/24cm

Black-crested Titmouse is found in drier areas than Tufted Titmouse, including mesquite and oak-juniper scrub. The two species hybridize where they overlap in east-central Texas; hybrids show a shadow of a black crest. **VOICE** Similar to Tufted but more monosyllabic; a quick *peeur*, 5 or more times.

adult

grayer auriculars than Tufted (also in juvenile)

whitish forehead, blackish crest

(considered a subspecies of Tufted Titmouse from 1983 to 2003)

Bridled Titmouse

Baeolophus wollweberi
L 5¼"/13cm   WS 8"/20cm

Bridled Titmouse prefers well-wooded areas, especially with oaks, in mountains and foothills. In winter it may form small flocks in lowland riparian groves or in mesquite. **VOICE** Song a fast series of sweet, staccato *ti* notes. Scolding call a low *schick-a-dee* or *dedededede*, with wrenlike quality.

adult

"harlequin" face pattern and crest unique among American passerines (Mountain Chickadee smaller and uncrested)

Oak Titmouse
Baeolophus inornatus
L 5¾"/15cm **WS** 9"/23cm

Nearly endemic to California, Oak Titmouse is a permanent resident in riparian areas with cottonwoods, oak-juniper woods and edges, and other wooded habitats with oaks. It forages for acorns and also searches the rough oak bark for insects, spiders, eggs, and larvae. **VOICE** Song a pleasant, rollicking *sri-ri, sri-ri, sri-ri, sri-ri* or similar; some sing rapid, paired phrases, apparently imitating other birds. Call a harsh *schick-a-dee-dee*.

adult
short crest (sometimes flattened and invisible)
only titmouse with brownish plumage, especially above
easy to confuse with many small juvenile passerines

juvenile
compare young Verdin, Bushtit
similar to adult but browner above

Juniper Titmouse
Baeolophus ridgwayi
L 5¾"/15cm **WS** 9"/23cm

Juniper Titmouse, found mainly in pinyon-juniper woods of the Great Basin, was once combined with Oak Titmouse as one species, called Plain Titmouse. The two overlap in northeasternmost California and apparently do not hybridize. After breeding, both species chase young from their territory and travel in pairs (unlike Tufted Titmouse, which maintains family groups). **VOICE** Song variable; a rapid, juncolike trill and a quick *suri-suri-suri-suri-suri*. Scold call *schick-a-dee,* similar to Bridled Titmouse.

adult
short crest
grayish overall, with little or no brown
(juvenile similar)

adult
slightly longer-billed than Oak Titmouse
juvenile Black-crested paler below, with longer crest and buffy sides (no overlap in range)

Black-capped Chickadee

Poecile atricapillus
L 5¼"/13cm **WS** 8"/20cm

Black-capped Chickadee is a familiar bird at backyard feeders and in varied woodlands. With its smart plumage and tame, curious nature (it comes readily to pishing), it has endeared birds to many people. Like other species of the northern forests, Black-capped sometimes moves southward in large flights, probably when food is scarce. **VOICE** Song a sweet, 2-part whistle, *see-bee,* first part higher; variations include *s-see-bee* or *see-bebee;* some Pacific birds may sound more like titmice. Call a nasal, harsh *schick-a-dee.*

paler adult

compare very similar Carolina Chickadee

entire cheek bright white

greater coverts edged in white

lower border of bib mottled

relatively long tail

darker adult

some populations show olive tones in back, strong rufous wash on sides and flanks

tertials darker than Carolina, with contrasting pale edges

Carolina Chickadee

Poecile carolinensis
L 4¾"/12cm **WS** 7½"/19cm

Carolina Chickadee replaces the very similar Black-capped Chickadee in southeastern woodlands. The two overlap along an irregular corridor from central New Jersey to southern Kansas, and some hybridization has been documented. Unlike Black-capped, Carolina is rarely seen far out of range. **VOICE** Song a singsong set of paired whistles, *see-day see-daw,* the first notes in each phrase higher in pitch. Calls like Black-capped but less hoarse and faster. Birds in contact zone with Black-capped sing either song or combinations.

adult, fresh

distinguished from Black-capped by smaller size, duller plumage, more uniform upperwings, grayish cast on rear of cheek, shorter tail, neat lower edge of bib; best told by song

adult, worn

molting and worn birds often show uneven border on lower edge of bib

less contrast in tertials and usually less tawny flanks than Black-capped

Mountain Chickadee

Poecile gambeli
L 5¼"/13cm **WS** 8½"/22cm

Mountain Chickadee inhabits mostly montane coniferous forests; like other chickadees it often joins mixed foraging flocks in the nonbreeding season. Although its populations are somewhat irruptive, as with Black-capped Chickadee, movements are mostly altitudinal; few birds have been recorded far out of range, but some do move into the western Great Plains after breeding. **VOICE** Song a plaintive *see-bee,* similar to Black-capped but often with additional *bee* notes on same pitch as first *bee* note. Calls also similar.

adult · uniformly gray above · occasional Black-capped and Carolina Chickadees show similar white feathering in cap

bib shape variable but typically narrow · darkness of underparts variable; some duskier

adult · areas of white feathering in black cap variable

white supercilium thinner or obscured in some individuals (especially worn birds in summer)

recalls Bridled Titmouse but lacks crest

Mexican Chickadee

Poecile sclateri
L 5"/13cm **WS** 8¼"/21cm

This small chickadee is found at elevations over 7,000' (2,100m) in pine and pine-oak forests of the Animas and Peloncillo Mountains of New Mexico, where it is local, and the Chiricahua Mountains of Arizona, where it is relatively common. A few move to slightly lower elevations in winter, but the species has never been recorded in valleys or deserts. **VOICE** Song unlike other chickadees: a variable, low, complex, gravelly *churdle-dee,* repeated in titmouselike phrases on one pitch. Call a hoarse, wiry *zzshh-zzshe-day.*

adult · dusky gray sides, flanks, vent

extensive bib, with lower sides mottled

only species of chickadee in range

adult · rear crown often appears raised

(some worn Mountain Chickadees similar but with narrower bib)

Boreal Chickadee
Poecile hudsonica
L 5½"/14cm   WS 8¼"/21cm

Boreal Chickadee is a permanent resident of northern spruce forests. It is less conspicuous than Black-capped Chickadee, as it forages closer to the tree trunk, usually in a quieter and more deliberate fashion. On rare occasions a few birds turn up well south of the boreal belt, usually during irruptions of Black-cappeds. When food is abundant, this species is known to cache food for winter consumption, mostly in rough bark or among spruce needle clusters. **VOICE** Song mostly a rapid trill of *dee* notes on one pitch. Call a rough, nasal *tsick-a-dee-dee,* slower than Black-capped.

Boreal Chickadee
paler adult

limited white on
face below eyes

brown
cap

overall dusty
gray tones

rusty
flanks

Boreal Chickadee
darker adult

easily told from
Gray-headed
Chickadee by sooty
face and coverts

lacks chestnut
back in all
plumages

Gray-headed Chickadee
Poecile cincta
L 5½"/14cm   WS 8½"/22cm

This little-known bird inhabits low, dense alder, willow, and spruce woods along stream basins in remote muskeg. It differs from the similar Boreal Chickadee, much as Black-capped differs from Carolina Chickadee, in its whiter cheek, pale-edged remiges and greater coverts, more mottled edge to the bib, and longer tail. **VOICE** Song not recorded in North America; Eurasian Gray-headed sings rapid set of hoarse *cheoow* calls. Calls an insistent, nasal *cheer* or *deer,* more forceful than Boreal, and a quick, hoarse *schik-a-day.*

Gray-headed
Chickadee adult

gray cast
to brown
cap

extensive white
cheek extends
to nape

frosty-edged
remiges; buffy-
tipped greater
coverts

small bib
with mottled
corners

Gray-headed
Chickadee
adult

worn birds
quite gray
overall

pale edges of
coverts and
remiges reduced,
but white cheek
always more
extensive than
Boreal

Chestnut-backed Chickadee

Poecile rufescens
L 4¾"/12cm   **WS** 7½"/19cm

The smallest and most brightly colored parid in North America, Chestnut-backed Chickadee is restricted to dense, humid coniferous and mixed forests in the northern part of its range and riparian willows and drier pine, oak, and pine-oak forests toward the southern end. It often feeds high in the canopy but readily eats at feeding stations. From the San Francisco Bay area southward, Chestnut-backeds are of the subspecies *barlowi*, which lacks the rich chestnut flanks of nominate northern birds. The southern *barlowi* is slowly expanding its range southward along the coast. **VOICE** Song an accelerating trill. Calls include a quick *sickadee*, very thin, buzzy, and wiry compared to other chickadees.

adult (nominate), fresh

brilliant white cheek

chestnut back and flanks

pale edges on remiges and coverts

adult (nominate), worn

cap and bib less neat than on fresh adults

paler chestnut on back and flanks (but still richer than rusty wash in Boreal, Black-capped Chickadees)

adult (*barlowi*)

subspecies from south side of Golden Gate Bridge in San Francisco to Santa Barbara has little or no rufous in flanks

some individuals have rich grayish belly

adult (*barlowi*)

some individuals quite gray, with little chestnut above

adults

as in other parids, courting males feed females, which flutter wings and call

adult

intermediate individuals with chestnut blotches in flanks seen often in northern California

White-breasted Nuthatch

Sitta carolinensis
L 5¾"/15cm   **WS** 11"/28cm

White-breasted Nuthatch is associated with mature oak forests in the East, southern Arizona, and the West Coast, but it prefers pine forests in much of the Interior West. Most remain in pairs year-round. Differences in habitat preference, plumage, measurements, and calls among subspecies lead some to suspect they might represent separate species. **VOICE** Song a nasal, drawn-out series of *wi* or *yeh* notes. Calls vary from a clear, nasal *yank* (eastern nominate subspecies), to a higher *beerb* (Pacific *aculeata*), to a rapid series of call notes (western mountains *nelsoni* and Great Basin *tenuissima*).

White-breasted Nuthatch adult, eastern (nominate)

paler blue above and paler below than western taxa, with slightly broader dark crown, less rusty plumage in vent

White-breasted Nuthatch adult, Arizona (*nelsoni*)

western taxa differ from eastern taxa in longer bill, much more richly colored underparts, blue-gray flanks, and more rusty vent

Pygmy Nuthatch

Sitta pygmaea
L 4¼"/11cm   **WS** 7¾"/20cm

Pygmy Nuthatch, the world's smallest nuthatch, has many disjunct western populations; it favors yellow, Monterey, and bristlecone pines, as well as pinyon-juniper habitats, usually in mountains and foothills. **VOICE** Song and call a short, high-pitched, piping *pip* or *peep*, often delivered by many birds at once.

Pygmy Nuthatch adult

remiges have pale edges

(some show pale spot on nape)

crown has grayish tones

buffy underparts and contrasting bluish gray flanks

Red-breasted Nuthatch

Sitta canadensis
L 4½"/11cm **WS** 8½"/22cm

Red-breasted Nuthatch breeds mostly in mature spruce, fir, and pine forests of the North, Pacific coast, and western mountains, but in the nonbreeding season it can turn up in almost any wooded habitat. It regularly eats at bird-feeding stations. Some individuals, presumably worn females, can be very pale below, but the white supercilium is always present. **VOICE** Song and calls higher than White-breasted Nuthatch; a single or rapid-fire, nasal *bheen* or similar.

adult male — dark eye line, white supercilium (compare White-breasted)

reddish orange below

female — weaker, more grayish head pattern than adult male

typically much paler underparts than adult male

Brown-headed Nuthatch

Sitta pusilla
L 4½"/11cm **WS** 7¾"/20cm

This diminutive nuthatch, endemic to pine and pine-oak woods of the Southeast, might be passed over for a small pinecone were it not for its distinctive vocalizations. Its diet includes insects and pine seeds; when cone crops fail, it sometimes strays from its core range. This is the only North American bird other than corvids that is documented to make regular use of tools: it uses pieces of bark to pry off loose bark and reach insects. **VOICE** Song and call a mirthful, high-pitched series of squeaks and squeals sounding like *kyew* or *kyew-dew;* foraging family group sounds like a room full of squeak toys.

adult

indistinct pale spot on nape

uniformly colored wings

nut brown crown bordered by dark eye line

adult

worn birds may lack eye line or have indistinct dark eye line

Wrentit

Chamaea fasciata
L 6½"/17cm   **WS** 7"/18cm

Wrentit is found in chaparral, scrub, and suburban underbrush and gardens. Like wrens and parids, it feeds heavily on insects and spiders in summer and also often on small berries. Pairs mate for life and might never stray from their territory of an acre or two. Some individuals have lived as long as 12 years, quite old for a small passerine. **VOICE** Song a crescendo series of clear whistles (sounding like a police whistle), accelerating like a bouncing ball coming to rest; singing males often wait to sing after Bewick's Wren.

distinguished from Bewick's Wren and Juniper and Oak Titmice by much longer tail and stark, pale eyes

rich brown above

grayish head, buffy throat

larger than Bushtit

darker adult

paler adult

pale mark above eyes

grayer birds still show buffy throat (some with pink cast) and breast

Brown Creeper

Certhia americana
L 5¼"/13cm   **WS** 7¾"/20cm

Brown Creeper inhabits mature deciduous and coniferous forests, where it makes a nest behind a loose strip of bark. To forage, it hitches woodpecker-like up one tree after another, usually in a spiraling pattern, starting at the base of the tree. Creepers join foraging groups of nuthatches, parids, and woodpeckers in winter and occasionally visit bird-feeding stations for suet. **VOICE** Song a 3- to 5-part series of thin, fluting notes, falling then rising. Call a modulated, sibilant *see,* similar to Golden-crowned Kinglet.

adult

decurved bill

mottled gray-brown above, including wings (well camouflaged against tree bark)

creeps up trees quickly

Bushtit

Psaltriparus minimus
L 4½"/11cm WS 6"/15cm

Bushtit, at 0.18 oz (5g), is one of the lightest of North American birds, weighing less than some hummingbirds. It is found in scrub, chaparral, and woodlands with brushy undergrowth. When not nesting, Bushtits forage in large flocks consisting of several family groups; they move rapidly through undergrowth, gleaning insects and larvae from small branches. Males of all subspecies are dark-eyed; females are pale-eyed after their first month. **VOICE** No song. Calls are high, wiry, rough notes, usually delivered by foraging flocks.

adult male, interior (*plumbeus* group)

tiny dark eyes

gray with brown auriculars

(black auriculars rare north of Mexico)

juvenile

plain mousy brown

travels with adults

adult female, coastal (*minimus* group)

brown crown

yellow eyes

sides washed pale brown

Verdin

Auriparus flaviceps
L 4½"/11cm WS 6½"/17cm

Verdin, the only North American bird in the family Remizidae (penduline tits), is found in mesquite and thorn scrub in desert washes and riparian areas, and occasionally in suburban areas with trees. It forages chickadee-like, hanging from small branches to glean insects and spiders and their eggs; it also feeds on nectar by piercing flowers at the base. Unusual among American birds, Verdin builds a bulky, spherical nest only for roosting. **VOICE** Song a sweet, high-pitched *sweet sweet sweet*. Call a weak, modulated *tseet;* also a loud, smacking *tchep.*

adult variably yellow head

chestnut lesser coverts can be hard to see

short, sharp, conical bill

juvenile

nondescript

short, sharp bill (compare warblers, vireos, flycatchers)

shorter tail than Bushtit

usually attended by adults

Wrens and Dipper

Wrens (family Troglodytidae) are small, mostly brown passerines with thin, decurved bills and often long tails that they hold cocked above the back. They occupy a wide array of habitats, from border deserts to the rocky Aleutian Islands, and spend most of their time near the ground. To many suburban dwellers, wrens are familiar visitors to backyard brambles, brush heaps, and feeding stations; several species readily accept nest boxes and will nest even in old boots, automobiles, or outhouses. Wrens are probably relatives of the gnatcatchers (and the tropical gnatwrens), which are most closely related to Old World warblers, but their relationships and phylogenetic placement have yet to be clearly determined.

Although this group's family name derives from the Latin for "cave-dweller," most of the nine species that breed in North America never enter caves. But wrens are expert foragers in tight spaces, including thickets, tangles, treefalls, and rocky crevices—any site that supports an abundance of insects, millipedes, spiders, and their eggs, which are a wren's chief foods. Some species also eat seeds and small fruits, especially in the cooler

American Dippers often submerge their heads to look for food before plunging into the water.

months, and a few eat snails, small frogs, lizards, or other small vertebrates. Their long, thin bills give them almost a surgeon's precision in plucking prey from crannies.

Wrens sing to attract mates and defend territories and are among the most musical of American birds. Their repertoires are variable among species: Cactus Wren seems to sing the same chugging song year after year, whereas Marsh Wren may sing more than 150 song types over the breeding season. Females sometimes counter-sing or duet with the males, especially in Carolina Wren, though their vocalizations are less varied and musical. Wrens build cup-shaped or spherical nests mostly in bushes or reeds, but some nest in crevices or cacti. Most of the wrens that nest in northern North America migrate southward in autumn or at least withdraw from northern parts of their range.

American Dipper (Cinclidae) is a gray, heavyset bird, about the size of a thrush. Dippers have short tails and pointed bills; their powerful legs and feet are adapted for doing something no other passerine does: swimming and walking underwater, where they forage for invertebrates. Dippers make round nests of mosses and various plants, placing them near streams, usually on a ledge, cliff, or underside of a bridge.

Wren populations in North America are thought to be stable, with a few exceptions: in the Southwest, Cactus and Rock Wrens may have lost ground to suburban development, and in the East, Bewick's Wren has declined sharply.

Male Cactus Wrens sing many subtle variations of a simple song; females deliver a quiet, higher-pitched song.

American Dipper
Cinclus mexicanus
L 8"/20cm **WS** 11"/28cm

American Dipper differs from its wren relatives in a more heavyset body, longer legs, uniformly gray plumage, and mostly aquatic lifestyle. It lives its entire life along mountain streams and rivers, where it wades and dives for insects and their larvae. Dippers descend to lower elevations in winter but are extremely rare out of range. "Water Ouzel" is a vernacular name for the species throughout its range. **VOICE** Song a series of sweet paired and trebled notes, in cadence very like a thrasher. Call wiry, single or double *dzit* notes.

adult
slate gray
short tail often cocked
bobs body often
always found near streams

juvenile
pale yellowish bill
narrow, pale edges to coverts and tertials
paler overall than adult, especially below

Cactus Wren
Campylorhynchus brunneicapillus
L 8½"/22cm **WS** 11"/28cm

This large wren is a permanent resident of arid regions, particularly cactus deserts and dry hilly country. It is often seen perched atop a cactus or other vegetation, delivering its unusual song or attending to its large stick nest. The threatened subspecies *sandiegense* of coastal southern California has sparser spotting below. **VOICE** Song a rapid series of guttural *ga* notes, sounding like a combustion engine that won't "turn over." Calls include low, growling, corvidlike *kraw*, *krot*, and *kok* notes, sometimes in series.

adult
long, broad supercilium
distinct white markings in coverts, mantle, remiges
spotted below
large and conspicuous

House Wren

Troglodytes aedon
L 4½"/11cm WS 6"/15cm

This is a familiar garden bird across most of southern Canada and the lower 48 states. It nests in many sorts of cavities and readily accepts nest boxes near wooded, brushy areas. Plumages vary from mousy gray to rufescent browns. Brown-throated Wren (several subspecies known collectively as the *brunneicollis* group) apparently inhabits the Chiricahua Mountains of Arizona. **VOICE** Song a series of rapid, bubbling trills, descending. Calls mostly short *chrrt* or *chik* notes; Brown-throated gives a shrill *tseeeer*.

brown adult
faint superciium
uniform plumage above and below
lacks ventral barring (compare shorter-tailed Winter Wren)

gray adult

adult (*brunneicollis* group)

southwestern subspecies rich buff below

Winter Wren

Troglodytes troglodytes
L 4"/10cm WS 5½"/14cm

Winter Wren is usually found foraging mouselike in brush piles, tree falls, or vine tangles with its tail cocked. This cavity nester breeds in boreal, montane, and Pacific coastal forests and winters in the Southeast and along the West Coast. **VOICE** Song a long series of fluting trills, higher than House Wren, sounding like a rapidly played piccolo. Call a nasal, rather loud *jimp-jimp* in East (like call of Song Sparrow), a drier *chek* or *tenk* note in West (like call of Wilson's Warbler).

adult
well-defined supercilium
smallest species of wren
very dark above
short tail
(Pacific/Northwestern *pacificus* group darker above than eastern, with buffier throat)

adult
eastern birds less richly colored than western birds

Carolina Wren

Thryothorus ludovicianus
L 5"/13cm **WS** 7"/18cm

A familiar sight and sound in the East, Carolina Wren is found in a variety of habitats, including suburban gardens, where it nests in cavities and nest boxes. Its range has gradually expanded northward during the past 100 years. Subspecies in southern Texas and Florida are more richly colored than nominate birds. **VOICE** Male's song a rollicking, remarkably varied set of repeated phrases, often expressed as *tea-kettle, tea-kettle, tea-kettle!* Female often delivers a harsh, trilled song/call antiphonally with male.

adult, fresh

black-bordered supercilium extends past nape

rusty above, buffy below

outer rectrices lack white tips (present in Bewick's)

adult, worn

juvenile and some adults whitish below

Bewick's Wren

Thryomanes bewickii
L 5"/13cm **WS** 7"/18cm

Bewick's Wren is an active, agile resident of dense thickets and brushy habitats. It is often seen foraging near the ground; there, its habit of twitching the tail from side to side distinguishes it from similar species. Populations in the East have declined greatly over the past century, possibly because of the spread of House Wren, which often destroys the eggs of Bewick's. **VOICE** Song a varied mix of dry trills and sweeter warbled phrases, most complex in eastern part of range. Call somewhat harsh *djik* or *pik* notes.

adult, western

long, thin supercilium lacks black border

unbarred above

pale gray belly and sides of neck

adult, eastern

some taxa warmer brown, even rusty brown above

Sedge Wren
Cistothorus platensis
L 4½"/11cm WS 6"/15cm

The tiny, pale Sedge Wren nests in moist fields and upland marshes and winters in similar habitats as well as saltmarsh edges. Though often difficult to see, it is easily detected by its distinctive voice. Because its breeding habitat is unpredictable in its availability, Sedge Wren is a nomadic nester and often renests or nests late in the season. **VOICE** Song a series of rich, distinct, husky *chip* notes; 1 or 2 introductory notes followed by a trilled set of similar notes. Call, frequently given, similar to introductory song notes.

adult
stippled crown; weakly defined supercilium
mottled wing pattern
buffy sides

adult
dark back streaked with straw yellow and dark brown

Marsh Wren
Cistothorus palustris
L 5"/13cm WS 6"/15cm

A rather dark wren of both freshwater and saltwater marshes, Marsh Wren is frequently seen singing its memorable song while perched on reeds and rushes. It builds spherical nests suspended above the water by several reed stalks. As many as 14 subspecies of Marsh Wren have been named. **VOICE** Song a rich, rapid mixture of gurgling, tinkling, and bubbling phrases, more grating and highly variable in western subspecies. Call a low, soft *tuk*.

adult
distinct white supercilium, back streaking
eastern birds more richly colored, with rusty flanks; black and white neck streaking
nesters often perch in view
adult
solid brown crown (compare Sedge Wren)
western and coastal southeastern birds gray below

Canyon Wren

Catherpes mexicanus
L 6"/15cm   WS 8"/20cm

The richly colored, long-billed Canyon Wren is a permanent resident in areas with vertical topography—rocky outcrops, cliffs, and canyons—where its sweet, cascading song seems a part of the western landscape. This species readily takes up residence in small southwestern towns where there are stone structures available. **VOICE** Song an unforgettable, loud, descending series of rich *tew* notes, slowing toward end, usually concluded with a nasal, scolding call. Call a sharp, electric *deeet!*, higher than Rock Wren.

darker adult
rusty tail
spots on back and wings
long bill

paler adult
some individuals paler gray-brown above
chestnut belly contrasts with white throat

Rock Wren

Salpinctes obsoletus
L 6"/15cm   WS 9"/23cm

Rock Wren, a rather plain species of the West, inhabits dry areas such as scrubland, arroyos, and rocky flats and slopes, where it typically sings from the ground or stone structures. Nesters in the north of the species' range withdraw southward in winter. Rock and Canyon Wrens are rather bold among humans; both species sway and bob when eyeing a person in their territory. **VOICE** Song a widely spaced series of 2 to 8 high-pitched, wiry trills, varying in pitch and speed. Call a distinctive, far-carrying *zdeeee*.

adult
gray above
buff-tipped gray tail
moderately long bill
spots on back and wings

adult
frequently bobs body when alert
cinnamon-colored rump (difficult to see)
flanks and supercilium washed with buff

Warblers, Kinglets, Gnatcatchers, and Allies

Adult male Canada Warbler with insect.

New World warblers (family Parulidae), Old World warblers (Sylviidae), kinglets (Regulidae), and Olive Warbler (Peucedramidae) are all small passerines with thin, pointed bills, active foraging habits, and usually colorful plumages, particularly in breeding adult males. The New World warblers are sometimes called "wood-warblers" to distinguish them from the Old World warblers, a family represented in North America by the gnatcatchers (genus *Polioptila*) and by Arctic Warbler. Until very recently, Olive Warbler was thought to be a parulid, but studies suggest a possible close relationship to finches (fringillids). Despite the many similarities in these groups, there are important differences. For example, like other oscine passerines of the Americas, parulids and Olive Warbler have nine primaries, while sylviids have ten; this means that American parulids appear to be more closely related to blackbirds and cardinals than to Old World warblers.

Warblers and their allies are tenacious, adaptable, hardy birds that have radiated into habitats as diverse as their jewel-like colors: from marshes and muskeg to thorn scrub and mangrove forests. Most species fare poorly, however, in developed urban and modern agricultural environments, which have too little in the way of insect life, nest sites, or both. Some warblers specialize to a greater degree than others in their choice of habitat: Kirtland's Warbler, for instance, nests almost entirely

in very young jack pine forests found in Michigan, and Golden-winged Warbler selects recently disturbed and early successional habitats (which are ephemeral and increasingly scarce in most parts of its range). Bachman's Warbler, probably extinct, was a species of southeastern swampwoods, apparently around stands of native cane; these habitats disappeared as flood regimes of many rivers were altered, although it is not known if this was a cause of the species' disappearance.

On migration, warblers, kinglets, and gnatcatchers will forage in habitats similar to their nesting areas when possible, but they readily take advantage of local abundances of insects or, in the case of the larger species, small fruits. Each species has a consistent manner of foraging. Yellow-rumped Warbler is perhaps the most flexible in its feeding techniques: it takes food by flycatching,

This rare photograph of a male Bachman's Warbler at Charleston, South Carolina, taken in 1958, documents one of the last verified records of this species.

gleaning, hover-gleaning, creeping (like a nuthatch), ground-sallying, and plucking. Most warblers and allies forage by just one or two of these methods, and some have quite specialized manners of hunting for insects and their larvae. Swainson's Warbler, for instance, walks through leaf litter and makes vibrations with its large feet, presumably to startle prey; Worm-eating Warbler seeks out insects in curled clusters of dead leaves; Black-and-white Warbler forages on trees, like nuthatches; and American Redstart flashes and fans its tail as it forages, flycatching the insects it flushes. Warblers seldom take vertebrate prey, although waterthrushes and other large species sometimes capture minnow-sized fish or small salamanders. Kinglets, with their tiny bills, are adept at removing tiny aphids and other arthropods and their eggs from tight cracks in bark and coniferous needle clusters; because these resources are available through the winter, many kinglets remain in the United States during the nonbreeding months.

For such large and diverse groups of birds as the sylviids, regulids, and parulids, it is surprising that mating systems are so uniform. Virtually all species are seasonally monogamous (although, as in many other passerine groups under study, there is increasing evidence of extra-pair copulations). Males arrive ahead of females on the breeding grounds and sing almost constantly, even as they forage. Courtship involves mostly singing, posturing, and in some species song flights. Males sing even after the young have fledged in some cases, but song activity drops sharply after the eggs hatch. In a few species, females are also known to sing, albeit usually quietly and infrequently. Many American warblers have a complex, rambling dawn or dusk song that is distinctly different from the day song(s) and appears to be intended for territorial maintenance. Parulids, sylviids, and regulids all build cup-shaped nests, including the cavity-nesting Lucy's and Prothonotary Warblers; some species place their nests on the ground, others quite high in trees or bushes. Soon after the young fledge, most warblers begin their long migrations to the New World tropics.

Populations of many warbler species have declined across large parts of North America as a result of clearcutting, development, and fragmentation of many types of forest. The same activities, however, have often produced local increases in species that utilize disturbed and regenerating habitats, such as Prairie Warbler and Common Yellowthroat. Bird conservationists are currently most concerned about localized species with very small populations (Kirtland's, Golden-cheeked, Lucy's, Hermit, and Colima Warblers) and about widespread species whose declines are well documented and appear to be steady (Cerulean, Golden-winged, and Prothonotary Warblers).

Blue-gray Gnatcatcher is the only gnatcatcher species that migrates. Like many other American passerines, it is currently expanding its range northward.

Ruby-crowned Kinglet's light body enables it to forage at the tips of branches, unlike many warblers, which are heavier.

Small Woodland Birds

Distinguishing between the many different small birds that inhabit a local park can be daunting. While woodpeckers, hummingbirds, and owls give themselves away quickly by their distinctive shapes and behaviors, the passerines—perching birds in the order Passeriformes, of which at least 402 species have been recorded in North America—have a remarkable number of look-alike species and families. These pages provide a thumbnail comparison of many types of small birds that might frequent a local birding spot with wooded areas or chaparral. (See also "Small Brown Landbirds," which covers mostly ground birds; pages 480–481.) When looking at an unfamiliar small bird, pay attention to its behavior, overall structure, calls, and bill shape.

Flycatchers can be difficult to identify, especially the smallest species of the genus *Empidonax* (pages 308–313). Like many woodland and scrubland birds, most flycatchers have eye rings, wing bars, and fairly plain plumages overall. Unlike other small woodland birds, flycatchers usually perch upright, watching for and then chasing passing insects, which they capture with an often audible snap of the bill. Many species twitch the wings and tail when perched.

Vireos (pages 326–333) are compact, mostly plain passerines with stout, slightly hooked bills and rather heavy legs. Vireos tend to move slowly and deliberately through trees and brush, looking for insects and their larvae and for fruit. The smallest species, however, forage quite actively, more like a kinglet or warbler, and have shorter and less bulbous bills than the larger species. The small Hutton's Vireo is very easily mistaken for a Ruby-crowned Kinglet, although it does not forage as actively as a kinglet.

Kinglets (page 356) are truly tiny birds with the smallest of bills. They forage almost continuously, Ruby-crowned often flicking its patterned wings as it moves through the trees, and can hover at the tips of branches to glean tiny insect larvae. Though superficially similar to warblers, vireos, and flycatchers, kinglets have even thinner bills, thinner legs, and shorter tails.

Warblers (pages 357–389) most resemble vireos, but nearly all warblers have thinner legs and thinner, pointed bills that lack the vireo's slight hook at the end. Warblers are rather active foragers and have many strategies for taking insects and larvae, including flycatching; most glean insects directly from branches, as vireos do. Warblers are most confusing when in their plainest plumages, whether streaky juvenal plumage (held only briefly) or first-fall plumage. Breeding females and nonbreeding adults can also be confusing, but in most species they have at least a hint of the head or wing pattern of the breeding male. Even the drabbest of warblers often have distinctive tail spots or a rump patch—plumage characteristics not shared with vireos, kinglets, or flycatchers in North America.

Yellow-bellied Flycatcher

Warbling Vireo

Blue-gray Gnatcatcher

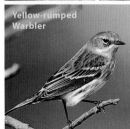

Yellow-rumped Warbler

Ruby-crowned Kinglet

House Wren

Boreal Chickadee

Oak Titmouse

Wrentit

Bushtit

Gnatcatchers (pages 358–359), with their long tails and active foraging habits, remind many observers of tiny mockingbirds. These very slender, tiny-billed birds chase insects in the air like flycatchers but move through the vegetation more rapidly, more like a kinglet, constantly flipping the tail to flush prey. Although distinctive, gnatcatchers can be confused with the even shorter-billed Bushtit, which travels in flocks most of the year. Pale females of the western gnatcatchers might also be taken for flycatchers but for their different foraging behaviors and very thin bills.

Chickadees (pages 338–341) are among the most familiar of woodland and backyard birds. They spend most of their time foraging actively in trees for tiny insects and larvae, often hanging upside down. In most cases, the dark cap and bib make them instantly recognizable, but some worn birds, especially of the brown-capped species, can have indistinct head patterns. Like their relatives the titmice, chickadees have short, stout bills and relatively heavy legs, but chickadees are smaller and slimmer than titmice.

Titmice (pages 336–337) and chickadees often form mixed-species foraging flocks in the nonbreeding season, announcing their presence with their similar calls. Titmice are mostly plainer and larger than chickadees, and some are plainer than small flycatchers; titmice lack wing

bars and eye rings, which many flycatchers have. Titmice are usually quickly recognized by their calls, active foraging behavior, short crests, and short, stout, pointed bills.

Bushtit (page 345) is not much more colorful than a titmouse but is likewise distinctive. Like a kinglet, Bushtit is a tiny bird with a very small bill, but it has a long tail for its size and often looks fluffed up. It is among the most active of birds, moving through brush quickly to glean insects and larvae. After the breeding season, Bushtits gather in large flocks; flockmates often follow one another single file as they cross an opening.

Wrens (pages 347–351) are small, brown birds of woodlands and many other habitats. They spend a good deal of time low in the vegetation or on the ground, using their long, thin, decurved bills to pluck spiders and other prey from crevices. Their tails can be short or long and are often held cocked as they forage. Although wrens do not form flocks, family groups sometimes remain together after the young fledge.

Wrentit (page 344) looks like a combination of a wren, a Bushtit, and perhaps a titmouse. Usually quite unobtrusive, Wrentit is found mainly in California chaparral. It forages low in the vegetation, using its tiny, slightly decurved bill to take small insects and berries. Though it does not flock with other species, it may eat at bird feeders.

Ruby-crowned Kinglet

Regulus calendula
L 4¼"/11cm   WS 7½"/19cm

Ruby-crowned Kinglet breeds in coniferous forests and winters in varied wooded and brushy habitats. When foraging, often in groups with other small birds, it moves restlessly through vegetation with nervous flicks of its wings, frequently delivering its distinctive call. This species regularly hover-gleans insects from the tips of branches. It is attracted to pishing and owl calls. **VOICE** Song a rollicking series of sweet, staccato notes on different pitches, ending with slower, syncopated phrases. Call a low *je-dit*.

adult

heavy eye ring, but thin at top and bottom

tiny and compact, smaller than warblers and vireos

adult male

little scarlet crown raised when agitated

thinner legs than vireos; soles of feet yellow

adult

very similar to Hutton's Vireo but with thinner bill, darker lores, dark secondary bases

Golden-crowned Kinglet

Regulus satrapa
L 4"/10cm   WS 7"/18cm

This tiny kinglet inhabits coniferous and mixed woods year-round and is often detected by its high, lisping call. It breeds mostly in boreal and high-mountain forests and forages in small flocks, often hanging upside down to glean insects and larvae from bark and needles. In winter small groups often join groups of foraging woodland birds. This species is easily drawn to pishing. **VOICE** Song a series of high *see* notes that accelerate and rise, then drop in chickadee-like jumble at close. Call similar to song.

adult male

tiny; smaller than warblers, with smaller bill

secondaries have dark bases, like Ruby-crowned but unlike vireos

male has orange feathers within golden crown, raised when agitated

adult

golden crown bordered with black

complex wing pattern

pale supercilium, black eye line

Arctic Warbler
Phylloscopus borealis
L 5"/13cm **WS** 8"/20cm

Arctic Warbler nests in thickets of dwarf birches, willows, and alders along streams in western Alaska, where it is locally common in summer; it migrates in fall across the Bering Sea to southern Asia. A few vagrants have reached California and northwestern Canada. Warblers of the genus *Phylloscopus* belong to the family Sylviidae, with gnatcatchers, and are not close relatives of American warblers. **VOICE** Song a rich, staccato, pulsating trill on one pitch. Call a sharp, modulated *dzzt*.

adult

olive-brown above

long supercilium extends to nape

narrow pale tips to coverts form very thin wing bar (lost when worn)

bill more blunt-tipped than in parulids

long primary projection

breeding adult male

often sings from top of willow, birch, or alder

pale legs usually conspicuous (compare Tennessee Warbler)

Dusky Warbler
Phylloscopus fuscatus
L 5¼"/13cm **WS** 7¼"/18cm

This Siberian species is an irregular migrant to Alaska's offshore islands, chiefly in fall, and has also visited California as a fall vagrant at least 6 times. A shy bird, it is usually located by its call note as it forages for insects in thickets and low, rank vegetation, flicking its wings. **VOICE** Call a sharp *shtek*, often compared to call of Lincoln's Sparrow.

adult/1st fall

pale supercilium

very short primary projection

short, thin bill

dusky brown or olive-brown upperparts; lacks wing bars (compare Arctic Warbler)

Golden-crowned Warbler
Basileuterus culicivorus
L 5"/13cm **WS** 7½"/19cm

Golden-crowned Warbler has visited Texas and New Mexico rarely, mostly in fall and winter. It forages in low scrub and riparian thickets. **VOICE** Song a set of distinct, rich *wee* and *chew* whistles, simple but varied, with upslurred ending. Call recalls a wren or Ruby-crowned Kinglet.

adult

yellow or gold-orange crown stripe with black borders (similar to Golden-crowned Kinglet, unlike other warblers)

unpatterned upperwings

deep yellow below

Blue-gray Gnatcatcher

Polioptila caerulea
L 4½"/11cm WS 6"/15cm

Blue-gray Gnatcatcher breeds in virtually any wooded or semiopen habitat. It is usually observed foraging through treetops or undergrowth while flicking its tail and giving a mewing call, reminding some of a tiny mockingbird. This species has expanded its range northeastward in recent decades, and spring vagrants are increasing on the Great Plains. **VOICE** Song an insistent series or jumble of thin notes punctuated by harsher notes and imitations. Call a very thin *speee* or *fszeeeee,* sounding like a begging nestling.

breeding adult male, western

stronger blue tones above than other gnatcatchers

primary projection longer than in other western gnatcatchers

adult female, eastern

prominent white eye ring

bright blue crown and back

white undertail (unlike other gnatcatchers)

brighter, clearer blue above than western Blue-grays

Black-tailed Gnatcatcher

Polioptila melanura
L 4½"/11cm WS 5½"/14cm

Black-tailed Gnatcatcher is a permanent resident of desert flats, washes, and ravines where acacia, mesquite, creosote, and paloverde dominate the landscape. It is found mostly in the Mojave and Sonoran Deserts and adjacent arid country. This species travels in pairs, staying mostly in vegetation and rarely flycatching as Blue-gray does. **VOICE** Song a complex, run-on mixture of different notes and imitations. Calls include a wrenlike fuss or chatter and many others, some probably imitations.

breeding adult male

grayer above than Black-capped Gnatcatcher

prominent eye ring

(nonbreeding birds lose cap and retain only black streak over eyes)

darker tones and less white in tail than Blue-gray Gnatcatcher

breeding adult male

rectrices black below with distinct white tips

adult female

shorter-billed than Black-capped

paler overall than California Gnatcatcher

California Gnatcatcher

Polioptila californica
L 4½"/11cm **WS** 5½"/14cm

This threatened species, found only in coastal sage scrub of southern California and Baja California, has become increasingly scarce as cities and suburbs expand. As of 2004 fewer than 5,000 pairs remained in the U.S. This species usually forages in pairs low in the scrub and interacts very little with Blue-gray Gnatcatcher, which winters in the same habitat. Nonbreeding males resemble females but have a dark streak over the eyes. **VOICE** Song a set of wiry, mewing notes on one pitch. Call a distinctive, shrill, nasal *rreeee-eer*, rising and falling; recalls a kitten.

breeding adult male — dark cap

gray-brown tertial edges (compare Blue-gray Gnatcatcher)

weak eye ring, most visible below eyes

duskier below than other gnatcatchers

breeding adult male

longer tail than Blue-gray

female

sootier overall than Black-tailed, with brownish tones, especially on belly

outer rectrices have narrower white tips than Black-tailed

Black-capped Gnatcatcher

Polioptila nigriceps
L 4¼"/11cm **WS** 6"/15cm

Black-capped Gnatcatcher is a rare and irregular year-round visitor to arid canyons and lowland scrub of southeastern Arizona. It is found in breeding pairs or in mixed pairs with Black-tailed Gnatcatcher. Because mixed pairs have produced hybrid young, use caution when identifying this species; some individuals may not be identifiable. **VOICE** Song most similar to Black-tailed. Call a scratchy, catlike *meeeer* or *reeeer*.

breeding adult male

longer bill than Blue-gray and Black-tailed Gnatcatchers

black crown (March–August) extends below eyes; reduced to few dark marks over eyes after breeding season

adult female

(nonbreeding male similar)

tail looks white from below (unlike Black-tailed)

told in all plumages from Black-tailed and Blue-gray by graduated white outer rectrices (tips widely spaced)

Blue-winged Warbler

Vermivora pinus
L 4¾"/12cm **WS** 7½"/19cm

Blue-winged Warbler is a well-studied species of diverse, brushy, second-growth habitats—from old fields to power-line cuts to woodland edges, especially where the understory is dense. It gleans insects from leaves, buds, and twigs, sometimes hanging upside down. Blue-winged has expanded its range in recent years, often into habitats where the related Golden-winged Warbler is found. The two species interbreed frequently and produce a wide variety of hybrids and backcrosses, which sing songs of either or both species. First-generation hybrids of pure parents are named "Brewster's Warbler"; the many backcrosses include "Lawrence's Warbler," the result of a pairing of "Brewster's" with Golden-winged. Studies of interactions between Blue-winged and Golden-winged Warblers reveal that in some areas Blue-winged is the dominant species, while in other places Golden-winged dominates. Blue-wingeds and hybrids usually winter in Mexico and northern Central America. **VOICE** Song a highly modulated *bzeeee bzzzzz*, second note lower. Call a sharp, flat *tsik* or *snik*.

adult male

bluish gray wings have prominent white wing bars

long, slender bill

vivid yellow face and breast

white or pale yellow undertail coverts

female

like male, but head and wing pattern and colors more muted

undertail coverts usually contrastingly white

wing bars narrow, often with yellow cast

adult male, Lawrence's Warbler

this backcross shows head pattern like Golden-winged Warbler, but underparts and wing pattern like Blue-winged

Brewster's Warbler

female and immature similar to Golden-winged but lack dusky auriculars and throat; usually show dark loral line

Brewster's Warbler

similar to Blue-winged but with dark gray back, white belly, yellow in wing bars

Golden-winged Warbler

Vermivora chrysoptera
L 4¾"/12cm WS 7½"/19cm

In a family of gems, Golden-winged Warbler stands out as one of the more striking members. Like Blue-winged Warbler, it inhabits brushy areas but prefers earlier stages of succession. To the north, it also inhabits alder bogs and areas with aspens, larches, and willows near spruce bogs. Like Blue-winged, this species forages like a chickadee, often hanging upside down to glean insects. **VOICE** Song a wiry *bzeeee bzzzz bzzzz bzzzz*, first note higher. Calls similar to Blue-winged.

adult male — brilliant lemon yellow crown and coverts

gray nape, mantle, tail; off-white underparts

black auriculars and throat

adult female — faint head and wing pattern always present

much paler gray than adult male

Olive Warbler

Peucedramus taeniatus
L 5¼"/13cm WS 9¼"/23cm

Olive Warbler looks like a warbler, but recent studies have shown that it is anatomically, genetically, and vocally different from warblers, and thus it is placed in its own family, Peucedramidae. This resident of montane pine forests forages like a warbler or kinglet, probing needle clusters and bark for insects and often flicking its long wings. As do finches, but not warblers, nestlings defecate on the rim of the nest. **VOICE** Song very similar to a titmouse's whistled *peeta peeta peeta*. Call a rich, descending *kyew*.

breeding adult male — gray above, pale gray below

broad, white wing bars; white primary bases

black auriculars; rather heavy bill

rich orange head and breast

1st fall female

faint trace of mask framed in buff

adult female/1st year male

dusky yellowish or tawny head; dark auriculars

Orange-crowned Warbler

Vermivora celata
L 5"/13cm **WS** 7¼"/18cm

Orange-crowned Warbler is a hardy warbler that is widespread in the North and West but scarce in the East. It inhabits brushy undergrowth in a great variety of habitats, from boreal forest to chaparral, and winters in thickets and tangles across the southern states and into Mexico, farther north than most warblers. This variable species is often confused with other warblers, particularly Tennessee and Yellow, though it tends to forage lower and more deliberately than those species. Orange-crowned varies from rich greenish yellow with blurry streaks to strikingly pale overall. Individuals differ according to age, sex, and subspecies: adult males of the Pacific coastal subspecies (*lutescens,* from southern Alaska to California, and *sordida* of southern California) are brighter yellow overall, and the nominate taiga subspecies and the Rocky Mountain subspecies *orestera* are much duller, some showing little yellow (particularly the first-fall females). Birds that nest farthest north migrate early in spring and quite late in fall. **VOICE** Song a listless, choppy trill, trailing off at end (similar to Yellow-rumped Warbler). Call a distinctive, sharp *stik*.

breeding adult male (*lutescens*)

indistinct head pattern with dark eye line

thinner, more decurved bill than Tennessee Warbler

yellow undertail coverts

greenish streaks below

pale adult (nominate)

orange crown usually concealed

shorter primary projection, longer tail than Tennessee Warbler

palest birds show very little yellow in undertail coverts

adult (*lutescens*)

yellowish throat and broken eye ring contrast with dusky crown

greenish cast above

usually dusky olive sides

usually yellowish undertail coverts

adult (likely female *lutescens*)

similar to male but colors more muted

1st fall (nominate)

pale throat, narrow eye arcs, hint of eye line

grayish green above, unlike bright yellow-green of Tennessee Warbler

Tennessee Warbler

Vermivora peregrina
L 4¾"/12cm   WS 7¾"/20cm

Tennessee Warbler breeds in open, boggy boreal forests and muskeg, usually where the understory is well developed and spruce budworm caterpillars are abundant, and winters in Central America and northern South America. As a long-distance migrant, it has long wings for its size, a feature accentuated by a short tail. **VOICE** Song a very loud, 3-part series of calls or phrases, increasing in tempo like a bouncing ball coming to rest and usually on different pitches. Call a rich, incisive *tik*.

breeding adult male
pewter crown and nape
moss green back
sharp bill
white supercilium
some are similar to Philadelphia Vireo, but bill fine and pointed

1st fall

similar to Orange-crowned Warbler but more vibrant yellow-green above; white undertail coverts in all plumages (faint yellow tint on some young birds); longer primary projection, shorter tail

Yellow Warbler

Dendroica petechia
L 5"/13cm   WS 7¾"/20cm

In riparian areas with abundant willows, from stunted tundra woods to the desert Southwest, Yellow Warbler's song seems to ring out from every other tree. The species also favors brushy fields—even clearcuts, strip mines, and abandoned orchards. In southernmost Florida, the subspecies *gundlachi* can be very plain and is often confused with *Vermivora*. **VOICE** Song a set of rich, sweet notes, last note highest, famously rendered *sweet sweet sweet I'm so SWEET!* Call a loud, sweet, full *chip*.

adult
reddish streaking below (absent or very faint in adult female)
rich yellow overall, brightest below

1st fall female
some individuals quite pale overall

female/1st year
yellowish overall, including tail spots

coverts and tertials have contrasting pale edges (unlike Orange-crowned)

first-year plumage remarkably plain, easily confused with *Vermivora*

Virginia's Warbler

Vermivora virginiae
L 4¾"/12cm   WS 7½"/19cm

On brushy slopes in dry mountain forests of the Great Basin and southern Rockies, Virginia's Warbler can be found singing from pines or oaks or foraging in undergrowth for insects. After breeding, it may form large flocks, often with other warblers, that forage rapidly up and down slopes. This bird's name honors the wife of William Anderson, who discovered the species in 1858. **VOICE** Song a loose set of up to 6 slurred, warbled notes; second or third set with different pitch and structure often follows. Call a loud *plik* or *spik* like Nashville Warbler.

adult male

rusty crown patch

often bobs tail

gray, with yellow breast patch and tail coverts

female/ 1st year

prominent white eye ring

pale gray overall (lacks Nashville Warbler's yellowish throat)

often has yellowish area on center of breast

yellow tail coverts above and below

Colima Warbler

Vermivora crissalis
L 5¾"/15cm   WS 7¾"/20cm

Colima Warbler is known in the U.S. only from the Chisos Mountains in Big Bend National Park, Texas. There, up to 150 birds breed in north-facing canyons and slopes with bunchgrasses, oaks, junipers, pinyon pines, and madrones at elevations of 6,000–7,000' (1,800–2,100m). **VOICE** Song a bright, staccato trill recalling Orange-crowned Warbler in pace, often descending, weakening, or lower at end (some close with a sharp, higher *tyew!*). Call a sharp *plik,* like *ridgwayi* Nashville Warbler.

adult

rusty crown patch often apparent

recalls Virginia's Warbler, but larger and darker above

adult

in fresh plumage shows extensive khaki-olive tones in back and flanks, unlike Virginia's

always lacks yellow in breast (compare Virginia's)

Nashville Warbler
Vermivora ruficapilla
L 4¾"/12cm   WS 7½"/19cm

Nashville Warbler breeds in open wood-lands with extensive brushy understory, often near spruce bogs, and in pine barrens and dry, successional habitats. The longer-tailed western subspecies *ridgwayi* bobs its tail frequently, unlike the eastern subspecies. **VOICE** Song usually 2 sets of sweet notes, first slower, second trilled, like Tennessee Warbler but less incisive: *seebit seebit seebit rititititi;* song richer in western birds, often lacking second part. Call a sharp *spik*, softer in eastern (nominate) birds.

Lucy's Warbler
Vermivora luciae
L 4¼"/11cm   WS 7"/18cm

Lucy's Warbler, the smallest American warbler, breeds in mesquite, salt-cedar, and low willow thickets and bosques (dense forests of low, thorny trees) along streams; unlike most warblers, it regularly nests in cavities. This shy but active forager gleans insects from twigs and foliage and nectar from desert plants, frequently bobbing its tail as it feeds. **VOICE** Song a series of loud, sweet notes on different pitches *(ti ti ti ti swee swee sweet)*, similar to Virginia's and Yellow Warblers. Call a sharp but vibrant *fink*.

Mourning Warbler
Oporornis philadelphia
L 5¼"/13cm   WS 7½"/19cm

Mourning Warbler breeds in disturbed habitats, especially berry brambles and fern-rich tangles that grow after burns or clearcuts in boreal or highland woods. It forages low in thickets and often hops rather than walks. Fall migrants are similar to yellowthroats but have a distinctive head pattern. Mourning returns from its tropical wintering grounds relatively late in spring. **VOICE** Song a rich, modulated *churry churry churry teri tri,* rising then falling, often garbled and complex. Call a rich *pwit,* similar to Common Yellowthroat.

breeding adult male

solid dark gray hood (weak eye ring rare)

blackish breast patch

(adult female similar but has paler gray head and lacks dark breast patch)

green above, vivid yellow below

1st fall

faint, nearly complete eye ring

paler lores than MacGillivray's

undertail coverts extend farther down tail than in MacGillivray's Warbler

faint hood but yellowish throat

MacGillivray's Warbler
Oporornis tolmiei
L 5¼"/13cm   WS 7½"/19cm

MacGillivray's Warbler is found in dense undergrowth, from blackberry tangles to willow-lined riparian thickets. Like Mourning Warbler, it forages low, but it is a more vocal species, uttering its distinctive call notes frequently; it is also more tractable, drawn to pishing and squeaking more than other *Oporornis.* **VOICE** Song similar to Mourning, but end variable, often more distinctively disyllabic and rising. Call a sharp *tchik.*

breeding adult male

like Mourning Warbler, but with shorter undertail coverts, longer tail

prominent white eye arcs

distinctly blackish lores extend over maxilla

adult female

strong eye arcs, gray hood, whitish throat

1st fall

like adult female but more muted

Common Yellowthroat

Geothlypis trichas
L 5"/13cm   WS 6¾"/17cm

This slim, long-tailed bird is widespread and common in wet brushy fields and marshes. More conspicuous than most ground-dwelling warblers, Yellowthroat twitches the tail like a wren and often forages in the open. Migrants can be numerous in varied habitats. North of Mexico, some 11 subspecies vary subtly, mostly in head pattern and in the extent of yellow below. **VOICE** Song a rolling, cheerful *ta-witchety,* repeated up to 6 times. Call a distinctive, full, flat *tchep;* also a wrenlike fuss.

breeding
adult male

olive-brown
above

distinctive
black mask
with pale
rear border

yellow throat
and breast

(first-fall male shows
trace of mask)

adult female

olive-brown
above

yellow throat
and undertail
coverts

1st fall female

dusky brown
above,
yellowish
below

Connecticut Warbler

Oporornis agilis
L 5¾"/15cm   WS 9"/23cm

Connecticut Warbler breeds in deciduous woodlands of poplar and aspen, in and around spruce and larch bogs, and locally in jack pine stands and mixed forests. It walks slowly along the ground and on branches (not hopping like other *Oporornis*) looking for insects, snails, and spiders. Migrants, because of their retiring habits, are especially hard to find. **VOICE** Song a rich, resonant, accelerating *sweet switcherit switcherit* or *beetcher batcher,* repeated. Call a flat, weak *pit.*

breeding
adult male

(adult female
similar but
paler)

pale gray
hood with
bold white
eye ring

duller above,
paler below than
other *Oporornis*

long,
strong legs

1st fall

large eyes
with eye ring

undertail coverts
extend much
farther down tail
than in Mourning
or especially
MacGillivray's
Warblers

long,
strong
bill

semblance of
adult pattern

Gray-crowned Yellowthroat

Geothlypis poliocephala
L 5½"/14cm WS 8¼"/21cm

Gray-crowned Yellowthroat is most closely related to Common Yellowthroat, but its heavier bill, longer tail, and dark lores suggest a chat (it was once called Ground Chat). It is a rare year-round visitor to southern Texas, where it was once resident and nested in grassy areas with scattered trees and shrubs. **VOICE** Songs include a garbled warble similar to a *Passerina* bunting and a cascade of sweet notes similar to Canyon Wren. Call a sweet, nasal *cheedleet*.

adult male | broken eye ring
larger than Common Yellowthroat
black lores and culmen; rest of bill pale
graduated tail longer than Common

immature/adult female
similar to adult male, but lores dusky (not blackish)
heavy, bicolored bill has curved culmen (unlike Common)

Wilson's Warbler

Wilsonia pusilla
L 4¾"/12cm WS 7"/18cm

Wilson's Warbler favors wet, well-vegetated areas with low undergrowth and shrubs, including bogs and muskeg with willows and alders, as well as slopes where the forest is broken. This species forages actively, flitting through brush or trees and capturing insects in flight, or hover-gleaning like a gnatcatcher, with much flicking of tail and wings. **VOICE** Song a series of rapid *che* notes, varying from staccato to soft in delivery (weaker and falling in eastern birds). Call a flat *timp* or *tchip*.

adult male
neat black cap (here raised slightly) does not reach bill
small, with tiny bill
yellow overall

female
smaller and smaller-billed than Hooded Warbler, with yellow (not dusky) lores, no white in tail
like adult male but cap smaller and less shiny

Kentucky Warbler
Oporornis formosus
L 5¼"/13cm **WS** 8½"/22cm

This handsome bird inhabits deep, moist deciduous woodlands with plenty of understory; it forages in leaf litter for insects and fallen berries, usually hopping, rarely walking. Males sing from thickets or saplings and occasionally in the forest canopy. Because of this species' preference for thick cover, it is seldom seen on migration. Some studies suggest it is related to yellowthroats. **VOICE** Song a richly burry set of rising *trrrreee* notes, often confused with Carolina Wren but less variable. Call a full *tchop*.

adult male
olive-green above
short tail
yellow below
dark crown, unique face pattern
rather long legs

adult female

very similar to male but browner above; crown and face pattern not as bold

(face pattern of first-fall female is duller olive-brown)

Hooded Warbler
Wilsonia citrina
L 5¼"/13cm **WS** 7"/18cm

Found in mature, moist, shady forests with dense undergrowth, Hooded Warbler forages on and just above the ground for insects and other arthropods, which it captures by pouncing, hovering, or gleaning, usually while fanning and quickly closing its long, white-spotted tail. Males sing through the day from concealed perches, usually at medium heights inside the canopy. **VOICE** Song a very rich, sweet *weeta weeta weet EE OO*, last notes rising then falling. Call a rich *tsit*.

yellow mask in jet black hood

adult female

most have yellow face with blackish frame in rear

much variation

olive above, yellow below

male

similar to adult female, but browner above and with weaker face pattern

white in outer rectrices (also in adults) often visible

1st fall female

eyes appear larger than Wilson's; usually has dusky loral spot

Prothonotary Warbler

Protonotaria citrea
L 5½"/14cm **WS** 8¾"/22cm

Prothonotary Warbler is named for the male's velvety saffron plumage, likened to the ceremonial yellow garments worn by Roman Catholic notaries. It nests in cavities, such as woodpecker holes, in wooded swamps, lining the nest with mosses and liverworts, a unique habit. Fledged young can usually swim if they fall into the water on leaving the nest. Migration is early in both spring and fall. **VOICE** Song a rich, sweet, pulsating set of *tswit* or *tsweet* notes, increasing in volume. Call a rich, loud *tsip!*

adult male

rich orange-yellow head and breast

green back, blue-gray wings

heavy, spikelike, black bill

female

similar to male but with more olive tones in crown and nape, paler bill

large, dark eyes

extensive white in tail

white undertail coverts

Yellow-breasted Chat

Icteria virens
L 7¾"/20cm **WS** 9¾"/25cm

The large, secretive Yellow-breasted Chat is so much larger than other warblers that it might be mistaken for a tanager. It inhabits scrubby brambles and sunny thickets where insects and berries are plentiful. Singing males frequently launch into song flights with slow, exaggerated wingbeats, tail-pumping, and dangling legs. **VOICE** Song a slow, mimidlike set of well-spaced calls, including a rich, deep *toop*, a low *kook*, jaylike fusses, and rapid, chattery *kookookoo* phrases. Calls a low *kuk* and a whiny *chup.*

adult male, eastern *(virens)*

dark eyes and lores surrounded by white

olive above

white crissum

heavy, black bill; black mouth-lining; short, white malar

vivid yellow throat and breast

adult, western *(auricollis)*

western subspecies shows longer white malar

grayish lores; pale mandible

rich yellow below, often shades toward orange in throat and upper breast of western subspecies

Swainson's Warbler

Limnothlypis swainsonii
L 5½"/14cm **WS** 9"/23cm

This shy but richly gifted singer breeds in canebrakes and swamp woods and Appalachian rhododendron thickets. Males remain still while they sing from a high, usually obscured perch. Foraging birds stay low, usually in deep leaf litter; there they search for insects and other arthropods with an odd, vibrating shuffle, often flipping over leaves. **VOICE** Similar to Louisiana Waterthrush. Song a rich, sweet, descending *teer teer teer whit-de-wheeow.* Call a strong *tchip.*

adult

pale supercilium, dark eye line

uniformly brown above with olive tones; crown has russet tones

long, heavy bill

adult

some individuals tinged with yellow below

pink legs, large feet

Worm-eating Warbler

Helmitheros vermivorum
L 5¼"/13cm **WS** 8½"/22cm

Worm-eating Warbler is a distinctive species of deciduous and mixed woodlands; it is usually found on slopes with a well-developed understory and in lowland pocosin habitats. It forages largely by hanging onto and probing dead leaf clusters and vine tangles for caterpillars and other insect larvae, extracting them with its long, pointed bill. **VOICE** Song a dry, even trill, usually less rich than Chipping Sparrow and drier than juncos or Pine Warbler (can vary tremendously). Call a sweet, loud *tsip.*

adult

uniformly brown above with olive tones

heavy bill

warm buff tones in head and breast

adult

head striped with black and rich buff

short tail, often partly opened

compare Ovenbird

Northern Parula

Parula americana
L 4½"/11cm WS 7"/18cm

The tiny, short-tailed Northern Parula breeds in southern woodlands, especially where Spanish moss (a bromeliad) is found, and in northern forests where old man's beard (a lichen) grows; both plants are important for nest building, although the species may also nest in moist woodlands and riparian areas that lack them. Parulas are active foragers, often hovering, hanging, and probing while working through trees and flowers or foraging low in weeds and tangles; they are very conspicuous warblers and tend to favor edges rather than deep woods. They are readily drawn to pishing and squeaking sounds. Most winter in eastern Mexico and on Caribbean islands. **VOICE** Song a rich, ascending trill that ends with a rising flourish—*zzzzzzeeeEEEUP!*—or a more complex fragmented song closer to Cerulean Warbler—*zree zree zree zree ZREEEIP!* Call a high *tsip*.

adult male — blue above with white eye arcs and olive-yellow mantle

yellow of throat and breast separated by mottled rufous band (often with black upper border)

(adult female similar but less richly colored)

1st fall female, bright — bluish malars border yellow throat

pattern like adult above, with semblance of eye arcs

short tail

lacks band below throat found in male

1st fall female, dull

many look greenish above, with little yellow below

Crescent-chested Warbler

Parula superciliosa
L 4¼"/11cm WS 6"/15cm

Crescent-chested Warbler, a Central American species related to parulas and to *Vermivora* warblers, has strayed several times to pine-oak woodlands in Arizona and western Texas. It forages much like Northern Parula, though often more slowly, methodically, and reclusively inside deep vegetation, often probing leaf clusters. **VOICE** Song a unique short, dry, electric buzz—*zzzzzzz*. Call a high, short *tsic*.

adult

striking white supercilium

olive back; bluish gray crown and nape and darker grayish auriculars

bright yellow below, with chestnut crescent below throat

Tropical Parula

Parula pitiayumi
L 4½"/11cm **WS** 6¼"/16cm

The colorful Tropical Parula is a scarce local resident in the coastal plain and Lower Rio Grande valley of Texas. Like Northern Parula, it builds pendulous nests in Spanish moss, usually near water. There are 14 named subspecies; *nigrilora* is found in Texas, but other taxa may account for rare records from Arizona, Colorado, and Louisiana. **VOICE** Song very similar to Northern Parula but drier, with buzzy ending flourish. Call similar to Northern.

adult male

like Northern Parula but lacks breastband and white around eyes; more extensively yellow below, with orange blush on breast

yellow malars (blue in Northern Parula)

adult female

similar to female Northern Parula but has usually darker lores, more extensive yellow below, and yellow (not bluish) malars

Black-throated Blue Warbler

Dendroica caerulescens
L 5¼"/13cm **WS** 7¾"/20cm

Black-throated Blue Warbler breeds in deciduous and mixed forests where the understory is rich in saplings and bushes, especially mountain laurels and rhododendrons; in the Virginias it also breeds in moist ravines with hemlocks and semiopen spruce woods, where it forages deliberately, mostly in the understory. **VOICE** Song a "lazy," ascending *zhur zhur zhur zreee,* very modulated. Call a quick, kissing *thsp,* most similar to a junco.

adult male

rich, deep blue above (duskier in Appalachian *cairnsi*)

first-fall male similar

black face and sides

snow white belly and primary bases

1st fall female
pattern like adult female but duller olive-brown above

white in primary bases often slight

dusky auriculars framed by paler malar, throat, supercilium

olive-brown above

white arc under eyes

adult female

very unlike male except for small amount of white in primary bases

American Redstart

Setophaga ruticilla
L 5¼"/13cm **WS** 7¾"/20cm

American Redstart breeds in moist mixed and deciduous woods with undergrowth and in swamp woods. When foraging, it droops its wings and fans and tosses its tail to flush insects with its movements and bright plumage. Redstarts, like small flycatchers, have well-developed rictal bristles. Males attain the definitive black and orange plumage in their second summer. **VOICE** Song a rapid series of up to 7 notes, variably sweet or modulated, usually ending with a quick, rich, downward flourish. Call a downward *tsek*.

adult male

"Halloween colors" unmistakable: velvety black with rich orange at sides and bases of remiges and rectrices

1st fall female

wing and tail pattern subtler than adult female, less yellow at sides of breas

adult female

often fans tail to show pattern (young male similar: patches of black plumage begin to appear in first summer)

yellow rather than orange in wings and tail

Painted Redstart

Myioborus pictus
L 5¾"/15cm **WS** 8¾"/22cm

Painted Redstart reaches the northern limit of its breeding range in the pine-oak mountain forests of Arizona and New Mexico; a few are found in Texas's Chisos Mountains. The species is partial to shady slopes with a closed canopy and a rich, diverse understory. It forages both low and high, flashing its wings and tail, like American Redstart, to startle insects with its bright plumage. **VOICE** Song a sweet, rhythmic *wheeta wheeta wheeta CHEW CHEW CHEW*. Call unique: a sweet, descending *tyeew*.

adult

white under eyes and in upperwing coverts and outer rectrices (compare Slate-throated Redstart)

scarlet belly contrasts with black plumage

juvenile

mostly sooty gray overall, with white arc under eyes and white wing patches

rosy belly acquired gradually during first molt

Red-faced Warbler
Cardellina rubrifrons
L 5½"/14cm   **WS** 8½"/22cm

Red-faced Warbler breeds in montane pine-oak forests north to Arizona and New Mexico. It forages chickadee-like in understory and canopy alike, often flipping its tail while feeding. **VOICE** Song a jumble of sweet, clear notes; like Canada Warbler but less hurried. Call a sharp, low *tsik*.

adult
cherry red face, throat, lower nape
black auriculars and crown
pale nape and rump

Fan-tailed Warbler
Euthlypis lachrymosa
L 5¾"/15cm   **WS** 7½"/19cm

Fan-tailed Warbler, a species of Mexico and Central America, is recorded rarely in mountains and canyons of extreme southeastern Arizona in spring. It forages like a redstart and is most closely related to *Myioborus* and to *Basileuterus* warblers. **VOICE** Song a clear, whistled *tyew tyew tyew tyew whee-ta-wee*, falling then rising. Call a distinctive, descending *tseeoo*.

adult
yellow, black-bordered crown patch
white loral spot and eye arcs
long, graduated, white-tipped tail
yellow below, almost orange on breast

Slate-throated Redstart
Myioborus miniatus
L 5¼"/13cm   **WS** 7¼"/18cm

Slate-throated Redstart, widespread in the Neotropics, has strayed to shady mountain canyons of Arizona, New Mexico, and Texas. Warblers in the tropical genus *Myioborus* are often called whitestarts. **VOICE** Song a variable, usually loose set of sweet notes, sometimes falling or rising in pitch or with accented ending. Call a sweet, quick *tik*.

adult male
gray above, rose-red below, with blackish throat, crimson central crown
long tail with extensive white; often fanned

Rufous-capped Warbler
Basileuterus rufifrons
L 5¼"/13cm   **WS** 7¼"/18cm

This rare visitor from Mexico to southern Arizona and Texas (with several records of nesting) forages slowly through vegetation of brushy slopes and canyons, cocking and twitching its tail like a wren. **VOICE** Song an accelerating, chippy trill, mostly on one pitch, sometimes ending with accented notes or a complex flourish. Call a staccato but soft *tsic*.

adult
unmarked olive-brown above
rufous rear auriculars and sides of crown
white malar
vivid yellow from chin to breast

Canada Warbler

Wilsonia canadensis
L 5¼"/13cm   WS 8"/20cm

Canada Warbler breeds in moist habitats with dense understory, from streamside thickets of alder in boreal forests to rhododendron-clad ravines in Appalachian forests. Although it hides in brush while foraging, it often investigates hikers, moose, or other invaders of its territory and responds vigorously to pishing. On migration, Canadas are usually found in low thickets. **VOICE** Song an irregular jumble of rich, sweet notes, with introductory *tchip* note and with syncopated rhythm. Call a sharp *tsik*.

breeding adult male

yellow throat and lores have black border

mostly white eye ring

unmarked bluish gray above

black "necklace" (weaker in younger males)

1st fall or adult female

lacks wing bars (unlike Magnolia Warbler)

gray above (unlike Nashville Warbler)

lacks black of breeding adult male

necklace pattern often faint

Cerulean Warbler

Dendroica cerulea
L 4¾"/12cm   WS 7¾"/20cm

The small, short-tailed Cerulean Warbler is a scarce species of deciduous woodlands, mostly riparian woods and mature and old-growth forests with a complex canopy. It forages high in trees, slowly gleaning insects. Males sing from a high perch, often for hours on end. The species appears to vacate breeding areas in July and early August; it is uncommonly observed as a fall migrant. **VOICE** Song a wiry, modulated, rapid *zheer, zheer, zhe-zhe-zhe zheee,* last part rising. Call a sharp *tzit*.

breeding adult male

vivid blue above

white wing bars

thin breastband borders throat

streaked flanks

adult female

(first-fall birds similar)

face and flanks often with buffy tint

unstreaked upperparts have blue-green tint (compare streaked back of first-fall female Blackburnian Warbler)

Kirtland's Warbler
Dendroica kirtlandii
L 5¾"/15cm **WS** 8¾"/22cm

This endangered warbler nests only in stands of young (5- to 15-year-old) jack pines on sandy soil with dense ground cover, a habitat found almost exclusively in north-central Michigan. Thanks to conservation efforts, the number of singing males rose from 167 in 1987 to 1,478 in 2006. Kirtland's forages mostly just above the ground, gleaning insects from pines and other plants, pumping the tail downward as it goes. The species winters in the southern Bahamas. **VOICE** Song a vigorous, rising, ringing *tup tup chee chee chee wee WEE!* Call a full, rich *tchip.*

breeding adult male

broken white eye ring

pale blue above and yellow below, with dark streaks in mantle and sides

1st fall

grayish brown above, with hint of broken eye ring; yellow underparts have tiny stipples across breast and flanks

adult female

similar to male but upperparts paler gray and lack strong blue tones

lores and streaking on underparts gray rather than black

Prairie Warbler
Dendroica discolor
L 4¾"/12cm   **WS** 7"/18cm

Prairie Warbler is abundant in semiopen, disturbed, and successional habitats, including scrubby, oak-clad dunes, pine woods, regenerating clear-cuts, and mangrove forests. This agile, active forager constantly pumps its tail as it gleans and chases insects. It is very inquisitive and readily attracted to pishing. Most winter in the Greater Antilles and Bahamas. **VOICE** Song a series of connected rising, modulated, wiry notes said to ascend the chromatic scale. Call a rich but flat *tsek.*

breeding adult male

adult female

black lower border to auriculars (moustachial crescent)

yellow below, with black flank streaks

similar to male but pattern and colors more muted

yellow-olive above, with reddish streaks on back

1st fall male

dark spot on neck

1st fall, duller

moustachial crescent and neck spot muted

pattern on face and flanks very faint

wags tail often

Pine Warbler
Dendroica pinus
L 5½"/14cm **WS** 8¾"/22cm

Pine Warbler is never found far from pinewoods, though it may forage in mixed woodlands, field edges, and wooded swamps, especially in winter. It tends to forage less actively than most *Dendroica* as it gleans insects from pines, and it is sometimes seen in mixed flocks with other forest birds. More than other warblers, Pine probes pine needle clusters, bark, and cones for small insects and larvae, sometimes creeping on bark to reach crannies almost like a Black-and-white Warbler. Like Yellow-rumped and Palm Warblers, Pine regularly forages on the ground for seeds and insects. When foraging terrestrially in the nonbreeding season, small groups of Pine Warblers may join Eastern Bluebirds or Chipping Sparrows. Most Pine Warblers are thought to be resident from the Carolinas southward. **VOICE** Song a rich trill, looser and more musical than Chipping Sparrow and Worm-eating Warbler. Call a sneezy, sweet *tsiw!*

breeding adult male

yellow "spectacles" recall Yellow-throated Vireo, but note thinner bill, longer tail, streaky breast

bright olive above, rich yellow below, with blurry olive streaking on breast

adult/ 1st fall male

grayish wings, white wing bars

yellowish around face, but dusky auriculars

yellowish below, sometimes bright, often mixed with olive (sometimes vaguely streaked)

1st fall

flanks sometimes have faint, diffuse streaks

sometimes mistaken for Bay-breasted Warbler; note larger bill, dusky auriculars, duller colors above and below, no blackish tone in wings

1st fall female

dullest birds recall Bay-breasted and Blackpoll Warblers, but note longer projection of tail past undertail coverts

1st fall female

very plain brown or gray-brown above

heavier bill than other *Dendroica*

wide wing bars

Palm Warbler

Dendroica palmarum
L 5½"/14cm **WS** 8"/20cm

Palm Warbler is easily identified by its constant tail-pumping. It breeds in open and semiopen boreal bogs ringed by larches, spruces, and sometimes pines, and also winters in open habitats. The yellow-bellied subspecies Yellow Palm Warbler *(hypochrysea)* is found from Quebec eastward, while the nominate Western Palm nests from Ontario westward; there is a zone of intergradation south of James Bay. **VOICE** Song a loose, pulsating, buzzy, rambling trill. Call a sharp, loud *tsip!*

breeding adult, Western Palm (nominate)
rusty crown
very little rusty or yellow below compared to Yellow Palm Warbler
often forages on the ground

breeding adult, Yellow Palm (hypochrysea)
rusty crown
extensively yellow underparts
variable rusty streaks below

nonbreeding, Yellow Palm (hypochrysea)
duller overall than spring birds, especially rusty crown

nonbreeding, Yellow Palm (hypochrysea)
pale yellow supercilium
some (probably young females) lack brown and rust tones
yellowish, lightly streaked underparts (compare Orange-crowned Warbler)

breeding adult
some individuals appear intermediate between Western and Yellow and may be intergrades

nonbreeding, Western Palm (nominate)
dark eye line, pale supercilium
brownish overall
prominent yellow undertail coverts
faintly streaked sides

Blackpoll Warbler

Dendroica striata
L 5½"/14cm WS 9"/23cm

Blackpoll Warbler breeds in moist coniferous woods, particularly spruce and balsam fir stands near bogs, and also frequents mixed woods with alder and willow, where it forages for insects and their larvae, especially caterpillars. This species makes a spectacular autumn migration, with millions flying out of the boreal forests and over the open Atlantic toward eastern South America. To accomplish this nonstop flight, birds double their body weight, gleaning insects at stopover sites. In spring they return across the Caribbean, Florida, and the Gulf states, where their distinctive, simple song seems to ring out from every tree. As long-distance migrants, they have especially long primaries, which project farther beyond the tertials than in less strongly migratory warbler species. **VOICE** Song a penetrating, high series of up to 20 well-spaced notes on one pitch, loudest in middle. Call a loud, sharp *tchip*.

breeding adult male

black cap and throat stripe border white face and connect to dark-streaked back and sides

very long wings

tail projects only slightly beyond very long white undertail coverts

1st fall

never shows rusty tones in sides like male Bay-breasted

like Bay-breasted Warbler, but with lightly streaked breast; white (not buffy) undertail; narrower wing bars; duller back; yellow soles of feet

adult female

faint trace of male's dark throat stripe and back and side streaking

face and breast sometimes washed with vanilla-buff or yellowish

1st spring female

some birds almost unstreaked below and very gray overall, without olive or yellow tones

spring birds of both sexes show yellow legs (black in Bay-breasted)

spring female

most are easily told from Bay-breasted by streaks below, white undertail coverts, yellow legs

Bay-breasted Warbler
Dendroica castanea
L 5½"/14cm **WS** 9"/23cm

Bay-breasted Warbler is a generally uncommon breeder in dense fir and spruce forests, especially near openings with undergrowth. Like Blackpoll, Cape May, Blackburnian, and Tennessee Warblers, Bay-breasted takes advantage of outbreaks of spruce budworm caterpillars. Its populations show strong fluctuations related to the availability of this prey and other food sources. Like many other Neotropical migrants, Bay-breasted crosses the Gulf of Mexico in passage to and from wintering grounds in Central and South America. During periods of inclement weather in spring, large numbers may be seen in "fallouts" with other migrants on the northern and western shores of the Gulf. **VOICE** Song a high, thin, lispy *thi thi thi thi thi thi thi* on one pitch, similar to Cape May, or *sew-see* notes like Black-and-white but less incisive and clear. Call similar to Blackpoll.

breeding adult male
black face
warm rusty (bay) throat, sides, crown
(adult female similar, but colors and pattern more muted)

nonbreeding male
greenish back, brighter than Blackpoll and Pine Warblers
very broad, white wing bars
bay-colored sides lack streaking (compare Blackpoll)

1st spring female
greenish tones in back
chestnut in crown sometimes absent
faint head pattern of adult female
very light bay or buff on breast

1st fall female, worn
young females on wintering grounds (shown) and on spring migration often whitish below (compare Pine Warbler)

1st fall female
smaller bill than Pine Warbler
greenish buff tones in back, neck, flanks
off-white or buffy-tinged, rather long undertail coverts
unstreaked underparts
usually dark legs

Chestnut-sided Warbler
Dendroica pensylvanica
L 5"/13cm WS 7¾"/20cm

Chestnut-sided Warbler normally breeds in early successional habitats, especially old pastures and orchards and riparian thickets at the edges of fields. It forages in trees, tail cocked and wings drooping, looking for insects on the underside of leaves. This confiding species is readily attracted to pishing. In fall migration, large numbers may be seen along eastern ridges, often with other *Dendroica*. **VOICE** Song often like Yellow Warbler but with snappy, descending flourish at end. Call a low, sometimes harsh *tschp* like Yellow.

breeding adult male

yellow crown bordered by black

black malar

chestnut sides

adult female or 1st spring male

markings muted and less extensive than adult male

1st fall female
yellow tint to wing bars (nonbreeding adult similar but with some chestnut on sides, especially male)

pale green above, gray below

white eye ring

Blackburnian Warbler
Dendroica fusca
L 5"/13cm WS 8½"/22cm

The breeding male Blackburnian Warbler, with its phosphorescent orange throat, is among the most striking of American passerines. It breeds in spruce, fir, and hemlock forests as well as mixed woodlands farther south. An active forager, it stays mostly in the canopy. **VOICE** Song a high, thin, rising series of *tsi* notes, accelerating into sharp *ti* notes and ending with a rising flourish or stuttering, downward turn; recalls Golden-crowned Kinglet's song. Call a sneezy *tschp*.

breeding adult male

black back has white "braces"

extensive white in coverts

head has complex pattern of orange and black

adult female

1st fall female

brown-streaked back (compare Cerulean Warbler)

similar to male but colors fainter and with gray auriculars

auriculars framed by buff-yellow

broad, white wing bars

Yellow-throated Warbler
Dendroica dominica
L 5½"/14cm **WS** 8"/20cm

Yellow-throated Warbler breeds in varied settings throughout its range: wooded swamps with cypress and tupelo in the South, pinewoods near water farther north, and riparian sycamores in the Midwest. The southeastern nominate subspecies has yellow lores, while the white-lored subspecies *albilora* nests roughly from the Appalachians westward. **VOICE** Song a series of rich, distinct sweet notes, descending stepwise, often with quick, upward flourish at end. Call a rich, sharp *tchip!*

adult *(albilora)* — long bill — black eye line and auriculars connect to side streaking — gray above with white wing bars — single white lower eye arc — egg-yolk yellow throat and breast; white belly

adult (nominate) — yellow tinge in lores (Gulf coast subspecies *stoddardi* also has yellow lores) — yellow chin (white in *albilora*)

Grace's Warbler
Dendroica graciae
L 5"/13cm **WS** 8"/20cm

Grace's Warbler breeds in montane pine forests and sometimes in mixed forests with large pines. It forages in pine needles, gleaning insects and rarely clambering around bark or clinging like Yellow-throated Warbler. The subspecies *graciae*, of northern Mexico and the U.S., is migratory; it returns to nesting grounds in April and May. **VOICE** Song a loose, ragged trill similar to Pine Warbler but accelerating toward end and with closing flourish. Call a very thin, high *tsip.*

adult male — short, yellow supercilium and yellow eye arc — (first-fall birds browner above but with strong yellow face pattern)

adult female — female and first-fall birds paler overall than adult male, with less black in face, crown, sides

Yellow-rumped Warbler

Dendroica coronata
L 5½"/14cm   WS 9¼"/23cm

The highly versatile Yellow-rumped Warbler forages from farm fields up to treetops. Birds of the white-throated northern/eastern subspecies (*hooveri* and nominate), called Myrtle Warbler, nest in coniferous and mixed boreal and highland forests. The western subspecies *auduboni*, Audubon's Warbler, nests in coniferous forests. **VOICE** Myrtle: song a loose, sweet, chippy or warbly trill, trailing off at end; call a rich but flat *tchip*. Audubon's: song similar to Myrtle but lower and slower; call a rough, rising *chwit*.

breeding adult male, Myrtle

yellow rump (all plumages)

black mask, white throat

yellow sides bordered by black streaks

breeding adult female, Audubon's

breeding adult male, Audubon's

like male but brown cast above, patterns reduced

similar to Myrtle, but with yellow throat, extensive black on chest, and no black mask

1st fall female, Myrtle

pale-bordered dark auriculars (absent in Audubon's and Cape May Warblers)

plain brown, streaked above and below

(Audubon's throat has yellow cast)

Black-throated Gray Warbler

Dendroica nigrescens
L 5"/13cm   WS 7¾"/20cm

This warbler breeds in arid interior habitats, especially pinyon-juniper woods and oak-clad slopes and canyons, as well as moist woodlands of the Pacific Northwest. An active, arboreal forager like other *Dendroica*, it often flutters out to glean insects from needles and twigs. **VOICE** Song recalls Chestnut-sided Warbler—rising, accelerating notes with a downward flourish—but with less tonal range and more modulated. Call a low, full *tchip*, recalling Myrtle (Yellow-rumped).

Black-throated Gray Warbler adult male

black crown, auriculars, throat separated by white

gray above with white wing bars

yellow loral spot

underparts white with black streaking

(all other plumages similar but paler and lack black throat)

Magnolia Warbler

Dendroica magnolia
L 5"/13cm **WS** 7½"/19cm

One might spend a long time looking for a Magnolia Warbler in a magnolia tree; it breeds in boreal and montane coniferous forests, often where there is dense young growth or areas with an edge or opening. The species forages in dense foliage, frequently fanning its patterned tail as it gleans insects and larvae. On migration it is tame and versatile, foraging in many habitats. **VOICE** Song a sweet, rich *weeta weeta weeto,* more rambling than Hooded Warbler, sometimes similar to a redstart. Call a sneezy, thin *tschif!*

breeding adult male

black mask

white greater coverts

black streaking below ends at throat

breeding adult female

like breeding adult male but pattern and color reduced; nonbreeding adult male similar

1st fall

olive-green back

streaked yellow underparts contrast with white undertail coverts (compare Canada and Prairie Warblers)

very plain gray face with eye ring

Cape May Warbler

Dendroica tigrina
L 4¾"/12cm **WS** 8¼"/21cm

Cape May Warbler breeds in coniferous, preferably black spruce, forests, usually nesting near a gap or edge, sometimes next to a bog. It forages actively, gleaning insects and their larvae from the outer parts of high branches, and can be elusive. These small, feisty birds often drive other birds from their territories. Spring migrants are often observed drinking nectar at flowering trees. **VOICE** Song a high, thin, sibilant, rising *thi thi thi thi thi* (sometimes with *si* or *ti-si* notes). Call a high, thin but sharp *tsi.*

breeding adult male

rufous face framed in yellow

starkly white greater coverts

neat streaks below

1st fall female

quite dull

breeding adult female

green tint in rump, remiges, sides of neck

diffuse streaking below

distinctive yellow face broken by dusky eye line and auriculars

greenish yellow rump in all plumages

(first-fall male similar)

Townsend's Warbler

Dendroica townsendi
L 5"/13cm   WS 8"/20cm

This hardy warbler of old-growth Pacific Northwest coniferous forests forages and nests often high in the boughs of spruce, pine, fir, or hemlock trees. It often hybridizes with Hermit Warbler. Townsend's has two separate winter ranges, one along the West Coast, the other in the mountains of Mexico. **VOICE** Song a variable set of high, modulated *zee* or *zoo* notes, often on one pitch, usually accelerating and with flourish at the end, rising or falling sharply. Call a sharp, flat *tip*.

adult male — black crown, auriculars, throat separated by yellow

yellow lower eye arc

back has dark streaks or spots

like breeding male but throat mottled with olive, back less strongly marked

nonbreeding adult male

female

more yellow on breast, darker auriculars than Black-throated Green Warbler

(first-fall male and adult female similar but with more streaking in back and breast)

Black-throated Green Warbler

Dendroica virens
L 5"/13cm   WS 7¾"/20cm

Black-throated Green Warbler breeds in open forested habitats, from white-cedar pocosins of the Carolina coast (*waynei* subspecies), to mixed forests with Virginia pine in the southern Appalachians, to spruce-fir stands in the boreal belt. It forages by gleaning, usually at mid-elevations in inner branches, less often in high and outer branches. **VOICE** Song a tuneful, wiry *zee zee zee zee zoo zee* or *zoo zee zoo zoo zee* (*zoo* notes always lower). Call a quiet, flat, kissing *tsik*.

adult male — yellow face bordered by black throat and vivid green upperparts

unstreaked back

auriculars tinged olive

1st fall female

adult female, molting

brighter green above than Townsend's, lacks distinct auricular patch, yellow on breast

face pattern more obscured in some individuals

lacks distinct dark auricular patch and yellow lower eye arc of Townsend's

Hermit Warbler

Dendroica occidentalis
L 5"/13cm **WS** 8"/20cm

Hermit Warbler, like Townsend's, occupies coniferous forests, but it is especially partial to Douglas-firs and true firs and prospers in younger forests. Both species nest in old-growth forests in the northern Cascade Range, where hybridization between the two is common. This species winters in montane pine-oak forests in Mexico and Guatemala. **VOICE** Song a rapid set of modulated, often rising *zee* notes similar to Prairie Warbler, or a more complex set of *we-see* notes, ending in a trilled flourish. Call like Townsend's.

adult male

grayish above with white wing bars

mostly yellow crown and face contrast with black throat

1st fall female

many show diffuse olive auriculars and olive back; note yellow eye ring

1st fall

grayish above like male but with little or no black on throat; dusky in auriculars

(adult female similar but has yellow chin and blackish throat)

Golden-cheeked Warbler

Dendroica chrysoparia
L 5"/13cm **WS** 7¾"/20cm

The endangered Golden-cheeked Warbler nests only in old-growth woodlands of oaks and Ashe juniper around the Edwards Plateau of central Texas. Like Black-throated Green Warbler, this species is a relatively early spring migrant, arriving in mid-March; it departs much earlier for its wintering grounds, however, usually by August. **VOICE** Song a set of rising, modulated but sweet *zer* notes, similar to Black-throated Green, usually with a higher, thin *zuur ti!* flourish at close. Call a flat *thip*.

breeding adult male

vivid yellow face surrounded by black crown, back, throat and broken by eye line

large, white wing bars

adult female

recalls Hermit Warbler but more streaked below and with neat eye line

faintly dusky lores and auriculars

(first-fall plumages similar but duller)

Ovenbird

Seiurus aurocapilla
L 6"/15cm WS 9½"/24cm

Ovenbird's resounding, crescendo song is heard in mature forested habitats where undergrowth is minimal and leaf litter abundant. This thrushlike warbler, named for its dome-shaped nest, walks slowly on the ground, head bobbing and tail often cocked, watching intently for insects, worms, snails, and small vertebrates. **VOICE** Song a resounding series of *CHER-tea* calls, each call louder than the previous; also a sputtering song, often given in flight at dusk and at night. Many calls, including loud *tchap* and *tsip* notes.

adult

patterned like a *Catharus* thrush but smaller, with more distinct and extensive streaking

bold white eye ring

nesting adult

adult

agitated birds raise black-bordered orange crown

(first-fall plumages similar)

sings from a perch but forages on the ground

Black-and-white Warbler

Mniotilta varia
L 5¼"/13cm WS 8¼"/21cm

This striking warbler breeds in mature and second-growth mixed and deciduous forests. It forages by probing with its thin, decurved bill into crannies in the bark for insects and larvae, creeping woodpecker-like around trees; this mode of locomotion is called "scansorial." It also takes small insect prey by gleaning foliage like other warblers. Like *Seiurus* warblers, it nests mostly on the ground. **VOICE** Song a series of high, thin *sewee* or *weesee* notes, usually on one pitch and with little variation in speed. Call a compact *stit*.

adult male

black auriculars

(breeding male has black throat)

unique pattern, lacking yellow in any plumage

female

like male but lacks black auriculars, throat, breast streaking

Northern Waterthrush

Seiurus noveboracensis
L 6"/15cm   **WS** 9½"/24cm

Northern Waterthrush is a hardy bird that breeds in wet boreal forests, usually near standing or slow-flowing water; it nests in thickets on the ground. This species forages on the ground, bobbing the rear portion of its body (like a Spotted Sandpiper) as it walks along shorelines and on muddy substrates in search of insects, worms, and snails. **VOICE** Song a 2- or 3-part series of sweet, staccato notes, descending and accelerating by degrees, rather like Kirtland's Warbler in quality but more hurried. Call a sharp *spik!*

adult — supercilium narrows at rear

smaller bill than Louisiana, and denser, finer streaking below that continues to throat

dull, dusky pink legs

adult — lower eye arc narrower than in most Louisianas

some adults and young show strong suffusion of yellow in face and underparts

---

Louisiana Waterthrush

Seiurus motacilla
L 6"/15cm   **WS** 10"/25cm

Unlike Northern Waterthrush, Louisiana Waterthrush nests in woodlands with relatively clear, fast-moving streams, especially areas lacking overly brushy borders. Its larger bill enables it to take larger prey, including small crayfish, frogs, mollusks, and fish. In many parts of the breeding range, this is the first warbler to return to the nesting grounds. **VOICE** Song a series of slurred, connected, sweet, descending notes with a rich, musical quality, often ending with a jumbled flourish. Call a rich, resonant, loud *tschip.*

adult

mostly whitish below with brownish buff cast on sides and flanks

adult — wide, white supercilium, broad at rear

vivid pink legs

throat unmarked white between submalar stripes

Thrushes, Mimids, Waxwings, and Allies

Thrushes (family Turdidae) are medium-sized, usually plump-looking passerines found around the world in a great diversity of habitats, from bleak, stony tundra to Pacific coastal rain forests to inner-city ball fields. Thrushes have sturdy, slim bills, rather long wings, and strong, moderately long legs that are well suited for their mostly terrestrial foraging habits. The larger American thrushes are usually found in woodlands, whereas the bluebirds and Townsend's Solitaire prefer open country with scattered trees.

Wood Thrush populations have declined tremendously in recent decades, a result of fragmented forests and acid rain.

Most thrushes hop on the ground looking for insects and other arthropods, which they capture with a quick pounce. The open-country species also flycatch or make quick sallies from a perch to the ground. Virtually all thrushes take fruit at some point during the year, usually in autumn and winter. In the nonbreeding season, some species, such as American Robin, form large, roving flocks that quickly strip trees of berries before moving on. Males arrive on the breeding grounds earlier than females and sing to mark and defend their territories. Thrushes are famous for their sublime songs, Hermit Thrush and Varied Thrush in particular. After nesting, spotted thrushes migrate to the American tropics, and Northern Wheatear and Bluethroat migrate to African and Eurasian wintering grounds. Most other species withdraw from northern parts of their range.

Mockingbirds, catbirds, and thrashers (Mimidae) are reminiscent of thrushes in overall build, but they have longer tails, shorter and less pointed wings, and bills that are either longer and decurved (most thrashers) or shorter and thinner. Like thrushes, mimids are fine songsters; in some cases, they imitate other birds' songs (hence the family name, which means "mimics"). Most mimids are terrestrial foragers that lurk in thickets, kicking back leaf litter in search of insects and the like; all species eat fruit as well.

Silky-flycatchers (Ptilogonatidae), waxwings (Bombycillidae), starlings and mynas (Sturnidae), and bulbuls (Pycnonotidae) have few North American representatives. All of these birds are comparable in size and shape to mimids and thrushes. Phainopepla is a silky-flycatcher found in the arid Southwest, usually near mistletoe or other small fruit; it makes seasonal movements but is apparently only a short-distance migrant. The two American waxwing species, Bohemian and Cedar Waxwings, are probably close relatives of Phainopepla and likewise wander in search of both insects and fruiting trees. European Starling and Red-whiskered Bulbul are both introduced species in North America; the former is one of the continent's most numerous bird species, while the latter is restricted largely to a small area in Florida.

Most mimids appear to be in a pattern of long-term decline, and several thrushes, especially Wood and Bicknell's Thrushes and Veery, also show diminished numbers. These declines are probably related to the fragmentation of habitat, which permits cowbirds and predators better access to nests, to deforestation in the tropics, and to acid rain, which may reduce the abundance of arthropods, snails, and other prey items.

Northern Wheatear

Oenanthe oenanthe
L 5¾"/15cm   WS 12"/30cm

Northern Wheatear is seen only rarely south of its breeding range, usually in autumn en route to its wintering grounds in Africa. It nests in open habitats, chiefly tundra and coastlines with rocky outcroppings; vagrants are often seen in similar open areas with low perches, such as fencerows or stony places, from which they hunt insects on the ground. **VOICE** Song a rapid, gargling mix of sweet and harsh notes. Call similar to song in tone, an alternating, repeated *seet ... tak*, last note dry and sharp.

breeding
adult male

small bill
(compare
shrikes)

short tail

long legs

breeding
adult female

lacks mask;
buffy throat
and breast
variable

buff in
supercilium
above lores

brown
above

cinnamon
wash below

nonbreeding
adult/1st fall

in flight, striking
tail pattern shows
black "T" at tip,
white base

Bluethroat

Luscinia svecica
L 5¾"/15cm   WS 9"/23cm

Bluethroat breeds in dense thickets of willows and dwarf birches on the tundra edge, where it sings from exposed perches and forages in vegetation and on the ground, mostly for insects. This Old World thrush migrates in autumn across the Bering Sea to winter in southern Asia. When not singing, Bluethroats tend to be shy and difficult to observe. **VOICE** Song a mimidlike set of varied phrases, often imitations of other birds. Call similar to Northern Wheatear.

breeding
adult male

blue and rufous
breastbands
unique among
American birds
(female shows
only faint bands)

breeding male often
cocks tail to show rufous
in uppertail coverts

nonbreeding
adult

strong
submalar
stripe

rufous bases in
uppertail coverts
and rectrices
(most obvious in
flying birds)

Eastern Bluebird

Sialia sialis
L 7"/18cm   WS 13"/33cm

In the 1960s, when Eastern Bluebird was in a sharp population decline, thousands of people began constructing and monitoring "bluebird trails" of nest boxes. This striking thrush is now a common sight in open woodlands and farms. It forages from perches for insects, snails, and worms and also eats berries in winter. Winter flocks sometimes huddle together in cavities on cold nights. **VOICE** Song a short, soft set of quick, warbled whistles. Call a quiet *chew-wee,* often given in flight.

adult male

paler above than Western Bluebird

rufous underparts extend to throat and sides of neck

white belly

juvenile

adult female

rufous wash extends to throat, neck, behind auriculars

white belly

(all juvenile thrushes heavily spotted)

Western Bluebird

Sialia mexicana
L 7"/18cm   WS 13½"/34cm

With its intense royal blue plumage, the male Western Bluebird ranks as one of North America's most attractive birds. This thrush frequents open woodlands and savannas during the nesting season, moving into deserts, riparian woods, farm fields, and pinyon-juniper woodlands in winter. Unlike Eastern Bluebird, Western may use nest helpers, usually unmated males, that feed nestlings. **VOICE** Song a series of alternating, rich *chup* and *chew* calls separated by brief pauses. Call a low *chew* and staccato chattering sounds.

adult male

chestnut on upper back, scapulars, coverts (rarely absent)

blue throat

more richly colored than Eastern Bluebird

adult female

gray head, neck, throat, belly

rusty wash only on breast and sides

Mountain Bluebird

Sialia currucoides
L 7½"/19cm   WS 14"/36cm

Mountain Bluebird breeds in remote habitats, from subalpine meadows, to high-elevation grasslands and aspen parkland, to sagebrush and pinyon-juniper woodlands of the Great Basin; most winter in farm fields and grasslands. Where range overlaps with Eastern Bluebird, hybrids are not uncommon. This bird hovers above insect prey and takes insects on the wing. **VOICE** Song a simple, harsh set of 5 to 7 low, throaty *chew* and *cher-oo* whistles, often sung on the wing; also a soft, rambling warble. Call a low *chewr*.

adult male

ultramarine above, paler below

thin bill

long wings, longer than other bluebirds

1st fall female

some show warmer tones below

adult female

pale gray, with blue in wings and tail

Townsend's Solitaire

Myadestes townsendi
L 8½"/22cm   WS 14½"/37cm

Solitaires are long-tailed montane thrushes renowned for their songs. Townsend's, the only solitaire recorded north of Mexico, inhabits open coniferous woodlands, especially in mountains, nesting in cavities on the ground; it winters in deserts, chaparral, and dry woodlands and is often seen perched atop a juniper watching for insects or eating berries. Unlike other woodland thrushes, it flycatches readily. **VOICE** Song a rich, rollicking warble similar to House Finch. Call a clear, high-pitched *peep*.

adult

white eye ring

soft gray plumage

white outer rectrices and buffy wing stripe (most visible when flying)

juvenile

dark gray with buffy tips on coverts, mantle, belly

American Robin

Turdus migratorius
L 10"/25cm   **WS** 17"/43cm

American Robin is the most widespread thrush in North America and a common nester in suburbs. It forages conspicuously on lawns, listening for earthworms and pouncing with precision to pull them from the ground. In winter robins form large flocks that wander in search of fruit. **VOICE** Song a series of 2 or 3 modulated whistles broken by brief pauses, often remembered as *cheery cheerily cheery-up,* repeated for hours. Common calls a low *tup* or a higher, emphatic *teep,* sometimes in rapid series.

adult male
broken eye ring
black head and white chin contrast with yellow bill
white vent

adult female

similar to male but more muted

juvenile

heavily spotted on breast, back, coverts

Varied Thrush

Ixoreus naevius
L 9½"/24cm   **WS** 16"/41cm

Varied Thrush's dreamy song is an unforgettable accompaniment to its misty, often fog-bound habitats: cool, humid coniferous forests and deciduous woods with dense alders. Vagrants to the east of typical range are occasionally seen with American Robins in woodlands (or at feeders, although they seldom forage on lawns). **VOICE** Song a well-spaced set of highly modulated whistles, varying in pitch, with an otherworldly quality. Call a deep *tchoop,* more emphatic than the *tchup* of Hermit Thrush.

adult male
dark breastband
rich orange belly, throat, supercilium, wing markings.

adult female

less intensely colored than male

diffuse gray breastband

Rufous-backed Robin
Turdus rufopalliatus
L 9½"/24cm **WS** 16"/41cm

This handsome thrush occasionally turns up as a winter vagrant in the Southwest. It is more retiring than American Robin, keeping to dense foliage of trees and thickets. It feeds on berries but unlike Clay-colored Robin does not frequent feeding stations. Like American Robin, Rufous-backed calls and sings mostly very early in the day, often before dawn. **VOICE** Song a series of rich, burry, warbled phrases, reminiscent of American Robin. Calls include a loud, descending, sibilant *sssiiuu*, a low *tuk* note (often in series), and a high, thin, lispy *si* in flight.

adult male
chestnut coverts and back
throat strongly streaked to upper breast
auburn underparts

adult female
dark lores in both sexes
paler than male
both sexes lack eye ring (unlike American Robin)

Clay-colored Robin
Turdus grayi
L 9"/23cm **WS** 15"/38cm

Clay-colored Robin is a scarce permanent resident in the Lower Rio Grande valley of Texas. Although often seen almost underfoot in tropical portions of its range, it is a shy bird in Texas, staying mostly in closed riparian vegetation and thickets and usually detected by its song. It occasionally visits suburban bird feeders for fruit. **VOICE** Song a thrasherlike series of slurred whistles, usually doubled. Call a far-carrying, rising *eeeeeurrah!* or *eeeurreee!* and agitated clucking.

adult
brown above, buff below
dusky red eyes
pale bill; streaked throat

Veery

Catharus fuscescens
L 7"/18cm **WS** 12"/30cm

Veery is a thrush of moist wooded habitats, especially poplar and aspen forests and riparian and other wetland areas with willow and alder thickets. Most populations are rusty-toned above, with sparser and less distinct spotting on the breast than other *Catharus*. The western subspecies *salicicolus* breeds from British Columbia to Colorado. **VOICE** Song a whirling, downward spiral of 4 to 7 fluting notes sounding, like Swainson's Thrush, as though sung through a pipe. Common call a nasal, downward *veer*.

eastern (nominate)   vivid rufous above

minimal breast spotting

western (salicicolus)

browner above, with only hints of rusty tones

(Pacific subspecies of Swainson's Thrush also have rusty tones)

Swainson's Thrush

Catharus ustulatus
L 7"/18cm **WS** 12"/30cm

Swainson's Thrush breeds in dense alder and willow thickets of muskegs, boreal spruce forests, western coniferous and aspen-poplar forests, and damp mixed eastern forests. The 6 subspecies of this variable thrush separate into the Olive-backed (*swainsoni*) group of the taiga and Rockies and the Russet-backed (*ustulatus*) group of the Pacific slope. **VOICE** Song a series of joined, fluting notes seeming to spiral upward. Calls include a spring peeper–like *peep,* a low *qurt,* and (in West) a liquid *whoit*.

Olive-backed (swainsoni)

olive tones above

more arboreal than other *Catharus*

strong eye ring; face has vivid buff cast

Russet-backed (ustulatus)

warm russet tones above (compare Hermit Thrush, Veery)

strong eye ring

less "spectacled" than Olive-backed, with less spotting below

Gray-cheeked Thrush

Catharus minimus
L 7¼"/18cm   WS 13"/33cm

This hardy thrush nests at the tree line and on tundra in stands of stunted spruce, alder, and willow trees. When migrating, it seeks out closed forests and moist thickets. *Catharus* thrushes are attracted to fruiting berry trees (especially mulberry) and may be closely observed there with patient watching. **VOICE** Song a thin, wiry, airy *twheew twhe-twhee, twhe-twheeeuw,* rising then falling, with hesitating pauses (descending pitch at close of full song differs from Bicknell's). Call an abrupt, rising *squear!* or *quear!*

adult — faint eye ring obscured in front of eye — heavier bill than Bicknell's — gray-brown sides — sparsely spotted breast has little or no buff

adult — incomplete eye ring — largely uniform plumage above — face subtly streaked, with little or no buffy tone

Bicknell's Thrush

Catharus bicknelli
L 6¾"/17cm   WS 11½"/29cm

Long considered a subspecies of Gray-cheeked Thrush, the smaller, more richly colored Bicknell's nests in stunted spruce and balsam fir forests often near ridge- and mountaintops. The two species overlap only during migration; they are distinguished by measurements and sometimes by their songs. Bicknell's winters in the Greater Antilles, Gray-cheeked in South America. **VOICE** Song differs from Gray-cheeked by ending on level pitch or clearly rising. Calls similar to but higher-pitched than Gray-cheeked.

adult — plain face like Gray-cheeked — shorter bill than Gray-cheeked, averaging more yellow in mandible — best told from Gray-cheeked by song

adult — tail usually has ruddy cast (compare Hermit Thrush)

Hermit Thrush

Catharus guttatus
L 6¾"/17cm   WS 11½"/29cm

Hermit Thrush breeds in boreal and high-elevation coniferous and mixed woods, where it forages mostly on the ground for invertebrates and berries. It is the only *Catharus* that regularly winters north of Mexico, in varied habitats, even shrubby suburban thickets. Northern and eastern taxa are rusty in wings and tail; birds are paler in the Interior West and darker in the Pacific Northwest. **VOICE** Song a flutelike series of rising notes. Common call a harsh *tchup*; alarm call (Interior West and Pacific) a rising, wheezy *chweeeEEE?*

1st fall, eastern (*faxoni*)

strong eye ring

reddish tail contrasts with back

heavily spotted below

often flicks wings and raises tail

adult, Pacific (nominate)

always shows complete eye ring

duller tones (more grayish brown) above than eastern

tail less rusty in some subspecies

Wood Thrush

Hylocichla mustelina
L 7¾"/20cm   WS 13"/33cm

Wood Thrush is almost an endemic breeder in the eastern U.S., found in mature deciduous forests, often moist woods with undergrowth. It forages terrestrially on snails, worms, insects, and other invertebrates. Its populations have undergone a rapid decline in recent decades, for reasons not yet clear. **VOICE** Song a varied, lively set of fluting phrases, both rising and falling, *oo-da-lee-oo*, introduced by 2 or 3 lower *doo* notes. Calls include a high, modulated *peet* and lower, liquid *wurt* and *wit*.

adult

pale, mostly complete eye ring

striped auriculars

large, with large bill

fledgling

can be confused with *Catharus*

adult

rufous nape

heavy spotting on flanks and belly (compare smaller *Catharus* thrushes)

Brown Thrasher

Toxostoma rufum
L 11½"/29cm **WS** 13"/33cm

The most widespread and richly colored of American thrashers, Brown Thrasher is also the only one associated with relatively moist habitats, especially brushy areas bordering deciduous or mixed woodlands east of the Rockies. In early spring males deliver varied songs (over 1,000 recorded variations) from a high, conspicuous perch, but for most of the year they remain hidden in dense cover. **VOICE** Song a long, musical series of doubled (sometimes trebled) notes or phrases. Calls include an abrupt *tchak* and an odd-sounding *chhzz*.

adult

coverts have black subterminal marks and white tips, making wing bars very distinct

longer tail and bill than Wood Thrush

intense rufous above, buffy cast below

fledgling

resembles thrushes, with short tail, spotted breast

trace of white wing bars (unlike thrushes)

Long-billed Thrasher

Toxostoma longirostre
L 11½"/29cm **WS** 12"/30cm

Long-billed Thrasher reaches its northern limit in southern Texas, from the Tamaulipan scrub of the Lower Rio Grande valley to the riparian woodlands and scrub of the southern hill country. It has strayed to New Mexico and Colorado but seems to be nonmigratory. When Brown Thrashers arrive to winter in Texas, the two species maintain separate feeding territories. **VOICE** Song much like Brown Thrasher but less musical and with less distinct pairing of phrases. Some calls similar to Brown; also a high *choop!* and quieter *keek*.

adult

longer, more decurved bill than Brown Thrasher

eyes more orange than Brown

shorter wings, less vivid underparts, weaker wing bars than Brown

streaking extends to undertail

adult

underparts whiter, with darker streaks, and face much grayer than Brown

Northern Mockingbird

Mimus polyglottos
L 10"/25cm **WS** 14"/36cm

This species is known for its nocturnal serenades as well as its habit of attacking people and pets in its territory. It inhabits open lowland areas from deserts to rangeland and can also be common in cities. Foraging birds flash white primary bases to startle insect prey. **VOICE** Song a series of repeated musical phrases separated by pauses, mostly imitations of birds and human sounds. Call a sharp *tchek.*

Northern Mockingbird adult

upperwing coverts edged in white

pale gray above; little head pattern

extensive white in tail and primaries, conspicuous in flight

Northern Mockingbird juvenile

pale gray, with limited spotting below (compare streaking of Sage Thrasher)

Gray Catbird

Dumetella carolinensis
L 8½"/22cm **WS** 11"/28cm

This retiring, sleek mimid is found in moist thickets and other dense, low vegetation, often near water. It typically sings from a concealed perch. Catbirds are less gifted mimics than mockingbirds, but patient listeners may hear a few imitations in their repertoire. In fall most of the population migrates eastward before heading to the southeastern coasts and into the tropics; hundreds might be observed after a cold front. **VOICE** Song a meandering series of sweet phrases, squeals, and nasal mewing notes (mewing call gives species its name); also gives a low *wurt* and an abrupt, rattling *kkkkk* alarm call, sounding like a mechanical noisemaker.

Gray Catbird

uniformly slaty gray, with darker crown (compare Townsend's Solitaire)

Gray Catbird

dark rusty undertail coverts flashed in courtship display

Sage Thrasher

Oreoscoptes montanus
L 8½"/22cm   WS 12"/30cm

The small, pale Sage Thrasher breeds only in sagebrush plains and foothills of the Great Basin; it winters in arid, open habitats farther south, especially pinyon-juniper woodlands and grasslands with bushes. The species is mostly terrestrial, but males sing from exposed perches. The overall appearance of this species seems to share qualities of both mockingbirds and thrashers; worn adults might be mistaken for Northern Mockingbird or Bendire's Thrasher, but the bill is intermediate between the two. **VOICE** Song a continuous, rather finchlike warble with a scratchy quality. Call a sharp, low *chuk*.

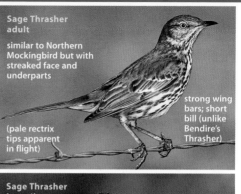

Sage Thrasher adult

similar to Northern Mockingbird but with streaked face and underparts

strong wing bars; short bill (unlike Bendire's Thrasher)

(pale rectrix tips apparent in flight)

Sage Thrasher juvenile

buffier breast and much less streaking below than adult

(worn adults also have minimal or indistinct streaks below)

Bendire's Thrasher

Toxostoma bendirei
L 9¾"/25cm   WS 13"/33cm

In the U.S. Bendire's Thrasher is largely restricted to deserts of the Southwest; it is found in areas with cacti, Joshua tree, creosote, yucca, or other tall vegetation and also inhabits agricultural land with native plant communities. Most appear to move southward in late summer to winter in Mexico, but many spend the winter in southern Arizona. **VOICE** Song a rapid series of harsh, warbled phrases, run together without pauses and repeated 1–3 times each. *Chuk* call similar to Curve-billed Thrasher.

Bendire's Thrasher adult

relatively straight mandible

flanks have buffy cast (compare Curve-billed Thrasher)

distinct, stippled spots below

Bendire's Thrasher duller adult

similar to young Curve-billed but smaller, with paler eyes and straighter, pale-based mandible

(juvenile similar but shorter-billed)

California Thrasher

Toxostoma redivivum
L 12"/30cm **WS** 12½"/32cm

Nearly endemic to California, California Thrasher breeds elsewhere only in a sliver of Baja California. This large, dark thrasher inhabits chaparral in coastal and foothill areas and wooded thickets near water. Like similar species, it uses its decurved bill to probe and dig for beetles, isopods, spiders, and other invertebrates; it also takes berries and seeds as large as acorns. **VOICE** Song a series of phrases repeated 2–3 times; deep-voiced and rather grating compared to smaller thrashers. Call a sweet *tluit*.

adult

most look brown above, buffy below

thick bill; dark eyes

adult

some individuals grayer (less buffy), but show stronger face pattern than Crissal Thrasher

Crissal Thrasher

Toxostoma crissale
L 11½"/29cm **WS** 12½"/32cm

This dark thrasher of the Southwest can be elusive in the brushy areas it inhabits, whether dense mesquite thickets along desert arroyos or chaparral foothills. In the Chihuahuan Desert, Crissal Thrasher is often seen as a dark streak running between bushes. Singing males perch high in vegetation early in the nesting season. **VOICE** Song a typical thrasher mix of repeated phrases, mellower and less grating than California Thrasher; less rushed and with distinct pauses, unlike Curve-billed. Call a querulous *purrrr-deee?*

adult

gray auriculars (not contrastingly darker, as in California Thrasher)

black submalar stripe separates pale throat and white malar

mostly medium gray overall

rusty undertail coverts

Curve-billed Thrasher

Toxostoma curvirostre
L 11"/28cm   WS 13½"/34cm

Curve-billed Thrasher is a large, conspicuous bird of southwestern deserts, including suburbs, favoring areas with abundant cholla and other cacti. Its loud call is one of the most familiar bird sounds from central Texas to central Arizona. In the U.S. several subspecies make up the *curvirostre* group, found from Arizona's Chiricahuas eastward; *palmeri* is found farther west. Vagrants have been discovered as far out of range as Wisconsin. **VOICE** Song a busy, skittering jumble of repeated phrases and staccato notes. Call a far-carrying *whit-WHEET!,* often with extra note at end, and a rich *chuk.*

adult
(*palmeri* group)

shorter bill and grayer, less distinctly spotted underparts than Texas population (adult and juvenile similar)

indistinct grayish wing bars (sometimes no wing bars)

adult
(*curvirostre* group)

pale rectrix tips

more distinctly spotted below

Le Conte's Thrasher

Toxostoma lecontei
L 8"/20cm   WS 13"/33cm

Le Conte's Thrasher specializes in some of the least hospitable habitats in the U.S.: very hot, arid desert scrub and washes with scattered saltbush and creosote. Uncommon and shy, it flees rapidly on foot from intruders; it is best observed in late winter and early spring when males sing from bush tops. Adults in fresh fall plumage are darker; the sun soon fades their plumage to a pale sandy gray. **VOICE** Song a precise series of resonant warbling phrases separated by pauses, usually with longer high, sweet slurred notes. Call a rising *wheep.*

adult

much paler overall than other thrashers, with remiges and rectrices slightly darker

juvenile

like adult but slightly browner, with weaker head pattern, shorter bill

bluish gray legs

Cedar Waxwing

Bombycilla cedrorum
L 7¼"/18cm   WS 12"/30cm

Cedar Waxwing is a habitat generalist, breeding in wooded and semiopen areas from the muskeg and boreal forest belt to Tennessee pinewoods; it requires only sufficient insect life to feed its young during the first days after hatching. After breeding, this species gathers in large, nomadic flocks that roam all manner of habitats, flycatching for insects, stripping trees of berries, and eating even sap and flowers. **VOICE** Song a series of high, sibilant *see* notes. Call a single song note; flocking birds often call simultaneously.

adult

innermost tertial has white edge

blackish mask and throat

adult waxwings have waxy red tips to secondaries

white undertail coverts

no white or yellow bars in primaries or coverts (compare Bohemian)

juvenile

trace of adult's mask and crest

blurry streaks below

yellow-tipped tail

Bohemian Waxwing

Bombycilla garrulus
L 8¼"/21cm   WS 14½"/37cm

Bohemian Waxwing breeds in northern boreal forests; it is an irruptive winter visitor across most of its nonbreeding range, appearing suddenly in great numbers after one or many years' absence to forage on berries of mountain ash and other fruits. A lone vagrant stands out in a flock of Cedars by its larger size, rusty undertail coverts, white in secondaries and greater coverts, and white or yellow primary tips. **VOICE** Much lower and slower than Cedar, with distinct notes creating an almost juncolike twitter.

adult

heavy body, grayish except for head

mask lacks white upper border (compare Cedar)

greater coverts and remiges have pale tips (here white)

cinnamon undertail coverts

1st winter

pale rust undertail coverts

lacks waxy red tips on secondaries

adult

some individuals browner overall, like Cedar

most adults show yellow in primary tips

European Starling
Sturnus vulgaris
L 8½"/22cm **WS** 16"/41cm

Introduced to Central Park, New York City, in 1890, European Starling quickly spread to become one of the most widespread of all North American birds. It is an astonishingly resourceful, omnivorous species, able to occupy just about any habitat—from urban downtown areas and landfills to open woodlands, where it displaces native species from cavities. Large roosts and feeding flocks of starlings form in fall and winter; they often forage among blackbirds in open fields. **VOICE** Song a grating, gargling concatenation of trills, squeals, whistles, and imitated sounds and songs of other species. Call a harsh, rolling *splllrr*.

adult, winter

remiges edged in rich brown

black bill gradually turns yellowish

regular pale spots on dark underparts

breeding adult

bright yellow bill

spots in body plumage wear off to produce high breeding plumage, with green and purple sheens

molting juvenile

gradually acquires blackish plumage

adult, fresh fall

neatly spotted underparts and scapulars; finely speckled face and throat

warm rusty edges to remiges and coverts

juvenile molting to 1st winter

resembles fall/winter adult; juvenal head feathers molt last

juvenile

dingy grayish brown overall, with paler throat

blurry streaks below

Red-whiskered Bulbul

Pycnonotus jocosus
L 7¼"/18cm WS 11"/28cm

Red-whiskered Bulbul (family Pycnonotidae) was introduced from southern Asia to southeastern Florida in the early 1960s. It is fairly uncommon south of Miami, most readily observed around Kendall. Its range does not appear to be expanding. The species is also found on occasion in Los Angeles County, California, where there is likely a very small breeding population. **VOICE** Song a sweet, fussing chatter, described as *chee-purdle-chee birdie-birdie*. Calls include a high *peet!* and quick *pettigrew*.

adult

dark crest
and crown

red in auriculars
often obscure
(absent or paler
in juvenile)

dark
breast
bar

red
undertail
coverts

Phainopepla

Phainopepla nitens
L 8"/20cm WS 11"/28cm

The only silky-flycatcher (family Ptilogonatidae) resident north of Mexico, Phainopepla is a sleek species of southwestern desert scrub, oak savannas, and riparian corridors, where, in fluttering flight, it flycatches insects and feeds on mistletoe and other small berries. Where food is abundant, this species often feeds and nests communally. **VOICE** Song a lackadaisical series of whistled and harsh notes, a cross between vireos and catbirds, including imitations of many species. Call a high, distinctive, nasal *woit?*

adult male

tall, wispy
crest

glossy
black

red eyes

(white in primaries
forms white patches,
apparent in flight)

immature   orange
              eyes

mousy gray-
brown

compare
mimids,
titmice

(fema
simila

Jays, Crows, and Kin

Ravens, crows, jays, magpies, and nutcrackers (family Corvidae) are a diverse group of medium-sized to large passerines with sturdy legs and bills, rounded wings, and often long tails. Their plumages can be simple shades of blue or black or quite stunning, as with the strikingly patterned magpies or the multicolored Green Jay. Corvids are found in every major habitat on the continent; Common Raven, the world's largest passerine, remains year-round even in northern Nunavut, enduring the brutal, dark winters.

Much of a corvid's success in difficult environments can be credited to its ingenuity in finding food and its ability to adapt to human-modified landscapes. Its gregariousness appears to be another advantage, birds of this group are quick to share new foraging techniques, whether raiding campsites and picnic baskets, dropping nuts on asphalt roads, or following toddlers for dropped food. Corvids are also among the few birds that appear to use tools, and experiments have shown that they are able to count, to remember the location of thousands of sites of cached nuts, and to find solutions to obstacles in procuring food. Most are omnivores, taking carrion, small animals, nestling birds and eggs, fruit, aquatic vertebrates and invertebrates, worms, waste grain, and other foods. Smaller corvids, especially jays, eat mostly seeds and nuts and also insects and other arthropods. Pinyon Jay feeds on pine nuts; flocks of this

Corvids frequently harass or "mob" birds of prey. Here a Fish Crow may be attempting to steal scraps of fish from an Osprey.

species and of Clark's Nutcracker travel widely in search of good cone crops.

Corvids are not known for their singing ability; their courtship is limited to quiet singing, animated posturing, and, in ravens, acrobatic paired flights. Jays and crows nest mostly in trees (ravens often nest on cliffs), making cup-shaped nests of twigs and sticks; magpies cover the nest with a dome of sticks. Corvids have rather complex breeding systems. For example, several pairs of Mexican Jays may hold a common territory and feed young in several nests regardless of their parentage. Florida Scrub-Jays assist their parents at the nest for at least a year, and in some areas crows also have nest helpers.

Other than Blue Jay, American corvids are not typically migratory, but many species make irregular movements out of the mountains or northern parts of range, especially when food supplies fail.

Among American corvids, Island Scrub-Jay and Florida Scrub-Jay are federally listed as threatened. Both species have very small populations and ranges and are thus potentially susceptible to diseases such as West Nile virus. Destruction of the fragile Florida scrub habitat has been the chief cause of Florida Scrub-Jay's decline.

Blue Jay nestlings, like the young of other jays, begin acquiring their feathers at age 2 weeks.

Blue Jay

Cyanocitta cristata
L 11"/28cm **WS** 16"/41cm

Blue Jay is a familiar sight in backyards and forests across most of eastern North America. It eats primarily acorns and other mast but also takes eggs and nestlings. This species is unique among American jays in that it migrates regularly in autumn, when flocks of hundreds move southward on the coast and through mountains in the East. **VOICE** Common call a strident, nasal *daaaay, daaaay;* also a short, mechanical rattling; imitations of raptors, especially Red-shouldered Hawk; and a sweet-sounding *doo-lim-pic!*

adult
unique combination of blue crest and dark collar and eye line
blue with white in coverts, secondaries, tail
only jay over most of range

fledgling
pale bill, short tail and crest; otherwise resembles adult

Steller's Jay

Cyanocitta stelleri
L 11"/28cm **WS** 18"/46cm

Steller's Jay is most common in forested areas of the Rocky Mountains and Pacific coast. It is bolder than Blue Jay, regularly approaching campsites to steal food. The two species sometimes hybridize where ranges meet. The subspecies *macrolopha* (southern Rockies) has a longer crest and different head markings than birds of the nominate group (Pacific coast, northern Rockies). **VOICE** Dozens of vocalizations; foraging birds deliver a raspy, rapid-fire *sh-ksh-ksh-ksh-ksh-ksh-k* and a drawn-out, descending *shhhhhhhhhrrrr.*

adult (*stelleri* group)
blue frontlet
sooty head, back, crest
barring in tail, like Blue Jay (compare other North American jays)
blue wings and tail

adult (*macrolopha*)
white frontlet and "eyebrow"

Mexican Jay
Aphelocoma ultramarina
L 11½"/29cm **WS** 20"/51cm

Mexican Jay, also called Gray-breasted Jay, is a relative of scrub-jays but has more muted plumage and a shorter tail. It forms flocks that fly swiftly and garrulously through the woods, foraging in trees and on the ground; in the morning and late afternoon, it often perches high to bask. Groups of up to 25 defend a single territory in which multiple females breed; young are fed by the group. **VOICE** Less strident than other jays; most common call a repeated, upwardly inflected *wenk?*, sounding querulous or inquisitive.

adult, Texas (couchii)

head lacks white markings (compare scrub-jays)

grayish brown back; gray breast

Texas birds a darker, richer blue

1st year

juvenile loses pink bill slowly

adult, Arizona (arizonae)

Arizona birds paler, with browner back

compare scrub-jays

Pinyon Jay
Gymnorhinus cyanocephalus
L 10½"/27cm **WS** 19"/48cm

Pinyon Jay is a specialist in pinyon pine and yellow pine habitats of the Great Basin and Rocky Mountains, where flocks of hundreds forage over great distances in search of pine nuts. This species is unique among jays in that it walks rather than hops when foraging on the ground and nests in colonies rather than defends a separate territory. At times of pinecone crop failure, Pinyon Jays may be found well out of their usual range. **VOICE** A quiet, quick *aye*, usually in rapid series; also various nasal, mewing notes and a harsh *kwa kwa kwa kwa!*

adult

gray cast to plumage

pale throat has faint streaking

adult, worn

long bill and short tail distinctive

looks like a small blue crow

juvenile

grayish overall, with touches of blue; paler throat

(wingbeats are rapid and steady, unlike scrub-jays)

long, dark bill and short tail differ from other jays in range

Western Scrub-Jay
Aphelocoma californica
L 11½"/29cm **WS** 16"/41cm

Western Scrub-Jay can be found in a wide variety of habitats, from semidesert scrub near sea level to dry mountain canyons high in the Rockies; but it favors brushy areas over open forest. Several brightly colored subspecies, known as the *californica* group, are found along the Pacific coast, where their confiding habits make them easily observed. A subspecies of the Interior West, Woodhouse's Scrub-Jay *(woodhouseii)*, is shier, quieter, and much duller in plumage. **VOICE** Most common call a harsh, rising *shrreeynk!*, repeated often. The two groups differ somewhat in their vocalizations.

adult, Pacific
(*californica* group)

Pacific coastal birds much brighter, with distinct blue collar

pale undertail coverts contrast with rich tan belly

adult, Interior West
(*woodhouseii*)

Interior birds duller, with indistinct or absent collar

white supercilium and breast (compare Mexican Jay)

undertail coverts washed grayish blue

loses pale bill in first year, but retains some sooty head feathers into second

older juvenile
(*californica* group)

adult

flies with undulating dips and short glides

juvenile, Pacific
(*californica* group)

gray above

pinkish yellow in bill base

unbarred tail (juvenile Steller's and Blue Jays have barred tails)

Island Scrub-Jay
Aphelocoma insularis
L 13"/33cm **WS** 17"/43cm

Of the endemic breeding bird species of temperate North America, Island Scrub-Jay has the most restricted range: it is found only on Santa Cruz Island off the coast of California, where some 8,000 individuals are resident in oak and mixed woodlands and chaparral. In its island isolation, this species has evolved to be larger and brighter than mainland scrub-jays, with a heavier bill. **VOICE** Very similar to Western Scrub-Jay but typically louder and harsher; includes a series of *shek* or *kwesh* notes, a sharp rattle, and a quick *chok*.

adult

vivid blue tones contrast with dark face and brown back

dark cheek tinged bluish

only jay in range

sky blue cast to undertail coverts

adult

heavier bill than mainland scrub-jays

Florida Scrub-Jay
Aphelocoma coerulescens
L 11½"/29cm **WS** 14"/36cm

Endemic to central Florida, Florida Scrub-Jay inhabits semiopen areas of oak scrub, an endangered habitat sustained by periodic fires. Fewer than 10,000 of these jays remain, their recent declines attributed to fragmentation and loss of habitat. Unlike other scrub-jays, nesting pairs use nest helpers, young from previous years that help defend the nest and territory and feed the young. **VOICE** Very harsh, short, raspy calls, lower and less inflected than other scrub-jays.

adult male

blue face and white forecrown (unlike other scrub-jays)

adult female

female and immature usually paler

Green Jay

Cyanocorax yncas
L 10½"/27cm **WS** 14"/36cm

The striking Green Jay is difficult to confuse with any other native North American bird. This Neotropical jay travels in small groups through the dense thickets and woodlands of southernmost Texas, feeding on both insects and plant matter. Flocks, made up of a pair and the previous year's young, defend the territory; however, the year-old birds do not feed nestlings. Although shy, Green Jay is attracted to bird-feeding stations in some areas. **VOICE** A harsh *ji-ji-ji-ji* and *shk-shk-shk-shk*, reminiscent of Blue and Steller's Jays.

adult

blue and black head contrasts with green body

adult

distinct black bib unique

tail appears yellow below (outer 2 tail feathers yellow)

Brown Jay

Cyanocorax morio
L 17"/43cm **WS** 26"/66cm

Brown Jay is a Neotropical species found in the U.S. in only a few spots along the Rio Grande in southern Texas, recently in Salineño and Chapeño, near Falcon Dam. It is typically seen in family groups that forage noisily through the brushy Tamaulipan woodlands, flying with labored wingbeats across openings. **VOICE** Most common call a strident, tremulous, raptorlike *clear!*, repeated often; also a mechanical hiccuping, produced through a bare, inflatable furcular sac on the chest.

adult

large, with long tail

brown, with pale belly

subadult

some yellow in bill

juvenile

yellow bill and eye ring

Gray Jay

Perisoreus canadensis
L 11"/28cm **WS** 18"/46cm

Gray Jay is closely associated with montane and boreal forests. It is retiring as a rule, but where habituated to humans it can become very confiding, stealing food from campsites or even taking it from the hand. In flight, Gray Jay flaps rapidly, then glides slowly to the next perch. Taxa vary from a very dark subspecies on the Pacific coast to almost white-headed birds in the Rockies. **VOICE** Some calls resemble Blue Jay's familiar *daaaay*, but mostly gentler *cook* calls; groups give chattering and fussing calls.

adult

no crest

dark gray above, pale gray below

(subspecies in Canada and Rockies have paler crowns)

(at a distance can be mistaken for a chickadee, but larger)

adult

unique dark cap with white forehead

very short bill

immature

sooty above

pale malar

(juvenile entirely gray below)

Clark's Nutcracker

Nucifraga columbiana
L 12"/30cm **WS** 24"/61cm

This handsome corvid occupies montane coniferous forests; it is more often heard than seen but is frequently observed singly, flying high over a valley or perched atop a pine; after breeding it may gather in large flocks. Like Pinyon Jay, nutcrackers have a long, pointed bill (an adaptation for feeding on pine nuts) and walk rather than hop. They cache nuts and seeds and can remember hundreds of cache locations for long periods. **VOICE** Most often a drawn-out, grating *krraaaaaaaa;* also a variety of rattles and other jaylike calls.

adult

long bill

gray body contrasts with black wings, white in tail

adult

distinctive black, white, and gray pattern

fledgling

mousy brownish gray, with shorter bill than adult

obvious white in secondaries and outer rectrices

Black-billed Magpie
Pica hudsonia
L 19"/48cm   WS 26"/66cm

Black-billed Magpie inhabits agricultural
land, ranches, and open parklands and
also suburban areas, provided there are
trees for roosting and nesting. It forages
mostly singly or in pairs but will gather
in groups where food is plentiful; it
often roosts communally. Magpies are
omnivores, taking a wide variety of food,
including carrion and refuse. **VOICE**
Most common call an upwardly inflected,
querulous *jeee!*, often repeated, followed
by harsher, jaylike chattering *shk-ksh-ksh-
ksh-ksh-k;* also grating, ternlike calls.

adult

black head,
breast, bill

white belly
and scapulars

secondaries
and elegant
long tail have
blue-green
sheen

adult

striking white in
primaries visible
in flight

Yellow-billed Magpie
Pica nuttalli
L 17"/43cm   WS 25"/64cm

Yellow-billed Magpie, known only from
the central valleys of California, is smaller
and more slender than Black-billed
Magpie, with a yellow bill and yellow
skin around the eyes. It tends to be
more gregarious, nesting in small, loose
colonies, often near human habitations,
and regularly forming flocks that forage
across the territories of several colonies.
A few recent records of this species from
southern Oregon probably pertain to wild
wanderers from California. **VOICE** Very
like Black-billed, perhaps higher-pitched.

adult

like Black-billed
but smaller and
more slender,
with yellow bill

adult

yellow skin
around eyes
variable

Common Raven

Corvus corax
L 24"/61cm **WS** 52"/1.3m

Common Raven is one of the most fascinating of passerines—and the world's largest. Ravens frequent remote habitats, from tundra to mountains to deserts, and can be found almost as far north as there is land. They are resourceful foragers, taking advantage of almost any source, including nestling birds, small mammals, and carrion. Often spotted in high, soaring flight, ravens "play" on the wing far more than crows do, executing full rolls and somersaults in paired and group displays. **VOICE** Highly varied, with dozens of calls, most commonly deep, hoarse cawing calls and throaty croaks; also almost human-sounding screams, whistles, and gargles.

Chihuahuan Raven

Corvus cryptoleucus
L 19"/48cm **WS** 45"/1.1m

Chihuahuan Raven is found mostly in dry grasslands, scrub, farms, and deserts of the southern Great Plains and Chihuahuan Desert; it is usually seen in pairs or small groups but sometimes forms large flocks. Chihuahuan closely resembles a small Common but has shorter wings, a less wedge-shaped tail, and nasal bristles that extend farther down the culmen. **VOICE** Similar to Common but less varied in tone and type and usually higher-pitched.

Common Raven adult

long wings

heavy bill

long wings and tail

heavy head and bill apparent in flight

Common Raven juvenile

inner edges of bill pinkish

tail spade-shaped when closed

body plumage lacks sheen of adult

Chihuahuan Raven adult

similar to Common Raven; more delicate in body and bill

heavy bill with long nasal bristles

Chihuahuan Raven adult

white bases of nape feathers (gray in Common) visible when preening or in strong winds

American Crow

Corvus brachyrhynchos
L 17"/43cm **WS** 38"/97cm

American Crow is widespread in many habitats but absent in the interior of dense forests and in most deserts. Its distinctive, familiar cawing is evocative of the American countryside, where it is often seen foraging on waste grain in harvested fields. Flocks are often seen mobbing much larger hawks and owls. Voice is usually the best clue to separating the four crow species. When perched, crows frequently flick their wings (ravens do not). **VOICE** Most frequent call the familiar *caaww, caaww;* also monkeylike jabbering and a mechanical rattle.

American Crow

black overall, with metallic bluish-violet gloss (strongest in upperparts)

heavy bill

American Crow

broad wings, shorter than ravens

wingtips usually appear more rounded and wider than Fish Crow in flight

American Crow

rounded tail, shorter than ravens

Northwestern Crow

Corvus caurinus
L 16"/41cm **WS** 35"/89cm

Northwestern Crow differs from American Crow chiefly in its slightly smaller size and lower, more ravenlike voice. Most birders identify this species by its range: it is the only crow inhabiting the Pacific coast from southern Alaska to northern Washington, where it is often seen scavenging along shorelines. **VOICE** Calls very similar to western American Crow but usually lower-pitched and rougher.

Northwestern Crow

very similar to American Crow but slightly smaller

only crow in range

Fish Crow

Corvus ossifragus
L 15"/38cm **WS** 35"/89cm

A small crow of the Southeast, Fish Crow is found in many lowland habitats, from open barrier islands to riparian forests, usually never far from water. It takes mostly animal prey, both vertebrate and invertebrate, and often forms large flocks at landfills, especially in the nonbreeding season. This species has expanded its range considerably in the 20th century, mostly along the Atlantic coast and major rivers such as the Mississippi. Fish Crow was once a strictly coastal species (like Northwestern Crow); its ability to adapt to human-modified environments may explain its expansion. Some authors suggest that the recovery of heron and tern populations has facilitated its spread; the species readily raids colonies for eggs and small nestlings. **VOICE** A distinctive, nasal *kah-uh* or *ehk;* much less jarring than American Crow (although juvenile American has similar call).

adult

more petite and smaller-billed than American Crow

appears shorter-legged than American

purple gloss on upperparts and breast visible in optimal light

adult

wings more pointed than American, with narrower, more pointed primaries

adult

overall wing area often appears smaller than American, body and tail slimmer

tail often appears longer and narrower than American

Tamaulipas Crow

Corvus imparatus
L 14"/36cm **WS** 29"/74cm

This rare species of lowland habitats in Tamaulipas, Mexico, is found in the U.S. only around Brownsville, in southernmost Texas. It generally builds a single nest (in Mexico it may nest in colonies), sometimes on a manmade structure. In the U.S., Tamaulipas Crow has declined in recent decades to a few pairs. The reasons for this decline are unknown; populations at the outer limits of range are ephemeral in many bird species. **VOICE** A low-pitched, froglike *gark* or *nark.*

adult

very petite (smallest North American crow)

strong blue tones in plumage

only crow in range

Blackbirds, Orioles, and Kin

Blackbirds and their kin (family Icteridae) are medium-sized passerines with straight, pointed bills (shorter and more conical on cowbirds and Bobolink) and relatively long, thick legs that are equally well adapted for perching and walking on the ground. Some species, such as Yellow-headed Blackbird, have large feet that help them balance on aquatic vegetation or mud. The plumages of icterids are often striking and colorful, ranging from brilliant orange and yellow in the long-tailed orioles and the short-tailed meadowlarks to glossy purple, green, and bronze in the grackles, cowbirds, and blackbirds. Bobolink males are mostly black during the breeding season, with a vivid buttercup nape and white in the wing coverts. In most species, females are less gaudily colored or less iridescent and often have brown rather than black tones.

Many species of icterid, especially the blackbirds, have adapted well to human-modified landscapes. Collectively, their breeding habitats extend from the tundra of eastern Alaska, where Red-winged Blackbirds sing from marshy swales, to the strip malls of southernmost Texas, where gangs of Great-tailed Grackles patrol parking lots for french fries. Blackbirds and grackles forage mostly on the ground for seeds, waste grain, mast, and invertebrates, but they eat a wide variety of other foods—fruits, blossoms, buds, and even other birds, birds' eggs, and nestlings. Orioles are much more arboreal in their foraging, and their diets, while also rich in insects and plant matter, feature more nectar. The longer-billed ground-foraging species, especially meadowlarks, frequently forage by inserting the bill into the ground or dense grasses and opening it to make a gap from which to take prey. Rusty Blackbird and Common Grackle employ this strategy in swamps, where they also sometimes wade into shallow water for aquatic invertebrates.

Breeding systems in blackbirds vary tremendously among the species. The larger grackles have polygynous systems that involve harems: large, dominant males defend a territory and mate with multiple females, a strategy seen frequently in mammals but very rarely in birds. Red-winged and Tricolored Blackbirds are also polygynous in their mating

Blackbirds, such as these Yellow-headeds, congregate in large flocks in the nonbreeding season.

but do not defend harems; Red-winged males defend distinct territories, whereas Tricolored males do not. Orioles are mostly monogamous. Cowbirds are brood parasites, laying their eggs in the nests of other songbirds and allowing the host species to feed the young birds. The newly hatched cowbird instinctively jettisons other eggs from the nest, leaving the host birds with just one cowbird fledgling.

Populations of blackbirds have been relatively stable and have even increased in some areas; the stark exception is Rusty Blackbird, whose populations may have decreased by as much as 90 percent in the latter part of the 20th century. Most oriole populations, on the other hand, have shown gradual declines in recent decades, probably because of habitat losses in both their breeding and wintering ranges. Bobolink has also suffered population declines, most likely a result of changes in agricultural practices.

Brown-headed Cowbird
Molothrus ater
L 7½"/19cm **WS** 12"/30cm

Brown-headed Cowbird is a common sight in most lowlands, from grasslands to forests; it is uncommon only in the extremes of the boreal forest and open desert. A versatile forager, it eats waste grain and insects in farm fields and birdseed at feeders. Cowbirds are brood parasites, laying eggs in other birds' nests to be raised by the hosts. **VOICE** Song a short, rising *tk-tk-klee,* first notes low and liquid, last note thin, high, and sweet. Calls include a sputtering rattle (female) and long sweet notes like close of song (male).

adult male

rich brown head contrasts with dark body (often green-glossed in good light)

stouter, smaller bill than other cowbirds

juvenile
streaky below

adult female

supercilium faint or absent

recalls a large sparrow

dark brown above, pale below; often has distinct pale malar and throat

---

Bronzed Cowbird
Molothrus aeneus
L 8¾"/22cm **WS** 14"/36cm

In the U.S. Bronzed Cowbird occurs mostly in summer in southern Texas and the Southwest. It has been recorded as far out of range as Nova Scotia and can be locally common in winter to western Florida. Two subspecies—the nominate form of southern Texas (dark-plumaged females) and *loyei* of the Southwest (females with pale brown heads and underparts)—may intergrade in western Texas near Big Bend. **VOICE** Song a long series of high, thin, sharp whistles, alternately rising and falling. Calls similar to Brown-headed Cowbird.

adult male

red eyes (unlike other U.S. icterids)

heavy neck, often "puffed up"

heavy, decurved bill

wings have bluish sheen; body plumage bronzy

adult female (nominate)

very dark blackish brown, without gloss on wings and tail seen on male

red eyes

(adult female *loyei* similar but less streaky below)

juvenile, western *(loyei)*

similar to Brown-headed but larger, with more arched culmen

(juvenile of nominate subspecies richer blackish brown overall)

Common Grackle

Quiscalus quiscula
L 12½"/32cm **WS** 17"/43cm

Common Grackle is widely distributed in open woodlands, agricultural lands, and suburbs. In optimal light, the iridescent hues of the Atlantic coastal subspecies *(stonei)*, Purple Grackle, are dazzling; this taxon is thought to be an intergrade between the nominate subspecies, Florida Grackle (which has a greenish back), and the northern/western subspecies *versicolor*, Bronzed Grackle (with a bronzy back). **VOICE** Song a harsh, creaking *hk-sheeee* or similar, usually rising. Calls a mechanical *kek, ki-kik, kiw, kyik, k-shrrr*, and others.

adult, Purple *(stonei)*
looks dark in shade but shows much iridescence in direct light
iridescent hues of blue, purple, bronze, and green

adult, Bronzed *(versicolor)*
purplish blue head (sometimes greenish)
bronze and violet hues in wings and body
(tail appears much shorter than body length in flight)

Shiny Cowbird

Molothrus bonariensis
L 7½"/19cm **WS** 11½"/29cm

Shiny Cowbird is a regular visitor to southern Florida, where small numbers occupy many semiopen habitats, and may be slowly spreading northward. Firm evidence of breeding in the U.S. has been elusive, largely because this species is a brood parasite. Vagrants have been noted as far out of range as Oklahoma and New Brunswick. **VOICE** Song like Brown-headed, starting with several low, liquid notes and ending with a rising, high, thin whistle; female's rattle call like Brown-headed, but male's sweet flight call, *ti-ti-ti-tyoo*, strikingly unlike Brown-headed.

adult male
rich brown eyes
unique, resplendent purple body plumage (in good light) similar to Purple Martin
bill less sparrowlike than Brown-headed Cowbird
longer tail than Brown-headed

adult female
faint supercilium
longer, more pointed bill than Brown-headed, with more uniform underparts from throat to vent
usually appears darker overall than female Brown-headed

Great-tailed Grackle
Quiscalus mexicanus
L 18"/46cm **WS** 23"/58cm (male)

A giant among blackbirds, Great-tailed Grackle may put observers in mind of Hitchcock's film *The Birds,* as flocks forage and roost noisily in highly urbanized areas. This species has recently spread northward in the Great Plains. Both males and females can have multiple partners, a reproductive strategy known as polygynandry. **VOICE** Song a loud, varied train of unusual sounds—muffled whistles, hisses, and rattles—that recall a ham radio being tuned. Call similar to Boat-tailed Grackle.

adult male
flat crown
purplish gloss

adult always pale-eyed

large bill and body

adult male

enormous tail often spread in flight

immature female

pale eyes (dark in female Boat-tailed)

lacks warm tones below of Boat-tailed Grackle

(adult female similar but has pale throat and supercilium set off by dusky auriculars)

Boat-tailed Grackle
Quiscalus major
L 16½"/42cm **WS** 23"/58cm (male)

Males of this conspicuous resident of coastal salt marshes often perform ostentatious group displays: they spread tails, rattle wings, puff out feathers, and make clattering calls with raised bills. Grackles eat just about anything, including other birds' eggs and nestlings; this species preys mostly on invertebrates and small vertebrates. **VOICE** Song of harsh *whee* notes that vary in length and inflection but not pitch; repeated in rapid series, often separated by quick, low gargling sounds. Call a low, sharp *chk.*

adult male, Atlantic *(torreyi)*
rounded crown

smaller than Great-tailed

bluish purple gloss on body

(tail appears nearly as long as body in flight)

yellow eyes in *torreyi* and in northern Gulf coast *alabamensis* (others brown-eyed)

adult female, Florida *(westoni)*

warm brown below

(Atlantic females have yellow eyes)

Brewer's Blackbird

Euphagus cyanocephalus
L 9"/23cm WS 15½"/39cm

Throughout the West and Midwest, Brewer's Blackbird can be seen strutting through farm fields and feedlots, eating waste grain and insects; but this highly adaptable species visits almost any open or semiopen habitat, from parking lots to picnic grounds, rest stops to montane meadows. In Atlantic coastal states, flocks of several dozen may sometimes gather locally around cattle or horse farms. **VOICE** Song an unremarkable, short, rising *ktzeee,* recalling a distant Red-winged Blackbird. Call a sharp, nasal *kut.*

adult male

head and breast have bluish purple gloss

in fall a few show brown feather edges in body plumage but never in coverts or upperwings

wings and back have green gloss

smaller than grackles, larger than cowbirds

adult female

longer legs and shorter, blunter bill than Rusty Blackbird

gray-brown overall, with darker wings and tail and dark eyes (rarely pale)

Rusty Blackbird

Euphagus carolinus
L 9"/23cm WS 14"/36cm

Rusty Blackbird nests in wet areas of the boreal forest and muskeg; it winters mostly in swamp woods, foraging on plant matter and insects, often while walking around the water's edge. Nonbreeding birds may join mixed blackbird flocks in farm fields to eat waste grain. Since the 1960s populations of this species are thought to have declined by as much as 90%. **VOICE** Song likened to a rusty door hinge: a squeaky *tklrrEEE!,* usually with gracklelike mutterings or series of *tk* call notes.

breeding adult male

plumage shows less green and purple iridescence than Brewer's

thinner, more pointed bill than Brewer's

dark plumage achieved by wear of rusty edges of fresh autumn plumage

nonbreeding adult female

buffy supercilium and throat

warm brown tones above

breeding adult female, worn

similar to female Brewer's, but with paler eyes, shorter legs and tail, and thinner bill

Red-winged Blackbird

Agelaius phoeniceus
L 8¾"/22cm **WS** 14"/36cm

This hardy species nests in moist pastures and wetlands and forages for seeds, insects, and grain in treetops, fields, and swamplands. In northern areas, it is often the first species to return in spring, the male's creaky song and flashing red epaulets foretelling winter's end. After breeding, Red-wingeds may form flocks in the millions. Bicolored Blackbird (2 California subspecies) has black median coverts. **VOICE** Song a harsh, rising *hark-a-rreee!* Calls include the usual blackbird *chk* and a higher *pyiu, tyiu, tzit,* and *tszeeur.*

adult male

black overall, with scarlet lesser coverts, yellow median coverts

(fresh fall plumage has rufous feather edges)

male, Bicolored Blackbird

no yellow in median coverts

adult female

often has buffy or pinkish tinge on throat

paler overall than Tricolored, and more distinctly marked

(worn females in some taxa almost blackish on belly, like Tricolored)

Tricolored Blackbird

Agelaius tricolor
L 8¾"/22cm **WS** 13"/33cm

Once a specialist of bulrush and cattail marshes in Pacific coastal states, the gregarious Tricolored Blackbird now also nests in a variety of agricultural habitats. The species is not migratory, although most disperse toward the coast in winter. Because of its limited range and small, declining numbers, this species is of conservation concern. **VOICE** Song like Red-winged Blackbird but lower, more nasal, less articulate and ringing, and descending rather than rising. Calls similar to Red-winged but lower.

adult male

"epaulets" a rich red in lesser coverts, whitish in median coverts

slightly thinner bill than Red-winged; plumage has more purplish gloss

(fresh fall male shows buffy gray feather edges, not rufous as in Red-winged)

adult female

(in flight shows longer, more pointed wings than Red-winged)

more solidly black below than Red-winged, with less tertial edging in fresh plumage

Yellow-headed Blackbird

Xanthocephalus xanthocephalus
L 9½"/24cm   **WS** 15"/38cm

Yellow-headed Blackbird appears to be related to meadowlarks. It nests only in freshwater marshes, especially cattail marshes, where its long legs and large feet are ideal for walking on mud and floating vegetation; it also forages in open fields and feedlots with grackles and other blackbirds. Males may have several mates, as is true of other marsh blackbirds. **VOICE** Song a bizarre assemblage of harsh, otherworldly calls of all sorts, compared by some to the robot R2D2 in the Star Wars films. Call a flat *kak*.

adult male

distinctive saffron yellow head against black body

white primary coverts eye-catching, especially in flight

adult female

dark brown, with variable amounts of yellow on breast, throat, brow

(first-winter male similar but darker, with primary coverts edged in white)

Bobolink

Dolichonyx oryzivorus
L 7"/18cm   **WS** 11¼"/29cm

The exuberant return of Bobolinks to meadows and pastures is a herald of spring: males arrive before females and fairly burst into song, even before landing on territories. The loss of native grasslands and destruction of nests during haying have reduced populations, but large flocks still stage locally in coastal wetlands in fall. **VOICE** Song a virtuoso set of varied, staccato, finchlike calls, most repeated several times, accelerating in tempo. Call a flat *chuk;* in flight a gentle *wenk*, often heard from migrants at night.

adult male

creamy yellow nape

white markings on scapulars, back, rump

mostly black below

nonbreeding adult

like breeding female but brighter buff body and bright, mostly pink bill

breeding adult female

boldly striped back

grayish bill

rich buff-yellow head and breast

Eastern Meadowlark

Sturnella magna
L 9½"/24cm **WS** 14"/36cm

This striking, plump icterid inhabits open areas such as meadows, prairies, farm fields, salt marshes, and grasslands. It is most often seen singing from a fence post or searching for insects and seeds on the ground. The pale southwestern subspecies *lilianae*, Lilian's Meadowlark, may represent a separate species. **VOICE** Song a variable low, whistled *tiooooo, tiierrrr,* second phrase lower, descending, and melancholy. Call a short, buzzy *dzzzit,* quite different from Western Meadowlark.

breeding adult (nominate)

strong contrast in head pattern

like Western Meadowlark but more richly rufous-tinged above (except Lilian's)

yellow throat separated from streaked auriculars by white malar

longer streaks in flanks than Western

nonbreeding, Lilian's

found in drier habitats than Western, unlike other taxa of Eastern

very similar to nonbreeding Western but outer rectrices show more white in flight and face pattern cleaner

white dominates outer rectrices; flies with rapid, choppy wingbeats, often gliding

Western Meadowlark

Sturnella neglecta
L 9½"/24cm   **WS** 14½"/37cm

Western Meadowlark is generally found in drier habitats with shorter grass than Eastern Meadowlark; it is more widespread, nesting well into the Canadian prairies, with vagrants recorded as far north as Alaska and Siberia. Meadowlarks are best distinguished by the male's song and call. **VOICE** Song a variable set of whistled phrases; usually begins with 1 or 2 sweet, clear notes and ends with more complex, contorted, slurred whistles (like a slide whistle). Call a flat *tuk,* never given by Eastern.

breeding adult

like Eastern but has paler flanks with shorter streaks, paler head and upperparts, less contrast in head pattern

bill usually appears longer, more decurved than Eastern

yellow of throat extends to malar, touching streaked auriculars (but not in all fall birds)

nonbreeding adult

upperpart feathers lack Eastern's dark shaft streak, showing simpler barred pattern (difficult to see)

Scott's Oriole

Icterus parisorum
L 9"/23cm **WS** 12½"/32cm

The glorious black and yellow Scott's Oriole nests mostly in arid grasslands and foothills with yuccas, plants that supply both nesting sites and materials, and also in deserts and canyons with pinyon-juniper, oak, and Joshua tree woodlands. It nests early, usually in April, and feeds mostly on insects and nectar. Scott's has recently been recorded as a vagrant to the Midwest, Canada, and Southeast. **VOICE** Song a variable set of slurred whistles recalling Western Meadowlark or titmice. Call a sweet, hollow *teet*. Also a flat *chuk* or *shak*.

adult male

black head, breast, back contrast with yellow body

adult female

back, chest, and often face heavily mottled with black

dingy yellow underparts

1st year

wing bars usually prominent

larger and grayer overall than Hooded Oriole, with straighter bill

can be uniformly gray-brown, with faint yellow on rump, tail, underparts

Audubon's Oriole

Icterus graduacauda
L 9½"/24cm **WS** 12"/30cm

Pairs of Audubon's Oriole are seen, usually year-round, in dense brushlands with mesquite along the lower Rio Grande. In the U.S. most are observed at feeding stations in Salineño, Texas, and vicinity. This retiring species is usually located by its distinctive song. Black-vented Oriole, a rare vagrant to U.S. border states, is smaller, with jet black wings, back, and undertail coverts. **VOICE** Song a tipsy-sounding set of slurred whistles, rising and falling erratically. Calls include a nasal *nyyee* and whistles similar to song notes.

adult male

greenish yellow back

large, long-tailed, and long-billed

single wing bar

black tail lacks yellow (compare Scott's Oriole)

black hood, tail, wings contrast with yellow underparts and back

immature

duller overall than adult, with less extensive black head (juvenile shows mostly pale yellowish head, lacking black, and unstreaked back)

Baltimore Oriole
Icterus galbula
L 8¾"/22cm WS 12"/30cm

Baltimore Oriole is often first noticed as a flash of tangerine and black in the trees, especially large shade trees by rivers and in villages, where its hanging nests are a common sight. In the Great Plains this species hybridizes with Bullock's Oriole (the two were once combined as Northern Oriole). Most migrate to Central and South America, but some winter in the Southeast. **VOICE** Song a brief, varied set of distinct, sweet whistles: *tyew, pyeer, teer, peededoo.* Calls include an odd nasal *veeer*, a low chatter, and a high *tyew-li* and *kleek.*

adult male

black head and back contrast with orange rump and underparts

zebra pattern in coverts and remiges

orange and black wing coverts and tail

adult female

back and scapulars appear mottled brown

mostly pale orange below (some grayer)

1st year

2 wing bars

head and back mottled medium to dark brown; white chin with dusky border

Bullock's Oriole
Icterus bullockii
L 8¾"/22cm WS 12"/30cm

Like Baltimore Oriole, Bullock's favors well-treed farmsteads and riparian habitats, especially with cottonwoods and willows; it is also seen in stands of sycamores and oaks or foraging in surrounding open countryside. In migration, single birds and small flocks may turn up in any lowland habitat. Most winter in Mexico, but a few remain and are often seen in groves of blooming eucalyptus. **VOICE** Song like Baltimore but more creaking, grating, and clipped and less variable; female sings a similar song. Calls raspier than Baltimore.

adult male

black eye line connects with black crown

much more white in wings than Baltimore Oriole

black chin

pale mandible and lower edge of maxilla

1st year male

like female but with throat stripe, eye line

adult female

grayish back

pale gray underparts

yellow-orange brightest on head, faint on breast (some young Baltimores very similar)

Orchard Oriole

Icterus spurius
L 7¼"/18cm   **WS** 9½"/24cm

A sign of spring in the East and Midwest is Orchard Oriole's cheerful syncopated song. This species nests in many open habitats with tall shade trees, including well-wooded suburbs, and also in shrubby areas rich in insects. During migration in late July, many cross the Gulf of Mexico, sometimes in flocks. **VOICE** Song a set of high, rich whistles changing quickly in tone, pitch, and timing, with punctuated stops. Calls a sweet descending *veer;* also a harsh *shk,* often in series (this call distinguishes it from Hooded Oriole).

adult male

brick orange underparts and coverts, darker than Baltimore

smaller and more slender than Baltimore Oriole, with little white in wings

1st year male

adult female

averages greener on back than Hooded Oriole

like female but with black throat and face

Hooded Oriole

Icterus cucullatus
L 8"/20cm   **WS** 10½"/27cm

Hooded Oriole inhabits generally arid environments; it is most numerous in wooded riparian areas or desert oases with palm trees, which it favors for nesting. It feeds on insects and, like other orioles, is readily attracted to backyards with offerings of fruit or of nectar at hummingbird and oriole feeders. Three subspecies occur north of Mexico: *sennetti* and the nominate in Texas and *nelsoni* farther west. Some females closely resemble Orchard Oriole but always have a longer bill. **VOICE** Song a contorted, catbirdlike set of mews, quick whistles, and harsh calls. Call a weak, rising *week.*

breeding adult male *(sennetti)*

white median coverts (compare Altamira Oriole)

extensively black face and throat

adult female

longer-tailed than Orchard

mostly pale mandible

grayish overall

juvenile

nonbreeding adult male *(nelsoni)*

back has black and olive barring (compare Streak-backed Oriole)

Altamira Oriole

Icterus gularis
L 10"/25cm **WS** 14"/36cm

In the U.S. Altamira Oriole is found year-round in southernmost Texas, usually in well-wooded areas near water. Its pendulous, woven nest sometimes measures more than 24" (61cm). Males sing frequently during the nesting season and also at other times; the species also chatters loudly year-round. Spot-breasted Oriole, introduced in southern Florida, is smaller and has a spotted breast. **VOICE** Song a set of deliberate, slurred whistles, rising and falling, with longer pauses than in other orioles. Call similar to song.

adult male

similar to Hooded Oriole but larger; less black on sides of throat; a heavier, mostly dark bill; and orange median coverts

immature

large

acquires black throat in first fall

strong orange tones in head and underparts (more yellowish in Hooded)

Streak-backed Oriole

Icterus pustulatus
L 8¼"/21cm **WS** 12½"/32cm

A vagrant species from Mexico, Streak-backed Oriole has been found in California in autumn and winter, with single records from Texas and Oregon. It is a rare nester in southern Arizona in tall cottonwoods along the San Pedro River in Santa Cruz and Pinal Counties. These birds are of the nominate subspecies group, which is otherwise endemic to western Mexico. **VOICE** Song similar to Bullock's Oriole but less complex, with more distinct phrases. Calls include a whistled *feet*, low *rank*, and short *wit*.

breeding adult male

strongly streaked back

heavier bill base than Hooded Oriole

extensive white in remiges and coverts' edges

breeding adult female

heavy bill with black tip

black throat surrounded by deep orange

distinct thick streaks on back

1st fall

heavier bill base than Hooded

back has dark stippling

Tanagers, Cardinals, and Kin

Cardinals and their relatives (family Cardinalidae) in North America include Northern Cardinal and Pyrrhuloxia (*Cardinalis*), the *Passerina* buntings, the *Pheucticus* grosbeaks, and Dickcissel (*Spiza*). A vagrant from Mexico, Crimson-collared Grosbeak, has also been recorded in Texas on a few dozen occasions. All cardinalids are small to medium-sized passerines. Breeding adult males often have dazzlingly colorful plumages, while females and young birds are cryptic and plain. Northern Cardinal and Pyrrhuloxia are long-tailed, crested, slender birds with heavy, short bills. The smaller *Passerina* buntings have more sparrowlike bills and shorter tails. The large Blue Grosbeak, while now considered a *Passerina*, has a much heavier bill, closer to those of the larger, heavyset *Pheucticus* grosbeaks. Dickcissel differs from the more typical cardinalids in its plumage and breeding system; it is treated with the Old World sparrows and Bananaquit (page 479).

Buntings, such as this male Indigo Bunting, appear to have simple songs, but there are countless subtle variations in note phrasing, pairing, and pitch among individuals.

Most cardinalids inhabit weedy fields, thickets, and edge habitats for at least some time during the year; they eat seeds, insects, fruit, flowers, and buds, and most are readily attracted to feeding stations stocked with seeds. The *Pheucticus* grosbeaks nest in mature forests but can often be found in brambles during migration. Courtship among cardinalids consists of energetic singing, feeding, and some posturing on the part of males. Unusual among songbirds, female Black-headed Grosbeaks and female *Cardinalis* sing fully developed songs during the breeding season. Despite the monogamous mating system of birds in this group, extra-pair copulation is not uncommon. Where ranges meet, hybridization, especially between Indigo and Lazuli Buntings and Rose-breasted and Black-headed Grosbeaks, is very common.

Most cardinalids are long-distance migrants to the tropics. Dickcissel, which has a polygynous mating system, migrates to the *llanos* (plains) of northern South America, where it forms enormous flocks in rice fields.

North American tanagers are probably best considered cardinalids, although they are currently placed in the family Thraupidae. They are robin-sized birds with moderately long tails and wings. Tanagers' bills seem intermediate between those of icterids and cardinalids: fairly heavy but also lengthy and somewhat pointed. The vivid red, yellow, and black plumages of breeding adult males rival those of the cardinalids; females are less striking in shades of olive and yellow.

As a rule, tanagers eat much less plant matter than cardinalids, taking mostly insects and their larvae; but they do consume berries and other small fruits in season. Summer and Hepatic Tanagers are avid bee-eaters, capturing bees on the wing and beating them on a branch to remove the stinger. Like cardinalids, *Piranga* tanagers form seasonally monogamous pairs and defend territories, and females in some species sing.

Cardinalids and tanagers are still relatively common; there have been declines in a few species of tanager, particularly Scarlet Tanager, and in Painted Bunting, the result of habitat loss and brood parasitism by cowbirds.

Identification of Female Tanagers

Adult male Scarlet and Western Tanagers, two of the more distinctive and attractive passerines in North America, are easy to identify. Male Hepatic and Summer Tanagers, depicted on page 432, are sometimes confused. Female tanagers, however, are much more difficult to identify than males.

Summer Tanager female

Hepatic Tanager female

Scarlet Tanager dull female

Western Tanager female

Flame-colored Tanager female

Hepatic and Summer Tanagers

Female Hepatic, Summer, and Scarlet Tanagers usually lack wing bars (although Scarlets with weak wing bars have been reported); their plumages are generally a faded yellowish below and darker above. In the Southwest, Hepatic Tanagers can occasionally be seen in the same groves as Summer Tanagers of the *cooperi* subspecies, especially on migration. Female *cooperi* birds have bills that are similar in size to the large bill of Hepatic Tanager; but the maxilla of Hepatic is typically darker and heavier, with more curve in the culmen, than that of *cooperi*. Female Hepatics also have dusky lores and gray-brown auriculars that divide the yellowish crown from the yellow throat and usually extend to the lores, a feature not seen in Summer Tanagers.

Summer and Scarlet Tanagers

Female Summer Tanagers in the East are smaller-billed than those in the Southwest, but they still have longer bills than female Scarlet Tanagers. Scarlets usually, but not always, have dusky bills, while Summers usually have pale bills. Scarlets usually have darker wings contrasting with an olive back, while Summers have more brownish upperparts (wings and back). But Scarlets with washed-out plumages showing little wing-back contrast are not unusual; such birds can be identified by bill structure (longer in Summer), by the tones of the back (greenish in Scarlet, brownish in Summer), by the color of the underside of the rectrices (grayer in Scarlet, greenish yellow in Summer), and by patterning in the face: Summer sometimes shows a faint dusky line through the eyes and/or under the eyes, while Scarlet looks plain-faced.

Western and Flame-colored Tanagers

Female Western and Flame-colored Tanagers are superficially similar: both have wing bars and are washed with yellow below. But female Flame-coloreds have darker bills; stippled backs, compared to the grayish or olive-gray backs of female Westerns; stronger, very white wing bars, without the yellowish tint of Westerns; and large white spots, rather than pale edges, on the tertials. In Arizona the two have hybridized; the suspected hybrid offspring have shown intermediate characteristics.

Summer Tanager
Piranga rubra
L 7¾"/20cm WS 12½"/30cm

Pine forests of the Southeast ring with the burry caroling of Summer Tanager, a bird also found in mixed oak woodlands and in riparian willow-cottonwood corridors in the Southwest. The western subspecies *cooperi* is larger and larger-billed than the nominate. This arboreal forager often sallies out after a bee or wasp, removing the stinger before eating. **VOICE** Song a set of modulated, whistled phrases likened to American Robin. Call a distinctive *PI-ti-tuk,* sometimes with more syllables.

adult male, eastern (nominate)

heavy, greenish yellow bill (usually longer and darker in *cooperi*)

rose-red overall

1st spring male
yellow and red mottling highly variable

adult female

lores not darker than face

little contrast between wings and back

variable: mostly yellowish, with orange or green tones (or blotches)

greenish yellow undertail (grayish in Scarlet Tanager)

Hepatic Tanager
Piranga flava
L 8"/20cm WS 12½"/32cm

In pine-oak forests of the Southwest, a singing Hepatic Tanager might be passed over for a Black-headed Grosbeak, so similar are their songs. Like Summer Tanager, Hepatic frequently forages in pairs that work carefully through pine boughs for insects and larvae; it often uses its bill to strike prey against a branch to soften it before eating. **VOICE** Song slower and lower than Summer, with longer pauses, almost seeming sluggish. Call a low *tchak.*

adult male

lores always grayish

very heavy bill has dark maxilla

less richly colored than Summer, with gray auriculars, flanks, and often back

adult female

yellowish crown and throat; pale gray-brown auriculars and lores

heavy, dark bill

plain gray-brown above

(juvenile similar but streaked overall)

Scarlet Tanager
Piranga olivacea
L 7"/18cm   **WS** 11½"/29cm

South of the boreal forest and north of the southern pinewoods, Scarlet Tanager nests in deciduous and mixed woods. Even where colorful warblers vie for the eye, the breeding male stands out as a singular beauty, its body plumage searing and luminescent in direct sunlight, glowing even in the shade of the canopy, where it forages slowly for fruit and insects. **VOICE** Song a simple set of about 5 burry, robinlike phrases. Call a distinctive *chip-burr,* accented on first syllable.

breeding
adult male

unmistakable, with bright red plumage, black wings and tail

(fall molting birds have large yellow-green patches)

immature male
like female but with blackish wings and tail

adult female

similar to Summer Tanager but darker olive-brown wings contrast more with belly; upperparts evenly greenish

faint wing bars rare

Western Tanager
Piranga ludoviciana
L 7¼"/18cm   **WS** 11½"/29cm

Western Tanager breeds in coniferous and mixed woodlands, especially with pines, spruces, firs, aspens, and oaks, often at high elevations. It is found in a great variety of habitats in migration, from desert scrub to backyard feeders. In winter this species turns up rarely but regularly at feeders in the Southeast. **VOICE** Song a 5-phrased set of burry whistles, very similar to Scarlet Tanager. Call a rattling *prttle-ik,* less incisive than Summer Tanager.

breeding
adult male

greater coverts tipped yellowish or off-white

head tinged variably with red

canary yellow body and median coverts

black back, tail, wings

pale female

grayer birds with little yellow are common

adult female

upper wing bar usually has some yellow

gray-brown back contrasts with yellowish head and rump

Flame-colored Tanager
Piranga bidentata
L 7¾"/20cm **WS** 12"/30cm

The well-named Flame-colored Tanager occasionally visits pine-oak forests of southeastern Arizona mountains, where it has nested on rare occasions and has hybridized with Western Tanager. Visitors are of the nominate subspecies, which nests in the mountains of western Mexico. Like other tanagers, Flame-colored tends to stay concealed in the foliage of larger trees while foraging or singing. **VOICE** Song similar to Western Tanager but burrier and more hesitant. Common call similar to Western, a low *prrrlek*.

adult male

dusky border around auriculars

rich red-orange head

large white spots at tips of coverts and tertials

Yellow Grosbeak
Pheucticus chrysopeplus
L 9¼"/23cm **WS** 14½"/37cm

A very large grosbeak of Mexico and Guatemala, Yellow Grosbeak has occasionally strayed to the Southwest, where it is usually observed in scrubby undergrowth, desert scrub, deciduous woodland edges, or thorn woods, and sometimes at feeders. Among North American birds, it is most closely related to Black-headed Grosbeak, but Yellow has a much larger bill and is vivid canary yellow below. **VOICE** Song similar to Black-headed but lower and less continuous. Call similar to Black-headed.

adult male

female

less white in coverts and remiges than male

bold black and white wing pattern

dusky crown and auriculars and streaked mantle, unlike male

Crimson-collared Grosbeak
Rhodothraupis celaeno
L 8¾"/22cm **WS** 13"/33cm

An unusual grosbeak endemic to brushlands of northeastern Mexico, Crimson-collared Grosbeak has strayed on rare occasions to southernmost Texas, mostly in winter. It is a shy bird that forages in thickets and thorn scrub, rarely perching for long in the open. This species may be more closely related to cardinals and the saltators of tropical America than to other so-called "grosbeaks." **VOICE** Song a sweet, modulated warbling, rising at end. Call a loud, slurred *psseuu*.

adult female

heavy bill has distinctive decurved culmen

adult male

black head surrounded by dark red

(young female similar but with more diffuse hood and duller gray and greenish yellow tones)

Painted Bunting
Passerina ciris
L 5½"/14cm **WS** 8¾"/22cm

Prized for centuries as cagebirds, male Painted Buntings are still trapped by the thousands in Mexico and Cuba. They are tireless singers, even in the heat of the day, but stay concealed in scrubby tangles or trees and are usually less conspicuous than Indigo Bunting. This species is declining along the southeastern coast; western populations appear to be stable. **VOICE** Song similar to Blue Grosbeak but with higher, clearer notes. Call a dry *spit,* less incisive and buzzy than Indigo.

adult male

deep blue "helmet"

neon green back

cardinal red throat, rump, eye ring, underparts

adult female

medium green above, paler below

no wing bars

(first-year male similar, often yellowish below)

Varied Bunting
Passerina versicolor
L 5½"/14cm **WS** 7¾"/20cm

This little-known Mexican species frequents densely vegetated areas of thorn scrub near water. The breeding male's plum, crimson, and deep azure tones, subtly blended through the wings and underparts, suggest a hastily sketched watercolor. Texas birds nest a bit earlier than those in southeastern Arizona, where breeding is timed to the summer monsoon rains. A few winter in the U.S., some in Big Bend. **VOICE** Song like Painted Bunting but lower, shorter, and less rich-toned. Call very similar to Painted.

breeding adult male

multicolored in shades of red and blue

culmen more curved than in other buntings

(nonbreeding plumage much browner overall)

adult female

remiges and coverts lack pale edges

uniformly colored

shorter wings than Indigo and Lazuli Buntings, with little primary projection

Blue Grosbeak
Passerina caerulea
L 6¾"/17cm   **WS** 11"/28cm

Of all the *Passerina* buntings found north of Mexico, Blue Grosbeak is by far the largest and heaviest-billed. Like its smaller relative Indigo Bunting, it is most common in disturbed and early successional habitats—brushy fields, hedgerows, thickets, and tangles on the edge of wooded areas. Such places produce the bounty of insects and seeds that form the diets of all *Passerina*. After the nesting season, Blue Grosbeak gathers into small flocks for migration and foraging; some are trans-Gulf migrants, while others move over land to their Central American wintering grounds. **VOICE** Song a jumbled, scratchy, indistinct warble, mostly on one pitch, lacking rich sweetness of Rose-breasted Grosbeak. Call a solid, sharp, very distinctive *spit* or *chink*.

Blue Grosbeak adult male
resplendent blue plumage
pale steely gray bill bordered with black
chestnut wing bars

Blue Grosbeak adult female
hints of chestnut and blue in upperwing coverts
warm brown above, paler below
(juvenile similar)

Blue Bunting
Cyanocompsa parellina
L 5½"/14cm   **WS** 8½"/22cm

Blue Bunting is a rare annual visitor to shadowy thickets in the Lower Rio Grande valley of southern Texas, most often seen in winter at bird-feeding stations among Indigo Buntings or sparrows. This retiring bird rarely sits in the open or in broad daylight; it does not form flocks. There is a single record from Louisiana in autumn, suggesting that northward dispersal could bring other records for the Gulf coast. In the nominate subspecies of eastern Mexico (and Texas), females are a rich cinnamon brown, very unlike the gray-brown *indigotica* of western Mexico. **VOICE** Song a cheery, sweet warble that begins hesitantly and trails off at end. Call a mellow *tsip*.

Blue Bunting adult male
very dark blue overall, with brighter blue on head, coverts, rump

Blue Bunting adult female
rich brown with cinnamon tone, darker above
dark bill has distinctly curved culmen

Indigo Bunting

Passerina cyanea
L 5½"/14cm   WS 8"/20cm

Indigo Bunting is abundant in open or semiopen habitats with weedy or brushy areas, particularly old-fashioned farmlands, power-line cuts, and early successional fields. In areas where buntings are abundant, birders may hear a dozen males singing at once as they perch conspicuously on utility wires and bushes. Migrating birds are frequently heard calling at night in the East as they pass overhead. **VOICE** Song a set of sweet, usually paired notes. Call a sharp, metallic *tik*.

adult male
deep blue overall, most intense on head
wings and tail often tinged blue
adult female/ 1st fall
much smaller bill than grosbeaks

nonbreeding adults
female faintly streaked below, with pale throat
nonbreeding male similar to breeding male but variably mottled with brown

Lazuli Bunting

Passerina amoena
L 5½"/14cm   WS 8½"/22cm

This bunting is found in open and semiopen habitats: lowland thickets, riparian tangles, sagebrush, chaparral, and scrubby areas with oak or pinyon-juniper. It is an early fall migrant and may be found in sizable flocks as early as July. Lazuli commonly hybridizes with Indigo Bunting where ranges overlap; males of these related species are territorial toward one another. **VOICE** Song and call strikingly similar to Indigo, but song less often has distinct pairings of notes.

adult male
deep turquoise upperparts and head (head paler than Indigo Bunting)
orange breast
white belly and wing bars (compare bluebirds)

adult female
mousy brown color similar to Indigo Bunting but breast more warmly colored and unstreaked, throat duskier, and wing bars usually more prominent
(juvenile similar but finely streaked below)

Rose-breasted Grosbeak

Pheucticus ludovicianus
L 8"/20cm   **WS** 12½"/32cm

This bird of deciduous and mixed woodlands is more often heard than seen as it feeds on berries, flowers, seeds, and insects in bushes and trees. In migration, loose flocks are found in varied habitats, especially near the Gulf and Atlantic coasts. With their finely streaked buffy underparts, immature birds can resemble Black-headed Grosbeak (with which this species hybridizes), but note the pinkish underwing coverts. **VOICE** Song a sweet caroling, robinlike but more measured and pure-toned. Call a nasal, squeaky *ik* or *fink*.

breeding adult male

ivory bill set off by black head

wings black above with white in primaries and coverts

cherry red triangle on breast

adult female

bold white supercilium and malar mark set off darker auriculars

very heavy bill, paler than Black-headed

whitish, neatly streaked breast

Black-headed Grosbeak

Pheucticus melanocephalus
L 8¼"/21cm   **WS** 12½"/32cm

Black-headed Grosbeak nests in most deciduous and mixed wooded habitats away from southwestern deserts. It is partial to oak and pine-oak habitats but also occurs in riparian lowlands with cottonwoods and dry pinyon-juniper slopes. This species preys on insects, including butterflies, and eats berries and seeds. Migrants may turn up in any wooded habitat. **VOICE** Song and calls similar to Rose-breasted Grosbeak but slightly higher; song more rapid, less flowing.

breeding adult male

dark head, tail, wings set off unique burnished orange body plumage

1st winter male

like female but head pattern stronger, underparts unstreaked and colorful

adult female

(vivid yellow underwing coverts, buffy in Rose-breasted)

resembles Rose-breasted but has more finely streaked flanks, darker maxilla, orange-buff in nape and breast

Northern Cardinal
Cardinalis cardinalis
L 8¾"/22cm **WS** 12"/30cm

Northern Cardinal (colloquially "red bird") is named for the male's color, said to resemble the robes of Roman Catholic cardinals. It lives in thickets, woodlands, suburbs, and city parks and locally in southwestern deserts and thorn scrub. Males are highly territorial, sometimes even attacking their own images in windows and car mirrors. Cardinals have been expanding their range northward for many years. **VOICE** Song a set of clear whistles, often rendered *bright bright bright, cheer cheer cheer.* Call a sharp, high *tik.*

adult male and female

black face surrounds orange-red bill

male has poppy red plumage

(desert nesters have longer crests, more bulbous bills)

heavy, orange bill (dark in juvenile)

female mostly brown with red in wings, tail, crest

Pyrrhuloxia
Cardinalis sinuatus
L 8¾"/22cm **WS** 12"/30cm

Pyrrhuloxia is a cardinal of brushy desert areas and ranchlands, especially near streams with mesquite, acacia, and hackberry. It is found in dry, open areas more often than Northern Cardinal and appears to better tolerate the extreme aridity and heat of the Chihuahuan and Sonoran Deserts. In the nonbreeding season, Pyrrhuloxia gathers in small flocks that may travel far from nesting areas in search of food (Northern Cardinal also disperses but not in flocks). **VOICE** Very similar to Northern Cardinal but higher.

adult male

soft gray plumage with carmine in wings, tail, crest, face, underwing coverts, breast

large, pale bill has curved culmen (compare Northern Cardinal)

adult female

resembles male but has pale brown rather than gray tones and usually duskier yellow bill

Finches

Finches (family Fringillidae) are small passerines that are sometimes confused with sparrows or buntings; this is particularly the case with the smaller species, which, like the other small, seed-eating passerines, have short, conical bills adapted for feeding on seeds. But finches differ from sparrows in many ways. Most have shorter tails that show a distinct, shallow fork. Finches are usually sexually dimorphic: males are usually brightly colored (brighter than sparrows) in reds, yellows, and rusts, and females and young of the smaller species are often mousy brown above and sometimes streaked below. Finches are more arboreal than sparrows, though most frequent open woodlands and edges rather than closed forests. Finches are often seen high overhead in the morning, in undulating flight; sparrows tend to stay low to the ground, flying overhead mainly during migration, at night.

During their periodic irruptions, finches (such as this female Pine Grosbeak) take advantage of bird-feeding stations and plantings, such as crabapple trees.

The nearest relatives of finches are probably the pipits and wagtails (family Motacillidae) and the Old World sparrows (Passeridae), both nine-primaried oscines, like finches. Other nine-primaried oscines—American warblers, tanagers, cardinalids, and icterids—are also probably closely related. Like the cardinalids, the larger finches have heavy, powerful bills. In the crossbills, the maxilla and mandible cross, like misaligned pincers, an adaptation for foraging on pine and spruce seeds.

Courtship among finches consists mostly of persistent singing, courtship feeding, and song flights around the female; females sometimes sing when building the nest, though less vigorously than males. Finches often nest rather close to one another and do not defend territories, but the male does guard the female against other males that approach too closely. After egg-laying, males sometimes form foraging flocks. Long after the young have fledged, the nests of finches are recognizable by their edges, which are covered with the feces of the nestlings; this is not seen in any other passerines except Olive Warbler (Peucedramidae).

Of all North American birds, the "winter finches"—Pine Siskin, White-winged and Red Crossbills, Pine and Evening Grosbeaks, and Common and Hoary Redpolls—are best known for their erratic wanderings and winter irruptions; many thousands may move south from the tundra and boreal forest and visit forests and feeding stations, where they can consume large amounts of birdseed. Such influxes are almost certainly the result of poor seed and cone crops in the core range.

The remoteness of their breeding grounds, the apparent stark fluctuations in breeding success, and their irregular movements make it difficult to assess the actual abundance and conservation status of most finches. Evening Grosbeak was quite rare in the East until the 1950s, when the species began nesting east of the Great Lakes in large numbers, apparently in response to a sustained outbreak of spruce budworms in the boreal forest. Its numbers have declined recently; it and Purple Finch are now less numerous in the East than they were a generation ago.

Common Redpoll

Carduelis flammea
L 5¼"/13cm **WS** 9"/23cm

This finch of tundra and muskeg forages much like goldfinches and siskins on seeds, buds, and insects. In winter redpolls may stage flights, or irruptions, well south of typical range, during which hundreds may descend on feeders stocked with thistle seed. A larger, darker subspecies, *rostrata,* winters in northern Canada and visits the Northeast. **VOICE** Song a continuous series of wiry trills and abrupt call notes. Calls a rising, nasal *jeeee?*; a sharp *ch-ch-cht* like White-winged Crossbill; and a wiry buzz like siskins.

adult male

darker on wings and back than Hoary Redpoll, with more extensive pink tint and streaking below

adult

adult

unusually pale birds told from Hoary by larger bill

female and some males lack pink wash below and have less black in face

Hoary Redpoll

Carduelis hornemanni
L 5½"/14cm **WS** 9"/23cm

Hoary Redpoll nests in bleak tundra to the northernmost point of North America. Where its range overlaps with Common Redpoll, Hoary often inhabits less brushy environments. In the lower 48 states it is found in northern Minnesota and North Dakota in winter and as a rare visitor elsewhere, usually in flocks of Common Redpoll. The nominate subspecies from Greenland is larger and snowier than the continental *exilipes* (shown here). **VOICE** Very similar to Common; perhaps lower and less modulated.

adult male

(often looks very whitish above)

tiny bill

little or no pink below

fine streaking below limited to sides (streaking usually absent in undertail coverts)

adult female

like male but bill even smaller, less black in face and less red in forecrown (or "poll"), browner auriculars and nape, no pink wash below

(juvenile similar but browner)

Cassin's Finch

Carpodacus cassinii
L 6¼"/16cm   WS 11½"/29cm

Cassin's Finch nests in montane pine, fir, and spruce forests, often right up to the tree line; in late fall and winter, most descend to lower elevations. Like Purple Finch, Cassin's is somewhat nomadic and irruptive; either species is capable of turning up at a backyard feeder in the western Great Plains. **VOICE** Song like other *Carpodacus* but more hurried; descending at first, with sweet, higher note at end. Some calls more complex than other *Carpodacus,* especially the rather flat *ki-ip* and *ki-di-ip* flight calls.

adult male

red most intense on crown

longer, less bulbous bill than Purple Finch, with straight culmen

flanks often streaked

longer primary projection than Purple Finch

juvenile

(adult female similar)

pale eye ring; face pattern more diffuse than in Purple Finch

neater streaking on back shows more contrast

underparts have neater, dark brown stippling than Purple Finch

Pine Siskin

Carduelis pinus
L 5"/13cm   WS 9"/23cm

Pine Siskin nests in boreal and mixed forests, where it feeds, like goldfinches, on seeds of weeds and composites and on conifer, birch, and alder seeds; it also forages for buds and insects. Like other *Carduelis* finches, siskins roam widely; they can be abundant some years, absent others. The sexes cannot be distinguished by plumage, although males tend to have more extensive and vivid yellow. **VOICE** Song an uninspired ramble of harsh buzzes, strained sweet notes, and faint imitations. Call a harsh, rising trill.

bright adult

thinner bill than other finches

strong yellow wing bars

yellow in bases of remiges and rectrices obvious in flight

finely streaked with brown above and below

duller adult/1st fall

(juvenile similar)

more limited yellow in bases of remiges and rectrices, little or none in covert edges

Purple Finch

Carpodacus purpureus
L 6"/15cm   WS 10"/25cm

The wine-and-rose-colored Purple Finch is a stolid species of coniferous and mixed woodlands. It feeds mostly on seeds, especially of elm and ash trees, and small fruits. Most move southward from the boreal forest in late fall, sometimes in large irruptive flights, at which time they are often observed at feeders. **VOICE** Song a rich, rambling, sweet, garbled warble reminiscent of Warbling Vireo. Call a very quiet, sharp *peek,* often unnoticed.

adult male

head and back suffused with rich rose red, often darkest in auriculars, crown, submalar

more bulbous bill than Cassin's Finch (culmen more curved)

forked tail

adult female

pale malar and supercilium contrast with dark crown and auriculars

heavy, bulbous bill

whitish, heavily streaked underparts

dull brown back, evenly streaked

House Finch

Carpodacus mexicanus
L 6"/15cm   WS 9½"/24cm

This common western finch of deserts and foothills was introduced in small numbers in New York in 1940; by the end of the 20th century it had become a common breeding bird of suburbs, cities, and agricultural areas throughout most of the eastern U.S., where it may compete with Purple Finch, at least in winter. It is abundant at feeders. **VOICE** Song a sweet, cheerful warble containing wiry notes (lower and less distinct in western birds). Calls a rich *chewp* and *sweep* like House Sparrow.

adult male

brown crown

curved culmen

(some individuals show orange or yellow rather than red tones)

distinct red breast, streaked belly (unlike Purple)

longer tail than Purple or Cassin's Finches

adult female

lacks head pattern of other *Carpodacus*

blurry streaking below

(juvenile similar; male acquires red in plumage in first fall)

Black Rosy-Finch

Leucosticte atrata
L 6¼"/16cm   **WS** 13"/33cm

Black Rosy-Finch nests in remote northern Great Basin alpine barrens and mountain summits, usually in snowfields and glaciers, and forages in adjacent grassy or rocky areas. As snow cover deepens, it descends to lower elevations and areas far from its breeding range, including Colorado and New Mexico. On winter nights, it may roost with Gray-crowned Rosy-Finch in manmade structures for warmth. **VOICE** Song similar to Gray-crowned but higher. Calls a sharp, low *cht* in staccato series and a higher *tyew*.

breeding adult

black bill

sooty forecrown, throat, cheek, back, breast

very little rose color below

nonbreeding adult, fresh

(younger birds show frosty charcoal tones instead of sooty back and breast)

yellow bill

Brown-capped Rosy-Finch

Leucosticte australis
L 6¼"/16cm   **WS** 13"/33cm

This finch has one of the most restricted and high-elevation breeding ranges of any North American passerine: alpine mountain barrens of Colorado, Wyoming, and New Mexico. After nesting, if snows are deep, it moves to lower elevations, sometimes into towns where it readily visits feeders. The species appears to have declined, but Colorado's Rocky Mountain National Park still has a few thousand breeding birds. **VOICE** Song a steady series of chirps, like House Sparrow but raspier. Calls harsh, like other rosy-finches.

breeding adult male

crown brown or slightly mottled with gray

warm brown overall

rosier below than Black Rosy-Finch

1st winter female

gray-brown crown (gray on other rosy-finches)

some quite drab

Gray-crowned Rosy-Finch

Leucosticte tephrocotis
L 6¼"/16cm   **WS** 13"/33cm

Gray-crowned Rosy-Finch is a hardy bird that inhabits some of the least hospitable places in the West, from stony tundra and offshore islands in Alaska to alpine barrens, scree, and snowfields of western mountains. Rosy-finches nest in rocky fields, caves, mines, cliffs, or dilapidated buildings, which provide protection from both the elements and predators. They forage on seeds and insects, especially where these are uncovered by melting snow. In winter many northern populations migrate into southwestern Canada, the Great Basin, and the southern Rockies; coastal Alaskan birds are sedentary. Gray-crowned is the most widespread and variable of the rosy-finches; subspecies include the large, dark *griseonucha* (Aleutians) and *umbrina* (Pribilofs), the intermediate *littoralis* (mainland Alaska through Cascades), and the nominate group—the similar *tephrocotis, dawsoni,* and *wallowa* (northern Alaska through northern Rockies and California's Sierra Nevada). **VOICE** Lower-pitched than other rosy-finches. Song a protracted series of burry chirps *(tchew),* often descending. Calls include very low, harsh, short scraping notes and a higher *tchew.*

breeding adult
(nominate)

brownish
above

dark forecrown
distinct from gray
hindcrown (some
Brown-cappeds have
gray-mottled crowns)

rosy mostly
in flanks
and coverts

nonbreeding
adult male
(littoralis)

full gray "helmet,"
with black throat
and central crown

(breeding male
similar but with
black bill)

1st winter
female *(littoralis)*

browner than
adult male,
lacking rosy tones

(Bering Sea taxa similar but
larger and darker brown)

breeding adult
(nominate)

younger males and some adult
females lack noticeable rosy tones

adult
(umbrina)

very
dark

heavy
body
and bill

bill yellow in
nonbreeding
season, black
in breeding

Lawrence's Goldfinch

Carduelis lawrencei

L 4¾"/12cm WS 8¼"/21cm

This goldfinch is an endemic nester in arid woodlands, chaparral, and brushy areas of northern Baja California and California's foothills and valleys. In nonbreeding months (August–March), sizable flocks may be observed in foothills and deserts of the Southwest, and a few visit western Texas on rare occasions. This species is regularly found around seeps, springs, cattle troughs, and other water sources in arid areas. **VOICE** Song a hurried set of warbled notes, mostly imitations of other birds. Calls include an inquisitive *doo-ler;* flight call an endearing *tink-oo.*

adult male

black face surrounds pale bill

yellow limited to breast and wings

adult female

extensive yellow in remiges and coverts

pale gray overall, with darker lores

(grayish juvenile similar but less yellow; compare Lucy's Warbler, Verdin)

Brambling

Fringilla montifringilla

L 6¼"/16cm WS 11"/28cm

Brambling is a migrant to the Aleutians and other Bering Sea islands and a rare fall and winter vagrant elsewhere in North America. It is almost always observed singly, usually at feeders or in weedy fields with goldfinches. Nonbreeding males are mottled on the head and mantle; these feather tips wear to satiny black for spring breeding plumage. **VOICE** Song a harsh, nasal, unmusical trill. Calls an almost jaylike *naaank,* a sweet *tseek,* and a low *toop.*

nonbreeding adult male

mostly pale bill (dark in breeding season)

black "helmet" and back

rusty orange breast, throat, lesser coverts, greater covert tips

nonbreeding adult male

like breeding male, but head and back mottled with black, brown, gray, rust

female

pale bill

white in rump and primary bases often visible

pale gray head with darker crown

rufous in wings and sides of breast

American Goldfinch

Carduelis tristis
L 5"/13cm **WS** 9"/23cm

American Goldfinch is often called "wild canary" for the breeding male's shimmering lemon yellow plumage. Goldfinches eat seeds at feeders and in weedy fields and also take seeds and buds of trees such as sweetgum, birch, and elm. Like other *Carduelis* finches, they irrupt southward irregularly, probably when food is scarce. **VOICE** Song a pleasant jumble of distinct, high, sweet, tinkling notes, usually with paired phrases. Flight call a sweet *pe-CHI-pee-pee*.

breeding
adult male

black forehead, wings, tail contrast with brilliant canary yellow body

nonbreeding female

very plain mousy brown, with yellow only in face; off-white or buffy wing bars; dark bill

breeding adult female

pinkish orange bill

brownish yellow back

white wing bars (lower bar can be buffy)

pale yellow below, with white crissum

Lesser Goldfinch

Carduelis psaltria
L 4½"/11cm **WS** 8"/20cm

Lesser Goldfinch occupies brushy, semiopen habitats from deserts through high mountains. It is partial to sunflower and thistle seeds, both in the wild and at feeders. In fall and winter, many withdraw from northern parts of their range; a few have turned up at feeders in the Midwest and East. **VOICE** Song more varied than American Goldfinch, with fewer sweet notes, often including imitations of other birds. Calls a rising *tee-dee* and a descending *teeer;* flight call a sharp, modulated *cht*, repeated.

adult male

dark cap

olive back with darker scapulars

pale wing bars and primary bases

(black-backed individuals seen in eastern part of range)

pale adult female

immature male

greenish back, pale primary bases

back has olive tint

some birds whitish below

mostly yellowish nape, underparts, vent

(some adult females similar but lack black in crown)

Pine Grosbeak

Pinicola enucleator
L 8¾"/22cm WS 14½"/37cm

Pine Grosbeak is a large, quiet finch of
montane and boreal coniferous forests,
especially of spruce, lodgepole pine,
and fir. In winter a few may venture well
south of range or into lowlands, where
they are often detected feeding on small
fruits such as crabapples. Like many bird
species that nest in remote regions, Pine
Grosbeaks can be quite tame. **VOICE**
Song a high, cheery, loose warbling,
tuneful but lackadaisical. Calls include a
House Finch–like *pur-peep* and a harsher
chi-chid (especially in West).

adult male

heavy bill has curved maxilla

soft gray body feathers have rosy tips except on flanks and vent (some males extensively gray below)

"russet" morph

some females and young males grayish overall with bronze-russet head

adult female

prominent white wing bars similar to male

gray with mustard-colored head and rump

Evening Grosbeak

Coccothraustes vespertinus
L 8"/20cm WS 14"/36cm

Evening Grosbeak began to spread
eastward from montane coniferous forests
of the Pacific Northwest in the early 20th
century; by the 1960s it had become a
staple in mixed forests and at feeders
throughout the Canadian Maritimes,
southeastern Canada, and New England.
Its spread appeared to have abated by the
late 1980s, perhaps because the spruce
budworm outbreak diminished, and it is
now rare again over much of the East and
Midwest. **VOICE** Song a high, metallic
keeer, repeated. Call a single song note.

adult male

olive-brown head, bright yellow "brow"

very heavy yellow bill (paler in winter)

white secondaries and coverts, yellow scapulars

rich burnished yellow below

adult female

like male but less white in primary bases and gray overall; yellow limited to nape, underwing coverts, sides

(juvenile similar)

Red Crossbill

Loxia curvirostra
L 6½"/16cm **WS** 11¼"/29cm

This finch of boreal and coniferous and mixed montane forests wanders widely year-round in search of pine nuts. The bird inserts its crossed bill, adapted for prizing open pinecones, between the scales and slowly opens it. Nine different groups of Red Crossbill (called "types") with different bill sizes and vocalizations may represent separate species in some cases. **VOICE** Song a staccato set of strained chirps, squeaks, and *chip* calls. Call notes vary widely among the 9 types, usually a sharp, doubled or trebled *kip* or *chip*.

adult male

brick red plumage with darker rectrices, remiges, auriculars

crossed bill distinctive

bill size and extent of red in plumage varies among individuals and taxa

subadult male

mixture of red and green in plumage

adult female

resembles male but plumage mottled gray and olive-yellow or dull green

(individuals with faint wing bars very rare)

White-winged Crossbill

Loxia leucoptera
L 6½"/16cm **WS** 10½"/27cm

White-winged Crossbill occupies northern spruce forests; it feeds mostly in spruce, larch, and hemlock trees, hanging upside down from the cones and quietly extracting the seeds. Crossbills occasionally eat at feeders, especially in winter. Juveniles of both species are heavily streaked below. **VOICE** Song a series of unmusical, electric trills on varying pitches, hitched together without pause. Some calls similar to Red Crossbill; also a distinctive electric *twww*, highly modulated, like redpolls but deeper.

adult male

auriculars sharply framed in dark gray

white wing bars

vivid rose pink body

female

bold wing bars

faint greenish yellow tones and blurry streaks below

(juvenile similar but streakier and duller)

Sparrows and Allies

Sparrows in North America include the New World sparrows (family Emberizidae) and the introduced Old World sparrows (Passeridae)—House Sparrow and Eurasian Tree Sparrow—which are distant relatives of Emberizidae. Emberizids are small, mostly brown birds with short, conical bills and moderately long tails. They typically have a straight-edged culmen (upper edge of the maxilla), whereas the passerids have a distinctly curved culmen, especially in males. An exception is White-collared Seedeater, a tiny emberizid whose range barely enters the United States in Texas, which also has a curved culmen. The curve-billed Bananaquit (Coerebidae) is also illustrated here; its relationships to other bird taxa are not well understood, but present research suggests kinship to the grassquits, tropical emberizids that have occasionally strayed to Florida and Texas.

Dusky Seaside Sparrow of Florida became extinct in the 1980s, a victim of pesticide spraying and loss of wetland habitat.

With a few exceptions, sparrows are birds of thickets and open brushy or marshy environments, where both seeds and insects, the mainstays of their diet, abound. A few species are found in open forests. Bill size differs subtly but importantly among sparrows and is a good clue as to the size of seed the species is likely to eat. Towhees and sparrows scratch both feet backward in rapid motion to move leaf litter and other material quickly, exposing insects and other arthropods as well as seeds.

Most sparrows have monogamous mating systems, with males singing to defend a territory and mate. Some are polygynous, notably Lark Bunting and Savannah Sparrow. Saltmarsh Sharp-tailed Sparrow has a very unusual mating system: the male does not defend a territory but wanders widely and attempts to mate with as many females as possible. A few species, such as Henslow's and Clay-colored Sparrows, maintain rather small territories (thus they seem almost colonial when habitat is optimal) or show little interest in territorial defense. Most sparrows build a cup-shaped nest of grasses on the ground or in a small tree or bush; a few species cover the cup with a dome of grasses for added concealment.

Unlike emberizids, passerids are generally colonial when nesting; males perform animated courtship displays, hopping around with cocked tail and drooped wings like windup toys. Passerids usually nest in cavities; they will accept virtually any cranny available (often in buildings), constructing a round nest of twigs and grasses within the cavity.

Conservation concerns for emberizids abound in North America, largely because their habitats—fields and grasslands in particular—have been heavily developed and modified for centuries. Among the most beleaguered species are Henslow's and Baird's Sparrows, which specialize in prairie habitats, and Bachman's Sparrow, a bird of longleaf pine savannas. These ecosystems have lost 97 to 99 percent of their precolonial extent. Conservation action came too late to save the distinctive Dusky Seaside Sparrow, a resident of western Florida marshes classified as a subspecies of Seaside Sparrow (but almost certainly a full species); the last of these birds died in 1987.

Spotted Towhee
Pipilo maculatus
L 8½"/22cm WS 10½"/27cm

Spotted Towhee breeds in montane thickets, dense forest understory, second-growth scrub, and chaparral-clad canyons and slopes. At least 9 subspecies occur north of Mexico. Spotted hybridizes with Eastern Towhee on the Great Plains; the two were once combined as Rufous-sided Towhee. **VOICE** Song similar to Eastern but buzzier, shorter, and often less rich-toned; or a more modulated *tweee* (lacking introductory note). Call a rough, whiny *drrreeeeeay* in some subspecies; others have a *chwee,* more like Eastern.

adult male

extensive white in wings and scapulars; but black primary bases

juvenile

spotted coverts

heavily streaked

adult female

most taxa have white in primaries but not in primary bases (unlike Eastern Towhee)

Eastern Towhee
Pipilo erythrophthalmus
L 8½"/22cm WS 10½"/27cm

Eastern Towhee inhabits gardens, fields, woodland thickets, and, in the Southeast, coastal dune scrub and palmetto scrub; migratory northern populations appear to be declining. Towhees forage with a "double-scratch," thrusting the body back and forth to reveal seeds and insects under leaf litter. Three subspecies in the Southeast often have whitish rather than red eyes. **VOICE** Song a cheerful, whistled tune remembered as *drink-your-TEEEEE!* or simply *drink-TEEE!,* last note higher and long. Call a nasal, burry *sha-WEEK!*

adult male (nominate)

black head and back

black wings with white in tips of outer rectrices and primary bases (rarely in scapulars or coverts)

rich rufous-orange sides, white belly

adult female

similar to male but black replaced by soft brown

(juvenile very similar to juvenile Spotted Towhee)

Green-tailed Towhee

Pipilo chlorurus
L 7¼"/18cm **WS** 9¾"/25cm

Green-tailed Towhee inhabits areas with sagebrush and antelope brush in the Great Basin (where populations have declined due to habitat loss) and also breeds widely in montane chaparral and dense shrubby slopes. It winters in similar habitats and more sparsely vegetated desert areas. A few stray eastward in late fall and winter. **VOICE** Song variable and more complex than other towhees: a short note, then a high whistle, then one or more raspy trills on different pitches, often falling at end. Call a rough, nasal *meeeah.*

adult

vivid rufous crown

moss green above, rich gray below and on head

white malar and throat

immature

very young birds densely streaked, gradually becoming grayer

Olive Sparrow

Arremonops rufivirgatus
L 6¼"/16cm **WS** 7¾"/20cm

Olive Sparrow, a relative of towhees, is resident in wooded habitats with extensive undergrowth, from Costa Rica to the brushlands and coastal prairie thickets of southern Texas. **VOICE** Song a series of rich, resonant, accelerating notes with cadence of a bouncing ball coming to rest. Call a very quiet *tik.*

adult

rust-brown eye line and crown stripes

broken eye ring

dull olive-brown above

pale gray below

large, pale legs and feet

Abert's Towhee

Pipilo aberti
L 9½"/24cm **WS** 11"/28cm

This scarce species is found in thickets, mesquite, and stands of willows and cottonwoods along water. **VOICE** Song a loud set of high, sweet, staccato notes followed by rapid-fire flat, staccato tones on much lower pitch. Calls include a high *seeeep* and notes like components of song.

adult

dark face with grayish pink to ivory bill distinctive

more richly colored crissum than other towhees

underparts sometimes show rose-rufous wash

California Towhee

Pipilo crissalis
L 9"/23cm   WS 11½"/29cm

This adaptable species is often found in gardens and parks but is most numerous in coastal sage scrub, pinyon-juniper woods with undergrowth, chaparral, and thickets of willows and other low vegetation near streams. In the past, California and Canyon Towhees were combined as Brown Towhee. **VOICE** Song an accelerating, stuttering series of sweet, staccato notes. Call a sharp, high *teek* or *chink;* interacting pairs give comical gabbling and squealing calls.

darker adult

face and vent washed with rich umber-brown

paler adult

less patterned overall, with more gray than brown

Canyon Towhee

Pipilo fuscus
L 9"/23cm   WS 11½"/29cm

As its name suggests, Canyon Towhee breeds in rocky, mostly arid environments with scattered shrubby vegetation. Like other towhees of hot environments, it forages quietly in shady spots; but it is relatively bold, often visiting rural parking lots or ranches to feed in the shade of vehicles or buildings. It is related to Abert's Towhee, which prefers wetter habitats. **VOICE** Song a simple whistled trill with distinct notes. Calls include a nasal, nuthatchlike *kittle,* a more yelping *kirr,* and a dry, fussing chatter.

adult

pale lores (darker in California Towhee)

distinct necklace pattern (and usually central breast spot in fresh plumage)

adult

usually distinctly rusty crown

markings of head and underparts often obscure or absent

Black-throated Sparrow

Amphispiza bilineata
L 5½"/14cm **WS** 7¾"/20cm

Black-throated Sparrow inhabits cactus-clad desert flats and hillsides, stark flatlands with creosote and saltbush, and pinyon-juniper slopes with brush. In winter it flocks with other sparrows in shrublands and deserts. Strays have been recorded well east and north of range. Juveniles lack the black throat and can be confused with Sage Sparrow. **VOICE** Song a bubbly tune (recalling Eastern Towhee but higher and more pure-toned). Calls include a rising, querulous *churr-HEE?* and high, faint, tinkling sounds.

adult, western (*deserticola*)

smaller, smaller-billed, and paler than Five-striped Sparrow, with wider white malar and supercilium, black throat

adult, Texas (nominate)

typically more richly colored than western subspecies but not separable in field

Five-striped Sparrow

Aimophila quinquestriata
L 6"/15cm **WS** 7¾"/20cm

In the U.S. Five-striped Sparrow breeds only in a few canyons of Arizona, notably Guadalupe Canyon and California Gulch. It is often found near water, but like other desert sparrows it can probably survive for long periods without drinking, taking moisture from insects and seeds. When not singing, this furtive species is difficult to spot, even in its open habitats. Some ornithologists think Five-striped is better placed in the genus *Amphispiza*. **VOICE** Song consists of single and doubled high, thin, often squeaky calls, with long pauses in between, sounding inattentive. Call a harsh *tchak*.

adult

rather dark overall

white supercilia, malars, and throat comprise 5 stripes

heavy bill

adult

black central breast spot

gray breast and flanks, whitish belly

Sage Sparrow
Amphispiza belli
L 6"/15cm **WS** 8¼"/21cm

Sage Sparrow occupies arid chaparral and sage scrub habitats. The sedentary nominate subspecies, Bell's Sparrow, which inhabits coastal California and Baja California, may be a separate species from the much paler interior subspecies (*nevadensis* and *canescens*), which disperse or migrate after nesting. Sage Sparrow runs rapidly through brush with its tail cocked. **VOICE** Song a short set of sweet but staticky notes or phrases, often falling then rising slightly. Call a soft, high *thp*, often in irregular series.

adult, interior (*canescens*)

pale gray head with striking white malar, eye ring, and white loral spot

this subspecies of interior California is slightly darker than Great Basin *nevadensis*

black throat stripe

adult, Pacific (nominate)

differs from interior birds in darker brown wings and back, darker gray head

White-collared Seedeater
Sporophila torqueola
L 4¼"/11cm **WS** 6¼"/16cm

The range of this Mexican relative of towhees and sparrows barely extends north over the Rio Grande into Texas, especially near Zapata and San Ygnacio; it is found in weedy fields, marsh margins, and tall stands of cane, mostly near water. It forages for seeds and insects in dense vegetation and can be difficult to find. **VOICE** Song a goldfinchlike set of whistled and trilled phrases of varying pitch, speed, and tone. Call an endearing high, nasal *queeyer!*

adult male

blackish "helmet" set off by buff-tan collar and throat

dark wings with white in primary bases and wing coverts

short tail

stubby bill has rounded culmen

female

small and nondescript

olive-brown above, paler tan-buff below, with very narrow wing bars

pale bill small but thick

Chipping Sparrow

Spizella passerina
L 5½"/14cm WS 8½"/22cm

Chipping Sparrow is a familiar sight in parks, golf courses, towns, farmlands, and open woods, especially pinewoods. This fairly tame, curious bird is easily drawn to pishing and often nests near buildings. In winter large flocks often gather in field edges and pinewoods, sometimes loosely associating with foraging bluebirds, warblers, or other sparrows. **VOICE** Song a loose, regular, "chipping" trill, richer than Worm-eating Warbler. Call a slight *tsip*.

breeding adult — neat rusty cap, thin black eye line

gray auriculars, paler throat and supercilium

nonbreeding adult

dark lores; pale gray rump; usually grayish below

1st winter

paler, less distinctly marked head pattern; sometimes brownish rump

Clay-colored Sparrow

Spizella pallida
L 5½"/14cm   WS 7½"/19cm

Clay-colored Sparrow breeds in open prairie and grasslands, often near water where small shrubs and thickets dot the landscape, and in parklands with breaks of birch, poplar, and alder; on the edges of its range, it often moves into early successional habitats, especially several years after a clear-cutting or fire, even into reclaimed strip mines and Christmas tree farms. Like other *Spizella*, it hops rather than walks. **VOICE** Song an insectlike set of up to 5 dry, buzzing sounds on one pitch. Call similar to Chipping Sparrow.

breeding adult

similar in structure to Chipping Sparrow, but lacks dark lores and rusty cap

overall rather pale and plain, with well-defined auriculars

adult — pale median stripe

stronger malar pattern than Chipping and Brewer's Sparrows

1st winter

elaborate head pattern

strong buffy tones

gray nape contrasts with pale brown back, pale buffy supercilium

Brewer's Sparrow
Spizella breweri
L 5½"/14cm   WS 7½"/19cm

The petite Brewer's Sparrow breeds in sagebrush plains of the Great Basin into the ramparts of the Rockies. An isolated subspecies, Timberline Sparrow *(taverneri)*, may represent a separate species; it breeds from northern British Columbia mountains into the Yukon in stunted birch, willow, and fir thickets. Brewer's winters in weedy fields in large flocks, often with other *Spizella*. **VOICE** Song a lovely, long set of run-on phrases, alternately sweet and trilling and dry and buzzy. Call similar to Chipping Sparrow.

adult (nominate)

grayish brown crown and nape often streaky; little or no central crown stripe

narrow, pale eye ring

small bill

mousy brown back has narrow dark streaks

adult, Timberline Sparrow *(taverneri)*

face pattern shows more contrast than nominate

larger than nominate

(darker, more contrasting back than nominate)

Black-chinned Sparrow
Spizella atrogularis
L 5¾"/15cm   WS 7¾"/20cm

The lovely, long-tailed Black-chinned Sparrow is found very locally in arid chaparral and on arid, rocky hillsides with scattered scrub oak or juniper and dense scrubby undergrowth. Like Brewer's Sparrow, it sometimes nests in what could be called loose, small colonies. In winter small numbers often flock with other sparrows in hillside habitats. **VOICE** Song a series of high, sweet notes that rise and accelerate rapidly into a wiry trill. Call a lispy, quiet *tsit*.

breeding adult

head and underparts soft gray, upperparts medium brown

pinkish bill surrounded by black plumage

long-tailed and rather slim overall

1st winter

similar to adult, but lacks black in face and has duskier bill

(streaky brown back, unstreaked in juncos)

American Tree Sparrow

Spizella arborea
L 6¼"/16cm **WS** 9½"/24cm

Most birders know American Tree Sparrow on its wintering grounds, where it flocks in fields, woodland edges, marshes, and hedgerows and often eats at feeders, especially in harsh weather. During the breeding season, its pure-toned warble rings sweetly through northern muskeg and brushy tundra, especially alder-willow thickets. **VOICE** Song a series of sweet, slurred notes that ascend and descend sharply but gracefully, with an echoing quality. Calls include a sweet but thin, sickly *tseup* and a peculiar rambling warble.

breeding adult

more robust than Field Sparrow, with more distinct rusty crown and eye line

dark maxilla, straw-colored mandible

lower wing bar stronger than in Field

nonbreeding adult

duller crown than breeding adult, usually broken by grayish center stripe

white outer rectrices

dark breast spot (lacking in Field Sparrow)

Field Sparrow

Spizella pusilla
L 5¾"/15cm **WS** 8"/20cm

Field Sparrow nests and winters in abandoned pastures and fields overgrown with broomsedge, blackberry brambles, sumac, and various bushes and saplings. It forages on seeds and insects, often in flocks in the nonbreeding season. In summer males sing their sweet, simple songs through the noonday heat, after many birds have fallen silent. **VOICE** Song a series of accelerating, whistled notes, very memorable. Call a rather robust, sweet *tsit*.

breeding adult

head pattern varies from mostly gray to extensively rufous on cap and behind eyes

more slender than American Tree Sparrow

pink bill

unmarked underparts (compare American Tree Sparrow)

adult

birds in western portion of range usually grayer overall, especially in face, but all have neat white eye ring

Rufous-crowned Sparrow

Aimophila ruficeps
L 6"/15cm   WS 7¾"/20cm

The secretive Rufous-crowned Sparrow spends most of its time on the ground. It is found on dry, rocky hillsides with scattered grass, bushes, and trees; in coastal sage scrub and chaparral; and around stony outcroppings. Its endearing nasal contact calls reveal its presence. This species often responds to pishing. **VOICE** Song a jumble of short, thin notes recalling House Wren. Calls include a sharp, high *tseet* and a high, nuthatchlike *deer,* usually repeated.

adult

grayish head with rusty crown and eye line

pale malar and throat divided by dark submalar stripe

very little primary projection

adult

eye ring usually distinct

most taxa have gray back with distinct rusty streaks

unstreaked below (juvenile has stippled breast)

long tail (appears rounded in flight)

Rufous-winged Sparrow

Aimophila carpalis
L 5¾"/15cm   WS 7½"/19cm

Rufous-winged Sparrow inhabits scrubby desert grasslands and washes with scattered mesquite, paloverde, hackberry, and cholla. Unlike other *Aimophila,* it often flushes into bushes or trees rather than running off through brush. Most birders see this species during the monsoon rains of July and August, when Arizona's deserts are often in bloom. **VOICE** Song a rich, sweet trill, often with introductory notes recalling Eastern Towhee. Call a high *tsip.*

adult

rufous crown; narrow eye line

rufous lesser coverts (can be hard to see)

neat dark streaks on back

adult

pale malar bordered by dark lines

dark culmen

Cassin's Sparrow
Aimophila cassinii
L 6"/15cm **WS** 7¾"/20cm

This nomadic sparrow of verdant grasslands may be abundant in an area when rains bring a bounty of insects and seeds but absent the next season. Breeding males sally up from their bush-top perches and deliver an unforgettable sweet song as they sail slowly downward. **VOICE** Song a rich, sweet trill, prefaced by 2 short, high notes and finished with 2 short whistles, the first lower, both seeming in minor key. Call a sharp, tinkling *tseek*.

gray adult

modest supercilium, eye ring, submalar stripe

pale outer corners of tail (dark in Botteri's Sparrow)

yellow wash on lores and bend of wing

faint streaks on flanks

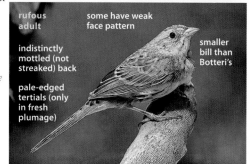

rufous adult

some have weak face pattern

indistinctly mottled (not streaked) back

pale-edged tertials (only in fresh plumage)

smaller bill than Botteri's

Botteri's Sparrow
Aimophila botterii
L 6"/15cm **WS** 7¾"/20cm

Botteri's Sparrow is found in grasslands with scattered mesquite or oak trees and in the coastal prairie of southernmost Texas. Singing birds perch conspicuously, but the species is otherwise difficult to find, as it forages and nests on the ground and often runs, mouselike, through dense cover rather than flushing. **VOICE** Song a rapidly accelerating trill recalling Olive Sparrow but more hesitant at opening. Call a sharp *tsip*, with quality like song notes.

adult

wings and face almost unpatterned

size and plumage similar to Cassin's Sparrow, but heavier bill; different song

adult

strongly streaked back

fresh tertials lack pale edges (compare Cassin's)

unstreaked flanks (unlike some Cassin's)

Bachman's Sparrow
Aimophila aestivalis
L 6"/15cm **WS** 7¼"/18cm

Bachman's Sparrow is classically a bird of longleaf pine savannas—a lowland, open-forest habitat with a grassy understory that once covered 90 million acres in the Southeast but now exists only in small patches. Bachman's is also found locally in recent cutovers, shortleaf pine forests, and palmetto scrub. It is a shy species that often runs instead of flushing. **VOICE** Song a high, thin, rising introductory note, sometimes with a buzzy quality, followed by a rich, resonant, musical trill. Call a high, quiet, thin *tsip*, sometimes in series.

bright adult

birds in fresh plumage show strong rufous tones in back, crown, eye line

some individuals washed with buff on breast, flanks, undertail coverts

worn adult

rusty crown and eye line

dark-streaked back

tertials tinged with rufous

Identification of *Aimophila* Sparrows

Cassin's, Botteri's, and Bachman's Sparrows (genus *Aimophila*) are similar in structure: large, long-tailed, and fairly heavy-billed. Bachman's, identified by its southeastern range and open pinewoods habitat, rarely strays northward. Cassin's and Botteri's Sparrows both inhabit desert grasslands; Cassin's is nomadic, occasionally straying as far out of range as eastern Canada (Botteri's has not been reported out of range). Many *Aimophila* are heavily worn, and thus difficult to identify, during the breeding season; their song is diagnostic. To identify a silent *Aimophila*, look at the back, uppertail coverts, bill, and head. In Cassin's, pale fringes on mantle and scapular feathers make the back look scaly; Botteri's and Bachman's show heavy gray and wine-rust streaks on the back. The uppertail coverts of Bachman's and Cassin's have dark subterminal marks; the coverts of Botteri's have long, dark shaft streaks. Botteri's has the largest bill of the three, Cassin's the smallest; Bachman's is in between. Bachman's shows a rusty crown and supercilium and ruddy stippling on the nape and sides of the breast. Botteri's has a similar though duskier and weaker head pattern and a very weak submalar mark (but lacks the nape and breast markings). Cassin's has only a weak head pattern, with the crown lightly stippled, but has a clear eye ring and submalar mark in fresh plumage.

Botteri's Sparrow

Cassin's Sparrow

Bachman's Sparrow

Dark-eyed Junco
Junco hyemalis
L 6¼"/16cm   **WS** 9¼"/23cm

One of the most variable of all American birds, Dark-eyed Junco is a familiar sparrow across the continent, rare only in subtropical areas of Florida and Texas. Dark-eyed nests in a wide variety of forested habitats, usually coniferous or mixed woodlands that have open ground for foraging; its pleasant, trilling song echoes into midday. This species' tolerance for harsh weather allows it to return to nesting areas early and to leave highland and boreal habitats later than most species. **VOICE** Song of all types a rich trill on one pitch, like Chipping Sparrow but not so dry. Call a short, flat *thtp,* similar to a hummingbird call.

Subspecies

Six different groups of subspecies of Dark-eyed Junco (called "types") breed in North America. Most are distinctive and have their own common names. (Where their ranges overlap—mostly in Nevada, California, and Idaho—most taxa interbreed freely.) **Slate-colored Junco** (subspecies group *hyemalis*) is common across Alaska, New England, and Appalachia as a breeding species, and in the lower 48 states in winter. It is essentially slate gray with a white belly and pink bill; females and young birds have varying amounts of brown above. **Oregon Junco** (subspecies group *oreganus*) is widespread west of the Great Plains but strays eastward often. Where Oregon and Slate-colored meet in the Canadian Rockies, intergrades (nicknamed "Cassiar Junco") are common. Four other western types of Dark-eyed Junco have limited ranges. **White-winged Junco** *(aikeni)* has a tiny breeding range in montane Wyoming, South Dakota, and Montana; it resembles a large, pale version

adult male, Oregon Junco *(oreganus* group)
the only subspecies with jet black hood contrasting with brown back

female, Oregon Junco *(oreganus* group)
similar to male but paler, with less contrast

1st winter, Oregon Junco *(oreganus* group)
pale trace of hood, usually with brownish hindcrown

juvenile, Oregon Junco *(oreganus* group)
briefly held juvenal plumage very streaky, as in other sparrows
usually accompanies adults at this age

adult, Gray-headed Junco *(caniceps)*
neat rufous back
dark eyes and lores; pink bill
pale gray overall
white belly, not distinctly defined

of Slate-colored with white wing bars. **Pink-sided Junco** *(mearnsi)* nests largely in central Montana and northern Wyoming and winters from Colorado into Mexico. It comes into contact with the distinctive **Gray-headed Junco** *(caniceps)* in southern Idaho and Wyoming and in Utah, where these two types interbreed. Gray-headeds interbreed with Oregon Juncos in eastern California and southern Nevada. **Red-backed Junco** *(dorsalis),* similar to Gray-headed, nests and winters in the mountains of central Arizona and New Mexico and also winters in western Texas.

adult male, Slate-colored Junco (nominate)

pink bill

slaty gray overall, lores only slightly darker

(bluish gray bill in Appalachian *carolinensis*)

white belly and outer rectrices

adult male, Pink-sided Junco (mearnsi)

slightly larger than Oregon Junco, with pale bluish gray hood, dark lores, rich orange-buff sides; recalls a bluebird

adult, White-winged Junco (aikeni)

dark lores and pale gray throat (unlike Slate-colored)

paler gray than Slate-colored (white wing bars rare in Slate-colored)

(female and immature juncos have brownish tones in plumage)

Yellow-eyed Junco

Junco phaeonotus
L 6¼"/16cm **WS** 10"/25cm

Yellow-eyed Junco is very like Dark-eyed Junco in habitat and most habits but differs in its song and its yellow eyes. Unlike Dark-eyed, it walks or shuffles rather than hops. This species is found mostly at elevations of about 6,000' (1,800m), in coniferous or mixed forests with underbrush and open areas; no other juncos nest in its range in Arizona. In winter it gathers in small groups, probably composed of families, that frequent parking lots and picnic sites. **VOICE** Song a rich, sweet, towheelike trill, quite variable, but usually introduced by several notes and sometimes closing with a second trill or set of notes on different pitch. Call a rich, sweet *tsip.*

adult

vivid yellow eyes

black maxilla, yellow mandible (pink in similar Red-backed subspecies of Dark-eyed Junco)

extensively black face

adult

rufous mantle distinctive

rufous in greater coverts and tertials (Red-backed has gray wings)

Grasshopper Sparrow

Ammodramus savannarum
L 5"/13cm **WS** 7¾"/20cm

This sparrow nests in fields and meadows, often with scattered bushes; the darker Florida subspecies *(floridanus)*, found in prairies with small oaks and palmetto, is listed as endangered. Elusive when foraging, Grasshopper stays mostly on the ground but may perch when flushed. It maintains territories, but nestlings are often fed by birds other than their parents. **VOICE** Song a high, tinkling, thin trill, like an insect's buzz, usually with 2 or 3 introductory notes; also a rapid jumble of squeaky notes. Call a high but soft *tp*.

adult

pale white central crown stripe

dark spot at rear edge of auriculars

white eye ring

heavy bill

chunky body

adult

upperparts marked with black, brown, rufous

yellow lores extend just to eyes (compare Le Conte's Sparrow)

flat crown

sides of breast have indistinct marks; otherwise pale buff below

---

Baird's Sparrow

Ammodramus bairdii
L 5½"/14cm **WS** 8¾"/22cm

Baird's Sparrow nests in the northern Great Plains, mostly in complex fields of native grasses such as wheatgrass, junegrass, needlegrass, a once vast habitat that has almost vanished. It can also survive in lightly grazed grasslands with scattered low shrubs, or in fields with dense exotic grasses. Like others in its genus, Baird's runs mouselike through the grasses when fleeing or when confronting a rival. **VOICE** Song an ethereal, high trill, varying in speed, usually introduced by 1–4 higher notes. Call a high, thin *tsee*.

adult

nape ocher-tinged (olive on Henslow's Sparrow), usually finely streaked

lines in face pattern more broken than in Henslow's

adult

face suffused with peach-buff (appears yellowish in some)

less rufous above and longer-tailed than Henslow's and Grasshopper Sparrows

Henslow's Sparrow

Ammodramus henslowii
L 5"/13cm   WS 6½"/17cm

This uncommon sparrow inhabits the few remaining fragments of native eastern prairie and has also adapted to reclaimed strip mines, abandoned pastures, and rank meadows. It winters in diverse grassy habitats, from longleaf pine savannas to rice fields. Singing males sometimes perch conspicuously and may sing well after dark. Nesting territories are so closely spaced that this species is nearly colonial. **VOICE** Song a short, fused twist of high, thin but rich notes sounding like *tsdlick,* with insectlike quality. Call a sharp *tsip* or *stit.*

adult

compact, with large head and rather short tail

tertials have rusty edges

narrow white eye ring

adult

rich russet tones of back and wings contrast with olive head

rather heavy bill

ocher-buff cast and limited, neat streaking on breast and sides

Savannah Sparrow

Passerculus sandwichensis
L 5½"/14cm   WS 6¾"/17cm

Savannah Sparrow is an abundant, variable species and is widespread as a nester in almost any wide-open habitat, from tundra to meadows to marsh margins to cultivated fields. It has several subspecies and is often mistaken for Song and Vesper Sparrows or for streaked *Ammodramus* species such as Baird's and young Grasshopper Sparrows. **VOICE** Song a pair of high, thin, airy trills, the first usually higher, introduced by accelerating, staccato *stit* or *ti* notes. Call a sharp *tsip,* like some *Ammodramus.*

adult

streaking below and facial markings typically neat and strong

(some subspecies show much more rufous in wings)

neat white eye ring, yellow lores

small bill

many show central breast spot

adult *(beldingi)*

Ipswich Sparrow *(princeps)*

very pale coastal Atlantic subspecies

darkest subspecies, found in coastal marshes of southern California

Nelson's Sharp-tailed Sparrow

Ammodramus nelsoni
L 5"/13cm WS 7"/18cm

Nelson's Sharp-tailed Sparrow inhabits wetlands year-round. Three subspecies breed in disjunct regions: *subvirgatus,* in coastal marshes of New England and southeastern Canada; *alterus,* in sedge bogs with dwarf willow and birch of the Hudson Bay coast; and the nominate, in freshwater marshes of the northern prairies. **VOICE** Song an unmusical, dry, staticky *tschyyy-drrrr,* second part lower, often likened to water hitting a hot skillet. Call a dry, hard *stik.*

adult (nominate or *alterus*)

sharp break between buff-yellow breast and white belly

adult, interior

worn birds can resemble Le Conte's but note unstreaked nape, grayish crown, larger bill, duller tertial edges

adult (subvirgatus)

similar to Saltmarsh Sharp-tailed Sparrow but indistinctly marked below and with shorter bill

Saltmarsh Sharp-tailed Sparrow

Ammodramus caudacutus
L 5¼"/13cm WS 7"/18cm

This sparrow has one of the most restricted breeding ranges of any North American songbird: narrow strips of coastal salt marsh with smooth cordgrass from Maine to Virginia. Because males apparently roam widely in search of females (rather than stake out a territory and sing day and night like Nelson's), the species can be difficult to find. **VOICE** Song a faint, raspy *tschee-dur,* like Nelson's but more musical, often repeated or with long concluding *schayyy.* Call a high, thin *tsit* or *tsik.*

adult

in fresh plumage rich buffy sides marked with distinct blackish streaking blends gradually into white belly

vivid orange-buff face contrasts with gray auriculars and pale throat

adult

looks very large-headed and long-billed at a distance, with very white underparts

juvenile

often mistaken for similar Seaside Sparrow but paler overall, and buffier tones on face

Le Conte's Sparrow

Ammodramus leconteii
L 5"/13cm WS 6½"/17cm

A good view of Le Conte's Sparrow reveals a beautiful palette of colors: a rich saffron face, blue-gray auriculars, and a nape spotted with straw and purplish maroon colors. This secretive sparrow breeds in wet meadows, sedge marshes, and freshwater marsh edges. Its breeding and winter ranges and habitat requirements coincide remarkably with those of Yellow Rail. **VOICE** Song an insectlike buzz with 1 or 2 brief, ticking introductory notes. Call a thin *steek*.

adult, fresh

bright yellow extends well beyond eyes (compare Grasshopper Sparrow)

white central crown stripe tinged yellow near bill

brighter, cleaner yellow face than sharp-tailed sparrows

adult, duller

auriculars sometimes streaked

purple-spotted nape

smaller bill than Nelson's Sharp-tailed Sparrow

yellow on sides and face often muted, strongest above gray lores and eyes

Seaside Sparrow

Ammodramus maritimus
L 6"/15cm WS 7½"/19cm

Seaside Sparrow nests and forages in the wettest, outer part of coastal salt marshes, where cordgrass and needlerush are regularly washed by tides. Of 9 subspecies, 2 are extinct—*nigrescens* and *pelonota*—both victims of the destruction of salt marshes. The distinctive Cape Sable Seaside Sparrow *(mirabilis)* of southern Florida is often considered a full species; with fewer than 3,000 birds left, this subspecies is listed as endangered. **VOICE** Song of 2 harsh, creaking, rising notes, recalling a distant Red-winged Blackbird but much less musical. Call a low *stipp*.

adult, Atlantic

large and dark

yellow above lores in all subspecies

heavy bill

distinct white throat and malar

juvenile

similar to Saltmarsh Sharp-tailed but darker above, yellow area above lores

Harris's Sparrow
Zonotrichia querula
L 7½"/19cm **WS** 10½"/27cm

Harris's Sparrow breeds entirely in muskeg of northern Canada; its somber song is one of the sweetest of this sparrow-rich habitat. Harris's winters in the southern Great Plains, foraging in weedy fields, hedgerows, and woodland edges; a few stray well east and west each year, sometimes turning up at feeders. **VOICE** Song usually 3 distinct whistles on same pitch, the first longest, the set then repeated at a different pitch. Call a rich, strong *pink*.

breeding adult

black face, throat, crown, and spot at rear of auriculars

heavy, pale pink bill

heavy body

variable black spotting on upper breast

1st winter

pink bill; black stippling around throat and breast

nonbreeding adult

bill duller but still pale pink

black in plumage reduced

Golden-crowned Sparrow
Zonotrichia atricapilla
L 7¼"/18cm **WS** 9½"/24cm

The large, long-tailed Golden-crowned Sparrow breeds mostly in alder and willow thickets along waterways, at the tree line, or in other low muskeg and tundra habitats. Males sing through the long summer days from a conspicuous perch. This species winters in brushy field edges, chaparral, and riparian thickets. **VOICE** Song a variable set of 3 or 4 plaintive whistles, central notes usually lower. Call a sharp *pink* or flatter *thcup*, different from White-crowned.

breeding adult

head pattern limited to black cap with golden central stripe

maxilla mostly dusky, contrasting with pale mandible

1st winter/dull nonbreeding adult

hint of gold in forecrown

face almost unmarked

bill mostly gray with duskier culmen

White-crowned Sparrow

Zonotrichia leucophrys
L 7"/18cm **WS** 9½"/24cm

This hardy sparrow is found in many habitats, from muskeg and recent burns in boreal forests to coastal sage scrub in California; migrants and wintering birds are found in brushy habitats. Five subspecies include the nominate form in the East and *gambelii, oriantha, pugetensis,* and *nuttalli* in the West. **VOICE** Song usually a series of scratchy whistled notes on one pitch, ending with several notes, one higher, one lower. Call a flat, low *pink* or *chink,* sharper and more ringing than Golden-crowned.

adult, western boreal range *(gambelii)*

lacks white throat and yellow in crown or lores (compare Golden-crowned, White-throated)

striking, neat head pattern and yellow bill (other subspecies show dark lores, pink bill)

1st winter

pale bill, unlike White-throated and Golden-crowned Sparrows

head pattern like adult but in buff and brown

White-throated Sparrow

Zonotrichia albicollis
L 6¾"/17cm **WS** 9"/23cm

White-throated Sparrow breeds in coniferous and mixed forests and muskeg, often in dense deciduous brush along streams, bogs, and beaver ponds. In winter it is common in thickets and backyards. Two color morphs differ in head color of breeding plumage: one tan-striped, one white-striped. **VOICE** Song a sad-sounding set of clear whistles on one pitch, introduced by single lower note, rendered *poor Sam Peabody, Peabody, Peabody.* Call a sweet, hard *pink.*

adult, white-striped morph

striking head pattern with yellow in lores, white throat (tan-striped morph similar but head more gray-brown, throat off-white)

1st winter

yellowish lores

always has tan-striped head

dark bill

trace of adult head pattern

Fox Sparrow
Passerella iliaca
L 7"/18cm **WS** 10½"/27cm

Fox Sparrow is a heavyset bird breeding in western mountains and northern muskeg, coastal forests, and streamside thickets. It has many distinctive subspecies, some of which have been considered separate species. **VOICE** Song a set of sweet, slurred whistles, rising and falling in pitch, with a pure-toned, oriole-like quality. Call a sharp, distinctive *sthlp* (a sharp *chink* in Thick-billed subspecies).

Subspecies
The northernmost type, **Red Fox Sparrow** (*iliaca* group), winters largely in the lower 48 states between the Great Plains and East Coast, where it is partial to dense thickets in deep woods. In coastal Alaska and British Columbia, the more uniformly brownish **Sooty Fox Sparrow** (*unalaschcensis* group) replaces Red; it winters mostly in tangles and chaparral along the coast south of Alaska. **Slate-colored Fox Sparrow** (*schistacea* group) and **Thick-billed Fox Sparrow** (*megarhycha* group) are similar in appearance but for the bill, which is much heavier in the latter. Slate-colored nests in Rocky Mountain and Great Basin thickets and winters mostly in California and the Southwest; Thick-billed nests to the west of Slate-colored, mostly in California and Oregon.

adult, Red Fox Sparrow (nominate)

large body and bill

gray nape and supercilium (more extensively gray in western Arctic)

vivid rust-red streaks and back color

1st winter, Red Fox Sparrow (nominate)

slightly browner than adult, with duller bill

Slate-colored Fox Sparrow (*schistacea*)

like Red in structure but only tail and wings rusty; rest of plumage lead gray

some birds, such as this one, appear intermediate in plumage and bill size between Slate-colored and Thick-billed and may be intergrades

Sooty Fox Sparrow (*unalaschcensis*)

uniformly brown above, very heavily marked below

Thick-billed Fox Sparrow (*megarhycha*)

like Slate-colored but with massive bill

Lark Sparrow

Chondestes grammacus
L 6½"/17cm WS 11"/28cm

The distinctive Lark Sparrow breeds in dry, open country and winters in large flocks in brushy deserts, prairies, pastures, and hedgerows. It forages on the ground, mostly for seeds. Strays are often seen in the East in early autumn, especially in bare fields near the coast. **VOICE** Song a bubbly, buntinglike carol of sweet notes and dry trills, varying in length and quality, usually with several sweet, high, incisive introductory notes. Call a high *tseep.*

adult

unique head pattern of red, black, and white

extensive white in tail (easily seen in flight)

large, slender sparrow with long tail

1st winter

shows clear trace of adult's head pattern

Lark Bunting

Calamospiza melanocorys
L 7"/18cm WS 10½"/27cm

This sparrow is restricted to sagebrush plains and especially shortgrass and mixed-grass prairies of the Great Plains, habitats that have been lost to agriculture over the past 150 years. It forms relatively large winter flocks that forage in dry plains and deserts. **VOICE** Song a long, slow, odd concatenation of cardinal-like, sweet notes; chatlike fusses, and dry, electric buzzes, often given in flight display. Calls include a sweet, low *tyew* or *tyew-ee* and a wiry buzz.

breeding adult male

pale, heavy bill has blue tint

jet black with white wing coverts and remiges' edges

(shows much white in tail in flight, like Lark Sparrow)

nonbreeding adult male

heavy, bluish bill unique

adult female

heavy, gray bill

white coverts

strong black submalar stripe

white in wing coverts and tail tip distinctive

Song Sparrow
Melospiza melodia
L 6¼"/16cm **WS** 8¼"/21cm

In many areas Song Sparrows are the familiar sparrows of backyards and hedgerows, seen pumping their tails in flight as they forage in flocks through areas of weeds and brush, often with other species. This is the most widespread of American sparrows, absent only from open tundra habitats. It is variable in voice and plumage, and more than 30 subspecies have been described, although few can be identified in the field. Song Sparrows that nest east of the Rocky Mountains (3 nearly identical subspecies) are often depicted as the "standard" Song Sparrow. **VOICE** Song varies greatly by region; usually a tuneful set of alternated bubbly trills and sweet notes. Call a thin, incisive *tsit* or *tseet*.

Song Sparrow adult, eastern

lightly marked birds sometimes lack breast spot

adult

Song Sparrow adult, California coast

most show obvious breast spot

rusty wings and coverts

heavy, blackish submalar and breast streaking

Song Sparrow adult, Pacific Northwest

some subspecies show rustier breast and sides

Vesper Sparrow
Pooecetes gramineus
L 6¼"/16cm **WS** 10"/25cm

This large sparrow is widespread in the West, scarce and local in the East; it nests in pastures, blueberry barrens, sagebrush and pinyon-juniper slopes, open pinewoods, and montane meadows; wintering birds flock in open lowlands. **VOICE** Song like Song and Lark Sparrows in its alternating trills and sweet notes, but more complex; opens with sweet notes and closes in chattering, reverberating trills. Call a short *tsip*.

Vesper Sparrow adult

dark auriculars have white spot in center

prominent white eye ring

rusty lesser coverts, pale-edged blackish median coverts

heavy body

long tail with white outer rectrices

Lincoln's Sparrow
Melospiza lincolnii
L 5¾"/15cm WS 7"/18cm

Lincoln's Sparrow breeds across the boreal forest and into the mountains of the West, favoring muskeg, regenerating clear-cuts or burns, and boggy thickets of willow and alder. It tends to skulk and can be difficult to find but responds well to pishing. In winter most seem to forage singly in dense cover. **VOICE** Song a series of distinctive, rising, reverberating trills, dropping sharply in pitch and volume. Call a sharp *stip* or flat *tic* (recalling Black-throated Blue Warbler).

adult

resembles Song Sparrow but with finer streaking; finer bill; and warm buff wash on breast, eye ring, and malar

adult

some show broad black submalar mark

fine streaking extends onto throat

Swamp Sparrow
Melospiza georgiana
L 5¾"/15cm WS 7½"/19cm

Swamp Sparrow commonly nests in freshwater marshes and bogs, often where cattails or bulrushes are dense. As a rule, it stays in cover, but it will leap to the top of a reed at the slightest squeak or pish. A distinctive subspecies of salt and brackish marshes from New Jersey to Virginia, *nigrescens*, has heavier black streaking on the back and a broader black band on the forehead. **VOICE** Song a rich trill of sweet notes on one pitch. Calls a sharp *tsit* (recalling Eastern Phoebe) and sweeter *tsink*.

breeding adult

darker below than Lincoln's Sparrow, with rust color in wings and back

neat rusty cap

unstreaked below

1st winter

similar to adult but with duller head pattern and darker, streaked breast

Chestnut-collared Longspur

Calcarius ornatus
L 6"/15cm **WS** 10½"/27cm

Male Chestnut-collared Longspurs deliver their lovely fluting songs over northern shortgrass and other prairies on spring mornings. The species winters on grasslands in large flocks, often mixing with other longspurs, larks, and pipits. Longspurs forage in the grass for insects and seeds. **VOICE** Song a rich, descending, fluting tune, compared to Western Meadowlark but shorter and less pure-toned. Call a disarming, nasal *kittle,* often repeated.

breeding adult male

chestnut nape

distinctive head pattern

extensive white in outer rectrices

black belly

1st winter female

like McCown's but with streaked breast, darker auriculars, gray bill

adult female

pale patch at rear of dusky auriculars; trace of rusty nape

Lapland Longspur

Calcarius lapponicus
L 6¼"/16cm **WS** 11½"/29cm

The hardy Lapland Longspur breeds in Arctic regions worldwide, where it nests both in dry, upland tundra and in lower, wet environments with higher dry areas; these preferred habitats are slowly shrinking, as warming temperatures allow the spread of shrubby plants farther and farther north. In late fall through winter, "Laps" gather in huge flocks on farm fields and prairies across the central lower 48 states. **VOICE** Song a complex, scratchy, somewhat mechanical but musical warble. Call a similarly scratchy *swit-chew.*

breeding adult male

rust-red nape

black crown, face, throat

outermost rectrix white

white supercilium and underparts

1st winter female

adult female

black-bordered auriculars; rusty nape and coverts

rufous coverts; strong head pattern

yellowish bill

McCown's Longspur

Calcarius mccownii
L 6"/15cm **WS** 11"/28cm

This uncommon sparrow breeds on semiarid shortgrass prairies of the northwestern Great Plains. In their flight display, males ascend about 30' (9m) and sing while floating down with spread wings and tail. McCown's winters mostly in dry lakebeds, arid farm fields, and high desert plains. **VOICE** Song a fluting, liquid ramble of sweet notes, sounding more like a flock than an individual. Calls include short, sweet *teep, kewp, dreet, tee-pip*, and *ki-pip* notes. All 4 longspurs give a dry rattle, especially in flight.

breeding adult male

(extensive white in outer rectrices)

black in breast, crown, malar

rufous in median coverts

pale gray overall

breeding adult female

1st winter female

paler face than Chestnut-collared Longspur, with larger, pink bill

heavy bill; faint rufous in coverts; dusky border around auriculars

Smith's Longspur

Calcarius pictus
L 6"/15cm **WS** 11¼"/29cm

Smith's Longspur breeds in a narrow band south of the open, grassy tundra and north of the boreal woods, where rocks and tiny, stunted trees provide song perches. It arrives in the southeastern Great Plains in late fall to winter on prairies, farm fields, and airports. **VOICE** Song a high, twisting warble recalling American Tree Sparrow (found in same habitat) but more rapid, with scratchy quality. Calls a sharp, dry *spik* and a short, sweet *sweek*.

breeding adult male

striking black and white head pattern

2 outer rectrices white

rich orange-buff nape and underparts

nonbreeding adult male

strong eye ring

(breeding adult female similar)

warm buff below

Snow Bunting
Plectrophenax nivalis
L 6¾"/17cm **WS** 13¾"/35cm

Snow Bunting breeds in remote dry tundra and rocky, barren areas. Like longspurs, it is a late-fall migrant that forms large flocks in open habitats, often mixing with larks and longspurs; buntings can also be found on rocky shorelines, dredge-spoil islands, and sand dunes. **VOICE** Song a grating but pleasant warble, similar to Lapland Longspur but with more distinct phrases. Calls include a sweet *tyew;* also a flight rattle similar to longspurs but softer.

breeding adult male

snow white with black mantle and scapulars

nonbreeding male

some black in primaries, lesser coverts, tail

like female but has more white in wings

breeding adult female

like male but white less stark; dark areas a streaky gray-brown, including crown

nonbreeding female

limited white in wings

bright orange-rust collar and auriculars

McKay's Bunting
Plectrophenax hyperboreus
L 6¾"/17cm **WS** 13¾"/35cm

McKay's Bunting, a close relative of Snow Bunting, nests on islands in the Bering Sea, chiefly Hall and St. Matthew, where the population totals several thousand. Most birders see this species in the Pribilofs, where it has sometimes hybridized with Snow Bunting, or on St. Lawrence Island. It winters along the coast of western Alaska, rarely in southern Alaska, and is a vagrant in the Pacific Northwest. **VOICE** Very similar to Snow Bunting.

breeding adult male

snow white with dark bill, legs, wingtips

breeding adult male

black tertials and wingtips in flight

nonbreeding male

mostly white head

dark wings and back

(nonbreeding female and first-winter male similar but with more orange-buff accents above)

Rustic Bunting

Emberiza rustica
L 6"/15cm WS 9½"/24cm

Rustic Bunting is one of many Eurasian *Emberiza* buntings that have been found in the Aleutian and other Alaskan islands as an uncommon spring and rare fall visitor. It is also a fall vagrant along the West Coast, found in brushy areas. Fall birds recall sparrows, but most show some rusty color in the rump and nape. **VOICE** Song a sweet, fluting warble recalling a longspur but more pure-toned. Call a very sharp, short, high *tsic* or *tic*.

breeding adult male

rusty nape; rich, rusty streaks on sides

black cheek and crown contrast with white throat and supercilium

1st winter female

pink bill

distinctive head pattern

rusty streaks on sides and flanks

Little Bunting

Emberiza pusilla
L 5"/13cm WS 8"/20cm

Little Bunting has been recorded in fall on Bering Sea islands, and 3 have turned up in California. This species forages on the ground in open field and edge habitats, where its cryptic plumage and small size make it easily overlooked. Other *Emberiza* species recorded rarely in Alaska include Pine, Yellow-breasted, Gray, Pallas's, and Reed Buntings. **VOICE** Song a rollicking but short, goldfinchlike warble of modulated trills and high, sweet notes. Call a very quick *tsit* or *tsik*.

neat white eye ring

black malar and crown

rust-brown central crown stripe, chin, face

black-bordered auriculars

breeding adult male

1st fall/winter

similar to adult but colors more muted (compare longspurs, Rustic Bunting)

House Sparrow

Passer domesticus
L 6¼"/16cm **WS** 9½"/24cm

House Sparrows were released in New York City in 1851 as part of a plan to have all the birds mentioned in Shakespeare's works nesting in Central Park. The species has since spread across the continent. It breeds in urban and suburban environments and on farms and ranches, never far from human habitation, and scavenges food from sidewalks and feedlots. **VOICE** Song a reedy, sweet but short *sreedip,* repeated in long series. Calls varied but similar in quality.

breeding adult male

chestnut nape reaches eyes, contrasts with gray crown

heavy black bill has curved culmen

black on breast extends to throat

median coverts have white tips (reduced or absent in nonbreeding and subadult males)

nonbreeding adult male

pale bill, trace of face pattern

adult female

pale supercilium; pale yellowish bill

unstreaked mousy brown below

Eurasian Tree Sparrow

Passer montanus
L 6"/15cm **WS** 8¾"/22cm

Eurasian Tree Sparrow, a widespread Old World sparrow, was introduced in St. Louis, Missouri, in 1870, as House Sparrow was spreading through the Midwest and beyond. It has remained a very local species, found along the Missouri–Illinois border and in extreme southeastern Iowa in farmland and rural suburbs, where it favors hedgerows and weedy fields. Vagrants have been recorded north to southern Manitoba and Ontario in recent years. **VOICE** Song quality similar to House Sparrow but comprised of harsher *chewr* calls. Calls like House, some more nasal and sputtering.

adult

like House Sparrow but smaller, with full chestnut cap and black cheek patch

juvenile

similar to adult, but paler, more muted plumage

bill has dull yellow base, dusky tip

Dickcissel

Spiza americana
L 6¼"/16cm **WS** 9¾"/25cm

A widespread bird of mixed prairies, pastures, and cultivated farm fields of many sorts, the colorful, sparrowlike Dickcissel wanders widely in search of optimal habitat. It is often found nesting east of Appalachia, hundreds of miles from its core range. In prime habitat, singing males may be abundant, perched conspicuously on fences, utility wires, and small shrubs, while the more cryptically patterned females stay hidden on the nest. Small numbers are regularly seen out of range, especially during fall migration. Drab first-winter birds are often found foraging with House Sparrows, which they resemble very closely. Dickcissel, currently classified as a cardinalid, was formerly considered an icterid, and some studies suggest it belongs in its own family. **VOICE** Song a short, rich, burry *dick-dick-SI-SI-slll* or similar, repeated vigorously through the day. Call a short, flat "Bronx cheer."

breeding adult male
gray crown and nape contrast with yellow-washed white malar and supercilium
vivid chestnut coverts
dark throat stripe
usually yellow breast

1st fall
like adult female but neatly streaked below

nonbreeding adult/1st winter
strong yellow in malar and supercilium (otherwise much like House Sparrow)

adult female
often some rust in coverts
trace of male's head pattern (white malar and supercilium, dark throat stripe)
yellow wash on breast

Bananaquit

Coereba flaveola
L 4½"/11cm **WS** 7¾"/20cm

The tropical Bananaquit strays into southern Florida in fall and winter, mostly to gardens and parks; in the tropics, the species is found from dry lowland scrub to high-mountain forests. It uses its decurved bill to probe and pierce flowers for nectar and readily accepts handouts of fruit, sugar, and nectar. This species is abundant on most islands of the Caribbean except Cuba, where it is quite rare. **VOICE** Song a series of dry, pulsating, insectlike trills or buzzes. Call a short, high *tsit*.

adult
striking face pattern
decurved bill, reddish at gape
white in primaries
yellow belly

Small Brown Landbirds

Many small, brownish, sparrowlike passerines from different families are found around the continent in open-country habitats. They can be troublesome to identify, but beginning birders can learn to pin them at least to family and/or genus by noting body and bill shapes, behavior (foraging and locomotion), basic field marks, and vocalizations, especially the songs (covered in individual species accounts). These pages provide a thumbnail comparison of many types of small, sparrowlike birds that frequent open fields, hedgerows, thickets, and other edge habitats. (See also "Small Woodland Birds," pages 354–355, which covers mostly arboreal species.)

Sparrows (pages 450–473) are small birds with conical bills that forage on or near the ground for seeds and insects; most are streaky brown above and paler below; some have streaks on the underparts. Their bills vary from short and delicate (Brewer's) to long and heavy (Seaside and Botteri's). Most areas have more than a dozen species, some of which remain in dense vegetation most of the time. In winter different species often flock together, flushing ahead of an observer, then quickly back into cover, which makes identification challenging.

Longspurs (pages 474–475) and their relatives the *Plectrophenax* buntings (Snow and McKay's, page 476) are short-legged, plump sparrows of open habitats such as tundra, shortgrass prairies, and beaches. Longspurs, named for the elongated nail on the hindtoe, are rather heavy-billed for their size, and all four have white in the outer rectrices. Like larks, pipits, and Snow Bunting, longspurs frequent farm fields in the nonbreeding season to forage for seeds, sometimes in mixed flocks.

Finches (pages 440–447) are often mistaken for sparrows; the smaller, sparrow-sized finches have conical bills, like those of sparrows, and some finches (Pine Siskin, female Purple, Cassin's, and House Finches, female redpolls) are brown above and streaky below like sparrows. The bills of finches differ: the siskins' bills are rather slender and finely pointed; redpolls' bills are very short and delicate; bills of Purple and House Finches have a subtle curvature in the culmen. Rosy-finches have very sparrowlike bills but usually show some rosy coloration in the plumage, unlike sparrows. Finches, other than the rosy-finches, are also usually more arboreal than sparrows; they tend to cling to weedstalks when feeding rather than perch on the ground, as sparrows often do. When flushed, finches usually fly up to the top of the vegetation but rarely fly into dense cover.

Female **buntings** of the genus *Passerina* (pages 435–437) are often mistaken for sparrows because of similar bill shape and brown plumages. While the bills show only

Song Sparrow

Smith's Longspur

Lazuli Bunting

Purple Finch

House Sparrow

Dickcissel

American Pipit

Red-winged Blackbird

Bobolink

Horned Lark

Palm Warbler

House Wren

subtle differences from the bills of sparrows, their plumages are much plainer, with little or no pattern in the wings and back.

Old World sparrows (page 478) are represented in North America by the introduced House and Eurasian Tree Sparrows. Males are distinguished from New World sparrows by their bills, which have a curved culmen. Female House Sparrow has a more conical bill and rather plain plumages similar to New World sparrows.

Dickcissel (page 479), when seen hopping among House Sparrows at a feeder, could easily be overlooked, especially a young female, which in plumage resembles a female House Sparrow. Dickcissel has a heavier bill, however, and usually has a thin submalar mark and sometimes faint streaking below.

Blackbirds (pages 422–425) are a diverse group; with exception of the meadowlarks, most have slender bodies, moderately long tails, and rather long bills that are heavier at the base. Only a few members of the family are regularly confused with sparrows. Bobolink has a deeper, more sparrowlike bill than larger blackbirds, and females and nonbreeding birds are quite sparrowlike; their richer colors and stronger plumage contrasts help to distinguish them from sparrows. Red-winged and Tricolored Blackbird females are streaky below, like sparrows, but their bills are much longer.

Pipits (pages 484–485) in North America are thin-billed terrestrial birds found in a wide variety of open habitats, from tundra to desert to lakeshores. Their plumage is sparrowlike, but their bodies and especially bills are much more slender. In agricultural fields, flocks of American Pipits amble actively back and forth, picking seeds and insects. Sprague's Pipit does not flock.

Horned Lark (page 486) can also often be found in agricultural fields. Like pipits, this species forages for seeds and can form large flocks. It is readily identified by its distinctive face pattern. Though larks have rather long legs, like pipits, they often feed more closely crouched to the ground, using a creeping shuffle more like that of the longspurs. Their bills are slimmer than those of longspurs but heavier and shorter than those of pipits.

Warblers (pages 357–389) are typically arboreal, but several species (Pine, Palm, and Yellow-rumped Warblers) regularly forage on the ground in open environments. Some of these are very plain brown above and paler below with a few streaks, rather like sparrows; in all cases their thin bills give them away.

Wrens (pages 347–351) also frequent field edges, where they stay mostly in thickets; their thin, often long bills, mottled plumages, and often cocked tails separate them easily from true "field birds."

Pipits, Wagtails, and Larks

Wagtails and pipits (family Motacillidae) and larks (Alaudidae) are only distant relatives, but they share habitat preferences, foraging strategies, and some structural and behavioral features. All are small to medium-sized, rather slim passerines that walk through shortgrass fields and other open habitats, often in groups, to feed on insects and seeds. They have strong legs, sometimes with elongated hind claws. All are ground-nesters, monogamous, and highly migratory. Motacillidae and Alaudidae are mainly Old World families: only two species of lark and four motacillids breed on this continent.

Wagtails are larger than pipits and have longer tails, which they constantly wag, and striking plumages. They are conspicuous, active foragers, chasing insects on the ground, flycatching, and even taking invertebrates in streams. Pipits forage less actively, usually walking

American Pipits and all wagtails, such as this Black-backed (see page 483), regularly forage along the edges of lakes and rivers, where insects and larvae are abundant.

erratically through fields. Larks and pipits perform splendid song-flight displays. American Pipit and Horned Lark form large flocks, often in association with longspurs and Snow Buntings, in the nonbreeding season. Pipits and larks have shown local declines in both wintering and breeding populations. Declines in Sprague's Pipit have been most severe.

Eastern Yellow Wagtail

Motacilla tschutschensis
L 6½"/17cm WS 10"/25cm

Until 2004 this summer resident of dwarf willow and birch thickets was considered a subspecies of *Motacilla flava* (now Western Yellow Wagtail). An Asian subspecies of Eastern Yellow, *simillima*, shows up occasionally in the Aleutians and Pribilofs; it is brighter green above and more richly yellow below. Gray Wagtail, which has a dark throat, is a vagrant to the Aleutians, Pribilofs, and Pacific coast. **VOICE** Song a monotonous set of squeaky notes, spaced evenly. Call an abrupt, buzzy *tswee!*, similar to song phrase.

breeding adult male

white supercilium

larger and longer-tailed than warblers

dark mask and crown

usually forages by walking on ground

breeding adult female

similar to male but with weaker head pattern

1st year

very plain brownish gray above

2 thin wing bars

off-white below (young White and Black-backed Wagtails have marks on breast)

White Wagtail

Motacilla alba

L 7¼"/18cm **WS** 10½"/27cm

This scarce and local bird usually builds its nest in manmade structures and debris near houses. When foraging it walks briskly along, sometimes rapidly chasing insects, all the while bobbing its tail. In Alaska, the Siberian subspecies *ocularis* nests from St. Lawrence Island to the state's northwestern coast. The eastern Asian subspecies *lugens*—which was given full species status as **Black-backed Wagtail** between 1982 and 2004—is a regular visitor to the western Aleutian Islands, where it has nested, and a vagrant to Pacific coast states (with one record also from North Carolina); males are strikingly different from White Wagtails, with largely white rather than dark remiges, snow white greater upperwing coverts, and a contrasting glossy black back and nape that extends to the lesser upperwing coverts. Other plumages are more difficult or impossible to distinguish from *ocularis*. Vagrants of the nominate subspecies, whose nearest nesting grounds are in Greenland and Iceland, have turned up in South Carolina, Quebec, and Newfoundland. **VOICE** Song a slow, stuttering or richer, warbling series of goldfinchlike notes, repeated in phrases or run together. Calls a short, sweet *tseelik* and harsher, metallic *tchchk*.

breeding adult male *(ocularis)*

black nape, hindcrown, and eye line

dusky remiges (unlike Black-backed)

black bib extends to bill (unlike similar female Black-backed)

nonbreeding adult (nominate)

similar to *ocularis* but lacks eye line in all plumages

juvenile (nominate)

faint trace of dusky bib and hindcrown

(juvenile Black-backed subspecies very similar, but has dark eye line)

nonbreeding adult female, Black-backed *(lugens)*

(adult male more extensively black on throat and breast)

differs from other subspecies in much darker back, whiter primaries, white chin

American Pipit

Anthus rubescens

L 6½"/17cm   **WS** 10½"/27cm

American Pipit breeds on barren mountaintops and tundra, where males perform ebullient flight displays, singing while gliding down from high in the air. After the nesting season, pipits form flocks in farm fields, shortgrass prairies, and shorelines. The more strongly marked Asian subspecies *japonicus* is a rare fall visitor to the Pacific coast. **VOICE** Song a series of sweet, clear, ringing or tinkling phrases, repeated continuously for up to 20 seconds. Call note a sibilant, rapid *sipip* or *sipipi.*

breeding adult, Rocky Mountains *(alticola)*

(most show more streaking in breast)

rich buff below

dark legs

nonbreeding adult *(japonicus)*

paler legs, heavier black markings below than other subspecies

nonbreeding adult

white eye ring and supercilium

neat dark streaking against white belly

paler legs than breeding birds

Sprague's Pipit

Anthus spragueii

L 6½"/17cm   **WS** 10"/25cm

This pipit breeds in native shortgrass prairies of the northern Great Plains; there, males sing suspended hundreds of feet in the air for a half-hour or more. In winter Sprague's is solitary, favoring prairies and open shortgrass habitats. Unlike American Pipit, it flushes rapidly upward, flies off, then drops sharply back into cover. **VOICE** Song a complex, modulated, spirally, descending trill of *tschiw* phrases lasting about 5 seconds, repeated every 5–10 seconds. Call a short, sharp, swallowlike *squit* or *jewt,* very different from American.

adult, worn

streaked back and crown

plumage cryptic in grasses; often found only when flushed

unpatterned face

pink legs

adult

some show pale, narrow eye ring

mandible mostly pale pink-orange

fine streaking on upper breast only

(juvenile similar but has much more strongly patterned back, prominent white wing bars)

Red-throated Pipit

Anthus cervinus
L 6¼"/16cm **WS** 10½"/27cm

On Alaska's Seward Peninsula and a few offshore islands, Red-throated Pipit breeds in dry, stony tundra adjacent to small wetlands. A few migrants turn up in autumn on Alaska's offshore islands and along the Pacific coast, mostly among flocks of American Pipits in farm fields and grassy areas. Careful scrutiny of American Pipit flocks could produce records of the species elsewhere. **VOICE** Song a continuous, pleasing series of varied phrases, most repeated in trilled fashion 2–5 times. Call a high, thin *spee!*

breeding adult

rich rusty orange wash on face and breast

heavily streaked below and on back (compare American Pipit)

1st year

rich buff wash on face and sides

strongly streaked on back and underparts

bold, dark submalar mark

pink legs

prominent white wing bar

Olive-backed Pipit

Anthus hodgsoni
L 6"/15cm **WS** 10"/25cm
This shy Eurasian species has reached Alaska's Bering Sea islands and Aleutian Islands and even California and Nevada during migration. Unlike other American pipits, it readily perches in bushes and trees and when flushed often flies to a perch or flies off some distance. **VOICE** Call, often given when flushed, a high, rough *speez*, much lower than Red-throated Pipit.

adult

white spot and black spot at rear of auriculars

pale olive-brown back faintly streaked

distinct deep buffy loral spot

white supercilium has black upper border

finely streaked flanks

Pechora Pipit

Anthus gustavi
L 5½"/14cm **WS** 9½"/24cm
Pechora Pipit, which breeds in Siberia and winters in Southeast Asia, has been recorded in North America only on Alaskan islands, but it is a long-distance migrant that may well show up on the Pacific coast in fall. Pechora Pipit skulks mouselike through low vegetation. **VOICE** Call a short, wiry *tdzip*, seldom heard, even from flushed birds.

adult/1st fall

primaries visible beyond tertials (unlike Red-throated)

more warmly colored and boldly marked than Red-throated, including nape

Sky Lark
Alauda arvensis
L 7¼"/18cm **WS** 13"/33cm

One of English literature's most celebrated
birds, Sky Lark was introduced on
Vancouver Island, British Columbia,
in the early 1900s. It is found there in
grassy habitats (especially at the airport)
and agricultural fields. Vagrants of the
more richly colored Asian subspecies
pekinensis have appeared in Pacific
coast states. **VOICE** Song a marvelous,
continuous jumble of sweet, scratchy
notes. Call note a modulated, chortling
trtltrk, sounding less musical and shorter
than call of Horned Lark.

adult, worn — short crest — pale-framed auriculars — short, blunt bill (unlike longspurs, pipits)

adult, fresh — warmer tones overall than in worn birds — "necklace" of neat stipples on breast — (white trailing edge to wings visible in flight) — white outer rectrices (best seen on flying birds)

Horned Lark
Eremophila alpestris
L 7¼"/18cm **WS** 12"/30cm

Horned Lark is the only native lark
that nests in North America. It breeds
in diverse open habitats: fields, dry
tundra, shortgrass prairies, and airports.
Displaying males give their ethereal
song on the wing. Larks eat insects and
in winter form large flocks that forage in
fields on the ground for seeds. **VOICE**
Song a rising, accelerating series of
tinkling notes, hesitant at first, then
gaining momentum. Call similar to song,
a sibilant, soft *see-lipi* or *see*.

adult male — black "horns," facial mark, breastband — upperparts vary in tone from pale sandy-buff to rich rust — most subspecies unstreaked below

juvenile — odd speckled plumage held briefly — easily confused with longspurs

adult female — similar to male but lacks "horns," less richly colored

Appendices

Staff for This Guide

Publisher: Andrew Stewart
Series Editor: Amy K. Hughes
Art Director: Drew Stevens
Project Editor: Pamela Nelson
Photo Editor: Ruth Jeyaveeran
Production: Arthur Riscen
Preproduction: Pre Tech Color, LLC
Copy Editor: Flynne Wiley
Photo/Editorial Assistant: Valerie Kenyon
Editorial Intern: Chloe Hanna
Illustrations: Ed Lam
Chief Map Consultant: Paul Lehman
Range Map Production: Mauricio Rodriguez
Endpaper Map: Ortelius Design

Editorial inquiries may be sent to:
NWF Field Guides
P.O. Box 479
Woodstock, VT 05091

editors@thefieldguideproject.com

Acknowledgments

This book was first suggested and developed by George Scott, past editor-in-chief of Chanticleer Press, with the support of his colleagues, publisher Andrew Stewart and associate publisher Alicia Mills, and in collaboration with Nathaniel Marunas of Barnes & Noble. Charles Nix conceived the beautiful design of the book. Sharp photographic material was provided by VIREO of the Academy of Natural Sciences, Philadelphia, Pennsylvania. VIREO's Douglas Wechsler and Matthew F. Sharp worked minor miracles in locating images of obscure plumages. The project brought together the talents of seasoned veterans in wildlife book publishing: graphic designer and art director Drew Stevens; photography researcher and editor Ruth Jeyaveeran; copy editor Flynne Wiley; production manager Arthur Riscen; series editor Amy K. Hughes; and project editor Pamela Nelson, who took great pains to research, polish, and pare what was often rough and dense prose. Patricia Fogarty and Lois Safrani provided additional editorial and photo research support, respectively. Mike Ferrari, Sharon Bosley, and Betsy Beier of Barnes & Noble offered many helpful suggestions and much encouragement and support. The book's text and captioning were read and edited carefully by consultants Alvaro Jaramillo, Louis R. Bevier, and Paul Lehman—fonts of knowledge about North American bird distribution and identification. Jonathan Alderfer, Jon L. Dunn, Brian L. Sullivan, and Craig Tufts were also kind enough to go through several early drafts of the manuscript and offer many constructive comments for its revision. The author would be happy to receive communication about this book at **campephilus@aol.com.**

Species Range Maps

Overall consultant/map researcher:
Paul Lehman

Regional Experts:
Alabama: Greg Jackson, Steve McConnell
Alaska: Steve Heinl
Arizona: Mark Stevenson
Baja California: Marshall Iliff
British Columbia: Chris Charlesworth, Rick Toochin
California: Don Roberson, John Wilson
Colorado: Peter Gent, Tony Leukering
Georgia: Giff Beaton, Paul W. Sykes, Jr.
Idaho: Charles Trost
Maine: Louis R. Bevier, Derek Lovitch, Bill Sheehan
Minnesota: Kim Eckert
Missouri: Bob Fisher, Mark Robbins

Montana: Terry McEneaney
Nebraska: Stephen J. Dinsmore
Nevada: Ted Floyd
New Brunswick: Brian Dalzell
New Hampshire: Stephen Mirick
New Mexico: John Parmeter
North Carolina: Ricky Davis, Harry LeGrand
North Dakota: Ron Martin
Ohio: Rob Harlan
Oklahoma: Jim Arterburn
Pennsylvania: Nick Pulcinella
Quebec: Pierre Bannon
Texas: Mark Lockwood
Utah: Jerry Ligouri
Washington: Steve Mlodinow
West Virginia: Gary Felton
Wisconsin: John Idzikowski, Larry Semo

Photo Credits

The photographs for each species account are credited clockwise, starting with the top image. Photographs on other pages are listed left to right, top to bottom. The photographs that appear in the table of contents (pp. 6–9) are credited to the page on which they appear in the species accounts.

All photographs are provided by VIREO, The Academy of Natural Sciences, except those indicated by an asterisk (*).

11 Arthur Morris

12 **a** Hanne and Jens Eriksen; **b** Steven Holt

13 **a** Dale and Marian Zimmerman; **b** Rob Curtis

14 **a** Greg Lasley; **b** Arthur Morris

15 Gerard Bailey

16 Arthur Morris

17 George L. Armistead

18 **a** Tom Vezo; **b** Brian Henry; **c** Rick and Nora Bowers

19 **a** Stephen J. Lang; **b** Arthur Morris

20 Arthur Morris

21 **a** Arthur Morris; **b** Garth McElroy

22 Arthur Morris

23 Dale & Marian Zimmerman

24 Michael Giannechini/Photo Researchers, Inc.*

25 Joe Fuhrman

26 Don Grall

27 Doug Wechsler

28 Jim Culbertson

34 **a** Arthur Morris; **b** Tom and Pat Leeson/Photo Researchers, Inc.*; **c** Arthur Morris

35 **a, b** Arthur Morris

36 **Black-bellied Whistling-Duck: a** Arthur Morris; **b** Jim Culbertson; **c** Doug Wechsler

36 **Fulvous Whistling-Duck: a** Arthur Morris; **b** Steven Holt

37 **Wood Duck: a** Joe Fuhrman; **b** Laura C. Gooch; **c** Joe Fuhrman

37 **Muscovy Duck: a** Doug Wechsler; **b** John Heidecker; **c** Rick and Nora Bowers

38 **Mallard: a, b** Arthur Morris; **c** Steven Holt; **d** Arthur Morris; **e** Alan and Sandy Carey

39 **American Black Duck: a** Stephen J. Lang; **b** Georges Dremeaux; **c** Dr. Michael Stubblefield; **d** Michael Godfrey

39 **Mottled Duck:** Tom Vezo

40 **Blue-winged Teal: a** Tom Vezo; **b** Russ Kerr; **c** Arthur Morris

40 **Cinnamon Teal: a** Arthur Morris; **b** Rob Curtis; **c** Arthur Morris

41 **Northern Shoveler: a, b** Tom Vezo; **c** Arthur Morris

41 **Garganey: a, b** Ray Tipper

42 **Gadwall: a** Doug Wechsler; **b** Rick and Nora Bowers

42 **Green-winged Teal: a** Arthur Morris; **b** David Tipling; **c** Mike Danzenbaker

43 **American Wigeon: a** Arthur Morris; **b** Richard Crossley; **c** Arthur Morris

43 **Eurasian Wigeon: a** Arthur Morris; **b** Bob de Lange; **c** Arthur Morris

44 **Northern Pintail: a** Richard and Susan Day; **b** Tom Vezo; **c** Doug Wechsler

44 **White-cheeked Pintail:** Arthur Morris

45 **Canvasback: a, b** John Heidecker

45 **Redhead: a, b** Arthur Morris

46 **Ring-necked Duck: a** Tom Vezo; **b** Arthur Morris

46 **Tufted Duck: a** Tom J. Ulrich; **b** Morten Strange

47 **Greater Scaup: a** Arthur Morris; **b** Johann Schumacher; **c** Arthur Morris

47 **Lesser Scaup: a, b** Arthur Morris; **c** John Heidecker

48 **Common Eider: a, b** Robert Royse; **c** Garth McElroy; **d** Jari Peltomäki; **e** Arthur Morris; **f** George L. Armistead

49 **King Eider: a** Kevin T. Karlson; **b** Earl H. Harrison; **c** Kevin T. Karlson

49 **Spectacled Eider:** Kevin T. Karlson

49 **Steller's Eider:** David Tipling

50 **White-winged Scoter: a** Brian E. Small; **b** Arthur Morris; **c** Dale and Marian Zimmerman

50 **Black Scoter: a** Arthur Morris; **b** George L. Armistead; **c** Arthur Morris

51 **Surf Scoter: a** Arthur Morris; **b** Rob Curtis; **c** Joe Fuhrman

51 **Harlequin Duck: a, b** Doug Wechsler

52 **Common Goldeneye: a, b** Garth McElroy

52 **Barrow's Goldeneye: a** Paul Bannick; **b** Brian E. Small

53 **Long-tailed Duck: a** Arthur Morris; **b** Jari Peltomäki; **c** Arthur Morris; **d, e** Jari Peltomäki; **f** Rob Curtis

54 **Common Merganser: a** Jim Culbertson; **b** John Heidecker

54 **Red-breasted Merganser: a** Arthur Morris; **b** Dr. Michael Stubblefield; **c** Arthur Morris

55 **Hooded Merganser: a** Garth McElroy; **b** Stephanie McCloskey

55 **Bufflehead: a** Tom Vezo; **b, c** Arthur Morris

56 **Ruddy Duck: a** Doug Wechsler; **b** Arthur Morris; **c** Sam Fried

56 **Masked Duck: a, b** Tom Vezo

57 **Brant: a** Doug Wechsler; **b** Stephanie McCloskey; **c** Arthur Morris; **d** Stephanie McCloskey; **e** Johann Schumacher

58 **Canada Goose: a** Arthur Morris; **b** Alan David Walther

58 **Cackling Goose: a** Stephanie McCloskey; **b** Robert Royse

59 **Greater White-fronted Goose: a** Rick and Nora Bowers; **b** Peter LaTourrette; **c** Joe Fuhrman

59 **Barnacle Goose:** Hanne and Jens Eriksen

60 **Snow Goose: a, b, c, d** Arthur Morris; **e** Edward S. Brinkley*

61 **Ross's Goose: a** Rick Mellon; **b, c** Arthur Morris; **d** Christie Van Cleve

61 **Emperor Goose:** Brian E. Small

62 **Tundra Swan: a** Arthur Morris; **b** Steven Holt; **c** David Tipling

62 **(box): a** Line Farr; **b** Sid Lipschultz; **c** Brian Gadsby

63 **Trumpeter Swan: a** Tom Vezo; **b** Rick and Nora Bowers

63 **Mute Swan: a** Steve Young; **b** Arthur Morris

64 **a** (top) Stephen J. Lang; **b** (bottom) Gary Nuechterlein

65 **a** Greg Lasley; **b** Rob Curtis; **c** Dr. Michael Stubblefield; **d** Brian Sullivan; **e** Ronald M. Saldino; **f** Edward S. Brinkley; **g** Jari Peltomäki

66 **Common Loon: a** Stephen J. Lang; **b** Arthur Morris; **c** Joe Fuhrman; **d** Paul Bannick

66 **Yellow-billed Loon: a** Eugene Potapov; **b** Greg Lasley

67 **Pacific Loon: a** Tom Vezo; **b** Arthur Morris; **c** Ronald M. Saldino

67 **Arctic Loon: a** Jari Peltomäki; **b** Rob Curtis; **c** David Tipling

68 **Red-throated Loon: a** Tom Vezo; **b, c** Dr. Michael Stubblefield

68 **Red-necked Grebe: a** Arthur Morris; **b** Kevin T. Karlson

69 **Western Grebe: a** Arthur Morris; **b** Gary Nuechterlein

69 **Clark's Grebe: a** Steven Holt; **b, c** Johann Schumacher

70 **Horned Grebe: a** Arthur Morris; **b** Joe Fuhrman; **c** Brian E. Small

70 **Eared Grebe: a** Arthur Morris; **b** Brian E. Small; **c** Mike Danzenbaker

71 **Pied-billed Grebe: a** Tom Vezo; **b** Arthur Morris

71 **Least Grebe: a** Greg Lasley; **b** Rick and Nora Bowers

72 **a, b** Steven Holt

73 **Black Guillemot: a** Tom J. Ulrich; **b** William Wilson/Photo Researchers, Inc.*; **c** Cathy and Allan Murrant

73 **Pigeon Guillemot: a** Steven Holt; **b** Mike Danzenbaker; **c** Brian Sullivan

74 **Common Murre: a** Arthur Morris; **b** Kevin Schafer; **c** Tom Vezo; **d, e** George L. Armistead

75 **Thick-billed Murre: a** Arthur Morris; **b** Brian E. Small; **c** Edward S. Brinkley

75 **Razorbill: a** David Tipling; **b** Helen Cruickshank; **c** Jari Peltomäki

76 **Marbled Murrelet: a** Casey Tucker; **b** Mike Danzenbaker; **c** Tim Zurowski

76 **Long-billed Murrelet:** Tony Leukering

77 **Dovekie: a** Dan Roby and Karen Brink; **b** Charles D. Duncan; **c** Steve Young

77 **Kittlitz's Murrelet: a** George L. Armistead; **b** Robert H. Day; **c** Tim Zurowski

78 **Xantus's Murrelet: a** Mike Danzenbaker; **b** Charles E. Newell; **c** Mike Danzenbaker

78 **Craveri's Murrelet: a** Don Roberson; **b, c** Brian E. Small

79 **Ancient Murrelet: a** Robert L. Pitman; **b** Mike Danzenbaker; **c** Rick and Nora Bowers

79 **Cassin's Auklet: a** William E. Townsend, Jr./Photo Researchers, Inc.*; **b** Brian Sullivan; **c** Brian E. Small

80 **Crested Auklet:** Arthur Morris

80 **Parakeet Auklet: a** Dan Roby and Karen Brink; **b** George L. Armistead; **c** Brian Sullivan

81 **Whiskered Auklet:** George Vernon Byrd

81 **Least Auklet: a, b** Arthur Morris

82 **Rhinoceros Auklet: a** Jake Faust; **b** Steven Holt

82 **Tufted Puffin: a** Arthur Morris; **b** Mike Danzenbaker

83 **Atlantic Puffin: a** Arthur Morris; **b** Brian Patteson

83 **Horned Puffin: a, b** Arthur Morris

84 **a** Arthur Morris; **b** Sam Fried

85 **a** Fred Truslow; **b, c** Arthur Morris; **d** Eric Preston; **e** Brian Sullivan; **f** Edward S. Brinkley

86 **Brown Pelican: a** Arthur Morris; **b** Brian K. Wheeler

86 **American White Pelican: a** Steven Holt; **b** Peter G. Connors

87 **Red-billed Tropicbird: a** Greg Lasley; **b** Brian Patteson*; **c** Rick and Nora Bowers

87 **White-tailed Tropicbird: a** Eric Preston; **b** Crawford H. Greenewalt; **c** Brian Patteson*

88 **Northern Gannet: a** Dan Roby and Karen Brink; **b** Tom Vezo; **c** George L. Armistead; **d** Edward S. Brinkley; **e** Fred Truslow

89 **Masked Booby: a** Hanne and Jens Eriksen; **b, c** Robert L. Pitman

89 **Blue-footed Booby: a** Tom J. Ulrich; **b** Brian E. Small; **c** Steve Metz

90 **Red-footed Booby: a, b** Robert L. Pitman; **c** Bruce Sorrie; **d, e** Robert L. Pitman; **f** Rick and Nora Bowers

91 **Brown Booby: a** Peter LaTourrette; **b, c** Robert L. Pitman

91 **Magnificent Frigatebird: a** John Cancalosi; **b** Rick and Nora Bowers; **c** Peter LaTourrette

92 **Double-crested Cormorant: a** Rick and Nora Bowers; **b, c, d** Arthur Morris

93 **Neotropic Cormorant: a** Rick and Nora Bowers; **b** Arthur Morris

93 **Great Cormorant: a** John Cancalosi; **b** Arthur Morris

94 **Pelagic Cormorant: a** Arthur Morris; **b** Robert L. Pitman

94 **Brandt's Cormorant: a** Joe Fuhrman; **b** Arthur Morris

95 **Red-faced Cormorant: a** Arthur Morris; **b** Mike Danzenbaker

95 **Anhinga: a; b** Tom Vezo

96 Kevin Schafer

97 **a** Ronald M. Saldino; **b** Edward S. Brinkley; **c** Robert L. Pitman; **d** Helen Cruickshank; **e** Arthur Morris; **f** Alan Tate; **g** Edward S. Brinkley

98 **Laysan Albatross: a, b** Robert L. Pitman

98 **Yellow-nosed Albatross: a** Robert L. Pitman; **b** Alan Tate

99 **Black-footed Albatross: a, b** Robert L. Pitman; **c** Glen Tepke

99 **Short-tailed Albatross: a** Peter Harrison; **b** Kevin Schafer; **c** Brian E. Small

100 **Black-capped Petrel: a, b, c** Brian Patteson

100 **Bermuda Petrel: a, b** Brian Patteson*

101 **Trinidade Petrel: a** George L. Armistead; **b, c** Brian Patteson

101 **Fea's Petrel: a, b** Brian Patteson*

102 **Galapagos/Hawaiian Petrel: a, b** George L. Armistead

102 **Murphy's Petrel: a** Brian E. Small; **b** Rich Pagen/Southwest Fisheries Science Center, NOAA Fisheries*

103 **Mottled Petrel: a, b** Greg Lasley

103 **Cook's Petrel: a** Todd McGrath*; **b** Brian Chudleigh

104 **Manx Shearwater: a, b** Brian Sullivan; **c** Mike Danzenbaker

104 **Audubon's Shearwater: a** Brian Patteson; **b** Robert L. Pitman; **c** Brian Patteson

105 Black-vented Shearwater: a, b Mike Danzenbaker

105 Wedge-tailed Shearwater: a Tony Palliser; **b** Ian Hutton; **c** Robert L. Pitman

106 Pink-footed Shearwater: a Ronald M. Saldino; **b** Greg Lasley

106 Cory's Shearwater: a Brian Patteson; **b** Brian Patteson*

107 Buller's Shearwater: a Tadao Shimba; **b** Mike Danzenbaker

107 Greater Shearwater: a Robert L. Pitman; **b** Serge LaFrance; **c** Rick and Nora Bowers

108 Sooty Shearwater: a Mike Danzenbaker; **b** Greg Lasley; **c** Don Hadden

108 Short-tailed Shearwater: a Rick and Nora Bowers; **b** Mike Danzenbaker

109 Flesh-footed Shearwater: a Don Hadden; **b** Brian E. Small; **c** Brian Sullivan

109 Northern Fulmar: a, b Robert L. Pitman

110 Band-rumped Storm-Petrel: a, b Brian Patteson*

110 Leach's Storm-Petrel: a, b, c Brian Patteson*

111 Wilson's Storm-Petrel: a William Wilson/Photo Researchers, Inc.*; **b, c** Brian Sullivan

111 White-faced Storm-Petrel: Mike Danzenbaker

112 Black Storm-Petrel: a, b Robert L. Pitman

112 Ashy Storm-Petrel: a Mike Danzenbaker; **b** Glen Tepke; **c** Eric Preston

113 Least Storm-Petrel: Brian Sullivan

113 Wedge-rumped Storm-Petrel: George L. Armistead

113 Fork-tailed Storm-Petrel: a, b, c Robert L. Pitman

114 Arthur Morris

115 a (top) Garth McElroy; **b, c** Arthur Morris; **d** Tom Vezo; **e** Greg Lasley

116 Parasitic Jaeger: a, b Arthur Morris; **c, d** Dr. Robert Ricklefs; **e** Herb Clarke

117 Long-tailed Jaeger: a Dan Roby and Karen Brink; **b** Tony Beck; **c** Brian Patteson; **d** Richard Crossley; **e** Brian Patteson; **f** Richard Crossley

118 Pomarine Jaeger: a, b Brian Patteson; **c** Robert L. Pitman; **d** Steve Young; **e, f** Brian Patteson

119 Great Skua: a Brian Patteson; **b** Steve Young; **c** Brian Patteson

119 South Polar Skua: a Rick and Nora Bowers; **b, c** Brian E. Small

120 a Tom Vezo; **b** Rick and Nora Bowers

121 a, b, c, d, e Arthur Morris; **f** Tom Vezo; **g** Arthur Morris; **h** Sam Fried; **i** Arthur Morris

122 Little Gull: a Jari Peltomäki; **b, c** Steve Young

122 Ross's Gull: a Tony Beck; **b** Joe Fuhrman; **c** Tom Vezo

123 Bonaparte's Gull: a Arthur Morris; **b** Tom Vezo; **c** Rick and Nora Bowers

123 Black-headed Gull: a Bob de Lange; **b** Fero Bednar; **c** Arthur Morris

124 Franklin's Gull: a Joe Fuhrman; **b** Brian E. Small; **c** Dr. Robert Ridgely

124 Laughing Gull: a Tom Vezo; **b** George L. Armistead; **c** Arthur Morris

125 Sabine's Gull: a Brian E. Small; **b** Mike Danzenbaker; **c** Peter LaTourrette

125 Black-legged Kittiwake: a Arthur Morris; **b** Andy Papadatos; **c** Arthur Morris

126 Ring-billed Gull: a, b, c Arthur Morris

126 Mew Gull: a Rick and Nora Bowers; **b** Thomas Grey; **c** Arthur Morris

127 California Gull: a Allan Cruickshank; **b** Brian E. Small; **c** Arthur Morris

127 Herring Gull: a Arthur Morris; **b** Mike Danzenbaker; **c** Arthur Morris

128 Glaucous Gull: a Arthur Morris; **b** George L. Armistead; **c** Marvin R. Hyett, M.D.

128 Glaucous-winged Gull: a Rob Curtis; **b** Martin Hale; **c** Rick and Nora Bowers

129 Iceland Gull: a Garth McElroy; **b** Marvin R. Hyett, M.D.; **c** Tony Beck

129 Thayer's Gull: a Robert Behrstock; **b** Mike Danzenbaker; **c** Earl W. Horn*

130 Western Gull: a, b, c Arthur Morris

130 Yellow-footed Gull: Tom Vezo

131 Great Black-backed Gull: a, b Arthur Morris

131 Lesser Black-backed Gull: a John Cancalosi; **b** Arthur Morris; **c** George L. Armistead

132 Ivory Gull: a Hanne and Jens Eriksen; **b** Alan Tate; **c** Harry Darrow

132 Heermann's Gull: a, b, c Arthur Morris

133 Rare Gulls: a Robin Chittenden; **b** George L. Armistead; **c** Brian E. Small; **d** Dr. Pyong-Oh Won

134 Brown Noddy: a Fred Truslow; **b** Robert L. Pitman

134 Black Noddy: a Mike Danzenbaker; **b** Robert L. Pitman

135 Sooty Tern: a Tom J. Ulrich; **b** Alan Tate; **c, d** Robert L. Pitman

135 Bridled Tern: a, b, c Brian Patteson

136 Black Tern: a Brian E. Small; **b** Tony Leukering; **c** Robert L. Pitman

136 White-winged Tern: a Garth McElroy; **b** Morten Strange; **c** Ray Tipper

137 a Tom Vezo; **b** Doug Wechsler; **c** Garth McElroy; **d** Arthur Morris

138 Royal Tern: a, b, c Arthur Morris

138 Elegant Tern: a Arthur Morris; **b** Frank Schleicher; **c** Stephanie McCloskey

139 Caspian Tern: a Helen Cruickshank; **b** Serge LaFrance; **c** Arthur Morris

139 Sandwich Tern: a Rick and Nora Bowers; **b, c** Arthur Morris

140 Common Tern: a, b, c, d Arthur Morris

140 Forster's Tern: a Gerard Bailey; **b, c** Arthur Morris

141 Arctic Tern: a Arthur Morris; **b** Barry Miller; **c** Arthur Morris; **d** Brian Chudleigh

141 Roseate Tern: a Dr. Michael Stubblefield; **b** Kevin T. Karlson; **c** Arthur Morris

142 Gull-billed Tern: a Jim Culbertson; **b** Hanne and Jens Eriksen; **c** Kevin T. Karlson

142 Aleutian Tern: a Dale R. Herter; **b** Doug Wechsler

143 Least Tern: a Marvin R. Hyett, M.D.; **b** Herb Clarke; **c** Arthur Morris

143 Black Skimmer: a Arthur Morris; **b** Tom Vezo; **c** Arthur Morris

144 a (top) John Heidecker; **b (bottom)** Dr. M. Philip Kahl

145 a (top) Doug Wechsler; **b (bottom)** Arthur Morris

146 Great Blue Heron: a Rob Curtis; **b, c, d, e** Arthur Morris; **f** Fred Truslow

147 Sandhill Crane: a, b, c Arthur Morris

147 Great Egret: Arthur Morris

148 Snowy Egret: a Arthur Morris; **b** Joe Fuhrman

148 Little Egret: a Peter Davey ARPS; **b** Hanne and Jens Eriksen; **c** Dr. Warwick Tarboton

149 Little Blue Heron: a, b, c Arthur Morris

149 Cattle Egret: a, b Arthur Morris; **c** Steve Young

150 Tricolored Heron: a, b, c Arthur Morris

150 Green Heron: a Tom Vezo; **b** James R. Woodward

151 Reddish Egret: a Tom Vezo; **b, c, d, e, f** Arthur Morris

152 American Bittern: a Gerard Bailey; **b** Dwight Sokoll

152 Least Bittern: a Tom Vezo; **b** Fred Truslow

153 Black-crowned Night-Heron: a Hanne and Jens Eriksen; **b** Arthur Morris; **c** Johann Schumacher

153 Yellow-crowned Night-Heron: a, b Arthur Morris

154 White Ibis: a, b, c Arthur Morris

154 Limpkin: Arthur Morris

155 Glossy Ibis: a James R. Woodward; **b** Dr. Michael Stubblefield; **c** Arthur Morris

155 White-faced Ibis: Arthur Morris

156 Roseate Spoonbill: a, b Arthur Morris

156 American Flamingo: a Patricio Robles Gil; **b** Frank Schleicher; **c** Dr. M. Philip Kahl

157 Wood Stork: a, b, c Arthur Morris

157 Whooping Crane: a Greg Lasley; **b, c** Joanne Williams

158 David Tipling

159 Black Rail: a Peter LaTourrette; **b** Mike Danzenbaker

159 Yellow Rail: a Jacques Brisson; **b** Matt White; **c** Brian E. Small

160 Sora: a Joe Fuhrman; **b** Rob Curtis

160 Virginia Rail: a Stephen J. Lang; **b** Harold Stiver; **c** Brian E. Small

161 Clapper Rail: a Scott Elowitz; **b** Rob and Ann Simpson; **c** Peter LaTourrette

161 King Rail: a Arthur Morris; **b** Earl H. Harrison

162 Common Moorhen: a, b, c Arthur Morris

162 American Coot: a Fred Truslow; **b** Arthur Morris; **c** Hugh P. Smith, Jr., and Susan C. Smith

163 Purple Gallinule: a, b Arthur Morris

163 Purple Swamphen: David Tipling

164 a (top) Rick and Nora Bowers; **b (bottom)** Kevin Smith

165 a Doug Wechsler; **b** Arthur Morris; **c** Jorge Sierra; **d** Arthur Morris

166 Northern Bobwhite: a, b Arthur Morris

166 Montezuma Quail: a Tom Vezo; **b** Sid and Shirley Rucker

167 Chukar: Andy Papadatos

167 Gray Partridge: Bob de Lange

168 Gambel's Quail: a Tom Vezo; **b** Dr. M. Philip Kahl

168 California Quail: a John Hoffman; **b** Hugh P. Smith, Jr., and Susan C. Smith

169 Scaled Quail: a, b Tom Vezo

169 Mountain Quail: a, b Ronald M. Saldino

170 Willow Ptarmigan: a, b Arthur Morris; **c** Richard and Susan Day; **d** Rick and Nora Bowers; **e** Peter G. Connors

171 Rock Ptarmigan: a Ronald M. Saldino; **b** Dr. Pete Myers

171 White-tailed Ptarmigan: a Tom J. Ulrich; **b** Georges Dremeaux

172 Spruce Grouse: a Warren Greene; **b** Michael Patrikeev

172 Dusky Grouse: a Brian E. Small; **b** Bob de Lange

173 Ruffed Grouse: a Frank Schleicher; **b** Michael Patrikeev; **c** Tom J. Ulrich

173 Himalayan Snowcock: James D. Bland

174 Greater Prairie-Chicken: a, b Richard and Susan Day

174 Lesser Prairie-Chicken: a Sam Fried; **b** Mike Danzenbaker

175 Sharp-tailed Grouse: a John Cancalosi; **b** Brian E. Small

175 Ring-necked Pheasant: a, b Tom Vezo

176 Greater Sage-Grouse: a John Cancalosi; **b** Tom Vezo

176 Gunnison Sage-Grouse: Lance Beeny

177 Wild Turkey: a Richard and Susan Day; **b** Andy Papadatos

177 Plain Chachalaca: a Earl H. Harrison; **b** Rick and Nora Bowers

178 a (top) John Cancalosi; **b (bottom)** William S. Clark

179 a (top) Rob Curtis; **b (bottom)** Tom J. Ulrich

180 a, b, c Brian K. Wheeler; **d** Brian E. Small; **e, f** Brian K. Wheeler

181 a, b, c, d, e, f Brian K. Wheeler

182 Turkey Vulture: a, b Arthur Morris; **c** Brian K. Wheeler

182 Black Vulture: a, b Brian K. Wheeler

183 California Condor: a Fred Truslow; **b** Christie Van Cleve; **c** Serge LaFrance

183 Osprey: a Dr. Michael Stubblefield; **b** Tom Vezo

184 Northern Harrier: a, b, c Brian K. Wheeler; **d** Jim Zipp; **e** Brian K. Wheeler

185 Crested Caracara: a Brian K. Wheeler; **b** Joanne Williams

185 Hook-billed Kite: a Mike Danzenbaker; **b, c** Brian K. Wheeler

186 Swallow-tailed Kite: a Brian K. Wheeler; **b** Kevin T. Karlson

186 Snail Kite: a, b Brian K. Wheeler; **c** Joanne Williams

187 Mississippi Kite: a Brian K. Wheeler; **b** Brian E. Small; **c** Brian K. Wheeler

187 White-tailed Kite: a Rick and Nora Bowers; **b** Brian K. Wheeler

188 Northern Goshawk: a Doug R. Herr; **b** Richard and Susan Day; **c** Brian K. Wheeler

189 Cooper's Hawk: a, b, c Brian K. Wheeler

189 Sharp-shinned Hawk: a, b, c Brian K. Wheeler

231 Rock Sandpiper: a, b Brian E. Small

231 Purple Sandpiper: a Doug Wechsler; **b** Dr. Michael Stubblefield

232 Dunlin: a Doug Wechsler; **b** Steve Greer

232 Curlew Sandpiper: a Michael P. Gage; **b** Steve Young; **c** Brian Chudleigh

233 Stilt Sandpiper: a Arthur Morris; **b** Rick and Nora Bowers; **c** Arthur Morris

233 Red Knot: a Doug Wechsler; **b, c** Arthur Morris

234 Red-necked Phalarope: a Arthur Morris; **b** Peter LaTourrette; **c** Arthur Morris

234 Wilson's Phalarope: a Arthur Morris; **b** Joseph Jehl, Jr.; **c** Arthur Morris

235 Red Phalarope: a Dan Roby and Karen Brink; **b** Peter LaTourrette; **c** Bob Steele

235 Sanderling: a Arthur Morris; **b** Philip D. Moylan; **c** Arthur Morris

236 Short-billed Dowitcher: (clockwise from top left) a John Heidecker; **b, c, d** Arthur Morris

236 Long-billed Dowitcher: a, b Arthur Morris; **c** Jim Culbertson

237 Wilson's Snipe: a Arthur Morris; **b** Alan David Walther

237 American Woodcock: a Rob Curtis; **b** Stephen J. Lang

238 American Avocet: a Tom Vezo; **b** Frank Schleicher; **c** Arthur Morris

238 Black-necked Stilt: Arthur Morris

239 Steven Holt

240 Band-tailed Pigeon: a Arthur Morris; **b** Hugh P. Smith, Jr., and Susan C. Smith; **c** Ronald M. Saldino

240 Rock Pigeon: a Hanne and Jens Eriksen; **b, c** Doug Wechsler

241 White-crowned Pigeon: a Ronald M. Saldino; **b** Paula Cannon

241 Red-billed Pigeon: a Harold Stiver; **b** Kevin T. Karlson

242 Mourning Dove: a, b Tom Vezo; **c** Arthur Morris

242 Spotted Dove: a Joe Fuhrman; **b** James Gallagher

243 White-winged Dove: a, b, c Tom Vezo

243 Eurasian Collared-Dove: a Kevin T. Karlson; **b** Jari Peltomäki; **c** Mike Danzenbaker

244 Common Ground-Dove: a Tom Vezo; **b** Rick and Nora Bowers; **c** Brian E. Small

244 Ruddy Ground-Dove: a Mike Danzenbaker; **b** Joe Fuhrman

245 Inca Dove: a Dale and Marian Zimmerman; **b** Gerald C. Kelley/Photo Researchers, Inc.*

245 White-tipped Dove: a Rob Curtis; **b** Marvin R. Hyett, M.D.

246 a (top) Steven Holt; **b (bottom)** Rob Curtis

247 Red-crowned Parrot: Herb Clarke

247 Red-lored Parrot: a Tom J. Ulrich; **b** Rick and Nora Bowers

247 Yellow-headed Parrot: a Gerald C. Kelley/Photo Researchers, Inc.*; **b** Rick and Nora Bowers

248 White-fronted Parrot: Patricio Robles Gil

248 Thick-billed Parrot: Rick and Nora Bowers

248 Monk Parakeet: Marvin R. Hyett, M.D.

249 Green Parakeet: Greg Lasley

249 White-winged Parakeet: Jany Sauvanet/Photo Researchers, Inc.*

249 Yellow-chevroned Parakeet: John Dunning

250 Michael Patrikeev

251 Groove-billed Ani: Jim Culbertson

251 Smooth-billed Ani: Steven Holt

252 Black-billed Cuckoo: a, b Arthur Morris

252 Yellow-billed Cuckoo: a Tom J. Ulrich; **b** Magill Weber

253 Mangrove Cuckoo: Marvin R. Hyett, M.D.

253 Greater Roadrunner: a Arthur Morris; **b** Rick and Nora Bowers

254 a (top) Warren Greene; **b (bottom)** Charles A. Heidecker

255 a (top) Rick and Nora Bowers; **b (bottom)** Brian E. Small

256 Barn Owl: a Marvin R. Hyett, M.D.; **b** Arthur Morris; **c** Carl D. Marti; **d** Tom Vezo

257 Short-eared Owl: a Warren Greene; **b** Garth McElroy

257 Long-eared Owl: Stephen J. Lang

258 Great Horned Owl: a, b Tom J. Ulrich; **c** Alan and Sandy Carey; **d** John Cancalosi

259 Great Gray Owl: Warren Greene

259 Snowy Owl: a Hanne and Jens Eriksen; **b, c** Warren Greene

260 Barred Owl: Warren Greene

260 Spotted Owl: John Cancalosi

261 Boreal Owl: a Warren Greene; **b** Dan Roby and Karen Brink

261 Northern Saw-whet Owl: a Warren Greene; **b** Alan Brady

262 Elf Owl: Rob Curtis

262 Flammulated Owl: a Alan and Sandy Carey; **b, c** Rick and Nora Bowers

263 Northern Pygmy-Owl: a Joe Fuhrman; **b** Alan and Sandy Carey

263 Ferruginous Pygmy-Owl: Tom Vezo

263 Northern Hawk Owl: Brian Henry

264 Eastern Screech-Owl: a Rob and Ann Simpson; **b** Brian Henry; **c** James R. Woodward

264 Burrowing Owl: a Arthur Morris; **b** Tom Vezo; **c** Sam Fried

265 Western Screech-Owl: Joe Fuhrman

265 Whiskered Screech-Owl: Joe Fuhrman

266 Common Nighthawk: a Allan Cruickshank; **b** Rob Curtis; **c** Steven Holt

266 Antillean Nighthawk: a Joe Fuhrman; **b** Mike Danzenbaker

267 Lesser Nighthawk: a Sam Fried; **b** Andy Papadatos; **c** Rob Curtis

267 Common Poorwill: a, b Rick and Nora Bowers

268 Whip-poor-will: a Warren Greene; **b** Arthur Morris; **c** Rick and Nora Bowers

268 Buff-collared Nightjar: Rick and Nora Bowers

269 Chuck-will's-widow: a Joe Fuhrman; **b** Rob and Ann Simpson

269 Common Pauraque: a Rick and Nora Bowers; **b** John Hoffman

270 (intro) Rick and Nora Bowers

270 Green Kingfisher: a John Dunning; **b** Rick and Nora Bowers

All photographs provided by VIREO (except those marked *).

271 Belted Kingfisher: a Rick and Nora Bowers; **b** John Heidecker; **c** Tom Vezo

271 Ringed Kingfisher: a, b Tom J. Ulrich

272 Elegant Trogon: a Rick and Nora Bowers; **b** Sid and Shirley Rucker; **c** Rick and Nora Bowers

272 Eared Quetzal: a Rick and Nora Bowers; **b** Brian E. Small

273 (intro) Fred Truslow

273 Ivory-billed Woodpecker: John Cancalosi

274 Acorn Woodpecker: a, b Tom Vezo

274 White-headed Woodpecker: a, b Brian E. Small

275 Red-headed Woodpecker: a Richard and Susan Day; **b** Arthur Morris

275 Lewis's Woodpecker: a, b Joe Fuhrman

276 Red-bellied Woodpecker: a Brian Henry; **b** Stephen J. Lang

276 Gila Woodpecker: a John Cancalosi; **b** Rick and Nora Bowers

277 Golden-fronted Woodpecker: a Tom Vezo; **b** Mike Danzenbaker

277 Arizona Woodpecker: a Mike Danzenbaker; **b** Ronald M. Saldino

278 Yellow-bellied Sapsucker: a Brian E. Small; **b** Richard and Susan Day; **c** James R. Woodward

278 Red-naped Sapsucker: a Joe Fuhrman; **b** Bob Steele

279 Red-breasted Sapsucker: a Betty Randall; **b** Paul Bannick; **c** Brian E. Small

279 Williamson's Sapsucker: a Betty Randall; **b** Joe Fuhrman

280 Hairy Woodpecker: a Richard and Susan Day; **b** Frank Schleicher; **c** Joe Fuhrman

281 Downy Woodpecker: a Richard and Susan Day; **b** Tom Vezo

281 Red-cockaded Woodpecker: a, b Stephen G. Maka

282 Black-backed Woodpecker: a, b Joe Fuhrman

282 American Three-toed Woodpecker: a George L. Armistead; **b** Brian E. Small

283 Nuttall's Woodpecker: a, b Hugh P. Smith, Jr., and Susan C. Smith

283 Ladder-backed Woodpecker: a, b Joe Fuhrman

284 Northern Flicker: a Arthur Morris; **b** Fred Truslow; **c** Joe Fuhrman; **d** Rick and Nora Bowers

285 Gilded Flicker: a, b Tom Vezo

285 Pileated Woodpecker: a Johann Schumacher; **b** Paul Bannick

286 Sidney W. Dunkle

287 a Robert Shantz; **b** Jim McKinney; **c** Brian Sullivan; **d** Scott Elowitz; **e** Kevin Smith

288 White-throated Swift: a Herb Clarke; **b** Brian E. Small; **c** Mike Danzenbaker

288 Black Swift: a Bill Schmoker; **b** Tom J. Ulrich; **c** Mike Danzenbaker

289 Chimney Swift: a Rick and Nora Bowers; **b** Julian Hough

289 Vaux's Swift: a Tony Beck; **b** Mike Danzenbaker

290 Purple Martin: a Tom Vezo; **b** Kevin T. Karlson; **c** Joe Fuhrman; **d** W. A. Paff

290 Barn Swallow: a Mike Danzenbaker; **b** Rob and Ann Simpson; **c** Marvin R. Hyett, M.D.; **d** Doug Wechsler

291 Cave Swallow: a Rick and Nora Bowers; **b** Brian Sullivan

291 Cliff Swallow: a Dale and Marian Zimmerman; **b** Peter LaTourrette; **c** Rolf Nussbaumer

292 Northern Rough-winged Swallow: a Greg Lasley; **b** Robert Shantz; **c** Joe Fuhrman

292 Bank Swallow: a Herb Clarke; **b** Joe Fuhrman; **c** Rob and Ann Simpson

293 Tree Swallow: a Arthur Morris; **b** Mike Danzenbaker; **c** Rick and Nora Bowers

293 Violet-green Swallow: a Joe Fuhrman; **b** Mike Danzenbaker; **c** Brian K. Wheeler

294 Richard and Susan Day

295 a Brian E. Small; **b** Kevin T. Karlson; **c** Rick and Nora Bowers; **d** Rob Curtis; **e, f** Rick and Nora Bowers

296 Ruby-throated Hummingbird: a Bob Steele; **b** Sid and Shirley Rucker; **c** Warren Greene

296 Black-chinned Hummingbird: a Dale and Marian Zimmerman; **b** Dan True; **c** Rick and Nora Bowers

297 Costa's Hummingbird: a Dan True; **b** Rick and Nora Bowers

297 Anna's Hummingbird: a, b, c Hugh P. Smith, Jr., and Susan C. Smith

298 Rufous Hummingbird: a Hugh P. Smith, Jr., and Susan C. Smith; **b** Dan True

298 Allen's Hummingbird: a Joe Fuhrman; **b** Rick and Nora Bowers; **c** Joe Fuhrman

299 Broad-tailed Hummingbird: a Dan True; **b** Crawford H. Greenewalt; **c** Sid and Shirley Rucker

299 Calliope Hummingbird: a Sid and Shirley Rucker; **b** Dale and Marian Zimmerman; **c** Sid and Shirley Rucker

300 Broad-billed Hummingbird: a Betty Randall; **b** Rick and Nora Bowers; **c** Betty Randall

300 White-eared Hummingbird: a, b Dan True

301 Violet-crowned Hummingbird: Dan True

301 Buff-bellied Hummingbird: Greg Lasley

301 Berylline Hummingbird: Sid and Shirley Rucker

302 Magnificent Hummingbird: a, b Robert Potts

302 Blue-throated Hummingbird: a Robert Potts; **b** Arthur Morris

303 Green Violet-ear: a Tom J. Ulrich; **b** Rick and Nora Bowers

303 Lucifer Hummingbird: a Rick and Nora Bowers; **b** Dan True

304 Brian Sullivan

305 a Brian E. Small; **b, c** Arthur Morris; **d** Joe Fuhrman; **e** John Dunning

306 Greater Pewee: a, b Rick and Nora Bowers

306 Olive-sided Flycatcher: a, b Brian E. Small; **c** O. S. Pettingill, Jr.

307 Eastern Wood-Pewee: a, b, c Arthur Morris

307 Western Wood-Pewee: a Joe Fuhrman; **b** Brian E. Small

308 Yellow-bellied Flycatcher: a, b, c Arthur Morris

308 Acadian Flycatcher: a Stephen J. Lang; **b** Doug Wechsler

309 Pacific-slope Flycatcher: a Brian E. Small; **b** Hugh P. Smith, Jr., and Susan C. Smith

309 Cordilleran Flycatcher: a Brian E. Small; **b** Rick and Nora Bowers

310 Least Flycatcher: a, b Greg Lasley

310 Northern Beardless-Tyrannulet: a, b Rick and Nora Bowers

311 Alder Flycatcher: a, b Fred Truslow

311 Willow Flycatcher: a Brian Henry; **b** Joe Fuhrman

312 Dusky Flycatcher: a Rick and Nora Bowers; **b** Betty Randall

312 Hammond's Flycatcher: a Brian E. Small; **b** Dale and Marian Zimmerman; **c** Dr. Michael Stubblefield

313 Gray Flycatcher: a Rick and Nora Bowers; **b** Brian E. Small

313 Buff-breasted Flycatcher: a Brian E. Small; **b** Rick and Nora Bowers

314 Eastern Phoebe: a Arthur Morris; **b** Philip D. Moylan

314 Black Phoebe: a Joe Fuhrman; **b** Alan David Walther

315 Say's Phoebe: Tom J. Ulrich

315 Vermilion Flycatcher: a Hugh P. Smith, Jr., and Susan C. Smith; **b** Dr. Michael Stubblefield; **c** Rick and Nora Bowers

316 Great Crested Flycatcher: a Warren Greene; **b** Arthur Morris

316 Brown-crested Flycatcher: a Greg Lasley; **b** Dr. Michael Stubblefield

317 Ash-throated Flycatcher: a Joe Fuhrman; **b** Hugh P. Smith, Jr., and Susan C. Smith

317 Dusky-capped Flycatcher: a, b Rick and Nora Bowers

318 Western Kingbird: a Brian E. Small; **b** Tony Beck

318 Cassin's Kingbird: a Rick and Nora Bowers; **b** Peter LaTourrette

319 Couch's Kingbird: a Arthur Morris; **b** Richard and Susan Day

319 Tropical Kingbird: a Joe Fuhrman; **b** Tom J. Ulrich

320 Eastern Kingbird: a Warren Greene; **b** Rick and Nora Bowers

320 Rose-throated Becard: a, b Brian E. Small; **c** Antonio Hidalgo

321 Gray Kingbird: a John Dunning; **b** Brian E. Small; **c** Kevin T. Karlson

321 Thick-billed Kingbird: a, b Brian E. Small

322 Fork-tailed Flycatcher: a Tom J. Ulrich; **b** Richard Crossley

322 Scissor-tailed Flycatcher: a Brian E. Small; **b** Greg Lasley

323 Great Kiskadee: a Tom Vezo; **b** Jim Culbertson

323 Sulphur-bellied Flycatcher: a Brian E. Small; **b** John Dunning

324 Rob Curtis

325 Loggerhead Shrike: a Johann Schumacher; **b** Kevin T. Karlson

325 Northern Shrike: a Dan Roby and Karen Brink; **b** Scott Elowitz; **c** Bob Steele

326 a (top) Arthur Morris; **b (bottom)** Sid Lipschultz

327 Bell's Vireo: a John Hoffman; **b** Robert Royse

327 Gray Vireo: a Greg Lasley; **b** Brian E. Small

328 Philadelphia Vireo: a Brian E. Small; **b** Garth McElroy

328 Warbling Vireo: a Joe Fuhrman; **b** Herb Clarke

329 Red-eyed Vireo: a Brian E. Small; **b** Arthur Morris

329 Yellow-green Vireo: Doug Wechsler

329 Black-whiskered Vireo: John Dunning

330 Blue-headed Vireo: a John Heidecker; **b** Warren Greene

330 (box): a Garth McElroy; **b** Brian E. Small; **c** Rick and Nora Bowers

331 Cassin's Vireo: a, b Brian E. Small

331 Plumbeous Vireo: a Rick and Nora Bowers; **b** Bob Steele

332 Yellow-throated Vireo: a John Dunning; **b** Rick and Nora Bowers

332 White-eyed Vireo: a Rob Curtis; **b** Brian E. Small

333 Black-capped Vireo: a Rick and Nora Bowers; **b** Greg Lasley

333 Hutton's Vireo: a Rick and Nora Bowers; **b** Joe Fuhrman; **c** Peter LaTourrette

334 Doug Wechsler

335 Brian Henry

336 Tufted Titmouse: a Tom Vezo; **b** Johann Schumacher

336 Black-crested Titmouse: Arthur Morris

336 Bridled Titmouse: Tom J. Ulrich

337 Oak Titmouse: a Joe Fuhrman; **b** Hugh P. Smith, Jr., and Susan C. Smith

337 Juniper Titmouse: a Georges Dremeaux; **b** Rick and Nora Bowers

338 Black-capped Chickadee: a Arthur Morris; **b** Tom Vezo

338 Carolina Chickadee: a, b Nathan Barnes

339 Mountain Chickadee: a, b Ronald M. Saldino

339 Mexican Chickadee: a Doug Wechsler; **b** Bob Steele

340 Boreal Chickadee: a Garth McElroy; **b** Jim Culbertson

340 Gray-headed Chickadee: a David Tipling; **b** Aaron Lang

341 Chestnut-backed Chickadee: a Tom J. Ulrich; **b** Arthur Morris; **c** Brian E. Small; **d** Rick and Nora Bowers; **e** Peter LaTourrette; **f** Brian E. Small

342 White-breasted Nuthatch: a Tom Vezo; **b** Rob Curtis

342 Pygmy Nuthatch: Rob Curtis

343 Red-breasted Nuthatch: a Warren Greene; **b** Richard Crossley

343 Brown-headed Nuthatch: a, b Fred Truslow

344 Wrentit: a Peter LaTourrette; **b** Brian E. Small

344 Brown Creeper: Brian Henry

345 Bushtit: a John Hoffman; **b** Rick and Nora Bowers; **c** Peter LaTourrette

345 Verdin: a Arthur Morris; **b** Rick and Nora Bowers

346 a (top) Rob Curtis; **b (bottom)** Rick and Nora Bowers

347 American Dipper: a Brian E. Small; **b** Kevin T. Karlson

347 Cactus Wren: Tom Vezo

348 House Wren: a James M. Wedge; **b** Richard and Susan Day; **c** Edward S. Brinkley

348 Winter Wren: a Arthur Morris; **b** Dr. Michael Stubblefield

349 Carolina Wren: a Gerard Bailey; **b** Crawford H. Greenewalt

349 Bewick's Wren: a Joe Fuhrman; **b** Sid and Shirley Rucker

350 Sedge Wren: a Brian E. Small; **b** Mike Danzenbaker

350 Marsh Wren: a James Zipp/Photo Researchers, Inc.*; **b, c** Steve Greer

351 Canyon Wren: a Rick and Nora Bowers; **b** Bob Steele

All photographs provided by VIREO (except those marked *).

351 Rock Wren: a, b Rick and Nora Bowers

352 a Bob Steele; **b** John Henry Dick

353 a Bob Steele; **b** John Heidecker

354 a Arthur Morris; **b** Brian E. Small; **c** Greg Lasley; **d** John Heidecker; **e** Bob Steele

355 a Johann Schumacher; **b** Garth McElroy; **c, d** Joe Fuhrman; **e** John Hoffman

356 Ruby-crowned Kinglet: a Dr. Michael Stubblefield; **b** Rob and Ann Simpson; **c** Joe Fuhrman

356 Golden-crowned Kinglet: a Brian E. Small; **b** Arthur Morris

357 Arctic Warbler: a Doug Wechsler; **b** Tom Vezo

357 Dusky Warbler: David Tipling

357 Golden-crowned Warbler: Steven Holt

358 Blue-gray Gnatcatcher: a Bob Steele; **b** Brian E. Small

358 Black-tailed Gnatcatcher: a Doug Wechsler; **b** Joe Fuhrman; **c** Doug Wechsler

359 California Gnatcatcher: a Herb Clarke; **b** Joe Fuhrman; **c** Brian E. Small

359 Black-capped Gnatcatcher: a, b Christian Artuso

360 Blue-winged Warbler: a Rob and Ann Simpson; **b** Gerard Bailey; **c** Jim Zipp; **d** Arthur Morris; **e** Rick and Nora Bowers

361 Golden-winged Warbler: a, b Barth Schorre

361 Olive Warbler: a John Hoffman; **b** Mike Danzenbaker; **c** Jim Culbertson

362 Orange-crowned Warbler: a Rick and Nora Bowers; **b** Rob Curtis; **c** Joe Fuhrman; **d** Brian E. Small; **e** Joe Fuhrman

363 Tennessee Warbler: a Barth Schorre; **b** Doug Wechsler

363 Yellow Warbler: a Arthur Morris; **b** Lee F. Snyder/Photo Researchers, Inc.*; **c** Joe Fuhrman

364 Virginia's Warbler: a, b Dale and Marian Zimmerman

364 Colima Warbler: a Rick and Nora Bowers; **b** Mike Danzenbaker

365 Nashville Warbler: a Herb Clarke; **b** Joe Fuhrman

365 Lucy's Warbler: a Rick and Nora Bowers; **b** Brian E. Small

366 Mourning Warbler: a, b Rick and Nora Bowers

366 MacGillivray's Warbler: a Rick and Nora Bowers; **b** Brian E. Small; **c** Joe Fuhrman

367 Common Yellowthroat: a Gerard Bailey; **b** Barth Schorre; **c** Johann Schumacher

367 Connecticut Warbler: a Rob Curtis; **b** John Dunning

368 Gray-crowned Yellowthroat: a Jim Culbertson; **b** Greg Lasley

368 Wilson's Warbler: a Peter LaTourrette; **b** Brian E. Small

369 Kentucky Warbler: a Nathan Barnes; **b** Gerard Bailey

369 Hooded Warbler: (clockwise from top left) a Rob and Ann Simpson; **b** Arthur Morris; **c** Brian E. Small

370 Prothonotary Warbler: a Brian Sullivan; **b** Gerard Bailey

370 Yellow-breasted Chat: a Arthur Morris; **b** Rick and Nora Bowers

371 Swainson's Warbler: a, b Doug Wechsler

371 Worm-eating Warbler: a Rob Curtis; **b** John Trott

372 Northern Parula: a Brian E. Small; **b** Gerard Bailey; **c** Johann Schumacher

372 Crescent-chested Warbler: E. F. Knights

373 Tropical Parula: a Brian E. Small; **b** Arthur Grosset

373 Black-throated Blue Warbler: a, b Gerard Bailey; **c** Brian E. Small

374 American Redstart: a Gerard Bailey; **b** John Heidecker; **c** Gerard Bailey

374 Painted Redstart: a Rick and Nora Bowers; **b** Sid and Shirley Rucker

375 Red-faced Warbler: Rick and Nora Bowers

375 Fan-tailed Warbler: Jim Zipp

375 Slate-throated Redstart: Rick and Nora Bowers

375 Rufous-capped Warbler: Rick and Nora Bowers

376 Canada Warbler: a Rick and Nora Bowers; **b** Barth Schorre

376 Cerulean Warbler: a Barth Schorre; **b** Brian E. Small

377 Kirtland's Warbler: a Robert Royse; **b** Dale and Marian Zimmerman; **c** Roger Eriksson

377 Prairie Warbler: (clockwise from top left) a Doug Wechsler; **b** Brian Henry; **c, d** Sam Fried

378 Pine Warbler: a Doug Wechsler; **b** James M. Wedge; **c** Doug Wechsler; **d, e** James M. Wedge

379 Palm Warbler: a Mike Danzenbaker; **b** Garth McElroy; **c** Dr. Michael Stubblefield; **d, e, f** Arthur Morris

380 Blackpoll Warbler: a Arthur Morris; **b** James M. Wedge; **c** Brian E. Small; **d** Robert Royse; **e** Brian E. Small

381 Bay-breasted Warbler: a Michael Patrikeev; **b** Doug Wechsler; **c** Brian E. Small; **d** Mike Danzenbaker; **e** John Dunning

382 Chestnut-sided Warbler: a, b Arthur Morris; **c** Gerard Bailey

382 Blackburnian Warbler: a Arthur Morris; **b** John Trott; **c** James M. Wedge

383 Yellow-throated Warbler: a Barth Schorre; **b** Brian E. Small

383 Grace's Warbler: a John Hoffman; **b** Rick and Nora Bowers

384 Yellow-rumped Warbler: a Arthur Morris; **b** Joe Fuhrman; **c** Rick and Nora Bowers; **d** Gerard Bailey

384 Black-throated Gray Warbler: Joe Fuhrman

385 Magnolia Warbler: a Arthur Morris; **b** Brian Henry; **c** Gerard Bailey

385 Cape May Warbler: a Robert Royse; **b** Arthur Morris; **c** Johann Schumacher

386 Townsend's Warbler: a Herb Clarke; **b** Joe Fuhrman; **c** Rick and Nora Bowers

386 Black-throated Green Warbler: a Arthur Morris; **b** John Heidecker; **c** Gerard Bailey

387 Hermit Warbler: a Brian Sullivan; **b, c** Brian E. Small

387 Golden-cheeked Warbler: a Greg Lasley; **b** Sid and Shirley Rucker

388 Ovenbird: a Brian E. Small; **b** Tom Vezo; **c** Gerard Bailey

388 Black-and-white Warbler: a Gerard Bailey; **b** Barth Schorre

389 Northern Waterthrush: a Brian E. Small; **b** Rick and Nora Bowers

389 Louisiana Waterthrush: a Rob Curtis; **b** Doug Wechsler

390 Steve Greer

391 Northern Wheatear: a, b Doug Wechsler; **c** Arthur Morris

391 Bluethroat: a Tom Vezo; **b** Doug Wechsler

392 Eastern Bluebird: a James M. Wedge; **b** Richard and Susan Day; **c** Brian Henry

392 Western Bluebird: a Arthur Morris; **b** Hugh P. Smith, Jr., and Susan C. Smith

393 Mountain Bluebird: a Tom Vezo; **b** Arthur Morris; **c** Peter LaTourrette

393 Townsend's Solitaire: a Joe Fuhrman; **b** Tony Leukering

394 American Robin: a Arthur Morris; **b** Marvin R. Hyett, M.D.; **c** Tom J. Ulrich

394 Varied Thrush: a Herb Clarke; **b** Joe Fuhrman

395 Rufous-backed Robin: a John Hoffman; **b** Rick and Nora Bowers

395 Clay-colored Robin: Greg Lasley

396 Veery: a Arthur Morris; **b** Brian E. Small

396 Swainson's Thrush: a Rob Curtis; **b** Brian E. Small

397 Gray-cheeked Thrush: a Gerard Bailey; **b** Nathan Barnes

397 Bicknell's Thrush: a Tim Laman; **b** Steve Faccio

398 Hermit Thrush: a Gerard Bailey; **b** Joe Fuhrman

398 Wood Thrush: a Gerard Bailey; **b** Charles E. Newell; **c** Jim Culbertson

399 Brown Thrasher: a Arthur Morris; **b** Hugh P. Smith, Jr., and Susan C. Smith

399 Long-billed Thrasher: a Andy Papadatos; **b** Arthur Morris

400 Northern Mockingbird: a Tom Vezo; **b** John Heidecker

400 Gray Catbird: a Gerard Bailey; **b** Jim Culbertson

401 Sage Thrasher: a Peter LaTourrette; **b** Mike Danzenbaker

401 Bendire's Thrasher: a Joe Fuhrman; **b** John Hoffman

402 California Thrasher: a Joe Fuhrman; **b** Frank Schleicher

402 Crissal Thrasher: Rick and Nora Bowers

403 Curve-billed Thrasher: a John Cancalosi; **b** Tom Vezo

403 Le Conte's Thrasher: a Joe Fuhrman; **b** Mike Danzenbaker

404 Cedar Waxwing: a Brian Henry; **b** Garth McElroy

404 Bohemian Waxwing: a Garth McElroy; **b** Brian K. Wheeler; **c** Steve Young

405 European Starling: a David Tipling; **b** Rick and Nora Bowers; **c** Brian Henry; **d** Hugh P. Smith, Jr., and Susan C. Smith; **e** Bob de Lange; **f** Doug Wechsler

406 Red-whiskered Bulbul: Martin Hale

406 Phainopepla: a Joe Fuhrman; **b** Bob Steele

407 a (top) Arthur Morris; **b (bottom)** Fred Truslow

408 Blue Jay: a, b Arthur Morris

408 Steller's Jay: a Steven Holt; **b** Tom Vezo

409 Mexican Jay: a Tom J. Ulrich; **b** Rick and Nora Bowers; **c** John Hoffman

409 Pinyon Jay: a Dale and Marian Zimmerman; **b** Joe Fuhrman; **c** Bob Steele

410 Western Scrub-Jay: a Alan David Walther; **b** Don Grall; **c** Hugh P. Smith, Jr., and Susan C. Smith; **d** Kevin Smith; **e** Dale and Marian Zimmerman

411 Island Scrub-Jay: a Joe Fuhrman; **b** Peter LaTourrette

411 Florida Scrub-Jay: a, b Arthur Morris

412 Green Jay: a Peter LaTourrette; **b** Arthur Morris

412 Brown Jay: a George L. Armistead; **b** Rick and Nora Bowers; **c** Jim Culbertson

413 Gray Jay: a Doug Wechsler; **b** Joe Fuhrman; **c** Michael Patrikeev

413 Clark's Nutcracker: a George L. Armistead; **b** Martin Meyers; **c** Marvin R. Hyett, M.D.

414 Black-billed Magpie: a Rob Curtis; **b** Helen Cruickshank

414 Yellow-billed Magpie: a Hugh P. Smith, Jr., and Susan C. Smith

415 Common Raven: a Tom Vezo; **b** Stephen J. Lang; **c** Tom Vezo; **d** Tom J. Ulrich

415 Chihuahuan Raven: a Rob Curtis; **b** Brian E. Small

416 American Crow: a Mike Danzenbaker; **b, c** Steven Holt

416 Northwestern Crow: Rob Curtis

417 Fish Crow: a, b Doug Wechsler; **c** George L. Armistead

417 Tamaulipas Crow: Jim Culbertson

418 Arthur Morris

419 Brown-headed Cowbird: a Mike Danzenbaker; **b** Robert Villani; **c** Barth Schorre

419 Bronzed Cowbird: a Joe Fuhrman; **b** Dale and Marian Zimmerman; **c** Robert Shantz

420 Common Grackle: a Tom Vezo; **b** Michael Patrikeev

420 Shiny Cowbird: a Joe Fuhrman; **b** Herb Clarke

421 Great-tailed Grackle: a John Hoffman; **b, c** Arthur Morris

421 Boat-tailed Grackle: a Doug Wechsler; **b** Jim Culbertson

422 Brewer's Blackbird: a Alan David Walther; **b** Dr. Michael Stubblefield

422 Rusty Blackbird: a Kevin T. Karlson; **b** Mike Danzenbaker; **c** Kevin T. Karlson

423 Red-winged Blackbird: a Tom Vezo; **b** Hugh P. Smith, Jr., and Susan C. Smith; **c** Tom Vezo

423 Tricolored Blackbird: a Joe Fuhrman; **b** Bob Steele

424 Yellow-headed Blackbird: a Tom Vezo; **b** Arthur Morris

424 Bobolink: a Brian Henry; **b** Stephen J. Lang; **c** Mike Danzenbaker

425 Eastern Meadowlark: a Arthur Morris; **b** Steven Holt; **c** Mike Danzenbaker

425 Western Meadowlark: a Doug Wechsler; **b** Arthur Morris

426 Scott's Oriole: a Rick and Nora Bowers; **b** Joe Fuhrman; **c** Rick and Nora Bowers

426 Audubon's Oriole: a Sam Fried; **b** Greg Lasley

427 Baltimore Oriole: a Johann Schumacher; **b, c** Tom Vezo

427 Bullock's Oriole: a Peter LaTourrette; **b** Joe Fuhrman; **c** Hugh P. Smith, Jr., and Susan C. Smith

428 Orchard Oriole: a Rob Curtis; **b** Barth Schorre; **c** Rob Curtis

All photographs provided by VIREO (except those marked *).

428 Hooded Oriole: a Arthur Morris; **b** Barth Schorre; **c** Hugh P. Smith, Jr., and Susan C. Smith; **d** Rick and Nora Bowers

429 Altamira Oriole: a Arthur Morris; **b** Steven Holt

429 Streak-backed Oriole: a Nick Kontonicolas; **b** Rick and Nora Bowers; **c** Brian E. Small

430 Garth McElroy

431 a Rob and Ann Simpson; **b** Rick and Nora Bowers; **c** Barth Schorre; **d** Joe Fuhrman; **e** Christie Van Cleve

432 Summer Tanager: a Rob Curtis; **b** Barth Schorre; **c** Arthur Morris

432 Hepatic Tanager: a, b Rick and Nora Bowers

433 Scarlet Tanager: a Rob and Ann Simpson; **b** Nathan Barnes; **c** Gerard Bailey

433 Western Tanager: a, b, c Joe Fuhrman

434 Flame-colored Tanager: Greg Lasley

434 Yellow Grosbeak: a Dale and Marian Zimmerman; **b** Marvin R. Hyett, M.D

434 Crimson-collared Grosbeak: a Rick and Nora Bowers; **b** Mike Danzenbaker

435 Painted Bunting: a Tom Vezo; **b** Barth Schorre

435 Varied Bunting: a, b Rick and Nora Bowers

436 Blue Grosbeak: a Rick and Nora Bowers; **b** Sid and Shirley Rucker

436 Blue Bunting: a, b Jim Culbertson

437 Indigo Bunting: (clockwise from top left) a Nathan Barnes; **b, c** Barth Schorre

437 Lazuli Bunting: a Peter LaTourrette; **b** Joe Fuhrman

438 Rose-breasted Grosbeak: a Barth Schorre; **b** James M. Wedge

438 Black-headed Grosbeak: a Tom Vezo; **b** Rick and Nora Bowers; **c** Joe Fuhrman

439 Northern Cardinal: Tom Vezo

439 Pyrrhuloxia: a Arthur Morris; **b** Kevin T. Karlson

440 Sidney Bahrt

441 Common Redpoll: a Gerard Bailey; **b** Doug Wechsler; **c** Brian Henry

441 Hoary Redpoll: a Tony Beck; **b** Gerard Bailey

442 Cassin's Finch: a Tom J. Ulrich; **b** Rick and Nora Bowers

442 Pine Siskin: a Alan David Walther; **b** Brian Henry

443 Purple Finch: a Rob Curtis; **b** Gerard Bailey

443 House Finch: a Arthur Morris; **b** Dale and Marian Zimmerman

444 Black Rosy-Finch: a Mike Danzenbaker; **b** Tom J. Ulrich

444 Brown-capped Rosy-Finch: a Rick and Nora Bowers; **b** Tom J. Ulrich

445 Gray-crowned Rosy-Finch: a, b Joe Fuhrman; **c** Mike Danzenbaker; **d** Arthur Morris; **e** Brian E. Small

446 Lawrence's Goldfinch: a Peter LaTourrette; **b** Joe Fuhrman

446 Brambling: a, b David Tipling; **c** Bob de Lange

447 American Goldfinch: a Gerard Bailey; **b, c** James M. Wedge

447 Lesser Goldfinch: a John Hoffman; **b** Joe Fuhrman; **c** Hugh P. Smith, Jr., and Susan C. Smith

448 Pine Grosbeak: a Rob Curtis; **b** Gerard Bailey; **c** Rob Curtis

448 Evening Grosbeak: a Warren Greene; **b** Brian Henry

449 Red Crossbill: a Steven Holt; **b, c** Joe Fuhrman

449 White-winged Crossbill: a, b Brian Henry

450 Paul W. Sykes, Jr.

451 Spotted Towhee: a Rick and Nora Bowers; **b** Peter LaTourrette; **c** Hugh P. Smith, Jr., and Susan C. Smith

451 Eastern Towhee: a Tom Vezo; **b** Arthur Morris

452 Green-tailed Towhee: a Don Grall; **b** Joe Fuhrman

452 Olive Sparrow: Peter LaTourrette

452 Abert's Towhee: Garth McElroy

453 California Towhee: a Hugh P. Smith, Jr., and Susan C. Smith; **b** Peter LaTourrette

453 Canyon Towhee: a Sam Fried; **b** Tom J. Ulrich

454 Black-throated Sparrow: a Garth McElroy; **b** Rick and Nora Bowers

454 Five-striped Sparrow: a, b Rick and Nora Bowers

455 Sage Sparrow: a Rick and Nora Bowers; **b** Greg Lasley

455 White-collared Seedeater: a Bill Schmoker; **b** Kevin T. Karlson

456 Chipping Sparrow: a Gerard Bailey; **b** Arthur Morris; **c** Tom Vezo

456 Clay-colored Sparrow: a Doug Wechsler; **b** Rick and Nora Bowers; **c** Arthur Morris

457 Brewer's Sparrow: a Rob Curtis; **b** Sam Fried

457 Black-chinned Sparrow: a Brian E. Small; **b** Dale and Marian Zimmerman

458 American Tree Sparrow: a Tom Vezo; **b** Dr. Michael Stubblefield

458 Field Sparrow: a Stephen J. Lang; **b** James R. Woodward

459 Rufous-crowned Sparrow: a Bob Steele; **b** Rick and Nora Bowers

459 Rufous-winged Sparrow: a Brian E. Small; **b** Rick and Nora Bowers

460 Cassin's Sparrow: a Greg Lasley; **b** Rick and Nora Bowers

460 Botteri's Sparrow: a, b Greg Lasley

461 Bachman's Sparrow: a Jim Zipp; **b** George L. Armistead

461 (box): a Greg Lasley; **b** Brian E. Small; **c** Robert Royse

462 Dark-eyed Junco: a Hugh P. Smith, Jr., and Susan C. Smith; **b** Arthur Morris; **c, d** Joe Fuhrman; **e** Don Grall

463 Dark-eyed Junco (cont'd): a Gerard Bailey; **b** Kathleen A. Niyo; **c** Robert Royse

463 Yellow-eyed Junco: a, b Rick and Nora Bowers

464 Grasshopper Sparrow: a Tom J. Ulrich; **b** Greg Lasley

464 Baird's Sparrow: a, b Greg Lasley

465 Henslow's Sparrow: a Rick and Nora Bowers; **b** Robert Royse

465 Savannah Sparrow: a Doug Wechsler; **b** Dr. Michael Stubblefield; **c** Joe Fuhrman

466 Nelson's Sharp-tailed Sparrow: a Gerard Bailey; **b** Brian E. Small; **c** Garth McElroy

466 Saltmarsh Sharp-tailed Sparrow: a Rob and Ann Simpson; **b** Michael P. Gage; **c** Tom Vezo

All photographs provided by VIREO (except those marked *).

467 **Le Conte's Sparrow: a** Rob Curtis; **b** Greg Lasley
467 **Seaside Sparrow: a** Doug Wechsler; **b** George L. Armistead
468 **Harris's Sparrow: a** Patricio Robles Gil; **b** Arthur Morris; **c** Rick and Nora Bowers
468 **Golden-crowned Sparrow: a** Doug Wechsler; **b** Joe Fuhrman
469 **White-crowned Sparrow: a** Hugh P. Smith, Jr., and Susan C. Smith; **b** Arthur Morris
469 **White-throated Sparrow: a** Tom Vezo; **b** Helen Cruickshank
470 **Fox Sparrow: a** Gerard Bailey; **b** Dr. Michael Stubblefield; **c** Brian E. Small; **d, e** Joe Fuhrman; **f** Glen Tepke
471 **Lark Sparrow: a** Tom Vezo; **b** Richard Crossley
471 **Lark Bunting: a** Greg Lasley; **b** Arthur Morris; **c** Helen Cruickshank
472 **Song Sparrow: a** Brian Henry; **b** Johann Schumacher; **c** Arthur Morris; **d** Tom Vezo
472 **Vesper Sparrow:** Rick and Nora Bowers
473 **Lincoln's Sparrow: a, b** Arthur Morris
473 **Swamp Sparrow: a** Dr. Michael Stubblefield; **b** John Heidecker

474 **Chestnut-collared Longspur: a** Brian E. Small; **b** Mike Danzenbaker; **c** Helen Cruickshank
474 **Lapland Longspur: a** Arthur Morris; **b** Steve Young; **c** Tom Vezo
475 **McCown's Longspur: a** Tom J. Ulrich; **b** Brian E. Small; **c** Mike Danzenbaker
475 **Smith's Longspur: a** Arthur Morris; **b** Richard Crossley
476 **Snow Bunting: a** Tom Vezo; **b** Steve Young; **c** Tom Vezo; **d** Crawford H. Greenewalt
476 **McKay's Bunting: a** Dr. Erica M. Brendel; **b** Jake Faust; **c** Mike Danzenbaker
477 **Rustic Bunting: a** Tadao Shimba; **b** Mike Danzenbaker
477 **Little Bunting: a** Hanne and Jens Eriksen; **b** Aurélien Audevard
478 **House Sparrow: a** Joe Fuhrman; **b** Arthur Morris; **c** David Tipling
478 **Eurasian Tree Sparrow: a** Hanne and Jens Eriksen; **b** Martin Meyers
479 **Dickcissel: a** Arthur Morris; **b** Barth Schorre; **c** Richard Crossley; **d** Richard and Susan Day

479 **Bananaquit:** Doug Wechsler
480 **a** Joe Fuhrman; **b** Richard Crossley; **c** Joe Fuhrman; **d** Gerard Bailey; **e** David Tipling; **f** Richard Crossley
481 **a** Herb Clarke; **b** Tom Vezo; **c** Mike Danzenbaker; **d** Tom Vezo; **e** Arthur Morris; **f** James M. Wedge
482 **(intro)** Mike Danzenbaker
482 **Eastern Yellow Wagtail: a, b** Tom Vezo; **c** William S. Peckover
483 **White Wagtail: a** Martin Hale; **b, c** Bob de Lange; **d** Joe Fuhrman
484 **American Pipit: a** Rick and Nora Bowers; **b** Martin Hale; **c** Peter LaTourrette
484 **Sprague's Pipit: a** Rick and Nora Bowers; **b** Brian E. Small
485 **Red-throated Pipit. a, b** Hanne and Jens Eriksen
485 **Olive-backed Pipit:** Tadao Shimba
485 **Pechora Pipit:** Brian Sullivan
486 **Sky Lark: a** Hanne and Jens Eriksen; **b** Bob de Lange
486 **Horned Lark: a** Alan David Walther; **b** Sam Fried; **c** Tom Vezo

Front cover: Indigo Bunting Adam Jones/DanitaDelimont.com*
Spine: Barn Owl Valentin Rodriguez/age fotostock*
Back cover: a White-eared Hummingbird Dan True; **b Tufted Titmouse** Tom Vezo; **c Long-billed Curlew** Arthur Morris; **d Mallard** Alan and Sandy Carey; **e Gilded Flicker** Tom Vezo; **f Red-shouldered Hawk** Brian K. Wheeler; **g Ring-necked Pheasant** Tom Vezo
How to Use This Book (front flap): a Arthur Morris; **b** David Tipling; **c** Mike Danzenbaker

VIREO

VIREO (Visual Resources for Ornithology), the international photograph collection of The Academy of Natural Sciences, is the world's most comprehensive source of bird photographs. VIREO includes photographs of more than two-thirds of all bird species, taken by many of the world's best bird photographers. Many of these photographs can be viewed on the VIREO website: www.acnatsci.org/vireo

VIREO (Visual Resources for Ornithology)
The Academy of Natural Sciences
1900 Benjamin Franklin Parkway
Philadelphia, PA 19103
Tel. (215) 299-1069
vireo@ansp.org

Glossary

aberrant Atypical; an aberrant bird differs strikingly in some aspect from most individuals of its species.

air sac As used in this guide, an expandable, featherless, often brightly colored and textured area on the sides of the neck in some birds; certain grouse and prairie-chickens inflate air sacs in courtship displays. In anatomical usage, the term refers to internal organs connected to the lungs in all birds.

albinism Congenital absence of pigmentation; in birds, results in white plumage and pink eyes.

alkaline Having a pH value greater than 7; alkaline lakes in the western United States support many bird species.

alpine barrens Areas above the timberline where vegetation is typically low, creeping, and sparse.

alternate plumage In most bird species, the plumage worn during the breeding season; often more vividly colored and patterned than the nonbreeding (or basic) plumage, particularly in males.

altitudinal migration Seasonal movement of birds along elevational gradients, normally downslope in the cooler months and upslope in the warmer.

altricial Referring to chicks that are naked, blind, and incapable of moving around on their own soon after hatching (compare "precocial").

alula Group of 2–7 feathers on the upper surface of the wing near the carpal joint ("wrist"); used for steering and "braking" in flight (and in some diving birds for underwater maneuvering).

antiphonal In bird songs, composed of phrases sung alternately by males and females.

arm Informal term for the inner portion of the wing between the body and the carpal joint; often used by hawk-watchers.

arroyo In arid regions, a water-carved gulch, deep gully, or small, narrow canyon that is often dry; in the United States, the term is used almost exclusively in the Southwest and California.

arthropod Invertebrate of the phylum Arthropoda, which includes insects, crustaceans, and arachnids.

aspect ratio In birds, the ratio of wing length to wing breadth.

asynchronous hatching Staggered hatching of birds in a single clutch (group of eggs), often over several days.

auriculars Feathers covering the center of the "cheeks" just behind the eyes, visible as a distinct patch in some species (such as Golden-winged Warbler); also called "ear coverts."

aviculture The breeding and raising of birds in captivity; when such species are cross-bred, new "strains," or types, are sometimes created that do not closely resemble their wild ancestors (as in Eurasian Collared-Dove and Rock Pigeon).

axillaries Group of stiff covert feathers located on the underwing next to the body (in the "armpit" region).

backcross Offspring resulting from the mating of a hybrid bird with one of its parental species.

barrier island Long, narrow island situated parallel to a shore and built by the action of waves and currents; a habitat often used by nesting and migrating waterbirds.

basic plumage In most bird species, the plumage worn during the nonbreeding season; often less strikingly patterned or colored than breeding (or alternate) plumage.

belly Section of a bird's underparts below the breast and before the vent.

bib Informal term for a distinctly pigmented area of the throat, usually a dark patch (as seen on many chickadees).

bog Area of soft, spongy, naturally waterlogged ground, typically having an acidic substrate of sphagnum moss and peat, in which characteristic shrubs and herbs and sometimes trees grow.

boreal forest Also called "taiga"; continuous belt of subarctic coniferous forest just below the tundra, in North America extending mostly from Alaska to eastern Canada.

borrow pit Area where soil has been excavated for use elsewhere; these pits often fill with water or are maintained as small ponds and lakes.

brackish Characterized by a mixture of salt and fresh water, as found in tidal areas such as bays, lagoons, and marshes.

breast Section of a bird's underparts below the throat and before the belly.

breastband Area of continuous, contrastingly pigmented plumage that extends across the breast (as in Semipalmated Plover).

brood parasite Bird that lays eggs in another bird's nest (sometimes a bird of another species).

brow line Line extending from the eye to the base of the maxilla (as in Razorbill).

call A usually brief vocalization birds use for contact, alarm, or warning or to solicit feeding, copulation, or gathering (compare "song").

canebrake Dense thicket of cane, in North America usually of the native species giant or switch cane (*Arundinaria gigantea*).

cap Informal term for the top a bird's head when it is contrastingly pigmented (as in chickadees); more extensive than the "crown."

Carolina sandhills A term for the longleaf pine–wiregrass ecosystem that once covered 90 million acres from the coastal plain of the Carolinas to eastern Texas but is now reduced to fewer than 3 million acres.

carpal joint The forward-projecting "wrist" of the wing, characterized by an obvious bend; a **carpal bar** is an area of contrastingly pigmented plumage that extends, usually diagonally, from this joint along the upperwing coverts toward the body (as in storm-petrels); a **carpal patch** is a distinct area of plumage near the joint, often on the underwing (as in Rough-legged Hawk).

cere Raised, fleshy area at the base of the maxilla, naked in diurnal raptors (Falconiformes), feathered in parrots, and covered with an operculum (flap) in pigeons.

chaparral Habitat dominated by a dense growth of mostly small-leaved evergreen shrubs that is found mainly in the West and Southwest and is characterized by hot, dry summers and cool, moist winters.

cheek Informal term for the area of a bird's head that includes the auriculars and surrounding feather tracts.

chin Informal term for the uppermost part of a bird's throat, adjacent to the mandible.

clear-cut Tract of woodland in which all trees have been removed.

clinal Showing gradual change in a character from one end of a species' (or population's) range to the other; this change typically is correlated with an environmental gradient, and forms at the endpoints may appear strikingly different.

closed forest Relatively dense forest that has a well-developed canopy (compare "open woodland").

coastal plain Area of flatland adjacent to a seacoast; the Atlantic Coastal Plain stretches some 2,200 miles (3,540km) from Cape Cod, Massachusetts, southward through the southeastern United States and Mexico to the Yucatán Peninsula.

Coast Ranges Mountain ranges that stretch along the western coast of North America from southeastern Alaska to Mexico.

collar Informal term for a distinctly pigmented area of plumage that encircles the neck and/or breast.

colony In birds, usually a group of the same species nesting together in close proximity; some birds, especially terns, herons, and egrets, nest in colonies comprised of several species, and some birds nest in widely scattered colonies.

coniferous forest Woodland composed of mostly evergreen, cone-bearing trees or shrubs with needlelike or scalelike leaves, including pines, spruces, and junipers.

contour feathers Feathers that form the outer layer of a bird's plumage, including remiges and rectrices.

corvid A bird of the family Corvidae.

cosmopolitan Having a nearly worldwide distribution.

coverts Contour feathers that lie over (or partly cover) other feathers and serve to protect them and to streamline the bird. **Uppertail** and **undertail coverts** cover the base of the tail on the upperside and underside of the body, respectively. **Wing coverts** are arranged in distinct tiers in many birds, especially larger species: **greater coverts** are the largest and closest to the remiges, **median coverts** form the next tier, **lesser coverts** the next, and **marginal coverts** are found along the very edge of the wing. Wing covert feathers may be further distinguished according to whether they cover primaries or secondaries and/or the upperside (upperwing coverts) or underside (underwing coverts): **greater**

underprimary coverts are the greater coverts that cover the bases of the primaries (but not the secondaries).

covey Group of game birds, especially smaller species such as quail.

cowl Informal term for a distinctly pigmented area of plumage that appears to drape from the upperparts to the sides of the breast.

crake Term for a small rail with a small bill.

crèche Group of precocial young birds of the same age from multiple nests in a colony; pelicans, terns, cormorants, and eiders of some species "pool" their young in crèches at an early stage.

crest Group of crown feathers that show a peak or elongation; adults of some species are always obviously crested, while others may raise a small crest only when alarmed.

crissum Area of feathers between the vent and rectrices that includes the undertail coverts.

crop In some birds, a saclike area between the throat and esophagus used to store food before regurgitation or digestion.

crown Area of feathers on top of the head above the eyes, bordered by the forehead and nape (less extensive than a "cap"); a **crown patch** is an area of distinctly pigmented feathers in the center of the crown; a **crown stripe** extends along the length of the crown, either down the center (median crown stripe) or along the sides of the center (lateral crown stripes).

culmen Ridge of the maxilla from base to tip.

culminicorn In albatrosses and some tubenose allies, a distinct bill plate that lies along the culmen up to the nail (as in Yellow-nosed Albatross).

deciduous woodland Woodland comprising mostly or solely trees that shed their foliage at the end of the growing season, usually autumn or winter.

decurved Curved downward; many birds' bills are decurved.

desert wash A usually dry desert streambed that flows only after periods of heavy rain.

dimorphic In a population or species, occurring in two forms that differ in size, shape, or coloration, frequently involving differences between male and female (sexual dimorphism) or color morphs.

dispersal Movement away from breeding areas by adults or young; usually distinguished from "migration" in being less regular or predictable.

display Innate, stylized activity or signal through which birds communicate.

diurnal Active by day.

dorsal Pertaining to the upperside of the body; in birds, refers especially to the tail, back, and wings.

dredge-spoil island Shoal or small island created by the deposition of sediment from dredging operations, usually in connection with the maintenance of ship channels.

early successional Referring to the first stages of regeneration of a (usually forested) disturbed habitat, during which grasses, shrubs, forbs, and saplings dominate.

eclipse plumage Plumage worn briefly by male waterfowl just after mating or after the breeding season; more muted than the plumage worn through most of the year and sometimes resembling that of the female.

endemic Native to or confined to a certain region and found nowhere else.

estuary Passage of the lower course of a river where its current meets the tides and the water is brackish.

eye arc Area of pale, arc-shaped plumage above and/or below the eye (as in MacGillivray's Warbler); thicker than "eye crescent."

eyebrow Stripe on the side of the head immediately above the eye.

eye-comb Thick, fleshy growth above the eye in certain galliforms; most noticeable when males are displaying or agitated but also seen in females of many species.

eye crescent Narrow area of contrasting plumage above and/or below the eye, of almost even thickness (as in Franklin's Gull).

eye line Line formed by dark plumage that extends through or behind the eye; also called an "eye stripe" (a term some sources use to indicate a thicker line).

eye patch Area of dark plumage around the eye.

eye ring Area of contrasting plumage encircling the eye (compare "orbital ring").

facial disc Group of feathers that surround the eyes of certain birds, particularly owls, in which the disc is often clearly defined.

facultative movements In birds, movements made in response to pressures or stresses in the immediate environment, such as food crop failures, drought, cold, or snow cover (compare "migration").

fen Low-lying, wet land with grassy vegetation; usually a flat, transitional area between land and water.

first-year bird Bird in its first 12 months of life; a **first-winter bird** is in its first winter, a **first-fall bird** in its first fall.

flanks Rear portion of the sides, from about the midpoint of the folded wing to the tail coverts.

fledge To grow a first set of contour feathers (as opposed to a coat of downy feathers), or juvenal plumage.

fledgling Bird that has fledged (acquired juvenal plumage) and left the nest; most birds begin to become independent of their parents at this time (compare "nestling"), although precocial birds leave the nest as downy chicks, long before acquiring their first set of contour feathers.

flight call Call used chiefly by flying birds, thought to function as a contact call among members of the same species, especially during nocturnal migration.

flycatch To capture flying insects while in flight.

forecrown Foremost part of the crown; a smaller area than the forehead.

forehead Front of the head, above the maxilla.

frontal shield Featherless, fleshy plate on the forehead, often brightly colored (as in Purple Gallinule).

frontlet Small area of distinctly delineated plumage near the foremost portion of the forehead.

furcular sac Pouch of skin lying just in front of the sternum that can be inflated to produce sounds in a few species (such as Brown Jay).

gadfly petrel Seabird of the genus *Pterodroma*, often simply called a "petrel," intermediate in size between storm-petrels and most shearwaters.

gape Angle of the bill where the maxilla meets the mandible.

glean To pick small food items singly, usually with delicate movements; warblers glean insects from leaves or needle clusters.

gonydeal angle Cusp on the outer portion of the mandible along the gonys; prominent on some birds, such as gulls.

gonys Ridge formed by the fusion of the two outer ridges of the mandible.

gorget Patch of brightly colored feathers on a hummingbird's throat.

grassland Area with extensive grass or grasslike vegetation, such as a prairie or meadow.

Greenland Current Ocean current that flows from the Arctic Ocean down the east side of Greenland, merging with the Labrador Current at the southern tip of Greenland.

grin patch Informal term for the appearance of the contrastingly dark cutting edges (tomia) near the base of the bill in Snow Goose.

gular pouch Patch, often colorful, of bare skin on the throat that may be distensible or inflatable (as in Magnificent Frigatebird).

gular skin Bare skin that surrounds the throat in some birds.

hammock Tract of forested land that rises above adjacent marshland, usually in the southeastern United States.

hand Informal term for the outer portion of the wing past the carpal joint; typically used by hawk-watchers.

High Arctic Area above the Low Arctic, where tundra vegetation is replaced by cushion plants, rock-brake ferns *(Cryptogramma),* prostrate shrubs, and rosette-forming herbs.

hindcrown Rear part of the crown, just forward of (above) the nape.

hover-glean To forage while fluttering in the air; kinglets often hover-glean insect larvae from the outer needle clusters of spruce trees.

humerals Feathers of the inner portion of the wing that lie along the humerus (wing bone nearest the body).

hybrid Offspring resulting from the breeding of different species (compare "intergrade"); certain bird species, including gulls, orioles, hummingbirds, and sapsuckers, regularly or occasionally hybridize.

icterid A bird of the family Icteridae.

immature Bird that is not yet an adult in plumage. (In this book, "immature" does not refer to a bird's ability to breed, as many species can breed in plumages other than definitive adult plumage.)

impoundment Body of water, such as a reservoir or marsh, contained by manmade boundaries, especially earthen dams.

intergrade Offspring resulting from the breeding of different subspecies (compare "hybrid").

Interior West Area of the western United States south of Canada that lies east of the Sierra Nevada and west of the Great Plains.

intertidal zone Area of a shoreline between the low- and high-tide points.

irruption Large-scale movement of a species outside its typical range, usually in autumn or winter; such movements do not occur in regular, predictable patterns, unlike migration.

juvenal plumage A bird's first covering of contour feathers; it is often brown or streaked.

juvenile Bird in juvenal plumage.

kite In bird flight, to hang in one position while facing into the wind with minimal or no flapping.

kleptoparasite Bird that forages by stealing food from other birds (such as Parasitic Jaeger).

Labrador Current Ocean current that flows southward between Canada and Greenland, extending down the U.S. East Coast to North Carolina, where its flow deflects the Gulf Stream eastward.

lagoon Sheltered, shallow body of water separated from deeper, more open water.

lek Site where males of some species (such as prairie-chickens) gather to perform group courtship displays for females; the term can also refer to the group of displaying males.

leucism Condition of plumage resulting from reduced pigment in feathers; leucistic birds vary from having a few stray whitish feathers to being nearly all white with just a trace of normal pigmentation (the latter resembling albino birds but with normally pigmented eyes).

lift Upward force exerted on a wing due to air flow across its surface.

lore Area between the eye and the base of the bill; some species have distinctively colored lores (such as White-throated Sparrow).

lowland Area of level land that is lower in elevation than surrounding land.

malar Small group of feathers, sometimes distinctively colored, that extends from the base of the bill downward and slightly backward along the throat (see "submalar stripe").

mandible Lower part of a bird's bill; sometimes called "lower mandible" (compare "maxilla").

mangrove forest Or mangrove swamp; low, dense woodland of tropical evergreen trees or shrubs that grow in coastal tropical and subtropical areas (of southern Florida and Texas in the scope of this guide); these plants, which grow in salt water, have stiltlike roots and stems and are important roosting and nesting sites for birds.

mantle In this guide, feathers of the upper back, not including the scapulars; in other publications, the term may also be used to include the scapulars and all visible upperwing coverts of the folded wing.

mask Informal term for an area of dark plumage extending from the base of the bill through and beyond the eyes (as in Loggerhead Shrike).

mast The nuts of forest trees accumulated on the ground.

maxilla Upper part of a bird's bill; sometimes called "upper mandible" (compare "mandible").

melanism In birds, a condition involving unusual dark pigmentation in the plumage.

mesquite Small, spiny trees or shrubs (genus *Prosopis*) that grow in hot, dry climates.

migration Regular movement of birds between nesting and wintering areas, generally stimulated by changes in the duration of daylight rather than a weather event or food shortage (compare "facultative movements").

mimid A bird of the family Mimidae.

mirror In gulls' remiges, an area of white plumage near the feather tip that is surrounded by dark plumage.

mob In birds, to gather around a perched predator (or pursue a flying predator) while calling vigorously ("scolding") and sometimes making swooping flights to strike; mixed flocks of small birds will often mob an owl in daylight.

molt The process of shedding old feathers and replacing them with new feathers, whether all or part of the plumage; most species have regular, predictable molts.

monogamy The condition of having only one mate during a breeding season or during the breeding life of a pair.

montane Of or found in mountainous environments.

morph In birds, a variation, usually in plumage, found within a population or an entire species; often called "color morph" (formerly "plumage phase," although the condition is permanent).

motte Copse or small stand of trees on a prairie, such as the oak mottes found on the coastal prairie of eastern Texas.

moustachial crescent Distinct area of dark plumage forming a curve along the lower border of the auriculars above the malar and somewhat resembling a mustache (as in Prairie Warbler).

mudflat Area of mud along rivers, lakes, or other water bodies usually exposed by receding tides or by drought; often important habitat for foraging shorebirds and waterbirds.

muskeg Habitat characterized by an acidic, very moist soil type common in Arctic and boreal areas that is made up of dead plants in various states of decomposition and often includes sphagnum moss and sedge peat; often found along the uneven interface of taiga and tundra, where there are few and stunted trees.

nail Distinct horny plate at the end of the maxilla or mandible, most pronounced and obvious in larger tubenoses (in the order Procellariiformes).

nape The back of the head, including the hindneck, just below the hindcrown.

nearshore waters Ocean waters between the low-tide point and a depth of about a hundred fathoms (200m).

Neotropical Of the New World tropics, which extend from southern Mexico through Central America into South America; a "Neotropical migrant" passes the nonbreeding season in this area.

nest box Box with an entrance hole set out specifically for cavity-nesting birds, such as wrens, woodpeckers, owls, and parids.

nestling Young bird that has not yet left the nest.

nominate subspecies In a species, the first subspecies to be described ("named") to science; nominate subspecies have the same scientific species and subspecies names (the nominate subspecies of Bell's Vireo is *Vireo bellii bellii*).

nonpasserine Any bird that is not in the order Passeriformes (passerines).

northern tier In the lower 48 United States, the states that border Canada.

oak scrub Open, fairly dry habitat consisting of shrubby, thicket-forming oaks.

offshore waters Open ocean waters, rather than nearshore waters; also called "pelagic waters" (see also "pelagic").

old-growth forest Mature woodland ecosystem characterized by the presence of old woody plants, especially old trees, and the wildlife and smaller plants associated with them.

open woodland Woodland community characterized by widely spaced trees or an open, broken canopy (such as a pine savanna).

orbital ring Ring of often brightly colored bare skin encircling the eye (as in Black-billed Cuckoo).

ornithologist Scientist who studies birds.

oscines Collective term for a suborder (Passeri) of the songbirds (passerines); see also "suboscines."

Pacific Slope The part of western North America that drains to the Pacific Ocean.

pack ice Floating sea ice that has been driven together into a mass.

parid A bird of the family Paridae.

passerine Any bird in the order Passeriformes; passerines are often called "perching birds."

peep Small shorebird of the genus *Calidris,* usually applied only to Least, Semipalmated, Western, Baird's, and White-rumped Sandpipers and not to larger *Calidris.*

pelagic Relating to deepwater ocean regions (see also "offshore waters").

permanent resident Nonmigratory species found year-round in a given area; sometimes refers to a species that makes short-distance (and/or facultative) movements, replacing local birds with birds of the same species from other areas in the nonbreeding months.

phenotype Observable physical properties of an organism.

phylogenetic Based on evolutionary history; used in the context of evolutionary relationships among taxa.

pine barren Area of infertile land that is dominated by pines and has limited understory vegetation (found in eastern North America).

pinyon-juniper woodland Habitat found on the lower slopes of mountains, consisting of short evergreen trees—mostly one or more species of pinyon pine *(Pinus)* and juniper *(Juniperus)*—mixed with desert and upland shrubs or open grasslands.

pishing Giving vocal imitations of parid calls (that sound a bit like steam escaping in quick bursts) to attract woodland birds.

plunge-dive To dive on aquatic prey from the air.

pocosin Freshwater bay swamp (bays are broadleaf evergreen trees of various families) in the Atlantic Coastal Plain.

polyandry The condition of a female having more than one mate in a breeding cycle.

polygyny The condition of a male having more than one mate in a breeding cycle.

polymorphic Having one or more distinct types within a population, usually referring to plumage types (or "morphs").

polynya Area of open water surrounded by sea ice.

prairie Extensive area of flat or rolling, mostly treeless grassland, especially the large tract or plain of central North America known as the Great Plains.

prairie pothole Depressional lake or pond formed by a stranded block of glacier and dependent for its water on rain or snow; these lakes are scattered through the northern Great Plains and into Canada and are important nesting areas as well as stopover sites for migrating waterfowl.

precocial Referring to chicks that are covered with down and capable of moving about when hatched, such as those of most shorebirds and galliforms (compare "altricial").

primaries The outermost and longest remiges, usually numbering between 9 and 12, that with their coverts form the outer portion of the wing.

primary projection The length of the primaries that projects past the tertials when the wing is folded (of particular use in the identification of certain passerines).

primary shaft The stiff central axis of the primary feather, sometimes distinctly visible in flying birds if the feather color is contrastingly dark (as in jaegers).

range Geographic area typically occupied by a species.

raptor Bird of prey, usually referring to a falcon, hawk, or owl.

rectrices (singular: **rectrix**) Tail feathers, not including the tail coverts.

recurved Curved upward (as in the bill of American Avocet).

remiges Flight feathers, including the primaries and secondaries but not their coverts.

resaca In southern Texas, a local name for an oxbow lake (formed when a meander of a river is cut off to form a crescent-shaped lake) of the Rio Grande.

resident Usually nonmigratory and present throughout the year.

rictal bristles Hairlike feathers that project from the gape area and are thought to aid in the capture of aerial insects by trapping them or serving a tactile function.

riparian Along the banks of a flowing natural watercourse such as a river; a riparian forest is found along a stream or river and does not extend far from the banks.

riverbottom swamp Bottomland hardwood forest with a river that moves very slowly through it (mostly southern United States); "bayou" is sometimes a local synonym.

rump Lower back above the uppertail coverts and below the mantle.

sage scrub Arid, mostly treeless habitat of the American West that is dominated by sage (*Salvia, Artemisia,* and other genera) and other low-growing plants; **coastal sage scrub,** found mostly in southern California, is a particular habitat that features species of sage and various shrubs, cacti, and grasses adapted to the semiarid climate of that region.

saltpan Shallow basin in a desert region containing salt and gypsum deposited by an evaporated salt lake; also a flat area of dry or drying salt water that opens or once opened onto tidal water.

savanna Ecosystem characterized by widely spaced overstory trees (often pines) and open expanses in the understory, which is usually grassy or herbaceous in patches; in this book, mostly refers to habitats of the southeastern United States involving loblolly and longleaf pines.

scansorial Adapted to or specialized for locomotion by climbing, especially on tree trunks.

scapulars Group of feathers that lies along the margins of the mantle or back and also overlaps the folded wing.

scree Loose rock debris covering a slope.

scrub Dry habitat (also called "scrubland") characterized by short or stunted vegetation, sometimes but not always with heavy undergrowth.

scrub oak Informal term applied to several species of thicket-forming shrubby oaks.

secondaries The remiges of the inner part of the wing.

second-growth woodland Trees that grow to cover an area after the original stand has been removed.

semi-precocial Referring to chicks that hatch open-eyed, covered with down, and capable of leaving the nest soon, but which stay at the nest and are fed by parents (as in tern and gull chicks).

shortgrass prairie Arid habitat of the western Great Plains, just east of the Rocky Mountains, characterized by sparse, low vegetation, little rainfall, and periods of severe drought.

shrub-steppe Habitat, found from eastern Washington and Oregon to western Wyoming and Colorado, characterized by grasses and shrubs, including big sagebrush, rabbitbrush, greasewood, bitterbrush, buckwheat, and hopsage.

sinkhole Natural depression that connects with a subterranean passage, generally occurring in limestone regions.

slough (Pronounced "slew" or "slou.") Marshy area, lake, or pond that lacks inflowing water; can be locally synonymous with "bayou" and "backwater."

song Vocalization used mostly by male birds to attract a mate or to define and defend a territory (compare "call").

spatulate Shaped like a spoon or a spatula.

speciation The process through which new species evolve from those in existence.

spectacles Informal term for a combination of contrastingly pigmented lores and eye rings, which resemble eyeglass frames (as in Plumbeous Vireo).

speculum Distinctively pigmented area on the upper surface of the secondaries, particularly in dabbling ducks (such as American Black Duck).

sphagnum moss Any of several mosses of the genus *Sphagnum* that grow in wet, acidic areas and whose decomposed remains form peat.

staging area Place where large numbers of birds traditionally gather en route to breeding or sometimes wintering areas, where they feed and/or roost before continuing onward.

stoop Characteristic aerial plunge of some falcons onto prey below.

subadult A bird that has not yet acquired definitive adult plumage but no longer has juvenal plumage.

Subarctic Area just below the Arctic Circle characterized by acidic soils and taiga forest vegetation.

submalar mark Or submalar stripe; mark or line of contrastingly dark plumage between the malar and the throat feathers.

suboscines Birds in the order Passeriformes other than those in the suborder Passeri (oscines); in North America (north of Mexico), flycatchers (suborder Tyranni) are the only representatives of the suboscines.

subterminal band The next-to-last tail band, adjacent to the terminal band.

subtropical Relating to areas adjacent to the tropics where summers are hot but winters are nontropical (southernmost Florida and southernmost Texas are the only subtropical regions in the United States).

succession The gradual development of an ecosystem caused by changes in community composition.

supercilium Area between the lower edge of the crown and the eye line, often contrasting in color with both.

swamp woods Type of freshwater wetland, often found along the floodplains of large rivers, that is filled with water most or all of the year.

taiga Also called "boreal forest"; continuous belt of subarctic coniferous forest just below the tundra, in North America extending mostly from Alaska to eastern Canada.

tailband Contrastingly pigmented area of the tail, perpendicular to the axis of the tail.

tallgrass prairie Grassland ecosystem of tall grasses (such as big bluestem, little bluestem, indiangrass, and switchgrass), once extending for tens of millions of acres from the Dakotas to Texas and east through Illinois, but now found only in tiny remnants.

talon Claw of a bird of prey.

Tamaulipan brushlands Ecosystem of the lower Rio Grande valley delta of southern Texas and northeastern Mexico (state of Tamaulipas), characterized by dense, thorny vegetation, mostly stunted trees and spiny shrubs.

taxon (plural: **taxa**) Broadly, a taxonomic category or group, such as a phylum, order, family, genus, or species; in this guide, "taxa" is often used as shorthand to refer to different subspecies.

terminal band Outermost tail band, at the tail's tip.

territoriality Behavior pattern in birds concerned with the occupation and defense of a territory, often characterized by intensive singing and clashes with rivals.

territory Area occupied by a single bird, mated pair, or group and often vigorously defended against intruders, especially those of the same species.

tertials Innermost secondaries (normally 3) that often have a different shape than other secondaries and are sometimes molted on a different schedule.

thorn scrub Dry habitat characterized by low-growing thorny vegetation.

thorn woods Any habitat where thorny trees dominate, usually in arid regions.

throat Area of the underparts bounded by the malars and the breast.

tideline Area where two different water masses or currents meet, often concentrating nutrients, prey items, and flotsam.

tomial notch Toothlike serration in the edge of the maxilla, as seen in shrikes and vireos.

tree line The elevation in a mountainous region above which trees do not grow or the northern (or southern) latitude beyond which trees do not grow; also called "timberline."

tremolo Rapid repetition of a single tone with a tremulous quality, similar to vibrato in human singing.

tropics The region of earth centered on the equator and lying between the Tropics of Capricorn and Cancer.

tundra In North America, the area north of the tree line in Canada and Alaska vegetated with low shrubs, dwarf heath shrubs, cottongrass communities, and various wetlands.

ulnar bar Area of dark plumage in the underwing coverts that extends from the humerals to the carpal joint, as seen in many gadfly petrel species.

vagrant Bird found outside its normal range, especially one quite far out of range.

vent Opening through which waste and reproductive products pass in birds; also the plumage located around this area between the legs.

ventral In birds, relating to the lower surface of the body from chin to undertail coverts.

wetland Low-lying area, such as a marsh or swamp, that is saturated with moisture for at least some period of time during a year or cycle.

wing bar Line of contrastingly pigmented (usually pale) plumage formed by the tips of the upperwing coverts, usually the median and/or greater coverts; many species of birds have two wing bars per wing.

wing-loading The weight of a bird divided by its wing area.

wing stripe Contrastingly pigmented (usually pale) lengthwise stripe on the upper surface of the extended wing, usually formed by the bases of the remiges (compare "carpal bar").

wrist Synonym for "carpal joint."

Resources and References

Web Sites

Alliance for Zero Extinction
www.zeroextinction.org

American Bird Conservancy
www.abcbirds.org

American Birding Association
www.americanbirding.org

American Bird Observatory List
www.nmnh.si.edu/BIRDNET/OBSERVATORY

American Ornithologists' Union
www.aou.org

Bird Conservation Alliance
www.birdconservationalliance.org

Bird Studies Canada/Études d'Oiseaux Canada
www.bsc-eoc.org

Boreal Songbird Initiative
www.borealbirds.org

Canadian Wildlife Service Migratory Birds Conservation
www.cws-scf.ec.gc.ca/mbc-com

Central Flyway Council
www.centralflyway.org
Conservation International
www.conservation.org
Cornell Lab of Ornithology
www.birds.cornell.edu
Ducks Unlimited
www.ducks.org
eBird
www.ebird.org
Hawk Mountain Sanctuary
www.hawkmountain.org
Manomet Center for Conservation Sciences
www.manomet.org
Migratory Bird Conservancy
www.conservebirds.org
National Audubon Society
www.audubon.org
National Fish and Wildlife Foundation
www.nfwf.org
National Wildlife Federation
www.nwf.org
Natural Resources Defense Council
www.nrdc.org
The Nature Conservancy
www.nature.org

NatureServe
www.natureserve.org
North American Bird Conservation Initiative
www.nabci-us.org
North American Waterfowl Management Plan
www.nawmp.ca
Partners In Flight
www.partnersinflight.org
The Peregrine Fund
www.peregrinefund.org
PRBO Conservation Science
www.prbo.org
Sierra Club
www.sierraclub.org
Smithsonian Migratory Bird Center
nationalzoo.si.edu/ConservationAndScience/
MigratoryBirds
U.S. Fish & Wildlife Service Division of Migratory Birds Management
www.fws.gov/migratorybirds
United States Shorebird Conservation Plan
www.fws.gov/shorebirdplan/
VIREO (Visual Resources for Ornithology)
www.acnatsci.org/vireo
Waterbird Conservation for the Americas
www.nawcp.org

Books

Alderfer, J., ed. 2005. *National Geographic Complete Birds of North America.* Washington, D.C.: National Geographic Society.

Beadle, D., and J. Rising. 2001. *Sparrows of the United States and Canada.* Princeton, NJ: Princeton University Press.

Beaman, M., and S. Madge. 1998. *The Handbook of Bird Identification for Europe and the Western Palearctic.* Princeton, NJ: Princeton University Press.

Dunn, J. L., and K. Garrett. 1997. *A Field Guide to Warblers of North America.* Boston: Houghton Mifflin.

Ehrlich, P. R., D. S. Dobkin, and D. Wheye. 1988. *The Birder's Handbook: A Field Guide to the Natural History of North American Birds.* New York: Simon & Schuster.

Howell, S. N. G. 2003. *Hummingbirds of North America.* Princeton, NJ: Princeton University Press.

Jaramillo, A., and P. Burke. 1999. *New World Blackbirds: The Icterids.* Princeton, NJ: Princeton University Press.

Leahy, C.W. 2004. *The Birdwatcher's Companion to North American Birdlife.* Princeton, NJ: Princeton University Press.

Madge, S., and H. Burn. 1988. *Waterfowl: An Identification Guide to the Ducks, Geese, and Swans of the World.* Boston: Houghton Mifflin.

Mullarney, K., L. Svensson, D. Zetterström, and P. J. Grant. 2000. *Birds of Europe.* Princeton, NJ: Princeton University Press.

O'Brien, M., R. Crossley, and K. Karlson. 2006. *The Shorebird Guide.* Boston: Houghton Mifflin.

Olsen, K. M., and H. Larsson. 2003. *Gulls of North America, Europe, and Asia.* Princeton, NJ: Princeton University Press.

---------. 1995. *Terns of Europe and North America.* Princeton, NJ: Princeton University Press.

Paulson, D. 2005. *Shorebirds of North America.* Princeton, NJ: Princeton University Press.

Pyle, P. 1997. *Identification Guide to North American Birds.* Bolinas, CA: Slate Creek Press.

Rising, J. D. 1996. *A Guide to the Identification and Natural History of the Sparrows of the United States and Canada.* Princeton, NJ: Princeton University Press.

Sibley, D. A. 2000. *The Sibley Guide to Birds.* New York: Knopf.

Taylor, D., and S. Message. 2006. *Shorebirds of North America, Europe, and Asia.* Princeton, NJ: Princeton University Press.

Wheeler, B. K. 2003. *Raptors of Eastern North America.* Princeton, NJ: Princeton University Press.

---------. 2003. *Raptors of Western North America.* Princeton, NJ: Princeton University Press.

Williamson, S. L. 2002. *A Field Guide to Hummingbirds of North America.* Boston: Houghton Mifflin.

Vagrant, Rare, and Extinct Birds

This list includes species of vagrant, rare, extinct, and non–North American species that are mentioned in the species accounts but do not have a dedicated species entry. The page number is given for each mention. An asterisk (*) indicates that the species is considered extinct.

Aztec Thrush (*Ridgwayia pinicola*), 23

Bachman's Warbler (*Vermivora bachmanii*)*, 352

Bahama Swallow (*Tachycineta cyaneoviridis*), 293

Baikal Teal (*Anas formosa*), 35

Baillon's Crake (*Porzana pusilla*), 158

Black-browed Albatross (*Thalassarche melanophris*), 97, 98

Black-hooded Parakeet (*Nendayus nenday*), 246

Black-vented Oriole (*Icterus wagleri*), 426

Blue-crowned Parakeet (*Aratinga acuticaudata*), 249

Brown Shrike (*Lanius cristatus*), 324

Brown Skua (*Stercorarius antarcticus*), 119

Budgerigar (*Melopsittacus undulatus*), 246

Carolina Parakeet (*Conuropsis carolinensis*)*, 246

Chestnut-fronted Macaw (*Ara severus*), 246

Chilean Flamingo (*Phoenicopterus chilensis*), 145

Cinnamon Hummingbird (*Amazilia rutila*), 301

Cockatiel (*Nymphicus hollandicus*), 246

Common Cuckoo (*Cuculus canorus*), 250

Common Sandpiper (*Actitis hypoleucos*), 228

Common Snipe (*Gallinago gallinago*), 237

Common Swift (*Apus apus*), 288

Corn Crake (*Crex crex*), 158

Dusky-headed Parakeet (*Aratinga weddellii*), 249

Dusky Seaside Sparrow (*Ammodramus maritimus nigrescens*)*, 450

Eskimo Curlew (*Numenius borealis*)*, 206

Eurasian Coot (*Fulica atra*), 158, 162

Eurasian Curlew (*Numenius arquata*), 221

Eurasian Hoopoe (*Upupa epops*), 12

Eurasian Oystercatcher (*Haematopus ostralegus*), 215

Falcated Duck (*Anas falcata*), 35

Far Eastern Curlew (*Numenius madagascariensis*), 221

Fork-tailed Swift (*Apus pacificus*), 288

Gray Bunting (*Emberiza variabilis*), 477

Gray-headed Swamphen (*Porphyrio poliocephalus*), 163

Gray-tailed Tattler (*Tringa brevipes*), 224

Gray Wagtail (*Motacilla cinerea*), 482

Great Auk (*Pinguinus impennis*)*, 27, 72

Greater Flamingo (*Phoenicopterus roseus*), 145, 156

Greater Sand-Plover (*Charadrius leschenaultii*), 213

Great Frigatebird (*Fregata minor*), 91

Great Knot (*Calidris tenuirostris*), 233

Great Tit (*Parus major*), 334

Great-winged Petrel (*Pterodroma macroptera*), 102, 109

Green-breasted Mango, (*Anthracothorax prevostii*), 303

Herald Petrel (*Pterodroma heraldica*), 101

Jabiru (*Jabiru mycteria*), 144, 145

Jack Snipe (*Lymnocryptes minimus*), 237

Kermadec Petrel (*Pterodroma neglecta*), 102

Labrador Duck (*Camptorhynchus labradorius*)*, 12

Lesser Flamingo (*Phoeniconaias minor*), 145

Lesser Frigatebird (*Fregata ariel*), 91

Little Ringed Plover (*Charadrius dubius*), 210

Long-toed Stint (*Calidris subminuta*), 228

Mitred Parakeet (*Aratinga mitrata*), 249

Nutting's Flycatcher (*Myiarchus nuttingi*), 317

Oriental Cuckoo (*Cuculus optatus*), 250

Paint-billed Crake (*Neocrex erythrops*), 158

Pallas's Bunting (*Emberiza pallasi*), 477

Parkinson's Petrel (*Procellaria parkinsoni*), 109

Passenger Pigeon (*Ectopistes migratorius*)*, 239

Pine Bunting (*Emberiza leucocephalos*), 477

Pin-tailed Snipe (*Gallinago stenura*), 237

Piratic Flycatcher (*Legatus leucophaius*), 323

Plain-capped Starthroat (*Heliomaster constantii*), 302

Red-masked Parakeet (*Aratinga erythrogenys*), 249

Reed Bunting (*Emberiza schoeniclus*), 477

Scarlet Ibis (*Eudocimus ruber*), 154

Solander's Petrel (*Pterodroma solandri*), 102

Spot-breasted Oriole (*Icterus pectoralis*), 429

Spotted Rail (*Pardirallus maculatus*), 158

Stejneger's Petrel (*Pterodroma longirostris*), 103

Steller's Sea-Eagle (*Haliaeetus pelagicus*), 178, 200

Streaked Shearwater (*Calonectris leucomelas*), 106

Strickland's Woodpecker (*Picoides stricklandi*), 277

Temminck's Stint (*Calidris temminckii*), 228

Variegated Flycatcher (*Empidonomus varius*), 323

West Indian Whistling-Duck (*Dendrocygna arborea*), 36

White-collared Swift (*Streptoprocne zonaris*), 288

White-faced Whistling-Duck (*Dendrocygna viduata*), 36

White-tailed Eagle (*Haliaeetus albicilla*), 200

White-throated Needletail (*Hirundapus caudacutus*), 288

Whooper Swan (*Cygnus cygnus*), 35, 63

Xantus's Hummingbird (*Hylocharis xantusii*), 301

Yellow-breasted Bunting (*Emberiza aureola*), 477

Zino's Petrel (*Pterodroma madeira*), 101

Endangered and Threatened Birds of North America

This list presents the birds of North America that are on the federal list of endangered and threatened wildlife (maintained by the U.S. Fish and Wildlife Service) and protected under the Endangered Species Act. For more information, visit the Fish and Wildlife Service Web site (www.fws.gov/endangered).

Status Key: E=Endangered, a species that is in danger of extinction throughout all or most of its range.
T=Threatened, a species that is likely to become endangered.

Family	Common name	Scientific name	Status
Anatidae	Steller's Eider	*Polysticta stelleri*	T
Anatidae	Spectacled Eider	*Somateria fischeri*	T
Phasianidae	Attwater's Prairie-Chicken	*Tympanuchus cupido attwateri*	E
Odontophoridae	Masked Bobwhite	*Colinus virginianus ridgwayi*	E
Diomedeidae	Short-tailed Albatross	*Phoebastria albatrus*	E
Procellariidae	Bermuda Petrel	*Pterodroma cahow*	E
Procellariidae	Hawaiian Petrel	*Pterodroma sandwichensis*	E
Pelecanidae	Brown Pelican	*Pelecanus occidentalis*	E
Ciconiidae	Wood Stork	*Mycteria americana*	E
Cathartidae	California Condor	*Gymnogyps californianus*	E
Accipitridae	Bald Eagle	*Haliaeetus leucocephalus*	T
Accipitridae	Everglades Snail Kite	*Rostrhamus sociabilis plumbeus*	E
Falconidae	Northern Aplomado Falcon	*Falco femoralis septentrionalis*	E
Rallidae	Light-footed Clapper Rail	*Rallus longirostris levipes*	E
Rallidae	California Clapper Rail	*Rallus longirostris obsoletus*	E
Rallidae	Yuma Clapper Rail	*Rallus longirostris yumanensis*	E
Gruidae	Whooping Crane	*Grus americana*	E
Gruidae	Mississippi Sandhill Crane	*Grus canadensis pulla*	E
Charadriidae	Western Snowy Plover	*Charadrius alexandrinus nivosus*	T
Charadriidae	Piping Plover	*Charadrius melodus*	E
Laridae	Least Tern	*Sternula antillarum*	E
Laridae	Roseate Tern	*Sterna dougallii dougallii*	E
Alcidae	Marbled Murrelet	*Brachyramphus marmoratus marmoratus*	T
Strigidae	Cactus Ferruginous Pygmy-Owl	*Glaucidium brasilianum cactorum*	E
Strigidae	Northern Spotted Owl	*Strix occidentalis caurina*	T
Strigidae	Mexican Spotted Owl	*Strix occidentalis lucida*	T
Picidae	Ivory-billed Woodpecker	*Campephilus principalis*	E
Picidae	Red-cockaded Woodpecker	*Picoides borealis*	E
Tyrannidae	Southwestern Willow Flycatcher	*Empidonax traillii extimus*	E
Laniidae	San Clemente Loggerhead Shrike	*Lanius ludovicianus mearnsi*	E
Vireonidae	Black-capped Vireo	*Vireo atricapilla*	E
Vireonidae	Least Bell's Vireo	*Vireo bellii pusillus*	E
Corvidae	Florida Scrub-Jay	*Aphelocoma coerulescens*	T
Sylviidae	Coastal California Gnatcatcher	*Polioptila californica californica*	T
Parulidae	Golden-cheeked Warbler	*Dendroica chrysoparia*	E
Parulidae	Kirtland's Warbler	*Dendroica kirtlandii*	E
Emberizidae	Cape Sable Seaside Sparrow	*Ammodramus maritimus mirabilis*	E
Emberizidae	Florida Grasshopper Sparrow	*Ammodramus savannarum floridanus*	E
Emberizidae	San Clemente Sage Sparrow	*Amphispiza belli clementeae*	T
Emberizidae	Inyo California Towhee	*Pipilo crissalis eremophilus*	T

Species Checklist

Ducks, Geese, and Swans (Anatidae)

_____ Black-bellied Whistling-Duck
_____ Fulvous Whistling-Duck
_____ Greater White-fronted Goose
_____ Emperor Goose
_____ Snow Goose
_____ Ross's Goose
_____ Brant
_____ Barnacle Goose
_____ Cackling Goose
_____ Canada Goose
_____ Mute Swan
_____ Trumpeter Swan
_____ Tundra Swan
_____ Muscovy Duck
_____ Wood Duck
_____ Gadwall
_____ Eurasian Wigeon
_____ American Wigeon
_____ American Black Duck
_____ Mallard
_____ Mottled Duck
_____ Blue-winged Teal
_____ Cinnamon Teal
_____ Northern Shoveler
_____ White-cheeked Pintail
_____ Northern Pintail
_____ Garganey
_____ Green-winged Teal
_____ Canvasback
_____ Redhead
_____ Ring-necked Duck
_____ Tufted Duck
_____ Greater Scaup
_____ Lesser Scaup
_____ Steller's Eider
_____ Spectacled Eider
_____ King Eider
_____ Common Eider
_____ Harlequin Duck
_____ Surf Scoter
_____ White-winged Scoter
_____ Black Scoter
_____ Long-tailed Duck
_____ Bufflehead
_____ Common Goldeneye
_____ Barrow's Goldeneye
_____ Hooded Merganser
_____ Common Merganser
_____ Red-breasted Merganser
_____ Masked Duck
_____ Ruddy Duck

Chachalacas and Kin (Cracidae)

_____ Plain Chachalaca

Partridges, Grouse, Turkeys, and Kin (Phasianidae)

_____ Chukar
_____ Himalayan Snowcock
_____ Gray Partridge
_____ Ring-necked Pheasant
_____ Ruffed Grouse
_____ Greater Sage-Grouse
_____ Gunnison Sage-Grouse
_____ Spruce Grouse
_____ Willow Ptarmigan
_____ Rock Ptarmigan
_____ White-tailed Ptarmigan
_____ Dusky/Sooty Grouse
_____ Sharp-tailed Grouse
_____ Greater Prairie-Chicken
_____ Lesser Prairie-Chicken
_____ Wild Turkey

New World Quail (Odontophoridae)

_____ Mountain Quail
_____ Scaled Quail
_____ California Quail
_____ Gambel's Quail
_____ Northern Bobwhite
_____ Montezuma Quail

Loons (Gaviidae)

_____ Red-throated Loon
_____ Arctic Loon
_____ Pacific Loon
_____ Common Loon
_____ Yellow-billed Loon

Grebes (Podicipedidae)

_____ Least Grebe
_____ Pied-billed Grebe
_____ Horned Grebe
_____ Red-necked Grebe
_____ Eared Grebe
_____ Western Grebe
_____ Clark's Grebe

Albatrosses (Diomedeidae)

_____ Yellow-nosed Albatross
_____ Laysan Albatross
_____ Black-footed Albatross
_____ Short-tailed Albatross

Shearwaters and Petrels (Procellariidae)

_____ Northern Fulmar
_____ Trinidade Petrel
_____ Murphy's Petrel
_____ Mottled Petrel
_____ Bermuda Petrel
_____ Black-capped Petrel
_____ Galapagos/Hawaiian Petrel
_____ Fea's Petrel
_____ Cook's Petrel
_____ Cory's Shearwater
_____ Pink-footed Shearwater
_____ Flesh-footed Shearwater
_____ Greater Shearwater
_____ Wedge-tailed Shearwater
_____ Buller's Shearwater
_____ Sooty Shearwater
_____ Short-tailed Shearwater
_____ Manx Shearwater
_____ Black-vented Shearwater
_____ Audubon's Shearwater

Storm-Petrels (Hydrobatidae)

_____ Wilson's Storm-Petrel
_____ White-faced Storm-Petrel
_____ Fork-tailed Storm-Petrel
_____ Leach's Storm-Petrel
_____ Ashy Storm-Petrel
_____ Band-rumped Storm-Petrel
_____ Wedge-rumped Storm-Petrel
_____ Black Storm-Petrel
_____ Least Storm-Petrel

Tropicbirds (Phaethontidae)

_____ White-tailed Tropicbird
_____ Red-billed Tropicbird

Boobies and Gannets (Sulidae)

_____ Masked Booby
_____ Blue-footed Booby
_____ Brown Booby
_____ Red-footed Booby
_____ Northern Gannet

Pelicans (Pelecanidae)

_____ American White Pelican
_____ Brown Pelican

Cormorants (Phalacrocoracidae)
_____ Brandt's Cormorant
_____ Neotropic Cormorant
_____ Double-crested Cormorant
_____ Great Cormorant
_____ Red-faced Cormorant
_____ Pelagic Cormorant

Darters (Anhingidae)
_____ Anhinga

Frigatebirds (Fregatidae)
_____ Magnificent Frigatebird

Bitterns, Herons, and Egrets (Ardeidae)
_____ American Bittern
_____ Least Bittern
_____ Great Blue Heron
_____ Great Egret
_____ Little Egret
_____ Snowy Egret
_____ Little Blue Heron
_____ Tricolored Heron
_____ Reddish Egret
_____ Cattle Egret
_____ Green Heron
_____ Black-crowned Night-Heron
_____ Yellow-crowned Night-Heron

Ibises and Spoonbills (Threskiornithidae)
_____ White Ibis
_____ Glossy Ibis
_____ White-faced Ibis
_____ Roseate Spoonbill

Storks (Ciconiidae)
_____ Wood Stork

New World Vultures (Cathartidae)
_____ Black Vulture
_____ Turkey Vulture
_____ California Condor

Flamingos (Phoenicopteridae)
_____ American Flamingo

Hawks, Kites, Eagles, and Kin (Accipitridae)
_____ Osprey
_____ Hook-billed Kite
_____ Swallow-tailed Kite
_____ White-tailed Kite
_____ Snail Kite

_____ Mississippi Kite
_____ Bald Eagle
_____ Northern Harrier
_____ Sharp-shinned Hawk
_____ Cooper's Hawk
_____ Northern Goshawk
_____ Gray Hawk
_____ Common Black-Hawk
_____ Harris's Hawk
_____ Red-shouldered Hawk
_____ Broad-winged Hawk
_____ Short-tailed Hawk
_____ Swainson's Hawk
_____ White-tailed Hawk
_____ Zone-tailed Hawk
_____ Red-tailed Hawk
_____ Ferruginous Hawk
_____ Rough-legged Hawk
_____ Golden Eagle

Caracaras and Falcons (Falconidae)
_____ Crested Caracara
_____ American Kestrel
_____ Merlin
_____ Aplomado Falcon
_____ Gyrfalcon
_____ Peregrine Falcon
_____ Prairie Falcon

Rails, Gallinules, and Coots (Rallidae)
_____ Yellow Rail
_____ Black Rail
_____ Clapper Rail
_____ King Rail
_____ Virginia Rail
_____ Sora
_____ Purple Gallinule
_____ Purple Swamphen
_____ Common Moorhen
_____ American Coot

Limpkin (Aramidae)
_____ Limpkin

Cranes (Gruidae)
_____ Sandhill Crane
_____ Whooping Crane

Lapwings and Plovers (Charadriidae)
_____ Northern Lapwing
_____ Black-bellied Plover
_____ European Golden-Plover
_____ American Golden-Plover

_____ Pacific Golden-Plover
_____ Lesser Sand-Plover
_____ Snowy Plover
_____ Wilson's Plover
_____ Common Ringed Plover
_____ Semipalmated Plover
_____ Piping Plover
_____ Killdeer
_____ Mountain Plover
_____ Eurasian Dotterel

Oystercatchers (Haematopodidae)
_____ American Oystercatcher
_____ Black Oystercatcher

Stilts and Avocets (Recurvirostridae)
_____ Black-necked Stilt
_____ American Avocet

Jacanas (Jacanidae)
_____ Northern Jacana

Sandpipers, Phalaropes, and Kin (Scolopacidae)
_____ Greater Yellowlegs
_____ Lesser Yellowlegs
_____ Spotted Redshank
_____ Wood Sandpiper
_____ Solitary Sandpiper
_____ Willet
_____ Wandering Tattler
_____ Spotted Sandpiper
_____ Upland Sandpiper
_____ Whimbrel
_____ Bristle-thighed Curlew
_____ Long-billed Curlew
_____ Black-tailed Godwit
_____ Hudsonian Godwit
_____ Bar-tailed Godwit
_____ Marbled Godwit
_____ Ruddy Turnstone
_____ Black Turnstone
_____ Surfbird
_____ Red Knot
_____ Sanderling
_____ Semipalmated Sandpiper
_____ Western Sandpiper
_____ Red-necked Stint
_____ Little Stint
_____ Least Sandpiper
_____ White-rumped Sandpiper
_____ Baird's Sandpiper
_____ Pectoral Sandpiper

Sandpipers, Phalaropes, and Kin (Scolopacidae), *continued*

_____ Sharp-tailed Sandpiper
_____ Purple Sandpiper
_____ Rock Sandpiper
_____ Dunlin
_____ Curlew Sandpiper
_____ Stilt Sandpiper
_____ Buff-breasted Sandpiper
_____ Ruff
_____ Short-billed Dowitcher
_____ Long-billed Dowitcher
_____ Wilson's Snipe
_____ American Woodcock
_____ Wilson's Phalarope
_____ Red-necked Phalarope
_____ Red Phalarope

Gulls, Terns, Skimmers, and Kin (Laridae)

_____ Great Skua
_____ South Polar Skua
_____ Pomarine Jaeger
_____ Parasitic Jaeger
_____ Long-tailed Jaeger
_____ Laughing Gull
_____ Franklin's Gull
_____ Little Gull
_____ Black-headed Gull
_____ Bonaparte's Gull
_____ Heermann's Gull
_____ Black-tailed Gull
_____ Mew Gull
_____ Ring-billed Gull
_____ California Gull
_____ Herring Gull
_____ Yellow-legged Gull
_____ Thayer's Gull
_____ Iceland Gull
_____ Lesser Black-backed Gull
_____ Slaty-backed Gull
_____ Yellow-footed Gull
_____ Western Gull
_____ Glaucous-winged Gull
_____ Glaucous Gull
_____ Great Black-backed Gull
_____ Kelp Gull
_____ Sabine's Gull
_____ Black-legged Kittiwake
_____ Ross's Gull
_____ Ivory Gull
_____ Gull-billed Tern
_____ Caspian Tern

_____ Royal Tern
_____ Elegant Tern
_____ Sandwich Tern
_____ Roseate Tern
_____ Common Tern
_____ Arctic Tern
_____ Forster's Tern
_____ Least Tern
_____ Aleutian Tern
_____ Bridled Tern
_____ Sooty Tern
_____ White-winged Tern
_____ Black Tern
_____ Brown Noddy
_____ Black Noddy
_____ Black Skimmer

Auks, Murres, and Puffins (Alcidae)

_____ Dovekie
_____ Common Murre
_____ Thick-billed Murre
_____ Razorbill
_____ Black Guillemot
_____ Pigeon Guillemot
_____ Long-billed Murrelet
_____ Marbled Murrelet
_____ Kittlitz's Murrelet
_____ Xantus's Murrelet
_____ Craveri's Murrelet
_____ Ancient Murrelet
_____ Cassin's Auklet
_____ Parakeet Auklet
_____ Least Auklet
_____ Whiskered Auklet
_____ Crested Auklet
_____ Rhinoceros Auklet
_____ Atlantic Puffin
_____ Horned Puffin
_____ Tufted Puffin

Pigeons and Doves (Columbidae)

_____ Rock Pigeon
_____ White-crowned Pigeon
_____ Red-billed Pigeon
_____ Band-tailed Pigeon
_____ Eurasian Collared-Dove
_____ Spotted Dove
_____ White-winged Dove
_____ Mourning Dove
_____ Inca Dove
_____ Common Ground-Dove
_____ Ruddy Ground-Dove
_____ White-tipped Dove

Parrots and Kin (Psittacidae)

_____ Monk Parakeet
_____ Green Parakeet
_____ Thick-billed Parrot
_____ White-winged Parakeet
_____ White-fronted Parrot
_____ Yellow-chevroned Parakeet
_____ Red-crowned Parrot
_____ Red-lored Parrot
_____ Yellow-headed Parrot

Cuckoos, Roadrunners, and Anis (Cuculidae)

_____ Black-billed Cuckoo
_____ Yellow-billed Cuckoo
_____ Mangrove Cuckoo
_____ Greater Roadrunner
_____ Smooth-billed Ani
_____ Groove-billed Ani

Barn Owls (Tytonidae)

_____ Barn Owl

Typical Owls (Strigidae)

_____ Flammulated Owl
_____ Western Screech-Owl
_____ Eastern Screech-Owl
_____ Whiskered Screech-Owl
_____ Great Horned Owl
_____ Snowy Owl
_____ Northern Hawk Owl
_____ Northern Pygmy-Owl
_____ Ferruginous Pygmy-Owl
_____ Elf Owl
_____ Burrowing Owl
_____ Spotted Owl
_____ Barred Owl
_____ Great Gray Owl
_____ Long-eared Owl
_____ Short-eared Owl
_____ Boreal Owl
_____ Northern Saw-whet Owl

Nighthawks and Nightjars (Caprimulgidae)

_____ Lesser Nighthawk
_____ Common Nighthawk
_____ Antillean Nighthawk
_____ Common Pauraque
_____ Common Poorwill
_____ Chuck-will's-widow
_____ Buff-collared Nightjar
_____ Whip-poor-will

Swifts (Apodidae)

_____ Black Swift
_____ Chimney Swift
_____ Vaux's Swift
_____ White-throated Swift

Hummingbirds (Trochilidae)

_____ Green Violet-ear
_____ Broad-billed Hummingbird
_____ White-eared Hummingbird
_____ Berylline Hummingbird
_____ Buff-bellied Hummingbird
_____ Violet-crowned Hummingbird
_____ Blue-throated Hummingbird
_____ Magnificent Hummingbird
_____ Lucifer Hummingbird
_____ Ruby-throated Hummingbird
_____ Black-chinned Hummingbird
_____ Anna's Hummingbird
_____ Costa's Hummingbird
_____ Calliope Hummingbird
_____ Broad-tailed Hummingbird
_____ Rufous Hummingbird
_____ Allen's Hummingbird

Trogons (Trogonidae)

_____ Elegant Trogon
_____ Eared Quetzal

Kingfishers (Alcedinidae)

_____ Ringed Kingfisher
_____ Belted Kingfisher
_____ Green Kingfisher

Woodpeckers and Allies (Picidae)

_____ Lewis's Woodpecker
_____ Red-headed Woodpecker
_____ Acorn Woodpecker
_____ Gila Woodpecker
_____ Golden-fronted Woodpecker
_____ Red-bellied Woodpecker
_____ Williamson's Sapsucker
_____ Yellow-bellied Sapsucker
_____ Red-naped Sapsucker
_____ Red-breasted Sapsucker
_____ Ladder-backed Woodpecker
_____ Nuttall's Woodpecker
_____ Downy Woodpecker
_____ Hairy Woodpecker
_____ Arizona Woodpecker
_____ Red-cockaded Woodpecker
_____ White-headed Woodpecker
_____ American Three-toed Woodpecker
_____ Black-backed Woodpecker
_____ Northern Flicker
_____ Gilded Flicker
_____ Pileated Woodpecker
_____ Ivory-billed Woodpecker

Tyrant Flycatchers (Tyrannidae)

_____ Northern Beardless-Tyrannulet
_____ Olive-sided Flycatcher
_____ Greater Pewee
_____ Western Wood-Pewee
_____ Eastern Wood-Pewee
_____ Yellow-bellied Flycatcher
_____ Acadian Flycatcher
_____ Alder Flycatcher
_____ Willow Flycatcher
_____ Least Flycatcher
_____ Hammond's Flycatcher
_____ Gray Flycatcher
_____ Dusky Flycatcher
_____ Pacific-slope Flycatcher
_____ Cordilleran Flycatcher
_____ Buff-breasted Flycatcher
_____ Black Phoebe
_____ Eastern Phoebe
_____ Say's Phoebe
_____ Vermilion Flycatcher
_____ Dusky-capped Flycatcher
_____ Ash-throated Flycatcher
_____ Great Crested Flycatcher
_____ Brown-crested Flycatcher
_____ Great Kiskadee
_____ Sulphur-bellied Flycatcher
_____ Tropical Kingbird
_____ Couch's Kingbird
_____ Cassin's Kingbird
_____ Thick-billed Kingbird
_____ Western Kingbird
_____ Eastern Kingbird
_____ Gray Kingbird
_____ Scissor-tailed Flycatcher
_____ Fork-tailed Flycatcher
_____ Rose-throated Becard

Shrikes (Laniidae)

_____ Loggerhead Shrike
_____ Northern Shrike

Vireos (Vireonidae)

_____ White-eyed Vireo
_____ Bell's Vireo
_____ Black-capped Vireo
_____ Gray Vireo
_____ Yellow-throated Vireo
_____ Plumbeous Vireo
_____ Cassin's Vireo
_____ Blue-headed Vireo
_____ Hutton's Vireo
_____ Warbling Vireo
_____ Philadelphia Vireo
_____ Red-eyed Vireo
_____ Yellow-green Vireo
_____ Black-whiskered Vireo

Jays and Crows (Corvidae)

_____ Gray Jay
_____ Steller's Jay
_____ Blue Jay
_____ Green Jay
_____ Brown Jay
_____ Florida Scrub-Jay
_____ Island Scrub-Jay
_____ Western Scrub-Jay
_____ Mexican Jay
_____ Pinyon Jay
_____ Clark's Nutcracker
_____ Black-billed Magpie
_____ Yellow-billed Magpie
_____ American Crow
_____ Northwestern Crow
_____ Tamaulipas Crow
_____ Fish Crow
_____ Chihuahuan Raven
_____ Common Raven

Larks (Alaudidae)

_____ Sky Lark
_____ Horned Lark

Swallows (Hirundinidae)

_____ Purple Martin
_____ Tree Swallow
_____ Violet-green Swallow
_____ Northern Rough-winged Swallow
_____ Bank Swallow
_____ Cliff Swallow
_____ Cave Swallow
_____ Barn Swallow

Chickadees and Titmice (Paridae)
_____ Carolina Chickadee
_____ Black-capped Chickadee
_____ Mountain Chickadee
_____ Mexican Chickadee
_____ Chestnut-backed Chickadee
_____ Boreal Chickadee
_____ Gray-headed Chickadee
_____ Bridled Titmouse
_____ Oak Titmouse
_____ Juniper Titmouse
_____ Tufted Titmouse
_____ Black-crested Titmouse

Verdin (Remizidae)
_____ Verdin

Bushtits (Aegithalidae)
_____ Bushtit

Nuthatches (Sittidae)
_____ Red-breasted Nuthatch
_____ White-breasted Nuthatch
_____ Pygmy Nuthatch
_____ Brown-headed Nuthatch

Creepers (Certhiidae)
_____ Brown Creeper

Wrens (Troglodytidae)
_____ Cactus Wren
_____ Rock Wren
_____ Canyon Wren
_____ Carolina Wren
_____ Bewick's Wren
_____ House Wren
_____ Winter Wren
_____ Sedge Wren
_____ Marsh Wren

Dippers (Cinclidae)
_____ American Dipper

Bulbuls (Pycnonotidae)
_____ Red-whiskered Bulbul

Kinglets (Regulidae)
_____ Golden-crowned Kinglet
_____ Ruby-crowned Kinglet

Old World Warblers and Gnatcatchers (Sylviidae)
_____ Dusky Warbler
_____ Arctic Warbler
_____ Blue-gray Gnatcatcher
_____ California Gnatcatcher
_____ Black-tailed Gnatcatcher
_____ Black-capped Gnatcatcher

Thrushes (Turdidae)
_____ Bluethroat
_____ Northern Wheatear
_____ Eastern Bluebird
_____ Western Bluebird
_____ Mountain Bluebird
_____ Townsend's Solitaire
_____ Veery
_____ Gray-cheeked Thrush
_____ Bicknell's Thrush
_____ Swainson's Thrush
_____ Hermit Thrush
_____ Wood Thrush
_____ Clay-colored Robin
_____ Rufous-backed Robin
_____ American Robin
_____ Varied Thrush

Babblers (Timaliidae)
_____ Wrentit

Mockingbirds, Catbirds, and Thrashers (Mimidae)
_____ Gray Catbird
_____ Northern Mockingbird
_____ Sage Thrasher
_____ Brown Thrasher
_____ Long-billed Thrasher
_____ Bendire's Thrasher
_____ Curve-billed Thrasher
_____ California Thrasher
_____ Crissal Thrasher
_____ Le Conte's Thrasher

Starlings (Sturnidae)
_____ European Starling

Wagtails and Pipits (Motacillidae)
_____ Eastern Yellow Wagtail
_____ White Wagtail
_____ Olive-backed Pipit
_____ Pechora Pipit
_____ Red-throated Pipit
_____ American Pipit
_____ Sprague's Pipit

Waxwings (Bombycillidae)
_____ Bohemian Waxwing
_____ Cedar Waxwing

Silky-Flycatchers (Ptilogonatidae)
_____ Phainopepla

Olive Warbler (Peucedramidae)
_____ Olive Warbler

New World Warblers (Parulidae)
_____ Blue-winged Warbler
_____ Golden-winged Warbler
_____ Tennessee Warbler
_____ Orange-crowned Warbler
_____ Nashville Warbler
_____ Virginia's Warbler
_____ Colima Warbler
_____ Lucy's Warbler
_____ Crescent-chested Warbler
_____ Northern Parula
_____ Tropical Parula
_____ Yellow Warbler
_____ Chestnut-sided Warbler
_____ Magnolia Warbler
_____ Cape May Warbler
_____ Black-throated Blue Warbler
_____ Yellow-rumped Warbler
_____ Black-throated Gray Warbler
_____ Golden-cheeked Warbler
_____ Black-throated Green Warbler
_____ Townsend's Warbler
_____ Hermit Warbler
_____ Blackburnian Warbler
_____ Yellow-throated Warbler
_____ Grace's Warbler
_____ Pine Warbler
_____ Kirtland's Warbler
_____ Prairie Warbler
_____ Palm Warbler
_____ Bay-breasted Warbler
_____ Blackpoll Warbler
_____ Cerulean Warbler
_____ Black-and-white Warbler
_____ American Redstart
_____ Prothonotary Warbler
_____ Worm-eating Warbler
_____ Swainson's Warbler
_____ Ovenbird
_____ Northern Waterthrush
_____ Louisiana Waterthrush
_____ Kentucky Warbler
_____ Connecticut Warbler
_____ Mourning Warbler
_____ MacGillivray's Warbler
_____ Common Yellowthroat

_____ Gray-crowned
     Yellowthroat
_____ Hooded Warbler
_____ Wilson's Warbler
_____ Canada Warbler
_____ Red-faced Warbler
_____ Painted Redstart
_____ Slate-throated Redstart
_____ Fan-tailed Warbler
_____ Golden-crowned Warbler
_____ Rufous-capped Warbler
_____ Yellow-breasted Chat

Bananaquit (Coerebidae)

_____ Bananaquit

Tanagers (Thraupidae)

_____ Hepatic Tanager
_____ Summer Tanager
_____ Scarlet Tanager
_____ Western Tanager
_____ Flame-colored Tanager

New World Sparrows (Emberizidae)

_____ White-collared Seedeater
_____ Olive Sparrow
_____ Green-tailed Towhee
_____ Spotted Towhee
_____ Eastern Towhee
_____ Canyon Towhee
_____ California Towhee
_____ Abert's Towhee
_____ Rufous-winged Sparrow
_____ Cassin's Sparrow
_____ Bachman's Sparrow
_____ Botteri's Sparrow
_____ Rufous-crowned Sparrow
_____ Five-striped Sparrow
_____ American Tree Sparrow
_____ Chipping Sparrow
_____ Clay-colored Sparrow
_____ Brewer's Sparrow
_____ Field Sparrow
_____ Black-chinned Sparrow
_____ Vesper Sparrow
_____ Lark Sparrow
_____ Black-throated Sparrow
_____ Sage Sparrow

_____ Lark Bunting
_____ Savannah Sparrow
_____ Grasshopper Sparrow
_____ Baird's Sparrow
_____ Henslow's Sparrow
_____ Le Conte's Sparrow
_____ Nelson's Sharp-tailed
     Sparrow
_____ Saltmarsh Sharp-tailed
     Sparrow
_____ Seaside Sparrow
_____ Fox Sparrow
_____ Song Sparrow
_____ Lincoln's Sparrow
_____ Swamp Sparrow
_____ White-throated Sparrow
_____ Harris's Sparrow
_____ White-crowned Sparrow
_____ Golden-crowned Sparrow
_____ Dark-eyed Junco
_____ Yellow-eyed Junco
_____ McCown's Longspur
_____ Lapland Longspur
_____ Smith's Longspur
_____ Chestnut-collared
     Longspur
_____ Little Bunting
_____ Rustic Bunting
_____ Snow Bunting
_____ McKay's Bunting

Cardinals and Kin (Cardinalidae)

_____ Crimson-collared
     Grosbeak
_____ Northern Cardinal
_____ Pyrrhuloxia
_____ Yellow Grosbeak
_____ Rose-breasted Grosbeak
_____ Black-headed Grosbeak
_____ Blue Bunting
_____ Blue Grosbeak
_____ Lazuli Bunting
_____ Indigo Bunting
_____ Varied Bunting
_____ Painted Bunting
_____ Dickcissel

Blackbirds, Orioles, and Kin
(Icteridae)

_____ Bobolink
_____ Red-winged Blackbird
_____ Tricolored Blackbird
_____ Eastern Meadowlark
_____ Western Meadowlark
_____ Yellow-headed Blackbird
_____ Rusty Blackbird
_____ Brewer's Blackbird
_____ Common Grackle
_____ Boat-tailed Grackle
_____ Great-tailed Grackle
_____ Shiny Cowbird
_____ Bronzed Cowbird
_____ Brown-headed Cowbird
_____ Orchard Oriole
_____ Hooded Oriole
_____ Streak-backed Oriole
_____ Bullock's Oriole
_____ Altamira Oriole
_____ Audubon's Oriole
_____ Baltimore Oriole
_____ Scott's Oriole

Finches and Kin (Fringillidae)

_____ Brambling
_____ Gray-crowned Rosy-Finch
_____ Black Rosy-Finch
_____ Brown-capped Rosy-Finch
_____ Pine Grosbeak
_____ Purple Finch
_____ Cassin's Finch
_____ House Finch
_____ Red Crossbill
_____ White-winged Crossbill
_____ Common Redpoll
_____ Hoary Redpoll
_____ Pine Siskin
_____ Lesser Goldfinch
_____ Lawrence's Goldfinch
_____ American Goldfinch
_____ Evening Grosbeak

Old World Sparrows (Passeridae)

_____ House Sparrow
_____ Eurasian Tree Sparrow

Species Index

Boldface type indicates a main species entry.

Quick Index

See the Species Index on page 518 for a complete listing of all species by common and scientific name.

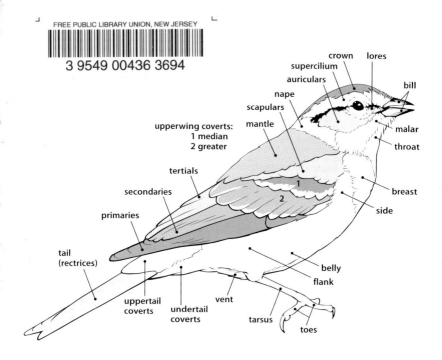

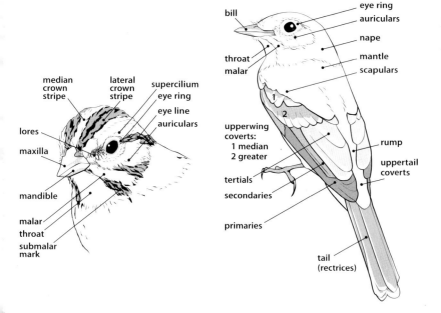